Alcoholism
SOURCEBOOK

Health Reference Series

First Edition

Alcoholism SOURCEBOOK

Basic Consumer Health Information about the Physical and Mental Consequences of Alcohol Abuse, Including Liver Disease, Pancreatitis, Wernicke-Korsakoff Syndrome (Alcoholic Dementia), Fetal Alcohol Syndrome, Heart Disease, Kidney Disorders, Gastrointestinal Problems, and Immune System Compromise, and Featuring Facts about Addiction, Detoxification, Alcohol Withdrawal, Recovery, and the Maintenance of Sobriety:

Along with a Glossary and Directories of Resources for Further Help and Information

Edited by
Karen Bellenir

615 Griswold Street • Detroit, MI 48226

Bibliographic Note

Because this page cannot legibly accommodate all the copyright notices, the Bibliographic Note portion of the Preface constitutes an extension of the copyright notice.

Each new volume of the *Health Reference Series* is individually titled and called a "First Edition." Subsequent updates will carry sequential edition numbers. To help avoid confusion and to provide maximum flexibility in our ability to respond to informational needs, the practice of consecutively numbering each volume will be discontinued.

Edited by Karen Bellenir

Health Reference Series

Karen Bellenir, *Series Editor*
Peter D. Dresser, *Managing Editor*
Joan Margeson, *Research Associate*
Dawn Matthews, *Verification Assistant*
Jenifer Swanson, *Research Associate*

EdIndex, Services for Publishers, *Indexers*

Omnigraphics, Inc.

Matthew P. Barbour, *Vice President, Operations*
Laurie Lanzen Harris, *Vice President, Editorial Dire*
Kevin Hayes, *Production Coordinator*
Thomas J. Murphy, *Vice President, Finance and Comp*
Peter E. Ruffner, *Senior Vice President*
Jane J. Steele, *Marketing Cooordinator*

Frederick G. Ruffner, Jr., Publisher

Library of Congress Cataloging-in-Publication Data

Alcoholism sourcebook : basic consumer health information about the physical and mental consequences of alcohol abuse, including liver disease, pancreatitis, Wernicke-Korsakoff syndrome (alcoholic dementia), fetal alcohol syndrome, heart disease, kidney disorders, gastrointestinal problems, and immune system compromise, and featuring facts about addiction, detoxification, alcohol withdrawal, recovery, and the maintenance of sobriety; along with a glossary and directories of resources for further help and information / edited by Karen Bellenir.--1st ed.
p. cm.-- (Health reference series)
Includes bibliographical references and index.
ISBN 0-7808-0325-6 (lib. bdg.)
1. Alcoholism--Popular works. 2. Consumer education. I. Bellenir, Karen. II Series.

RC565 .A4493 2000
616.86'1--dc21

00-034024

∞

This book is printed on acid-free paper meeting the ANSI Z39.48 Standard. The infinity symbol that appears above indicates that the paper in this book meets that standard.

Printed in the United States

Table of Contents

Part II: Alcohol's Physical Effects

Part III: Alcohol and Pregnancy

Part IV: Alcohol and the Brain

Part V: Treatment and Recovery

Part VI: Prevention

Part VII: Additional Help and Information

Preface

About This Book

According to statistics compiled by the U.S. Department of Health and Human Services about 14 million Americans—almost 10 percent of adults—meet the diagnostic criteria for alcohol abuse. Although per capita alcohol consumption has declined over the past decade, alcohol-related illnesses and deaths remain significant problems. As many as 44 percent of the more than 40,000 traffic crash fatalities each year involve alcohol. Heavy drinking also contributes to other killers: liver cirrhosis, heart disease, stroke, and some cancers. The National Institute on Alcohol Abuse and Alcoholism estimates that the economic cost of alcohol abuse in 1992, the most recent year for which sufficient data are available, was $148 billion.

This *Sourcebook* presents information about alcohol use and abuse. It describes alcohol's effects on the brain and other organs of the body, including how heavy drinking can damage the liver, pancreas, kidneys, heart, gastrointestinal tract, and immune system. A special section offers facts about alcohol and pregnancy. For people interested in treatment for alcoholism, individual chapters discuss topics such as detoxification, alcohol withdrawal, medications used to help maintain abstinence, and relapse and recovery. Readers seeking information on alcohol prevention programs will find a section detailing a wide variety of strategies and approaches. A glossary and directories of different types of resources are also provided.

How to Use This Book

This book is divided into parts and chapters. Parts focus on broad areas of interest. Chapters are devoted to single topics within a part.

Part I: Alcohol Use and Abuse describes the differences between the use of alcohol and its abuses, including alcohol dependency and alcoholism. The concept of moderate drinking is defined, and facts are presented about a wide variety of alcohol-related problems.

Part II: Alcohol's Physical Effects provides information about how alcohol impacts various organs and systems of the body, including the liver, pancreas, kidneys, cardiovascular system, and immune system. It also includes facts about the relationship between alcohol and sleep patterns and describes how alcohol consumption can lead to the development of some types of cancer.

Part III: Alcohol and Pregnancy offers a description of the physical, behavioral, and cognitive effects maternal drinking—even in moderate quantities—can have on the developing fetus. Information is also included about the life-long consequences of those effects.

Part IV: Alcohol and the Brain explains how alcohol works in the brain and describes the structural brain changes associated with alcohol abuse. Related topics, including alcohol-related dementia and the relationship between alcoholism and memory function, are also presented.

Part V: Treatment and Recovery provides tips on reducing alcohol consumption, receiving treatment for alcoholism, and maintaining abstinence.

Part VI: Prevention describes the many different types of programs and strategies used to prevent alcohol abuse.

Part VII: Additional Help and Information includes a glossary of alcohol-related terms, a list of resources for people seeking help with recovery, a directory of general information resources, a directory of resources for information on underage drinking, and a list of state substance abuse agencies.

Bibliographic Note

This volume contains documents and excerpts from publications issued by the following U.S. government agencies: Agency for Health Care

Policy and Research (AHCPR), Center for Substance Abuse Prevention (CSAP), National Clearinghouse for Alcohol and Drug Information (NCADI), National Institute on Aging (NIA), National Institute on Alcohol Abuse and Alcoholism (NIAAA), and the U.S. Department of Justice, Office of Juvenile Justice and Delinquency Prevention (OJJDP).

In addition, this volume contains copyrighted documents from the following organizations: American Academy of Family Physicians, Center for Alcohol Studies, Clinical Reference Systems, Connecticut Clearinghouse, Family Caregiver Alliance, Indiana Prevention Resource Center/Indiana University, Internet Alcohol Recovery Center/ University of Pennsylvania Health System, National Council on Alcoholism and Drug Dependence, Inc. (NCADD), New York Online Access to Health (NOAH), and the Research Institute on Addictions. Copyrighted articles from *Behavioral Health Management*, *Brown University Digest of Addiction Theory and Application*, *Geriatrics*, *Journal of the American Medical Association (JAMA)*, and *Postgraduate Medicine* are also included.

Full citation information is provided on the first page of each chapter. Every effort has been made to secure all necessary rights to reprint the copyrighted material. If any omissions have been made, please contact Omnigraphics to make corrections for future editions.

Acknowledgements

In addition to the organizations listed above, special thanks are due to document engineer Bruce Bellenir, researchers Jenifer Swanson and Joan Margeson, verification assistant Dawn Matthews, and permissions specialist Maria Franklin.

Note from the Editor

This book is part of Omnigraphics' *Health Reference Series*. The series provides basic information about a broad range of medical concerns. It is not intended to serve as a tool for diagnosing illness, in prescribing treatments, or as a substitute for the physician/patient relationship. All persons concerned about medical symptoms or the possibility of disease are encouraged to seek professional care from an appropriate health care provider.

Our Advisory Board

The *Health Reference Series* is reviewed by an Advisory Board comprised of librarians from public, academic, and medical libraries. We would like to thank the following board members for providing guidance to the development of this series:

Health Reference Series *Update Policy*

The inaugural book in the *Health Reference Series* was the first edition of *Cancer Sourcebook* published in 1992. Since then, the *Series* has been enthusiastically received by librarians and in the medical community. In order to maintain the standard of providing high-quality health information for the lay person, the editorial staff at Omnigraphics felt it was necessary to implement a policy of updating volumes when warranted.

Medical researchers have been making tremendous strides, and it is the purpose of the *Health Reference Series* to stay current with the most recent advances. Each decision to update a volume will be made on an individual basis. Some of the considerations will include how much new information is available and the feedback we receive from people who use the books. If there is a topic you would like to see added to the update list, or an area of medical concern you feel has not been adequately addressed, please write to:

Editor
Health Reference Series
Omnigraphics, Inc.
615 Griswold Street
Detroit, MI 48226

The commitment to providing on-going coverage of important medical developments has also led to some format changes in the *Health Reference Series*. Each new volume on a topic is individually titled and called a "First Edition." Subsequent updates will carry sequential edition numbers. To help avoid confusion and to provide maximum flexibility in our ability to respond to informational needs, the practice of consecutively numbering each volume has been discontinued.

Part One

Alcohol Use and Abuse

Chapter 1

Moderate Drinking

Introduction

Although the benefits and risks associated with moderate drinking have gained increasing attention in recent years from both researchers and the general public, no universal definition of moderate drinking exists. Most currently used definitions are based on a certain number of drinks consumed in a specific time period. Defining a "drink," however, also is difficult because alcoholic beverages can differ substantially in their alcohol content, even within the same beverage category (for example, beer, wine, or distilled spirits). Because international differences in drink definitions also exist, comparing studies from different countries is difficult. The development of a universal definition of moderate drinking is hampered further by variations in the way alcohol consumption levels and drinking patterns are being assessed. Despite these problems, definitions of moderate drinking and drinking guidelines have been developed in the United States and other countries.

Growing Interest in Moderate Drinking

As documented by ancient texts, people have long been aware of both the harmful and beneficial effects of drinking alcohol. Research into alcohol's effects, however, is relatively new, as evidenced by the

Excerpted from "What Is Moderate Drinking? Defining "Drinks" and Drinking Levels," by Mary C. Dufour, in *Alcohol Research and Health*, Vol. 23, No. 9, 1999. To order a copy of the publication with the entire article and references, contact the U.S. Government Printing Office; (202) 512-1800.

fact that the National Institute on Alcohol Abuse and Alcoholism (NIAAA) was not created until 1971. Initially, alcohol researchers focused primarily on understanding alcoholism and on identifying effective prevention and treatment strategies. In recent years, however, moderate drinking also has become a topic of great interest and lively debate as researchers and the media have reported on the health benefits of moderate alcohol consumption. For example, studies have indicated that moderate drinking may be associated with reduced risk of heart attack, atherosclerosis, and certain types of strokes as well as a reduced risk of brittle bones (osteoporosis) in postmenopausal women.

To discuss adequately the potential benefits and risks associated with moderate drinking one must first answer the question, What is moderate drinking? The meaning of the term “moderate” is highly subjective, however, and what one person considers to be moderate drinking, another person may view as heavy drinking.

Many current definitions of moderate drinking are based on a specific number of drinks consumed during a designated time period (for example, per day or per week). This definition, however, raises the obvious question, What is a “drink”? Another important question is, Why does it matter how a drink is defined?

What Is a Drink?

Both the definition and standardization of the term “drink” are relevant primarily in two settings: (1) commercial establishments that serve alcohol (e.g., restaurants and bars) and (2) alcohol research. The standardization of drink sizes has been a long-standing practice in alcohol-serving establishments. Commercial measures of alcoholic beverages, however, are heavily influenced by local drinking customs and regulations. In some countries, the serving sizes for various alcoholic beverages are mandated by law and, consequently, are uniform from one establishment to another. In the United States, however, each bar, restaurant, or other establishment that serves alcoholic beverages can set its own standards, although establishments generally are consistent in the sizes of the drinks they serve.

In private homes, drink sizes may vary even further. For beer, wine coolers, and similar alcoholic beverages, the serving size is most likely to be consistent across different households because a “serving” or drink often corresponds to one (standard size) can or bottle. For wine and distilled spirits (for example, vodka and whiskey), however, the size of one drink is entirely up to the person pouring it and may vary from occasion to occasion.

Surprisingly, even in alcohol research no universally accepted standard-drink definition exists, although such a definition would be helpful for comparing the results of different studies. The lack of a definition is, to some extent, historically based. When alcohol-use surveys of the general population were first instituted, they focused primarily on the distinction between drinkers and nondrinkers. As alcohol survey research progressed and investigators became interested in assessing the consequences of various levels and patterns of alcohol consumption, scientists had to develop methods to quantify consumption more accurately.

The definition of a standard drink is further complicated by the fact that in most studies of alcohol consumption, researchers are interested primarily in the effects of the alcohol contained in alcoholic beverages and not so much in the individual effects of various beverages. However, alcoholic beverages differ substantially in their alcohol content. Accordingly, a drink should be defined in terms of alcohol content, so that a drink of beer contains approximately the same amount of alcohol as a drink of wine or spirits. At first glance, this requirement appears to be a simple mathematical problem of comparing the alcohol contents of several beverages. In fact, however, such comparisons are rather complicated, because even within one beverage category, the alcohol contents may differ considerably.

To calculate and compare the alcohol contents of various beverages, however, scientists must select one conversion factor (or average alcohol content) for each category to reflect the alcohol contents of beer, wine, and spirits. One set of conversion factors that frequently is used in the United States defines average alcohol contents as follows:

- Beer: 4.5 percent alcohol
- Wine: 12.9 percent alcohol
- Spirits: 41. 1 percent alcohol.

In the United States, the U.S. Department of Health and Human Services (DHHS) and the U.S. Department of Agriculture (USDA) have developed a commonly used definition of a standard drink that has been published in *Nutrition and Your Health: Dietary Guidelines for Americans* (DHHS and USDA 1995). According to that definition, a standard drink contains approximately 0.5 fl oz (or approximately 12 grams) alcohol and corresponds to the following beverage amounts:

- 12 fluid ounces regular beer
- 5 fluid ounces wine
- 1.5 fluid ounces 80-proof distilled spirits.

What Is Moderate Drinking?

Not surprisingly, given the variability in the definitions of one drink, the numerous approaches to assessing alcohol consumption, and the subjective interpretation of the word "moderate," definitions of "moderate drinking" vary considerably among researchers. In the English language, "moderate" can be used as both a qualitative and a quantitative term, but it generally carries strong qualitative connotations. For example, *Webster's* dictionary (1966) defines moderate as "characterized by an avoidance of extremes of behavior; observing reasonable limits, showing discretion and self control" (p. 145 1). Based on this definition, most people who consume alcohol would likely consider themselves moderate drinkers, regardless of the actual alcohol amounts they consume.

Despite the rather vague definition of "moderate," alcohol survey researchers use the term to describe certain drinking levels. In their surveys, scientists must classify the wide range of alcohol consumption found in the population into a manageable number of drinking categories. One commonly used scheme includes the categories of abstainer, light drinker, moderate drinker, and heavy or heavier drinker. The definitions of each category, however, can vary among studies. For example, Dawson and colleagues (Dawson, D.A.; Grant, B.F.; and Chou, P.S. Gender differences in alcohol intake. In: Hunt, W.A., and Zakhari, S., eds. *Stress, Gender, and Alcohol-Seeking Behavior*. National Institute on Alcohol Abuse and Alcoholism Research Monograph No. 29. NIH Pub. No. 95-3893. Bethesda, MD: the Institute, 1995. pp. 1-21) proposed the following definitions, where one drink is equivalent to 0.5 fluid ounce (fl oz) alcohol:

- Abstainer: drinks less than 0.01 fl oz alcohol per day (i.e., fewer than 12 drinks in the past year)
- Light drinker: drinks 0.01 to 0.21 fl oz alcohol per day (i.e., 1 to 13 drinks per month)
- Moderate drinker: drinks 0.22 to 1.00 fl oz alcohol per day (i.e., 4 to 14 drinks per week)
- Heavier drinker: drinks more than 1.00 fl oz alcohol per day (i.e., more than 2 drinks per day).

To some degree, discrepancies in the definition of moderate drinking may result from the fact that some people confuse the term with "social drinking"—that is, drinking patterns that are accepted by the society in which they occur. Depending on the society, however, those drinking levels may not be moderate or risk free. Even when a definition of moderate drinking has been developed, that definition may not apply equally to all people or under all circumstances. For example, although it may not be harmful for a party's host to consume three or four drinks during the evening, the same amount of alcohol when consumed by a guest who plans on driving home could place the guest at risk for being in a car crash. Similarly, a healthy woman will likely experience no negative effects from drinking one drink per day; however, if the woman is pregnant, the same drinking level may lead to adverse effects (fetal impairment).

In addition to the circumstances under which drinking occurs, alcohol's effects on the drinker (for example, on the ability to drive a car) depend to a large extent on the blood alcohol levels (BALs) achieved after alcohol consumption. The same number of drinks, however, will result in different BALs in a 150 pound (lb) and a 250 lb person. Even people with identical body weights can achieve different BALs because of variations in the levels of water and fat in the body, which primarily depend on the drinker's age and gender. Alcohol is a small, water-soluble molecule that is distributed throughout the body water. Women tend to have proportionately less body water and more body fat than do men and therefore may achieve higher BALs than do men with the same body weight after drinking the same alcohol amount. Similarly, body water generally decreases and body fat increases with increasing age. As a result of these physiological differences, the same number of drinks will result in different BALs in a 140 lb woman and a 140 lb man, or in a 20-year-old man and a 60-year-old man with identical body weights.

Moderate Drinking Guidelines

One of the most compelling reasons for collecting data on alcohol consumption and for developing models of alcohol-related risks and benefits is the desire to determine "safe" or "low-risk" levels and patterns of alcohol consumption—that is, consumption levels below which drinking is not strongly associated with negative consequences. In fact, when people ask, "What is moderate drinking?" what they often really want to know is how much alcohol is safe or sensible to drink or how much they can drink without being at high risk of incurring negative consequences.

Analyses of safe or low-risk drinking levels can help formulate public health policies, such as moderate drinking guidelines, which have been developed in many countries around the world. In the United States, such guidelines are included in the publication *Nutrition and Your Health: Dietary Guidelines for Americans*, a document produced jointly by DHHS and USDA. The *Dietary Guidelines*, which are updated every 5 years, are designed to inform the American public about food choices that promote health and prevent disease. With respect to alcohol consumption, the most recent edition states, "If you drink alcoholic beverages, do so in moderation" (DHHS and USDA 1995). Moderation is defined as no more than one drink per day for women and no more than two drinks per day for men. A drink is considered to be 12 ounces regular beer, 5 ounces wine, or 1.5 ounces 80-proof distilled spirits. Those drinking levels are considered a "ceiling," not a "floor"—that is, one can drink less than those levels and still consider oneself a moderate drinker.

The *Dietary Guidelines* also list several categories of people who should not drink at all. Those categories include children and adolescents, people who cannot keep their consumption moderate, women who are pregnant or trying to conceive, people who plan to drive or participate in activities that require attention or skill, and people using over-the-counter and prescription medications that interact with alcohol. Finally, the *Dietary Guidelines* provide specific recommendations for recovering alcoholics and for people who have family members with alcohol problems.

About the Author

Mary C. Dufour, MD, MPH, is deputy director of the National Institute on Alcohol Abuse and Alcoholism, Bethesda, Maryland.

Chapter 2

Gender Differences in Moderate Drinking Effects

Research has confirmed the observation that women become more impaired than men after drinking similar quantities of alcohol. In addition, women appear to be more susceptible than men to alcohol's long-term health effects (for example, alcoholic liver disease). The prevalence of chronic alcohol-related problems is significantly lower among women, however, perhaps in part because only 2 percent of American women are heavy drinkers, compared with 9 percent of men (Substance Abuse and Mental Health Services Administration 1998).

Studies report adverse effects in men and women at even moderate drinking levels. Among those effects are disturbances of sensory information processing, short-term memory, reaction time, and eye-hand coordination. These deficits can impair the ability to drive a motor vehicle and may persist to the following day, impeding one's performance at work. The potential influence of gender on the acute effects of alcohol is therefore of importance for the large number of women who are social drinkers.

Excerpted from "Gender Differences in Moderate Drinking Effects," by Martin S. Mumenthaler, Joy L. Taylor, Ruth O'Hara, and Jerome A. Yesavage, in *Alcohol Research and Health*, Vol. 23, No. 9, 1999. To order a copy of the publication with the entire article and references, contact the U.S. Government Printing Office; (202) 512-1800.

Overview of Alcohol Pharmacokinetics

Blood alcohol concentration (BAC) is determined by the rate of alcohol absorption from the gastrointestinal (GI) tract into the bloodstream, the volume of distribution in the body, and the rate of elimination. Absorption and distribution determine the proportion of an ingested drug or other chemical substance that reaches the organs (alcohol bioavailability) where it may subsequently exert its effects. Alcohol is eliminated from the body largely by a metabolic process called oxidation, which occurs mostly in the liver. Some oxidation of alcohol also occurs during the absorption phase, thereby affecting the bioavailability of alcohol.

Absorption and Distribution

Alcohol consumed by mouth is rapidly absorbed into the bloodstream from the stomach and small intestine. The rate of absorption of alcohol depends on several factors, including the amount and concentration of alcohol ingested and the quantity and composition of food in the stomach. Alcohol absorbed from the small intestine flows through the portal vein directly to the liver, where a portion of the alcohol is metabolized. The process by which a substance is metabolized before entering the general circulation is called first-pass metabolism (FPM).

The portion of alcohol that is absorbed from the gastrointestinal system and that escapes FPM enters the general circulation and is rapidly distributed throughout the body, preferentially in body water (within the bloodstream and in the fluid within and between cells). Studies on alcohol pharmacokinetics must therefore take into account subjects' body compositions, a significant factor in gender-related studies.

Gender Differences

Significant gender differences in alcohol pharmacokinetics appear to include increased bioavailabiliy and faster disappearance rates in women.

- Women have proportionally more body fat and less water than do men of the same body weights. Because alcohol is dispersed in body water, women reach higher peak BACs than men after consuming equivalent doses of alcohol, even when doses are adjusted for body weight.

- Evidence suggests that women eliminate more alcohol per volume of blood per hour than do men.

Influence of the Menstrual Cycle

As a possible explanation for gender differences in alcohol pharmacokinetics, researchers have suggested that the physiological responsiveness of women to alcohol may vary throughout the menstrual cycle as a result of changes in levels of sex steroid hormones. The mechanism for such a possible effect is unclear.

Of 18 studies reviewed, 5 found menstrual cycle effects on alcohol pharmacokinetics. The results of these studies are conflicting.

Influence of Sex Hormones

Testing women on different days of the menstrual cycle is only one way to investigate the relationship of sex hormones to drug action. Researchers have adopted other strategies, such as administering supplemental steroid hormones (animal studies), choosing ovariectomized [women who have had their ovaries removed] or pregnant subjects, or recruiting females who use oral contraceptives.

In some human studies, women taking oral contraceptives, which suppress the natural monthly hormonal cycle, reached significantly lower blood alcohol concentrations and eliminated alcohol more slowly than women not taking oral contraceptives. Other researchers reported no effect of oral contraceptive use on alcohol absorption, peak blood alcohol concentration, or elimination rates.

Conclusions

Women achieve higher BACs than do men after drinking equivalent amounts of alcohol, even when doses are adjusted for body weight. Women may be more susceptible than men to alcohol's effects on cognitive functions (for example, divided attention and memory). In contrast, impairment of psychomotor performance (e.g., eye-brain-hand coordination and body sway) does not seem to be affected by gender, Evidence suggests that men and women eliminate approximately the same total amount of alcohol per unit body weight per hour (same alcohol elimination rate), but that women eliminate significantly more alcohol per unit of lean body mass per hour (higher alcohol disappearance rate) than do men. Research has not determined whether this specific difference in disappearance rate may lead to faster recovery of alcohol-induced cognitive performance impairment in women. Additional studies might shed further light on this matter by testing subjects under heavy workload conditions (for example, in-flight simulators) to increase the chance of identifying slight gender differences that may have escaped detection in previous studies.

Some data have prompted the speculation that hormonal fluctuations associated with the menstrual cycle might influence alcohol pharmacokinetics and alcohol's effects on women. Critical review of the current literature, however, implies that the menstrual cycle is unlikely to affect alcohol pharmacokinetics and has little biological significance with respect to alcohol's effects on performance.

About the Authors

Martin S. Mumenthaler, PhD, is a research associate; Joy L. Taylor, PhD, is a research associate; Ruth O'Hara, PhD, is a senior research scholar; and Jerome A. Yesavage, MD, is a professor at the Department of Psychiatry and Behavioral Sciences, Stanford University School of Medicine, Stanford, California.

Chapter 3

Alcohol Consumption among Racial and Ethnic Minorities

Much of the research on alcohol-related issues in the United States has been conducted with samples of whites and has ignored the potential influence of cultural factors, such as race and ethnicity. For example, although nationwide household alcohol surveys in the United States have been administered since 1964, the first national alcohol survey with an emphasis on blacks and Hispanics was implemented only in 1984. Over the past decade, however, considerable advances—primarily in the quality of the research—have been made in alcohol studies among ethnic minorities in the United States.

The importance of conducting alcohol research among minorities is underscored by findings that members of many ethnic minorities in the United States report higher rates of heavy drinking and alcohol-related problems than do whites. Consequently, it is imperative, from a public health perspective, to better understand ethnic-specific drinking patterns and their associated problems.

A dominant theme that has emerged in analyses of drinking patterns among members of various ethnic minorities is the influence of stressors related to social adjustment to the dominant U.S. culture. Those stressors include the following:

Excerpted from "Alcohol Consumption Among Racial/Ethnic Minorities: Theory and Research," by Raul Caetano, Catherine L. Clark, and Tammy Tam, in *Alcohol Research and Health*, Vol. 22, No. 4, 1998. To order a copy of the publication with this entire article and references, contact the U.S. Government Printing Office: (202) 512-1800.

- Acculturative stress (the adaptation to or acquisition of the beliefs and values of the dominant culture) which is most typically felt by immigrants who are faced with the turmoil of leaving their homeland and adapting to a new society
- Socioeconomic stress, which is often experienced by ethnic minorities who feel disempowered because of inadequate financial resources and limited social class standing
- Minority stress, which refers to the tensions that minorities encounter resulting from racism.

Although some overlap exists among these stressors, they are conceptually and empirically distinct forces and often require specific coping strategies.

A second fundamental theme emerging from recent ethnicity-focused alcohol research is that tremendous variability exists within each ethnic group, posing significant theoretical and methodological challenges to researchers. As a result of this heterogeneity, broad categorizations of ethnicity, such as "Hispanic" and "Native American," may lead to inaccurate generalizations and invalid findings.

Drinking Patterns and Underlying Causes among Hispanics

The history of alcohol research among Hispanics in the United States exemplifies the difficulties in studying a heterogeneous minority population. Most analyses have treated Hispanics as a single group, despite the fact that traditional alcohol use patterns vary among Hispanics with different countries of origin. In addition, studies among Hispanics typically have focused on male drinking patterns. Although such studies are useful for providing an overview, they gloss over subgroup and gender differences in drinking patterns by referring to "standard" Hispanic cultural norms that promote male alcohol consumption and female abstention. More recent research, however, has demonstrated that drinking patterns and rates of alcohol-related problems often differ among Hispanic subgroups, as follows:

- According to the Hispanic Health and Nutrition Examination Survey (a large-scale survey of Hispanics residing in the Southwest; the Northeast; and Dade County, Florida), Mexican-American and Puerto Rican men have higher rates of heavy drinking than do Cuban-American men.

- According to the same survey, Mexican-American women have higher rates of both abstinence and frequent heavy drinking than do Cuban-American and Puerto Rican women.
- In other nationwide studies, Mexican Americans exhibited more alcohol-related problems than did Cuban-Americans and Puerto Ricans.
- The prevalence of alcohol dependence is higher among U.S.-born Mexican-American women than among Puerto Rican and immigrant Mexican-American women.

One traditional explanation for heavy drinking patterns among Hispanic men, particularly Mexican-Americans, is the concept of "exaggerated machismo." This concept, which has been neither well defined nor measured empirically, implies that Hispanic men strive to appear strong and masculine and that the ability to drink large amounts of alcohol exemplifies their masculinity. To date, however,

Table 3.1. Drinking Patterns of U.S. Drinkers by Gender, Ethnicity, Income, and Education (1990)

	Drinking Pattern (% of respondents)		
Respondent Characteristic	**Current**	**Weekly**	**Heavy***
Gender			
Female (1,189)**	59.4	18.8	1.4
Male (869)	71.2	40.0	6.5
Ethnicity			
Black (261)	61.6	25.8	3.5
White (1570)	65.9	30.2	3.5
Hispanic (150)	66.6	26.5	8.9
Other (77)	57.0	21.6	1.4
Income			
> Median	73.8	31.7	2.5
< Median	56.1	25.5	4.9
Education			
Less than high school	50.4	23.5	6.3
High school	66.3	26.4	3.8
Some college	70.2	30.6	3.1
College	75.4	39.8	1.8

*Heavy drinkers are those who reported having five or more drinks on one occasion at least once per week during the previous year.
**Numbers in parentheses indicate the number of respondents in each category.
SOURCE: Adapted from National Institute on Alcohol Abuse and Alcoholism 1997.

no convincing association between "exaggerated machismo" and drinking patterns has been demonstrated.

Drinking Patterns and Underlying Causes among Blacks

As with Hispanics, much of the discussion on alcohol consumption patterns among blacks (U.S.-born African-Americans as well as immigrants from the Caribbean, Africa, and Europe) has focused on the prevalence of heavy drinking and ignored patterns of abstention and lighter drinking. Drinking patterns among blacks traditionally have been thought to result from social disorganization (for example, family breakdown and psychological dysfunction). Heavy drinking was considered a dominant characteristic of the "black" way of life, and early sociocultural studies characterized blacks' attitudes toward alcohol as more permissive and liberal than those of whites. Furthermore, scholars have argued that alcohol advertising targeting the black community has promoted heavier alcohol consumption, particularly of malt liquor, among members of this ethnic group.

More recent examinations of historical trends and empirical data have provided a broader view of black drinking. Other research also has indicated that the attitudes of blacks toward drinking and drunkenness are not overly permissive and, in some cases, tend to be more conservative than those of whites. For example, many studies have documented relatively high abstention rates among black women compared with white women.

In summary, recent research has contradicted many of the stereotypes of alcohol consumption patterns among blacks. Most likely, blacks' drinking patterns and alcohol-related problems result from a complex interplay of individual attributes, environmental characteristics, and historical and cultural factors that shape the life history of blacks in the United States. Alcohol researchers have begun to identify those factors and determine their relative importance.

Drinking Patterns and Underlying Causes among Asian-Americans

In contrast to Hispanics and blacks, Asian-Americans typically have been considered a "model minority," with high rates of abstention and low rates of heavy alcohol use. This image likely results from the fact that few Asian-Americans enter alcoholism treatment and from the lack of research on alcohol consumption patterns among

Asian-Americans who might be at risk for alcohol problems, such as refugees from Cambodia and Vietnam. Despite the generally low drinking rates among Asian-Americans, however, substantial variations in drinking behavior exist among different Asian subgroups. For example, in a study among four Asian ethnic groups in Los Angeles, there were more drinkers than abstainers among Japanese-Americans and Chinese-Americans and more abstainers than drinkers among Filipino-Americans and Korean-Americans. The rates of heavy drinking also differed greatly among Asian subgroups, with the highest proportions of heavy drinkers found among Japanese-Americans, followed by Filipino-Americans, Korean-Americans, and Chinese-Americans. Likewise, in an assessment of alcohol and other drug service needs among Asian-Americans in California, those of Vietnamese and Chinese-Vietnamese origin had higher alcohol consumption levels than did those of Japanese, Chinese, Korean, and Filipino origin. Overall, however, the lifetime alcohol use among all Asian-American subgroups in that study was lower than the national average.

Pronounced gender differences in alcohol consumption also exist among Asian-Americans, with Asian-American women being much more likely to abstain or consume lesser amounts of alcohol than their male counterparts. Again, substantial differences exist among drinking behaviors of various ethnic subgroups. Thus, drinking rates range from as high as 67 percent among Japanese-American women and 52 percent among Cambodian-American women to as low as 18 percent among Korean-American women and 20 percent among Filipino-American women.

Researchers have developed several theories to explain the stereotyped drinking patterns of low alcohol consumption among Asian-Americans. A popular explanation is the flushing response that many Asians experience. This response is a physiological reaction to alcohol ingestion that includes flushing of the skin, especially in the face and torso, and an increase in skin temperature. Other unpleasant symptoms associated with the flushing response include nausea, dizziness, headache, fast heartbeat, and anxiety. Various researchers have considered this physiological sensitivity to alcohol a protective factor against excessive alcohol use. Some studies suggest, however, that flushing may only be protective for people who develop the flushing response rapidly after ingesting alcohol. Still other studies have detected no significant association between consumption level and the flushing response. Fin ally, some researchers have argued that the unpleasant symptoms are related to the amount of alcohol consumed, not to flushing itself.

Researchers also have argued that low alcohol consumption levels among Asians are related to cultural values, such as the influence of ancient Confucian and Taoist philosophies on Chinese and Japanese drinking styles. The emphasis on conformity and harmony in those philosophies is believed to promote a moderate drinking style. Similarly, traditional Japanese culture focuses on interdependence, restraint, and group achievement and may thereby contribute to controlled drinking. Finally, drinking in most Asian cultures takes place in prescribed social situations, which may limit the likelihood of alcohol abuse.

Most likely, no conceptual model that focuses on only one facet of the phenomenon can account for the complex drinking patterns among Asian-Americans. Future research should take an integrative approach to address the differences among various Asian-American ethnic groups and to identify the interactive effects of the physiological, cultural, and social factors specific to each subgroup.

Drinking Patterns and Underlying Causes among Native Americans

As with Hispanics and blacks, much of the literature on Native American alcohol consumption has focused on heavy drinking or binge drinking. Many of the discussions are based on the "Firewater Myth," which suggests that Native Americans are predisposed to heavy alcohol consumption and are unable to control their drinking and their behavior when intoxicated. This myth dates back to the late 1600s, when British settlers, French trappers, and other colonial observers in North America (including Benjamin Franklin, the Jesuits, and members of the Lewis and Clark exploration party) noted the presumed insistence of Native Americans on drinking to the point of intoxication and the resulting alcohol-induced debauchery and violence. That myth still persists, and many people, including many Native Americans, still consider heavy binge drinking to be representative of the "Indian way of drinking."

However, as with single-variable explanations of alcohol consumption patterns among other ethnic groups, the Firewater Myth is insufficient to describe and explain drinking among Native Americans for two main reasons. First, no evidence exists to demonstrate increased physiological or psychological reactivity to alcohol among Native Americans compared with other ethnic groups. Second, Native Americans are a highly heterogeneous ethnic group of more than 500 tribes who speak more than 200 distinct languages. Alcohol use varies widely among those tribes. For example, the Navajo tend to view social drinking as acceptable, whereas the Hopi consider drinking irresponsible. In fact, many Native Americans abstain from alcohol use.

Still, some Native Americans do engage in heavy and dangerous alcohol consumption, and numerous hypotheses have attempted to explain this phenomenon. Some theories focus on societal factors, such as poverty, unemployment, lack of opportunity, and lack of integration into either traditional Native American or Western culture. Other theories posit that Native Americans drink to cope with various negative emotions, including low self-esteem, anxiety, frustration, boredom, powerlessness, isolation, hopelessness, and despair. Finally, some theories are more specific to Native American culture, suggesting that Native Americans drink rapidly to induce an altered state of consciousness, a practice congruent with some traditional Native American practices.

Conclusions

The study of alcohol consumption among ethnic minorities in the United States has been maturing in recent years. Researchers in the field are moving away from single-factor explanations of drinking and are beginning to develop and test theories focusing on the complex interplay of psychological, historical, cultural, and social factors that describe and explain alcohol use among minority groups. Likewise, other factors—for example, sociodemographic characteristics (such as age, income, and education); attitudes toward drinking; norms regulating drinking behavior; and alcohol availability as determined by taxation, number of alcohol outlets in the community, and hours of sale—likely predict various kinds of ethnic-specific drinking patterns. By recognizing the heterogeneity within each ethnic group, it will be easier for researchers and clinicians to identify the subpopulations that are truly at risk and which should be targeted by prevention and intervention programs. Furthermore, researchers must publicize factual reports of the drinking behaviors of ethnic minority groups, so that inaccurate stereotypes—such as the "macho Hispanic" and "drunken Indian"—are not perpetuated. Such stereotypes continue to undermine efforts of ethnic communities to find acceptance in society at large.

About the Authors

Raul Caetano, MD, PhD, is a professor and assistant dean of the Dallas Master in Public Health Program, School of Public Health,

University of Texas, Dallas, Texas. Catherine L. Clark, PhD, is an associate scientist and Tammy Tam, Ph.D., is a scientist at the Alcohol Research Group, Public Health Institute, Berkeley, California.

Chapter 4

Alcohol Metabolism

Metabolism is the body's process of converting ingested substances to other compounds. Metabolism results in some substances becoming more, and some less, toxic than those originally ingested. Metabolism involves a number of processes, one of which is referred to as oxidation. Through oxidation, alcohol is detoxified and removed from the blood, preventing the alcohol from accumulating and destroying cells and organs. A minute amount of alcohol escapes metabolism and is excreted unchanged in the breath and in urine. Until all the alcohol consumed has been metabolized, it is distributed throughout the body, affecting the brain and other tissues. As this text explains, by understanding alcohol metabolism, we can learn how the body can dispose of alcohol and discern some of the factors that influence this process. Studying alcohol metabolism also can help us to understand how this process influences the metabolism of food, hormones, and medications.

The Metabolic Process

When alcohol is consumed, it passes from the stomach and intestines into the blood, a process referred to as absorption. Alcohol is then metabolized by enzymes, which are body chemicals that break down

---

Excerpted from *Alcohol Alert*, National Institute on Alcohol Abuse and Alcoholism (NIAAA), No. 35, PH 371, January 1997. The full text of this document, including references, is available on NIAAA's website at http://www.niaaa.nih.gov. Copies are also available free of charge from the National Institute on Alcohol Abuse and Alcoholism (NIAAA) Publications Distribution Center, Attn.: *Alcohol Alert*, P.O. Box 10686, Rockville, MD 20849-0686.

other chemicals. In the liver, an enzyme called alcohol dehydrogenase (ADH) mediates the conversion of alcohol to acetaldehyde. Acetaldehyde is rapidly converted to acetate by other enzymes and is eventually metabolized to carbon dioxide and water. Alcohol also is metabolized in the liver by the enzyme cytochrome P450IIE1 (CYP2E1), which may be increased after chronic drinking. Most of the alcohol consumed is metabolized in the liver, but the small quantity that remains unmetabolized permits alcohol concentration to be measured in breath and urine.

The liver can metabolize only a certain amount of alcohol per hour, regardless of the amount that has been consumed. The rate of alcohol metabolism depends, in part, on the amount of metabolizing enzymes in the liver, which varies among individuals and appears to have genetic determinants. In general, after the consumption of one standard drink, the amount of alcohol in the drinker's blood (blood alcohol concentration, or BAC) peaks within 30 to 45 minutes. (A standard drink is defined as 12 ounces of beer, 5 ounces of wine, or 1.5 ounces of 80-proof distilled spirits, all of which contain the same amount of alcohol.) The BAC curve provides an estimate of the time needed to absorb and metabolize different amounts of alcohol [approximately 2 hours for one drink; 4½ hours for two drinks; 6 hours for three drinks; and 7 hours for four drinks]. Alcohol is metabolized more slowly than it is absorbed. Since the metabolism of alcohol is slow, consumption needs to be controlled to prevent accumulation in the body and intoxication.

Factors Influencing Alcohol Absorption and Metabolism

Food

A number of factors influence the absorption process, including the presence of food and the type of food in the gastrointestinal tract when alcohol is consumed. The rate at which alcohol is absorbed depends on how quickly the stomach empties its contents into the intestine. The higher the dietary fat content, the more time this emptying will require and the longer the process of absorption will take. One study found that subjects who drank alcohol after a meal that included fat, protein, and carbohydrates absorbed the alcohol about three times more slowly than when they consumed alcohol on an empty stomach.

Gender

Women absorb and metabolize alcohol differently from men. They have higher BACs after consuming the same amount of alcohol as men and are more susceptible to alcoholic liver disease, heart muscle damage, and brain damage. The difference in BACs between women and men has been attributed to women's smaller amount of body water, likened to dropping the same amount of alcohol into a smaller pail of water. An additional factor contributing to the difference in BACs may be that women have lower activity of the alcohol metabolizing enzyme ADH in the stomach, causing a larger proportion of the ingested alcohol to reach the blood. The combination of these factors may render women more vulnerable than men to alcohol-induced liver and heart damage.

Effects of Alcohol Metabolism

Body Weight

Although alcohol has a relatively high caloric value, 7.1 calories per gram (as a point of reference, 1 gram of carbohydrate contains 4.5 calories, and 1 gram of fat contains 9 calories), alcohol consumption does not necessarily result in increased body weight. An analysis of data collected from the first National Health and Nutrition Examination Survey (NHANES I) found that although drinkers had significantly higher intakes of total calories than nondrinkers, drinkers were not more obese than nondrinkers. In fact, women drinkers had significantly lower body weight than nondrinkers. As alcohol intake among men increased, their body weight decreased. An analysis of data from the second National Health and Nutrition Examination Survey (NHANES II) and other large national studies found similar results for women, although the relationship between drinking and body weight for men is inconsistent. Although moderate doses of alcohol added to the diets of lean men and women do not seem to lead to weight gain, some studies have reported weight gain when alcohol is added to the diets of overweight persons.

When chronic heavy drinkers substitute alcohol for carbohydrates in their diets, they lose weight and weigh less than their nondrinking counterparts. Furthermore, when chronic heavy drinkers add alcohol to an otherwise normal diet, they do not gain weight.

Sex Hormones

Alcohol metabolism alters the balance of reproductive hormones in men and women. In men, alcohol metabolism contributes to testicular injury and impairs testosterone synthesis and sperm production. In a study of normal healthy men who received 220 grams of alcohol daily for 4 weeks, testosterone levels declined after only 5 days and continued to fall throughout the study period. Prolonged testosterone deficiency may contribute to feminization in males, for example, breast enlargement. In addition, alcohol may interfere with normal sperm structure and movement by inhibiting the metabolism of vitamin A, which is essential for sperm development. In women, alcohol metabolism may contribute to increased production of a form of estrogen called estradiol (which contributes to increased bone density and reduced risk of coronary artery disease) and to decreased estradiol metabolism, resulting in elevated estradiol levels. One research review indicates that estradiol levels increased in premenopausal women who consumed slightly more than enough alcohol to reach the legal limit of alcohol (BAC of 0.10 percent) acutely. A study of the effect of alcohol on estradiol levels in postmenopausal women found that in women wearing estradiol skin patches, acute alcohol consumption significantly elevated estradiol levels over the short term.

Medications

Chronic heavy drinking appears to activate the enzyme CYP2E1, which may be responsible for transforming the over-the-counter pain reliever acetaminophen (Tylenol™) and many others into chemicals that can cause liver damage, even when acetaminophen is taken in standard therapeutic doses. A review of studies of liver damage resulting from acetaminophen-alcohol interaction reported that in alcoholics, these effects may occur with as little as 2.6 grams of acetaminophen (four to five "extra-strength" pills) taken over the course of the day in persons consuming varying amounts of alcohol. The damage caused by alcohol-acetaminophen interaction is more likely to occur when acetaminophen is taken after, rather than before, the alcohol has been metabolized. Alcohol consumption affects the metabolism of a wide variety of other medications, increasing the activity of some and diminishing the activity, thereby decreasing the effectiveness, of others.

A Commentary by NIAAA Director Enoch Gordis, M.D.

The study of metabolism has both practical and broader scientific implications. On the practical side, information on how the body metabolizes alcohol permits us to calculate, for example, what our blood alcohol concentration (BAC) is likely to be after drinking, including the impact of food and gender differences in the rate of alcohol metabolism on BAC. This information, of course, is important when participating in activities for which concentration is needed, such as driving or operating dangerous machinery.

With respect to its broader scientific application, metabolism, which has long been studied, is emerging with new implications for the study of alcoholism and its medical consequences. For instance, how is metabolism related to the resistance of some individuals to alcoholism? We know that some inherited abnormalities in metabolism (for example, flushing reaction among some persons of Asian descent) promote resistance to alcoholism. Recent data from two large-scale NIAAA-supported genetics studies suggest that alcohol dehydrogenase genes may be associated with differential resistance and vulnerability to alcohol. These findings are important to the study of why some people develop alcoholism and others do not. Studies of metabolism also can identify alternate paths of alcohol metabolism, which may help explain how alcohol speeds up the elimination of some substances (for example, barbiturates) and increases the toxicity of others (for example, acetaminophen). This information will help health care providers in advising patients on alcohol-drug interactions that may decrease the effectiveness of some therapeutic medications or render others harmful.

Chapter 5

Alcohol: What You Don't Know Can Harm You

If you are like many Americans, you may drink alcohol occasionally. Or, like others, you may drink moderate amounts of alcohol on a more regular basis. If you are a woman or someone over the age of 65, this means that you have no more than one drink per day; if you are a man, this means that you have no more than two drinks per day. Drinking at these levels usually is not associated with health risks and can help to prevent certain forms of heart disease. But did you know that even moderate drinking, under certain circumstances, is not risk free? And that if you drink at more than moderate levels, you may be putting yourself at risk for serious problems with your health and problems with family, friends, and coworkers? This text explains some of the consequences of drinking that you may not have considered.

What Is a Drink?

A standard drink is:

- One 12-ounce bottle of beer or wine cooler (Note: Beer ranges considerably in its alcohol content, with malt liquor being higher in its alcohol content than most other brewed beverages.)
- One 5-ounce glass of wine
- 1.5 ounces of 80-proof distilled spirits.

National Institute on Alcohol Abuse and Alcoholism (NIAAA), NIH Pub. No. 99-4323, 1999.

Drinking and Driving

It may surprise you to learn that you don't need to drink much alcohol before your ability to drive becomes impaired. For example, certain driving skills—such as steering a car while, at the same time, responding to changes in traffic—can be impaired by blood alcohol concentrations (BACs) as low as 0.02 percent. (The BAC refers to the amount of alcohol in the blood.) A 160-pound man will have a BAC of about 0.04 percent 1 hour after consuming two 12-ounce beers or two other standard drinks on an empty stomach. And the more alcohol you consume, the more impaired your driving skills will be. Although most States set the BAC limit for adults who drive after drinking at 0.08 to 0.10 percent, impairment of driving skills begins at much lower levels.

Interactions with Medications

Alcohol interacts negatively with more than 150 medications. For example, if you are taking antihistamines for a cold or allergy and drink alcohol, the alcohol will increase the drowsiness that the medication alone can cause, making driving or operating machinery even more hazardous. And if you are taking large doses of the painkiller acetaminophen and drinking alcohol, you are risking serious liver damage. Check with your doctor or pharmacist before drinking any amount of alcohol if you are taking any over-the-counter or prescription medications.

Interpersonal Problems

The more heavily you drink, the greater the potential for problems at home, at work, with friends, and even with strangers. These problems may include: Arguments with or estrangement from your spouse and other family members; strained relationships with coworkers; absence from or lateness to work with increasing frequency; loss of employment due to decreased productivity; and committing or being the victim of violence.

Alcohol-Related Birth Defects

If you are a pregnant woman or one who is trying to conceive, you can prevent alcohol-related birth defects by not drinking alcohol during your pregnancy. Alcohol can cause a range of birth defects, the most serious being fetal alcohol syndrome (FAS). Children born with alcohol-related birth defects can have lifelong learning and behavior problems. Those born with FAS have physical abnormalities, mental impairment, and behavior problems. Because scientists do not know exactly how much alcohol it takes to cause alcohol-related birth defects, it is best not to drink any alcohol during this time.

Long-Term Health Problems

Some problems, like those mentioned above, can occur after drinking over a relatively short period of time. But other problems—such as liver disease, heart disease, certain forms of cancer, and pancreatitis—often develop more gradually and may become evident only after long-term heavy drinking. Women may develop alcohol-related health problems after consuming less alcohol than men do over a shorter period of time. Because alcohol affects many organs in the body, long-term heavy drinking puts you at risk for developing serious health problems, some of which are described below.

Alcohol-Related Liver Disease

More than 2 million Americans suffer from alcohol-related liver disease. Some drinkers develop alcoholic hepatitis, or inflammation of the liver, as a result of long-term heavy drinking. Its symptoms include fever, jaundice (abnormal yellowing of the skin, eyeballs, and urine), and abdominal pain. Alcoholic hepatitis can cause death if drinking continues. If drinking stops, this condition often is reversible. About 10 to 20 percent of heavy drinkers develop alcoholic cirrhosis, or scarring of the liver. Alcoholic cirrhosis can cause death if drinking continues. Although cirrhosis is not reversible, if drinking stops, one's chances of survival improve considerably. Those with cirrhosis often feel better, and the functioning of their liver may improve, if they stop drinking. Although liver transplantation may be needed as a last resort, many people with cirrhosis who abstain from alcohol may never need liver transplantation. In addition, treatment for the complications of cirrhosis is available.

Heart Disease

Moderate drinking can have beneficial effects on the heart, especially among those at greatest risk for heart attacks, such as men over the age of 45 and women after menopause. But long-term heavy drinking increases the risk for high blood pressure, heart disease, and some kinds of stroke.

Cancer

Long-term heavy drinking increases the risk of developing certain forms of cancer, especially cancer of the esophagus, mouth, throat, and voice box. Women are at slightly increased risk of developing breast cancer if they drink two or more drinks per day. Drinking may also increase the risk for developing cancer of the colon and rectum.

Pancreatitis

The pancreas helps to regulate the body's blood sugar levels by producing insulin. The pancreas also has a role in digesting the food we eat. Long-term heavy drinking can lead to pancreatitis, or inflammation of the pancreas. This condition is associated with severe abdominal pain and weight loss and can be fatal.

Help Is Available

If you or someone you know has been drinking heavily, there is a risk of developing serious health problems. Because some of these health problems are both reversible and treatable, it is important to see your doctor for help. Your doctor will be able to advise you about both your health and your drinking.

For more information, contact:

Al-Alon Family Group Headquarters, Inc.
1600 Corporate Landing Parkway
Virginia Beach, VA 23454-5617
Phone: (757) 563-1600
Toll Free: (888) 4AL-ANON (for meeting information, M-F, 8a-6p ET; except holidays)
Fax: (757) 563-1655
Web site: www.al-anon-alateen.org
E-mail: wso@al-anon.org

Makes referrals to local Al-Anon groups, which are support groups for spouses and other significant adults in an alcoholic person's life. Also makes referrals to Alateen groups, which offer support to children of alcoholics. Locations of Al-Anon or Alateen meetings worldwide can be obtained by calling 1-888-4AL-ANON Monday through Friday, 8 a.m.-6 p.m. (e.s.t.). Free informational materials can be obtained by calling the toll-free numbers (operating 7 days per week, 24 hours per day): U.S.: (800) 356-9996 Canada: (800) 714-7498

Alcoholics Anonymous
P.O. Box 459
Grand Central Station
New York, NY 10163
Phone (212) 870–3400
Web site: www.alcoholics-anonymous.org

Makes referrals to local AA groups and provides informational materials on the AA program. Many cities and towns also have a local AA office listed in the telephone book.

National Council on Alcoholism and Drug Dependence, Inc.
12 West 21 Street, Seventh Floor
New York, New York 10010
Toll Free: (800) NCA-CALL (800-622-2255) (24-hour affiliate referral)
Phone: (212) 206-6770
Fax: (212) 645-1690
E-mail: national@ncadd.org
Web site: http://www.ncadd.org

Provides telephone numbers of local NCADD affiliates (who can provide information on local treatment resources) and educational materials on alcoholism via the above toll-free number.

National Institute on Alcohol Abuse and Alcoholism
National Institutes of Health
Willco Building
6000 Executive Boulevard
Bethesda, MD 20892-7003
Phone: (301) 443-0786
Web site: www.niaaa.nih.gov

Makes available free publications on all aspects of alcohol abuse and alcoholism. Many are available in Spanish. Call, write, or search the World Wide Web site for a list of publications and ordering information.

Chapter 6

A Sobering Look at Alcohol-Related Problems

Alcoholism and Alcohol-Related Problems

- Alcohol, the most widely used psychoactive drug in the United States, has unique pharmacological effects on the person drinking it.
- Alcohol contributes to 100,000 deaths annually, making it the third leading cause of preventable mortality in the United States, after tobacco and diet/activity patterns.
- Among 9,216 deaths attributed to non-medical use of other drugs in 1995, 39% also involved alcohol
- In 1992, more than seven percent of the population ages 18 years and older—nearly 13.8 million Americans—had problems with drinking, including 8.1 million people who are alcoholic. Almost three times as many men (9.8 million) as women (3.9

The information in this chapter was compiled from the following publications produced by the National Council on Alcoholism and Drug Dependence, Inc. (NCADD): "Alcoholism and Alcohol Related Problems: A Sobering Look," August 1998; "Use of Alcohol and Other Drugs Among Women," January 1998; "Youth, Alcohol, and Other Drugs: An Overview," February 1998; "FYI: Impaired Driving," undated; "FYI: Alcohol and Crime," 1998; and "Alcohol and Other Drugs in the Workplace," undated; © NCADD, reprinted with permission. For the full text of these documents, including all source citations, please visit NCADD's web site at www.ncadd.org.

million) were problem drinkers, and prevalence was highest for both sexes in the 18-to-29-years-old age group.

- About 43% of US adults—76 million people—have been exposed to alcoholism in the family: they grew up with or married an alcoholic or a problem drinker or had a blood relative who was ever an alcoholic or problem drinker.
- 64% of high school seniors report that they have been drunk; more than 31% say that have had five or more drinks in a row during the last two weeks.
- People who begin drinking before age 15 are four times more likely to develop alcoholism than those who begin at age 21.
- From 1985 to 1992, the economic costs of alcoholism and alcohol-related problems rose 42% to $148 billion. Two-thirds of the costs related to lost productivity, either due to alcohol-related illness (45.7%) or premature death (21.2%). Most of the remaining costs were in the form of health care expenditures to treat alcohol use disorders and the medical consequences of alcohol consumption (12.7%), property and administrative costs of alcohol-related motor vehicle crashes (9.2%), and various additional costs of alcohol-related crime (8.6%). Based on inflation and population growth, the estimated costs for 1995 total $166.5 billion.
- Nearly one-fourth of all persons admitted to general hospitals have alcohol problems or are undiagnosed alcoholics being treated for the consequences of their drinking.
- On average, untreated alcoholics incur general health care costs at least 100% higher than those of nonalcoholics, and this disparity may exist as long as 10 years before entry into treatment.
- Based on victim reports, each year 183,000 (37%) rapes and sexual assaults involve alcohol use by the offender, as do just over 197,000 (15%) of robberies, about 661,000 (27%) aggravated assaults, and nearly 1.7 million (25%) simple assaults.
- Alcohol is typically found in the offender, victim or both in about half of all homicides and serious assaults, as well as in a high percentage of sex-related crimes, robberies, and incidents of domestic violence, and alcohol-related problems are disproportionately found among both juvenile and adult criminal offenders.

- Fetal alcohol syndrome (FAS), which can occur when women drink during pregnancy, is the leading known environmental cause of mental retardation in the Western World.

A Preventable Disease

- Alcohol-related problems are not likely to be reduced by strategies involving single interventions directed solely at the individual; economic, political, social and environmental forces that work together to encourage and perpetuate these problems must also be addressed.
- Price increases on alcoholic beverages may be especially effective at reducing addictive consumption by younger, poorer, and less educated consumers, while information on the long-term health impacts of drinking may have a greater effect on addictive consumption by older, richer, and more educated consumers.
- School-based prevention programs that focus on social influences, such as peer resistance training or attempts to change perceived norms about alcohol, show more promise for changing alcohol use patterns than programs that emphasize the development of personal capabilities such as self-esteem, skill in making decisions and solving problems, and understanding how alcohol use can interfere with personal values and goals.
- Nations banning the advertising of distilled spirits, compared to nations with no bans, had approximately 16% lower alcohol consumption; countries banning beer and wine ads had 11% lower alcohol consumption than those prohibiting only the advertising of spirits. The reductions in motor vehicle fatality rates were 10% and 23% respectively.
- 3.4 million Americans—approximately 1.6% of the population ages 12 and older—received treatment for alcoholism and alcohol-related problems in 1994; treatment peaked among people between the ages 26-34.
- A study examining the relative cost effectiveness of 33 specific treatment modalities for alcoholism suggested that more costly treatments are not necessarily more effective; of the six treatment modalities classified as having "good evidence of effect," all appear in the minimal-, low-, or medium-low-cost categories.

- Providing heavy drinkers who are not alcohol-dependent with self-help materials relating to alcoholism can, by itself, be an effective method of brief intervention.

Environmental Influences

- Parenting practices, parental alcohol use, and peer drinking can influence a person's alcohol use and the associated problems that can stem from drinking.
- Content analyses of alcohol advertisements on television show that the ads link drinking with highly valued personal attributes such as sociability, elegance, and physical attractiveness, and with desirable outcomes such as success, relaxation, romance, and adventure.
- Alcohol advertising may influence adolescents to be more favorably predisposed to drinking.

Negative Consequences

- The regular consumption of large amounts of alcohol (defined as more than three drinks per day) is undesirable from the standpoint of health for almost all people and drinking low-to-moderate amounts can be desirable or undesirable, depending on individual characteristics.
- Although there are fewer deaths from alcohol-related causes than from cancer or heart disease, alcohol-related deaths tend to occur at much younger ages.
- Studies of suicide victims in the general population show that about 20% of such suicide victims are alcoholic.
- Heavy and chronic drinking:
  - can harm virtually every organ and system in the body.
  - is the single most important cause of illness and death from liver disease (alcoholic hepatitis and cirrhosis).
  - is associated with cardiovascular diseases such as cardiomyopathy, hypertension, arrhythmias, and stroke.
  - contributes to approximately 65% of all cases of pancreatitis.
  - depresses the immune system and results in a predisposition to infectious diseases, including respiratory infections, pneumonia, and tuberculosis.

- increases risk for cancer, with an estimated 2-4% of all cancer cases thought to be caused either directly or indirectly by alcohol. The strongest link between alcohol and cancer involves cancers of the upper digestive tract, including the esophagus, the mouth, the pharynx, and the larynx. Less consistent data link alcohol consumption and cancers of the liver, breast and colon.
- can lead to inadequate functioning of the testes and ovaries, resulting in hormonal deficiencies, sexual dysfunction and infertility.
- is related to a higher rate of early menopause and a higher frequency of menstrual irregularities (duration, flow, or both) in women.

- Each year 4,000 to 12,000 babies are born with the physical signs and intellectual disabilities associated with FAS, and thousands more experience the somewhat lesser disabilities of fetal alcohol effects.
- An association has been established in both homosexual and heterosexual populations between alcohol use, drug use, and behavior that increases the risk for contracting HIV and other sexually transmitted diseases, but underlying processes and mechanisms that explain this relationship have not been definitively identified.
- Separated and divorced men and women were three times as likely as married men and women to say they had been married to an alcoholic or problem drinker.
- An estimated 6.6 million children under the age of 18 years live in households with at least one alcoholic parent.
- 41% of all traffic fatalities (the leading cause of accidental death) are alcohol-related; alcoholics are nearly five times more likely than others to die in motor vehicle crashes.
- One study showed that half of all boating fatalities had a blood alcohol content (BAC) of .04; BACs of .10 or more were found in 31% of the fatalities.
- Alcoholics are 16 times more likely than others to die in falls, and 10 times more likely to become fire or burn victims.
- Estimates suggest that alcohol is associated with between 47% and 65% of adult drownings.

- Up to 40% of industrial fatalities and 47% of industrial injuries can be linked to alcohol consumption and alcoholism.

Consumption Patterns and Practices

- From 1994 to 1995, annual per capita consumption of alcohol in the US declined 1.8% to 2.17 gallons, the lowest it has been since 1964.
- Two-thirds of the population drink, but 10% of all drinkers (those who drink most heavily) drink half of all alcohol consumed.

Gender Differences

- Study findings suggest that women metabolize alcohol less efficiently than men, a difference that leads to higher blood alcohol concentrations in women over a shorter period of time. This difference may make women more vulnerable than men to alcohol-induced liver damage.
- Alcohol-related problems more prominent for women than men include serious reproductive and sexual dysfunctions; rapid development of dependence; more serious liver disease among those who are patients; victimization by others, particularly spouses; and sexual victimization.

Use of Alcohol and Other Drugs among Women

Consumption Rates, Patterns, and Trends

- 44% of females age 12 or older report current (past month) alcohol use; 8.7% are binge drinkers (defined as 5 or more drinks on the same occasion at least once in the past month); and 1.9% drink heavily (5 or more drinks on the same occasion on at least 5 different days in the past month).
- Current use of alcohol is highest among women ages 26 to 34; binge and heavy drinking are highest among 18- to 25-year-olds.
- While significantly fewer adult women than men use alcohol, cigarettes or illicit drugs, among 12- to 17-year olds, rates of female and male use are similar.

- Never-married, divorced, and separated women generally have the highest rates of heavy drinking and drinking-related problems; widowed women, the lowest rates, and married women, intermediate rates.
- Four times as many pregnant women drank frequently (7 or more drinks per week or 5 or more drinks on at least one occasion) in 1995 (3.5%) as in 1991 (0.8%).

Alcohol and Other Drug-Related Problems

- Research suggests that women may be at higher risk for developing alcohol-related problems at lower levels of consumption than men.
- Nearly 4 million American women ages 18 and older can be classified as alcoholic or problem drinkers, one-third the number of men; of these women, 58% are between the ages of 18 to 29.
- Compared with men, women with drinking problems also are at increased risk for depression, low self-esteem, alcohol-related physical problems, marital discord or divorce, spouses with alcohol problems, a history of sexual abuse, and drinking in response to life crises.
- Among the personal and environmental factors that increase women's risks for problem drinking are: the influence of husbands' or partners' drinking; the relationship of depression and alcohol abuse or alcohol dependence in women; sexual experience, including alcohol expectancies and reported effects of drinking on sexual behavior, sexual orientation and sexual dysfunction; and violent victimization, including physical and sexual victimization in childhood as well as in adulthood.
- Among drug-using women, 70% report having been abused sexually before the age of 16; and more than 80% had at least one parent addicted to alcohol or one or more illicit drugs.
- Alcohol or other drug use may make women more vulnerable to rape. A 1988 survey of female college students found that 53% of rape victims had used alcohol or both alcohol and other drugs beforehand. 64% reported alcohol or other drug use by the rapist.

- Alcohol is present in more than one-half of all incidents of domestic violence, with women most likely to be battered when both partners have been drinking.

Health Issues

- The death rate among women alcoholics is higher than among males because of their increased risk for suicide, alcohol-related accidents, cirrhosis and hepatitis.
- Women develop cirrhosis of the liver at a much lower cumulative dose of alcohol than do men; moreover, women remain at increased risk of disease progression even after abstinence.
- The frequency of menstrual disturbances, spontaneous abortions and miscarriages increases with level of drinking; problem drinking has adverse effects on fertility and sexual function.
- In one large study, the death rate from breast cancer was 30% higher among middle-aged and elderly women reporting at least one drink daily than among nondrinkers.

Treatment Issues

- Women with alcohol problems are less likely than men to seek help initially in alcoholism or other chemical dependency services; instead, women prefer consulting physicians or mental health clinics staff, settings in which their drinking problem is less likely to be diagnosed.
- 29.5% or 363,127 of the clients admitted for treatment of alcohol or drug-related problems in 1995 were women; alcohol, or alcohol in combination with another drug, was the primary reason for admission in 42% of these cases; smoked cocaine in 18%; and heroin in 16%. Distinct patterns of use also are evident among certain ethnic/age groups: 50% of African American women ages 30 to 34 smoked cocaine/crack; 63% of Mexican-American origin women ages 40 to 44 used heroin; 16% of women from other racial/ethnic groups, which includes Asian American women, ages 20-24 used methamphetamine.
- Women make up 33% of the Alcoholics Anonymous (AA) membership. Among AA members ages 30 and under, 40% are women.

Youth and Alcohol

An Overview

- About 9.5 million Americans between ages 12-20 had at least one drink last month; of these 4.4 million were "binge" drinkers (consuming five or more drinks in a row on a single occasion) including 1.9 million heavy drinkers (consuming five or more drinks on the same occasion on at least five different days).
- 82% of high school seniors have used alcohol; in comparison, 65% have smoked cigarettes; 50% have used marijuana; and 9% have used cocaine.
- Purchase and public possession of alcohol by people under the age of 21 is illegal in all 50 states.
- Approximately 2/3 of teenagers who drink report that they can buy their own alcoholic beverages.
- Use of alcohol and other drugs is associated with the leading causes of death and injury (e.g., motor-vehicle crashes, homicides, and suicides) among teenagers and young adults.
- Use of alcohol or other drugs at an early age is an indicator of future alcohol or drug problems; people who begin drinking before age 15 are four times more likely to develop alcoholism than those who begin at 21.

Usage Rates and Patterns

- First use of alcohol typically begins around the age 13; marijuana around 14.
- Among high school seniors, current use of alcohol is higher for whites and Hispanics than blacks; the same is true for marijuana, but with greater similarity in the rates of use.
- Approximately 8% of the nation's eighth graders; 22% of tenth graders; and 34% of twelfth graders have been drunk during the last month; 13%, 23% and 26%, respectively, have used an illicit drug.
- Among teenagers who binge drink, 39% say they drink alone; 58% drink when they are upset; 30% drink when they are bored; and 37% drink to feel high.

- Junior/middle and senior high school students drink 35% of all wine coolers sold in the United States; they also consume 1.1 billion cans of beer.
- 38% of college students have "binged" on alcohol during the past two weeks.
- Among college students in one survey, rates of binge drinking were highest among Caucasians, 43.3% for males and 24.4% for females; among African-Americans the rates were 24.8% for males and 5.4% for females; and among Asians, 32% for males and 20% for females.
- Young adults ages 18-25 are most likely to binge or drink heavily. About half of the drinkers in this age group binge and about one in five are heavy drinkers.

Negative Consequences

- Drivers under the age of 25 were more likely than those 25 or older to be intoxicated [when involved] in a fatal crash.
- Drivers ages 21-24 had the highest intoxication rates (27%) for fatal crashes in 1996.
- In 1995, 21.5% (262,112) of the clients admitted to alcohol or other drug treatment programs were under age 24, including 18,194 under age 15.
- A clear relationship exists between alcohol use and grade-point average among college students: students with GPAs of D or F drink three times as much as those who earn As.
- 31.9% of youth under 18 in long-term, state-operated juvenile institutions in 1987 were under the influence of alcohol at the time of the arrest.
- Almost half of college students who were victims of campus crimes said they [were] drinking or using other drugs when they were victimized.
- Researchers estimate that alcohol use is implicated in one- to two-thirds of sexual assault and acquaintance or "date" rape cases among teens and college students.
- Among sexually active teens, those who average five or more drinks daily were nearly three times less likely to use condoms,

thus placing them at greater risk for HIV infection. Among all teens who drink, 16% use condoms less often after drinking.

Attitudes, Perceptions, and Influences

- 80% of teenagers don't know that a 12 oz. can of beer has the same amount of alcohol as a shot of whiskey; similarly, 55% don't know that a 5 oz. glass of wine and a 12 oz. can of beer have the same amount of alcohol.
- 56% of students in grades 5 to 12 say that alcohol advertising encourages them to drink.
- 30% of children in grades four through six report that they have received "a lot" of pressure from their classmates to drink beer; 31% to try marijuana; and 34% to try cigarettes.
- A survey of high school students found that 18% of females and 39% of males say it is acceptable for a boy to force sex if the girl is stoned or drunk.

Impaired Driving

Overview

- Motor-vehicle crashes are the leading cause of death in the United States for persons ages 1-34 (1994).
- 41% (17,126) of U.S. traffic fatalities in 1996 were alcohol-related; on average, drinking and driving killed a human being every 31 minutes.
- About 3 in every 10 Americans will be involved in an alcohol-related crash at some time in their lives.
- During 1990, the economic impact of alcohol-related crashes was $46.1 billion, including $5.1 billion in medical expenses; this represents approximately 33% of all economic costs attributed to motor-vehicle crashes.
- In general, holiday periods are characterized by an increased rate of traffic fatalities and a higher proportion of deaths involving impaired driving; the increase may be related, in part, to higher rates of travel—especially at times of greatest risk (e.g., nighttime and weekends, when drivers are most likely to be drinking).

- Approximately 1.4 million drivers were arrested in 1995 for driving under the influence of alcohol or narcotics.
- Persons arrested for driving while impaired (DWI) are at substantially greater risk for future death in a motor-vehicle crash involving alcohol than those who have not been arrested for DWI, and this risk increases directly in relation to the number of DWI arrests.
- Of convicted DWI offenders, 61% reported drinking beer only, while 2% reported drinking wine only, 18% liquor only and 20% had been drinking more than one type of alcoholic beverage.
- To prevent injuries and deaths in alcohol-related crashes, additional and stronger state legislation (e.g., mandatory substance abuse assessment and treatment) should be directed toward persons arrested for or convicted of DWI.

Blood Alcohol Content

- The proportion of alcohol to blood in the body is expressed as the blood alcohol concentration (BAC). In the field of traffic safety, BAC is expressed as the percentage of alcohol in deciliters of blood—for example, .10% (i.e., 0.10 grams per deciliter).
- Compared with drivers who have not consumed alcohol, the risk of a single-vehicle fatal crash for drivers with BACs between .02% and .04% is estimated to be 1.4 times higher; for those with BACs between .05% and .09%, 11.1 times higher; for drivers with BACs between .10% and .14%, 48 times higher and for those with BACs at or above .15%, the risk is estimated to be 380 times higher.
- Fatally injured drivers with BAC levels of .10 or greater were 7 times as likely to have a prior conviction for DWI compared to fatally injured sober drivers.
- The implementation of .08% BAC laws and other associated activities (such as public information campaigns drawing attention to the change) are associated with reductions in fatal crash driver alcohol involvement.

Trends

- From 1986 to 1996, intoxication rates decreased for drivers of all age groups; drivers 16-20 experienced the largest decrease (41%), followed by drivers 21-24 (25%).

- Factors that may have contributed to the decline in both impaired driving and total alcohol-related traffic fatalities among young persons include prompt license suspension for persons who drive while impaired; increasing the minimum drinking age (since 1988, the minimum drinking age has been 21 in all states); and the initiation of public education, community awareness and media campaigns about the dangers of alcohol-involved driving.
- From 1977 to 1994, the number of male drivers involved in alcohol-related fatal traffic crashes decreased 25%; for females there was a 12% increase; possible explanations include changing roles for women, increased social acceptability of women as both drinkers and drivers and increased exposure for women during times of high risk as well as an emphasis on males in impaired driving prevention and intervention programs (e.g., nighttime and weekends).

Alcohol and Crime

The vast majority of people who consume alcoholic beverages do not engage in criminal behavior. However, since nonoffending behavior is not typically measured, little statistical information exists upon which to base any estimate of the likelihood of committing a criminal act when drinking or following a period of drinking.

The Role of Alcohol in Crime Victimization

- About three million violent crimes (including rapes and sexual assaults; robberies; and aggravated and simple assaults) occur each year in which the victims perceive the offender to have been drinking at the time of the offense; about two-thirds of these crimes are characterized as simple assaults.
- Based on victim reports, on average each year about 183,000 (37%) rapes and sexual assaults involve alcohol use by the offender, as do just over 197,000 (15%) robberies, about 661,000 (27%) aggravated assaults, and nearly 1.7 (25%) million simple assaults.
- Among violent crimes the offender is far more likely to have been drinking than under the influence of other drugs, with the exception of robberies where other drugs are as almost as likely to have been used as alcohol.

- Alcohol is more likely to be a factor in violence where the attacker and the victim know one another: two-thirds of victims who were attacked by an intimate (including a current or former spouse, boyfriend or girlfriend) reported that alcohol had been involved whereas only 31% of victimizations by strangers are alcohol-related.
- Nearly half a million incidents of violence between intimates involve offenders who have been drinking; in addition, 118,000 incidents of family violence (excluding spouses) involve alcohol, as do 744,000 incidents among acquaintances.
- Individuals under age 21 were the victims in just over 13% of incidents of alcohol-related violence, and the offenders in nearly 9%.
- 70% of alcohol-related incidents of violence occur in the home and begin with the greatest frequency at 11 p.m.; 20% of these incidents involve the use of a weapon other than hands, fists, or feet.
- Victims were injured in 60% of alcohol-related incidents of violence, with men and women equally represented, but with men more than twice as likely to have sustained a major injury due to a greater number of severe lacerations.

Use of Alcohol by Convicted Offenders

- Among the 5.3 million convicted offenders under the jurisdiction of corrections agencies in 1996, more than 36% were estimated to have been drinking at the time of the offense for which they had been convicted. This translates into just under 2 million convicted offenders nationwide on an average day, including 1.3 million individuals on probation; 85,000 in local jails; 360,000 in state and federal prisons; and more than 200,000 under parole supervision.
- Male offenders are more likely to have been drinking than female offenders when they committed their crimes, except among inmates of state prisons where women were more likely to have been drinking.
- Four in ten violent crimes involve alcohol use by the offender; alcohol use is even more common in public order crimes (such as driving while intoxicated, weapons offenses and commercial vice) and assault.

- State prisoners convicted of murder reported that alcohol was a factor in about half of the murders they committed; those who murdered intimates reported drinking the largest quantity for the longest period prior to the offense.
- Among convicted offenders, beer is the most commonly used alcoholic beverage, by itself and in combination with distilled spirits; 30% of probationers, 32% of local jail inmates and 23% of state prisoners had been drinking beer before committing their crimes.
- Inmates of state prisons reported drinking the equivalent of as many as 15 beers up to eight hours before committing their crimes.
- 30% of state prisoners described themselves as daily drinkers; this population began drinking before age 17 and were the most intoxicated at the time of their arrests.
- About half of all state inmates who described themselves as daily drinkers prior to entering prison had received some form of treatment—most often participation in a self-help group—at some point in their lives.
- Among the 1,196 confinement facilities nationwide in 1995, 192 (16%) indicated that providing treatment for alcoholism and other drug addictions was central to their missions; 39 prisons described their primary function as providing treatment.

Alcohol and Crime in College

- College students reported about 463,000 (31%) alcohol-related incidents of violence in 1995.
- 90% of alcohol-related incidents of violence involving college students occurred off campus.
- Per capita arrest rates for alcoholic beverage law violations (including prohibited manufacture, sale or possession of alcohol, and maintaining illegal drinking places but excluding public drunkenness and driving-related offenses) are highest at public, four-year colleges.
- Just over half of campus law enforcement agencies at four-year universities and colleges with at least 2,500 students report that they operate alcohol education programs; public universities (59%) more often reported the availability of such programs and services than private colleges (43%).

Alcohol in the Workplace

- 7.5% of Americans employed in full-time jobs report heavy drinking, defined as drinking five or more drinks per occasion on five or more days in the past 30 days; 6.6% of part-timers and 10.8% of unemployed workers also report heavy drinking; across all three categories, heavy drinkers are most likely to be found in the 18 to 25 year old age group.
- Up to 40% of industrial fatalities and 47% of industrial injuries can be linked to alcohol consumption and alcoholism.
- In 1990, problems resulting from use of alcohol and other drugs cost American business an estimated $81.6 billion in lost productivity due to premature death ($37 billion) and illness ($44.6 billion); 86% of these combined costs can be attributed to drinking problems alone.
- Employees who were in serious trouble with alcohol showed significant improvement in drinking behavior and job adjustment during the months immediately following an intervention to confront problem drinking that was intruding on their work.

The Risks

- Work roles with little or no supervision, and those characterized by high mobility, are associated with increased rates of problem drinking.
- Numerous studies suggest a significant relationship between work stress and the development of drinking problems.
- In general, unmarried workers (divorced, separated, or never married) had about twice the rate of illicit drug and heavy alcohol use as married workers.
- 75% of workers paid on an hourly basis at one manufacturing plant reported that it was easy for them to drink at their work stations. This group included assembly line workers, electricians and machinists.

Gender Differences

- Studies have shown that the drinking patterns of employed women are different from those of women not employed outside the home, with less abstinence, increased consumption, and greater frequency of drinking occasions observed among employed women.

- Theories about job stress, job conflict, or role overload (i.e., working women who also are married) as factors influencing alcohol consumption among women in paid employment have found little support; in fact, some studies associate a lack of roles with increased drinking and problem drinking. Drinking patterns of employed women instead seem to be influenced by greater accessibility to alcohol and by complex issues surrounding the gender balance of a workplace or occupation.

Prevalence by Occupation

- The highest rates of current and past year illicit drug use are reported by workers in the following occupations: construction, food preparation, and waiters and waitresses. Heavy alcohol use followed a similar pattern, although auto mechanics, vehicle repairers, light truck drivers and laborers also have high rates of alcohol use.
- The lowest rates of illicit drug use are found among workers in the following occupations: police and detectives, administrative support, teachers, and child care workers. The lowest rates of heavy alcohol use are among data clerks, personnel specialists and secretaries.

The Cost

- Individuals with drinking problems or alcoholism at any time in their lives suffer income reductions ranging from 1.5% to 18.7% depending on age and sex compared with those with no such diagnosis.
- Absenteeism among alcoholics or problem drinkers is 3.8 to 8.3 times greater than normal and up to 16 times greater among all employees with alcohol and other drug-related problems. Drug-using employees take three times as many sick benefits as other workers. They are five times more likely to file a worker's compensation claim.
- Non-alcoholic members of alcoholics' families use ten times as much sick leave as members of families in which alcoholism is not present.

- 43% of CEOs responding to one survey estimated that use of alcohol and other drugs cost them 1% to 10% of payroll.

Employee Assistance Programs

- For every dollar they invest in an Employee Assistance Program (EAP), employers generally save anywhere from $5 to $16. The average annual cost for an EAP ranges from $12 to $20 per employee.
  - General Motors Corporation's EAP saves the company $37 million per year — $3,700 for each of the 10,000 employees enrolled in the program.
  - United Airlines estimates that it has a $16.95 return for every dollar invested in employee assistance.
  - Northrop Corporation saw a 43% increase in the productivity of each of its first 100 employees to enter an alcohol treatment program. After three years' sobriety, the average savings for each was nearly $20,000.
  - Philadelphia Police Department employees undergoing treatment reduced their sick days by an average of 38% and their injured days by 62%.
  - Oldsmobile's Lansing, Michigan plant saw the following results in the year after its alcoholic employees underwent treatment: lost man-hours declined by 49%, health care benefits by 29%, leaves by 56%, grievances by 78%, disciplinary problems by 63% and accidents by 82%.
- 45% of full-time employees who were not self-employed had access to an EAP provided by their employers but within a single year only 1.5% used an EAP because of alcohol or other drug-related problems.
- While roughly 90% of the Fortune 500 companies have established EAPs, this percentage is much lower among smaller companies. Only 9% of businesses with fewer than 50 employees have EAP programs. 90% of U.S. businesses fall into this category.

Treatment Issues

- Studies suggest that employees who are pressured into treatment by their employers are slightly more likely to recover from their alcoholism and improve their performance than those who are not so pressured.

- Research indicates that alcoholism treatment can yield significant reductions in total health care costs and utilization for an alcoholic and his or her family.
- Less than 1/3 of one percent of employed persons are receiving treatment for alcoholism and other drug dependence.
- One survey reports that nearly nine in ten employers limit benefits for alcoholism, other drug dependence and mental disorders despite the fact that 52% of the survey participants could not say how much it cost them to provide treatment for these diseases.

Chapter 7

Alcoholism: An Overview

What Is Alcoholism?

Alcoholism is a chronic, progressive, and often fatal disease; it is a primary disorder and not a symptom of other diseases or emotional problems. The chemistry of alcohol allows it to affect nearly every type of cell in the body, including those in the central nervous system. In the brain, alcohol interacts with centers responsible for pleasure. After prolonged exposure to alcohol, the brain adapts to the changes alcohol makes and becomes dependent on it. For people with alcoholism, drinking becomes the primary means through which they can deal with people, work, and life. Alcohol dominates their thinking, emotions, and actions. The severity of this disease is influenced by factors such as genetics, psychology, culture, and response to physical pain.

Alcoholism can develop insidiously; often there is no clear line between problem drinking and alcoholism. In addition to alcohol dependence, experts are now defining alcohol use by levels of harm that it may be causing. This information is useful to determine possible interventions at earlier stages. The only early indications of alcoholism may be the unpleasant physical responses to withdrawal that occur during even brief periods of abstinence. Sometimes people experience long-term depression or anxiety, insomnia, chronic pain, or personal or work stress that lead to the use of alcohol for relief, but often no extraordinary events have occurred that account for the drinking problem.

Alcoholics have little or no control over the quantity they drink or the duration or frequency of their drinking. They are preoccupied with drinking, deny their own addiction, and continue to drink even though they are aware of the dangers. Over time, some people become tolerant to the effects of drinking and require more alcohol to become intoxicated, creating the illusion that they can "hold their liquor." They have blackouts after drinking and frequent hangovers that cause them to miss work and other normal activities. Alcoholics might drink alone and start early in the day. They periodically quit drinking or switch from hard liquor to beer or wine, but these periods rarely last. Severe alcoholics often have a history of accidents, marital and work instability, and alcohol-related health problems. Episodic violent and abusive incidents involving spouses and children and a history of unexplained or frequent accidents are often signs of drug or alcohol abuse.

Alcohol Use and Abuse

Experts now define levels of alcohol use by how harmful it is as well as how dependent a person is on it (with a drink defined as 12-oz of beer, 6 oz of wine, or 1.5 oz of 90-proof liquor).

Moderate Drinking: Equal to or less than two drinks a day for men and equal to or less than one drink a day for women.

Heavy Drinking: More than 14 drinks per week or 4 drinks at one sitting for men and more than seven drinks a week or three drinks at one sitting for women. (Drinking over this amount puts a person at risk for adverse health events.)

Hazardous Drinking: Hazardous drinking is an average consumption of 21 drinks or more per week for men (or 7 or more drinks per occasion at least 3 times a week) and 14 or more drinks per week for women (or more than 5 drinks per occasion at least 3 times a week). Hazardous drinking is considered to place individuals at risk for adverse health events.

Harmful Drinking: Harmful drinking occurs when alcohol consumption has actually caused physical or psychological harm. This is determined if there is clear evidence that alcohol is responsible for such harm, the nature of that harm can be identified, alcohol consumption has persisted for at least a month or has occurred repeatedly for the past year, and the individual is not alcohol dependent.

Alcohol Abuse: One or more of the following alcohol-related problems over a period of one year: failure to fulfill work or personal obligations; recurrent use in potentially dangerous situations; problems with the law; and continued use in spite of harm being done to social or personal relationships.

Alcohol Dependence: The individual experiences three or more of the following alcohol-related problems over a period of one year: increased amounts of alcohol needed to produce an effect; withdrawal symptoms or drinking alcohol to avoid these symptoms; drinking more over a given period than intended; unsuccessful attempts to quit or cut down; giving up significant leisure or work activities; continuing drinking in spite of the knowledge of its physical or psychological harm to oneself or others.

What Causes Alcoholism?

People have been drinking alcohol for perhaps 15,000 years. Just drinking steadily and consistently over time can produce dependence and cause withdrawal symptoms during periods of abstinence; this physical dependence, however, is not the sole cause of alcoholism. To develop alcoholism, other factors usually come into play, including biology genetics, culture, and psychology.

Genetic Factors

Genetic factors play a significant role in alcoholism and may account for about half of the total risk for alcoholism. They effect men and women equally. Researchers are investigating a number of inherited traits that make particular individuals susceptible to this disorder. Even if genetic factors can be identified, however, they are unlikely to explain all cases of alcoholism. In fact, it may be a natural lack of genetic protection that plays a major role in alcoholism. Because alcohol is not found easily in nature, genetic mechanisms to protect against excessive consumption may not have evolved in humans as they frequently have for protection against natural threats. It is important to understand that, whether they inherit the disorder or not, people with alcoholism are still legally responsible for their actions. Inheriting genetic traits does not doom a child to an alcoholic future. Environment, personality, and emotional factors also play a strong role.

Brain Chemicals

Alcohol has widespread effects on the brain. Of particular interest to researchers are a number of brain chemicals that include gamma aminobutyric acid (GABA), dopamine, serotonin, glutamate, norepinephrine, and opioid peptides. Genetic factors that cause imbalances in one or more of these brain chemicals and which may increase the risk for alcohol dependency are under intense scrutiny. Long-term use of alcohol itself, however, can cause adaptations that change the brain's chemistry and cause cravings, pain on withdrawal, and addiction. Such changes include depletion of gamma-aminobutyric acid (which inhibits impulsivity), an increase in glutamate (which produces an over-excited nervous system), and higher levels of norepinephrine and corticotropin releasing factor (which causes stress and tension). When a person with alcoholism stops drinking, the hyperactivity in the brain caused by these events produces an intense need to calm down with the use of yet more alcohol. In addition, the patient continues to seek euphoria and pleasure produced by other chemicals. Serotonin and opioid peptides are important for feelings of well being. A rapid release in the brain of alcohol-induced dopamine causes euphoria, and repeated alcohol administration increases the sensitivity to these dopamine pathways. Animal studies indicate, however, that heavy drinking depletes the stores of dopamine and serotonin over time. Cravings for alcohol which lead to dependency or relapse then appear to be produced by two effects: the need to reduce agitation caused by an overexcited nervous system and the desire to restore pleasurable feelings that have been reduced by lower activity of dopamine and serotonin. One recent study suggested that agitation may be the more important factor in causing a relapse than mood shifts.

Levels of Response to Alcohol

A number of studies on twins and population groups at risk for alcoholism, such as Native Americans, have suggested that genetic factors may determine one's level of response to alcohol. Such studies have found that people with a family history of alcohol tend to be able to drink more to achieve a level of intoxication than other people experience with less liquor. In other words, they "hold their liquor" better. Experts suggest such people may inherit a lack of those warning signals that ordinarily make people stop drinking. Some research suggests this factor may contribute to between 40% and 60% of alcoholism cases related to genetic factors.

Factors Affecting Aldehyde or Alcohol Dehydrogenase

Alcohol is metabolized in a two-stage process. It is first converted to acetaldehyde by a chemical called alcohol dehydrogenase (ADH), which is then converted into acetate by another chemical called aldehyde dehydrogenase (ALDH). Genes that affect either ADH or ALDH are under intense scrutiny for either their protective or harmful roles or both. For example, many Asians and possibly many Jewish people, are less likely to become alcoholic because of a genetic factor that makes them deficient in ALDH. In its absence, acetate, which is toxic, builds up after drinking alcohol and rapidly leads to flushing, dizziness, and nausea. People with this genetic susceptibility, then, are likely to experience adverse reactions to alcohol and therefore more likely not to become alcoholic. (This deficiency is not completely protective against drinking, however, particularly if there is added social pressure, such as among college fraternity members.) Investigators are looking for variants in the ALDH gene that may increase production of this enzyme, which in turn may make people genetically susceptible to alcoholism.

Social and Emotional Causes of Alcoholic Relapse

Between 80% and 90% of people treated for alcoholism relapse, even after years of abstinence. Patients and their caregivers should understand that relapses of alcoholism are analogous to recurrent flare-ups of chronic physical diseases. One study found that three factors placed a person at high risk for relapse: frustration and anger, social pressure, and internal temptation. Another study suggests that impaired sleep is also an important predictor of relapse.

Mental and Emotional Stress. Alcohol blocks out emotional pain and is often perceived as a loyal friend when human relationships fail. It is also associated with freedom and a loss of inhibition that offsets the tedium of daily routines. When the alcoholic tries to quit drinking, the brain seeks to restore what it perceives to be its equilibrium. The brain's best weapons against abstinence are depression and anxiety (the emotional equivalents of physical pain) that continue to tempt alcoholics to return to drinking long after physical withdrawal symptoms have abated. Even intelligence is no ally in this process, for the brain will use all its powers of rationalization to persuade the patient to return to drinking. According to an interesting 1999 study, however, although a person's IQ had no effect on abstinence, a high verbal ability appeared to aid the alcoholic in remaining sober. It is important to realize that any life change may cause temporary grief and anxiety, even changes for the better. With time and the substitution of healthier pleasures, this emotional turmoil weakens and can be overcome.

Codependency. One of the most difficult problems facing a person with alcoholism is being around people who are able to drink socially without danger of addiction. A sense of isolation, a loss of enjoyment, and the ex-drinker's belief that pity, not respect, is guiding a friend's attitude can lead to loneliness, low self-esteem, and a strong desire to drink. Close friends and even intimate partners may have difficulty in changing their responses to this newly sober person and, even worse, may encourage a return to drinking. To preserve marriages to alcoholics, spouses often build their own self-images on surviving or handling their mates' difficult behavior and then discover that they are threatened by abstinence. Friends may not easily accept the sober, perhaps more subdued, comrade. In such cases, separation from these "enablers" may be necessary for survival. It is no wonder that, when faced with such losses, even if they are temporary, a person returns to drinking. The best course in these cases is to encourage close friends and family members to seek help as well. Fortunately, groups such as Al-Anon exist for this purpose.

Social and Cultural Pressures. The media portrays the pleasures of drinking in advertising and programming. The medical benefits of light to moderate drinking are frequently publicized, giving ex-drinkers the spurious excuse of returning to alcohol for their health. These messages must be categorically ignored and acknowledged for what they are, an industry's attempt to profit from potentially great harm to individuals.

Who Becomes an Alcoholic?

General Risks and Age

Some population studies indicate that in a single year, between 7.4% and 9.7% of the population are dependent on alcohol, and between 20% and 25% of Americans identify themselves as heavy drinkers when they visit their physician. A 1996 national survey reported that 11 million Americans are heavy drinkers and 32 million engaged in binge drinking (five or more drinks on one occasion) in the month previous to the survey. People with a family history of alcoholism are more likely to begin drinking before the age of 20 and to become alcoholic. Such adolescent drinkers are also more apt to underestimate the effects of drinking and to make judgment errors, such as going on binges and driving after drinking, than young drinkers without a family history of alcoholism. But anyone who begins drinking in adolescence is at risk for developing alcoholism. Currently 1.9 million young people between the ages of 12 and 20 are considered heavy drinkers and 4.4 million are binge drinkers.

Although alcoholism usually develops in early adulthood, the elderly are not exempt. A survey of 5,000 adults over 60 reported that 15% of men and 12% of women were hazardous drinkers, and 9% of men and 3% of women were alcohol dependent. In another study, the prevalence of problem drinking was as high as 49% among nursing home patients. Alcohol also affects the older body differently; people who maintain the same drinking patterns as they age can easily develop alcohol dependency without realizing it. Physicians may overlook alcoholism when evaluating elderly patients, mistakenly attributing the signs of alcohol abuse to the normal effects of the aging process.

Gender

Most alcoholics are men, but the incidence of alcoholism in women has been increasing over the past 30 years. About 9.3% of men and 1.9% of women are heavy drinkers, and 22.8% of men are binge drinkers compared to 8.7% of women. In general, young women problem drinkers follow the drinking patterns of their partners, although they tend to engage in heavier drinking during the premenstrual period. Women tend to become alcoholic later in life than men, and it is estimated that 1.8 million older women suffer from alcohol addiction. Even though heavy drinking in women usually occurs later in life, the medical problems women develop because of the disorder occur at about the same age as men, suggesting that women are more susceptible to the physical toxicity of alcohol.

Family History and Ethnicity

The risk for alcoholism in sons of alcoholic fathers is 25%. The familial link is weaker for women, but genetic factors contribute to this disease in both genders. In one study, women with alcoholism tended to have parents who drank. Women who came from families with a history of emotional disorders, rejecting parents, or early family disruption had no higher risk for drinking than women without such backgrounds. A stable family and psychological health were not protective in people with a genetic risk. Unfortunately, there is no way to predict which members of alcoholic families are most at risk for alcoholism.

Some population groups, such as Irish and Native Americans, have an increased incidence in alcoholism while others, such as Jewish and Asian Americans, have lower risk. Overall, there is no difference in alcoholic prevalence between African Americans, whites, and Hispanic people. Although the biological causes of such different risks are not known, certain people in these population groups may be at higher or lower risk because of the way they metabolize alcohol.

Emotional Disorders

Severely depressed or anxious people are at high risk for alcoholism, smoking, and other forms of addiction. Major depression, in fact, accompanies about one-third of all cases of alcoholism. It is more common among alcoholic women (and women in general) than men. Depression and anxiety may play a major role in the development of alcoholism in the elderly, who are often subject to dramatic life changes, such as retirement, the loss of a spouse or friends, and medical problems. Problem drinking in these cases may be due to self-medication of the anxiety or depression. It should be noted, however, that it is not always clear whether people with emotional disorders are self-medicating with alcohol or whether long-term alcoholism itself causes chemical changes that produce anxiety and depression.

Personality Traits

Studies are finding that alcoholism is strongly related to impulsive, excitable, and novelty-seeking behavior, and such patterns are established early on, if not inherited. People with attention deficit hyperactivity disorder, a condition that shares these behaviors, have a higher risk for alcoholism. In a test of mental functioning, alcoholics (mostly women) did not show any deficits in thinking but they were less able to inhibit their responses. Children who later become alcoholics or who abuse drugs are more likely to have less fear of new situations than others, even if there is a greater risk for harm than in nonalcoholics. On the other hand, studies are also finding an association between alcohol use and having social phobia, a form of anxiety in which the individual has an intense fear of being publicly scrutinized and humiliated. Such individuals may use alcohol as a way to become less inhibited in public situations.

Socioeconomic Factors

It has been long thought that alcoholism is more prevalent in people with lower educational levels and in those who are unemployed. A thorough 1996 study, however, reported that the prevalence of alcoholism among adult welfare recipients was 4.3% to 8.2%, which was comparable to the 7.4% found in the general population. There was also no difference in prevalence between poor African Americans and poor whites. People in low-income groups did display some tendencies that differed from the general population. For instance, as many women as men were heavy drinkers. Excessive drinking may be more dangerous in lower income groups; one study found that it was a major factor in the higher death rate of people, particularly men, in lower socioeconomic groups compared with those in higher groups.

Geographic Factors

Although 54% of urban adults use alcohol at least once a month compared to 42% in nonurban areas, living in the city or the country does not affect the risks for bingeing or heavy alcohol use. One study reported that people in the north central United States are at highest risk for heavy drinking (6.4% heavy use and 19% binge drinking) and those in the Northeast have the lowest risk (4.5% heavy use and 13% binge drinking).

Smokers

Researchers are finding common genetic factors in alcohol and nicotine addiction, which may explain, in part, why alcoholics are often smokers. Alcoholics who smoke compound their health problems. More alcoholics die from tobacco-related illnesses, such as heart disease or cancer, than from chronic liver disease, cirrhosis, or other conditions that are more directly tied to excessive drinking.

Sugar Cravings

People who crave sugar may also be at higher risk for alcoholism. In one recent study, 62% of male alcoholics enjoyed a sweet sugar solution compared with only 21% of those without a drinking problem.

It is not known, however, whether having a "sweet tooth" can be an early predictor of alcoholism or whether alcohol abusers simply develop a taste for sweetness as a result of their chronic alcohol abuse.

How Serious Is Alcoholism?

About 100,000 deaths a year can be wholly or partially attributed to drinking, and alcoholism reduces life expectancy by 10 to 12 years. Next to smoking, it is the most common preventable cause of death in America. Although studies indicate that adults who drink moderately (about one drink a day) have a lower mortality rate than their non-drinking peers, their risk for untimely death increases with heavier drinking. The earlier a person begins drinking heavily, the greater their chance of developing serious illnesses later on. Alcoholism can kill in many different ways, and, in general, people who drink regularly have a higher rate of deaths from injury, violence, and some cancers.

Overdose

Alcohol overdose can lead to death. This is a particular danger for adolescents who may want to impress their friends with their ability to drink alcohol but cannot yet gauge its effects.

Accidents, Suicide, and Murder

Alcohol plays a major role in more than half of all automobile fatalities. Less than two drinks can impair the ability to drive. Alcohol also increases the risk of accidental injuries from many other causes. One study of emergency room patients found that having had more than one drink doubled the risk of injury, and more than four drinks increased the risk eleven times. Another study reported that among emergency room patients who were admitted for injuries, 47% tested positive for alcohol and 35% were intoxicated. Of those who were intoxicated, 75% showed evidence of chronic alcoholism. This disease is the primary diagnosis in one quarter of all people who commit suicide, and alcohol is implicated in 67% of all murders.

Domestic Violence and Effects on Family

Domestic violence is a common consequence of alcohol abuse. Research suggests that for women, the most serious risk factor for injury from domestic violence may be a history of alcohol abuse in her male partner. Alcoholism in parents also increases the risk for violent behavior and abuse toward their children. Children of alcoholics tend to do worse academically than others, have a higher incidence of depression, anxiety, and stress and lower self-esteem than their peers. One study found that children who were diagnosed with major depression between the ages of six and 12 were more likely to have alcoholic parents or relatives than were children who were not depressed. Alcoholic households are less cohesive, have more conflicts, and their members are less independent and expressive than households with nonalcoholic or recovering alcoholic parents. In addition to their own inherited risk for later alcoholism, one study found that 41% of children of alcoholics have serious coping problems that may be life long. Adult children of alcoholic parents are at higher risk for divorce and for psychiatric symptoms. One study concluded that the only events with greater psychological impact on children are sexual and physical abuse.

The Effect of Alcohol on Mental Functioning

Drinking too much alcohol can cause mild neurologic problems in anyone, including insomnia and headache (especially after drinking red wine). Long-term alcohol use appears to have major effects upon the hippocampus, an area in the brain associated with learning and memory and the regulation of emotion, sensory processing, appetite, and stress. Brain scans of people with long-term alcoholism have shown atrophy in different parts of the brain and reduced brain activity, which fortunately seems to be reversible with continued abstinence. In a 1999 study, loss of verbal memory and slower reaction times were associated with a higher incidence of recent alcohol use (i.e., within the last 3 months). A history of lifetime alcohol use, however, did not seem to impair mental functioning of patients with mild to moderate alcoholism. One study that uses imaging techniques to scan the brains of inebriated subjects suggested that while alcohol stimulates those parts of the brain related to reward and induces euphoria, it does not appear to impair cognitive performance (the ability to think and reason). Except in severe cases, any neurologic damage is not permanent and abstinence nearly always leads to recovery of normal mental function. Severely alcoholic patients, however, often have co-existing psychiatric or neurologic problems, and habitual use of alcohol eventually produces depression and confusion.

Medical Problems

Alcohol can affect the body in so many ways that researchers are having a hard time determining exactly what the consequences are from drinking. It is well known, however, that chronic consumption leads to many problems, some of them deadly. Frequent heavy drinking is associated with a higher risk for alcohol-related medical disorders (pancreatitis, upper gastrointestinal bleeding, nerve damage, and impotence) than is episodic drinking or continuous drinking without intoxication. As people age, it takes fewer drinks to become intoxicated, and organs can be damaged by smaller amounts of alcohol than in younger people. Also, up to one-half of the 100 most prescribed drugs for older people react adversely with alcohol. Alcohol abusers who require surgery also have an increased risk of postoperative complications, including infections, bleeding, insufficient heart and lung functions, and problems with wound healing. Alcohol withdrawal symptoms after surgery may impose further stress on the patient and hinder recuperation.

Liver Disorders. The liver is particularly endangered by alcoholism. About 10% to 35% of heavy drinkers develop alcoholic hepatitis, and 10% to 20% develop cirrhosis. In the liver, alcohol converts to toxic chemicals, such as acetaldehyde, which trigger the production of immune factors called cytokines. In large amounts, these agents cause inflammation and tissue injury and are proving to be major culprits in the destructive process in the liver. Not eating when drinking and consuming a variety of alcoholic beverages are also factors that increase the risk for liver damage. People with alcoholism are also at higher risk for hepatitis B and C, potentially chronic liver diseases than can lead to cirrhosis and liver cancer. People with alcoholism should be immunized against hepatitis B; they may need a higher-than-normal dose of the vaccine for it to be effective.

Gastrointestinal Problems. Alcohol can cause diarrhea and hemorrhoids. Alcohol abuse can cause ulcers, particularly in people taking the painkillers known as nonsteroidal anti-inflammatory drugs (such as aspirin or ibuprofen). Alcohol can contribute to serious and chronic inflammation of the pancreas (pancreatitis) in people who are susceptible to this condition.

Heart Disease and Stroke. The effects of alcohol on heart disease vary depending on consumption. Evidence strongly suggests that light to moderate alcohol, particularly grape wine, consumption (one or two drinks a day) protects the heart. The benefits are strongest in people at high risk for heart disease and may be fairly small in those at low risk. Light to moderate alcohol intake may even reduce the risk of sudden cardiac death. Large doses of alcohol, however, can trigger irregular heartbeats and raise blood pressure even in people with no history of heart disease. A major study found that those who consumed more than three alcoholic drinks a day had higher blood pressure than teetotalers. The more alcohol someone drank, the greater the increase in blood pressure, with binge drinkers (people who have nine or more drinks once or twice a week) being at greatest risk. One study found that binge drinkers had a risk for a cardiac emergency that was two and a half times that of nondrinkers. Alcohol abuse has also been associated with and may actually be one cause of idiopathic dilated cardiomyopathy, a condition in which the heart enlarges and its muscles weaken, putting the patient at risk for heart failure. Alcohol may also increase the risk for hemorrhagic stroke (caused by bleeding in the brain), although, as with heart disease, it may protect against stroke caused by narrowed arteries.

Cancer. Alcohol may not cause cancer, but it probably does increase the carcinogenic effects of other substances, such as cigarette smoke. One study indicated that alcohol, in combination with tobacco smoke, causes genetic damage that is associated with the development of cancer in the upper airways, the esophagus, and liver; abstaining from alcohol appeared to reverse this damage. Moderate use of alcohol has been associated with a higher risk for breast cancer because of increased estrogen levels or possibly because the liver overproduces certain carcinogenic growth factors in response to alcohol.

Pneumonia and Other Infections. Acute alcoholism is strongly associated with very serious pneumonia. One study on laboratory animals suggests that alcohol specifically damages the bacteria-fighting capability of lung cells. Chronic alcoholism also causes changes in the immune system, although in people without any existing medical problems these changes do not appear to be significant.

Skin, Muscle, and Bone Disorders. Severe alcoholism is associated with osteoporosis (loss of bone density), muscular deterioration, skin sores, and itching. Alcohol-dependent women seem to face a higher risk than men for damage to muscles, including muscles of the heart, from the toxic effects of alcohol.

Hormonal Effects. Alcoholism increases levels of the female hormone estrogen and reduces levels of the male hormone testosterone, factors that contribute to impotence in men.

Pregnancy and Infant Development. Even moderate amounts of alcohol may have damaging effects on the developing fetus, including low birth weight and an increased risk for miscarriage. High amounts can cause fetal alcohol syndrome, which can result in mental and growth retardation. One study indicates a significantly higher risk for leukemia in infants of women who drink any type of alcohol during pregnancy.

Diabetes. Moderate alcohol consumption may help protect the hearts of adults with older-onset, also called type 2, diabetes. It should be noted, however, that alcohol can cause hypoglycemia, a drop in blood sugar, which is especially dangerous for people with diabetes who are taking insulin. Intoxicated diabetics may not be able to recognize symptoms of hypoglycemia, a particularly hazardous condition.

Malnutrition and Wernicke-Korsakoff Syndrome. A pint of whiskey provides about half the daily calories needed by an adult, but it has no nutritional value. In addition to replacing food, alcohol may also interfere with absorption of proteins, vitamins, and other nutrients. Of particular concern in alcoholism is a severe deficiency in the B-vitamin thiamine, which can cause a serious condition called Wernicke-Korsakoff syndrome. Symptoms of this syndrome include severe loss of balance, confusion, and memory loss. Eventually, it can result in permanent brain damage and death. Another serious nutritional problem among alcoholics is deficiency of the B vitamin folic acid, which can cause severe anemia.

Acute Respiratory Distress Syndrome. One study indicated that intensive care patients with a history of alcohol abuse have a significantly higher risk for developing acute respiratory distress syndrome (ARDS) during hospitalization. ARDS is a form of lung failure that can be fatal. It can by caused by many of the medical conditions common in chronic alcoholism, including severe infection, trauma, blood transfusions, pneumonia, and other serious lung conditions.

Drug Interactions. The effects of many medications are strengthened by alcohol, while others are inhibited. Of particular importance is its reinforcing effect on antianxiety drugs, sedatives, antidepressants, and antipsychotic medications. Alcohol also interacts with many drugs used by diabetics. It interferes with drugs that prevent seizures or blood clotting. It increases the risk for gastrointestinal bleeding in people taking aspirin or other nonsteroidal inflammatory drugs including ibuprofen and naproxen. In other words, taking almost any medication should preclude drinking alcohol.

How Is Alcoholism Diagnosed?

Even when people with alcoholism experience withdrawal symptoms, they nearly always deny the problem, leaving it up to coworkers, friends, or relatives to recognize the symptoms and to take the first steps toward treatment.

Family members cannot always rely on a physician to make an initial diagnosis. Although 15% to 30% of people who are hospitalized suffer from alcoholism or alcohol dependence, physicians often fail to screen for the problem. In addition, doctors themselves often cannot recognize the symptoms. In one study, alcohol problems were detected by the physician in less than half of patients who had them. It is particularly difficult to diagnose alcoholism in the elderly, where symptoms of confusion, memory loss, or falling may be attributed to the aging process alone. Heavy drinkers may be more likely to complain to their doctors about so-called somatization symptoms, which are vague ailments such as joint pain, intestinal problems, or general weakness, that have no identifiable physical cause. Such complaints should signal the physician to follow-up with screening tests for alcoholism. Alcoholism is particularly less likely to be recognized in elderly women. In fact, only 1% of older women who need treatment for alcoholism are diagnosed accurately and treated appropriately. Instead, they are often diagnosed with depression and may even be prescribed anti-anxiety drugs or antidepressants that can have dangerous interactions with alcohol. Even when physicians identify an alcohol problem, however, they are frequently reluctant to confront the patient with a diagnosis that might lead to treatment for addiction.

Screening for Alcoholism

A physician who suspects alcohol abuse should ask the patient questions about current and past drinking habits to distinguish moderate from heavy drinking. If alcohol abuse or dependency is indicated, the physician will usually perform a screening test. Many are available for diagnosing alcoholism, usually either standardized questionnaires that the patient can take on their own or that are conducted by the physician. Because people with alcoholism often deny their problem or otherwise attempt to hide it, the tests are designed to elicit answers related to problems associated with drinking rather than the amount of liquor consumed or other specific drinking habits. The quickest test takes only one minute; it is called the CAGE test, an acronym for the following questions: (C) attempts to Cut down on drinking; (A) Annoyance with criticisms about drinking; (G) Guilt about drinking; and (E) use of alcohol as an eye-opener in the morning. This test and another called the Self-Administered Alcoholism Screening Test (SAAST), appear to be most useful in detecting alcoholism in white middle-aged males. They are not very accurate for identifying alcohol abuse in older people, white women, and African- and Mexican-Americans. A more effective test for such individuals may be the Alcohol Use Disorders Identification Test (AUDIT), which asks three questions about amount and frequency of drinking, three questions about alcohol dependence, and four questions about problems related to alcohol consumption. AUDIT is an important component in screening for alcoholism in anyone, because it is the only test specifically designed to identify hazardous or harmful drinking. Other short screening tests are the Michigan Alcoholism Screening Test (MAST) and The Alcohol Dependence Scale (ADS).

Laboratory and Other Tests

Tests for alcohol levels in the blood are not useful for diagnosing alcoholism because they reflect consumption at only one point in time and not long-term usage. A mean corpuscular volume (MCV) blood test is sometimes used to measure the size of red blood cells, which increase with alcohol use over time. A test for a factor known as carbohydrate-deficient transferrin may prove to be fairly accurate indicator of heavy drinking. A physical examination and other tests should be performed to uncover any related medical problems. Sometimes the results of tests that detect other problems, such as blood tests reporting liver damage or low testosterone levels in men, can persuade alcoholics to seek help.

What Are the General Guidelines for Treating Alcoholism?

Getting the Patient to Seek Treatment

Once a diagnosis of alcoholism is made, the next major step is getting the patient to seek treatment. One study reported that the main reasons alcoholics do not seek treatment are lack of confidence in successful therapies, denial of their own alcoholism, and the social stigma attached to the condition and its treatment. The best approaches for motivating a patient to seek treatment are group meetings between people with alcoholism and their friends and family members who have been affected by the alcoholic behavior. Using this interventional approach, each person affected offers a compassionate but direct and honest report describing specifically how he or she has been specifically hurt by their loved one's or friend's alcoholism. Children may even be involved in this process, depending on their level of maturity and ability to handle the situation. The family and friends should express their affection for the patient and their intentions for supporting the patient through recovery, but they must strongly and consistently demand that the patient seek treatment. Employers can be particularly effective. Their approach should also be compassionate but strong, threatening the employee with loss of employment if he or she does not seek help. Some large companies provide access to inexpensive or free treatment programs for their workers.

The alcoholic patient and everyone involved should fully understand that alcoholism is a disease and that the responses to this disease, need, craving, and fear of withdrawal, are not character flaws but symptoms, just as pain or discomfort are symptoms of other illnesses. They should also realize that treatment is difficult and sometimes painful, just as treatments for other life-threatening diseases, such as cancer, are, but that it is the only hope for a cure.

Treatment Options

A number of treatment options now exist for alcoholism, including psychotherapy, medications that target brain chemicals involved in addiction, and social support groups such as Alcoholics Anonymous. Studies are suggesting the cognitive therapies and medications, such as naltrexone, may be very effective for some people. Even brief intervention by a family doctor can be helpful for reducing alcohol intake in many heavy drinkers.

People with mild to moderate withdrawal symptoms are usually treated as outpatients and assigned to support groups, counseling, or both. Inpatient treatment can be performed in a general or psychiatric hospital or in a center dedicated to treatment of alcohol and other substance abuse. It is recommended for patients with a coexisting medical or psychiatric disorder and those who may harm themselves or others, who have not responded to conservative treatments, or who have a disruptive home environment. A typical inpatient regimen may include a physical and psychiatric work-up, detoxification, treatment with medications and psychotherapy or cognitive-behavioral therapy, and an introduction to Alcoholics Anonymous. Because of the high cost of inpatient care, its advantages over outpatient care are being questioned. One study compared employed alcoholics who were either hospitalized, treated as outpatients with compulsory attendance at AA meetings, or allowed to choose their own treatment option, including none at all. After two years, everyone experienced fewer job problems, but those in the inpatient group had significantly fewer rehospitalizations and remained abstinent longer than people in the other two groups. Another study analyzing drug and alcohol treatment programs found that 75% of inpatients completed therapy compared to only 18% of outpatients. Other studies, however, have shown no difference in results between inpatient and outpatient programs. Given the current economic climate, it seems unlikely that most care providers will choose inpatient treatment for alcoholics who are not a threat to others or themselves if there are alternatives.

Treatment for the Medically or Mentally Ill Alcoholic. Severe alcoholism is often complicated by the presence of serious medical or mental illnesses. A program called integrated outpatient treatment (IOT) has been designed specifically for medically ill alcoholics. The patient visits a clinic once a month for both intensive alcohol treatment and a physical check-up, which includes tracking factors, such as liver function, that are affected by drinking. Patients are motivated through discussions of benefits and costs of drinking and by reporting any barriers to changing their habits and learning strategies to overcome them. One study showed that IOT significantly increased abstinence and the number of treatment visits. IOT may even improve survival rates. Interestingly, however, drinking also significantly decreased in a comparison group of patients who were treated only for their medical conditions.

Treatment for patients with both alcoholism and mental illness is particularly difficult. The greater the psychiatric distress a person is experiencing, the more he or she is tempted to drink, particularly in negative situations. Antidepressants or anti-anxiety medications in addition to support services may help people with depression and anxiety. People with alcoholism and more severe problems, such as schizophrenia or severe bipolar disorder probably need more intense help. AA groups are underused by patients with a double-diagnosis of mental illness and alcoholism because the focus of the organization is on addiction not psychiatric problems. Some AA members have even been known to discourage patients with dual disorders to go off their medications. In one survey 54% of AA members felt that such patients would do better in groups designed especially for dual disorders. Unfortunately, no such programs are available.

Treatment Goals

The ideal goals of long-term treatment by many physicians and organizations such as AA are total abstinence and replacement of the addictive patterns with satisfying, time-filling behaviors that can fill the void in daily activity that occurs when drinking has ceased. Because abstinence is so difficult to attain, many professionals choose to treat alcoholism as a chronic disease; that is, they expect and accept relapse but they aim for as long a remission period as possible. Even reducing alcohol intake can lower the risk for alcohol-related medical problems. Studies suggest, however, that patients who secure total abstinence have better survival rates, mental health, and marriages and they are more responsible parents and employees than those who continue to drink or relapse. There is also no way to determine which people can stop after one drink and which ones cannot. Alcoholics Anonymous and other alcoholic treatment groups whose goal is strict abstinence are greatly worried by the publicity surrounding these studies, since many people with alcoholism are eager for an excuse to start drinking again. At this time, seeking total abstinence is the only safe route.

What Is the Treatment for Alcohol Withdrawal?

Symptoms of Withdrawal

When a person with alcoholism stops drinking, withdrawal symptoms begin within six to 48 hours and peak about 24 to 35 hours after the last drink. During this period the inhibition of brain activity caused by alcohol is abruptly reversed. Stress hormones are over-produced and the central nervous system becomes over-excited. Seizures occur in about 10% of adults during withdrawal, and in about 60% of these patients, the seizures are multiple. The time between the first and last seizure is usually six hours or less. About 5% of alcoholic patients experience delirium tremens, which usually develops two to four days after the last drink. Symptoms include fever, rapid heart beat, either high or low blood pressure, extremely aggressive behavior, hallucinations, and other mental disturbances. Although it is not clear if older people with alcoholism are at higher risk for more severe symptoms than younger patients, several studies have indicated that they may suffer more complications during withdrawal, including delirium, falls, and a decreased ability to perform normal activities.

Initial Assessment

Upon entering a hospital because of alcohol withdrawal, patients should be given a physical examination for any injuries or medical conditions and should be treated for any potentially serious problems, such as high blood pressure or irregular heartbeat. The immediate goal of treatment is to calm the patient as quickly as possible. Patients are usually given one of the anti-anxiety drugs known as benzodiazepines, which relieve withdrawal symptoms and help prevent progression to delirium tremens. An injection of the B vitamin, thiamine, may be given to prevent Wernicke-Korsakoff syndrome. Patients should be observed for at least two hours to determine the severity of withdrawal symptoms. Physicians may use assessment tests, such as the Clinical Institute Withdrawal Assessment Scale (CIWA), to help determine treatment and whether the symptoms will progress in severity.

Treatment for Withdrawal Symptoms

About 95% of people have mild to moderate withdrawal symptoms, including agitation, trembling, disturbed sleep, and lack of appetite. In 15% to 20% of people with moderate symptoms, brief seizures and hallucinations may occur, but they do not progress to full-blown delirium tremens. Such patients can nearly always be treated as outpatients. After being examined and observed, the patient is usually sent home with a four-day supply of anti-anxiety medication, scheduled for follow-up and rehabilitation, and advised to return to the emergency room if withdrawal symptoms become severe. If possible, a family member or friend should support the patient through the next few days of withdrawal.

Benzodiazepines. Benzodiazepines are anti-anxiety drugs that inhibit nerve-cell excitability in the brain and help reduce the risk for seizures. They also relieve withdrawal symptoms, and make it easier for patients to remain in treatment. They include diazepam (Valium), lorazepam (Ativan), midazolam (Versed), and oxazepam (Serax). These drugs vary in how long they are effective. Diazepam has a longer duration of action than lorazepam or midazolam, for example. Typically, the physician may give the patient an initial, or loading, intravenous dose of diazepam with additional doses given every one to two hours thereafter over the period of withdrawal. This regimen can cause very heavy sedation. Lorazepam and oxazepam are easier for the liver to metabolize than other benzodiazepines and often prove useful for treating alcoholic patients. Some physicians question the use of any anti-anxiety medication for mild withdrawal symptoms. Others believe that repeated withdrawal episodes, even mild forms, that are inadequately treated may result in increasingly severe and frequent seizures with possible brain damage. Benzodiazepines may be administered intravenously or orally, depending on the severity of symptoms. One study reported that when a single, intravenous dose, lorazepam, was given within several hours of a first alcohol-related seizure, it reduced the risk for subsequent ones.

Benzodiazepines are usually not prescribed for more than two weeks or administered for more than three nights per week. Tolerance to these drugs may develop after as little as four weeks of daily use. Physical dependence may develop after just three months of normal dosage. People who discontinue benzodiazepines after taking them for long periods may experience rebound symptoms, sleep disturbance and anxiety, which can develop within hours or days after stopping the medication. Some patients experience withdrawal symptoms from the drugs, including stomach distress, sweating, and insomnia, that can last from one to three weeks. Common side effects are day-time drowsiness and a hung-over feeling. Respiratory problems may be exacerbated. Benzodiazepines are potentially dangerous when used in combination with alcohol. They should not be used by pregnant women or nursing mothers unless absolutely necessary.

Other Drugs for Mild to Moderate Withdrawal. Beta-blockers, such as propranolol (Inderal) and atenolol (Tenormin), may sometimes be used in combination with a benzodiazepine. This class of drugs is effective in slowing heart rate and reducing tremor. Other drugs being tested are clonidine (Catapres) and carbamazepine (Tegretol). When used by themselves, they do not, however, appear to be effective in reducing seizures or delirium. Chlormethiazole, a derivative of vitamin B_1, is presently used in Europe and is showing promise in reducing agitation and seizures.

Treatment for Delirium Tremens, Seizures, and Other Severe Symptoms

People with symptoms of delirium tremens must be treated immediately. Untreated delirium tremens has a fatality rate that can be as high as 20%. Symptomatic patients are usually given intravenous anti-anxiety medications. It is extremely important that fluids be administered. Restraints may be necessary to prevent injury to themselves or others.

Seizures are usually self-limited and treated with a benzodiazepine. Intravenous phenytoin (Dilantin) along with a benzodiazepine may be used in patients who have a history of seizures, who have epilepsy, or in those whose seizures cannot be controlled. Because phenytoin may lower blood pressure, the patient's heart should be monitored during treatment. For hallucinations or extremely aggressive behavior, antipsychotic drugs, particularly haloperidol (Haldol), may be administered. Lidocaine (Xylocaine) may be given to people with disturbed heart rhythms.

What Are the Long-Term Treatments for Alcoholism to Prevent Relapse?

Psychotherapy and Cognitive-Behavioral Therapy

The two usual forms of therapy for alcoholics are cognitive-behavioral and interactional group psychotherapy based on the Alcoholics Anonymous 12-step program. In one study, all treatment approaches were, on average, equally effective as long as the individual program was competently administered. Those with fewer psychiatric problems, however, did best with the AA approach. This confirms an earlier study in which researchers categorized alcoholics as either Type A or Type B. Type A individuals became alcoholic at a later age, had less severe symptoms or fewer psychiatric problems, and had a better outlook on life than those with Type B. The people in the Type A group did well with the 12-step approach. They did not do as well with cognitive-behavioral therapy. Type B people became alcoholic at an early age, had a high family risk for alcoholism, more severe symptoms, and a negative outlook on life. This group did poorly with interactional group therapy but tended to do better with cognitive-behavioral therapy. This difference in response to the two forms of treatments held up after two years.

Interactional Group Psychotherapy (12-Step Program). Alcoholics Anonymous (AA), founded in 1935, is an excellent example of interactional group psychotherapy and remains the most well-known program for helping people with alcoholism. It offers a very strong support network using group meetings open seven days a week in locations all over the world. A buddy system, group understanding of alcoholism, and forgiveness for relapses are AA's standard methods for building self-worth and alleviating feelings of isolation. AA's 12-step approach to recovery includes a spiritual component that might deter people who lack religious convictions. Prayer and meditation, however, have been known to be of great value in the healing process of many diseases, even in people with no particular religious assignation. AA emphasizes that the "higher power" component of its program need not refer to any specific belief system. Associated membership programs, Al-Anon and Alateen, offer help for family members and friends.

Cognitive-Behavioral Therapy. Cognitive-behavioral therapy uses a structured teaching approach and may be better than AA for severe alcoholism. People with alcoholism are given instruction and homework assignments intended to improve their ability to cope with basic living situations, control their behavior, and change the way they think about drinking. For example, patients might write a history of their drinking experiences and describe what they consider to be risky situations. They are then assigned activities to help them cope when exposed to "cues," places or circumstances that trigger their desire to drink. Patients may also be given tasks that are designed to replace drinking. An interesting and successful example of such a program was one that enlisted patients in a softball team; this gave them the opportunity to practice coping skills, develop supportive relationships, and engage in healthy alternative activities. In one study of patients with both depression and alcoholism, this therapeutic approach achieved 47% abstinence rates after six months compared to only 13% abstinence in patients who received standard treatments and relaxation techniques. It appears to be especially effective when used in combination with opioid antagonists, such as naltrexone.

Medications to Aid in Abstinence

Opioid Antagonists. Opioid antagonists are drugs that reduce the intoxicating effects of alcohol and the urge to drink. One of these agents, naltrexone (ReVia), has been found to be very effective for people with low- to moderate alcohol dependency when used with cognitive behavioral therapy. In one 1999 study, for example, 62% of patients taking naltrexone and undergoing such therapy did not relapse into heavy drinking compared with 40% of patients taking a placebo (a "dummy" pill). It does not appear to improve abstinent rates, however. Taking the drug consistently as prescribed by the doctor is very important for its success. The most common side effect of naltrexone is nausea, which is usually mild and temporary. High doses cause liver damage.

The drug should not be administered to anyone who has used narcotics within a week to 10 days. An oral form of nalmefene, an opioid antagonist currently available only by injection, is also proving to be effective in preventing relapse in heavy drinkers. Nalmefene blocks more opioid receptors than naltrexone does and may have less of an adverse effect on the liver.

Aversion Medications. Some drugs have properties that interact with alcohol to produce distressing side effects. Disulfiram (Antabuse) causes flushing, headache, nausea, and vomiting if a person drinks alcohol while taking the drug. The symptoms can be triggered after drinking half a glass of wine or half a shot of liquor and last from half an hour to two hours, depending on dosage of the drug and the amount of alcohol consumed. One dose of disulfiram is usually effective for one to two weeks. Overdose can be dangerous, causing low blood pressure, chest pain, shortness of breath, and even death. Studies have not shown the use of disulfiram to have any effect on staying abstinent, although it does reduce the frequency of drinking. One study indicated that the drug may be more effective in patients with spouses or other family members or caregivers, including AA "buddies," who are close by and vigilant to ensure that they take it. (Such support, however, probably improves the effectiveness of any treatment.) Another aversion drug, calcium carbimide, was withdrawn from the market.

Acamprosate. Acamprosate (Campral) calms the brain and reduces cravings by inhibiting the transmission of the neurotransmitter gamma aminobutyric acid (GABA). Studies in Europe indicate that it reduces the frequency of drinking. Although it is not clear whether it can improve abstinence, one study reported that 60% of patients remained abstinent for 12 weeks, and in another 43% were still abstinent after nearly a year. The drug may cause occasional diarrhea and headache. It also can impair certain memory functions but does not alter short-term working memory or mood. People with kidney problems should use it cautiously. Combination therapy with naltrexone or disulfiram may be possible.

Antidepressant and Anti-Anxiety Drugs. Depression is common among alcohol-dependent people and can lead to a higher relapse rate. Antidepressants may be helpful, particularly for patients who suffer from both depression and alcoholism. Because of their effect on serotonin, the antidepressants selective serotonin reuptake inhibitors (SSRIs) were of particular interest. They include fluoxetine (Prozac), sertraline (Zoloft), paroxetine (Paxil), citalopram (Celexa), and fluvoxamine (Luvox). Studies indicate they may be useful for reducing alcohol intake in heavy drinkers even if they are not depressed, although these drugs appear to have no significant affect on alcoholism itself. Another small study reported that people given the tricyclic antidepressant desipramine (Norpramin, Pertofrane), whether or not they exhibited other symptoms of depression, had fewer drinking days and a longer period between relapses than those not taking the drug. A unique anti-anxiety drug, buspirone (BuSpar), may also be beneficial for alcoholics, particularly if they also suffer from anxiety. The drug has few side effects and a low potential for abuse. It not only reduces anxiety, but also appears to have modest effects on alcohol cravings. In one study, alcoholics who took it had a slow return to alcohol consumption and fewer drinking days than those not on the drug. Another study, however, found no significant effect on alcoholism.

Other Drugs. Under investigation are drugs that affect dopamine, the neurotransmitter (chemical messenger in the brain) that produces a sense of reward after drinking. Among these, tiapride, which blocks dopamine, is showing some modest benefits in small European studies. In one small study, isradipine, a calcium channel blocker, reduced cravings more effectively than naltrexone and the antidepressant paroxetine (Paxil). Calcium channel blockers are ordinarily used to treat high blood pressure and other medical conditions. Another drug being investigated for withdrawal and abstinence is gamma-hydroxybutyric acid (GHB). In one small study, 58% of subjects remained abstinent during a six-month period. It should be noted that GHB is sold illegally as a street drug because of its euphoric effects at high doses, which can have serious side effects, including seizures, coma, and respiratory arrest.

Where Can Help Be Obtained for Alcoholism?

Al-Anon Family Group Headquarters, Inc.
1600 Corporate Landing Parkway
Virginia Beach, VA 23454-5617
Toll Free: (888) 4AL-ANON (for meeting information, M-F, 8a-6p ET; except holidays)
Fax: (757) 563-1655
Web site: http://www.Al-Anon-Alateen.org
E-mail: wso@al-anon.org

Alcoholics Anonymous
P.O. Box 459
Grand Central Station
New York, NY 10163
Phone (212) 870–3400
Web site: www.alcoholics-anonymous.org

Hazelden Foundation
P.O. Box 11
Center City, MN 55012-0011
Toll Free (800) 257-7800; or 1-651-257-4010 outside the U.S.
E-mail: info@hazelden.org
Web site: http://www.hazelden.org

National Clearinghouse for Alcohol and Drug Information (NCADI)
P.O. Box 2345
Rockville, MD 20847-2345
Toll Free: (800) 729-6686
Toll Free: (800) 487-4889 (TDD)
Fax: (301) 468-6433
E-Mail: info@health.org
Web site: www.health.org

National Council on Alcoholism and Drug Dependence, Inc.
12 West 21 Street, Seventh Floor
New York, New York 10010
Toll Free: (800) NCA-CALL (800-622-2255) (24-hour affiliate referral)
Phone: (212) 206-6770
Fax: (212) 645-1690
E-mail: national@ncadd.org
Web site: http://www.ncadd.org

National Institute on Alcohol Abuse and Alcoholism (NIAAA)
National Institutes of Health
Willco Building
6000 Executive Boulevard
Bethesda, MD 20892-7003
Phone: (301) 443-0786
Web site: www.niaaa.nih.gov

National Organization on Fetal Alcohol Syndrome
418 'C' Street North East
Washington, DC 20002
Phone: (202)785-4585
Fax: (202) 466-6456
E-mail: nofas@erols.com
Web site: http://www.nofas.org

Recovery
P.O. Box 1412
Herndon, VA 20172-1412
Web site: http://www.recovery.org/aa

Web of Addictions
Web site: http://www.well.com/user/woa

NOTE: Additional resources are listed in the end section of this book.

Chapter 8

Alcohol Dependence: Possible Causes

Definition of Alcohol Dependence

When does someone cross that boundary between recreational alcohol use and dependence? Three main symptom clusters have been used to help draw this distinction.

Loss of Control. Some people have defined addiction by focusing on the degree of control over alcohol. In the past, addiction experts called this psychological dependence. For example, a business executive may plan to have 1 or 2 beers after work, but he ends up having 5 or 6. Loss of control also becomes evident when a person makes repeated, but unsuccessful, attempts to cut down or stop drug use. Finally, loss of control is marked by compulsive thoughts and actions. Much of the day is spent either thinking about getting high again or recovering from a previous high.

Maladaptive Consequence. A second measure of alcohol dependence is the presence of negative psychological, social, and medical consequences. Alcohol dependence is the leading cause of missed days at work. Alcohol dependence is also associated with severe medical

---

Excerpted from "Alcohol Dependence: Diagnosis, Clinical Aspects, and Biopsychosocial Causes," by Joseph R. Volpicelli, M.D., Ph.D., from the Internet Alcohol Recovery Center (www.med.upenn.edu/recovery), © 1999 University of Pennsylvania Health System; reprinted with permission. The full text of this document is available on the internet at www.med.upenn.edu/recovery/pros/dependence.html.

problems which we will discuss in more detail below. People who continue to use alcohol despite adverse effects on their health, occupational or social functioning show symptoms of alcohol dependence.

Biological Adaptation. Finally, some substance abuse experts define dependence solely with physiological adaptation to alcohol. In the past this has been referred to as physical dependence. Physical dependence is shown by either tolerance or withdrawal. Tolerance is defined as a decrease in the response to alcohol as use continues over time. Thus, it takes a progressively larger amounts of alcohol to produce the same effect. Chronic alcohol users may also experience withdrawal symptoms such as rapid heart rates or excessive sweating when they stop or decrease alcohol drinking. People who show either physical tolerance or symptoms of withdrawal are said to be physically adapted to the drug.

Causes of Alcohol Dependence

Psychosocial Theories

All the psychological theories of drug dependence assume that alcohol satisfies some important need. Psychoanalytic theories focus on unconscious needs while behavioral theories focus on the role of tension reduction to account for alcohol abuse.

Psychoanalytic. One early psychoanalytic theory suggested that children who are fixated at the oral stage are more prone to abuse alcohol later in life. Psychoanalysts theorize that oral fixation results when children are either frustrated in their oral dependent needs (unloving mother) or too easily satisfied by oral stimulation (overprotective mother). When stressed as adults, oral-dependent people are more likely to turn to alcohol to cope.

Adams (1978) suggests that it is not deprived infants who develop oral traits but rather children (particularly boys) with overprotective mothers. Later in life such men will have a strong need to remain dependent on either their mother or another woman. When their needs become frustrated, they become angry. Unable to deal with anger assertively, these people find that alcohol provides an effective way to reduce aggressive impulses. It has the additional advantage of hurting those people around them.

Psychoanalytic theories make some intuitive sense since many alcoholics have immature social skills. They often turn to alcohol to help cope with life stresses. Despite this intuitive appeal, there are little prospective data to support these theories. An alcohol dependent person may exhibit dependent traits, however, these traits are just as likely to result from chronic alcohol use as they are to lead to it. Even if correlations exist between alcohol abuse and dependent personalities, it is not clear which is the cause and which is the effect. In summary, there is little evidence to support the oral fixation theory.

Tension Reduction. Another important theory for alcohol abuse is that alcohol drinking is reinforced because alcohol reduces tension. Conger (1951) proposed the Tension Reduction Hypothesis as a model for alcohol drinking. The model assumes that alcohol can reduce tension and people learn to drink alcohol to avoid or reduce unpleasant stress. Clinical observations and studies appear to support this theory.

First, alcohol dependence and anxiety symptoms often coexist. Many anxious patients say that drinking alcohol helps them reduce anxiety. This is especially true of phobic patients who often use alcohol to help face their fears. One patient could only travel over bridges after drinking five or more beers. Another patient needed to drink before attending any social function. She would have one or two drinks while getting dressed and another two or three at the social function to help her feel more relaxed.

Alcohol relapse often occurs following a negative life event such as loss of a job or death of a spouse. For example, one patient had a very severe relapse following the breakup with his girlfriend. Stress from the breakup may have increased the patient's desire to use alcohol to relieve this stress. Epidemiological studies also support the Tension Reduction Hypothesis, since alcohol drinking is associated with cultural stress. States with high rates of divorce, births, unemployment and other stressful life events also have high rates of alcohol abuse.

While clinical and epidemiological studies support the Tension Reduction Hypothesis, experimental studies fail to show that increased tension leads to increased drinking. If people drink alcohol to reduce tension, we would expect that alcohol drinking would increase during tension-arousing situations. This prediction led to many conflicting results. For example, in laboratory studies, subjects who are threatened with an electric shock or who receive feedback that they have done poorly on a test do not increase drinking.

How can we account for these conflicting results? The tension reducing properties of alcohol may be specific to certain situations. Alcohol may reduce tension only for social stress but not for other sorts of stresses. Also, alcohol may reduce tension only in particular doses (low doses but not high doses) and under certain conditions (in naturalistic but not experimental situations). In addition, alcohol may reduce tension only for some individuals who carry a gene for alcoholism. Finally, alcohol may not reduce tension but may dampen the impact of a stressful situation. The results of several studies support this hypothesis. Experienced male drinkers who are threatened with electric shock or social evaluation show less subjective and physiological signs of anxiety when intoxicated than when sober.

Recent reviews suggest yet another view of the relationship between stress and alcohol drinking. According to this analysis people do not drink alcohol to reduce tension. Rather, they drink once tension has stopped and a sense of relief has set in. This is known as the "happy hour" effect. It accounts for the frequent observation that anxiety and alcohol drinking often go together. However, it is the sudden removal of stress that sets the occasion for drinking, rather than the situation causing stress. For example, Volpicelli et al. (1990) found that rats increased their alcohol drinking following, but not during, uncontrollable stress. In another study, rats living in a fearful environment tended to drink less alcohol than rats removed from the fearful environment and placed in a safe, home cage. One study of college students showed similar results. After completing a difficult (stressful) test, half the students were told they did poorly, scoring in the lower 15th percentile of their peers. The other half were told they did well, scoring in the upper 15th percentile. The relieved subjects—who thought they did well on the test — drank more alcohol than subjects who believed they did poorly.

Biological

Genetics. Researchers have discovered that alcohol dependence runs in families. A classic study by Goodwin (1974), compared the adopted children of alcohol-dependent parents to the adopted children of non-alcohol-dependent parents. In the children of alcohol-dependent biological parents, the risk of becoming alcohol dependent increased. In contrast, if the adoptive parents were alcohol-dependent, there was no increased risk of alcoholism. In general, if one biological parent is alcoholic, the likelihood of a child becoming dependent increases nearly three times. If both parents are alcoholic, the likelihood of alcohol dependence increases about five times. However, the likelihood of alcohol dependence does not increase in children whose nonbiological parent is dependent on alcohol. This work shows that genetic factors affect the risk of alcohol dependence more than the family environment.

In an attempt to determine what specific inherited factor(s) increase their risk of alcohol abuse, researchers have conducted a series of studies comparing the biological children of alcohol dependent parents to the biological children of non-alcoholic parents. Several differences emerge between these two groups.

One source of biological vulnerability suggests that high risk subjects have some instability in their nervous system that can be counteracted by drinking alcohol. For example, sons of alcohol dependent fathers are less able to hold their body still when asked to stand at attention, compared to sons of nonalcoholic fathers. Typically, people without alcoholic fathers sway more when intoxicated. However, when sons of alcoholic fathers drink alcohol, there is less body sway. Also, patients who have an inherited disorder in which their hand shakes, familial essential tremor, are more likely to abuse alcohol. When they drink alcohol, the tremor vanishes.

Another biological mechanism that may put people at risk for alcohol dependence is increased sensitivity to the pleasure producing effects of alcohol. Alcohol dependent patients will often report that they noticed a wonderful calm high the very first time they drank alcohol. Alcohol dependent patients also show pain relief, analgesia, following a small dose of alcohol. These studies suggest that alcoholics receive more pleasure or obtain more pain relief compared to non-alcohol abusing people.

Similarly people who are not abusing alcohol, but have alcohol dependent parents, are more sensitive to the pleasure producing effects from alcohol. They report more pleasure associated with their first drink. Also, high risk people show increased alpha waves (a measure of relaxation) after a small dose of alcohol. Finally, studies show that in subjects with alcoholic parents, small doses of alcohol increase peripheral levels of beta-endorphin by 170 percent. In contrast, subjects without alcoholic parents do not have this large increase in beta-endorphin.

Chapter 9

New Findings in the Genetics of Alcoholism

This chapter reviews recent research on the importance of genetic influences on alcohol abuse and dependence. The ultimate goal of those studies was to identify genetically influenced characteristics, or phenotypes, that affect alcoholism risk. This might then facilitate the search for social and environmental influences that are more directly useful in prevention and treatment.

The contribution of genetic influences in alcoholism is supported by the 3-to 4-fold higher prevalence of this disorder in first-degree relatives of alcoholics, a rate that increases another 2-fold in identical twins of alcoholics.[1-4] Adoption-type studies reveal that the increased risk remains strong for children of alcoholics adopted and raised by nonalcoholics.[5,6]

The genetic influences appear to be, in large part, separate from a generic predisposition toward dependence on other drugs.[7-9] These influences might involve multiple genes or incomplete expression of several major genes, along with environmental influences.[10] This complexity produces many challenges in the search for specific genes that contribute to the risk.[11] One useful approach in this situation is to focus on endophenotypes, more easily measured characteristics that contribute to the risk but do not explain the entire disorder. Subsequent investigations then can use genetic linkage studies, or genome

---

"New Findings in the Genetics of Alcoholism," by Marc A. Schuckit and Thomas C. Jefferson in *JAMA, The Journal of the American Medical Association*, May 26, 1999, Vol. 281, Issue 20, p. 1875, © 1999 American Medical Association, all rights reserved; reprinted with permission.

scans, to identify more powerful, usually Mendelian, genetic traits, and/or use case-control or candidate gene studies.[11,12] The following sections describe some of these methods as they have been applied to alcoholism.

Alcohol Metabolizing Enzymes

Alcohol is first broken down primarily by alcohol dehydrogenase (ADH), an enzyme for which two genetically controlled variants (ADH2, ADH3) produce a faster rate of metabolism.[13-15] The ADH actions create acetaldehyde which, at higher blood levels, causes an increased heart rate, skin flushing, and possible nausea and vomiting.

Acetaldehyde blood levels are usually low because this substance is rapidly destroyed by a form of the enzyme, aldehyde hydrogenase (ALDH2). However, a genetically controlled variation of ALDH2 called ALDH2-2 is biologically inactive, with the result that the 10% of Asians who carry 2 genes of this form (i.e., homozygotes) have an intense adverse reaction to even low doses of alcohol, and subsequently carry no risk for alcohol dependence. The 40% of Asian men and women who are heterozygotes have a more intense reaction to alcohol than persons with all active ALDH2-1, a finding that is associated with a lower risk for alcoholism in heterozygotes. Less than 10% of alcoholics in Japan are heterozygotes compared with 40% of the Japanese population.[15] Among Asian men and women, and possibly among several other ethnic groups including Jewish people, a lower alcoholism risk is also associated with ADH2 or ADH3 isoenzymes, although the impact of these ADH genotypes is not as strong as that for ALDH.[16]

The Level of Response to Alcohol

The intensity of response to most drugs has genetic components. Many alcoholics report an ability to consume large amounts of alcohol with relatively little effect from early in their drinking careers. Thus, the relationship between the level of response (LR) to alcohol and alcoholism risk has been studied.[7,10] Identical twins are more similar on LR than are fraternal twin pairs, and LR is genetically influenced in animals. A lower LR (or a need for higher levels of alcohol to produce an effect) is associated with higher levels of alcohol intake in some murine lines.

These data led to comparisons of children of alcoholics with controls on the effects of alcohol on the intensity of changes in subjective feelings, brain wave measures, standing steadiness, and several biological markers. Relatively low intensities of reaction to alcohol have been found in about 40% of the children of alcoholics compared with less than 10% of controls. Follow-up studies revealed that a low LR at age 20 years predicted alcoholism by age 35 years, thus explaining the majority of the relationship between family history and alcohol abuse and dependence.[3,10] Thus, a low LR to alcohol might he one genetically influenced phenotype that contributes to 40% to 60% of the variance of the alcoholism risk related to genetic factors.

While no specific gene has yet been identified as responsible for this relatively low intensity of response to alcohol, both genome scan (classical linkage) and candidate gene studies are under way. For example, in a pilot study, 17 men with low LR scores at age 20 years were compared with 24 demographically similar men who had much higher LRs.[17] As part of a larger study, these 41 individuals had also been followed up at about age 35 years to determine their rates of alcoholism. The high LR and low LR groups were then evaluated for the patterns of five candidate genes relating to serotonin and gamma-aminobutyric acid functioning. The results indicated that the LL allele of the serotonin transporter gene and the gamma-aminobutyric $\text{acid}_{\text{alpha-6}}$ receptor gene were associated, in an additive fashion, with both a low LR at age 20 years and a higher risk for alcoholism by age 35 years. These results are offered as examples of how the candidate gene approach can be used, but the real importance of these two markers, if any, will await replication. Other potential candidate genes possibly related to both a low LR and a higher alcohol intake include neuropeptide Y, additional serotonin receptors, and cellular second messenger systems.

Additional Phenotypes of Interest

Several genetically influenced brain wave characteristics have been observed in alcohol-dependent people and in their children at higher rates than expected from chance alone.[18,19] One is a low-amplitude, positive-polarity wave observed approximately 300 milliseconds after a rare, but anticipated, stimulus as part of an event-related potential (a P300 wave). Recent linkage studies have identified hot spots for P300 on both chromosomes 2 and 6. These findings might lead to testing specific candidate genes, using P3 amplitude as an endophenotype related to the risk of alcoholism. A second set of genetically influenced brain wave markers possibly associated with the risk of alcoholism relate to prominent alpha and beta bands of the background cortical encephalogram result.[19]

Studies have also evaluated the potential importance of the brain's dopamine neurochemical system in the risk for substance use disorders, including alcoholism.[20] A 1990 report noted a relationship between the gene controlling the D_2 dopamine receptor gene (DRD2) and alcoholism, although the majority of attempts at replication have been negative. Additional data point toward the potential importance of a gene related to the DRD4 receptor gene. Regarding other receptors, while a study of polymorphism related to the micro-opioid receptor gene was negative, the possible impact that opioid antagonist drugs have in alcohol treatment and the relationship between alcohol and opioid intake in some animals highlights the need for further evaluations.[21] Similar conclusions can be drawn regarding the potential importance of genes influencing some cellular mechanisms of the effects of alcohol, including those related to adenelyl cyclase and associated systems.

Implications for Treatment

A number of combined genetic factors appear to explain approximately half of the alcoholism risk, and the search for genes that have an effect on (not definitively cause) risk has important implications. The range of potential causes seen in genetic studies implies that there might not be a single definitive treatment that will work for everyone. Prevention and treatment will probably require a variety of interventions. Regarding prevention, the genetic data reinforce the wisdom of teaching children of alcoholics that they carry a heightened vulnerability toward a serious disorder, which can be avoided by abstinence or diminished by adhering to limited levels of alcohol intake.

The identification of specific genes associated with phenotypes that affect the risk of alcoholism can facilitate prospective studies of predisposed individuals who were resilient and did not express the disorder. For example, there are preliminary indications that people with a low LR are more likely to develop alcohol dependence in the presence of personality characteristics of enhanced susceptibility to boredom and more impulsive behaviors.[10] If corroborated, once genes related to LR are identified young people with the genotype might benefit from interventions that help them to deal with boredom and diminish their impulsive behavior.

The potential impact of our burgeoning knowledge of genetic influences in alcoholism also extends to possible treatments. For example, some alcoholics might carry a predisposition through the dopamine system, while the risk for others might be related to opioid receptors. Specific treatments more relevant to some alcohol dependent individuals than to others might he developed and tested.

Funding and Support

This work was supported by the Veterans Affairs Research Service and National Institute on Alcohol Abuse and Alcoholism grants AA05526 and 5U10AA08403.

References

1. Prescott CA, Kendler KS. Genetic and environmental contributions to alcohol abuse and dependence in a population-based sample of male twins. *Am J Psychiatry*. 1999;156:34-40.

2. Pickens RW, Svikis DS, McGue M, Lykken DT, Heston LL, Clayton PJ. Heterogeneity in the inheritance of alcoholism. *Arch Gen Psychiatry*. 1991;48:19-28.

3. Heath AC, Bucholz KK, Madden PAF, et al. Genetic and environmental contributions to alcohol dependence risk in a national twin sample. *Psychol Med*. 1997;27:1381-1396.

4. Kendler KS, Prescott CA, Neale MC, Pedersen NL. Temperance board registration for alcohol abuse in a national sample of Swedish male twins born 1902-1949. *Arch Gen Psychiatry*. 1997;54:178-184.

5. Goodwin DW, Schulsinger R, Hermansen L, Guze SB, Winokur G. Alcohol problems in adoptees raised apart from alcoholic biological parents. *Arch Gen Psychiatry*. 1973;28:238-255.

6. Schuckit MA, Goodwin DW, Winokur G. A study of alcoholism in half-siblings. *Am J Psychiatry*. 1972;128:1132-1136.

7. Schuckit MA, Smith TL. An 8-year follow-up of 450 sons of alcoholic and control subjects. *Arch Gen Psychiatry*. 1996;53:202-210.

8. Bierut LJ, Dinwiddie SH, Begleiter H, et al. Familial transmission of substance dependence. *Arch Gen Psychiatry*. 1998;55:982-988.

9. Tsuang MT, Lyons MJ, Meyer JM, et al. Co-occurrence of abuse of different drugs in men. *Arch Gen Psychiatry*. 1998;55:967-972.

10. Schuckit MA. Biological, psychological, and environmental predictors of the alcoholism risk: a longitudinal study. *J Stud Alcohol*. 1998;59:485-494.

11. Baumeister M. Complex genetics and implications for psychiatry. *Biol Psychiatry*. 1999;45:522-532.

12. Malhotra AK, Goldman D. Benefits and pitfalls encountered in psychiatric genetic association studies. *Biol Psychiatry*. 1999:45:544-550.

13. Wall TL, Ehlers CL. Genetic influences affecting alcohol use among Asians. *Alcohol Health Res World*. 1995;19:184-189.

14. Chao HM. Alcohol and the mystique of flushing. *Alcohol Clin Exp Res*. 1995;19:104-109.

15. Murayama M, Matsushita S, Muramatsu T, Higuchi S. Clinical characteristics and disease course of alcoholics with inactive aldehyde dehydrogenase-2. *Alcohol Clin Exp Res*. 1998;22:524-527.

16. Neumark YD, Friedlander Y, Thomasson HR, Li TK. Association of the ADH2-2 allele with reduced ethanol consumption in Jewish men in Israel: a pilot study. *J Stud Alcohol*. 1998;59:133-139.

17. Schuckit MA, Mazzanti C, Smith TL, et al. Selective genotyping for the role of the 5-HT^{2A}, 5-HT^{2C}, and $GABA_{alpha\text{-}6}$ receptors and the serotonin transporter in the level of response to alcohol: a pilot study. *Biol Psychiatry*. 1999;45:647-651.

18. Begleiter H, Porjesz B, Reich T, et al. Quantitative trait loci analysis of human event-related brain potentials: P3 voltage. *Electroencephalogr Clin Neurophysiol*. 1998;108:244-250.

19. Ehlers CL, Garcia-Andrade C, Wall TL, Cloutier D, Phillips E. Encephalographic responses to alcohol challenge in Native American mission Indians. *Biol Psychiatry*. 1999;45:776-787.

20. Edenberg HJ, Foroud T. Koller DL, et al. A family-based analysis of the association of the dopamine 02 receptor (DRD2) with alcoholism. *Alcohol Clin Exp Res*. 1998;22:505-512.

21. Sander T, Gscheidel N, Wendel B, et al. Human micro-opioid receptor variation and alcohol dependence. *Alcohol Clin Exp Res*. 1998;22:2108-2110.

Author Affiliations: Department of Psychiatry, School of Medicine, University of California, San Diego, and the Alcohol and Drug Treatment Program, San Diego Veterans Affairs Medical Center, San Diego, California.

Chapter 10

Youth Drinking: Risk Factors and Consequences

Introduction

Despite a minimum legal drinking age of 21, many young people in the United States consume alcohol. Some abuse alcohol by drinking frequently or by binge drinking—often defined as having five or more drinks in a row. (A standard drink is 12 grams of pure alcohol, which is equal to one 12-ounce bottle of beer or wine cooler, one 5-ounce glass of wine, or 1.5 ounces of 80-proof distilled spirits.) A minority of youth may meet the *Diagnostic and Statistical Manual of Mental Disorders, Fourth Edition (DSM-IV)* criteria for alcohol dependence. The progression of drinking from use to abuse to dependence is associated with biological and psychosocial factors. This *Alcohol Alert* examines some of these factors that put youth at risk for drinking and for alcohol-related problems and considers some of the consequences of their drinking.

Prevalence of Youth Drinking

Thirteen- to fifteen-year-olds are at high risk to begin drinking. According to results of an annual survey of students in 8th, 10th, and 12th grades, 26 percent of 8th graders, 40 percent of 10th graders,

---

From *Alcohol Alert*, No. 37, July 1997, National Institute on Alcohol Abuse and Alcoholism (NIAAA). The full text of this publication, including references, is available on NIAAA's World Wide Web site at http://www.niaaa.nih.gov. Copies are also available free of charge from the National Institute on Alcohol Abuse and Alcoholism (NIAAA) Publications Distribution Center, Attn.: *Alcohol Alert*, P.O. Box 10686, Rockville, MD 20849-0686.

and 51 percent of 12th graders reported drinking alcohol within the past month. Binge drinking at least once during the 2 weeks before the survey was reported by 16 percent of 8th graders, 25 percent of 10th graders, and 30 percent of 12th graders.

Males report higher rates of daily drinking and binge drinking than females, but these differences are diminishing. White students report the highest levels of drinking, blacks report the lowest, and Hispanics fall between the two.

A survey focusing on the alcohol-related problems experienced by 4,390 high school seniors and dropouts found that within the preceding year, approximately 80 percent reported either getting "drunk," binge drinking, or drinking and driving. More than half said that drinking had caused them to feel sick, miss school or work, get arrested, or have a car crash.

Some adolescents who drink later abuse alcohol and may develop alcoholism. Although these conditions are defined for adults in the *DSM*, research suggests that separate diagnostic criteria may be needed for youth.

Drinking and Adolescent Development

While drinking may be a singular problem behavior for some, research suggests that for others it may be an expression of general adolescent turmoil that includes other problem behaviors and that these behaviors are linked to unconventionality, impulsiveness, and sensation seeking.

Binge drinking, often beginning around age 13, tends to increase during adolescence, peak in young adulthood (ages 18-22), then gradually decrease. In a 1994 national survey, binge drinking was reported by 28 percent of high school seniors, 41 percent of 21- to 22-year-olds, but only 25 percent of 31- to 32-year-olds. Individuals who increase their binge drinking from age 18 to 24 and those who consistently binge drink at least once a week during this period may have problems attaining the goals typical of the transition from adolescence to young adulthood (e.g., marriage, educational attainment, employment, and financial independence).

Risk Factors for Adolescent Alcohol Use, Abuse, and Dependence

Genetic Risk Factors. Animal studies and studies of twins and adoptees demonstrate that genetic factors influence an individual's vulnerability to alcoholism. Children of alcoholics are significantly more likely than children of nonalcoholics to initiate drinking during adolescence and to develop alcoholism, but the relative influences of environment and genetics have not been determined and vary among people.

Biological Markers. Brain waves elicited in response to specific stimuli (e.g., a light or sound) provide measures of brain activity that predict risk for alcoholism. P300, a wave that occurs about 300 milliseconds after a stimulus, is most frequently used in this research. A low P300 amplitude has been demonstrated in individuals with increased risk for alcoholism, especially sons of alcoholic fathers. P300 measures among 36 preadolescent boys were able to predict alcohol and other drug (AOD) use 4 years later, at an average age of 16.

Childhood Behavior. Children classified as "under-controlled" (i.e., impulsive, restless, and distractible) at age 3 were twice as likely as those who were "inhibited" or "well-adjusted" to be diagnosed with alcohol dependence at age 21. Aggressiveness in children as young as ages 5-10 has been found to predict AOD use in adolescence. Childhood antisocial behavior is associated with alcohol-related problems in adolescence and alcohol abuse or dependence in adulthood.

Psychiatric Disorders. Among 12- to 16-year-olds, regular alcohol use has been significantly associated with conduct disorder; in one study, adolescents who reported higher levels of drinking were more likely to have conduct disorder.

Six-year-old to seventeen-year-old boys with attention deficit hyperactivity disorder (ADHD) who were also found to have weak social relationships had significantly higher rates of alcohol abuse and dependence 4 years later, compared with ADHD boys without social deficiencies and boys without ADHD.

Whether anxiety and depression lead to or are consequences of alcohol abuse is unresolved. In a study of college freshmen, a *DSM-III* diagnosis of alcohol abuse or dependence was twice as likely among those with anxiety disorder as those without this disorder. In another study, college students diagnosed with alcohol abuse were almost four times as likely as students without alcohol abuse to have a major depressive disorder. In most of these cases, depression preceded alcohol abuse. In a study of adolescents in residential treatment for AOD dependence, 25 percent met the *DSM-III-R* criteria for depression, three times the rate reported for controls. In 43 percent of these cases, the onset of AOD dependence preceded the depression; in 35 percent, the depression occurred first; and in 22 percent, the disorders occurred simultaneously.

Suicidal Behavior. Alcohol use among adolescents has been associated with considering, planning, attempting, and completing suicide. In one study, 37 percent of eighth-grade females who drank heavily reported attempting suicide, compared with 11 percent who did not drink. Research does not indicate whether drinking causes suicidal behavior, only that the two behaviors are correlated.

Psychosocial Risk Factors

Parenting, Family Environment, and Peers. Parents' drinking behavior and favorable attitudes about drinking have been positively associated with adolescents' initiating and continuing drinking. Early initiation of drinking has been identified as an important risk factor for later alcohol-related problems. Children who were warned about alcohol by their parents and children who reported being closer to their parents were less likely to start drinking.

Lack of parental support, monitoring, and communication have been significantly related to frequency of drinking, heavy drinking, and drunkenness among adolescents. Harsh, inconsistent discipline and hostility or rejection toward children have also been found to significantly predict adolescent drinking and alcohol-related problems.

Peer drinking and peer acceptance of drinking have been associated with adolescent drinking. While both peer influences and parental influences are important, their relative impact on adolescent drinking is unclear.

Expectancies. Positive alcohol-related expectancies have been identified as risk factors for adolescent drinking. Positive expectancies about alcohol have been found to increase with age and to predict the onset of drinking and problem drinking among adolescents.

Trauma. Child abuse and other traumas have been proposed as risk factors for subsequent alcohol problems. Adolescents in treatment for alcohol abuse or dependence reported higher rates of physical abuse, sexual abuse, violent victimization, witnessing violence, and other traumas compared with controls. The adolescents in treatment were at least 6 times more likely than controls to have ever been abused physically and at least 18 times more likely to have ever been abused sexually. In most cases, the physical or sexual abuse preceded the alcohol use. Thirteen percent of the alcohol dependent adolescents had experienced posttraumatic stress disorder, compared with 10 percent of those who abused alcohol and 1 percent of controls.

Advertising. Research on the effects of alcohol advertising on adolescent alcohol-related beliefs and behaviors has been limited. While earlier studies measured the effects of exposure to advertising, more recent research has assessed the effects of alcohol advertising awareness on intentions to drink. In a study of fifth- and sixth-grade students' awareness, measured by the ability to identify products in commercials with the product name blocked out, awareness had a small but statistically significant relationship to positive expectancies about alcohol and to intention to drink as adults. This suggests that alcohol advertising may influence adolescents to be more favorably predisposed to drinking.

Consequences of Adolescent Alcohol Use

Drinking and Driving. Of the nearly 8,000 drivers ages 15-20 involved in fatal crashes in 1995, 20 percent had blood alcohol concentrations above zero. For more information about young drivers' increased crash risk and the factors that contribute to this risk, see *Alcohol Alert* No. 31: Drinking and Driving.

Sexual Behavior. Surveys of adolescents suggest that alcohol use is associated with risky sexual behavior and increased vulnerability to coercive sexual activity. Among adolescents surveyed in New Zealand, alcohol misuse was significantly associated with unprotected intercourse and sexual activity before age 16. Forty-four percent of sexually active Massachusetts teenagers said they were more likely to have sexual intercourse if they had been drinking, and 17 percent said they were less likely to use condoms after drinking.

Risky Behavior and Victimization. Survey results from a nationally representative sample of 8th and 10th graders indicated that alcohol use was significantly associated with both risky behavior and victimization and that this relationship was strongest among the 8th-grade males, compared with other students.

Puberty and Bone Growth. High doses of alcohol have been found to delay puberty in female and male rats, and large quantities of alcohol consumed by young rats can slow bone growth and result in weaker bones. However, the implications of these findings for young people are not clear.

A Commentary by NIAAA Director Enoch Gordis, M.D.

Alcohol, the most widely used and abused drug among youth, causes serious and potentially life-threatening problems for this population. Although alcohol is sometimes referred to as a "gateway drug" for youth because its use often precedes the use of other illicit substances, this terminology is counterproductive; youth drinking requires significant attention, not because of what it leads to but because of the extensive human and economic impact of alcohol use by this vulnerable population.

For some youth, alcohol use alone is the primary problem. For others, drinking may be only one of a constellation of high-risk behaviors. For these individuals, interventions designed to modify high-risk behavior likely would be more successful in preventing alcohol problems than those designed solely to prevent the initiation of drinking. Determining which influences are involved in specific youth drinking patterns will permit the design of more potent interventions. Finally, we need to develop a better understanding of the alcohol treatment needs of youth. Future questions for scientific attention include, what types of specialized diagnostic and assessment instruments are needed for youth; whether treatment in segregated, "youth only" programs is more effective than in general population programs; and, irrespective of the setting, what types of specific modalities are needed by youth to increase the long-term effectiveness of treatment.

Chapter 11

Aging and Alcohol Abuse

Anyone at any age can have a drinking problem. Great Uncle George may have always been a heavy drinker—his family may find that as he gets older the problem gets worse. Grandma Betty may have been a teetotaler all her life, just taking a drink "to help her get to sleep" after her husband died—now she needs a couple of drinks to get through the day. These are common stories. Drinking problems in older people are often neglected by families, doctors, and the public.

Physical Effects of Alcohol

Alcohol slows down brain activity. Because alcohol affects alertness, judgment, coordination, and reaction time—drinking increases the risk of falls and accidents. Some research has shown that it takes less alcohol to affect older people than younger ones. Over time, heavy drinking permanently damages the brain and central nervous system, as well as the liver, heart, kidneys, and stomach. Alcohol's effects can make some medical problems hard to diagnose. For example, alcohol causes changes in the heart and blood vessels that can dull pain that might be a warning sign of a heart attack. It also can cause forgetfulness and confusion, which can seem like Alzheimer's disease.

Mixing Drugs

Alcohol, itself a drug, is often harmful if mixed with prescription or over-the-counter medicines. This is a special problem for people over

National Institute on Aging (NIA), March 1999.

65, because they are often heavy users of prescription medicines and over-the-counter drugs. Mixing alcohol with other drugs such as tranquilizers, sleeping pills, pain killers, and antihistamines can be very dangerous, even fatal. For example, aspirin can cause bleeding in the stomach and intestines; when it is combined with alcohol, the risk of bleeding is much higher.

As people age, the body's ability to absorb and dispose of alcohol and other drugs changes. Anyone who drinks should check with a doctor or pharmacist about possible problems with drug and alcohol interactions.

Who Becomes a Problem Drinker?

There are two types of problem drinkers—chronic and situational. Chronic abusers have been heavy drinkers for many years. Although many chronic abusers die by middle age, some live well into old age. Most older problem drinkers are in this group.

Other people may develop a drinking problem late in life, often because of "situational" factors such as retirement, lowered income, failing health, loneliness, or the death of friends or loved ones. At first, having a drink brings relief, but later it can turn into a problem.

How to Recognize a Drinking Problem

Not everyone who drinks regularly has a drinking problem. You might want to get help if you:

- Drink to calm your nerves, forget your worries, or reduce depression
- Lose interest in food
- Gulp your drinks down fast
- Lie or try to hide your drinking habits
- Drink alone more often
- Hurt yourself, or someone else, while drinking
- Were drunk more than three or four times last year
- Need more alcohol to get "high"
- Feel irritable, resentful, or unreasonable when you are not drinking
- Have medical, social, or financial problems caused by drinking

Getting Help

Older problem drinkers have a very good chance for recovery because once they decide to seek help, they usually stay with treatment programs. You can begin getting help by calling your family doctor or clergy member. Your local health department or social services agencies can also help.

Resources

Alcoholics Anonymous (AA) is a voluntary fellowship of alcoholics who help themselves and each other get and stay sober. Check the phone book for a local chapter or write the national office at:

Alcoholics Anonymous
P.O. Box 459
Grand Central Station
New York, NY 10163
Phone (212) 870–3400
Web site: www.alcoholics-anonymous.org

The National Institute on Alcohol Abuse and Alcoholism (NIAAA) provides information on alcohol abuse and alcoholism. Contact:

National Institute on Alcohol Abuse and Alcoholism (NIAAA)
National Institutes of Health
Willco Building
6000 Executive Boulevard
Bethesda, MD 20892-7003
Phone: (301) 443-0786
Web site: http://www.niaaa.nih.gov

The National Council on Alcoholism and Drug Dependence, Inc. can refer you to treatment services in your area. Contact:

National Institute on Alcohol Abuse and Alcoholism (NIAAA)
National Institutes of Health
Willco Building
6000 Executive Boulevard
Bethesda, MD 20892-7003
Phone: (301) 443-0786
Web site: http://www.niaaa.nih.gov

The National Institute on Aging offers a variety of resources on health and aging. Contact:

NIA Information Center
P.O. Box 8057
Gaithersburg, MD 20898-8057
Toll-Free: (800) 222-2225; (800) 222-4225 TTY

Additional resources are listed in the end section of this book.

Chapter 12

Alcohol Doses, Measurements, and Blood Alcohol Levels

The punchline to an often told joke suggests that the reason medical journals use technical jargon is to make sure that only doctors understand the message. With regard to recent medical journal discussions of alcoholic beverage doses and blood alcohol levels, however, a not-so-funny result of the latest extreme in technical jargon is that even doctors often don't understand the message. In an attempt to develop an "international standard" for measurements described in scientific publications, the so-called Systeme Internationale requires that journals describe doses of beverage alcohol in terms of "grams," rather than "ounces," and the blood levels are described in terms of "millimoles per liter," instead of the usual "percent of alcohol by volume" measurement.

This means that, instead of describing the ingestion of two, twelve ounce beers containing one ounce of absolute alcohol, the medical journal speaks about ingestion of 28.5 grams alcohol. Instead of describing the level of alcohol in a patient's blood as 0.10% (or 100 mg/dL) the level is described as 22 mmol/L. This system certainly is confusing for the layperson, and is likely to create comprehension problems for many physicians as well.

A "millimole" is one one-thousandth of a "mole." A "mole" is defined as the amount of a substance contained in exactly 6.02×10^{23} (NOTE:

"Factline on Alcohol Doses, Measurements, and Blood Alcohol Levels," by William J. Bailey, M.P.H., *Factline* Number 11, November, 1995, updated August 1, 1998, Indiana Prevention Resource Center at Indiana University, © 1995, 1998 The Trustees of Indiana University; reprinted with permission.

This number is and should be reading as "ten to the twenty-third power.") molecules of a substance (6.02×10^{23} is called "Avogadro's number," and is the number of atoms in 12 grams of pure Carbon). What that has to do with a person's level of intoxication is beyond most people's comprehension. Any physician whose mind makes such a logical connection is likely to be unable to communicate on a level his or her patients can understand. Anyone who orders drinks by the gram will probably be presumed to be intoxicated and refused service.

Add to this discussion the differences between measures of the percentage of alcohol "by volume" versus "by weight," different systems of measuring the "proof" of an alcoholic beverage, medical versus legal standards for measuring blood alcohol levels, and discussions of calorie content and specific gravity. If you are confused, you are not alone.

Alcohol Doses

Further complicating discussions of amounts of alcohol is the difference between potency measures based upon "percent of alcohol by volume" and measures based upon "percent of alcohol by weight." Since alcohol weighs less than water, any discussion about the proportion of alcohol in a beverage must specify whether the comparison is "by weight" or "by volume." A pint of water weights about one pound (16 ounces). A pint of pure alcohol weighs about 12.8 ounces. If one pint of pure alcohol is mixed with one pint of water, the result is a beverage that is 50% alcohol "by volume." If one pound of pure alcohol is mixed with one pound of pure water, the result is a beverage that is 50% alcohol "by weight." Since one pound of water 16 fluid ounces, and one pound of alcohol is about 20 fluid ounces, the 36 total fluid ounces in a resulting beverage is about 55.5% alcohol "by volume," although it is 50% "by weight." As an example of the importance of specifying the system used to measure the percentage of alcohol in a beverage, Coors Brewing Company promotional materials describe "Zima" as containing 3.7% alcohol by weight; 4.6% alcohol by volume. To convert measures by weight into measures by volume (or visa versa), use a conversion factor of 0.79.

Measures of Potency: "Proof"

The strength of an alcoholic beverage is usually expressed as either the percentage of absolute alcohol by volume, or as "proof." In the United States, proof is a measure of the amount of absolute alcohol in distilled spirits, and is calculated as the number of parts of alcohol in 200 parts of beverage at 60 degrees Fahrenheit (a beverage that is 50% alcohol is "100 proof;" a beverage that is 43% alcohol is "86 proof"). Under the American system, one "proof" is equal to one-half percent of alcohol by volume.

The concept of "proof" emerged prior to the 18th century, when few people had the equipment necessary to make precise measurements of the percentage of alcohol in a beverage. Exotic formulas, such as igniting a mixture of equal parts of the beverage and gunpowder, were used to test the proof of distilled spirits.

A different system for measuring proof is used in England, In England, proof is measured by comparing equal volumes of water and the beverage at 51 degrees Fahrenheit. 100 proof is set at the point at which the beverage weighs 12/13th as much as water. This means that a beverage that is said to be 100 proof under the British system is 114.2 proof under the American system. A beverage that is 100 proof under the American system is said to be 87.6 proof under the British system.

Alcohol Doses

The dose of alcohol is calculated by multiplying the volume of an alcoholic beverage by the percentage of alcohol by volume. For example, twelve ounces of beer that is 4% alcohol by volume would have a dose of 0.48 ounces of alcohol. Pure alcohol (100% alcohol) is called "absolute alcohol." Absolute alcohol is alcohol without any water molecules in it. Alcohol produced by distillation contains water molecules that are very hard to remove. The strongest readily available alcoholic beverage, often called "neutral grain spirits" is about 95% absolute alcohol (190 proof). It is possible to manufacture absolute alcohol, also called "scientific alcohol," by synthesis.

Table 12.1. Examples of Drink Equivalence: These servings have approximately 0.50 ounces of absolute alcohol.

Drink	Alcohol Content
12 ounces of 4% beer	0.48 ounces of absolute alcohol
5 ounces of 10% wine	0.50 ounces of absolute alcohol
1.25 ounces of 40% vodka (80 proof)	0.50 ounces of absolute alcohol
1.25 ounces of 43% whiskey (86 proof)	0.52 ounces of absolute alcohol

The dose of alcohol in a typical 12 ounce can of beer, is approximately equal to the dose of alcohol in a 4 to 5 ounce serving of wine, or in a "shot" of whiskey. This average-sized dose of alcohol is equal to one-half ounce of absolute alcohol, and is sometimes called a "drink equivalent."

Alcohol Measurements

Measurements and Equivalents

One fluid ounce (U.S.) of alcohol equals:

- 1.805 cubic inches
- 29.573 milliliters
- 1.041 British fluid ounces
- and weighs 0.79 ounces avoirdupois

Common measurements of alcoholic beverages (U.S.):

- **pony shot:** 0.5 jigger; 0.75 fluid ounces
- **shot:** 0.666 jigger; 1 fluid ounce
- **large shot:** 1.25 ounces
- **jigger:** 1.5 shots; 1.5 fluid ounces
- **pint:** 16 shots; 0.625 fifths
- **fifth:** 25.6 shots; 25.6 ounces; 1.6 pints; 0.8 quarts; 0.75706 liters
- **quart:** 32 shots; 32 ounces; 1.25 fifths
- **magnum:** 2 quarts; 2.49797 wine bottles
- **bottle wine:** 0.800633 quarts; 0.7577 liters

Calorie Content of Alcoholic Beverages

One gram of ethyl alcohol yields 7 calories of energy when metabolized by the body. That converts of approximately 200 calories per ounce of absolute alcohol, or about 100 calories per drink equivalent (one-half ounce of absolute alcohol). The total calorie content of an alcoholic beverage includes the calories from the alcohol itself, and calories from other components of the beverage (residual sugars or grains in beers and wines, for example). A typical serving of regular beer yields about 150 calories (about 100 calories from the alcohol and about 50 calories from the residual carbohydrates). A typical serving of light beer has a lower alcohol content and less residual carbohydrates, so the total calorie content could be about 100 calories (about

80 calories from the alcohol and about 20 calories from the residual carbohydrates).

Blood Alcohol Levels

Conversion Factors for Alternative Measurements

The most common system for measuring and reporting Blood Alcohol Levels (BAL) is calculated using the weight of alcohol (milligrams) and the volume of blood (deciliter). This yields a Blood Alcohol Concentration that can be expressed as a percentage (i.e. 0.10% alcohol by volume), or as a proportion (i.e. 100 mg. per deciliter). This system is the one prescribed by almost every state, and is sometimes referred to as the "weight by volume" or "w/v" method.

A few states prescribe a "weight by weight" or "w/w" method (milligrams of alcohol in milligrams of blood). For forensic evidence purposes, the w/w can be calculated by dividing the w/v by a factor or 1.055 (the average specific gravity of blood).

Although most evidentiary rules specify that the proportion of alcohol in the whole blood by used to measure the level of intoxication, most hospitals routinely calculate the proportion of a drug in the plasma portion of the blood. While this measurement is the most useful one for medical purposes, it is not the appropriate one for most legal purposes. Since the addition of red and white blood cells would

Table 12.2. Examples of Drink Non-Equivalence: These typical servings of other alcoholic beverages do NOT contain a single drink equivalent. They may contain more or less alcohol than is found in an "average-sized" dose of alcohol.

Dose of Alcoholic Beverage	Amount of absolute alcohol	Number of drink equivalents
40 ounce bottle of 8% malt liquor	3.2 oz.	6.4 drink equivalents
12 ounce bottle of 2.5% low alcohol beer	0.3 oz.	0.6 drink equivalents
1.25 ounce shot of 151 proof rum	0.94 oz.	1.9 drink equivalents
12.5 ounce bottle of 20% fortified wine cooler	2.5 oz.	5.0 drink equivalents

add to the blood volume that dilutes the alcohol, using only the plasma fraction would result in a percentage of alcohol that is higher than would be found in whole blood. Although there is some variation from person to person, depending upon the density of their bloods, the average adjustment factor is 1.16. In other words, to estimate the alcohol level in whole blood using the alcohol level in blood plasma, divide by 1.16. For example, a plasma alcohol level of 0.15% would convert to a blood alcohol level of 0.13%.

Chapter 13

Alcohol and Medication Interactions

Introduction

Many medications can interact with alcohol, thereby altering the metabolism or effects of alcohol and/or the medication. Some of these interactions can occur even at moderate drinking levels and result in adverse health effects for the drinker. Two types of alcohol-medication interactions exist:

1. pharmacokinetic interactions, in which alcohol interferes with the metabolism of the medication, and
2. pharmacodynamic interactions, in which alcohol enhances the effects of the medication, particularly in the central nervous system (for example, sedation).

Most people who consume alcohol, whether in moderate or large quantities, also take medications, at least occasionally. As a result, many people ingest alcohol while a medication is present in their body or vice versa. A large number of medications—both those available only by prescription and those available over the counter (OTC)—have the potential to interact with alcohol, resulting in potentially serious medical consequences. For example, the sedative effects of both alcohol

---

Excerpted from "Alcohol and Medication Interactions," by Ron Weathermon and David W. Crabb, in *Alcohol Research and Health*, Vol. 23, No. 1, 1999. To order a copy of the publication with this entire article and references, contact the U.S. Government Printing Office: (202) 512-1800.

and sedative medications can enhance each other, thereby seriously impairing a person's ability to drive or operate other types of machinery.

Most studies assessing alcohol-medication interactions focus on the effects of chronic heavy drinking. Relatively limited information is available, however, on medication interactions resulting from moderate alcohol consumption (one or two standard drinks per day; a standard drink is defined as one 12-ounce can of beer or bottle of wine cooler, one 5-ounce glass of wine, or 1.5 ounces of distilled spirits and is equivalent to approximately 0.5 ounce, or 12 grams of pure alcohol). Researchers, physicians, and pharmacists must therefore infer potential medication interactions at moderate drinking levels based on observations made with heavy drinkers. In addition, moderate alcohol consumption may directly influence some of the disease states for which medications are taken.

Alcohol-Medication Interactions

Alcohol Absorption, Distribution, and Metabolism

[To understand how alcohol-medication interactions can occur, it will be helpful to understand how alcohol is metabolized by the body.]

When alcohol is ingested through the mouth, a small amount is immediately broken down (metabolized) in the stomach. Most of the remaining alcohol is then absorbed into the bloodstream from the gastrointestinal tract, primarily the stomach and the upper small intestine. Alcohol absorption occurs slowly from the stomach but rapidly from the upper small intestine. Once absorbed, the alcohol is transported to the liver through the portal vein. A portion of the ingested alcohol is metabolized during its initial passage through the liver; the remainder of the ingested alcohol leaves the liver, enters the general (systemic) circulation, and is distributed throughout the body's tissues.

Alcohol metabolism (or the metabolism of any other substance) that occurs in the gastrointestinal tract and during the substance's initial passage through the liver is called "first-pass metabolism."

Alcohol that has not been eliminated by first-pass metabolism enters the systemic circulation and is distributed throughout the body water (the blood and the watery fluid surrounding and inside the cells). Alcohol does not dissolve in fat tissues.

The liver is the primary site of alcohol metabolism. Alcohol circulating in the blood is transported to the liver, where it is broken down by several enzymes, the most important of which are ADH [alcohol dehydrogenase] and cytochrome P450. The activities of these enzymes may vary from person to person, contributing to the observed variations in alcohol elimination rates among individuals.

ADH converts alcohol into acetaldehyde in a reaction called oxidation. Acetaldehyde, which is a toxic substance that may contribute to many of alcohol's adverse effects, is broken down further by an enzyme called aldehyde dehydrogenase (ALDH).

Antibiotics

The package inserts for most antibiotics include a warning for patients to avoid using alcohol with those medications. The rationale for these warnings is not entirely clear, however, because only a few antibiotics appear to interact with alcohol. For example, although some antibiotics induce flushing [a reaction that can include facial flushing, nausea, and vomiting], most antibiotics do not. The antibiotic erythromycin may increase alcohol absorption in the intestine (and, consequently, increase blood alcohol levels) by accelerating gastric emptying. Furthermore, people taking the antituberculosis drug isoniazid should abstain from alcohol, because isoniazid can cause liver damage, which may be exacerbated by daily alcohol consumption. Aside from these effects, however, moderate alcohol consumption probably does not interfere with antibiotic effectiveness.

Antidepressants

Several classes of antidepressant medications exist, including tricyclic antidepressants (TCAs), selective serotonin reuptake inhibitors (SSRIs), monoamine oxidase (MAO) inhibitors, and atypical antidepressants. These classes differ in their mechanism of action in that they affect different brain chemicals. All types of antidepressants, however, have some sedative as well as some stimulating activity.

TCAs with a higher ratio of sedative-to-stimulant activity (amitriptyline, doxepin, maprotiline, and trimipramine) will cause the most sedation. Alcohol increases the TCAs' sedative effects through pharmacodynamic interactions. In addition, alcohol consumption can cause pharmacokinetic interactions with TCAs. For example, alcohol appears to interfere with the first-pass metabolism of amitriptyline in the liver, resulting in increased amitriptyline levels in the blood. In addition, alcohol-induced liver disease further impairs amitriptyline breakdown and causes significantly increased levels of active medication in the body. High TCA levels, in turn, can lead to convulsions and disturbances in heart rhythm.

SSRIs (fluvoxamine, fluoxetine, paroxetine, and sertraline), which are currently the most widely used antidepressants, are much less sedating than are TCAs. In addition, no serious interactions appear to occur when these agents are consumed with moderate alcohol doses. In fact, SSRIs have the best safety profile of all antidepressants, even when combined in large quantities with alcohol (for example, in suicide and overdose situations).

Conversely, people taking MAO inhibitors or atypical antidepressants can experience adverse consequences when simultaneously consuming alcohol. Thus, MAO inhibitors (for example, phenelzine and tranylcypromine) can induce severe high blood pressure if they are consumed together with a substance called tyramine, which is present in red wine. Accordingly, people taking MAO inhibitors should be warned against drinking red wine. The atypical antidepressants (nefazodone and trazodone) may cause enhanced sedation when used with alcohol.

Antihistamines

These medications, which are available both by prescription and OTC, are used in the management of allergies and colds. Antihistamines may cause drowsiness, sedation, and low blood pressure (hypotension), especially in elderly patients. Through pharmacodynamic interactions, alcohol can substantially enhance the sedating effects of these agents and may thereby increase, for example, a person's risk of failing or impair his or her ability to drive or operate other types of machinery. As a result of these potential interactions, warning labels on OTC antihistamines caution patients about the possibility of increased drowsiness when consuming the medication with alcohol. Newer antihistamines (certrizine and loratidine) have been developed to minimize drowsiness and sedation while still providing effective allergy relief. However, these newer medications may still be associated with an increased risk of hypotension and falls among the elderly, particularly when combined with alcohol. Consequently, patients taking nonsedating antihistamines still should be warned against using alcohol.

Barbiturates

These medications are sedative or sleep-inducing (hypnotic) agents that are frequently used for anesthesia. Phenobarbital, which is probably the most commonly prescribed barbiturate in modern practice, also is used in the treatment of seizure disorders. Phenobarbital activates some of the same molecules in the central nervous system (CNS) as does alcohol, resulting in pharmacodynamic interactions between the two substances. Consequently, alcohol consumption while taking phenobarbital synergistically enhances the medication's sedative side effects. Patients taking barbiturates therefore should be warned not to perform tasks that require alertness, such as driving or operating heavy machinery, particularly after simultaneous alcohol consumption.

Benzodiazepines

Like barbiturates, benzodiazepines (BZDs) are classified as sedative-hypnotic agents and act through the same brain molecules as do barbiturates. Accordingly, as with barbiturates, concurrent consumption of BZDs and moderate amounts of alcohol can cause synergistic sedative effects, leading to substantial CNS impairment. It is worth noting that both barbiturates and benzodiazepines can impair memory, as can alcohol. Consequently, the combination of these medications with alcohol would exacerbate this memory-impairing effect.

Histamine H_2 Receptor Antagonists (H_2RAs)

H_2RAs (for example, cimetidine, ranitidine, nizatidine, and famotidine), which reduce gastric acid secretion, are used in the treatment of ulcers and heartburn. These agents reduce ADH activity in the stomach mucosa and cimetidine also may increase the rate of gastric emptying. As a result, alcohol consumed with cimetidine undergoes less first-pass metabolism, resulting in increased blood alcohol levels (BALs). For example, in a study of people who consumed three or four standard drinks over 135 minutes while taking cimetidine, BALs rose higher and remained elevated for a longer period of time than in people not taking cimetidine. Not all H_2RAs, however, exert the same effect on BALs when taken with alcohol. Thus, cimetidine and ranitidine have the most pronounced effect, nizatidine has an intermediate effect, and famotidine appears to have no effect (that is, appears not to interact with alcohol). In addition, because women generally appear to have lower first-pass metabolism of alcohol, they may be at less risk for adverse interactions with H_2PAs.

Muscle Relaxants

Several muscle relaxants (for example, carisoprodol, cyclobenzaprine, and baclofen), when taken with alcohol, may produce a certain narcotic-like reaction that includes extreme weakness, dizziness, agitation, euphoria, and confusion. For example, carisoprodol is a commonly abused and readily available prescription medication that is sold as a street drug. Its metabolism in the liver generates an anxiety-reducing agent that was previously marketed as a controlled substance (meprobamate). The mixture of carisoprodol with beer is popular among street abusers for creating a quick state of euphoria.

Nonnarcotic Pain Medications and Anti-Inflammatory Agents

Many people frequently use nonnarcotic pain medications and anti-inflammatory agents (for example, aspirin, acetaminophen, or ibupro fen) for headaches and other minor aches and pains. In addition, arthritis and other disorders of the muscles and bones are among the most common problems for which older people consult physicians. Nonsteroidal anti-inflammatory drugs (NSAIDs) (for example, ibuprofen, naproxen, indomethacin, and diclofenac) and aspirin are commonly prescribed or recommended for the treatment of these disorders and are purchased over-the-counter in huge amounts. Several potential interactions exist between alcohol and these agents:

- NSAIDs have been implicated in an increased risk of ulcers and gastrointestinal bleeding in elderly people. Alcohol may exacerbate that risk by enhancing the ability of these medications to damage the stomach mucosa.
- Aspirin, indomethacin, and ibuprofen cause prolonged bleeding by inhibiting the function of certain blood cells involved in blood clot formation. This effect also appears to be enhanced by concurrent alcohol use.
- Aspirin has been shown to increase blood alcohol levels after small alcohol doses, possibly by inhibiting first-pass metabolism.

An important pharmacokinetic interaction between alcohol and acetaminophen can increase the risk of acetaminophen-related toxic effects on the liver. To prevent liver damage, patients generally should not exceed the maximum doses recommended by the manufacturers (4 grams, or up to eight extra-strength tablets of acetaminophen per day). In people who drink heavily or who are fasting, however, liver injury may occur at doses as low as 2 to 4 grams per day. The specific drinking levels at which acetaminophen toxicity is enhanced are still unknown. Because acetaminophen is easily available over-the-counter, however, labels on the packages warn people about the potentially dangerous alcohol-acetaminophen combination. Furthermore, people should be aware that combination cough, cold, and flu medications may contain aspirin, acetaminophen, or ibuprofen, all of which might contribute to serious health consequences when combined with alcohol.

Opioids

Opioids are agents with opium-like effects (for example, sedation, pain relief, and euphoria) that are used as pain medications. Alcohol accentuates the opioids' sedating effects. Accordingly, all patients receiving narcotic prescriptions should be warned about the drowsiness caused by these agents and the additive effects of alcohol. Overdoses of alcohol and opioids are potentially lethal because they can reduce the cough reflex and breathing functions; as a result, the patients are at risk of getting foods, fluids, or other objects stuck in their airways or of being unable to breathe.

Certain opioid pain medications (for example, codeine, propoxyphene, and oxycodone) are manufactured as combination products containing acetaminophen. These combinations can be particularly harmful when combined with alcohol because they provide "hidden" doses of acetaminophen. As described in the previous section, alcohol consumption may result in the accumulation of toxic breakdown products of acetaminophen.

Warfarin

The anticoagulant warfarin is used for the prevention of blood clots in patients with irregular heart rhythms or artificial heart valves; it is also used to treat clots that form in extremities such as legs, arms, or sometimes the lungs. Its anticoagulant effect is acutely altered by even small amounts of alcohol. In people taking warfarin and ingesting a few drinks in one sitting, anticlotting effects may be stronger than necessary for medical purposes, placing these people at risk for increased bleeding. This excessive warfarin activity results from alcohol-related inhibition of warfarin metabolism by cytochrome P450 in the liver. Conversely, in people who chronically drink alcohol, long-term alcohol consumption activates cytochrome P450 and, consequently, warfarin metabolism. As a result, warfarin is broken down faster than normal, and higher warfarin doses are required to achieve the desired anticoagulant effect. Thus, alcohol consumption can result in dangerously high or insufficient warfarin activity, depending on the patient's drinking pattern. Therefore, patients taking warfarin generally should avoid alcohol.

Herbal Medications

Herbal medications currently are widely used, and many people assume that because these products are "natural," they also are safe to use. This assumption may not always be correct, however. For example, chamomile, echinacea, and valerian commonly are used as sleep aids, and like prescription and OTC products that cause sedation, these herbal products may produce enhanced sedative effects in the central nervous system when combined with alcohol. In addition, liver toxicities caused by various natural products have now been identified, and their combination with alcohol may enhance potential adverse effects. To date, limited documentation of such interactions exists because of a lack of scientific studies on this subject.

Alcohol's Influences on Various Disease States

Many people who are being treated for chronic health problems, such as diabetes and high blood pressure (hypertension), consume alcohol, whether occasionally or regularly. As described above, alcohol consumption, even at moderate levels, may interfere with the activities of many medications prescribed for such conditions. In addition, however, alcohol use may contribute to or exacerbate certain medical conditions.

Diabetes

In people with diabetes, control of the levels of the sugar glucose in the blood is severely impaired, either because these people lack the hormone insulin, which plays a central role in blood sugar regulation, or because their body does not respond appropriately to the insulin they produce. Alcohol consumption in diabetics can result either in higher-than-normal blood sugar levels (hyperglycemia) or in lower-than-normal blood sugar levels (hypoglycemia), depending on the patient's nutritional status.

Diabetics who consume alcohol also must be alert to the fact that the symptoms of mild intoxication closely resemble those of hypoglycemia. Accordingly, diabetics should check their blood glucose levels whenever they are uncertain about whether their symptoms are caused by hypoglycemia or alcohol intoxication. Finally, patients using certain diabetes medications (for example, chlorpropamide) should be cautioned that the medications can cause a disulfiram-like reaction when alcohol is consumed. [Disulfiram is a medication designed to discourage people from drinking. When alcohol is consumed by a person taking disulfiram, it makes them sick.]

Hyperlipidemia

In people with hyperlipidemia, the levels of fat molecules in the blood—particularly molecules called triglycerides—are higher than normal. This condition can be associated with an increased risk of various health problems, the most serious of which is cardiovascular disease. Alcohol consumption may exacerbate hyperlipidemia, because the same metabolic alcohol effects that inhibit gluconeogenesis also inhibit fat metabolism. As a result, the production of certain molecules called very low density lipoprotein (VLDL) particles is increased. Thus, people with elevated triglyceride levels in the blood should probably abstain from alcohol to determine if alcohol consumption is contributing to their elevated lipid levels.

Hypertension

Elevated blood pressure is a risk factor for cardiovascular disease, including heart attacks. Alcohol is known to cause a dose-dependent elevation in blood pressure. Researchers do not yet know exactly what levels of alcohol consumption cause hypertension. However, all patients who are diagnosed with high blood pressure should be questioned regarding their alcohol intake before being started on antihypertensive therapy. In some of those patients, cessation of drinking alone may reduce blood pressure and thus obviate the need for pharmacological treatment. Furthermore, patients taking certain kinds of cardiac medications (for example, isosorbide—Isordil® and Ismo®, terazosin—Hytrin®, doxazosin—Cardura®) should be warned that alcohol consumption in combination with those medications may cause lower-than-normal blood pressure. These important potential risks associated with even moderate alcohol consumption (one or two standard drinks per day) must be considered when discussing the cardiovascular benefits associated with moderate drinking (for example, reduced risk of heart attacks and certain kinds of strokes.)

Hepatitis C Infection

Infection with the hepatitis C virus, which can result in serious and even fatal liver damage, is common in the United States and around the world. The only effective treatment to date involves a substance called interferon-alpha, often in combination with an agent called ribavirin, and has a cure rate of approximately 40 percent. Heavy alcohol use in patients infected with hepatitis C accelerates the rate of liver damage and increases the risk of cirrhosis. Moreover, heavy alcohol use appears to reduce the number of hepatitis C-infected people who respond to treatment with interferon-alpha. Researchers do not yet know how alcohol consumption exacerbates disease progression and interferes with treatment. Nevertheless, people infected with the hepatitis C virus probably should avoid using alcohol, particularly during interferon-alpha treatment.

Conclusions

Given the variety and complexity of observed interactions between alcohol and numerous medications, it is difficult to recommend an alcohol consumption level that can be considered safe when taking medications. As a rule, people taking either prescription or over-the-counter medications should always read the product warning labels to determine whether possible interactions exist. Similarly, health care providers should be alert to the potential for moderate alcohol use to either enhance medication effects or interfere with the desired therapeutic actions of a medication.

About the Authors

Ron Weathermon, PharmD, is an assistant professor at the School of Pharmacy and Pharmaceutical Services, Purdue University, Indianapolis, Indiana.

David W. Crabb, MD, is a Professor in the Departments of Medicine and Biochemistry and Molecular Biology, Indiana University School of medicine, Indianapolis, Indiana.

Chapter 14

Alcohol and Tolerance

Alcohol consumption interferes with many bodily functions and affects behavior. However, after chronic alcohol consumption, the drinker often develops tolerance to at least some of alcohol's effects. Tolerance means that after continued drinking, consumption of a constant amount of alcohol produces a lesser effect or increasing amounts of alcohol are necessary to produce the same effect. Despite this uncomplicated definition, scientists distinguish between several types of tolerance that are produced by different mechanisms.

Tolerance to alcohol's effects influences drinking behavior and drinking consequences in several ways. This chapter describes how tolerance may encourage alcohol consumption, contributing to alcohol dependence and organ damage; affect the performance of tasks, such as driving, while under the influence of alcohol; contribute to the ineffectiveness or toxicity of other drugs and medications; and may contribute to the risk for alcoholism.

Functional Tolerance

Humans and animals develop tolerance when their brain functions adapt to compensate for the disruption caused by alcohol in both their

From *Alcohol Alert*, No. 28 PH 356, April 1995, National Institute on Alcohol Abuse and Alcoholism (NIAAA). The full text of this publication, including references, is available on NIAAA's World Wide Web site at http://www.niaaa.nih.gov. Copies are also available free of charge from the National Institute on Alcohol Abuse and Alcoholism (NIAAA) Publications Distribution Center, Attn.: *Alcohol Alert*, P.O. Box 10686, Rockville, MD 20849-0686.

behavior and their bodily functions. This adaptation is called functional tolerance. Chronic heavy drinkers display functional tolerance when they show few obvious signs of intoxication even at high blood alcohol concentrations (BACs), which in others would be incapacitating or even fatal. Because the drinker does not experience significant behavioral impairment as a result of drinking, tolerance may facilitate the consumption of increasing amounts of alcohol. This can result in physical dependence and alcohol-related organ damage.

However, functional tolerance does not develop at the same rate for all alcohol effects. Consequently, a person may be able to perform some tasks after consuming alcohol while being impaired in performing others. In one study, young men developed tolerance more quickly when conducting a task requiring mental functions, such as taking a test, than when conducting a task requiring eye-hand coordination, such as driving a car. Development of tolerance to different alcohol effects at different rates also can influence how much a person drinks. Rapid development of tolerance to unpleasant, but not to pleasurable, alcohol effects could promote increased alcohol consumption.

Different types of functional tolerance and the factors influencing their development are described below. During repeated exposure to low levels of alcohol, environmental cues and processes related to memory and learning can facilitate tolerance development; during exposure to high levels of alcohol, tolerance may develop independently of environmental influences.

Acute Tolerance

Although tolerance to most alcohol effects develops over time and over several drinking sessions, it also has been observed within a single drinking session. This phenomenon is called acute tolerance. It means that alcohol-induced impairment is greater when measured soon after beginning alcohol consumption than when measured later in the drinking session, even if the BAC is the same at both times.

Acute tolerance does not develop to all effects of alcohol but does develop to the feeling of intoxication experienced after alcohol consumption. This may prompt the drinker to consume more alcohol, which in turn can impair performance or bodily functions that do not develop acute tolerance.

Environment-Dependent Tolerance

The development of tolerance to alcohol's effects over several drinking sessions is accelerated if alcohol is always administered in the same environment or is accompanied by the same cues. This effect has been called environment-dependent tolerance. Rats that regularly received alcohol in one room and a placebo in a different room demonstrated tolerance to the sedative and temperature-lowering effects of alcohol only in the alcohol-specific environment. Similar results were found when an alcohol-induced increase in heart rate was studied in humans. When the study subjects always received alcohol in the same room, their heart rate increased to a lesser extent after drinking in that room than in a new environment.

Environment-dependent tolerance develops even in "social" drinkers in response to alcohol-associated cues. In a study analyzing alcohol's effects on the performance of an eye-hand coordination task, a group of men classified as social drinkers received alcohol either in an office or in a room resembling a bar. Most subjects performed the task better (i.e., were more tolerant) when drinking in the bar-like environment. This suggests that for many people, a bar contains cues that are associated with alcohol consumption and promote environment-dependent tolerance.

Learned Tolerance

The development of tolerance also can be accelerated by practicing a task while under the influence of alcohol. This phenomenon is called behaviorally augmented (i.e., learned) tolerance. It first was observed in rats that were trained to navigate a maze while under the influence of alcohol. One group of rats received alcohol before their training sessions; the other group received the same amount of alcohol after their training sessions. Rats that practiced the task while under the influence of alcohol developed tolerance more quickly than rats practicing without prior alcohol administration.

Humans also develop tolerance more rapidly and at lower alcohol doses if they practice a task while under the influence of alcohol. When being tested on a task requiring eye-hand coordination while under the influence of alcohol, people who had practiced after ingesting alcohol performed better than people who had practiced before ingesting alcohol. Even subjects who only mentally rehearsed the task after drinking alcohol showed the same level of tolerance as those who actually practiced the task while under the influence of alcohol.

The expectation of a positive outcome or reward after successful task performance is an important component of the practice effect on tolerance development. When human subjects knew they would receive money or another reward for successful task performance while under the influence of alcohol, they developed tolerance more quickly than if they did not expect a reward. The motivation to perform better contributes to the development of learned tolerance.

Learned and environment-dependent tolerance have important consequences for situations such as drinking and driving. Repeated practice of a task while under the influence of low levels of alcohol, such as driving a particular route, could lead to the development of tolerance, which in turn could reduce alcohol-induced impairment. However, the tolerance acquired for a specific task or in a specific environment is not readily transferable to new conditions. A driver encountering a new environment or an unexpected situation could instantly lose any previously acquired tolerance to alcohol's impairing effects on driving performance.

Environment-Independent Tolerance

Exposure to large quantities of alcohol can lead to the development of functional tolerance independent of environmental influences. This was demonstrated in rats that inhaled alcohol vapors. In another study, mice demonstrated tolerance in environments different from the one in which the alcohol was administered. Significantly larger alcohol doses were necessary to establish this environment-independent tolerance than to establish environment-dependent tolerance.

Metabolic Tolerance

Tolerance that results from a more rapid elimination of alcohol from the body is called metabolic tolerance. It is associated with a specific group of liver enzymes that metabolize alcohol and that are activated after chronic drinking. Enzyme activation increases alcohol degradation and reduces the time during which alcohol is active in the body, thereby reducing the duration of alcohol's intoxicating effects.

However, certain of these enzymes also increase the metabolism of some other drugs and medications, causing a variety of harmful effects on the drinker. For example, rapid degradation of sedatives (e.g., barbiturates) can cause tolerance to them and increase the risk for their use and abuse. Increased metabolism of some prescription medications, such as those used to prevent blood clotting and to treat diabetes, reduces their effectiveness in chronic drinkers or even in recovering alcoholics. Increased degradation of the common painkiller acetaminophen produces substances that are toxic to the liver and that can contribute to liver damage in chronic drinkers.

Tolerance and the Predisposition to Alcoholism

Animal studies indicate that some aspects of tolerance are genetically determined. Tolerance development was analyzed in rats that were bred to prefer or not prefer alcohol over water. The alcohol-preferring rats developed acute tolerance to some alcohol effects more rapidly and/or to a greater extent than the nonpreferring rats. In addition, only the alcohol-preferring rats developed tolerance to alcohol's effects when tested over several drinking sessions. These differences suggest that the potential to develop tolerance is genetically determined and may contribute to increased alcohol consumption.

In humans, genetically determined differences in tolerance that may affect drinking behavior were investigated by comparing sons of alcoholic fathers (SOAs) with sons of nonalcoholic fathers (SONAs). Several studies found that SOAs were less impaired by alcohol than SONAs. Other studies found that, compared with SONAs, SOAs were affected more strongly by alcohol early in the drinking session but developed more tolerance later in the drinking session. These studies suggest that at the start of drinking, when alcohol's pleasurable effects prevail, SOAs experience these strongly; later in the drinking session, when impairing effects prevail, SOAs do not experience these as strongly because they have developed tolerance. This predisposition could contribute to increased drinking and the risk for alcoholism in SOAs.

A Commentary by NIAAA Director Enoch Gordis, M.D.

Tolerance can be a useful clue for clinicians in identifying patients who may be at risk for developing alcohol-related problems. For example, younger patients who are early in their drinking histories and who report that they can "hold their liquor well" may be drinking at rates that will place them at risk for medical complications from alcohol use, including alcoholism. The fact that tolerance to all of alcohol's effects does not develop simultaneously is also important; people who are mildly tolerant may exhibit more symptoms of impairment when faced with unfamiliar activities, such as driving in an unknown area, than when they are engaged in routine actions, such as driving home from work. Lastly, although we know that initial sensitivity to alcohol may play a role in the development of alcoholism, the role of tolerance in maintaining addiction to alcohol needs further exploration.

Chapter 15

Alcohol and Stress

The term "stress" often is used to describe the subjective feeling of pressure or tension. However, when scientists refer to stress, they mean the many objective physiological processes that are initiated in response to a stressor. As this chapter explains, the stress response is a complex process; the association between drinking and stress is more complicated still. Because both drinking behavior and an individual's response to stress are determined by multiple genetic and environmental factors, studying the link between alcohol consumption and stress may further our understanding of drinking behavior.

The Stress Response

The maintenance of the body's relatively steady internal state, or homeostasis, is essential for survival. The body's delicate balance of biochemical and physiological function is constantly challenged by a wide variety of stressors, including illness, injury, and exposure to extreme temperatures; by psychological factors, such as depression and fear; and by sexual activity and some forms of novelty-seeking. In response to stress, or even perceived stress, the body mobilizes an

---

From *Alcohol Alert*, No. 32 PH 363, April 1996, National Institute on Alcohol Abuse and Alcoholism (NIAAA). The full text of this publication, including references, is available on NIAAA's World Wide Web site at http://www.niaaa.nih.gov. Copies are also available free of charge from the National Institute on Alcohol Abuse and Alcoholism (NIAAA) Publications Distribution Center, Attn.: *Alcohol Alert*, P.O. Box 10686, Rockville, MD 20849-0686.

extensive array of physiological and behavioral changes in a process of continual adaptation, with the goal of maintaining homeostasis and coping with the stress.

The stress response is a highly complex, integrated network involving the central nervous system, the adrenal system, and the cardiovascular system. When homeostasis is threatened, the hypothalamus gland, at the base of the brain, initiates the stress response by secreting corticotropin-releasing factor (CRF). CRF coordinates the stress response by triggering an integrated series of physiological and behavioral reactions. CRF is transported in blood within the brain and in seconds triggers the pituitary gland to release adrenocorticotropin hormone (ACTH), also referred to as corticotropin. ACTH then triggers secretion of glucocorticoid hormones (i.e., "steroids") by the adrenal glands, located at the top of the kidneys. Glucocorticoid hormones play a key role in the stress response and its termination.

Activation of the stress response affects smooth muscle, fat, the gastrointestinal tract, the kidneys, and many other organs and the body functions that they control. The stress response affects the body's regulation of temperature; appetite and satiety; arousal, vigilance, and attention; mood; and more. Physical adaptation to stress allows the body to redirect oxygen and nutrients to the stressed body site, where they are needed most.

Both the perception of what is stressful and the physiological response to stress vary considerably among individuals. These differences are based on genetic factors and environmental influences that can be traced back to infancy.

Stress is usually thought of as harmful; but when the stress response is acute and transient, homeostasis is maintained and no adverse effects result. Under chronic stress, however, when the body either fails to compensate or when it overcompensates, damage can occur. Such damage may include suppression of growth, immune system dysfunction, and cell damage resulting in impaired learning and memory.

Does Stress Influence Drinking?

Human research to clarify the connection between alcohol and stress usually has been conducted using either population surveys based on subject self-reports or experimental studies. In many but not all of these studies, individuals report that they drink in response to stress and do so for a variety of reasons. Studies indicate that people drink as a means of coping with economic stress, job stress, and marital problems, often in the absence of social support, and that the more severe and chronic the stressor, the greater the alcohol consumption. However, whether an individual will drink in response to stress appears to depend on many factors, including possible genetic determinants of drinking in response to stress, an individual's usual drinking behavior, one's expectations regarding the effect of alcohol on stress, the intensity and type of stressor, the individual's sense of control over the stressor, the range of one's responses to cope with the perceived stress, and the availability of social support to buffer the effects of stress. Some researchers have found that high levels of stress may influence drinking when alternative resources are lacking, when alcohol is accessible, and when the individual believes that alcohol will help to reduce the stress.

Numerous studies have found that stress increases alcohol consumption in animals and that individual animals may differ in the amount of alcohol they consume in response to stress. Such differences may be related in part to an animal's experiencing chronic stress early in life: Prolonged stress in infancy may permanently alter the hormonal stress response and subsequent reactions to new stressors, including alcohol consumption. For example, monkeys who were reared by peers, a circumstance regarded as a stressor compared to mother-rearing, consumed twice as much alcohol as monkeys who were mother-reared. According to Viau and colleagues, adult rats handled for the first 3 weeks of life demonstrate markedly reduced hormonal responses to a variety of stressors compared with rats not handled during this time. In humans, Cloninger reported an association between certain types of alcoholism and adverse early childhood experiences.

Animal studies reporting a positive correlation between stress and alcohol consumption suggest that drinking may take place in response to chronic stress perceived as unavoidable. For instance, rats chronically exposed to unavoidable shock learn to be helpless or passive when faced with any new stressor—including shock that is avoidable—and to demonstrate increased alcohol preference compared with rats that received only avoidable shock. The rats exposed to unavoidable shock exhibit the hormonal changes indicative of the stress response, including increased levels of corticosteroid hormones.

Whether humans drink in response to uncontrollable stress is less clear, according to Pohorecky. In a review investigating the connection between alcohol consumption and stress, Pohorecky notes several studies in which researchers sampled individuals from areas affected by natural disaster. One study found that alcohol consumption increased by 30 percent in the 2 years following a flood at Buffalo Creek, West Virginia. Similarly, there was evidence of increased drinking in the towns surrounding Mount St. Helens following eruption of the volcano. Following the nuclear plant accident at Three Mile Island, however, alcohol consumption was infrequently used by those sampled as a means of coping with the resulting stress.

In both humans and animals, drinking appears to follow stress. Some human research, however, shows that drinking may take place in anticipation of or during times of stress.

Does Drinking Reduce or Induce Stress?

Some studies have reported that acute exposure to low doses of alcohol may reduce the response to a stressor in animals and humans. For example, low doses of alcohol reduced the stress response in rats subjected to strenuous activity in a running wheel. In humans, a low dose of alcohol improved performance of a complex mental problem-solving task under stressful conditions. However, in some individuals, at certain doses, alcohol may induce rather than reduce the body's stress response.

Much research demonstrates that alcohol actually induces the stress response by stimulating hormone release by the hypothalamus, pituitary, and adrenal glands. This finding has been demonstrated in animal studies. In one study with rats, the administration of alcohol initiated the physiological stress response, measured by increased levels of corticosterone. In addition to stimulating the hormonal stress response, chronic exposure to alcohol also results in an increase in adrenaline.

Stress, Alcoholism, and Relapse

Stress may be linked to social drinking, and the physiological response to stress is different in actively drinking alcoholics compared with nonalcoholics. Researchers have found that animals preferring alcohol over water have a different physiological response to stress than animals that do not prefer alcohol. Nonetheless, a clear association between stress, drinking behavior, and the development of alcoholism in humans has yet to be established.

There may, however, in the already established alcoholic, be a clearer connection between stress and relapse: Among abstinent alcoholics, personally threatening, severe, and chronic life stressors may lead to alcohol relapse. Brown and colleagues studied a group of men who completed inpatient alcoholism treatment and later experienced severe and prolonged psychosocial stress prior to and independent of any alcohol use. The researchers found that subjects who relapsed experienced twice as much severe and prolonged stress before their return to drinking as those who remained abstinent. In this study, severe psychosocial stress was related to relapse in alcoholic males who expected alcohol to reduce their stress. Those most vulnerable to stress-related relapse scored low on measures of coping skills, self-efficacy, and social support. Stress-related relapse was greatest among those who had less confidence in their ability to resist drinking and among those who relied on drinkers for social support. Although many factors can influence a return to drinking, Brown and colleagues note that stress may exert its greatest influence on the initial consumption of alcohol after a period of abstinence.

A Commentary by NIAAA Director Enoch Gordis, M.D.

Stress is commonly believed to be a factor in the development of alcoholism (alcohol dependence). However, current science is more informative about the relationship between drinking and stress than about the relationship between stress and alcohol dependence.

Drinking alcohol produces physiological stress, that is, some of the body's responses to alcohol are similar to its responses to other stressors. Yet, individuals also drink to relieve stress. Why people should engage in an activity that produces effects similar to those they are trying to relieve is a paradox that we do not yet understand. One hypothesis is that stress responses are not exclusively unpleasant; the arousal associated with stress itself may be rewarding. This might explain, for example, compulsive gambling or repeated participation in "thrill-seeking" activities. Current studies may illuminate genetic variations in the physiological response to stress that are important in drinking or other activities with the potential to become addictive.

Training clinical staff to accurately appraise patients' drink-provoking stressors may help staff to identify individuals at risk for relapse. One route to relapse prevention is the teaching of coping skills where patients learn how to deal with these stressors without drinking. How this treatment approach compares with others remains of special interest.

Chapter 16

Alcohol and Risky Sexual Behavior

Risky sexual behavior such as sex with multiple partners, or unprotected sex, has long been thought to be influenced by the use of alcohol. There is some scientific evidence that heavy alcohol consumption effects sexual arousal and may provide an excuse for greater sexual activity. In fact, according to a recent study by Research Institute on Addictions (RIA) scientists Maria Testa, Ph.D., and R. Lorraine Collins, Ph.D., women are more likely to have sex with men they have just met that day when they have consumed alcohol than when they were not drinking.

Despite the fact that women suffer negative consequences from their sexual behavior, very little research has examined the role of alcohol in women's sexual behavior. Testa and Collins' study was designed to understand the role of alcohol in the behavior of women who are at a higher than average risk of negative consequences of sexual behavior as a result of their high levels of sexual activity and alcohol use. The risks faced by such women include unwanted pregnancy; acquired immune deficiency syndrome (AIDS), which is increasing at a higher rate among women than among men (Centers for Disease Control, 1994); and sexually transmitted diseases (STDs), which may result in infertility, ectopic pregnancy, and cervical cancer (Hatcher et al., 1994).

This chapter contains text from the June 1998 issue of *Research in Brief* (ISSN 1047-8418), a newsletter published six times a year by the Research Institute on Addictions, a component of the New York State Office of Alcoholism and Substance Abuse Services; reprinted with permission.

The effect of alcohol consumption on sexual behavior was examined in a sample of 123 non-monogamous, heterosexually-active single women who were moderate to heavy drinkers. The researchers employed event-based methodology, wherein women were asked to describe two recent sexual encounters with a new or occasional partner, one involving alcohol and one not involving alcohol.

Considerations

In studying sexual behaviors among women, it is important to recognize that sexual behavior often occurs within a context of unequal power and different role expectations for women (Amaro, 1995). For example, although condom use is commonly used to assess HIV prevention, women cannot make the final decision to use a condom. Women must convince their partner to use a condom or refuse to have sex without a condom, both behaviors which are difficult because they may elicit anger or rejection from the man, as well as the possibility of the end of the relationship. (Mays & Cochran, 1988; Weinstock, Lindan, Bolan, Kegeles, & Hearts, 1992).

The issues considered in this particular study included the following: In sexual encounters involving alcohol, would women be likely to have sex with men they knew less well? Would intoxicated women perceive fewer negative consequences (such as AIDS or pregnancy) from their sexual behavior? Would the sexual encounter involving alcohol be any more likely to involve pressure or force from the men? Would women feel more regret immediately after an encounter involving alcohol?

Current Findings

The results showed that women were more likely to have sex with men they had just met in the encounter involving alcohol than in the encounter not involving alcohol. A substantial number of sexual encounters with new or occasional partners that included alcohol, particularly with partners met that day, occurred after time spent in a bar rather than time spent at home. In contrast, the majority of sexual encounters not involving alcohol followed time spent at home.

Women were no less likely to discuss birth control or AIDS prevention during the alcohol encounter, nor did they perceive less risk of pregnancy, HIV, or sexually transmitted diseases immediately before sex in the alcohol encounter. In fact, virtually all of the discussions about AIDS and STD prevention occurring within the alcohol encounter were initiated solely or partly by the woman. The results gave no indication that women's sexual communication was influenced by lack of power, either in general or as a result of alcohol consumption. Although women were more likely to use condoms if they had discussed birth control or HIV prevention, condom use was not affected by alcohol consumption.

These findings suggest that there may be qualitative differences between sexual encounters involving alcohol versus those not involving alcohol, with the former more likely to involve bar encounters and "one-night stands" and the latter marking the sexual beginning of a developing relationship. Consistent with several other recent event-based studies, alcohol use was not associated with condom use or other forms of birth control. Further, alcohol did not inhibit discussion of AIDS or pregnancy prevention.

Future Directions

Failure to find an effect between alcohol and birth control may reflect the fact that this group of women reached maturity after information about AIDS prevention had been widely disseminated and condom use may therefore be firmly ingrained. Furthermore, this study focused on sexual encounters involving new or occasional partners, where condoms are more likely to be used. To better understand how alcohol influences sexual encounters, ongoing research with this sample of women will explore the association between alcohol consumption and factors related to sexual partner, such as who initiates sex, intimacy with the partner at the time of intercourse, and continuance of the relationship beyond the first sexual encounter.

References

Amaro, H. (1995). Love, sex, and power. *American Psychologist*, 50, 437-447.

Centers for Disease Control. (1994). HIV/AIDS surveillance report. *HIV/AIDS Surveillance Report*, 6, 8-12.

Hatcher, R. A., Trussell, J., Stewart, F., Stewart, G. K., Kowal, D., Guest, F., Cates, W., & Policar, M. S. (1994). *Contraceptive technology (16th ed.)*. New York: Irvington.

Mays, V. M., & Cochran, S. D. (1988). Issues in the perception of AIDS risk and risk reduction activities by Black and Hispanic/Latina women. *American Psychologist*, 43, 949-957.

Weinstock, H. S., Lindan, C., Bolan, G., Kegeles, S. M., & Hearts, N. (1992). Factors associated with condom use in a high risk heterosexual population. *Sexually Transmitted Diseases*, 20, 14-20.

About the Authors

Maria Testa, Ph.D., and R. Lorraine Collins, Ph.D., are senior research scientists with the Research Institute on Addictions in Buffalo, NY. This research was supported by a National Institute on Alcohol Abuse and Alcoholism grant to Maria Testa, Ph.D., and can be found in *Psychology of Addictive Behaviors*, 12 (3), 190-201, 1997.

Chapter 17

Alcohol, Violence, and Aggression

Scientists and nonscientists alike have long recognized a two-way association between alcohol consumption and violent or aggressive behavior. Not only may alcohol consumption promote aggressiveness, but victimization may lead to excessive alcohol consumption. Violence may be defined as behavior that intentionally inflicts, or attempts to inflict, physical harm. Violence falls within the broader category of aggression, which also includes behaviors that are threatening, hostile, or damaging in a nonphysical way. This chapter explores the association between alcohol consumption, violence, and aggression and the role of the brain in regulating these behaviors. Understanding the nature of these associations is essential to breaking the cycle of alcohol misuse and violence.

Extent of the Alcohol-Violence Association

Based on published studies, Roizen summarized the percentages of violent offenders who were drinking at the time of the offense as follows: up to 86 percent of homicide offenders, 37 percent of assault offenders, 60 percent of sexual offenders, up to 57 percent of men and 27 percent of women involved in marital violence, and 13 percent of

From *Alcohol Alert*, No. 38, October 1997, National Institute on Alcohol Abuse and Alcoholism (NIAAA). The full text of this publication, including references, is available on NIAAA's World Wide Web site at http://www.niaaa.nih.gov. Copies are also available free of charge from the National Institute on Alcohol Abuse and Alcoholism (NIAAA) Publications Distribution Center, Attn.: *Alcohol Alert*, P.O. Box 10686, Rockville, MD 20849-0686.

child abusers. These figures are the upper limits of a wide range of estimates. In a community-based study, Pernanen found that 42 percent of violent crimes reported to the police involved alcohol, although 51 percent of the victims interviewed believed that their assailants had been drinking.

Alcohol-Violence Relationships

Several models have been proposed to explain the complex relationships between violence or aggression and alcohol consumption. To avoid exposing human or animal subjects to potentially serious injury, research results discussed below are largely based on experiments on nonphysical aggression. Other studies involving humans are based on epidemiological surveys or data obtained from archival or official sources.

Alcohol Misuse Preceding Violence

Direct Effects of Alcohol. Alcohol may encourage aggression or violence by disrupting normal brain function. According to the disinhibition hypothesis, for example, alcohol weakens brain mechanisms that normally restrain impulsive behaviors, including inappropriate aggression. By impairing information processing, alcohol can also lead a person to misjudge social cues, thereby overreacting to a perceived threat. Simultaneously, a narrowing of attention may lead to an inaccurate assessment of the future risks of acting on an immediate violent impulse.

Many researchers have explored the relationship of alcohol to aggression using variations of an experimental approach developed more than 35 years ago. In a typical example, a subject administers electric shocks or other painful stimuli to an unseen "opponent," ostensibly as part of a competitive task involving learning and reaction time. Unknown to the subject, the reactions of the nonexistent opponent are simulated by a computer. Subjects perform both while sober and after consuming alcohol. In many studies, subjects exhibited increased aggressiveness (e.g., by administering stronger shocks) in proportion to increasing alcohol consumption.

These findings suggest that alcohol may facilitate aggressive behavior. However, subjects rarely increased th eir aggression unless they felt threatened or provoked. Moreover, neither intoxicated nor sober participants administered painful stimuli when nonaggressive means of communication (e.g., a signal lamp) were also available.

These results are consistent with the real-world observation that intoxication alone does not cause violence. The following subsections explore some mechanisms whereby alcohol's direct effects may interact with other factors to influence the expression of aggression.

Social and Cultural Expectancies. Alcohol consumption may promote aggression because people expect it to. For example, research using real and mock alcoholic beverages shows that people who believe they have consumed alcohol begin to act more aggressively, regardless of which beverage they actually consumed. Alcohol-related expectancies that promote male aggressiveness, combined with the widespread perception of intoxicated women as sexually receptive and less able to defend themselves, could account for the association between drinking and date rape.

In addition, a person who intends to engage in a violent act may drink to bolster his or her courage or in hopes of evading punishment or censure. The motive of drinking to avoid censure is encouraged by the popular view of intoxication as a "time-out," during which one is not subject to the same rules of conduct as when sober.

Violence Preceding Alcohol Misuse

Childhood Victimization. A history of childhood sexual abuse or neglect is more likely among women with alcohol problems than among women without alcohol problems. Widom and colleagues found no relationship between childhood victimization and subsequent alcohol misuse in men. Even children who only witness family violence may learn to imitate the roles of aggressors or victims, setting the stage for alcohol abuse and violence to persist over generations. Finally, obstetric complications that damage the nervous system at birth, combined with subsequent parental neglect such as might occur in an alcoholic family, may predispose one to violence, crime, and other behavioral problems by age 18.

Violent Lifestyles. Violence may precede alcohol misuse in offenders as well as victims. For example, violent people may be more likely than nonviolent people to select or encounter social situations and subcultures that encourage heavy drinking. In summary, violence may contribute to alcohol consumption, which in turn may perpetuate violence.

Common Causes for Alcohol Misuse and Violence

In many cases, abuse of alcohol and a propensity to violence may stem from a common cause. This cause may be a temperamental trait, such as a risk-seeking personality, or a social environment (e.g., delinquent peers or lack of parental supervision) that encourages or contributes to deviant behavior.

Another example of a common cause relates to the frequent co-occurrence of antisocial personality disorder (ASPD) and early-onset (i.e., type II) alcoholism. ASPD is a psychiatric disorder characterized by a disregard for the rights of others, often manifested as a violent or criminal lifestyle. Type II alcoholism is characterized by high heritability from father to son; early onset of alcoholism (often during adolescence); and antisocial, sometimes violent, behavioral traits. Type II alcoholics and persons with ASPD overlap in their tendency to violence and excessive alcohol consumption and may share a genetic basis.

Spurious Associations

Spurious associations between alcohol consumption and violence may arise by chance or coincidence, with no direct or common cause. For example, drinking is a common social activity for many adult Americans, especially those most likely to commit violent acts. Therefore, drinking and violence may occur together by chance. In addition, violent criminals who drink heavily are more likely than less intoxicated offenders to be caught and consequently are over-represented in samples of convicts or arrestees. Spurious associations may sometimes be difficult to distinguish from common-cause associations.

Physiology of Violence

Although individual behavior is shaped in part by the environment, it is also influenced by biological factors (e.g., hormones) and ultimately planned and directed by the brain. Individual differences in brain chemistry may explain the observation that excessive alcohol consumption may consistently promote aggression in some persons, but not in others. The following subsections highlight some areas of intensive study.

Serotonin

Serotonin, a chemical messenger in the brain, is thought to function as a behavioral inhibitor. Thus, decreased serotonin activity is associated with increased impulsivity and aggressiveness as well as with early-onset alcoholism among men.

Researchers have developed an animal model that simulates many of the characteristics of alcoholism in humans. Rhesus macaque monkeys sometimes consume alcohol in sufficient quantities to become intoxicated. Macaques with low serotonin activity consume alcohol at elevated rates; these monkeys also demonstrate impaired impulse control, resulting in excessive and inappropriate aggression. This behavior and brain chemistry closely resemble that of type II alcoholics. Interestingly, among both macaques and humans, parental neglect leads to early-onset aggression and excessive alcohol consumption in the offspring, again correlated with decreased serotonin activity.

Although data are inconclusive, the alcohol-violence link may be mediated by chemical messengers in addition to serotonin, such as dopamine and norepinephrine. There is also considerable overlap among nerve cell pathways in the brain that regulate aspects of aggression, sexual behavior, and alcohol consumption. These observations suggest a biological basis for the frequent co-occurrence of alcohol intoxication and sexual violence.

Testosterone

The steroid hormone testosterone is responsible for the development of male primary and secondary sexual characteristics. High testosterone concentrations in criminals have been associated with violence, suspiciousness, and hostility. In animal experiments, alcohol administration increased aggressive behavior in socially dominant squirrel monkeys, who already exhibited high levels of aggression and testosterone. Alcohol did not, however, increase aggression in subordinate monkeys, which exhibited low levels of aggression and testosterone.

These findings may shed some light on the life cycle of violence in humans. In humans, violence occurs largely among adolescent and young adult males, who tend to have high levels of testosterone compared with the general population. Young men who exhibit antisocial behaviors often "burn out" with age, becoming less aggressive when they reach their forties. By that age, testosterone concentrations are decreasing, while serotonin concentrations are increasing, both factors that tend to restrain violent behavior.

Conclusion

No one model can account for all individuals or types of violence. Alcohol apparently may increase the risk of violent behavior only for certain individuals or subpopulations and only under some situations and social/cultural influences.

Although much remains to be learned, research suggests that some violent behavior may be amenable to treatment and some may be preventable. One study found decreased levels of marital violence in couples who completed behavioral marital therapy for alcoholism and remained sober during followup. Results of another study suggest that a 10-percent increase in the beer tax could reduce murder by 0.3 percent, rape by 1.32 percent, and robbery by 0.9 percent. Although these results are modest, they indicate a direction for future research. In addition, preliminary experiments have identified medications that have the potential to reduce violent behavior. Such medications include certain anticonvulsants (e.g., carbamazepine); mood stabilizers (e.g., lithium); and antidepressants, especially those that increase serotonin activity (e.g., fluoxetine). However, these studies either did not differentiate alcoholic from nonalcoholic subjects or excluded alcoholics from participation.

A Commentary by NIAAA Director Enoch Gordis, M.D.

Both alcohol use and violence are common in our society, and there are many associations between the two. Understanding the nature of these associations, including the environmental and biological antecedents of each and the ways in which they may be related, is essential to developing effective strategies to prevent alcohol-related violence as well as other social problems, such as domestic violence, sexual assault, and childhood abuse and neglect. Because no area of science stands apart from another, understanding more about alcohol-related violence also will shed light on violence in general and produce information that may be useful to reducing it.

Science has made progress on elucidating the environmental and biological antecedents of alcohol abuse and alcoholism; less progress has been made toward understanding the causes of violence. Understanding the biology of violence will help us to clearly define the role of the environment in increasing the risk for violence and increase our understanding of who is at risk for violent behavior. This understanding also will help us to develop effective interventions—both social and medical where intended—to help those whose violence has caused trouble for themselves and others.

Chapter 18

Violence and Crime

"In both animal and human studies, alcohol, more than any other drug, has been linked with a high incidence of violence and aggression." *Seventh Special Report to the U.S. Congress on Alcohol and Health* (Secretary of Health and Human Services, January 1990)

Crime is inextricably related to alcohol and other drugs (AOD). More than 1.1 million annual arrests for illicit drug violations, almost 1.4 million arrests for driving while intoxicated, 480,000 arrests for liquor law violations and 704,000 arrests for drunkenness come to a total of 4.3 million arrests for alcohol and other drug statutory crimes. That total accounts for over one-third of all arrests in this country.[1,2]

The impaired judgment and violence induced by alcohol contribute to alcohol-related crime. Rapes, fights, and assaults leading to injury, manslaughter, and homicide often are linked with alcohol because the perpetrator, the victim, or both, were drinking. The economic cost of AOD-related crime is $61.8 billion annually.[3]

Many perpetrators of violent crime were also using illicit drugs. Some of these drugs, such as PCP and steroids, may induce violence. These drugs can also be a catalyst for aggressive-prone individuals who exhibit violent behavior as a result of taking them.

"Violence and Crime and Alcohol and Other Drugs," *Making the Link Series*, National Clearinghouse for Alcohol and Drug Information (NCADI), NCADI Inventory Number ML002, Spring 1995.

The need for preventing alcohol and other drug problems is clear when the following statistics are examined:

- Alcohol is a key factor in up to 68 percent of manslaughters, 62 percent of assaults, 54 percent of murders/attempted murders, 48 percent of robberies, and 44 percent of burglaries.[4]
- Among jail inmates, 42.2 percent of those convicted of rape reported being under the influence of alcohol or alcohol and other drugs at the time of the offense.[5]
- Over 60 percent of men and 50 percent of women arrested for property crimes (burglary, larceny, robbery) in 1990, who were voluntarily tested, tested positive for illicit drug use.[2]
- In 1987, 64 percent of all reported child abuse and neglect cases in New York City were associated with parental AOD abuse.[6]

We cannot put a monetary value on the human lives and suffering associated with alcohol and other drug problems. But we know the child welfare and court costs needed to deal with the consequences of these problems are substantial. The cost to arrest, try, sentence, and incarcerate those found guilty for these 4.3 million alcohol- and other drug-related offenses is a tremendous drain on our Nation's resources.

References

All statistics cited in this *Making the Link* fact sheet come from the following sources:

1. U.S. Department of Justice, Bureau of Justice Statistics, *Crime in the United States 1991*, Washington, DC, 1992.
2. U.S. Department of Justice, Bureau of Justice Statistics, *Drugs, Crime, and the Justice System: A National Report*, Washington, DC, 1992.
3. Institute for Health Policy, Brandeis University, *Substance Abuse: The Nation's Number One Health Problem: Key Indicators for Policy*. The Robert Wood Johnson Foundation, October 1993.
4. U.S. Department of Health and Human Services, National Institute on Alcohol abuse and Alcoholism, *Alcohol and Health:*

Sixth Special Report to Congress on Alcohol and Health from the Secretary of Health and Human Services, 1987.

5. Collins, J.J. and Messerschmidt, M.A., Epidemiology of Alcohol-Related Violence, *Alcohol Health and Research World*, 17(2): 93-100, 1993, National Institute on Alcohol Abuse and Alcoholism.

6. Chasnoff, I.J., Drugs, *Alcohol, Pregnancy and Parenting*, Northwestern University Medical School, Departments of Pediatrics and Psychiatry and Behavioral Sciences, Hingham, MA, Kluwer Academic Publishers, 1988.

Chapter 19

Alcohol and Suicide

> "They [researchers] cite a wide range of potential suicide triggers, from loss of employment or loved ones, to aging and physical impairment. But, in almost all cases, they agree there is an underlying psychiatric illness—primarily depression, followed by alcoholism and substance abuse." "The Mystery of Suicide," *Newsweek*, April 18, 1994

Authorities agree that many suicides are not reported, but the National Center for Health Statistics records between 25,000 and 30,000 self-inflicted deaths in the U.S. annually. For every death from suicide, experts estimate that eight other suicide attempts are made. Suicide is now the second leading cause of death among persons 15 to 24 years of age. It is increasingly a problem among adolescents and elderly people.[1]

No cause-and-effect relationship between use of alcohol and/or other drugs and suicide has been established, but such use often is a contributing factor. Research indicates several possible explanations. Drinking, use of other drugs, or both may reduce inhibitions and impair the judgment of someone contemplating suicide, making the act more likely. And use of AOD also may aggravate other risk factors for suicide such as depression or other mental illness.[1]

"Alcohol and Other Drugs and Suicide," *Making the Link Series*, National Clearinghouse for Alcohol and Drug Information (NCADI), NCADI Inventory Number ML009, Spring 1995.

High rates of alcohol involvement have been found among suicide victims who use firearms. Recent studies suggest that alcohol tends to be associated with impulsive rather than premeditated suicides.[2]

Other research findings underscore the importance of alcohol/other drug problem prevention in reducing suicides:

- Between 20 and 35 percent of suicide victims had a history of alcohol abuse or were drinking shortly before their suicides.[2]
- In one study of youthful suicide, drug and alcohol abuse was the most common characteristic of those who attempted suicide; fully 70 percent of these young people frequently used alcohol and/or other drugs.[3]
- Nearly 24 percent of suicide victims in another study had blood alcohol concentrations (BACs) of .10 or greater (the legal level for intoxication in many jurisdictions).[4]

Similarly, an analysis of 100,000 deaths in 1989 found positive BACs in 35 percent of suicide fatalities.[4]

In 1989, the cost of providing health care for people who had attempted suicide was estimated at $116.4 million annually.[1]

As the fifth leading cause of years of potential life lost, suicide claims an estimated total of 900,000 years of life in America every year.[1] Yet, the value of lives lost to suicide and the impact on those they leave behind cannot be measured.

References

All statistics cited in this *Making the Link* fact sheet come from the following sources:

1. National Committee for Injury Prevention and Control, "Injury Prevention: Meeting the Challenge," 1993.
2. *Seventh Special Report to the U.S. Congress on Alcohol and Health*, January 1990.
3. U.S. Department of Education, "Youth & Alcohol: Selected Reports to the Surgeon General," 1993.
4. *Eighth Special Report to the U.S. Congress on Alcohol and Health*, September 1993.

Part Two

Alcohol's Physical Effects

Chapter 20

The Effects of Alcohol

The Origins of Alcohol

Ethyl alcohol, or ethanol, is a clear, thin, odorless liquid that boils at 173 degrees F (78 degrees C). It can burn, it can be mixed with water in any proportion, and it is one of the few alcohols that is made for consumption; however, it never exists full-strength in any alcoholic beverage. Ethyl alcohol is the subject of this chapter, and from now on will be referred to simply as "alcohol."

Alcohol is produced during a natural process called fermentation, which occurs when yeast, a microscopic plant that floats freely in the air, reacts with the sugar in fruit or vegetable juice, creating alcohol and releasing carbon dioxide. The process stops naturally when about 11% to 14% of the juice is alcohol; the product of this fermentation is wine. A similar process is used to make beer.

Distillation is the process used to make beverages with a higher alcohol content. In this process the fermented liquid is heated until it vaporizes, and then the vapor is cooled until it condenses into a liquid again. Distilled alcoholic beverages (e.g., whiskey, gin, vodka, and rum) contain 40% to 50% alcohol. They are sometimes referred to as "spirits" or "hard liquor."

"Facts on: The Effects of Alcohol," Fact Sheet No. 15, by Gail Gleason Milgram, Ed.D., Center of Alcohol Studies, Rutgers, The State University of New Jersey, © 1996. Reproduced with permission from the Rutgers University Center of Alcohol Studies, 607 Allison Rd., Piscataway, NJ 08854-8001.

Alcohol in the Body

When someone drinks an alcoholic beverage it flows into the stomach. While it is in the stomach, the drinker does not feel the effects of the alcohol, but alcohol does not remain in the stomach very long. Some of it is absorbed through the stomach walls into the bloodstream, but most alcohol passes into the small intestine and then into the bloodstream, and this circulates throughout the body. Once alcohol is in the bloodstream it reaches the brain and the drinker begins to feel its effects. The reason that a large person does not feel the effects of a drink as quickly as a small person is because the large person has more blood and other body fluids and will not have as high a level of alcohol in the blood after drinking the same amount of alcohol.

The body disposes of alcohol in two ways: elimination and oxidation. Only about 10% of the alcohol in the body leaves by elimination from the lungs and kidneys. About 90% of the alcohol leaves by oxidation. The liver plays a major role in the body's oxidation of alcohol. When alcohol enters the liver, some of it is changed to a chemical called acetaldehyde. When acetaldehyde is combined with oxygen, acetic acid is formed. When the acetic acid is further combined with oxygen, carbon dioxide and water are formed.

The oxidation of alcohol produces calories. One ounce of pure alcohol contains about 163 calories (or about 105 calories in a 1 1/2 ounce glass of whiskey or gin), but it does not contain vitamins or other physically beneficial nutrients. The liver can oxidize only a certain amount of alcohol each minute; the oxidation rate of alcohol in a person weighing 150 pounds, for example, is about 7 grams of alcohol per hour. This is equivalent to about 3/4 of an ounce of distilled spirits, 2 1/2 ounces of wine, or 7 3/4 to 8 ounces of beer per hour. If a person drank no more than 3/4 of an ounce of whiskey or half a bottle of beer every hour, the alcohol would never accumulate in the body, the person would feel little of the effects of the alcohol, and would not become intoxicated.

Oxidation continues until all the alcohol has left the body. Since the body can remove only a small amount of alcohol at a time, those who choose to drink are advised to drink slowly.

The Effects of Alcohol

The effects of alcohol on an individual depend on a variety of factors. These include:

- *How one feels before drinking:* If a person is upset and tense, very excited, sad, nervous, or even extremely happy, he or she may tend to gulp drinks and actually consume more alcohol than planned.
- *What the drinker expects alcohol to do:* Some people expect a drink to help them feel relaxed, happy, angry or sad. Quite naturally, these feelings can be produced by the drink; how you want to feel helps you feel that way.
- *How much one drinks:* A person who has one drink during dinner is not likely to feel the effects of alcohol. But having six drinks before and during dinner means the individual might not make it through dessert.
- *How long one takes to drink:* This is a critical factor: four drinks in one hour will have an obvious effect on the drinker, but the same four drinks over a four-hour period will probably have a very slight, if any, effect.
- *Type of alcoholic beverage:* Some beverages have more alcohol in them than others. Beer has about 4.5% alcohol, "table wines" average from 11% to 14%, "fortified" or "dessert wines" (such as sherry or port) have 16% to 20%, and distilled spirits range from 40% to 50%. However, in normal size, each drink (i.e., 12 ounces of beer, 5 ounces of wine, and 1 1/2 ounces of distilled spirits) contains approximately the same amount of alcohol.
- *Size of the drinker:* Because of the way alcohol circulates in the body, the size of the drinker also relates to the effects of alcohol. A person weighing 220 pounds will not feel the effects of a drink as much as a person weighing 120 pounds.
- *Food in the stomach:* The alcohol consumed does not affect the drinker until it has been absorbed into the bloodstream. Food in the stomach slows the alcohol's absorption, so that a person who has a drink after eating a meal will feel less effect than a person who has a drink on an empty stomach.
- *Experience in using alcoholic beverages:* Someone drinking a glass of wine may experience light-headedness the first time, but will probably not experience that effect on subsequent occasions. However, most individuals who drink know what to expect from various amounts of alcohol because of their prior experience with drinking.

Alcohol acts directly on the brain, and affects its ability to work. The effects of alcohol on the brain are quite complex, but alcohol is usually classified as a depressant. Judgment is the first function of the brain to be affected; the ability to think and make decisions becomes impaired. As more alcohol is consumed, the motor functions of the body are affected.

The effects of alcohol are directly related to the concentration (percentage) of alcohol in the blood; however, the effects vary among individuals and even in the same individual at different times. In the following description, the blood alcohol concentrations (BAC) are those that would probably be found in a person weighing about 150 pounds:

- At a BAC of 0.03% (after about one cocktail, one glass of wine, or one bottle of beer), the drinker will feel relaxed and experience a slight feeling of exhilaration.
- At 0.06% (after two cocktails, two glasses of wine, or two bottles of beer), the drinker will experience a feeling of warmth and relaxation; there will be a decrease of fine motor skills and he or she will be less concerned with minor irritations.
- At 0.09% (after three cocktails, three glasses of wine, or three bottles of beer), reaction time will be slowed, muscle control will be poor, speech will be slurred and the legs will feel wobbly.
- At 0.12% (after four cocktails, four glasses of wine, or four bottles of beer), his or her judgment will be clouded, inhibitions and self-restraint lessened, and the ability to reason and make logical decisions will be impaired.
- At 0.15% (after five cocktails, five glasses of wine, or five bottles of beer), vision will be blurred, speech unclear, walking will be unsteady, and coordination impaired.
- At 0.18% (after six cocktails, six glasses of wine, or six bottles of beer), all of the drinker's behavior will be impaired, and he or she will find it difficult to stay awake.
- At a BAC of about 0.30% alcohol in the blood (after 10 to 12 drinks), the drinker will be in a semi-stupor or deep sleep. Most people are not able to stay awake to reach a BAC higher than 0.30%.
- If the BAC reaches 0.50% the drinker is in a deep coma and in danger of death. As the alcohol level reaches 1% in the blood, the breathing center in the brain becomes paralyzed and death occurs.

In many states a BAC of 0.10% is considered legal evidence that a driver is intoxicated; some states use a BAC of 0.08%. In some European countries the legal BAC is as low as 0.05%.

About the Author

Gail Gleason Milgram, Ed.D., is a Professor and Director of the Education and Training Division at the Rutgers University Center of Alcohol Studies:

Rutgers Center for Alcohol Studies
607 Allison Road
Piscataway, NJ 08854-8001
Phone: (732) 445-2190
Fax: (732) 445-3500
E-mail: chrouse@rci.rutgers.edu
Web site: http://www.rci.rutgers.edu/~cas2/

Chapter 21

Medical Effects of Heavy Drinking in Late Life

As many as 15% of community-dwelling older persons are heavy drinkers,[1] but their alcoholism is often hidden from their physicians. The atypical or non-specific presentation of illness that is common in later life may mask the concomitant [occurring at the same time] effects of alcohol abuse. Moreover, patients are unlikely to admit to having a problem with alcohol during history-taking at a routine office visit.

It comes as no surprise, therefore, that physicians have not demonstrated a great track record for identifying patients who are problem drinkers. For example:

- Less than one-half the primary care physicians in a study supported by the Agency for Health Care Policy and Research included alcohol abuse in the diagnosis of patients who drank four or more drinks per day.[2]
- Medical staff correctly identified only 33 of 99 problem drinkers in a study of 265 older persons with a history of substance abuse.[3]

To help recognize alcohol abuse in late life, this chapter discusses the physiologic and psychological characteristics of older persons that predispose them to this problem.

 Although this document was written for physicians, concerned family members and friends may find the information useful. Bracketed comments have been added to assist the lay reader.

Patterns of Alcoholism in the Older Patient

Few realize the true extent of substance abuse by older Americans. The prevalence of alcohol abuse alone is 3 to 15% among those living in the community[1] and as high as 18 to 44% in general medical[4] and psychiatric[5] inpatients, respectively. In a study of 1,150 older men (mean age, 73.7 years), 10.4% reported they had been "heavy" drinkers at some time during their lives.[6]

Depression, loneliness, and lack of social support are the most frequently cited antecedents [previous circumstances] to drinking for older alcoholics.[7] Drinking in secrecy is common, as are attempts to minimize the true extent of alcohol use when pressed by family or physicians.

Alcohol abuse in later life is often associated with psychiatric disorders, such as depression and anxiety. A study in Canada of 3,258 randomly selected household residents over age 65 reported a lifetime prevalence of drug abuse/dependence of 6.9%, with a male:female ratio of 3 to 1. These authors noted that 80.3% of those with substance abuse/dependence also had a lifetime diagnosis of another psychiatric disorder.[8]

More than 50% of older persons experience either depression or serious anxiety at some time during later life. Blazer and Williams reported significant depression in about 15% of a population of community-dwelling elderly.[9]

The prevalence of dementia is 10% in persons over age 70 and as high as 22 to 47% in persons over age 80. Symptoms of dementia may be confused with those of alcohol abuse, thus delaying proper diagnosis. Chronic alcohol abuse may also result in cognitive decline.

Patterns of Alcoholism

There appear to be two patterns of alcohol abuse in older persons:

- *Early-onset alcoholics* began drinking in their younger years, have had a lifetime pattern of drinking, and continue to drink in late life.
- *Late-onset alcoholics* have developed alcoholic drinking patterns for the first time late in life.

A family history of alcoholism is much more common in individuals who began abusing alcohol earlier in life. Early-onset drinkers more frequently have a personality disorder, schizophrenia, poor socioeconomic status, malnutrition, and history of multiple physical injuries (e.g., from alcohol-related accidents or behavioral problems).

The late-onset drinker usually has a history of stable early adjustment and positive work history and is more likely than the early-onset alcoholic to live with family in later years.

The Older Alcoholic: Physiologic Changes

Clinically, the same amount of alcohol once consumed in prior years with impunity may cause clinical symptoms in late life. Physiologic changes seen with normal aging make older patients particularly susceptible to problems from acute alcohol toxicity (Table 21.1).

Table 21.1. Acute Alcohol Ingestion: Medical complications in older adults.

- Cognitive impairment and confusion, even with moderate intake
- Increased cardiac rate and output; increased blood pressure
- Hypothermia from cutaneous vasodilation and loss of body heat
- Acute gastritis and acute pancreatitis
- Alcohol-induced hypoglycemia
- Inhibition of antidiuretic hormone, leading to volume depletion, electrolyte disturbance, and dehydration

Source: Prepared for Geriatrics *by Steven R. Gambert, MD*

Volume of Distribution

Alcohol consumed as a beverage is distributed to the fluid compartment of the body. The decline in extra-cellular and intracellular fluid and the higher proportion of body fat to muscle associated with normal aging result in a decreased volume of distribution.

As a result, the alcohol load from a drink that reaches the central nervous system (CNS) is increased with age. This makes older persons particularly vulnerable to alcohol's acute effects, including altered cognition and behavior and an increased tendency for accidents and falls. The elderly alcoholic may be mistakenly diagnosed with dementia or a tumor rather than a subdural hematoma [a swelling from a mass of blood under the dura, which covers the brain and spinal column] resulting from a fall during a bout of drinking.

Cognitive Changes

The number of brain cells also declines with normal aging, further increasing the alcohol-to-brain-cell ratio in older persons who drink. The basal ganglion [a part of the brain involved with movement], hippocampus [part of the brain system that is involved with motivation and emotion], reticular activating system [directs attention and maintains wakefulness], and neocortex [involved with the processing of some types of sensory information] undergo neuronal loss with aging at faster rates than do other regions of the brain. These changes may result in altered cognition and motor skills. Even moderate drinking will take an additional toll on these processes.

Cognitive deficits resulting from alcohol abuse magnify other age-related changes or disease. Alcohol-related confusion may be confounded by underlying illness, such as mild dementia. When evaluating an elderly patient, be aware that a confused, disoriented older patient might be drunk rather than demented. Any change in mental status warrants evaluation.

Cardiac Effects

Alcohol exerts an acute effect on cardiac muscle, increasing cardiac rate and output. Systolic blood pressure [the "top" number] may be increased and blood shunted from the splanchnic circulation [for vital organs] to the periphery, resulting in cutaneous vasodilation [dilation of the skin blood vessels] and loss of body heat. These effects—when coupled with other age-related problems in maintaining thermoneutrality and generating heat through shivering—can put the older person who drinks at increased risk of hypothermia [low body temperature].

Gastrointestinal (GI) Changes

Alcohol increases acid production by the stomach's parietal [wall] cells. Although aging results in decline in parietal cell mass, there may be a breakdown in the mucosal lining due to other pathology [conditions produced by diseases]. Alcohol consumption increases the risk of hyperemia [too much blood in a body part], increased mucus production, and decreased acid secretion leading to acute gastritis. The resultant nausea and vomiting may predispose the older alcoholic to electrolyte disturbances and dehydration.

Pancreatic Changes

Alcohol may stimulate the production of secretin by the pancreas, resulting in increased pancreatic enzyme output. These proteolytic enzymes may lead to autodigestion [digestion of tissue by its own secretions] of pancreatic tissue and acute pancreatitis. Alcohol may cause inflammation of the duodenum, with resulting edema and spasm at the sphincter of Oddi of the common bile duct [where the common bile duct opens into the duodenum], leading to an obstruction of pancreatic flow.

Ketoacidosis

Acute alcohol ingestion may result in alcoholic ketoacidosis [an increase in the blood's acidity due to the presence of ketones], a particularly serious problem for older patients due to decreased reserve capacity and the likelihood of co-existing illness. Arterial blood pH is reduced with a high anion gap [measurement of the difference between positively and negatively charged ions]. Test results for serum ketones are usually only weakly positive, because beta-hydroxy butyrate, the predominant ketone of ethyl alcohol, is not detected by standard tests for ketones.

Patients with alcoholic ketoacidosis may be alert yet ill or frankly comatose. Supportive care, with particular attention to fluid and electrolytes, is essential until metabolic balance returns.

Hypoglycemia

Older persons with poor dietary habits or anorexia associated with chronic disease are particularly susceptible to alcohol-induced hypoglycemia. Glycogen stores are impaired by periods of low caloric intake and alcohol's inhibition of hepatic gluconeogenesis [the formation of glycogen in the liver].

Hypoglycemia will have a greater impact on older persons, because they have less efficient counter-regulatory mechanisms and fewer brain, cardiac, and renal cells. This decreased reserve may result in more significant tissue damage and altered physiologic damage from the hypoglycemia.

Alcohol-induced hypoglycemia can also increase the risk of confusion, tachycardia [rapid heart beat], falls, and other autonomic [independently-functioning] and neuroglucopenic [system that delivers glucose to the brain] symptoms, especially when coupled with age-prevalent post-prandial [after eating] hypoglycemia or the use by patients with type II diabetes of oral hypoglycemic agents.

Diuresis

Alcohol inhibits anti-diuretic hormone secretion from the posterior pituitary gland, leading to prompt water diuresis [large amounts of urine]. This may result in urinary incontinence, volume depletion, electrolyte disturbances, and changes in mental status.

Other Effects

Central nervous system (CNS) depression secondary to acute alcohol ingestion is well known. Tendon reflexes may be hyperactive due to reduced inhibitory spinal motor neuronal activity.

Chronic Metabolic Effects of Alcohol Abuse

Much like the aging process, chronic alcohol abuse can affect almost every cell, organ, and tissue of the body (see Table 21.2).

Hepatic [Liver] Effects

Perhaps the most studied complication of chronic alcohol abuse is liver toxicity. Liver disease may range from fatty metamorphosis to cirrhosis. Consequences may include systemic complaints of fatigue, anorexia, and weight loss. Until jaundice is noted, these vague complaints may not be ascribed to alcoholic liver disease in patients with other age-prevalent disorders.

On examination, patients may show typical clinical signs, including spider angioma [a pattern of thin red lines created by dilated capillaries], icterus [jaundice], ecchymosis [irregular patches of blue-black discoloration of the skin], gynecomastia [in men, the enlargement of breast tissue], testicular atrophy, muscle wasting, palmar erythema [red palms], and Dupuytren's contracture [a condition in which the ring finger and little finger bend toward the palm and cannot be straightened]. However, these findings may be easily mistaken for other disorders or wrongly blamed on advanced age. Even laboratory testing may be misleading, as liver function tests may be normal even as the liver fails and production of hepatic enzymes is diminished.

In the primary care setting, increased prothrombin times [the time it takes for blood clots to form] and reduced serum albumin [the main protein found in blood] are highly suggestive of advanced liver disease. Once liver disease is detected, advise patients to abstain from alcohol while consuming sufficient calories and vitamins. Doses of medications cleared through the liver must be adjusted. Severe disease will require protein and sodium restriction.

Impotence

Impotence is common among older men with vascular disorders and particularly among chronic drinkers. Age itself is not a cause of impotence, and a man's quality of life is affected by impotence, regardless of his age.

The liver is the major site of binding globulin production and catabolism of testosterone and conjugation of its metabolites with sulfuric or glucuronic acid [that is, metabolic processes in the liver effect

Table 21.2. Chronic Alcohol Ingestion: Medical complications in older adults.

Hormonal	Increased ratio of free estrogen to free testosterone, worsening age-related decline in testosterone
Cardiac	Cardiomyopathy; Cardiomegaly; Cardiac fibrosis; Microvascular infarction with associated reduced myocardial contractility and tachycardia
Oral	Glossitis; Stomatitis; Parotid gland enlargement
Gastrointestinal	Chronic gastritis
Blood disorders	Mixed anemias secondary to multiple deficiencies (i.e., iron, folate, vitamin B_{12}); Thrombocytopenia; Granulocytopenia
Hepatic	Fatty metamorphosis; Cirrhosis
Nutritional deficiencies	Protein-calorie malnutrition; Hypomagnesemia; Hypophosphatemia; Hypocalcemia; Hypovitaminosis; Thiamine deficiency

Source: Prepared for Geriatrics *by Steven R. Gambert, MD*

the male hormone testosterone]. Therefore, alcoholic changes may result in an increase in the ratio of physiologically free estrogen to free androgen, leading to testicular atrophy, spider angioma, palmar erythema, and gynecomastia.

An increased rate of conversion of adrenocorticosteroid [a hormone] precursors to estrogen has also been reported. This is thought to result from decreased uptake of androstenedione by the diseased liver, with a resultant increase in estrone production. Decreased concentrations of plasma testosterone, decreased testosterone production, increased testosterone clearance, and an altered hypothalamic pituitary axis [the hypothalmus and pituitary gland are both involved with hormone regulation in the body] have all been noted following alcohol ingestion, even in the absence of liver disease.

Discontinuation of alcohol may lead to improved liver function and return of normal testosterone levels. However, once liver disease has upset the hormonal balance necessary for sexual function, these changes may be permanent.

Testosterone replacement therapy may correct the abnormality, but this therapy is not without risk. Testosterone may worsen the symptoms of prostatic hypertrophy, and there is concern that the hormone may stimulate prostate cancer growth.

Heart Disease

Chronic alcohol ingestion has both a direct and indirect effect on the cardiovascular system. Care must be taken not to blame cardiomyopathy on atherosclerotic disease when, in fact, it is alcohol-induced. Alcohol has been associated with cardiomegaly [enlarged heart], cardiac fibrosis [abnormal fibrous tissue], microvascular infarcts, and swelling and altered subcellular myocardial [heart muscle] components, glycogen, and lipid deposition. Clinically, chronic alcoholism has been associated with reduced myocardial contractility and output and with tachycardia.

Gastrointestinal (GI) Disorders

Older persons who abuse alcohol chronically have higher rates of glossitis [inflammation of the tongue], stomatitis [inflammation of the mouth], and parotid gland [located near the ear] enlargement. An increased incidence of squamous cell carcinoma [a type of cancer] of the oral pharynx may be further exacerbated by tobacco use, which is often seen with alcoholism.

Chronic gastritis [inflammation of the stomach] may lead to iron deficiency anemia. Anemia may also result from a deficiency in folate or vitamin B_{12}. Sideroblastic and hemolytic anemia are also more common in alcoholics than in nonalcoholics.

Alcohol is the most common cause of thrombocytopenia [decrease in blood platelets], which may occur with or without granulocytopenia [decrease in granulocytes, which are a type of white blood cell]. Failure of these parameters to return to normal within one week of abstinence usually indicates another etiologic factor [cause] or a chronic complication of alcohol use.

Nutritional Deficiencies

Protein-calorie malnutrition, select vitamin deficiencies, hypomagnesemia, hypophosphatemia, and hypocalcemia [low amounts of magnesium, phosphate, and calcium] are seen in older alcoholics. Cirrhotic changes related to chronic alcoholism may impair the ability of the liver to hydroxylate vitamin D to 25-hydroxy-vitamin D (calcifediol). It is calcifediol that is hydroxylated primarily in the kidney to 1, 25-dihydroxy-vitamin D (calcitriol), the most active form of vitamin D_3 in stimulating intestinal calcium and phosphate transport. [In other words, chronic alcoholism may damage the liver in way that causes problems with the body's ability to metabolize vitamin D. This results in an impairment of the body's ability to properly absorb calcium and phosphate in the intestines.]

Deficiencies in dietary intake of vitamin D, malabsorption of fat, and the concomitant use [use at the same time] of phenytoin or phenobarbital may also impair vitamin D metabolism. The result may be osteomalacia [soft bones], with increased risk of bone pain and fractures.

Wernicke-Korsakoff syndrome is associated with thiamine deficiency commonly found in alcoholism. Its cognitive symptoms can easily be mistaken as a delirium or a dementia if the patient's alcohol abuse is unrecognized. The typical patient has been living alone with no documented history of a cognitive impairment and is admitted to the hospital for a medical problem. During hospitalization, their cognitive impairment is usually very obvious and may be thought to be dementia of acute onset or delirium related to medication or some other etiology, such as infection.

EEG tracing may demonstrate a diffuse slowing pattern or be normal. Cerebrospinal fluid and laboratory profiles are usually within normal range. Thiamine treatment is quite effective at rapid restoration of thiamine levels, although the memory deficit often remains.

Management of Alcoholism in Older Patients

Identification of alcoholism as a problem is the first step to evaluation and treatment of the older patient. A useful warning sign is the daily use of alcohol. However, some patients are reluctant or embarrassed to admit a problem, and others with cognitive deficits may not remember drinking. Interviewing family members or acquaintances is often useful when you suspect alcohol abuse.

It is often not possible to apply the usual diagnostic criteria of alcohol abuse to the elderly alcoholic. For example, those who are retired would not have a record of work-related absenteeism, and those who no longer drive would not accumulate a pattern of traffic offenses.

The CAGE questionnaire is a practical and reliable tool that can be used in the primary care office to screen for alcohol abuse. Alcohol abuse is considered to exist if a person answers "yes" to two or more of four simple questions that start with, "Have you ever. . .":

- tried to **C**ut down on your drinking?
- been **A**nnoyed by anybody criticizing your drinking?
- felt **G**uilty about your drinking?
- had an **E**ye-opener (drink) in the morning?[10]

In some cases, addiction to alcohol occurs unknowingly. Patients may be unaware that some over-the-counter medications (e.g., antitussive preparations [cough medicine]) contain potentially harmful and addicting amounts of alcohol. A medication review may provide insight into potentially addictive preparations your patients may be using.

Medical Treatment

Many older alcoholics do not realize how greatly alcohol affects their cognition. For some patients, a direct discussion may be all that is needed to convince them to stop drinking. In most cases, however, it is not this simple.

The goal of treatment must be total abstinence. Older alcoholics are at least as likely as younger alcoholics to make treatment contact, remain in treatment, and recover.[11] Programs tailored to the older person may have the highest success rate in this population. In a study of 137 older alcoholic patients randomly assigned to either an "older alcoholic rehabilitation" program or a conventional program, those in the special program were 2.1 times more likely to report abstinence at 1 year.[12]

Older patients may also benefit from participating in programs such as Alcoholics Anonymous, although members of this organization tend to be younger than age 65. AA chapters that meet at local senior centers may be helpful.

For patients whose alcohol use has led to dietary deficiencies and vitamin inadequacy, replacement therapy is essential. Medical support for alcohol-induced conditions is also warranted. Specific measures include the use of thiamine supplements (100 mg/d) for at least the first week of treatment. In certain cases, hospitalization may be necessary to treat acute illness or chronic changes in need of careful evaluation and therapy.

Summary

Late-life alcohol abuse can lead to reduced function, quality of life, and premature institutionalization. Physicians need to be alert to the possibility of occult [hidden] alcohol abuse in the routine workup of older patients. Detection of problem drinking can improve the diagnostic accuracy of concomitant disease and open the door for interventions to help patients recover from alcohol dependence.

References

1. Myers JK, et al. Six month prevalence of psychiatric disorders in three communities. *Arch Gen Psychiatry* 1984; 41:959.

2. Wenrich MD, Paauw DS, Carline JD, et al. Do primary care physicians screen patients about alcohol intake using the CAGE questions? *J Gen Intern Med* 1995; 10:631-4.

3. McInnes E, Powell J. Drug and alcohol referrals: Are elderly substance abuse diagnoses and referrals being missed? *BMJ* 1994; 308:444-6.

4. McCusher J, Cherubin CE, Zimberg S. Prevalence of alcoholism in general municipal hospital population. *New York State J Med* 1971; 71:751.

5. Moore RA. The diagnosis of alcoholism in a psychiatric hospital: A trial of the Michigan Alcoholism Screening Test. *Am J Psychiatry* 1972; 128:1565.

6. Colsher PL, Wallace RB. Elderly men with histories of heavy drinking: Correlates and consequences. *J Stud Alcohol* 1990; 51:528-35.

7. Schonfeld L, Dupree LW. Antecedents of drinking for early-and late-onset elderly alcohol abusers. *J Stud Alcohol* 1991; 52:587-92.

8. Russell JM, Newman SC, Bland RC. Epidemiology of psychiatric disorders in Edmonton. Drug abuse and dependence. *Acta Psychiatr Scand* 1994; 376 (suppl):54-62.

9. Blazer D, Williams CD. Epidemiology of dysphonia and depression in an elderly population. *Am J Psychiatry* 1980; 137:439.

10. Ewing JA. Detecting alcoholism: The CAGE questionnaire. *JAMA* 1984; 252:1905.

11. Fitzgerald JL, Mulford HA. Elderly vs. younger problem drinker "treatment" and recovery experiences. *Br J Addiction* 1992; 87:1281-91.

12. Kashner TM, Rodell DE, Ogden SR, Guggenheim FG, Karson CN. Outcomes and costs of two VA inpatient treatment programs for older alcoholic patients. *Hosp Community Psychiatry* 1992; 43:985-9.

About the Author

Dr. Steven R. Gambert is professor and vice chairman for academic affairs, department of medicine, UMDNJ-New Jersey Medical School, Newark, and a member of *Geriatrics*' Editorial Board.

Chapter 22

Alcohol Hangover

What Is a Hangover?

A hangover is characterized by the constellation of unpleasant physical and mental symptoms that occur after a bout of heavy alcohol drinking (see Table 22.1). Physical symptoms of a hangover include fatigue, headache, increased sensitivity to light and sound, redness of the eyes, muscle aches, and thirst. Signs of increased sympathetic nervous system activity can accompany a hangover, including increased systolic blood pressure, rapid heartbeat (i.e., tachycardia), tremor, and sweating. Mental symptoms include dizziness; a sense of the room spinning (i.e., vertigo); and possible cognitive and mood disturbances, especially depression, anxiety, and irritability. The particular set of symptoms experienced and their intensity may vary from person to person and from occasion to occasion. In addition, hangover characteristics may depend on the type of alcoholic beverage consumed and the amount a person drinks. Typically, a hangover begins within several hours after the cessation of drinking, when a person's blood alcohol concentration (BAC) is falling. Symptoms usually peak about the time BAC is zero and may continue for up to 24 hours thereafter.

Excerpted from, "Alcohol hangover: mechanisms and mediators," by Robert Swift and Dena Davidson, in *Alcohol Health & Research World*, Winter 1998, Vol. 22, No. 1, p. 54(7). A complete copy of this publication may be ordered from the U.S. Government Printing Office. Call (202) 512-1800 for information on price and availability.

Table 22.1. Symptoms of Hangover

Class of Symptoms	Type
Constitutional	Fatigue, weakness, and thirst
Pain	Headache and muscle aches
Gastrointestinal	Nausea, vomiting, and stomach pain
Sleep and biological rhythms	Decreased sleep, decreased REM (rapid eye movements), and increased slow-wave sleep
Sensory	Vertigo and sensitivity to light and sound
Cognitive	Decreased attention and concentration
Mood	Depression, anxiety, and irritability
Sympathetic hyperactivity	Tremor, sweating, and increased pulse and systolic blood pressure

Overlap exists between hangover and the symptoms of mild alcohol withdrawal (AW), leading to the assertion that hangover is a manifestation of mild withdrawal. Hangovers, however, may occur after a single bout of drinking, whereas withdrawal occurs usually after multiple, repeated bouts. Other differences between hangover and AW include a shorter period of impairment (i.e., hours for hangover versus several days for withdrawal) and a lack of hallucinations and seizures in hangover.

People experiencing a hangover feel ill and impaired. Although a hangover may impair task performance and thereby increase the risk of injury, equivocal data exist on whether hangover actually impairs complex mental tasks. When subjects with a BAC of zero were tested following alcohol intoxication with peak BACs in the range of 50 to 100 milligrams per deciliter (mg/dL), most of them did not show significant impairments in the performance of simple mental tasks, such as reaction time. Similarly, several studies that investigated the hangover effects on a more complex mental task (i.e., simulated automobile driving) did not report impaired performance. In contrast, a study of military pilots completing a simulated flying task revealed significant decrements in some performance measures (particularly among older pilots) 8 to 14 hours after they had consumed enough alcohol to be considered legally drunk.

Prevalence of Hangover

Generally, the greater the amount and duration of alcohol consumption, the more prevalent is the hangover, although some people report experiencing a hangover after drinking low levels of alcohol (i.e., one to three alcoholic drinks), and some heavy drinkers do not report experiencing hangovers at all. A survey by Harburg and colleagues (1993) on the prevalence of hangovers found that approximately 75 percent of the subjects who drank to intoxication reported experiencing a hangover at least some of the time. In a study of 2,160 Finnish men, researchers found an association between increased weekly alcohol consumption and the frequency of hangover: 43.8 percent of the group of heaviest drinkers (i.e., study subjects who drank more than 106 grams [g] of alcohol per week or approximately 9 drinks) reported experiencing a hangover monthly or more often, compared with 6.6 percent of the remaining study subjects. Similarly, in a study of 1,041 drinkers in New York State, 50 percent of the subjects who drank two or more drinks per day reported experiencing hangovers in the previous year, whereas subjects who consumed lower levels of alcohol reported fewer hangovers. Other reports, however, claim that hangovers occur less often in heavy drinkers. In a study of 43 alcoholic drinkers admitted for inpatient treatment, 50 percent of the subjects reported experiencing no hangovers within the previous year and 23 percent reported never experiencing a hangover.

Physiologocal Factors Contributing to Hangover

Hangover symptoms have been attributed to several causes, including the direct physiological effects of alcohol on the brain and other organs; the effects of the removal of alcohol from these organs after alcohol exposure (i.e., withdrawal); the physiological effects of compounds produced as a result of alcohol's metabolism (i.e., metabolites), especially acetaldehyde; and nonalcohol factors, such as the toxic effects of other biologically active chemicals (i.e., congeners) in the beverage, behaviors associated with the alcohol-drinking bout (e.g., other drug use, restricted food intake, and disruption of normal sleep time), and certain personal characteristics (e.g., temperament, personality, and family history of alcoholism). Although current evidence suggests that more than one factor most likely contributes to the overall hangover state, the following sections address each of the postulated causes in turn.

Direct Alcohol Effects

Alcohol may directly contribute to a hangover in several ways, including the following.

Dehydration and Electrolyte Imbalance. Alcohol causes the body to increase urinary output (i.e., it is a diuretic). The consumption of 50 g of alcohol in 250 milliliters (mL) of water (i.e. approximately 4 drinks) causes the elimination of 600 to 1,000 mL (or up to 1 quart) of water over several hours. Alcohol promotes urine production by inhibiting the release of a hormone (i.e., antidiuretic hormone, or vasopressin) from the pituitary gland. In turn, reduced levels of antidiuretic hormone prevent the kidneys from reabsorbing (i.e., conserving) water and thereby increase urine production. Additional mechanisms must be at work to increase urine production, however, because antidiuretic hormone levels increase as BAC levels decline to zero during hangover. Sweating, vomiting, and diarrhea also commonly occur during a hang-over, and these conditions can result in additional fluid loss and electrolyte imbalances. Symptoms of mild to moderate dehydration include thirst, weakness, dryness of mucous membranes, dizziness, and lightheadedness—all commonly observed during a hangover.

Gastrointestinal Disturbances. Alcohol directly irritates the stomach and intestines, causing inflammation of the stomach lining (i.e., gastritis) and delayed stomach emptying, especially when beverages with a high alcohol concentration (i.e., greater than 15 percent) are consumed. High levels of alcohol consumption also can produce fatty liver, an accumulation of fat compounds called triglycerides and their components (i.e., free fatty acids) in liver cells. In addition, alcohol increases the production of gastric acid as well as pancreatic and intestinal secretions. Any or all of these factors can result in the upper abdominal pain, nausea, and vomiting experienced during a hangover.

Low Blood Sugar. Several alterations in the metabolic state of the liver and other organs occur in response to the presence of alcohol in the body and can result in low blood sugar levels (i.e., low glucose levels, or hypoglycemia). Alcohol metabolism leads to fatty liver (described earlier) and a buildup of an intermediate metabolic product, lactic acid, in body fluids (i.e., lactic acidosis). Both of these effects can inhibit glucose production.

Alcohol-induced hypoglycemia generally occurs after binge drinking over several days in alcoholics who have not been eating. In such a situation, prolonged alcohol consumption, coupled with poor nutritional intake, not only decreases glucose production but also exhausts the reserves of glucose stored in the liver in the form of glycogen, thereby leading to hypoglycemia. Because glucose is the primary energy source of the brain, hypoglycemia can contribute to hangover symptoms such as fatigue, weakness, and mood disturbances. Diabetics are particularly sensitive to the alcohol-induced alterations in blood glucose. However, it has not been documented whether low blood sugar concentrations contribute to hangover symptomatically.

Disruption of Sleep and Other Biological Rhythms. Although alcohol has sedative effects that can promote sleep onset, the fatigue experienced during a hangover results from alcohol's disruptive effects on sleep. Alcohol-induced sleep may be of shorter duration and poorer quality because of rebound excitation after BACs fall, leading to insomnia. Furthermore, when drinking behavior takes place in the evening or at night (as it often does), it can compete with sleep time, thereby reducing the length of time a person sleeps. Alcohol also disrupts the normal sleep pattern, decreasing the time spent in the dreaming state (i.e., rapid eye movement [REM] sleep) and increasing the time spent in deep (i.e., slow-wave) sleep. In addition, alcohol relaxes the throat muscles, resulting in increased snoring and, possibly, periodic cessation of breathing (i.e., sleep apnea).

Alcohol interferes with other biological rhythms as well, and these effects persist into the hangover period. For example, alcohol disrupts the normal 24-hour (i.e., circadian) rhythm in body temperature, inducing a body temperature that is abnormally low during intoxication and abnormally high during a hangover. Alcohol intoxication also interferes with the circadian nighttime secretion of growth hormone, which is important in bone growth and protein synthesis. In contrast, alcohol induces the release of adrenocorticotropic hormone from the pituitary gland, which in turn stimulates the release of cortisol, a hormone that plays a role in carbohydrate metabolism and stress response; alcohol thereby disrupts the normal circadian rise and fall of cortisol levels. Overall, alcohol's disruption of circadian rhythms induces a "jet lag" that is hypothesized to account for some of the deleterious effects of a hangover.

Alcohol and Headache. In a large epidemiological survey of headache in Danish 25- to 64-year-olds, the lifetime prevalence of hangover headache was 72 percent, making it the most common type of headache reported. Alcohol intoxication results in vasodilatation, which may induce headaches. Alcohol has effects on several neurotransmitters and hormones that are implicated in the pathogenesis of headaches, including histamine, serotonin, and prostaglandins. However, the etiology of hangover headache remains unknown.

Effects of Alcohol Withdrawal (AW)

The AW syndrome following the cessation of excessive drinking results from compensatory changes in the central nervous system that take place in response to chronically administered depressant substances (in this case, alcohol, or more specifically, ethanol). These changes include alterations in two types of receptors embedded in nerve cell membranes. One receptor type binds with an important chemical messenger (i.e., neurotransmitter) called gamma-aminobutyric acid (GABA), and the other type binds with another neurotransmitter, glutamate. Both GABA and glutamate are critical in regulating nerve cell activity: GABA is the body's primary means of inhibiting nerve cell activity, and glutamate is the primary means of exciting it.

Following chronic alcohol exposure, the body decreases (i.e., downregulates) the number or sensitivity of GABA receptors and increases (i.e., upregulates) the number or sensitivity of glutamate receptors in an effort to counterbalance alcohol's sedative effects. When alcohol is removed from the body, however, the central nervous system and the portion of the nervous system that coordinates response to stress (i.e., the sympathetic nervous system) remain in an unbalanced "overdrive" state. Sympathetic nervous system hyperactivity accounts for the tremors, sweating, and tachycardia observed in both hangover and AW syndrome.

Several lines of evidence suggest that a hangover is a mild manifestation of the AW syndrome in non-alcohol-dependent drinkers. First, the signs and symptoms of hangover and mild AW overlap considerably. The revised Clinical Institute Withdrawal Assessment for Alcohol scale, an instrument widely used to assess the severity of a withdrawal episode in alcohol-dependent patients, measures 10 withdrawal-associated items: nausea and vomiting; tremor; sweating; anxiety; agitation; headache; disturbances in the sense of touch, hearing, and vision (e.g., hallucinations); and orientation (e.g., awareness of the date and location). Several of these items also are usually present during a hangover, including nausea and vomiting, tremor, sweating, anxiety, headache, and sensory disturbances.

Second, Begleiter and colleagues (1974) present evidence that the hangover condition is actually a state of central nervous system excitation, despite the perceived sedation and malaise. Support for this view comes from the research of Pinel and Mucha (1980), which shows that single doses of alcohol decrease seizure thresholds in animals several hours later. Their finding indicates rebound excitation, a phenomenon noted to occur after short-term administration of some sedatives that can quickly clear the body, including alcohol and certain benzodiazepine drugs.

Third, the observation that alcohol readministration alleviates the unpleasantness of both AW syndrome and hangovers suggests that the two experiences share a common process.

Effects of Alcohol Metabolites

Alcohol undergoes a two-step process in its metabolism. First, an enzyme (i.e., alcohol dehydrogenase) metabolizes alcohol to an intermediate product, acetaldehyde; then a second enzyme (aldehyde dehydrogenase [ALDH]) metabolizes acetaldehyde to acetate. Acetaldehyde is a chemically reactive substance that binds to proteins and other biologically important compounds. At higher concentrations, it causes toxic effects, such as a rapid pulse, sweating, skin flushing, nausea, and vomiting. In most people, ALDH metabolizes acetaldehyde quickly and efficiently, so that this intermediate metabolite does not accumulate in high concentrations, although small amounts are present in the blood during alcohol intoxication. In some people, however, genetic variants of the ALDH enzyme permit acetaldehyde to accumulate. Those people routinely flush, sweat, and become ill after consuming small amounts of alcohol.

Because of the similarity between the acetaldehyde reaction and a hangover, some investigators have suggested that acetaldehyde causes hangovers. Although free acetaldehyde is not present in the blood after BACs reach zero, the toxic effects of acetaldehyde produced during alcohol metabolism may persist into the hangover period.

Effects of Factors Other Than Alcohol

Factors other than alcohol also may contribute to a hangover. These factors include the following possibilities.

Congeners. Among other reasons, people consume alcoholic beverages for their ethanol content. Most alcoholic beverages contain smaller amounts of other biologically active compounds, however, including other alcohols. These compounds, known as congeners, contribute to the taste, smell, and appearance of alcoholic beverages. Congeners may be produced along with ethanol during fermentation, generated during aging or processing through the degradation of the beverage's organic components, or added to the beverage during the production process. Investigators now believe that congeners may contribute to a beverage's intoxicating effects and to a subsequent hangover. Research has shown that beverages composed of more pure ethanol, such as gin or vodka, induce fewer hangover effects than do beverages containing a large number of congeners, such as whiskey, brandy, or red wine. A hangover also may occur when pure ethanol is administered, however.

One specific congener implicated in hangover effects is methanol, which is an alcohol compound found in alcoholic beverages along with ethanol. The two compounds differ slightly in chemical structure in that methanol contains one less carbon atom and two fewer hydrogen atoms than ethanol. The same enzymes that metabolize ethanol, alcohol dehydrogenase, and aldehyde dehydrogenase also metabolize methanol; however, the products of methanol metabolism (i.e., formaldehyde and formic acid) are extremely toxic and in high concentrations may cause blindness and death.

Support for methanol's contribution to hangovers comes from several sources. For example, distilled spirits that are more frequently associated with the development of a hangover, such as brandies and whiskeys, contain the highest concentrations of methanol. Moreover, in an experimental study with four subjects who consumed red wine containing 100 milligrams per liter (mg/L) of methanol, Jones (1987) found that elevated blood levels of methanol persisted for several hours after ethanol was metabolized, which corresponded to the time course of hangover symptoms. Methanol lingers after ethanol levels drop, because ethanol competitively inhibits methanol metabolism. The fact that ethanol readministration fends off hangover effects may be further evidence of methanol's contribution to the hangover condition, given ethanol's ability to block methanol metabolism and thereby slow the production of formaldehyde and formic acid.

Certain people develop headaches soon after drinking red wine but not after drinking white wine or vodka. Recent research finds that red wine, but not white wine or vodka, can increase plasma serotonin and plasma histamine levels. The specific agents in wine responsible for these increased levels are not known. Increased plasma serotonin and histamine can trigger headaches in susceptible people.

Use of Other Drugs. The use of other drugs often accompanies heavy alcohol consumption. Most heavy drinkers smoke cigarettes, and some also use marijuana, cocaine, or other drugs. Although certain drugs can themselves produce hangover symptoms and affect alcohol intoxication, the effects of the various alcohol and other drug combinations on alcohol hangover are unknown.

Personal Influences. Some evidence exists that increased hangover symptoms occur more often in people possessing certain personality traits, such as neuroticism, anger, and defensiveness. Negative life events and feelings of guilt about drinking also are associated with experiencing more hangovers. In addition, Earleywine (1993) reports greater hangover symptoms in people who have a higher personality risk for the development of alcoholism. Those studies suggest that people who have an elevated personality risk for alcoholism experience more acute withdrawal and hangover symptoms and may initiate further drinking in an effort to find relief.

Research has shown that a history of alcoholism in a person's family (i.e., a positive family history) is associated with a decreased sensitivity to the intoxicating effects of alcohol and a greater risk for developing alcoholism. Newlin and Pretorius (1990) suggested that a positive family history for alcoholism may be associated with a tendency for increased hangover symptoms as well. Their research compared the self-reported hangover symptoms in college-age sons of alcoholic fathers with symptoms in sons of nonalcoholic fathers and found that the subjects with a positive family history for alcoholism had had greater hangover symptoms during the previous year. The amount of drinking was comparable between the two groups, although the subjects with a positive family history reported consuming significantly more mixed drinks than the group with a negative family history.

Treatments for Hangover

Many treatments are described to prevent hangover, shorten its duration, and reduce the severity of its symptoms, including innumerable folk remedies and recommendations. Few treatments have undergone rigorous investigation, however. Conservative management offers the best course of treatment. Time is the most important component, because hangover symptoms will usually abate over 8 to 24 hours.

Certain medications may provide symptomatic relief for hangover symptoms. For example, antacids may alleviate nausea and gastritis. Aspirin and other nonsteroidal anti-inflammatory medications (e.g., ibuprofen or naproxen) may reduce the headache and muscle aches associated with a hangover but should be used cautiously, particularly if upper abdominal pain or nausea is present. Anti-inflammatory medications are themselves gastric irritants and will compound alcohol-induced gastritis. Although acetaminophen is a common alternative to aspirin, its use should be avoided during the hangover period, because alcohol metabolism enhances acetaminophen's toxicity to the liver.

About the Authors

Robert Swift, M.D., Ph.D., is associate professor in the Department of Psychiatry and Human Behavior at Brown University, Providence, Rhode Island, and associate chief of staff for research and education at Providence Veterans Affairs Medical Center.

Dena Davidson, Ph.D., is assistant professor of psychiatry at Indiana University of Medicine, Indianapolis, Indiana.

Chapter 23

Alcohol's Effects on Liver Function

Alcohol-Induced Liver Injury

Alcohol abuse is the leading cause of liver-related mortality in the United States. Excessive alcohol consumption leads to two serious types of liver injury: In some instances it causes hepatic inflammation (alcoholic hepatitis), and in others it induces progressive liver scarring (fibrosis or cirrhosis). Frequently, alcoholic hepatitis and fibrosis co-occur in the same individual. The exact prevalence of alcoholic liver disease in the United States is difficult to assess because alcohol consumption is often underreported, but current health statistics suggest that the number of people suffering some form of alcoholic liver disease likely exceeds 2 million. An estimated 900,000 people have cirrhosis, and of the 26,000 who die each year, at least 40 percent and perhaps as many as 90 percent have a history of alcohol abuse.

The mechanisms leading from chronic alcohol consumption to serious liver disease are not completely clear. The sections below review numerous possibilities supported by current investigation. Following this review is a discussion of hereditary and environmental factors that may affect the susceptibility of certain people to alcoholic liver disease or that may modify the progression of liver disease.

Excerpted from *Ninth Special Report to the U.S. Congress on Alcohol and Health,* U.S. Department of Health and Human Services, National Institute on Alcohol Abuse and Alcoholism, June 1997. Bracketed comments have been added to assist the lay reader.

Possible Mechanisms of Alcoholic Liver Injury

Free Radical Formation

Alcohol metabolism by hepatocytes [liver cells] requires oxygen. As alcohol and oxygen are consumed, the body often produces free radicals. These compounds are highly reactive and can interact with proteins, lipids, and deoxyribonucleic acid (DNA), thereby causing damage or death to liver cells. When free radicals attack unsaturated lipids [fats] in cell membranes, the result is a deleterious chain reaction of lipid radical formation known as lipid peroxidation. Some evidence suggests that alcoholic liver disease occurs more frequently in populations that consume a diet high in polyunsaturated fat.

Inflammatory cells that reside in the liver also may produce free radicals in response to alcohol. For example, Kupffer cells (liver macrophages [a type of cell that plays a role in the immune system]) produce superoxide anion [a free radical that is an oxygen atom with an extra electron] in response to either acute or chronic alcohol exposure. Chronic alcohol consumption also causes circulating white blood cells known as neutrophils to migrate to the liver. If activated by an inflammatory substance such as endotoxin (a component of bacterial outer cell membranes), neutrophils may contribute to liver pathology [disease] by releasing large amounts of superoxide.

Impaired Antioxidant Defense

Liver cells are normally equipped with an array of antioxidants that can neutralize free radicals. However, chronic alcohol consumption diminishes the levels of these antioxidants, thereby creating oxidative stress, a condition that renders liver cells more susceptible to injury induced by free radicals.

The antioxidant vitamins A and E also are normally present in the liver, but their levels are reduced with chronic alcohol consumption. In rats, depletion of vitamin E enhances alcohol-induced lipid peroxidation and exacerbates liver injury. Despite these known effects, vitamin E has shown no substantial benefit in preventing or reversing alcoholic liver injury in experimental animals, perhaps because it is a fat-soluble vitamin, which limits its absorption. Similarly, studies of vitamin A supplementation in animals have yielded somewhat disappointing results, in part because vitamin A has an inherent liver toxicity that restricts its therapeutic dose range. However, given the potential importance of antioxidants for reducing liver injury, antioxidant therapy will likely continue as an active area of study.

Hypoxia

Blood enters the liver via the portal vein and traverses long channels called sinusoids [small, irregular blood vessels found in the liver] before exiting via the central vein. Because liver cells continuously extract oxygen from sinusoidal blood, the blood nearest the central vein contains less oxygen than that in the portal vein. Under normal circumstances, the amount of oxygen delivered to liver cells in the central vein region (the pericentral zone) is sufficient to support cellular metabolism; however, chronic alcohol ingestion increases oxygen consumption by liver cells. This increased demand for oxygen may not be met by the relatively oxygen-poor pericentral blood and may lead to hypoxia (oxygen deficiency).

Eicosanoid Effects

Eicosanoids are metabolites of arachidonic acid [an essential fatty acid] that exhibit a wide range of biological activity. They comprise several classes of compounds, including prostaglandins [a group of compounds that play a role in such functions as blood pressure, muscle contraction, and body temperature], thromboxanes [compounds related to prostaglandins], and leukotrienes [compounds that may play a role in allergic reactions an inflammation]. Prostaglandins (especially prostaglandin E_2) are known for their protective effects on liver cells. In contrast, thromboxanes (such as thromboxane B_2) cause vasoconstriction [constriction of the blood vessels] and can be directly toxic to hepatocytes. Leukotrienes may cause liver injury by attracting and activating neutrophils [a type of white blood cell]. Chronic alcohol consumption has been shown to reduce production of protective eicosanoids by liver cells and enhance synthesis of thromboxane B_2.

Acetaldehyde Effects

Acetaldehyde, the first oxidative metabolite of alcohol, is a highly reactive compound that may promote hepatic injury and fibrosis. Acetaldehyde normally is metabolized rapidly to acetate, but acetaldehyde accumulates at higher levels in alcoholics. If its concentrations become high enough, acetaldehyde can become a substrate [a compound acted upon by an enzyme] for aldehyde oxidase and other enzymes that produce free radicals as byproducts of this reaction. Acetaldehyde also can react with specific amino acid residues on cellular proteins to form acetaldehyde-protein adducts [molecules formed by one molecule attaching to another]. These adducts can be demonstrated in the livers of human alcoholics and alcohol-fed animals. In most instances, the adducts localize preferentially to the pericentral zone, where liver injury is often greatest. Acetaldehyde-protein adducts also may stimulate liver cells to produce collagen, which may result in fibrosis and, ultimately, cirrhosis.

In addition, acetaldehyde may form adducts with the proteins that form the cellular microstructure. These proteins provide mechanical support and are essential to a variety of intracellular activities. Reaction with acetaldehyde can impair assembly of this support system, which may in turn disturb important transport processes in liver cells. These processes include uptake of extracellular compounds and secretion of proteins. Acetaldehyde-induced impairment of protein secretion has been implicated in the swelling ("ballooning") of liver cells observed in alcoholic liver disease.

Cytokine Effects

Cytokines are a diverse group of substances with inflammatory, fibrogenic, and growth-promoting properties. Many are associated with alcoholic liver disease and are under active investigation as mediators of liver injury. Patients with alcohol-induced liver inflammation (alcoholic hepatitis) frequently have high circulating levels of the cytokines interleukin-1 (IL-1), interleukin-6 (IL-6), interleukin-8 (IL-8), and tumor necrosis factor-alpha (TNF-alpha) [interleukins and tumor necrosis factor alpha play a role in immune responses]. IL-8 and TNF-alpha, in particular, correlate negatively with prognosis of liver disease. Transforming growth factor-beta (TGF-beta), another cytokine found in the livers of alcoholics, plays a critical role in hepatic fibrosis.

Role of Kupffer Cells and Endotoxin

Kupffer cells [a type of cell found in the liver that plays a role in immune responses] are emerging as important contributors to alcoholic liver injury. In addition to their role in free radical-induced and hypoxic liver damage, these cells produce cytokines (including TNF-alpha and TGF-beta) in response to alcohol. TNF-alpha and TGF-beta may cause direct tissue damage, enhance alcohol-induced hepatic inflammation, or both. Kupffer cells may also influence the rate of alcohol metabolism by liver cells. Experiments in alcohol-fed rats whose Kupffer cells were selectively eliminated have shown that these rats consumed as much alcohol as their corresponding controls but, unlike their corresponding controls, exhibited no signs of alcohol-induced liver injury. These findings demonstrate a central role for Kupffer cells in alcoholic liver injury.

Although the mechanisms whereby alcohol activates Kupffer cells are unknown, several studies point to endotoxin as an important cofactor. Endotoxin is a component of the bacterial cell membrane that acts as a potent stimulus of many inflammatory cells. Chronic alcohol ingestion is thought to allow endotoxin, which is derived presumably from bacteria that normally reside in the gut, to enter the circulation by increasing intestinal permeability. Several studies have shown that endotoxin interacts with alcohol to stimulate Kupffer cells.

Immune Responses to Altered Hepatocellular Proteins

Chronic alcohol ingestion may lead to autoimmune liver injury. One autoimmune process involves antibodies that bind to liver cells and target them for destruction by inflammatory cells. To be recognized as "foreign" by the immune system, liver cells first must be altered. Acetaldehyde and hydroxyethyl radicals can accomplish this task by forming adducts with proteins on the liver cell surface; indeed, antibodies directed against such modified proteins are detectable in the blood of alcoholic patients and may even serve as markers of alcohol abuse in some people.

Mechanisms of Alcoholic Liver Fibrosis

Among the many adverse effects of alcohol on the liver, fibrosis (scarring) is of major importance because it leads to irreversible cirrhosis. Chronic alcohol consumption induces liver fibrosis by stimulating the fat-storing cells of the liver, known as Ito cells, to differentiate into stellate cells, which produce collagen. The precise stimuli that initiate and regulate this process are unknown. However, other compounds with known roles in alcoholic liver injury may contribute to fibrosis through effects on stellate cells.

Hereditary and Environmental Cofactors Implicated in Alcoholic Liver Injury

Hereditary Variations in Alcohol Metabolism

In an effort to explain why only a small proportion of alcoholics develop serious liver disease, investigators have suggested that hereditary variations in enzymes that metabolize alcohol may contribute to risk. Polymorphisms (or genetic variants) in alcohol dehydrogenase (ADH), CYP2EI [an enzyme that plays a role in alcohol metabolism and also produces free radicals], and aldehyde dehydrogenase (ALDH) are under study. Numerous polymorphisms exist for ADH; these result in large differences in the rates of alcohol metabolism among different ethnic groups. Despite these findings, no single ADH allele [a different form of the same gene] has been firmly linked to the development of alcoholic liver injury.

A polymorphism in CYP2EI has been identified in a region of the gene that controls transcription [a process whereby genetic information in a strand of DNA is communicated]. People who have this rare allele, called c2, have higher baseline CYP2EI activity than those who do not. This higher activity may contribute to liver damage through increased generation of toxic free radical byproducts of alcohol metabolism.

ALDH polymorphisms also have been implicated in the development of alcoholic liver injury. An allele known as $ALDH2^2$ is present in about 50 percent of the Chinese and Japanese; it encodes an enzyme that is completely inactive toward acetaldehyde. People with two copies of this allele ($ALDH2^2$ homozygotes) generally have an aversion to alcohol because they rapidly develop acetaldehyde toxicity (flushing and nausea) after drinking. However, some people with only one copy of the gene ($ALDH2^2$ heterozygotes) are habitual drinkers and develop liver injury with higher frequency and at a lower cumulative dose than people with a normal ALDH phenotype.

Gender

Women seem to be more susceptible to serious alcoholic liver injury; they develop cirrhosis at a lower cumulative dose of alcohol than men do. In addition, compared with men, women who have alcoholic liver injury remain at substantially higher risk of disease progression even with abstinence.

Two hypotheses have been proposed to explain gender-specific differences in the risk of alcoholic liver disease. The first implicates gastric ADH as a causative factor. Although ADH is present in high levels in the liver, it also is found in the stomach and intestine, and metabolism of alcohol by gastric ADH limits the amount of ingested alcohol that ultimately reaches the liver. Some studies have shown that women have lower levels of gastric ADH activity than men, which suggests that dose for dose, women may deliver more concentrated levels of alcohol to the liver and therefore may exhibit earlier signs of liver toxicity. However, other investigators have found no such gender differences in gastric ADH activity, and some researchers question whether the stomach plays a significant role in first-pass metabolism of alcohol.

The second hypothesis holds that accelerated alcoholic liver injury in women may be related to gender differences in the metabolism of fatty acids. Using animal models to study liver injury, researchers have consistently shown an important role for fat in the disease process. Chronic alcohol consumption inhibits beta-oxidation of fatty acids by hepatic mitochondria. Disruption of this process may lead to an accumulation of nonmetabolized fatty acids in liver cells and ultimately to liver cell injury. This problem may be circumvented by diversion of fatty acids to alternate, compensatory metabolic routes. Recent studies have shown that one compensatory pathway is efficiently stimulated in alcohol-fed male rats but not in alcohol-fed female rats. In addition, the binding capacity of fatty acid binding proteins, which assist in fatty acid metabolism, also is reduced in alcohol-fed female rats relative to alcohol-fed male rats; this finding provides additional support for fatty acid toxicity in causing liver injury in alcoholic women.

Diet and Nutrition

Studies in baboons indicate that alcohol induces liver injury despite adequate protein-calorie and vitamin nutrition; these studies indicate that alcohol alone has some inherent toxicity regardless of nutritional status. In humans, however, alcoholic liver injury is strongly associated with nutrition. Numerous dietary factors may facilitate or precipitate alcoholic liver injury. For example, depletion of antioxidant vitamins and glutathione [a sulfur-containing compound] can enhance oxidative stress in the liver. A diet high in polyunsaturated fat increases levels of CYP2EI, which may permit accumulation of substrates for alcohol-induced lipid peroxidation in the liver and thereby contribute to oxidative stress. Chronic alcohol ingestion promotes absorption of iron from the intestine and increases hepatic iron stores. In view of its role in free radical production, increased hepatic iron might be expected to contribute to oxidative alcoholic liver injury.

Coexistent Viral Hepatitis

Infection with the hepatitis C virus (HCV) acts at least additively, if not synergistically [an enhancing effect], with alcohol to increase risk of liver injury. Roughly 18 to 25 percent of alcoholics exhibit signs of HCV infection. In alcoholics with liver injury, this proportion can increase to more than 40 percent. Although this percentage is lower in some studies, there is general agreement that alcoholics infected with HCV develop liver injury at a younger age and at a lower cumulative dose of alcohol than noninfected alcoholics do. These findings may be related to observed effects of alcohol in enhancing HCV replication, in depressing the host immune response to the virus, or both.

Hepatitis B virus infection also increases the incidence of chronic liver injury in alcoholics. Epidemiologic data suggest that this virus poses an additive, rather than a synergistic, risk of liver injury in combination with alcohol.

Coffee Drinking and Cigarette Smoking

Alcoholics who smoke more than one pack of cigarettes per day have three times the risk of cirrhosis than those who do not smoke. By contrast, alcoholics who consume four or more cups of coffee daily have a five-fold lower incidence of cirrhosis than those who do not drink coffee. The reason for the synergistic effect of smoking and the protective effect of coffee is uncertain; the effect of coffee may be unrelated to caffeine, as drinking tea does not appear to afford the same benefit.

Chapter 24

Alcohol-Related Pancreatic Damage

An association between alcohol abuse and pancreatic injury was reported as early as 1878 (Friedreich 1878). Alcoholic pancreatitis is a potentially fatal illness that may be short term (acute) or long term (chronic). The relationship between acute and chronic pancreatitis is complex. Symptoms shared by acute and chronic pancreatitis include disabling abdominal pain and interference with normal pancreatic functions. This chapter discusses the extent of the problem, clinical aspects, diagnosis, development, and treatment of both acute and chronic alcohol-related pancreatitis.

The Healthy Pancreas

The pancreas lies deep within the abdomen, behind the stomach. The pancreas serves two major functions. First, certain cells (islet cells) dispersed throughout the pancreas play the role of an endocrine gland by producing two crucial hormones that regulate blood-sugar (glucose) levels: insulin and glucagon. Poorly regulated blood glucose can produce symptoms associated with diabetes. The hormones produced by these cells are released directly into the bloodstream. Second, another specialized group of cells (acinar cells) secrete digestive

---

Excerpted from "Alcohol-Related Pancreatic Damage: Mechanisms and Treatment," by Minoti V. Apte, M.D., M. Med. Sci., Jeremy S. Wilson, M.D., Ph.D., and Mark A. Korsten, M.D., *Alcohol Health and Research World*, Winter 1997, Vol. 21, No, 1, p. 13(8). A complete copy of this publication may be ordered from the U.S. Government Printing Office. Call (202) 512-1800 for information on price and availability.

enzymes into the small intestine through tubes (ducts). In support of its digestive function, the pancreas also secretes bicarbonate through these same ducts. Pancreatic bicarbonate, a chemical similar to household baking soda, helps adjust and maintain the relatively weak acidity required for the action of intestinal digestive enzymes.

Pancreatitis arises in the acinar cells. However, inflammatory damage can destroy all parts of the pancreas—the islet cells as well

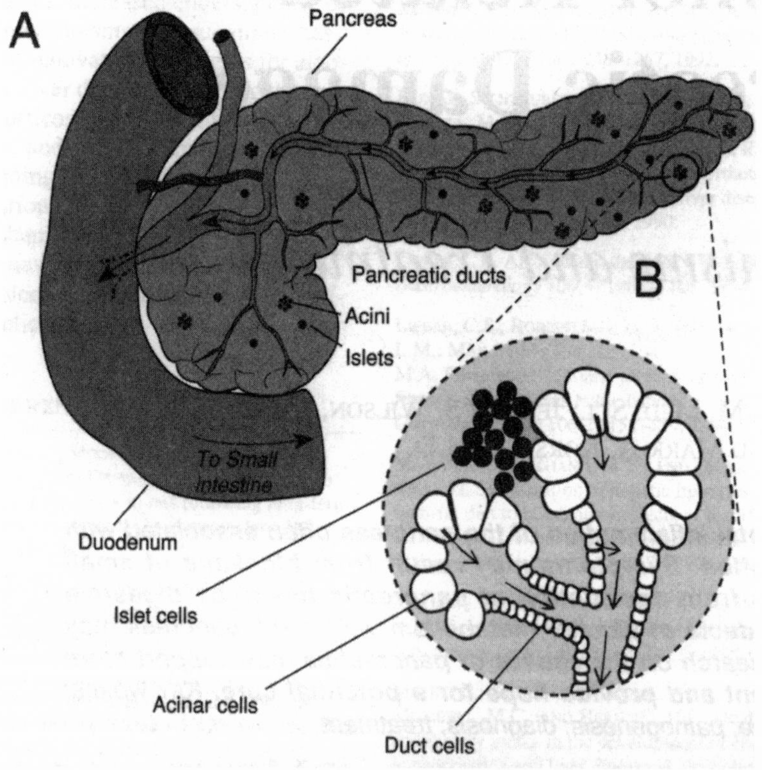

Figure 24.1. *The human pancreas. (A) View of the pancreas showing clusters of acinar cells (acini), islet cells (islets), and pancreatic ducts. (B) An enlargement of a secretory region of the pancreas. Acini secrete digestive enzymes into the small intestine, islets secrete the hormones insulin and glucagon into the bloodstream to regulate blood glucose concentration, and duct cells secrete bicarbonate to regulate small intestine acidity.*

as the acinar cells Any disorder that affects the digestion of food or the subsequent metabolism of digested food in the bloodstream is likely to have serious consequences for the entire body.

The Extent of the Problem

Since Friedreich's initial observation, many studies have confirmed that excessive alcohol intake is associated with pancreatic damage. However, the proportion of cases of pancreatitis attributed to alcohol varies widely among countries and even among different studies in the same country. In the United States, for instance, the reported incidence of pancreatitis attributed to alcohol ranges from 5 to 90 percent. This huge variation may be related to the difficulties in accurately identifying alcohol abuse and to differences in the populations studied.

The mortality rate of patients with alcoholic pancreatitis is about 36 percent higher than that of the general population. Approximately 50 percent of patients with alcoholic pancreatitis die within 20 years of onset of the disease. Only 20 percent of deaths occurring before a patient's life expectancy are attributed to pancreatitis or its complications; most of these deaths are attributed to the effects of alcohol or smoking on other organs such as the liver.

Medical Aspects

Alcoholic pancreatitis usually occurs in men in their forties. Initial symptoms include vomiting as well as acute abdominal pain, which may be localized to the back and upper abdomen and is relieved by leaning forward. In mild cases, the pain may last 2 to 3 days; the short-term prognosis in such cases is very good. In severe cases, however, the pain may persist for several weeks and the risk of death rises to about 30 percent. Less commonly, pancreatitis can be completely painless and is only diagnosed from symptoms of insufficient pancreatic function, such as diabetes and steatorrhea (excess fat in feces).

One complication of pancreatitis is localized masses of dead tissue and old blood walled off between the pancreas and surrounding organs (pseudocysts). If a pseudocyst becomes infected, it can invade the pancreas and become an abscess.

Approximately 5 to 6 years after the onset of the disease (especially in patients who continue to drink), evidence of chronic pancreatic disease develops as a result of progressive destruction of pancreatic tissue (parenchyma). Patients seek medical attention for persistent pain, weight loss, diabetes, and maldigestion of food (a result of inadequate production of digestive enzymes by the pancreas). Abstinence from alcohol has been shown to slow the rate of progression of the disease and decrease the severity of abdominal pain.

Until recently, it was generally accepted that alcoholic pancreatitis began as a chronic disease with occasional episodes, or acute "flare-ups." This notion was based on results of tissue analyses and x-ray studies taken from alcoholics during their first attack of pancreatitis that seemed to reveal signs of already existing chronic pancreatitis. Among these signs were shrinkage of tissue (atrophy), replacement of healthy tissue by scar tissue (fibrosis), and hardening of tissue caused by calcium deposits (calcification). Furthermore, autopsy studies demonstrated evidence of pancreatic fibrosis in alcoholics who had no history of clinical pancreatitis.

In recent years, the view that alcoholic pancreatitis is a form of chronic pancreatitis has been challenged. Opinion is now reverting to the hypothesis first put forward in 1946 by Comfort and colleagues, who suggested that repeated attacks of acute pancreatic inflammation resulted in chronic pancreatitis. This hypothesis is supported by both clinical and experimental studies. A large prospective study has reported that changes in the pancreas related to chronic pancreatitis were more likely to occur in alcoholics who had recurrent acute inflammation of the pancreas.

Diagnosis of Alcoholic Pancreatitis

A clinical diagnosis of pancreatitis is usually made on the basis of an attack of severe abdominal pain and tenderness, accompanied by a rise in the blood level of a pancreatic enzyme that digests starch (amylase) to more than three times the normal limit. Increased amylase in the blood has been the "gold-standard" diagnostic test for acute pancreatitis for more than 50 years. However, recent studies indicate that up to one-third of patients with alcoholic pancreatitis may fail to show any significant rise in amylase levels. In such circumstances, measurement of blood levels of a pancreatic enzyme that digests fats (lipase) can be helpful, because serum lipase levels remain elevated for a longer period than do amylase levels.

The cause of a case of pancreatitis can be attributed to alcohol based on a patient's history of alcohol abuse. Attempts are under way to find a biochemical marker that would help distinguish alcoholic from nonalcoholic pancreatitis. One report has suggested that the ratio of serum lipase to serum amylase levels may be helpful in this regard. Subsequent investigations, however, have found that this ratio is not sufficiently sensitive or specific for determining the cause of pancreatitis.

Another potentially useful biochemical test has been described recently. A Belgian study demonstrated that elevated activity of trypsin, a pancreatic enzyme that digests protein, is specifically associated with acute alcoholic pancreatitis. These researchers found that activity of trypsin in the blood increased in every study subject with alcoholic pancreatitis, even when the amylase and lipase levels were normal. Conversely, serum trypsin activity did not differ between healthy controls, alcoholic controls, and patients with nonalcoholic pancreatitis. However, this was a small study, with only 32 patients in the experimental group. Larger studies are needed to confirm the usefulness of serum trypsin as a specific marker of alcohol-related pancreatic disease.

Treatment of Alcoholic Pancreatitis

The mainstays of treatment for an acute attack of alcoholic pancreatitis are bed rest, pain relief, fasting, and administration of intravenous fluids. Other treatment measures, such as the administration of enzyme inhibitors (to reduce the corrosive effects of digestive enzymes on the pancreas) and the administration of chemicals that protect against dangerously reactive molecular fragments (antioxidants) are not yet of proven benefit. Similarly, it is not yet known whether protective (prophylactic) antibiotics have any place in the routine treatment of acute pancreatitis. Two controlled trials of prophylactic antibiotic treatment in severe pancreatitis have demonstrated a significant reduction in secondary systemic infection (septic episodes), although the treatment did not alter the death rate or the need for surgery in these patients. Surgery is required to manage complications such as pseudocysts and pancreatic abscesses and is sometimes needed for the treatment of chronic pain.

The treatment of chronic alcoholic pancreatitis is difficult. Abstinence from alcohol reduces the frequency of acute attacks as well as decreases pain. The pain of chronic pancreatitis can be controlled by medication (preferably nonnarcotics). The clinician first must rule out other possible causes of pain in these patients, such as pseudocysts, tumors, or ulcers. In some cases, intractable pain can be temporarily relieved by chemically blocking the nerves that supply sensation to the pancreas. Poor pancreatic function (for example, impaired enzyme excretion) is often treated by administering pancreatic enzyme preparations in tablets or capsules, whereas diabetes is treated with oral hypoglycemic agents or insulin.

How Alcoholic Pancreatitis May Develop

Despite decades of research, the pathogenesis of alcoholic pancreatitis remains elusive. Studies have been hampered because little is known about the earliest effects of alcohol on the human pancreas and because obtaining human pancreatic tissue for examination during life is difficult, because of its relatively inaccessible position within the abdomen. The slow progress in this field also can be attributed to the lack of a suitable animal model. Nonetheless, significant advances have been made, particularly with respect to the direct toxic effects of alcohol on acinar cells.

Early theories regarding the development of alcoholic pancreatitis focused on the main pancreatic duct, which carries pancreatic juices to the small intestine, and a muscular structure where the pancreatic duct opens into the small intestine (the sphincter of Oddi). In the 1970's, the research emphasis shifted to the small ducts that lead to the main pancreatic duct. In recent years, however, the focus has changed again, with most research centering on the alcohol's direct effects on acinar cells.

Alcohol and the Large Pancreatic Duct. One early theory postulated that pancreatic injury is caused by alcohol-induced spasm of the sphincter of Oddi, leading to backup of pancreatic enzymes into the unprotected tissues of the pancreas. Therefore, instead of entering the intestine to digest food, the enzymes "digest" the pancreatic cells themselves. Another theory postulated that backflow of bile or the contents of the duodenum into the pancreatic duct led to pancreatic damage. However, studies to date have failed to provide convincing data to support these theories.

Effects of Alcohol on Small Ducts. Small pancreatic ducts begin at the acini and drain into the large pancreatic duct. In the early 1970's researchers hypothesized that alcohol induces pancreatitis by causing small pancreatic ducts to be blocked by protein plugs. According to this hypothesis, the acini that secrete into the blocked ducts would then undergo fibrosis, while the plugs would eventually enlarge and calcify. Research has not clearly demonstrated that protein deposition within pancreatic ducts precedes acinar damage. It is therefore uncertain whether protein plugs are a cause or an effect of pancreatic injury. Nonetheless, it is generally accepted that protein plugs may play an important role in the progression, if not the initiation, of the disease.

Direct Toxic Effects of Alcohol on Acinar Cells. Most recent research into the pathogenesis of alcoholic pancreatitis has centered on the direct toxic effects of alcohol on acinar cells. This direction of research is not unreasonable given that the acinar cell synthesizes large amounts of digestive enzymes, which have the potential to cause cell injury when activated.

Factors Influencing Individual Susceptibility

An apparent clinical paradox exists with respect to the occurrence of pancreatitis in alcoholics. Although it is well established that the risk of developing pancreatitis rises with increasing alcohol consumption (suggesting the presence of constant dose-related effects of alcohol on the pancreas), it is also clear that only a small proportion of heavy drinkers develop clinically significant pancreatitis. The latter observation raises the possibility that a factor (or factors) other than alcoholism influence the susceptibility of an alcoholic to pancreatitis. A number of factors that may distinguish alcoholics who develop pancreatitis from those who do not have been investigated. These factors include diet, amount and type of alcohol consumed, the pattern of alcohol consumption, hereditary factors (for example, blood group), fat intolerance, and smoking. Many studies have provided conflicting results, probably because they compared subjects with alcoholic pancreatitis (the experimental group) with subjects from the general population (the control group). Thus, the control and experimental groups differed from each other with respect to two of the factors under study: alcoholism and pancreatitis.

Chapter 25

Alcohol's Role in Gastrointestinal Disorders

Among the many organ systems that mediate alcohol's effects on the human body and its health, the gastrointestinal (GI) tract plays a particularly important part. Several processes underlie this role. First, the GI tract is the site of alcohol absorption into the bloodstream and, to a lesser extent, of alcohol breakdown and production. Second, the direct contact of alcoholic beverages with the mucosal that lines the upper GI tract can induce numerous metabolic and functional changes. These alterations may lead to marked mucosal damage, which can result in a broad spectrum of acute and chronic diseases, such as acute gastrointestinal bleeding (from lesions in the stomach or small intestine) and diarrhea. Third, functional changes and mucosal damage in the gut disturb the digestion of other nutrients as well as their assimilation into the body, thereby contributing to the malnutrition and weight loss frequently observed in alcoholics. Fourth, alcohol-induced mucosal injuries—especially in the upper small intestine—allow large molecules, such as endotoxin and other bacterial toxins, to pass more easily into the blood or lymph. These toxic substances can have deleterious effects on the liver and other organs.

Excerpted from "Alcohol's Role in Gastrointestinal Tract Disorders," by Christiane Bode, Ph.D. and J. Christian Bode, M.D., *Alcohol Health and Research World*, Winter 1997, Vol. 21, No, 1, p. 78(8). A complete copy of this publication may be ordered from the U.S. Government Printing Office. Call (202) 512-1800 for information on price and availability.

The GI Tract—An Overview

The GI tract's functions are to physically and chemically break down ingested food, allow the absorption of nutrients into the bloodstream, and excrete the waste products generated. The GI tract can be viewed as one continuous tube extending from the mouth to the anus (Figure 25.1), which is subdivided into different segments with specific functions.

In the mouth, or oral cavity, the teeth mechanically grind the food into small pieces. Moreover, saliva excreted by the salivary glands

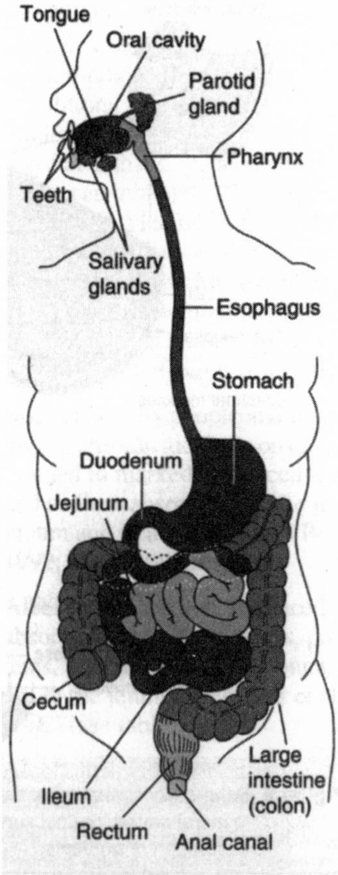

***Figure 25.1.** Schematic representation of the human gastrointestinal tract. The small intestine comprises the duodenum, the ileum, and the jejunum.*

initiates the food's chemical degradation. From the oral cavity, the food passes through the throat (pharynx) into the esophagus. The coordinated contraction and relaxation of the muscles surrounding the esophagus propels the food into the stomach.

In the stomach, the chemical degradation of the food continues with the help of gastric acid and various digestive enzymes. Excessive gastric acid production can irritate the mucosa, causing gastric pain, and result in the development of gastric ulcers. Two bands of muscle fibers (sphincters) close off the stomach to the esophagus and the intestine. Weakness of the sphincter separating the stomach from the esophagus allows the stomach content to flow back into the esophagus. This process, which is called gastroesophageal reflux, can lead to heartburn as well as inflammation (reflux esophagitis) and even to the development of ulcers in the lower part of the esophagus.

From the stomach, the food enters the small intestine, which is divided into three segments: the duodenum, the jejunum, and the ileum. Like the esophagus and stomach, the intestine is surrounded by layers of muscles, the rhythmic movements of which help mix the food mass and push it along the GI tract. The intestine's inner mucosal surface is covered with small projections called villi, which increase the intestinal surface area (Figure 25.2). As the food mass moves through the small intestine, digestive enzymes secreted by the intestinal cells complete the chemical degradation of nutrients into simple molecules that can be absorbed through the intestinal wall into the bloodstream. What finally remains in the intestine are primarily indigestible waste products. These products progress into the large intestine, where the waste is compacted and prepared for excretion through the anus. Like the small intestine, the large intestine can be divided into three segments: the cecum; the colon, which constitutes about 80 percent of the large intestine; and the rectum. The following sections review alcohol's effect on the different regions of the GI tract.

The Oral Cavity and the Esophagus

The oral cavity, pharynx, esophagus, and stomach are exposed to alcohol immediately after its ingestion. Thus, alcoholic beverages are almost undiluted when they come in contact with the mucosa of these structures. It is therefore not surprising that mucosal injuries (lesions) occur quite frequently in people who drink large amounts of alcohol. (The alcohol amount necessary to cause mucosal injury varies significantly among individual drinkers and depends, for example, on whether alcohol consumption occurs on an empty stomach or is accompanied by a meal. Thus, no clear threshold exists above which alcohol exerts its adverse effects. However, the risk for adverse effects such as tissue damage generally increases following the consumption of more than 2 ounces of alcohol, which corresponds to approximately four standard drinks).

Chronic alcohol abuse damages the salivary glands and thus interferes with saliva secretion. In alcoholics this damage commonly manifests itself as an enlargement (hypertrophy) of the parotid gland, although the mechanisms leading to this condition are unknown. Moreover, alcoholics may suffer from inflammation of the tongue (glossitis)

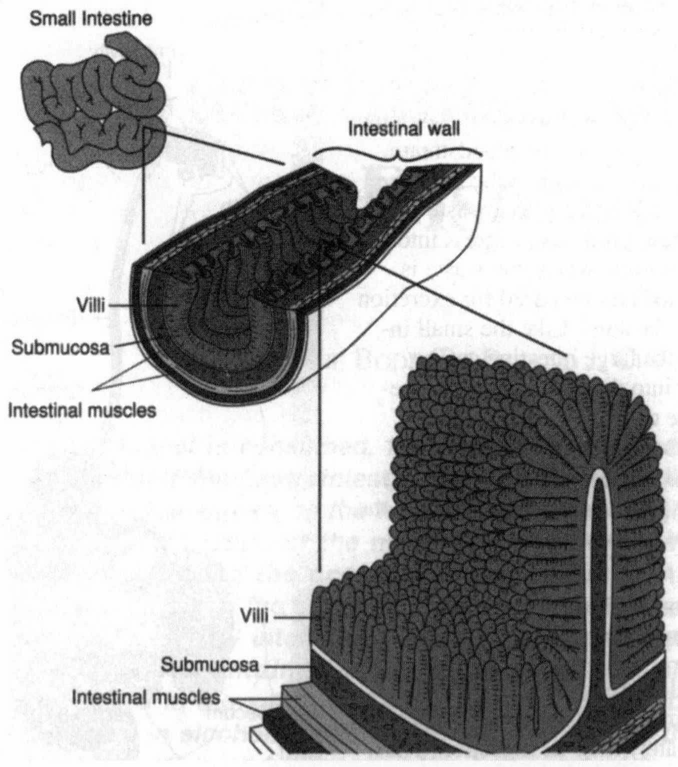

Figure 25.2. *Schematic illustration of the villi lining the small intestine. These villi serve to increase the internal surface area of the intestine and thus enhance the absorption of nutrients.*

and the mouth (stomatitis). It is unclear, however, whether these changes result from poor nutrition or reflect alcohol's direct effect on the mucosa. Finally, chronic alcohol abuse increases the incidence of tooth decay, gum disease, and loss of teeth.

Alcohol consumption can affect the esophagus in several ways. For example, alcohol distinctly impairs esophageal motility, and even a single drinking episode (acute alcohol consumption) significantly weakens the lower esophageal sphincter. As a result, gastroesophageal reflux may occur, and the esophagus' ability to clear the refluxed gastric acid may be reduced. Both of these factors promote the occurrence of heartburn. Moreover, some alcoholics exhibit an abnormality of esophageal motility known as a "nutcracker esophagus," which mimics symptoms of coronary heart disease. ('The term "nutcracker esophagus" refers to the painful, spasmodic contractions of the esophagus that the patients who suffer the disorder describe as feeling as though the esophagus were being squeezed by a nutcracker.)

Chronic alcohol abuse leads to an increased incidence not only of heartburn but also of esophageal mucosal inflammation (esophagitis) and other injuries that may induce mucosal defects (esophagitis with or without erosions). In addition, alcoholics make up a significant proportion of patients with Barrett's esophagus. This condition, which occurs in 10 to 20 percent of patients with symptomatic gastroesophageal reflux disease, is characterized by changes in the cell layer lining the esophagus (the epithelium) that lead to abnormal acid production. A diagnosis of Barrett's esophagus is an important indicator of an increased risk of esophageal cancer, because in some patients the altered epithelial cells become cancerous.

Another condition affecting alcoholics is Mallory-Weiss syndrome, which is characterized by massive bleeding caused by tears in the mucosa at the junction of the esophagus and the stomach. The syndrome accounts for 5 to 15 percent of all cases of bleeding in the upper GI tract. In 20 to 50 percent of all patients, the disorder is caused by increased gastric pressure resulting from repeated retching and vomiting following excessive acute alcohol consumption.

The Stomach

Both acute and chronic alcohol consumption can interfere with stomach functioning in several ways. For example, alcohol—even in relatively small doses—can alter gastric acid secretion, induce acute gastric mucosal injury, and interfere with gastric and intestinal motility.

The Small Intestine

As described previously, the small intestine is the organ in which most nutrients are absorbed into the bloodstream. Studies in humans and animals as well as in tissue culture have demonstrated that alcohol can interfere with the absorption of several nutrients. Alcohol itself, however, also is rapidly absorbed in the small intestine. In the human jejunum, for example, the alcohol concentration can drop from 10 percent to just 1.45 percent over a distance of only 30 centimeters (12 inches, about a quarter of the total length of the jejunum).

Therefore, alcohol's effects on nutrient absorption may vary throughout the small intestine, and tissue-culture experiments with constant alcohol concentrations may not always reflect the conditions in the body. Studies in laboratory animals have demonstrated that acute alcohol consumption can inhibit the absorption of water, sodium, glucose, and certain amino acids and fatty acids in the small intestine. Several studies in humans have analyzed the effects of chronic alcohol consumption with the following results:

- Both in healthy people and in alcoholics, chronic alcohol consumption led to markedly reduced water and sodium absorption in the jejunum and ileum.
- Alcoholics exhibited a reduced absorption of carbohydrates, proteins, and fats in the duodenum, but not in the jejunum.
- Alcoholics without confounding disorders, such as cirrhosis or impaired pancreatic function, exhibited malabsorption of fat and protein.
- Alcoholics showed malabsorption of xylose, a sugar frequently used to study the function of the digestive tract. The proportion of alcoholics who experienced this malabsorption ranged from 18 to 76 percent in various studies. This variation may reflect differences in the nutritional status, the mean daily alcohol intake, or the presence of alcohol-related liver disease among the studies' subjects.
- After chronic alcohol consumption, the absorption of thiamine (vitamin B^{1}), folic acid, and vitamin B^{12} was either unchanged or decreased. Folic acid deficiency, which frequently occurs in alcoholics, can result in various disorders of the GI tract as well as in anemia. However, this deficiency is more likely to result

from a diet containing insufficient folic acid than from poor folic acid absorption.

In summary, alcohol inhibits absorption of a variety of nutrients. The importance of these absorption disorders in the development of nutritional disturbances in alcoholics, however, is unclear. In alcoholics with limited pancreatic function or advanced liver disease, digestion of nutrients may be a more significant problem than impaired absorption disorders.

The Large Intestine

Until recently, alcohol's effects on the large intestine had received only minor attention. Studies in dogs found that acute alcohol administration depressed the colon's impeding motility but enhanced its propulsive motility. In healthy humans, alcohol administration also significantly reduced the frequency and strength (amplitude) of the muscle contractions in a segment of the rectum. These effects could reduce the transit time and thus the compaction of the intestinal contents and thereby contribute to the diarrhea frequently observed in alcoholics.

Medical Consequences

Alcohol-induced digestive disorders and mucosal damage in the GI tract can cause a variety of medical problems. These include a loss of appetite and a multitude of abdominal complaints, such as nausea, vomiting, feelings of fullness, flatulence, and abdominal pain. Diseases of the liver and pancreas may contribute to and aggravate these complaints. Thus, about 50 percent of alcoholics with an initial stage of liver damage (fatty liver) and 30 to 80 percent of patients with an advanced stage of alcohol-induced liver injury (alcoholic hepatitis) report some symptoms of abdominal discomfort. These abdominal complaints can lead to reduced food intake, thereby causing the weight loss and malnutrition commonly observed in alcoholics.

In addition to causing abdominal complaints, alcohol plays a role in the development of cancers of the GI tract. It is likely, however, that alcohol does not cause GI-tract cancers by itself but acts in concert with other cancer-inducing agents (as a cocarcinogen). Alcohol abuse, like smoking, is associated with the development of cancers of the tongue, larynx (the organ of voice), and pharynx; both alcohol consumption and smoking independently increase the risk for these tumors.

Epidemiological studies also strongly indicate that chronic alcohol consumption, especially of distilled spirits, markedly contributes to the development of esophageal cancer. Thus, after adjusting for smoking habits, heavy beer drinkers have a 10 times greater risk and heavy whisky drinkers a 25 times greater risk of developing esophageal cancer, compared with people who consume less than 30 g of alcohol (about 2 standard drinks) daily. The differences between beer and whisky drinkers remain even if they consume the same amount of pure alcohol. In drinkers who also smoke 20 cigarettes or more daily, the risk of esophageal cancer increases about 45-fold.

Heavy alcohol consumption also is associated with the development of tumors in the colon and rectum. However, the relative risk of cancer is higher for rectal cancer than for colon cancer. Moreover, the increased risk of rectal cancer appears to result mainly from heavy beer consumption, whereas distilled spirits appear to have no effect.

Summary

Alcohol consumption can interfere with the function of all parts of the gastrointestinal tract. Acute alcohol ingestion induces changes in the motility of the esophagus and stomach that favor gastroesophageal reflux and, probably, the development of reflux esophagitis. Alcohol abuse may lead to damage of the gastric mucosa, including hemorrhagic lesions. Beverages with a low alcohol content stimulate gastric acid secretion, whereas beverages with a high alcohol content do not.

In the small intestine, alcohol inhibits the absorption of numerous nutrients. The importance of these absorption disorders for the development of nutritional disturbances in alcoholics, however, is unclear. In alcoholics with other digestive disorders (for example, advanced liver disease or impaired pancreatic function), impaired digestion likely is more significant. Acute alcohol consumption also damages the mucosa in the upper region of the small intestine and may even lead to the destruction of the tips of the villi. The findings of human and animal studies suggest that these mucosal defects favor the following sequence of events: Alcohol-induced mucosal damage in the small intestine increases the mucosa's permeability, facilitating the transport of large molecules, such as bacterial endotoxin and/or other toxins, into the blood or lymph. This results in the release of potentially toxic cytokines by certain white blood cells and

Kupffer cells. These cytokines, in turn, exert multiple injurious effects on membranes and the microcirculation. The result is possible cell damage and even cell death in the liver and other organs.

Motility disorders, maldigestion, and malabsorption in alcoholics can result in digestive problems, such as anorexia, nausea, and abdominal pain. Alcohol abuse also promotes the development of cancers of the tongue, larynx, pharynx, and esophagus. Finally, the results of recent epidemiological studies indicate an association between alcohol consumption and the development of colorectal cancer.

Chapter 26

Alcohol's Impact on Kidney Function

Kidney Structure and Function

Cushioned in fatty tissue near the base of the spinal column, the kidneys are efficiently designed organs that perform two primary tasks in the body: excretion of metabolic end products and precise regulation of body fluid constituents. As they accomplish these tasks, the kidneys form and collect urine, which exits through the ureters to the bladder.

Each of the 2 million functional units (nephrons) in a pair of normal kidneys forms urine as it filters blood plasma of substances not needed by the body. Of the 48 gallons of filtrate processed through the nephrons of the kidneys each day, only about 1 to 1.5 quarts exit as urine. During this filtering process, substances are reabsorbed or secreted to varying degrees as the filtrate passes through the distinct segments of the nephron tubule.

Regulating Electrolyte Levels and Fluid Volume

The kidney tubules play an important role in keeping the body's water and electrolyte levels in equilibrium. In many cases, control

Excerpted from "Kidney Structure and Function," by Mary Beth de Ribeaux, and "Alcohol's Impact on Kidney Function," by Murray Epstein, M.D., in *Alcohol Health and Research World*, Winter 1997, Vol. 21, No, 1, p. 91(2) and 84(8). A complete copy of this publication may be ordered from the U.S. Government Printing Office. Call (202) 512-1800 for information on price and availability.

mechanisms govern the rate of reabsorption or secretion in response to the body's fluctuating needs. Under the influence of antidiuretic hormone (ADH), for example, the tubules can create either a concentrated urine, to discharge excess solutes and conserve water, or a dilute urine, to remove extra water from body fluids.

In addition to their role in regulating the body's fluid composition, the kidneys produce hormones that influence a host of physiological processes, including blood pressure regulation, red blood cell production, and calcium metabolism. Besides producing hormones, the kidneys respond to the actions of regulatory hormones produced in the brain, the parathyroid glands in the neck, and the adrenal glands located atop the kidneys.

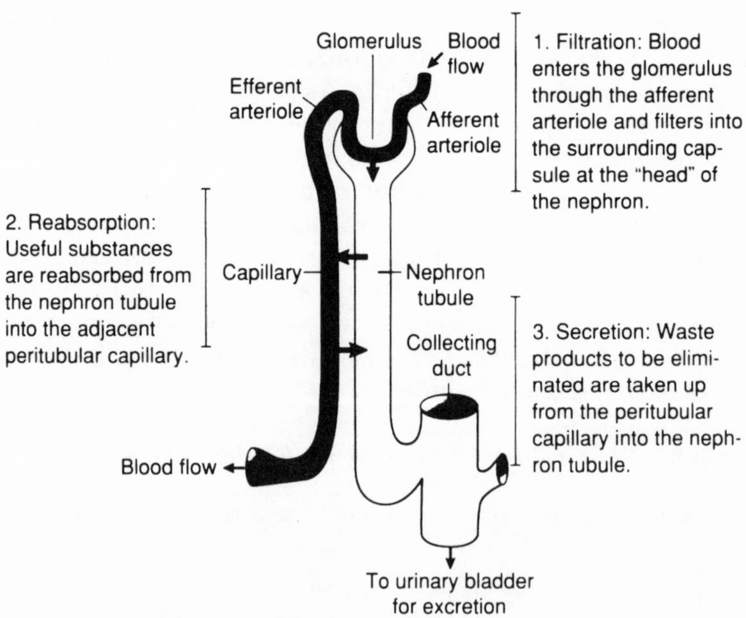

***Figure 26.1.** Urine Formation. Three basic processes—glomerular filtration, tubular reabsorption, and tubular secretion—contribute to urine formation.*

Alcohol's Impact

Because of the kidneys' important and varied role in the body, impairment of their function can result in a range of disorders, from mild variations in fluid balance to acute kidney failure and death. Alcohol, one of the numerous factors that can compromise kidney function, can interfere with kidney function directly, through acute or chronic consumption, or indirectly, as a consequence of liver disease.

Gross and Microscopic Changes

One way in which alcohol directly affects the kidneys is by altering the form and structure of this pair of organs. For example, in an early study on dogs, investigators observed several striking alterations after chronic alcohol administration. The basement membrane of the glomerulus became abnormally thickened and was characterized by cell proliferation. Further changes included enlarged and altered cells in the kidney tubules. Another study compared kidney structure and function in alcohol-fed and control rats. The alcohol-fed group experienced kidney swelling and significantly reduced kidney function; in addition, under microscopic examination, the kidneys of alcohol-fed rats were found to have cells enlarged with increased amounts of protein, fat, and water, compared with those of the control animals.

Blood-Flow Changes

Normally the rate of blood flow, or perfusion, (hemodynamics) through the kidneys is tightly controlled, so that plasma can be filtered and substances the body needs can be reabsorbed under optimal circumstances. Established liver disease impairs this important balancing act, however, by either greatly augmenting or reducing the rates of plasma flow and filtration through the glomerulus. Investigators have not yet fully explained the mechanisms underlying this wide range of abnormalities, though, and have devoted little attention to alcohol's effects on kidney hemodynamics in people who do not have liver disease.

The few studies focusing on alcohol's direct effects on perfusion in human kidneys suggest that regulatory mechanisms retain control over this component of kidney function despite alcohol consumption. Even at high blood alcohol levels, only minor fluctuations were found in the rates of plasma flow and filtration through the kidneys. Additional studies are needed to confirm these observations, however.

Effects on Fluid and Electrolyte Balance

One of the main functions of the kidneys is to regulate both the volume and the composition of body fluid, including electrically charged particles (ions), such as sodium, potassium, and chloride ions (electrolytes). However, alcohol's ability to increase urine volume (its diuretic effect) alters the body's fluid level (hydration state) and produces disturbances in electrolyte concentrations. These effects vary depending on factors such as the amount and duration of drinking, the presence of other diseases, and the drinker's nutritional status.

Fluid. Alcohol can produce urine flow within 20 minutes of consumption; as a result of urinary fluid losses, the concentration of electrolytes in blood serum increases. These changes can be profound in chronic alcoholic patients, who may demonstrate clinical evidence of dehydration.

Sodium. The serum sodium level is determined by the balance of fluid in relation to that of sodium: Not enough fluid in the body results in a sodium concentration that is too high (hypernatremia), whereas excessive amounts of fluid produce a sodium concentration that is too low (hyponatremia). Hyponatremia does not constitute merely a biochemical abnormality but most likely has clinical consequences as well (for example, impaired mental activity, neurological symptoms, and, in extreme instances, seizures).

Potassium. Normally the kidneys are a major route of potassium ion excretion and serve as an important site of potassium regulation. Alcohol consumption historically has been found to reduce the amount of potassium excreted by the kidneys, although the body's hydration state may help determine whether potassium excretion will increase or decrease in response to alcohol. Levels of potassium, like those of sodium, also can affect the way the kidneys handle fluid elimination or retention. In addition, potassium depletion has been proposed to exacerbate hyponatremia through any of several mechanisms: For example, potassium losses may stimulate ADH activity, thereby increasing the amount of fluid reabsorbed and causing the body's sodium concentration to decrease as a result. Alternatively, potassium losses may increase thirst, also through hormonal mechanisms, thereby promoting increased fluid intake.

Phosphate. Low blood levels of phosphate commonly occur acutely in hospitalized alcoholic patients, appearing in more than one-half of severe alcoholism cases. Indeed, when the condition does not appear, clinicians treating alcoholic patients should suspect that another problem is masking the recognition of low phosphate levels, such as ongoing muscle dissolution, excess blood acidity (acidosis), inadequate blood volume, or kidney failure.

Magnesium. Chronic alcoholism is the leading cause of low blood levels of magnesium (hypomagnesemia) in the United States. Often it occurs simultaneously with phosphate deficiencies, also frequently encountered among alcoholic patients. Hypomagnesemia responds readily to magnesium supplementation treatment, however.

Calcium. Early studies showed that alcohol consumption markedly increases calcium loss in urine. In severely ill alcoholic patients, low blood levels of calcium occur about as often as low blood levels of phosphate and can cause convulsions or potentially life-threatening muscle spasms when respiratory muscles are involved. Alcoholic patients with liver disease often have abnormally low levels of a calcium-binding protein, albumin, and also may have impaired vitamin D metabolism; either of these two factors could result in reduced blood levels of calcium (hypocalcemia). Muscle breakdown and magnesium deficiency are other potential causes of hypocalcemia in alcoholic patients.

Body Fluid Volume and Blood Pressure

Chronic alcohol consumption may cause both fluid and solutes to accumulate, thereby increasing the overall volume of body fluids. In turn, such expansion of body fluid volume can contribute to high blood pressure, a condition often seen among chronic alcoholic patients.

Clinical studies of hypertensive patients have demonstrated that reducing alcohol intake lowers blood pressure and resuming consumption raises it. Although the mechanisms responsible for these effects have not been established, an experimental study by Chan and Sutter (1983) offers some insight. In this study, male rats given 20-percent alcohol in their drinking water for 4 weeks experienced decreased urinary volume and sodium excretion as well as increased blood concentrations of hormones that raise blood pressure by constricting blood vessels. The results of this study suggest that alcohol's influence on blood pressure may be attributable, at least in part, to its effects on the production of hormones that act on the kidneys to regulate fluid balance or that act on blood vessels to constrict them.

Acid-Base Balance Effects

Most of the metabolic reactions essential to life are highly sensitive to the acidity (hydrogen ion concentration) of the surrounding fluid. The kidneys play an important role in regulating acidity, thereby helping determine the rate at which metabolic reactions proceed. Alcohol can hamper the regulation of acidity, thus affecting the body's metabolic balance.

Like the kidneys, the liver plays an important role in maintaining acid-base balance. Liver diseases-including alcohol-induced liver problems disrupt this function and can contribute directly or indirectly to a wide range of acid-base disturbances.

Regulatory Effects

To keep the kidneys functioning optimally and to maintain functional stability (homeostasis) in the body, a variety of regulatory mechanisms exert their influence. Alcohol can perturb these controls, however, to a degree that varies with the amount of alcohol consumed and the particular mechanism's sensitivity.

As an example, Puddey and colleagues (1985) evaluated the effects of hormones that regulate kidney function. Their results show not only how alcohol disrupts homeostasis but also how the body reacts to restore it. Following moderate alcohol consumption—about 24 oz—of nonalcoholic beer with 1 milliliter of alcohol per kilogram of body weight added, the investigators noted several effects. Alcohol-induced urination reduced the subjects' plasma volume, resulting in an increased concentration of plasma sodium. In addition, the subjects' blood pressure and plasma potassium concentration decreased. These changes in fluid volume, electrolyte balance, and blood pressure may have stimulated the activity of hormones to return body fluid volume and composition back to normal, which occurred soon after consumption.

Alcohol consumption also is known to induce a state of low blood sugar (hypoglycemia) and activate the portion of the nervous system that coordinates the body's response to stress (the sympathetic nervous system). Both of these factors affect hormones that regulate kidney function, just as changes in fluid volume and electrolyte balance do.

Indirect Effects

Physicians have recognized an interrelationship between kidney and liver disorders at least since the time of Hippocrates. Although a disorder in one organ can complicate a primary problem in the other (or a pathological process may involve both organs directly), kidney dysfunction complicating a primary disorder of the liver (for example, cirrhosis) is the most clinically significant scenario. Frequently, such kidney dysfunction results from liver problems related to alcohol. In fact, most patients in the United States diagnosed with both liver disease and associated kidney dysfunction are alcohol dependent. Three of the most prominent kidney function disturbances that arise in the presence of established liver disease are impaired sodium handling, impaired fluid handling, and acute kidney failure unexplained by other causes (hepatorenal syndrome).

Impaired Sodium Handling. Patients with alcohol-induced liver cirrhosis show a great tendency to retain salt (sodium chloride), and their urine frequently is virtually free of sodium. A progressive accumulation of extracellular fluid results, and this excess fluid is sequestered primarily in the abdominal region, where it manifests as marked swelling (ascites). In addition, excess fluid accumulates in spaces between cells, clinically manifested as swelling (edema) of the lower back and legs. As long as cirrhotic patients remain unable to excrete sodium, they will continue to retain the sodium they consume in their diet. Consequently, they will develop increasing ascites and edema and experience weight gain. In some cases, vast amounts of abdominal fluid may collect, occasionally more than 7 gallons.

Impaired Fluid Handling. In many patients with liver cirrhosis, the kidneys' ability to create dilute urine is compromised, leading to a state of abnormally low sodium concentration (hyponatremia). In hyponatremic patients, the amount of fluid retained by the kidneys is disproportionately greater than the amount of sodium retained. In other words, the kidneys' ability to excrete excess fluid by way of dilute urine is impaired, and too much fluid is reabsorbed. Hyponatremia probably is the single most common electrolyte disturbance encountered in the management of patients with cirrhosis of the liver. This abnormality may reflect the severity of liver disease, but the available data do not allow correlation of kidney impairment with the degree of clinical signs of liver disease, such as ascites or jaundice.

Hepatorenal Syndrome. Hepatorenal syndrome may appear in patients afflicted with any severe liver disease, but in the United States, studies most often have identified alcoholic cirrhosis as the underlying disorder. Major clinical features of hepatorenal syndrome include a marked decrease in urine flow, almost no sodium excretion and, usually, hyponatremia and ascites. Blood urea nitrogen (BUN) levels and serum concentrations of the waste product creatinine are somewhat elevated, but rarely to the degree seen in patients with end-stage kidney failure when kidney disease is the primary disorder. Judgments based on such relatively modest BUN and serum creatinine increases often underestimate kidney dysfunction in patients with hepatorenal syndrome, however, because malnourished cirrhotic patients tend to have low levels of urea and creatinine.

Chapter 27

Alcohol and Hormone Balance

Along with the nervous system, the endocrine, or hormonal, system is the primary regulatory mechanism for virtually the entire human body. Hormones are chemical messengers that control and coordinate the function of tissues and organs. Each hormone is secreted from a particular gland and distributed throughout the body to act on different tissues.

Hormones are released as a result of nerve impulses or in response to specific physiological or biochemical events. Following their release, hormones instigate a cascade of reactions within the body, the end result of which can include synthesis and release of enzymes and changes in cell membranes. Highly sensitive feedback mechanisms reduce or increase the amount of different hormones being released at any given time.

The effects of alcohol on endocrine function are multiple and complex. Several variables, including the type, length, and pattern of alcohol exposure; level of intoxication; and coexisting medical problems, such as malnutrition and liver dysfunction, must be considered when assessing the impact of alcohol on hormonal status.

Excerpted from "The Endocrine System: Alcohol Alters Critical Hormonal Balance," by Nicholas Emanuele, M.D. and Mary Ann Emanuele, M.D., in *Alcohol Health and Research World*, Winter 1997, Vol. 21, No, 1, p. 53(12). A complete copy of this publication may be ordered from the U.S. Government Printing Office. Call (202) 512-1800 for information on price and availability.

Hypothalmic-Pituitary-Adrenal Axis

The hypothalamus is the control center for most of the body's hormonal systems. Located deep within the brain, the hypothalamus receives nerve impulses stemming from both physical and psychological stimuli and releases hormones in response to those signals. Hypothalamic activity thus governs numerous body functions, including reproduction, metabolism, use of nutrients, and growth.

The hypothalamus, the anterior pituitary gland, and the adrenal glands function together as a well-coordinated unit known as the hypothalamic-pituitary-adrenal (HPA) axis. Cells in the hypothalamus produce most of a key hormone called corticotropin-releasing factor (CRF) in humans. The hypothalamus secretes CRF into the hypothalamic-pituitary portal system, the network of blood vessels that functionally connects the hypothalamus and the anterior pituitary gland. At the pituitary gland, CRF binds to specific receptors on special pituitary cells called corticotropes, which produce adrenocorticotropic hormone (ACTH). Upon CRF stimulation, ACTH production and secretion is enhanced. ACTH is then transported through the general blood circulation to its target tissue, the adrenal gland, where it stimulates production of adrenal hormones, primarily glucocorticoids. Glucocorticoids then feed back in a negative fashion to both the hypothalamus and the pituitary gland to decrease CRF and ACTH release, respectively.

Glucocorticoids have many physiological effects; they influence carbohydrate, lipid, protein, and nucleic acid metabolism; the cardiovascular system; bone and calcium metabolism; the central nervous system; and growth, development, and reproduction. Notably, glucocorticoids also modify immunological responses, underscoring the important interrelationship between the endocrine and immune systems. In addition to their functions within the HPA, both CRF and ACTH have independent effects on the immune system, reproduction, and temperature regulation. Although increases in ACTH and glucocorticoids are usually short-lived, this stimulation has far-reaching consequences for numerous other organ systems.

One manifestation of alcohol's effect on the HPA axis resembles a disorder called Cushing's syndrome, a disease stemming from an excess of cortisol. Clinical signs of the syndrome include obesity of the torso (with purplish stretch marks); a round, red face; high blood pressure; muscle weakness; easy bruisability; acne; diabetes; osteoporosis; and a variety of psychological disturbances. Women also may develop facial hair (hirsutism) and menstrual disturbances. About two-thirds of the cases of Cushing's syndrome are caused by ACTH-producing pituitary tumors.

Some drinkers develop a condition called alcohol-induced pseudo-Cushing's syndrome. It is indistinguishable from true Cushing's syndrome, although it tends to be clinically more mild. Proof that the pseudo-Cushing's syndrome results from alcohol consumption and not from tumorous overproduction of ACTH or cortisol derives from the observation that its symptoms and signs disappear with abstinence from alcohol, usually within 2 to 4 months. The prevalence of this syndrome among alcoholics is unknown, but clinical experience indicates that most alcoholics do not have the full-blown syndrome.

Based on alcohol's ability to activate the HPA axis in animals, the existence of alcohol-induced pseudo-Cushing's syndrome should not be surprising. Whether the syndrome results from alcohol's effects on the brain or at the pituitary or adrenal levels, however, is not clear. Nonetheless, the existence of alcohol-induced pseudo-Cushing's syndrome indicates that alcohol consumption somehow leads to a clinically significant activation of the HPA axis in humans.

Hypothalmic-Pituitary-Gonadal Axis

The hypothalamic-pituitary-gonadal axis is a complex system involving feedback from the target organs, the gonads (the testes and ovaries), to the hypothalamus, where a key reproductive hormone, luteinizing hormone-releasing hormone (LHRH), is released into the portal blood system. Upon reaching the pituitary gland, LHRH attaches to specific receptors and activates a complicated cascade of biochemical events that results in the synthesis and release of the two gonadotropin hormones, luteinizing hormone (LH) and follicle-stimulating hormone (FSH).

LH is largely responsible for gonadal production of androgens, which are hormones that have masculinizing effects (for example, testosterone). FSH is important for normal development and maturation of sperm in the male and ovarian follicles in the female. The gonadal hormones—including testosterone in the male and estrogen and progesterone in the female—then circulate back to the hypothalamic-pituitary unit and encourage or discourage further release of LHRH, LH, and FSH in a finely tuned system.

Although the products of the gonads are essential to reproduction, testosterone, estrogen, and progesterone, like the glucocorticoids, all have actions throughout the body. These effects include roles in carbohydrate and lipid metabolism, the cardiovascular system, and normal bone growth and development. In addition, gonadal hormones are important mediators of the central nervous system and play a role in the immune system. A disturbance of the hypothalamic-pituitary-gonadal axis thus can result not only in altered fertility but also in problems such as osteoporosis, muscle weakness and impaired immune function.

Men

Diminished sexual function in alcoholic men has been clinically noted over many years; early studies largely attributed this problem to liver disease. However, when young, healthy, nonalcoholic volunteers were exposed acutely to alcohol, a fall in serum testosterone was consistently demonstrated. A central defect in the human hypothalamic-pituitary unit was first suggested when it was noted that LH levels in adult men failed to increase as expected for the concomitant decrease in testosterone levels, and both LH and FSH failed to increase after stimulation with clomiphene citrate, a drug that acts at the hypothalamus level to increase LHRH production. Interestingly, in younger men who were given alcohol and LHRH to stimulate their pituitary glands' production of LH, testosterone levels actually increased, suggesting enhanced sensitivity.

Women

Because of female reproductive cyclicity, the hormonal physiology is more complex in women than in men. The 28-day human reproductive cycle can be divided into two phases: a 14-day follicular phase, which begins with the first day of menses, followed by a 14-day luteal phase. Ovulation, the release of the egg from the ovary, occurs at the midpoint of the 28-day cycle

Even moderate drinking in healthy women can lead to significant reproductive problems, including delayed ovulation and failure to ovulate (anovulation). Shortening of the luteal phase also was observed. Menstrual problems did not appear to occur in the women who were occasional drinkers or who were moderate drinkers consuming fewer than two drinks per day. A dose-response relationship appears to exist between alcohol consumption and the frequency of menstrual problems. This notion also is supported by epidemiological surveys showing that prevalence of menstrual disturbances grows with increasing alcohol consumption.

The mechanism of these problems is not entirely clear. However, it is of interest that acute alcohol administration has been reported to raise estrogen levels. Whether this rise is due to an increased estrogen secretion, enhanced conversion of estrogen from precursor substances, decreased metabolism, or a combination of these factors is uncertain. Nonetheless, it has been demonstrated that estrogen administration can disrupt the reproductive cycle, at least in part because estrogen can suppress FSH. This knowledge gives rise to the idea that alcohol intake could lead to increased estrogen, inhibiting FSH and disrupting folliculogenesis and subsequent corpus luteum function. In addition, alcohol has been shown to suppress progesterone, the main secretory product of the corpus luteum. Thus, even moderate amounts of alcohol may cause infertility (through suppressing ovulation) and an increased risk for spontaneous abortion (through interfering with the pregnancy-maintaining function of the corpus luteum).

Prolactin

The hormone prolactin, secreted by the anterior pituitary gland, supports lactation and breast feeding. For most of the other anterior pituitary hormones, the net effect of the hypothalamus is stimulatory; for prolactin, however, the action of the hypothalamus is inhibitory. Much of this inhibitory effect on prolactin synthesis and release is mediated by dopamine, a neurotransmitter delivered from the hypothalamus, although many other hypothalamic regulatory factors may modify prolactin release to a lesser extent. Also in contrast to the other anterior pituitary hormones, which stimulate discrete target organs, no single peripheral tissue clearly feeds back negatively on prolactin release.

Human and animal studies on both sexes have demonstrated that both acute and chronic alcohol exposure leads to a stimulation of prolactin release. Alcohol-induced reduction of dopamine's inhibitory effect may underlie this phenomenon; however, alcohol's influence on other hypothalamic factors that modify prolactin release also may account for prolactin stimulation. In addition, data from several laboratories show that alcohol applied to the anterior pituitary can stimulate prolactin release, indicating a direct effect of alcohol on the pituitary. Whatever the cause, elevated prolactin frequently is associated with reproductive deficits in both males and females. High prolactin levels can cause impotence in males and disruption of normal ovulatory cycles in females. Clearly, however, elevated prolactin levels are not the only cause for impaired reproductive capabilities: Alcoholic females can have reproductive abnormalities with or without excessive prolactin.

The suckling of infants is well known to induce prolactin release; although alcohol normally stimulates an increase in prolactin, the suckling effect is actually diminished in alcohol-ingesting women, impairing breast feeding and leading to negative consequences for infant health.

Growth Hormone

The hypothalamic-pituitary-growth hormone (GH) axis functions in a manner similar to the other integrated neuroendocrine systems previously described. The hypothalamus produces large amounts of growth hormone releasing factor (GRF), which is secreted into the hypothalamic-pituitary portal system and then to the anterior pituitary, where it binds to GRF receptors on the pituitary gland. Under GRF stimulation, pituitary GH production is enhanced. Another important hormone in this system is somatostatin. Hypothalamic somatostatin arrives at the pituitary through the portal system, where it activates somatostatin receptors. Somatostatin then inhibits GH secretion. Thus the interplay between hypothalamic GRF and somatostatin tightly regulates the amount of GH being produced by the pituitary gland.

Once pituitary GH has been synthesized and released, a key target for this hormone is the liver, which produces insulin-like growth factor 1 (IGF-1), a chemical that carries out many of the actions of GH (for example, protein formation and cell growth) at the tissue level. IGF-1 also feeds back at the hypothalamus and the pituitary to reduce GH synthesis and secretion

Both acute and chronic alcohol exposure consistently have been shown to diminish serum GH and IGF-1 levels in animals and humans of both sexes. This lowering of GH and IGF-1 is particularly deleterious to adolescents, who are dependent on these hormones for the normal pubertal process to occur. Older people, however, also suffer negative consequences from a loss of these hormones, such as impaired immune function and muscle weakness.

Hypothalmic-Pituitary Thyroid Axis

The hypothalamic-pituitary-thyroid (HPT) axis is of paramount importance. Because the metabolic processes of every cell in the body depend on normal amounts of thyroid hormone, disruption of this unit has widespread negative effects on tissue function.

The hypothalamus produces and secretes thyrotropin-releasing hormone (TRH) into the hypothalamic-pituitary portal system. TRH stimulates the thyrotrope cells of the anterior pituitary gland to produce thyroid-stimulating hormone (TSH), which then stimulates the synthesis and secretion of thyroid hormones. The principal thyroid hormones are thyroxine (T4) and triiodothyronine (T3). Although the thyroid gland secretes both of these hormones following TSH stimulation, most (about 70 percent) of the circulating T3 is derived from the liver's conversion of T4. The circulating thyroid hormones, primarily T3, feed back in a negative fashion at both the hypothalamic and the anterior pituitary level.

When abstinent alcoholics were studied, baseline T3 and, sometimes, T4 levels were lower than in nonalcoholic control subjects. The decline in thyroid hormones might not result from alcohol consumption itself but rather from an attendant illness. The fall in T3 and T4 is a common adaptation of thyroid hormone economy in acute or chronic nonthyroidal illness, a situation known as the euthyroid sick syndrome. (For example, the euthyroid sick syndrome occurs in situations such as sepsis, burns, and major trauma.) In any case, the TSH response to TRH remains blunted in abstinent alcoholics, as during alcohol withdrawal, but the prolactin response normalizes. The reason for this effect is not clear. It does not seem to be caused by excessive dopaminergic inhibition, as it is during alcohol withdrawal; if this were the case, the prolactin response would be impaired as well. Psychologically depressed individuals also have blunted TSH responses to TRH, but associated depression is not the mechanism here, because no relationship exists between personal or family history of depression and blunted TSH responsiveness in alcoholics. Whatever the reason, it is of great interest that young nonalcoholic men with alcoholic fathers (who are at high risk for alcoholism themselves) also tend to have abnormal TSH responsiveness to TRH, usually a blunted response. This finding suggests that TSH change might be a marker for vulnerability to alcohol and might point to some neurobiological abnormality that predisposes people to that disease.

Alcohol, Calcium Balance, and Bone

To form bone that is structurally sound, normal calcium and phosphorous balance is essential. Active vitamin D (cholecalciferol) is formed primarily in the skin in the presence of sunlight; smaller amounts are obtained through diet. The active form of vitamin D next is metabolized to a more active form in the liver (25-hydroxycholecalciferol), then to an even more potent form in the kidney, (1,25-dihydroxycholecalciferol) under the control of parathyroid hormone (PTH). The most active form of vitamin D, 1,25-dihydroxycholecalciferol, is responsible for normal calcium absorption from the intestinal tract. The impact of alcohol on calcium metabolism has been explored, and studies generally have confirmed that alcohol will impair calcium absorption from the upper part of the gastrointestinal (GI) tract (the jejunum and ileum). This impairment in calcium absorption leads to a fall in serum calcium levels, which feeds back to the parathyroid glands, resulting in an increase in secretion by this gland of parathyroid hormone (PTH). Elevated PTH, in turn, leads to calcium resorption or calcium withdrawal from bone, leading to demineralization of the bone and bone disease (osteoporosis). Another school of thought suggests that the most important deleterious effect of alcohol on bone is not mediated through PTH but rather by direct inhibition of the function of bone-forming cells called osteoblasts.

Contributing to the problem of bone demineralization is alcohol-induced testosterone suppression. The importance of androgens for maintaining bone mass in adult males is well established. Androgens also appear to increase bone formation at critical areas in the long bones of the body and at areas of the bones (cortical) that promote normal bone growth. Several lines of evidence firmly correlate reduced skeletal mass with reduced testosterone levels in men: Men who experience testosterone deprivation for any reason throughout their life have decreased bone mass. Thus, low testosterone levels resulting from alcohol ingestion can result in osteoporosis, causing increased risk of bone fractures. A reduction in bone mass of 50 percent has been reported in chronic alcoholics, confirming the magnitude of this problem. Thus, the problem with accelerated osteoporosis in males exposed to alcohol seems to be related to calcium malabsorption with subsequent PTH elevation and low testosterone levels.

Coupled with the problem of osteoporosis is the fact that the increase in PTH release not only encourages more avid calcium absorption from the GI tract but also results in enhanced phosphorous excretion into the urine, with the resultant effect of low serum phosphorous levels (hypophosphatemia). Hypophosphatemia has profound effects on muscles, resulting in weakness of the shoulder and pelvic girdle muscles, making it difficult for patients to perform simple maneuvers such as rising from a sitting position and climbing stairs.

Pancreatic Function

Control of blood glucose is a finely tuned process involving the key hormone insulin, which is produced by special cells of the pancreas.

Insulin synthesis and secretion are controlled by a complex cascade of hormonal signals and enzymes, resulting in the release of insulin into the blood circulation. Once insulin reaches its appropriate target cells, especially liver, muscle, and bone, it binds to a receptor and activates a process by which proteins called glucose transporters are produced and brought to the surfaces of the various target cells. They then facilitate entry of glucose into these cells, which can be used immediately for energy or stored for the cells' future use.

In the fed state, chronic alcohol consumption raises blood glucose; in the fasted state, alcohol can produce low blood glucose (hypoglycemia) in both diabetics and nondiabetics. (A fed state is one in which a person has consumed normal quantities of food over the 8 hours preceding measurement of blood components or other physiological factors; a fasted state is one in which a person has consumed no food for at least the 8 hours preceding measurements.) In addition to simply not eating, alcoholic hypoglycemia occurs for two main reasons. In the fasting state, the body has two major defense mechanisms to prevent hypoglycemia: glycogenolysis and gluconeogenesis. Glycogen, a chemical made up of glucose molecules linked together, is stored primarily in the liver. Glycogenolysis is the process by which glycogen is broken down into its constituent glucose molecules and secreted into the circulation; it is the body's first line of defense against fasting-state hypoglycemia. Glycogen reserves, however, last only for several hours; when depleted, the body turns to gluconeogenesis, its second line of defense. Gluconeogenesis is the formation of new glucose from amino acids and other chemical substances, a process occurring primarily in the liver. In conditions of alcoholic hypoglycemia, patients are usually starved, and their glycogen reserve has already been depleted. Furthermore, the metabolism of alcohol shuts down the process of gluconeogenesis; consequently, no glucose can be formed. Because of depleted glycogen reserves and impaired gluconeogenesis, the person becomes hypoglycemic. Some of the most profound hypoglycemia seen clinically is alcoholic hypoglycemia, which can lead to permanent neurological consequences, such as paralysis, seizures, coma, or even death.

Conclusion

The effects of alcohol on the endocrine system have far-reaching consequences not only for hormone production but also for the function of virtually every organ system. Alcohol-related problems include immune dysfunction as a result of disturbances in cortisol, testosterone,

GH, and prolactin; reproductive problems; cardiovascular abnormalities stemming from disrupted glucose and lipid balance; and bone disease, among others. The role of hormones, such as TRH, in the genesis of alcoholism is an exciting area of research; findings in this area may produce innovative treatments for the disorder.

Chapter 28

Alcohol's Effect on Blood Cells

People who abuse alcohol are at risk for numerous alcohol-related medical complications, including those affecting the blood (the blood cells as well as proteins present in the blood plasma) and the bone marrow, where the blood cells are produced. In this chapter, the terms "chronic alcohol abuse" or "chronic excessive alcohol consumption" refer to the ingestion of 1 pint or more of 80- to 90-proof alcohol (about 11 drinks) per day. However, alcohol-related hematological problems can occur at much lower consumption levels. The drinker's risk for developing these problems grows with increasing alcohol consumption.

Alcohol's adverse effects on the blood-building, or hematopoietic, system are both direct and indirect. The direct consequences of excessive alcohol consumption include toxic effects on the bone marrow; the blood cell precursors; and the mature red blood cells (RBCs), white blood cells (WBCs), and platelets. Alcohol's indirect effects include nutritional deficiencies that impair the production and function of various blood cells.

These direct and indirect effects of alcohol can result in serious medical problems for the drinker. For example, anemia resulting from diminished RBC production and impaired RBC metabolism and function can cause fatigue, shortness of breath, lightheadedness, and even reduced mental capacity and abnormal heartbeats. A decrease in the

---

Excerpted from "The Hematological Complications of Alcoholism," by Harold S. Ballard, M.D., in *Alcohol Health and Research World*, Winter 1997, Vol. 21, No, 1, p. 42(9). A complete copy of this publication may be ordered from the U.S. Government Printing Office. Call (202) 512-1800 for information on price and availability.

number and function of WBCs increases the drinker's risk of serious infection, and impaired platelet production and function interfere with blood clotting, leading to symptoms ranging from a simple nosebleed to bleeding in the brain (hemorrhagic stroke). Finally, alcohol-induced abnormalities in the plasma proteins that are required for blood clotting can lead to the formation of blood clots (thrombosis).

Alcohol's Effects on the Bone Marrow and on Red Blood Cell Production

Alcohol is the most commonly used drug whose consequences include the suppression of blood cell production, or hematopoiesis. Because its toxic effects are dose dependent, however, significantly impaired hematopoiesis usually occurs only in people with severe alcoholism, who also may suffer from nutritional deficiencies of folic acid and other vitamins that play a role in blood cell development. Chronic excessive alcohol ingestion reduces the number of blood cell precursors in the bone marrow and causes characteristic structural abnormalities in these cells, resulting in fewer-than-normal or nonfunctional mature blood cells. As a result, alcoholics may suffer from moderate anemia, characterized by enlarged, structurally abnormal RBCs; mildly reduced numbers of WBCs, especially of neutrophils; and moderately to severely reduced numbers of platelets. Although this generalized reduction in blood cell numbers (pancytopenia) usually is not progressive or fatal and is reversible with abstinence, complex aberrations of hematopoiesis can develop over time that may cause death.

Many bone marrow abnormalities occurring in severe alcoholics affect the RBC precursor cells. These abnormalities most prominently include precursors containing fluid-filled cavities (vacuoles) or characteristic iron deposits.

Development of Vacuoles in RBC Precursors

The most striking indication of alcohol's toxic effects on bone marrow cells is the appearance of numerous large vacuoles in early RBC precursor cells. It is unknown whether these vacuoles affect the cell's function and thus the drinker's health; however, their appearance generally is considered an indicator of excessive alcohol consumption.

Sideroblastic Anemia

Sideroblastic anemia is a common complication in severe alcoholics: Approximately one-third of these patients contain ringed sideroblasts (cells containing ferritin—an iron complex—which cannot mature into functional RBCs) in their bone marrow. Alcohol may cause sideroblastic anemia by interfering with the activity of an enzyme that mediates a critical step in hemoglobin synthesis. Abstinence can reverse this effect: The ringed sideroblasts generally disappear from the bone marrow within 5 to 10 days, and RBC production resumes. In fact, excess numbers of young RBCs called reticulocytes can accumulate temporarily in the blood, indicating higher-than-normal RBC production.

Megaloblastic Anemia

Megaloblasts (large immature and nonfunctional cells) occur frequently in the bone marrow of alcoholics; they are particularly common among alcoholics with symptoms of anemia, affecting up to one-third of these patients. These alcoholics generally also have reduced folic acid levels in their RBCs. The most common cause of this deficiency is a diet poor in folic acid, a frequent complication in alcoholics, who often have poor nutritional habits. In addition, alcohol ingestion itself may accelerate the development of folic acid deficiency by altering the absorption of folic acid from food.

Alcohol-Related RBC Disorders

Alcohol-related abnormalities in RBC production manifest themselves not only in the bone marrow but also through the presence of defective RBCs in the blood. For example, grossly enlarged RBCs can occur in the blood—a condition called macrocytosis—as well as oddly shaped RBCs that are subject to premature or accelerated destruction (hemolysis) because of their structural abnormalities. As a result, alcoholics frequently are diagnosed with anemia

Macrocytosis

People who drink excessive amounts of alcohol can develop macrocytosis even in the absence of other factors associated with RBC enlargement, such as alcoholic liver disease or folic acid deficiency. In fact, alcohol abuse is the disorder most commonly associated with macrocytosis: Up to 80 percent of men and 46 percent of women with macrocytosis have been found to be alcoholics. The precise mechanism underlying macrocytosis still is unknown. However, alcohol appears to interfere directly with RBC development, because the macrocytes disappear within 2 to 4 months of abstinence.

Hemolytic Anemia

Hemolysis can be an underlying cause of anemia, and several types of hemolytic anemia may be caused by chronic heavy alcohol consumption. Two of these disorders are characterized by the presence of malformed RBCs—stomatocytes and spur cells—whereas one alcohol-related hemolytic anemia is caused by reduced phosphate levels in the blood (hypophosphatemia). Diagnosing hemolysis in alcoholic patients is not easy, because these patients frequently exhibit confounding conditions, such as alcohol withdrawal, abnormal folic acid levels, bleeding, or an enlarged spleen.

Alcohol's Effects on Iron Metabolism

In addition to interfering with the proper absorption of iron into the hemoglobin molecules of red blood cells (RBCs), alcohol use can lead to either iron deficiency or excessively high levels of iron in the body. Because iron is essential to RBC functioning, iron deficiency, which is commonly caused by excessive blood loss, can result in anemia. In many alcoholic patients, blood loss and subsequent iron deficiency are caused by gastrointestinal bleeding. Iron deficiency in alcoholics often is difficult to diagnose, however, because it may be masked by symptoms of other nutritional deficiencies (for example, folic acid deficiency) or by coexisting liver disease and other alcohol-related inflammatory conditions. For an accurate diagnosis, the physician must therefore exclude folic acid deficiency and evaluate the patient's iron stores in the bone marrow.

Conversely, alcohol abuse can increase iron levels in the body. For example, iron absorption from the food in the gastrointestinal tract may be elevated in alcoholics. Iron levels also can rise from excessive ingestion of iron-containing alcoholic beverages, such as red wine. The increased iron levels can cause hemochromatosis, a condition characterized by the formation of iron deposits throughout the body (for example, in the liver, pancreas, heart, joints, and gonads). Moreover, patients whose chronic alcohol consumption and hemochromatosis have led to liver cirrhosis are at increased risk for liver cancer.

Alcohol's Effects on White Blood Cells

Since the 1920's, clinicians have noted an association between excessive alcohol ingestion and the development of infections. These observations suggest that alcohol interferes with the normal production and/or function of WBCs, which form the body's defense against microorganisms and other foreign substances. Because alcoholics commonly develop bacterial infections, much research has focused on alcohol's effects on neutrophils, the primary cell of defense against bacterial invasion. However, alcohol also impairs the function of monocytes and macrophages, which attack bacteria and other microorganisms, and of lymphocytes, which mediate the immune response.

Neutrophils

When a severe bacterial infection occurs, the body's response usually includes an increase in the number of WBCs—specially neutrophils—in the blood, a condition called leukocytosis. In contrast, alcoholics suffering from bacterial infections often exhibit a reduced number of neutrophils in the blood (neutropenia).

Monocytes and Macrophages

The monocyte-macrophage system, like neutrophils, constitutes an important line of defense against infections. Monocytes and macrophages clear invading microorganisms as well as foreign or defective proteins from the blood by engulfing and subsequently destroying them. Alcohol interferes with the function of the monocyte-macrophage system, with clinically significant consequences. For example, compared with healthy people, alcoholics are less resistant to infections by microorganisms that normally are eradicated by monocytes and macrophages, such as the bacteria that cause tuberculosis and various forms of pneumonia.

Alcohol's Effects on the Blood Clotting System

Blood clotting, or coagulation, an important physiological process that ensures the integrity of the vascular system, involves the platelets, or thrombocytes, as well as several proteins dissolved in the plasma. When a blood vessel is injured, platelets are attracted to the site of the injury, where they aggregate to form a temporary plug. The platelets secrete several proteins (clotting factors) that—together with other proteins either secreted by surrounding tissue cells or present in the blood—initiate a chain of events that results in the formation of fibrin. Fibrin is a stringy protein that forms a tight mesh in the injured vessel; blood cells become trapped in this mesh, thereby plugging the wound. Fibrin clots, in turn, can be dissolved by a process that helps prevent the development of thrombosis (fibrinolysis).

Alcohol can interfere with these processes at several levels, causing, for example, abnormally low platelet numbers in the blood (thrombocytopenia), impaired platelet function (thrombocytopathy), and diminished fibrinolysis. These effects can have serious medical consequences, such as an increased risk for strokes.

Summary

Numerous clinical observations support the notion that alcohol adversely affects the production and function of virtually all types of blood cells. Thus, alcohol is directly toxic to the bone marrow, which contains the precursors of all blood cells, as well as to the mature cells circulating in the bloodstream. Moreover, long-term excessive alcohol consumption can interfere with various physiological, biochemical, and metabolic processes involving the blood cells. The medical consequences of these adverse effects can be severe. They include anemia, which in severe cases can have debilitating effects; an increased risk of serious bacterial infections; and impaired blood clotting and fibrinolysis, which can cause excessive bleeding and place the drinker at increased risk of strokes. These direct effects may be exacerbated by the presence of other alcohol-related disorders, such as liver disease and nutritional deficiencies. Abstinence can reverse many of alcohol's effects on hematopoiesis and blood cell functioning.

Chapter 29

Alcohol Consumption and Blood Pressure

African-American alcoholics may run a greater risk than white alcoholics for blood pressure elevations as the drinking career lengthens, according to researchers James York, Ph.D. and Judith Ann Hirsch, Ph.D. at the Research Institute on Addictions.

The risk of death from stroke increases continuously with systolic blood pressures (SBPs) greater than 112 mm Hg or diastolic blood pressures (DBPs) greater than 78 mm Hg in men, with African-Americans being at risk more than whites. Findings such as these emphasize the importance of studying factors, such as alcohol intake, that are associated with increases in blood pressure (BP). Although numerous empirical and epidemiological studies have suggested a positive association between BP and recent alcohol consumption in moderate drinkers, there is still considerable controversy over the exact relationships that exist between current or past alcohol intake, SBP or DBP, and modifying or confounding variables such as age, sex, race, adiposity, smoking, and physical activity.

The decision to assess alcohol intake over the entire drinking career was motivated by the expectation that the probability of tissue or organ system toxicities should increase as a function of the cumulative dose. To test this hypothesis, two-hundred fifty-three alcoholic subjects,

"Lifetime Alcohol Consumption Related to Increases in Blood Pressure in Alcoholics," in the January 1997 issue of *Research in Brief* (ISSN 1047-8418), a newsletter published six times a year by the Research Institute on Addictions, a component of the New York State Office of Alcoholism and Substance Abuse Services; reprinted with permission. For more information, contact: RIA Public Communications, 1021 Main Street, Buffalo, N.Y. 14203-1016.

between 20 and 59 years of age, were recruited from local alcoholism treatment centers and screened for other drug use or medical problems, including hypertension. An average of 35 days passed from the subjects' cessation of drinking to the beginning of the testing. Subjects completed questionnaires detailing their level of physical activity, socioeconomic status, medical problems, and alcohol dependency. Each subject was then interviewed to assess lifetime alcohol consumption in terms of quantity, frequency, and type of beverage, as well as the point at which they began drinking at least one drink per month. BPs were first corrected for the influence of confounding or modifying variables (age, activity, body mass index, health score, socioeconomic status, cigarettes per day) before regression against alcohol consumption measures.

Relationship of Alcohol Intake to Blood Pressure

Dr. York, principal investigator on the study, explained, "The strongest associations were between diastolic blood pressure and the duration (years) of the drinking career," and were most noticeable in black alcoholics, both men and women. The effect accounted for a rise in diastolic blood pressure of about 7% for every ten years of drinking, and was independent of the total amount of alcohol consumed over the lifetime of the subjects. A 7% rise in diastolic blood pressure can be expected to increase the risk of death from stroke by approximately 50%. Measures of lifetime total alcohol dose were also significantly correlated with DBP in black males, but only a few measures of recent alcohol consumption were correlated with DBP, and the correlations were small.

The finding that the duration of drinking, independent of the lifetime total dose, was most highly correlated with blood pressure, suggests somewhat of an equivalency in the biological impact of drinking episodes among alcoholic subjects, although the subjects varied considerably in alcohol intake over the career. The results of this study appear in *Hypertension* 28:133-138, 1996.

References

Neaton JD, Kuller L, Stamler J, Wentworth DN. Impact of systolic and diastolic blood pressure on cardiovascular mortality. In Laragh JH, Brenner BM (eds). *Hypertension: pathophysiology, diagnosis and management*. New York: Raven Press, 1995, pp 127-145.

Klatsky AL. Blood pressure and alcohol intake. In Laragh JH and Brenner BM (eds). *Hypertension: pathophysiology, diagnosis and management. 2nd ed*, New York: Raven Press, 1995; 2649-67.

Chapter 30

Alcohol and the Heart

Cardiovascular Effects of Alcohol

An association between excessive alcohol consumption and cardiac dysfunction has been recognized for more than a century, but the direct role of alcohol as opposed to accompanying nutritional deficiencies has come into focus only recently. Some degree of subclinical depression of heart function is apparent in a large proportion of alcoholics. Heavy alcohol drinking (more than four drinks per day) has been associated with a variety of detrimental effects on the heart and vascular system; by contrast, moderate alcohol consumption (up to two drinks per day) may have some beneficial effects.

At the level of the heart muscle, long-term heavy consumption of alcohol can lead to alcoholic cardiomyopathy, which is characterized by loss of contractile function and enlargement of the heart. In addition, defects in the electrical conduction properties of the heart brought on by acute or chronic alcohol abuse can result in arrthythmias, or disturbances in the rhythm and synchronization of the heartbeat.

Cardiomyopathy

Any intrinsic degenerative disease of the heart muscle may be referred to as "cardiomyopathy." Alcoholic cardiomyopathy reflects low-output

---

Excerpted from *Ninth Special Report to the U.S. Congress on Alcohol and Health,* U.S. Department of Health and Human Services, National Institute on Alcohol Abuse and Alcoholism, June 1997.

congestive heart failure with clinical symptoms and pathology that are indistinguishable from other forms of dilated cardiomyopathy. This disease progresses from an asymptomatic stage in which the contractile function of the heart is compromised. These initial deficiencies are compensated by a variety of mechanisms, including dilation of the ventricles (the pumping chambers of the heart), an increase in the bulk of heart muscle (cardiac hypertrophy), and an increase in blood volume. Eventually, the compensatory mechanisms break down; as a result, the heart cannot pump enough blood to meet the body's normal requirements. In this phase, known as cardiac decompensation, patients experience shortness of breath and fatigue, and deficiencies in oxygenation are exacerbated by increased blood volume. Finally, heart failure may progress to a point at which cardiac output can no longer sustain life.

Chronic alcohol abuse is thought to be the underlying cause in an estimated 20 to 50 percent of all cases of dilated cardiomyopathy. Alcoholic cardiomyopathy usually develops over years (more than 10) of excessive drinking; clinical symptoms most often become evident between 30 and 60 years of age. The disease appears to be more common in men than in women, but this observation may simply reflect the greater prevalence of alcoholism in men. Recent studies comparing the deleterious effects of alcohol on heart function in alcoholic women and men indicate that women are at least as sensitive as men to alcohol's cardiotoxic effects. Although nutritional deficiencies may exacerbate some cardiovascular effects of alcoholism, it is now clear that alcohol has direct toxic effects on heart muscle and that this is the primary cause of alcoholic cardiomyopathy. One study found reduced ejection fractions (the proportion of blood ejected from the heart at each beat) in one-third of a group of well-nourished alcoholics. These investigators also found that the depression of cardiac contractile function and the observed increase in heart mass correlated with total lifetime consumption of alcohol; their finding indicates that there may be a dose-dependent component to alcohol's effect. Alcoholic cardiomyopathy may be reversible with abstinence if the disease is not too far advanced; that is, while it remains in a subclinical state. However, even with abstinence, patients with severe symptoms may progress to congestive heart failure and death.

In recent years, considerable progress has been made in understanding how alcohol interferes with the mechanical function of the heart. Effects of alcohol may be acute (changes that are dependent on the immediate presence of alcohol) or chronic (changes that develop over an extended period of regular alcohol consumption). Establishing experimental models that reproduce the low output form of congestive cardiomyopathy seen in long-term alcoholics has been an elusive goal; however, changes occurring over relatively shorter times can be studied in animals fed alcohol as part of their diet. In addition, whereas overt responses of the heart to acute alcohol exposure reverse rapidly once alcohol is no longer present, repeated episodes of acute alcohol exposure can lead to cumulative damage and adaptation of the cardiovascular system that likely contribute to the development of alcoholic heart disease. Therefore, investigations of both acute and chronic actions of alcohol on heart biochemistry and physiology are important for defining the basis of alcohol-induced heart disease.

How Alcohol Effects Heart Muscles

Acute alcohol exposure causes a direct depression of the contractile function of heart muscle. This effect may be masked somewhat by an indirect stimulation of the heart resulting from an alcohol-induced elevation of catecholamines, such as adrenaline. (Catecholamines are compounds having actions in the body that mimic actions of the sympathetic nervous system, which controls automatic processes such as heart rate.) At one time, direct suppressive effects of alcohol were thought to result from alterations in energy metabolism of the heart, but recent evidence suggests alcohol also interferes with steps controlling contraction.

Heart muscle contraction is triggered by electrical impulses that pass rapidly through the heart. The impulses cause an increase in the concentration of calcium ions within the heart muscle cells; in turn, calcium ions activate the proteins responsible for contraction. Recent technical advances have allowed investigation of this excitation-contraction process at the cellular level. Such studies have shown that changes in the concentration of calcium ions responsible for muscle contraction are reduced in the presence of high levels of alcohol. Targets for alcohol's action in producing this effect have been identified as specific channels in the cell membrane that control entry of calcium ions and the sarcoplasmic reticulum, an intracellular organelle that serves as a calcium storage unit. In addition, contractile proteins of the heart muscle appear to be less sensitive to calcium ion activation in the presence of alcohol, even at low concentrations.

Arrhythmia

The heartbeat is driven by the sinoatrial node, a group of intrinsic pacemaker cells in which fluxes of cellular ions initiate electrical depolarization of the cell membrane. Once initiated, this depolarization propagates rapidly through the heart to produce an essentially synchronous contraction of the entire organ. The synchronization and frequency of heart muscle contraction are critical for efficient pump function.

Arrhythmias can involve irregular beating (dysrhythmia) or asynchronous contractions of the heart muscle cells (fibrillation). Sustained loss of pump function, particularly that associated with ventricular fibrillation, can lead to sudden death. Both acute alcohol intoxication and chronic alcohol consumption are associated with arrhythmias; the most common rhythm disturbances observed are atrial fibrillation and ventricular dysrhythmia. In most cases, atrial fibrillation brought on by acute alcohol consumption reverses within 24 hours after drinking stops.

Alcoholics may have an enhanced sensitivity to short-term arrhythmogenic effects of acute alcohol exposure, and they may experience arrhythmias during alcohol withdrawal. The term "holiday heart" has been used to refer to arrhythmias associated with binge drinking in alcoholics. Arrhythmia is considered to be one of the major factors precipitating sudden death in alcoholics. A recent survey of 156 published papers demonstrated that heavy drinking is associated with increased risk for cardiac arrhythmias, cardiomyopathy, and sudden coronary death. Others have reported that electrocardiographic abnormalities in alcoholic patients are associated with an adverse prognosis and indicate dysfunction that may predispose these patients to sudden cardiac death.

Several potential mechanisms have been implicated in alcohol-induced arrhythmias, including disturbances in the initiation of electrical depolarization, interference in the propagation of electrical impulses, and alterations in the normal path and sequence of electrical excitation. Both acute and chronic alcohol exposure can modify the electrical properties of heart cells responsible for impulse initiation and propagation. Alcohol inhibits the sodium-potassium pump, which is a membrane protein that maintains the basal ion composition inside cardiac cells. Alcohol also modifies the time course of electrical depolarization and subsequent repolarization (known as the action potential) in atrial and ventricular muscle preparations, including Purkinje fibers (specialized conducting cells of the myocardium).

Chapter 31

Alcohol and Coronary Heart Disease

Heart attacks and other forms of coronary heart disease (CHD) result in approximately 500,000 deaths annually, accounting for 25 percent of the nation's total mortality. Research has revealed an association between moderate alcohol consumption and lower risk for CHD. (Definitions of moderate drinking vary among studies. The U.S. Department of Agriculture and the U.S. Department of Health and Human Services define moderate drinking as not more than two drinks per day for men and no more than one drink per day for women. A standard drink is 12 grams of pure alcohol, which is equivalent to one 12-ounce bottle of beer, one 5-ounce glass of wine, or 1.5 ounces of distilled spirits.) This chapter reviews epidemiologic evidence for this association, explores lifestyle factors and physiological mechanisms that might suggest ways to explain alcohol's apparent protective effects, and presents available data on the balance between alcohol's beneficial and harmful effects on health.

Epidemiologic Evidence

With few exceptions, epidemiologic data from at least 20 countries in North America, Europe, Asia, and Australia demonstrate a 20- to

From *Alcohol Alert*, No. 45, October 1999, National Institute on Alcohol Abuse and Alcoholism (NIAAA). The full text of this publication, including references, is available on NIAAA's World Wide Web site at http://www.niaaa.nih.gov. Copies are also available free of charge from the National Institute on Alcohol Abuse and Alcoholism (NIAAA) Publications Distribution Center, Attn.: *Alcohol Alert*, P.O. Box 10686, Rockville, MD 20849-0686.

40-percent lower CHD incidence among drinkers compared with nondrinkers. Moderate drinkers exhibit lower rates of CHD-related mortality than both heavy drinkers and abstainers. Such studies range from comparisons of nationwide population data to retrospective analyses of health and drinking patterns within communities.

The most persuasive epidemiologic evidence for alcohol's possible protective effects on CHD comes from prospective studies, in which participants provide information on their drinking habits and health-related practices before the onset of disease. Participants' subsequent health histories are evaluated through a series of follow-up interviews. Large-scale prospective investigations confirm an association between moderate drinking and lower CHD risk. The specific studies described here represent a total population of more than one million men and women of different ethnicities. Follow-up periods average 11 years, the longest being the 24-year prospective phase of the Framingham CHD mortality study. (The mean study duration is calculated from the date of the first intake interview and unadjusted for the number of participants or premature mortality.) The two largest of these studies were conducted by the American Cancer Society, one including 276,800 men and the other including 490,000 men and women.

Other large prospective investigations that associate moderate drinking with lower risk for CHD include a series of studies by Kaiser-Permanente analyzing CHD hospitalization and death rates in both men and women; studies of CHD incidence and mortality among female nurses; and studies of CHD incidence and mortality among male physicians. Results of these American studies are confirmed by data from similar investigations conducted in England, Denmark, China, and other countries. In addition, a smaller 12-year study found an association between moderate drinking and lower risk of CHD-related death among older persons (average age of 69) with late-onset diabetes, a population at high risk for CHD. However, a recent 21-year prospective study from Scotland found no association between moderate drinking and lower risk for CHD among 6,000 working men ages 35 to 64.

Is Alcohol's Role Causal or Incidental?

An association between moderate drinking and lower risk for CHD does not necessarily mean that alcohol itself is the cause of the lower risk. For example, a review of population studies indicates that the higher mortality risk among abstainers may be attributable to shared traits other than participants' nonuse of alcohol. Substantial evidence has discounted speculation that abstainers include a large proportion of former heavy drinkers with pre-existing health problems ("sick quitters"). Nevertheless, health-related lifestyle factors that correlate consistently with drinking level could account for some of the association between alcohol and lower risk for CHD. Among the most widely studied of these factors are exercise and diet.

Few studies have adjusted for subjects' levels of physical activity, despite evidence that exercise protects against CHD occurrence and mortality. In a comprehensive review of published studies, Berlin and Colditz (Berlin, J.A., and Colditz, G.A. A meta-analysis of physical activity in the prevention of coronary heart disease. *Am J Epidemiol* 132(4):612-628, 1990.) concluded that risk for CHD was proportionately lower at higher exercise levels. Measures of activity level vary among studies. Studies evaluate factors such as job-related physical requirements, frequency of participation in unspecified sports, estimated vigorousness of given activities, calculations of energy expended, and tests of cardiovascular fitness. Results of a community survey indicated that the prevalence of regular exercise was higher among moderate and heavy drinkers than among nondrinkers. Regular exercise was defined as any form of nonoccupational physical activity performed at least three times per week. The role of exercise in the alcohol-CHD association requires additional study.

Diet is one of the strongest influences on CHD-related death among men ages 50 to 70. International comparisons, laboratory data, and prospective studies suggest that diets high in saturated fat and cholesterol increase the risk for CHD. Epidemiologic data suggest that moderate drinkers may consume less fat and cholesterol than heavier drinkers and abstainers, potentially accounting for a portion of the lower CHD risk associated with alcohol. However, results of other prospective studies indicate that alcohol's association with lower CHD risk is independent of nutritional factors.

The Role of Beverage Choice

Some studies report that wine (particularly red wine) affords more CHD protection than beer or liquor at equivalent levels of alcohol consumption. This finding suggests that the association between alcohol consumption and CHD risk may result from the effects of beverage ingredients other than alcohol itself. Epidemiologic and laboratory studies investigating this hypothesis have produced conflicting results.

A comparison of data from 21 developed countries concluded that wine consumption was more strongly correlated with lower CHD risk than was consumption of other alcoholic beverages. However, large-scale prospective studies have not found any difference in the incidence of CHD associated with beverage type. Red wine has been shown to contain certain nonalcoholic ingredients that could hypothetically interfere with the progression of CHD. However, research has not yet demonstrated a significant role for these chemicals in arresting CHD development in humans.

Evidence suggests that a preference for wine over other alcoholic beverages is associated with a lifestyle that includes other favorable health-related practices. For example, drinkers who prefer wine tend to smoke less and drink less and have a more healthful diet than those who prefer beer or liquor.

How Might Alcohol Lower Risk for CHD?

To function normally, the muscle tissue that constitutes the bulk of the heart requires a constant supply of oxygen-containing blood. Blood is delivered to the heart muscle through the coronary arteries. Cholesterol and other fatty substances can accumulate within the coronary arteries, partially impeding the flow of blood. This condition underlies the clinical manifestations of CHD, which may range from episodic chest pain to sudden death. The most common serious manifestation of CHD is the heart attack. Heart attacks are generally triggered by the formation of a blood clot within a constricted coronary artery, obstructing blood flow and depriving a portion of the heart muscle of oxygen. The resulting impairment of the heart's pumping ability may cause permanent disability or death, either immediately or through the progressive development of medical complications.

Researchers have investigated several theories to explain how alcohol itself might lower risk for CHD. For example, alcohol may protect the heart by preventing the constriction of the coronary arteries, inhibiting clot formation, and enhancing recovery following a heart attack. Most of the evidence supporting these potential mechanisms is derived from experiments using animals or cells isolated from artery walls and grown in the laboratory. Controlled clinical experiments are needed to confirm that the effects observed in such studies can alter the development or progression of CHD in humans.

Results of laboratory research indicate that alcohol administration may help prevent arterial narrowing in mice. Such an effect could stem from changes in the blood concentrations of certain fatty substances that influence the deposition of cholesterol within the coronary arteries. However, human and animal studies indicate that less than one-half of the lower risk for CHD associated with alcohol consumption can be explained by altered blood levels of these fatty substances. Therefore, researchers are investigating additional explanations for alcohol's apparent protective effects.

Alcohol may help prevent clot formation within already narrowed coronary arteries. Clotting occurs partly in response to chemicals released into the blood from the arterial wall. Exposure of these cells to alcohol in the laboratory suppresses the production of substances that promote clotting and stimulates the production and activity of substances that inhibit clotting. In addition, analyses of blood samples drawn from human volunteers indicate that alcohol consumption increases blood levels of anticlotting factors and decreases the "stickiness" of the specialized blood cells (platelets) that clump together to form clots.

Results of laboratory research suggest that alcohol might help protect against reperfusion injury, a form of damage caused by the sudden restoration of blood flow to heart muscle weakened by previous oxygen deprivation. Alcohol's effects on reperfusion injury have been studied in guinea pigs and rats, but not in humans. Heavy alcohol consumption by humans can cause rapid and irregular heartbeat and can impair the heart's pumping ability, two of the major causes of death following a heart attack. Alcohol may also interact harmfully with medications prescribed to treat heart diseases. Thus, although alcohol may help protect against CHD, drinking may increase the risk of adverse health effects after a heart attack.

Risks and Benefits

The apparent benefits of moderate drinking on CHD mortality are offset at higher drinking levels by increasing risk of death from other types of heart disease; cancer; liver cirrhosis; and trauma, including trauma from traffic crashes. Moderate drinking is not risk free. The trade-offs between risks and benefits can be exemplified by the fact that alcohol's anticlotting ability, potentially protective against heart attack, may increase the risk of hemorrhagic stroke, or bleeding within the brain.

A Commentary by NIAAA Director Enoch Gordis, M.D.

We last visited the issue of the effect of moderate drinking on risk for coronary heart disease (CHD) in 1992 (*Alcohol Alert* No. 16). Since that time, research findings continue to confirm an association between moderate drinking and a lower risk for CHD. While there is an association between moderate drinking and lower CHD risk, science has not confirmed that alcohol itself causes the lower risk. It also is plausible that the lower risk might result from some as yet unidentified factor or surrogate associated both with alcohol use and lower CHD risk, such as lifestyle, diet and exercise, or additives to alcoholic beverages. Research is now in progress to answer these questions. The distinction between an association and a cause is important, particularly when considering what advice to give to the public. Further, even if we find that alcohol itself is responsible for the lower risk, still to be considered would be the trade-offs between the benefits and risks, particularly for specific subsets of the population. For example, moderate drinking by older persons may lower CHD but increase risk for other alcohol-related health conditions, such as adverse alcohol-drug interactions; trauma, including falls and automobile crashes; or hemorrhagic stroke.

Until these issues are clarified, we continue to believe that the most prudent advice is the following: (1) Individuals who are not currently drinking should not be encouraged to drink solely for health reasons, because the basis for health improvements has not yet been established as deriving from alcohol itself; (2) individuals who choose to drink and are not otherwise at risk for alcohol-related problems should not exceed the one- to two-drink-per-day limit recommended by the U.S. Dietary Guidelines (Individuals at risk for alcohol-related problems include pregnant or nursing women, operators of automobiles and other potentially dangerous machinery, individuals taking medications where alcohol use is contraindicated, individuals with a family history of alcoholism, and individuals who are recovering from alcoholism.); and (3) individuals who currently are drinking beyond the U.S. Dietary Guidelines' recommended limits should be advised to lower their daily alcohol intake to these limits.

Chapter 32

Alcohol and Compromised Immunity

The immune system serves as the body's defense against infections by microorganisms; damage caused by other foreign substances; and the uncontrolled, tumorous growth of the body's own cells. Impairment of this system can increase a person's risk for developing various illnesses, including infectious diseases, such as tuberculosis, and certain types of cancer. Alcohol can modulate this defense, and clinicians have known for a long time that chronic alcohol abusers have an impaired immune system. This impairment manifests itself in several ways. For example, alcoholics are prone to infections by various disease-causing microorganisms (pathogens); have a decreased ability to fight these infections; and have an increased risk of developing tumors, particularly in the head, neck, and upper gastrointestinal tract. Although alcohol-induced malnutrition—including vitamin deficiencies—and advanced liver cirrhosis likely contribute to some abnormalities in the immune system of alcoholics, alcohol itself also is a potent modulator of immune functions. Interestingly, not only chronic alcohol abuse but also single-episode (acute) and/or moderate alcohol consumption can affect the immune system.

Excerpted from "Alcohol's Contribution to Compromised Immunity," by Gyongyi Szabo, M.D. Ph.D., in *Alcohol Health and Research World*, Winter 1997, Vol. 21, No, 1, p. 30(9). A complete copy of this publication may be ordered from the U.S. Government Printing Office. Call (202) 512-1800 for information on price and availability.

The Immune System: An Overview

The immune system has two main arms: innate (or nonspecific) immunity and acquired (or specific) immunity. Innate immunity exists before the body is exposed to a pathogen for the first time. Moreover, this system does not respond to specific pathogens but instead responds to any pathogen it encounters. For example, the cells involved in innate immunity immediately attack any kind of bacterium or virus that enters the body, whether it is the first or second infection by that organism. Acquired immunity, in contrast, is activated only after the body is exposed to a pathogen for the first time. In addition, the acquired response is specific to one particular pathogen. For example, when *Mycobacterium tuberculosis*, the bacterium that causes tuberculosis, enters the body, the contact with that pathogen activates cells involved in acquired immunity. These activated cells attack only *M. tuberculosis* and no other bacteria or viruses. The activated cells also generate a kind of immune "memory" that allows the body to fight a second infection by the same pathogen even faster and more efficiently.

Innate Immunity

The elements of innate immunity include white blood cells that ingest and destroy microorganisms (phagocytes); certain proteins that circulate in the blood, called the complement system; and signaling molecules (cytokines) that are produced and secreted by some of the phagocytes. Several different types of phagocytes exist, with specific functions as follows:

- Neutrophils ingest and thereby destroy pathogens, primarily invading bacteria.
- Monocytes that circulate in the blood or that have entered the tissues ingest and destroy a variety of foreign substances and microorganisms. (Cells that ingest foreign substances and that have left the bloodstream and reside in tissues are called macrophages). Monocytes also exhibit pathogen-derived proteins and other molecules (antigens) on their surfaces in order to activate other cells in the immune system. Finally, monocytes and macrophages secrete cytokines that help regulate immune system activity.
- Natural killer (NK) cells recognize and eliminate cells in the body that have been infected by parasites or that have turned into cancer cells.

Acquired Immunity

The elements of acquired immunity include numerous cell types and molecules that function cooperatively to mount a complex host defense and thereby amplify and focus the protection offered by the innate immunity. The most important cells involved in acquired immunity are T lymphocytes (or T cells) and B lymphocytes (or B cells). These cells circulate in the blood or reside in special lymphoid tissues (for example, the spleen, lymph nodes, and tonsils), where they can encounter antigens and initiate an immune response.

T cells and B cells are the cornerstones of two types of immune responses, the cell-mediated immunity and the antibody-mediated (humoral) immunity. The cell-mediated immunity relies primarily on T cells that are activated by exposure to antigen-presenting cells (for example, monocytes, macrophages, and B cells). Each antigen-presenting cell displays only one antigen (for example, a viral protein) on its surface and thus stimulates only T cells that recognize this specific antigen. The activated T cell then can bind to other cells carrying the same antigen (for example, virus-infected cells) and initiate their destruction. Several subpopulations of T cells have specific functions in the complex chain of events occurring during an immune response:

- Helper T cells produce and secrete cytokines that stimulate the activity of other immune cells.
- Cytotoxic T cells recognize antigens on the surface of virus-infected or transplanted cells and destroy these cells.
- Suppressor T cells inhibit other immune responses, thereby preventing overreaction of the immune system.
- Delayed-type hypersensitivity T cells produce cytokines that induce a localized inflammatory response and attract macrophages and cytotoxic T cells to that site to eliminate the antigen.

The B cells produce the humoral immunity. These cells carry immune proteins (antibodies, or immunoglobulins) on their surface that recognize and bind to antigens. Like T cells, each B cell also recognizes only one specific antigen and becomes activated when it comes into contact with it. Most activated B cells develop into so-called plasma cells, which secrete their antibodies into the blood or lymph. There the antibodies can bind to their target antigens (for example, a virus or a virus-infected cell) and thus mark them for destruction.

Other B cells become memory cells, which help the body fight a second infection by the same pathogen more expeditiously.

The T-cell and B-cell responses are not independent of each other, however, but are intricately intertwined. Thus, B cells that have bound an antigen serve as antigen-presenting cells that can activate a T-cell response. Moreover, B cells and T cells communicate with each other and with other immune cells by secreting numerous cytokines that can influence various components of both the nonspecific and specific immune responses.

Alcohol's Effects on the Immune Defense

The body's response to an invading pathogen can be divided into two phases. The first phase is an inflammatory reaction, which protects the body from the immediate effects of the infection. The inflammatory response primarily involves phagocytic cells that help eliminate the pathogen, cytokines secreted mainly by these phagocytes, and other molecules (for example, oxygen radicals) that assist in killing the pathogen. The second phase, the development of immunity to the pathogen, is mediated by T cells and B cells. Alcohol can interfere with both phases of the immune response.

Alcohol's Effects on the Inflammatory Response

Effects on Phagocytic Cells. During an inflammatory response, chemical substances released by cells at the site of the infection induce phagocytes to migrate from their normal locations in the bloodstream or the tissues to the site of the inflammation. This process is called chemotaxis.

Chronic as well as acute alcohol consumption reduces the ability of phagocytes to ingest and break down pathogenic bacteria. For example, cultured human monocytes exposed to alcohol showed reduced phagocytic functions; moreover, the cells produced less of a receptor protein that is required for the ingestion of antibody-coated particles. In mice, both short-term and long-term alcohol feeding reduced the phagocytic ability of macrophages residing in the membrane lining the abdominal cavity. Thus, abnormal neutrophil adherence and chemotaxis, as well as reduced phagocytic function of macrophages, may contribute to the impaired defense against microorganisms observed after alcohol consumption.

Effects on Inflammatory Cytokines. Phagocyte contact with pathogens induces the release of cytokines by the phagocytes that help initiate and maintain the inflammatory response and thus play a pivotal role in the body's immune defense. The most common inflammatory cytokines—tumor necrosis factor alpha (TNF-[Alpha]), IL-1, and IL-6—are primarily produced by monocytes and macrophages. During an overwhelming inflammatory response, however, neutrophils, lymphocytes, and other tissue cells also can be sources of inflammatory cytokines. Excessive levels of these cytokines may cause tissue damage, whereas reduced levels may result in an insufficient immune response.

In chronic alcohol abusers, particularly those with alcoholic liver disease, the levels of TNF-[Alpha], IL-1, and IL-6 in the blood are significantly elevated. These increased cytokine levels may contribute to most of the signs and symptoms observed in patients with alcoholic hepatitis for example, generally increased metabolism, fever, weight loss, elevated levels of proteins produced in the liver, and markers of malnutrition). It is unknown, however, which cells cause the elevated inflammatory cytokine production in alcoholics.

The other cytokine controlling inflammatory reactions and T-cell proliferation is TGF-[Beta]. Elevated TGF-[Beta] levels may have multiple implications for immune-system functioning, including inhibition of inflammatory cytokine production by monocytes and other cells, inhibition of T-cell proliferation, and augmentation of the humoral immune response. As a result, the drinker becomes more susceptible to infections and exhibits decreased immune system activity in eliminating infections. In addition, elevated TGF-[Beta] levels promote collagen production. Collagen molecules normally form the fibers making up tendons and ligaments. However, excessive collagen production resulting from alcohol-induced TGF-[Beta] may result in abnormal collagen deposits in the liver that have been implicated in the development of some types of alcoholic liver disease.

Alcohol also increases the production of nonprotein regulatory molecules that inhibit the antigen-presenting capacity of monocytes, inflammatory cytokine production, and T-cell proliferation.

By increasing the levels of these substances as well as of IL-10 and TGF-[Beta], alcohol can interfere with the body's normal defense against invading microorganisms in two ways: by reducing inflammatory-cytokine production and by inhibiting T-cell proliferation.

Effects on Oxygen-Radical Production. Oxygen radicals (for example, superoxide anions and hydrogen peroxide) are unstable oxygen-containing molecules that readily interact with other molecules in a cell. Oxygen radicals produced by macrophages and other phagocytes play a crucial role in destroying microorganisms, especially in the lungs. The alcohol-induced decreases in the macrophages' production of oxygen radicals and nitric oxide could undermine the body's defense against bacteria. This mechanism could contribute to the high incidence of tuberculosis in alcoholics.

Alcohol-induced overproduction of oxygen radicals in the liver, in contrast, may contribute to the development of alcoholic liver damage. Together, these observations imply that alcohol may have a dual negative effect on the body's oxygen-radical production. First, alcohol may inhibit oxygen-radical and nitric oxide production in macrophages in the lung, where these substances are essential for killing microorganisms. Second, alcohol may increase oxygen-radical production in the liver, where these molecules may cause tissue damage.

Alcohol's Effects on Immunity

Effects on T Cells. Alcoholics and laboratory animals chronically ingesting alcohol have lower-than-normal numbers of all subpopulations of T cells in the blood, in the thymus—the gland where T cells mature—and in the spleen, where immune reactions are initiated. The mechanism underlying the alcohol-induced decrease in T-cell numbers still is unknown. Some researchers have suggested that acute alcohol exposure induces programmed cell death, or apoptosis, in immature T cells in the thymus. Acute alcohol exposure also results in increased apoptosis of mature lymphocytes and monocytes in the blood.

Overall, the effects of both acute and chronic alcohol exposure result in a weakened cell-mediated immune response. This shift in the immune response likely impairs the body's defense against bacterial infections requiring a predominantly cell-mediated immune response, such as infections with *M. tuberculosis* or *Listeria monocytogenes*.

Effects on B Cells. A characteristic immune-system aberration observed in alcoholics is the elevation of antibody levels in the blood. Similarly, acute alcohol consumption in mice increased antibody production in response to certain chemical substances. Because antibodies are produced by B cells, these observations indicate that alcohol alters either the number or function of B cells. To date, conflicting results exist regarding these two alternatives.

One possible explanation for these conflicting findings is that alcohol interferes only with some aspects of B-cell functioning. For example, B cells do not respond to all antigens in the same manner. In response to some antigens, B cells require the assistance of cytokines secreted by T cells (T-cell–dependent responses), whereas in response to other antigens, T-cell activation is not required (T-cell-independent responses). Alcohol appears to affect these responses differently, because B cells in the spleens of alcohol-consuming animals showed impaired proliferation during a T-cell-dependent response but normal proliferation during a T-cell-independent response. Similarly, alcoholics exhibited an intact T-cell-independent antibody response after administration of a specific antigen. Thus, alcohol may interfere with antibody production indirectly by inhibiting the production of certain T-cell-derived cytokines required for B-cell function. The complexity of alcohol's effects on B cells is underscored further by findings that alcohol impairs B-cell proliferation in response to the T-cell-derived cytokine IL-4 but not in response to the T-cell-derived cytokine IL-2.

Effects on Natural Killer Cells. NK cells are a type of white blood cell involved in the destruction of virus-infected and cancerous cells. Consequently, NK cells play an important role in preventing tumor development. Chronic alcohol consumption is associated with increased incidence of tumors, suggesting that NK cell activity may be impaired. In laboratory animals, chronic alcohol administration reduced the number and activity of NK cells. Tissue-culture experiments, in contrast, produced conflicting results, demonstrating that alcohol had either an inhibitory effect or no effect on NK cell activity. Finally, acute alcohol consumption temporarily reduced the ability of rats to eliminate certain tumor cells and prevent the development of tumor metastases.

Effects on Cytokines. Cytokines produced by lymphocytes (lymphokines, such as IL's and interferons [IFN's]) regulate the functions of immune cells as well as nonimmune cells (for example, nerve cells and cells of hormone-producing organs). The effects of either chronic or acute alcohol use on cytokine production and function, however, are only partially understood. IL-2 is one of the most important T-cell-produced cytokines; it promotes the proliferation and survival of certain T-cell subpopulations. Although alcohol in tissue culture experiments had no effect on the ability of T cells to produce IL-2, it likely interferes with the T-cell response to IL-2. The potential intracellular mechanisms underlying these effects, however, remain unknown.

Consequences of Alcohol's Effects on the Immune System

Increased Susceptibility to Bacterial Infections

Alcoholics are considered "immunocompromised hosts" because the incidence and severity of infections are increased in these patients. Infections with pathogens that reside within the host's cells and cause diseases such as pneumonia or tuberculosis are especially prevalent. Thus, alcoholics have an increased incidence of pneumococcal pneumonia compared with the general population, and despite the use of antibiotics, the mortality among these patients remains disturbingly high (15 to 77 percent).

Alcohol use also impairs the body's defense against pathogens infecting the lungs, such as pneumonia-causing bacteria (for example, pneumococci, *Klebsiella pneumoniae*, and *Legionella pneumophila*) and *M. tuberculosis*. For example, in rats infected with pneumococci, the animals' susceptibility to lethal pneumonia increased if they received alcohol for 1 week before the infection. Moreover, the alcohol-fed rats experienced an increased spread of the pneumococci from the lungs through the bloodstream compared with non-alcohol-treated rats and also failed to eliminate the pneumococci from the blood. Other studies investigating alcohol's effects on the susceptibility to infections with *Klebsiella pneumoniae* and *Legionella pneumophila* indicated that chronic alcohol treatment suppressed the production and/or function of neutrophils and macrophages. Moreover, treatment with a protein factor that stimulates neutrophil production ameliorated the alcohol-induced immunosuppression by recruiting more neutrophils to the lungs.

Increased Susceptibility to HIV

The relationship between alcohol use and susceptibility to infections with the human immunodeficiency virus (HIV), which causes acquired immune deficiency syndrome (AIDS), is an actively evolving area of research. Although ample data are available on the immunological abnormalities caused by alcohol use and HIV infection, respectively, knowledge concerning their combined immunosuppressive effects is more limited. Some researchers have proposed that alcohol's modulatory effects on the immune system may increase the risk of initial HIV infection as well as accelerate the infection's progression. Although this hypothesis still awaits formal confirmation, several findings support alcohol's proposed influence.

Current knowledge strongly suggests that alcohol use—potentially both acute and chronic—can increase a person's susceptibility to HIV infection and contribute to alterations in the immune system that may result in an accelerated progression of the infection. However, further research is needed to elucidate the mechanism by which alcohol may modulate the biology of HIV infection. In addition to its biological effects, alcohol use may increase the risk of HIV infection by modifying the drinker's behavior. For example, factors such as increased risk taking and uninhibited sexual behavior, which are associated with both acute and chronic alcohol use, can contribute to an increased risk for HIV infection.

Consequences of Traumatic Injuries

Traumatic injuries frequently are associated with severe suppression of the immune system, which can lead to overwhelming infections and may result in multiple organ failure and even death. Alcohol intoxication not only increases the risk of sustaining traumatic injuries (for example, in motor vehicle accidents) but also may exacerbate trauma-induced immunosuppression. Thus, one study found that acutely intoxicated patients (those with blood alcohol levels greater than 0.2 percent) who had sustained severe abdominal injuries had a 2.6 times greater incidence of infections than did patients who had not consumed alcohol.

Conclusions and Future Directions

Numerous research efforts have confirmed that both acute and chronic alcohol use have profound regulatory effects on the immune system. Studies in laboratory animals and in humans have demonstrated that even acute, moderate alcohol consumption can impair the body's defense against bacteria and viruses, although these effects are likely only transient. The clinical implications of such a transient immunodepression still need to be studied further. For certain types of infections (for example, HIV and mycobacteria), however, the failure of an appropriate initial immune response to pathogens can have profound and potentially prolonged effects on the immune system and the drinker's health.

Researchers and clinicians are gaining further insight into the complex mechanisms and consequences of immunosuppression in chronic alcoholics. It is important, however, to dissect the effects caused by the body's chronic exposure to alcohol itself and the effects of other alcohol-related immunomodulatory conditions, such as malnutrition, vitamin deficiencies, and alcoholic liver disease. Moreover, a better understanding of the specific immune system alterations caused by chronic alcohol consumption is necessary for designing effective therapeutic approaches to ameliorating immunosuppression in chronic alcoholics.

Researchers also are investigating the mechanisms underlying the differential effects of chronic and acute alcohol use on the immune system. For example, the increased levels of inflammatory cytokines observed in alcoholics contrast with the decreased inflammatory response seen after acute alcohol treatment. Finally, additional research is needed to delineate some of the intracellular signaling events in immune cells that are affected by acute and chronic alcohol use in order to better understand alcohol's regulatory effects on the complex interactions of the immune system.

Chapter 33

Alcohol and Sleep

The average adult sleeps 7.5 to 8 hours every night. Although the function of sleep is unknown, abundant evidence demonstrates that lack of sleep can have serious consequences, including increased risk of depressive disorders, impaired breathing, and heart disease. In addition, excessive daytime sleepiness resulting from sleep disturbance is associated with memory deficits, impaired social and occupational function, and car crashes. Alcohol consumption can induce sleep disorders by disrupting the sequence and duration of sleep states and by altering total sleep time as well as the time required to fall asleep (sleep latency). This chapter explores the effects of alcohol consumption on sleep patterns, the potential health consequences of alcohol consumption combined with disturbed sleep, and the risk for relapse in those with alcoholism who fail to recover normal sleep patterns.

Sleep Structure, Onset, and Arousal

Before discussing alcohol's effects on sleep, it is helpful to summarize some basic features of normal sleep. A person goes through two alternating states of sleep, characterized in part by different types of

---

From *Alcohol Alert*, No. 41, July 1998, National Institute on Alcohol Abuse and Alcoholism (NIAAA). The full text of this publication, including references, is available on NIAAA's World Wide Web site at http://www.niaaa.nih.gov. Copies are also available free of charge from the National Institute on Alcohol Abuse and Alcoholism (NIAAA) Publications Distribution Center, Attn.: *Alcohol Alert*, P.O. Box 10686, Rockville, MD 20849-0686.

brain electrical activity (brain waves). These states are called slow wave sleep (SWS), because in this type of sleep the brain waves are very slow, and rapid eye movement (REM) sleep, in which the eyes undergo rapid movements although the person remains asleep.

Most sleep is the deep, restful SWS. REM sleep occurs periodically, occupying about 25 percent of sleep time in the young adult. Episodes of REM normally recur about every 90 minutes and last 5 to 30 minutes. REM sleep is less restful than SWS and is usually associated with dreaming. Although its function is unknown, REM appears to be essential to health. In rats, deprivation of REM sleep can lead to death within a few weeks. In addition, a transitional stage of light sleep occurs at intervals throughout the sleep period.

Sleep was formerly attributed to decreased activity of brain systems that maintain wakefulness. More recent data indicate that sleep, like consciousness, is an active process. Sleep is controlled largely by nerve centers in the lower brain stem, where the base of the brain joins the spinal cord. Some of these nerve cells produce serotonin, a chemical messenger associated with sleep onset and with the regulation of SWS. Certain other nerve cells produce norepinephrine, which helps regulate REM sleep and facilitates arousal. The exact roles and interactions of these and other chemical messengers in orchestrating sleep patterns are not known. Significantly, however, alcohol consumption affects the function of these and other chemical messengers that appear to influence sleep.

Alcohol and Sleep in Those without Alcoholism

Alcohol consumed at bedtime, after an initial stimulating effect, may decrease the time required to fall asleep. Because of alcohol's sedating effect, many people with insomnia consume alcohol to promote sleep. However, alcohol consumed within an hour of bedtime appears to disrupt the second half of the sleep period. The subject may sleep fitfully during the second half of sleep, awakening from dreams and returning to sleep with difficulty. With continued consumption just before bedtime, alcohol's sleep-inducing effect may decrease, while its disruptive effects continue or increase. This sleep disruption may lead to daytime fatigue and sleepiness. The elderly are at particular risk, because they achieve higher levels of alcohol in the blood and brain than do younger persons after consuming an equivalent dose. Bedtime alcohol consumption among older persons may lead to unsteadiness if walking is attempted during the night, with increased risk of falls and injuries.

Alcoholic beverages are often consumed in the late afternoon (for example, at "happy hour" or with dinner) without further consumption before bedtime. Studies show that a moderate dose of alcohol consumed as much as 6 hours before bedtime can increase wakefulness during the second half of sleep. By the time this effect occurs, the dose of alcohol consumed earlier has already been eliminated from the body, suggesting a relatively long-lasting change in the body's mechanisms of sleep regulation. (Terms such as "light," "moderate," or "heavy" drinking are not used consistently by alcoholism researchers. A standard drink is generally considered to be 12 ounces of beer, 5 ounces of wine, or 1.5 ounces of distilled spirits, each drink containing approximately 0.5 ounce of alcohol.)

The adverse effects of sleep deprivation are increased following alcohol consumption. Subjects administered low doses of alcohol following a night of reduced sleep perform poorly in a driving simulator, even with no alcohol left in the body. Reduced alertness may potentially increase alcohol's sedating effect in situations such as rotating sleep-wake schedules (foe example, shift work) and rapid travel across multiple time zones (jet lag). A person may not recognize the extent of sleep disturbance that occurs under these circumstances, increasing the danger that sleepiness and alcohol consumption will co-occur.

Alcohol and Breathing Disorders

Approximately 2 to 4 percent of Americans suffer from obstructive sleep apnea (OSA), a disorder in which the upper air passage (the pharynx, located at the back of the mouth) narrows or closes during sleep. The resulting episode of interrupted breathing (apnea) wakens the person, who then resumes breathing and returns to sleep. Recurring episodes of apnea followed by arousal can occur hundreds of times each night, significantly reducing sleep time and resulting in daytime sleepiness. Those with alcoholism appear to be at increased risk for sleep apnea, especially if they snore. In addition, moderate to high doses of alcohol consumed in the evening can lead to narrowing of the air passage causing episodes of apnea even in persons who do not otherwise exhibit sym ptoms of OSA. Alcohol's general depressant effects can increase the duration of periods of apnea, worsening any preexisting OSA.

OSA is associated with impaired performance on a driving simulator as well as with an increased rate of motor vehicle crashes in the absence of alcohol consumption. Among patients with severe OSA, alcohol consumption at a rate of two or more drinks per day is associated with a five-fold increased risk for fatigue-related traffic crashes compared with OSA patients who consume little or no alcohol. In addition, the combination of alcohol, OSA, and snoring increases a person's risk for heart attack, arrhythmia, stroke, and sudden death.

Age-Related Effects and the Impact of Drinking

Little research has been conducted on the specific effects of alcohol on sleep states among different age groups. One study investigated the effects of prenatal alcohol exposure on sleep patterns in infants. Measurements of brain electrical activity demonstrated that infants of mothers who consumed at least one drink per day during the first trimester of pregnancy exhibited sleep disruptions and increased arousal compared with infants of nondrinking women. Additional studies revealed that infants exposed to alcohol in mothers' milk fell asleep sooner but slept less overall than those who were not exposed to alcohol. The exact significance of these findings is unclear.

Normal aging is accompanied by a gradual decrease in SWS and an increase in nighttime wakefulness. People over 65 often awaken 20 times or more during the night, leading to sleep that is less restful and restorative. Age-related sleep deficiencies may encourage the use of alcohol to promote sleep, while increasing an older person's susceptibility to alcohol-related sleep disturbances. Potential sources of inconsistency among study results include different doses of alcohol employed and failure to screen out subjects with preexisting sleep disorders.

Effects of Alcohol on Sleep in Those with Alcoholism

Active Drinking and Withdrawal

Sleep disturbances associated with alcoholism include increased time required to fall asleep, frequent awakenings, and a decrease in subjective sleep quality associated with daytime fatigue. Abrupt reduction of heavy drinking can trigger alcohol withdrawal syndrome, accompanied by pronounced insomnia with marked sleep fragmentation. Decreased SWS during withdrawal may reduce the amount of restful sleep. It has been suggested that increased REM may be related to the hallucinations that sometimes occur during withdrawal. In patients with severe withdrawal, sleep may consist almost entirely of brief periods of REM interrupted by numerous awakenings.

Recovery and Relapse

Despite some improvement after withdrawal subsides, sleep patterns may never return to normal in those with alcoholism, even after years of abstinence. Abstinent alcoholics tend to sleep poorly, with decreased amounts of SWS and increased nighttime wakefulness that could make sleep less restorative and contribute to daytime fatigue. Resumption of heavy drinking leads to increased SWS and decreased wakefulness. This apparent improvement in sleep continuity may promote relapse by contributing to the mistaken impression that alcohol consumption improves sleep. Nevertheless, as drinking continues, sleep patterns again become disrupted.

Researchers have attempted to predict relapse potential using measures of sleep disruption. One study measured REM sleep in patients admitted to a 1-month alcoholism treatment program. Higher levels of REM predicted those who relapsed within 3 months after hospital discharge in 80 percent of the patients. A review of additional research concluded that those who eventually relapsed exhibited a higher proportion of REM and a lower proportion of SWS at the beginning of treatment, compared with those who remained abstinent. Although additional research is needed, these findings may facilitate early identification of patients at risk for relapse and allow clinicians to tailor their treatment programs accordingly.

A Commentary by NIAAA Director Enoch Gordis, M.D.

According to recent news reports, Americans are at risk for a variety of sleep-related health problems. Alcohol use affects sleep in a number of ways and can exacerbate these problems. Because alcohol use is widespread, it is important to understand how this use affects sleep to increase risk for illness. For example, it is popularly believed that a drink before bedtime can aid falling asleep. However, it also can disrupt normal sleep patterns, resulting in increased fatigue and physical stress to the body. Alcohol use can aggravate sleeping disorders, such as sleep apnea; those with such disorders should be cautious about alcohol use. Many nursing mothers are still regularly advised by their physicians to have a drink to promote lactation (so-called let-down reflex). Babies who receive alcohol in breast milk are known to have disrupted sleeping patterns. Because researchers do not yet know what effect this disruption has on nursing infants, physicians should reconsider this advice.

Alcoholism treatment also can be complicated by sleep problems during withdrawal and during subsequent behavioral treatment, where sleeping problems experienced by many recovering alcoholics may increase their risk for relapse. Because it is likely that alcohol may act on the same neurotransmitters involved in sleep, increased knowledge of alcohol's effects on the brain will help to promote new therapeutic techniques for alcohol-related sleep disorders and, perhaps, improve the chance for long-term sobriety.

Chapter 34

Alcohol and Cancer

Cancer kills an estimated 526,000 Americans yearly, second only to heart disease. Considerable evidence suggests a connection between heavy alcohol consumption and increased risk for cancer, with an estimated 2 to 4 percent of all cancer cases thought to be caused either directly or indirectly by alcohol.

A strong association exists between alcohol use and cancers of the esophagus, pharynx, and mouth, whereas a more controversial association links alcohol with liver, breast, and colorectal cancers. Together, these cancers kill more than 125,000 people annually in the United States.

Two types of research link alcohol and cancer:

- Epidemiologic research has shown a dose dependent association between alcohol consumption and certain types of cancer. As alcohol consumption increases, so does risk of developing certain cancers.
- More tenuous results have come from research into the mechanism by which alcohol could contribute to cancer development.

The strongest link between alcohol and cancer involves cancers of the digestive tract.

- Chronic heavy drinkers have a higher incidence of esophageal cancer than does the general public. The risk appears to increase as

---

An undated fact sheet distributed by Connecticut Clearinghouse, 334 Farmington Avenue, Plainville, CT 06062 (800) 232-4424 or (860) 793-9791, web site http://www.ctclearinghouse.org; reprinted with permission.

alcohol consumption increases. An estimated 75 percent of esophageal cancers in the U.S. are attributed to chronic, excessive alcohol consumption.

- Nearly 50 percent of cancers of the mouth, pharynx, and larynx are associated with heavy drinking. People who drink large quantities of alcohol over time have an increased risk of these cancers as compared with abstainers.
- The risk increases dramatically when heavy drinkers also smoke.

Prolonged, heavy drinking has been associated in many cases with primary liver cancer. However, it is liver cirrhosis, whether caused by alcohol or another factor, that is thought to induce the cancer.

- In areas of Africa and Asia, liver cancer afflicts 50 or more people per 100,000 per year, usually associated with cirrhosis caused by hepatitis viruses.
- In the United States, liver cancer is relatively uncommon, afflicting approximately 2 people per 100,000, but excessive alcohol consumption is linked to as many as 36 percent of these cases by some investigators.
- The association between alcohol use and liver cancer is difficult to interpret because liver cirrhosis and hepatitis B and C virus infections often confound data.

Less consistent data link alcohol consumption and other cancers.

- Chronic alcohol consumption has been associated with a small (averaging 10 percent) increase in a woman's risk of breast cancer. According to these studies, the risk appears to increase as the quantity and duration of alcohol consumption increases. Other studies, however, have found no evidence of such a link.
- Epidemiologic studies have found a small but consistent dose-dependent association between alcohol consumption and colorectal cancer even when controlling for fiber and other dietary factors. Despite the large number of studies, however, causality cannot be determined from the available data.
- A few studies have linked chronic heavy drinking with cancers of the stomach, pancreas, and lungs. However, the association is consistently weak and the majority of studies have found no association.

Research is being conducted to shed light on alcohol's role in developing cancers.

- Preliminary studies show that alcohol may affect cancer development at the genetic level by affecting oncogenes (genes that normally promote cell division) at the initiation and promotion stages of cancer.
- Although there is no evidence that alcohol itself is a carcinogen, alcohol may act as a cocarcinogen by enhancing the carcinogenic effects of other chemicals. In humans, the risk for mouth, tracheal, and esophageal cancer is 35 times greater for people who both smoke and drink than for people who do neither, implying a cocarcinogenic interaction between alcohol and tobacco-related carcinogens.
- Chronic alcohol abuse may result in abnormalities in the way the body processes nutrients and may subsequently promote certain types of cancer. A recent study indicates that as few as two drinks per day negates any beneficial effects of a "correct" diet on decreasing risk of colon cancer.

In summary, the evidence for alcohol's role in promoting some cancers (for example, cancers of the mouth and throat) is stronger than the evidence linking alcohol use to other cancers, such as breast cancer. According to Dr. Enoch Gordis, Director of the National Institute on Alcohol Abuse and Alcoholism, "Public health policy should reflect the strength of the evidence of alcohol's role in promoting various cancers. Convincing evidence of alcohol's effects on common cancers—even when these effects are minor—has important public health implications. However, it is equally important that the public not be subjected to undue alarm when evidence for an increased risk for cancer due to alcohol use is weak or inconclusive."

Chapter 35

Breast Cancer Risk Linked to Level of Alcohol Consumption

Women who consume 2-5 alcoholic drinks per day may increase their risk of breast cancer by 30-50%, according to a study published in the *Journal of the American Medical Association.*

Investigators Stephanie A. Smith-Warner, Ph.D., and colleagues from the Harvard School of Public Health conducted a meta-analysis of seven prospective studies that investigated the connection between nutritional intake and breast cancer. Each of the studies included at least 200 women who were evaluated for up to 11 years. The combined studies had a sample size of 322,647 women who developed 4,335 cases of invasive cancer.

The investigators pooled and analyzed data from the studies for possible breast cancer risk factors, including level of alcohol consumption, pre- or post-menopausal status, maternal history of breast cancer, use of hormone replacement therapy, weight, age at menarche, and other factors.

The investigators found that 22.5% to 55.3% of women participating in the seven studies were nondrinkers. Among those who did drink, mean alcohol consumption ranged from 3.22 to 12.58 grams per day.

Analyses indicated that "alcohol consumption was positively associated with the risk of invasive breast cancer." Women who drank

---

"Breast Cancer Risk Linked to Level of Alcohol Consumption," *The Brown University Digest of Addiction Theory and Application*, July 1998 Vol. 17, No. 7, p. 1(2), an average of 30 to 60 grams of alcohol per day (about 2-5 drinks) had "a relative risk of 1.41 compared with nondrinkers"—a 41% increased risk. For women who consumed 60 g/day (four or more drinks per day) the association was slightly weaker.

Among women who consumed 2-5 drinks per day, risk of breast cancer increased roughly 8% for each 10 gram (0.75-1 drink per day) increase in alcohol consumption.

The interaction of alcohol consumption with other known risk factors for breast cancer was not statistically significant, indicating that alcohol consumption operated independently in this study. Other risk factors included:

- menopausal status;
- use of hormone replacement or oral contraceptives;
- maternal or fraternal history of breast cancer;
- obesity;
- fiber and fat intake;
- smoking history;
- age of menarche;
- age at first pregnancy and number of children;
- education level; and
- history of benign breast disease.

Study Limits

The investigators note that only information about women's current baseline alcohol consumption was available for inclusion in this study. It is possible that the group of nondrinkers may, therefore, have included former drinkers.

Lifetime alcohol consumption and consumption during early adulthood were not examined. In addition, alcohol consumption may have been under-reported.

Authors' Conclusions

"These analyses indicate that alcohol consumption and risk of invasive breast cancer are positively associated in women." Women consuming 2 to 5 drinks per day increased their risk of breast cancer by 41%; women who consumed five or more drinks per day increased their risk by 31%.

The authors note that alcohol consumption is a modifiable risk factor for breast cancer. While further investigation of the association between alcohol and cancer is needed, they say that "reduction of regular alcohol consumption in women is likely to reduce breast cancer risk."

Suggested Readings

Ginsburg, E.S., Mello, N.K., et al. Effects of alcohol ingestion on estrogens in postmenopausal women. *Journal of the American Medical Association*, 276:1747-1751, 1996.

Longnecker, M.P. Alcohol beverage consumption in relation to risk of breast cancer: Meta-analysis and review. *Cancer Causes Control*, 5:73-82, 1994.

Stephanie A. Smith-Warner, Donna Spiegelman, Shiaw-Shyuan Yaun, Piet A. van den Brandt, Aaron R. Folson, R. Alexandra Goldbohm, Saxon Graham, Lars Holmberg, Geoffrey R. Howe, James R. Marshall, Anthony B. Miller, John D. Potter, Frank E. Speizer, Walter C. Willett, Alicia Wolk, and David J. Hunter. Alcohol and breast cancer in women: A pooled analysis of cohort studies. *Journal of the American Medical Association*, 279:535-540, 1998.

Part Three

Alcohol and Pregnancy

Chapter 36

Drinking and Your Pregnancy

When You Are Pregnant, Drinking Can Hurt Your Baby

When you are pregnant, your baby grows inside you. Everything you eat and drink while you are pregnant affects your baby. If you drink alcohol, it can hurt your baby's growth. Your baby may have physical and behavioral problems that can last for the rest of his or her life. Children born with the most serious problems caused by alcohol have fetal alcohol syndrome.

Children with fetal alcohol syndrome may:

- Be born small.
- Have problems eating and sleeping.
- Have problems seeing and hearing.
- Have trouble following directions and learning how to do simple things.
- Have trouble paying attention and learning in school.
- Have trouble getting along with others and controlling their behavior.
- Need medical care all their lives.
- Need special teachers and schools.

"Drinking and Your Pregnancy," National Institute on Alcohol Abuse and Alcoholism (NIAAA), NIH Pub. No. 96-4101, September 1998.

Questions You May Have about Alcohol and Drinking while You Are Pregnant

Can I drink alcohol if I am pregnant?

No. Do not drink alcohol when you are pregnant. Why? Because when you drink alcohol, so does your baby. Think about it. Everything you drink, your baby also drinks.

Is any kind of alcohol safe to drink during pregnancy?

No. Drinking any kind of alcohol when you are pregnant can hurt your baby. Alcoholic drinks are beer, wine, wine coolers, liquor, or mixed drinks. A glass of wine, a can of beer, and a mixed drink all have about the same amount of alcohol.

What if I drank during my last pregnancy and my baby was fine?

Every pregnancy is different. Drinking alcohol may hurt one baby more than another. You could have one child that is born healthy, and another child that is born with problems.

Will these problems go away?

No. These problems will last for a child's whole life. People with severe problems may not be able to take care of themselves as adults. They may never be able to work.

What if I am pregnant and have been drinking?

If you drank alcohol before you knew you were pregnant, stop drinking now. You will feel better and your baby will have a good chance to be born healthy. If you want to get pregnant, do not drink alcohol. You may not know you are pregnant right away. Alcohol can hurt a baby even when you are only 1 or 2 months pregnant.

How can I stop drinking?

There are many ways to help yourself stop drinking. Do not have a drink when other people drink. If someone gives a drink and says it is OK say no. Stay away from people or places that may keep alcohol.

If you cannot stop drinking, GET HELP. You may have a disease called alcoholism. There are programs that can help you stop drinking. They are called alcohol treatment programs. Your doctor or nurse can find a program to help you. Even if you have been through a treatment program before, try it again. There are programs just for women.

For Help and Information

You can get help from a doctor, nurse, social worker, pastor, or clinics and programs near you. For confidential information, you can contact:

Alcoholics Anonymous
P.O. Box 459
Grand Central Station
New York, NY 10163
Phone (212) 870–3400
Web site: www.alcoholics-anonymous.org

National Council on Alcoholism and Drug Dependence, Inc.
12 West 21 Street, Seventh Floor
New York, New York 10010
Toll Free: (800) NCA-CALL (800-622-2255) (24-hour affiliate referral)
Phone: (212) 206-6770
Fax: (212) 645-1690
E-mail: national@ncadd.org
Web site: http://www.ncadd.org

National Institute on Alcohol Abuse and Alcoholism (NIAAA)
National Institutes of Health
Willco Building
6000 Executive Boulevard
Bethesda, MD 20892-7003
Phone: (301) 443-0786
Web site: http://www.niaaa.nih.gov

National Organization on Fetal Alcohol Syndrome
418 'C' Street North East
Washington, DC 20002
Phone: (202)785-4585
Fax: (202) 466-6456
E-mail: nofas@erols.com
Web site: http://www.nofas.org

Chapter 37

Alcohol-Related Birth Defects

Definitions and Symptoms

- Fetal alcohol syndrome (FAS), the leading known cause of mental retardation, is caused by maternal alcoholism or heavy drinking during pregnancy.
- Features of FAS include growth deficiency before and after birth; effects on the central nervous system such as intellectual impairment, developmental delays, and behavioral problems; and changes in facial features such as a flattened midface, a small jaw, and a thin upper lip.
- Fetal alcohol effects (FAE) is used to describe individuals exposed to alcohol in the womb who exhibit only some of the attributes of FAS and do not fulfill the diagnostic criteria for FAS.
- Children with FAS commonly have problems with learning, attention, memory, and problem solving, along with incoordination, impulsiveness, and speech and hearing impairments.
- Although many of the physical characteristics associated with FAS become less prominent after puberty, intellectual problems

---

The information in this chapter was taken from "Alcohol- and Other Drug-Related Birth Defects" National Council on Alcoholism and Drug Dependence, Inc. (NCADD), © March 1998; reprinted with permission. For the full text, including all source citations, please visit NCADD's web site at www.ncadd.org.

endure and behavioral, emotional, and social problems become more pronounced.

Use of Alcohol during Pregnancy

- In the first nationally representative survey of drug use among pregnant women, 18.8 percent or 757,000 women reported drinking alcohol.
- The proportion of frequent drinkers increased as smoking level increased, and was more than three times higher among women receiving no prenatal care than among those who received prenatal care.
- The rate of alcohol use among white women was significantly higher than the rate for Hispanics. In regard to age, rates of alcohol use for women ages 25-29 and 30 and older were both significantly greater than the rate for women under age 25.

Incidence and Prevalence of Alcohol-Related Birth Defects

- Each year 4,000 to 12,000 babies are born with the physical signs and intellectual disabilities associated with FAS, and thousands more experience the somewhat lesser disabilities of FAE.
- Estimates of the prevalence of FAS vary from 0.2 to 1.0 per 1,000 live births.
- Making a diagnosis of FAS/FAE at birth is difficult because facial characteristics are difficult to discern and some features such as behavioral and cognitive functioning problems are not observable at birth. As a result, data on FAS/FAE incidence based on use of medical records and registry of birth defects are low.

Risks and Consequences

- The extent of damage caused by prenatal alcohol exposure depends on the stage of fetal development, biological and environmental variables, and the amount and timing of the mother's alcohol consumption.
- Maternal age, ethnic and/or socioeconomic differences, genetic influences and the severity of alcoholism in women while pregnant

are factors that may make their children more vulnerable to FAS.

- Once a woman bears a child with FAS, the probability that subsequent children will have FAS is 70 percent.
- Pregnant women consuming between one and two drinks per day are twice as likely as nondrinkers to have a growth-retarded infant weighing less than 5.5 pounds.
- Newborns whose mothers drink heavily (an average of five drinks per day, especially during the last three months of pregnancy) may show signs of alcohol withdrawal such as tremors, sleeping problems, inconsolable crying, and abnormal reflexes.

Costs

- Newborns with perinatal alcohol and other drug exposure have hospital stays three times longer than those born to mothers who are drug-free.
- The economic costs associated with FAS were estimated at $2.1 billion for 1990.
- The total annual cost of treating the birth defects caused by FAS was estimated at $1.6 billion in 1985. For persons over 21 years the cost was $1.3 billion. Neonatal intensive care for growth retardation due to FAS accounted for $118 million.

Chapter 38

The Effects of Prenatal Alcohol Exposure

Pregnant alcoholic women risk the health of their offspring in multiple ways: (1) Exposure to alcohol during gestation may lead to fetal alcohol syndrome (FAS) or fetal alcohol effects; (2) the physical consequences of alcoholism in the mother (for example, falls or malnutrition) may independently affect the developing fetus; (3) genetic vulnerability to alcoholism in the fetus may increase the effects of prenatal exposure; and (4) the lifestyle of an alcoholic parent may lead to negative consequences for the fetus, the pregnancy, and the developing child. This chapter addresses the first of these issues—the effects of exposure to alcohol during gestation—in detail. However, any or all of the other issues listed may exacerbate the adverse effects of prenatal alcohol exposure.

As a teratogen [something that interferes with normal fetal development], alcohol is capable of directly inducing developmental abnormalities in a fetus. Alcohol use during pregnancy is one of the most common known causes of preventable birth defects, and its results can persist as long-term deficits in physical and cognitive growth and development.

The dangers of fetal alcohol exposure, initially identified in the late 1960's, are entirely preventable if women abstain from drinking during

---

Excerpted from "The Effects of Prenatal Alcohol Exposure," by Cynthia Larkby, M.S.W. and Nancy Day, Ph.D. M.P.H., in *Alcohol Health and Research World*, Summer 1997, Vol. 21, No, 3, p. 192(7). A complete copy of this publication may be ordered from the U.S. Government Printing Office. Call (202) 512-1800 for information on price and availability.

pregnancy. Given this fact, in 1981 the U.S. Surgeon General issued the first health advisory recommending that women who are pregnant or planning a pregnancy should not drink alcohol, and this advisory was repeated in 1990 and 1995.

FAS Definition and Diagnosis

At the extreme end of the spectrum of prenatal exposure effects, FAS is a clinical diagnosis applied to children who have been exposed to alcohol during gestation and exhibit deficits in growth, physical structure (morphology), and the central nervous system (CNS). To meet the clinical case definition, the child must have symptoms in each of the following three categories: (1) growth deficiency in both the prenatal and postnatal periods: (2) abnormalities in facial and skull structure, including small eye openings, alterations in nose and forehead structure, an absent or elongated groove between the upper lip and nose (philtram), a thin upper lip, a flattened midface, and underdevelopment of the upper or lower jaw; and (3) CNS deficits, such as mental retardation and behavioral problems. Of these symptoms, the facial abnormalities are the most characteristic of FAS, whereas the CNS anomalies have the most significant effect on overall development. Separately, each of these features is defined as an alcohol-related birth defect (ARBD) or a fetal alcohol effect.

The features associated with FAS may change with age, complicating the diagnosis. Before age 2, CNS dysfunction is difficult to assess, and the classic facial abnormalities may not be clearly evident. At older ages, growth deficits are offset by the adolescent growth spurt as well as normal changes in facial length and width associated with maturation. Because of these changes, growth deficits and facial features become less apparent after puberty, and without prepubertal photographs and reliable growth records, FAS may be difficult to diagnose in adolescents or adults.

Accurately assessing fetal alcohol exposure may prove even more difficult. To obtain correct information regarding the quantity of alcohol consumed as well as the timing and duration of alcohol use during pregnancy, clinicians and researchers need reliable methods to determine alcohol exposure. Although biological tests are available to measure the amount of alcohol consumed, these tests reflect use over a very short time period and do not allow estimates of the pattern or duration of use to be made. In general, clinicians and researchers rely on the mother's self-report of alcohol use. Self-reports may be inaccurate, however, because social pressures, fear of being labeled, and anxiety about losing custody of her child may lead a woman to underreport her alcohol consumption during pregnancy. Problems recalling the frequency and quantity of alcohol consumed also can lead to erroneous estimates. In the absence of an accurate report, clinicians and caretakers, such as foster and adoptive parents, will not know whether or to what extent the child was exposed to alcohol during gestation.

Because of the difficulty in reliably ascertaining fetal alcohol exposure, a committee convened by the Institute of Medicine to study FAS recently reviewed the diagnostic criteria currently in use and recommended revisions. The committee members proposed a diagnostic classification system with five categories: (1) FAS with confirmed maternal alcohol exposure, (2) FAS without confirmed maternal alcohol exposure, (3) partial FAS with confirmed maternal alcohol exposure, (4) ARBD with a history of maternal alcohol exposure, and (5) alcohol-related neurodevelopmental disorder (ARND) with a history of maternal alcohol exposure. The last two categories are used for offspring who have morphologic and neurologic alcohol-related effects, respectively, without the full features of FAS, and they may co-occur in the same individual.

FAS Epidemiology

Alcoholism and Alcohol Use among Women

In a nationwide household survey conducted in 1992, 4.08 percent of the women who were interviewed met the criteria for alcohol abuse and/or dependence within the 12 months preceding the survey. (The criteria used in this study corresponded to the criteria for alcohol abuse and dependence listed in the American Psychiatric Association's *Diagnostic and Statistical Manual of Mental Disorders, Fourth Edition*. In general, the terms "alcoholic" and "alcoholism," as used in this article, encompass both diagnoses.) The highest prevalence rates for alcohol abuse and/or dependence were found among women of child-bearing age (9.84 percent for women ages 18 to 29 and 3.98 percent for women ages 30 to 44).

Women who are alcoholic typically experience several other problems, including comorbid medical or psychiatric disorders (for example, depression) and social problems (for example, unstable marriages; spouses with drinking problems; and child-care responsibilities, often as single mothers). This multiplicity of problems complicates the pregnancy of an alcoholic woman, because her fetus is exposed not only to the teratogenic effects of alcohol, but also to the negative effects of the other factors that coexist in her life. By comparing birth outcomes in upper middle class and lower class alcoholic mothers, on study showed that economic or lifestyle factors play a role in the rate of FAS. They found that, although the intake of absolute alcohol was equivalent in the two groups, 2.7 percent of the upper middle class mothers had a child with FAS, compared with 40.5 percent of the lower class mothers.

The problem of alcohol exposure during pregnancy is not limited to alcoholic women, however. A majority of women drink, as evidenced by a national household survey in which 64 percent of the women surveyed were drinkers (drank at least once a year), 4 percent reported daily drinking, 6 percent drank five or more drinks on occasion at least weekly, and 1 percent reported drinking enough to feel drunk at least weekly. Age, race, social class, and occupation all predicted drinking patterns among women. For example, younger women were most likely to drink, and white women drank more than their black or Hispanic counterparts. Drinkers had a higher education level and income than nondrinkers and were more likely to work full time outside the home. These same four characteristics also described women who were heavy drinkers. (In this study, "heavy drinkers" were defined as people who consumed eight or more drinks per day as often as three times per week.)

Despite the fact that women's drinking rates have remained relatively constant since the 1960's, the rate of drinking during pregnancy appears to be increasing. For example, the Behavioral Risk Factor Surveillance System reported that among pregnant women, the rate of drinking increased from 12.4 percent in 1991 to 16.3 percent in 1995 and that the rate of frequent drinking was four times higher in 1995 than in 1991, increasing from 0.8 percent in 1991 to 3.5 percent in 1995. ("Frequent drinking" was defined in this study as consuming seven or more drinks per week or five or more drinks on an occasion in the past month.)

Prevalence of FAS

Among the general population, a national surveillance program known as the Birth Defects Monitoring Program reported a rate of 5.2 FAS cases per 10,000 live births. Similarly, a recent summary of findings from prospective studies estimated the overall rate of FAS to be 3.3 cases per 10,000 live births. The rate of FAS is likely to be considerably underestimated, however, because of the difficulty in making the diagnosis and the reluctance of clinicians to label children and mothers.

Relationship of Exposure and Effects

Fetal development is a sequential, multistaged process. To determine the effects of prenatal exposure on child development, factors such as the timing, dose, and pattern of alcohol exposure must be considered, because growth, morphologic abnormalities, and CNS deficits occur at different points during gestation. Major morphologic abnormalities result from exposure early in pregnancy, growth is most affected by late exposure, and CNS deficits occur throughout gestation. Thus, offspring who are exposed to alcohol throughout pregnancy will not have the same outcome as offspring who are exposed only during early pregnancy or only at specific times during pregnancy.

Identifying the nature of the relationships between prenatal alcohol exposure and outcome is also important for research and clinical reasons. Exposure to a toxin may affect fetal outcome in two ways: The effect may be directly related to the amount of exposure (a linear relationship), or exposure may be problematic only above a certain level (a threshold relationship). A linear relationship between alcohol exposure and child development means that no "safe" level of drinking during pregnancy exists, because even a small amount of alcohol could produce an effect. In contrast, the threshold model implies that a "safe" level of drinking does exist, below which negative effects do not occur. Data from studies to date demonstrate that the relationship between alcohol exposure and outcome varies depending on the type of outcome under consideration, however. For example, reports from the animal and human literature support a threshold relationship between prenatal alcohol exposure and CNS development, whereas the data on physical growth indicate that the effect of gestational exposure to alcohol is linear. Therefore, no "safe" level of consumption exists, and the best policy for women continues to be abstinence during pregnancy to avoid any negative effects on their offspring.

Specific Effects of Prenatal Exposure

People with FAS demonstrate growth deficits, morphologic abnormalities, mental retardation, and behavioral difficulties. A systematic follow-up study examined 61 subjects identified as having FAS or fetal alcohol effects to determine adolescent and adult manifestations of the syndrome. The study results give an overview of the long-term impact of prenatal alcohol exposure. At adolescence and adulthood, the subjects were short in stature and small in head circumference; they also exhibited a high rate of abnormal facial features, although these characteristics were not as pronounced as they had been at younger ages. The subjects' IQ scores ranged from 20 to 105 with a mean of 68. Six percent of the subjects took regular school classes, but the remainder of the study participants were unable to achieve this schooling level or maintain regular outside employment. In addition, the subjects demonstrated poor concentration and attention, an inability to live independently in adulthood, stubbornness, social withdrawal, and conduct problems, such as lying, cheating, and stealing. Their characteristics and long-term outcome predict the expected outcome for people who were prenatally exposed to alcohol but do not have the full syndrome. At lower levels of exposure, a subset of fetal alcohol effects, rather than the full extent of FAS features, is most likely to occur.

The following sections describe the effects of prenatal alcohol exposure on growth, morphology, and CNS development in turn. Many of the examples are taken from the Maternal Health Practices and Child Development (MHPCD) project, a longitudinal study of the long-term effects of prenatal alcohol exposure. In this study, researchers recruited adult women in their fourth month of pregnancy from a prenatal clinic. All women who consumed an average of three or more drinks per week during their first trimester, plus a random sample of one-third of the women who drank alcohol less often, were selected as study subjects. In general, alcohol use during pregnancy was light to moderate among the women participating in the study, although subjects who represented the entire spectrum of use were included in the sample.

Growth Deficits

Children with FAS are small for their age—indeed, such smallness is one of the criteria for diagnosis, although growth deficits also are found among children who were exposed to alcohol during pregnancy but do not fulfill the full criteria for FAS. As noted previously, however, growth retardation is somewhat ameliorated at puberty. In the MHPCD project, these growth deficits are symmetrical, affecting height, weight, and head circumference to the same degree, and remain significant through age 10. The relationship between prenatal exposure and growth deficits is linear (the greater the prenatal alcohol exposure, the more pronounced the effect on postnatal growth).

Postnatal environment and maternal characteristics influence the relationship between prenatal alcohol exposure and growth, however. Whereas studies of disadvantaged populations have found that prenatal alcohol exposure continues to affect growth at follow-up, studies of more advantaged cohorts have found that growth deficits are not maintained as the children get older. Another study found that alcohol exposure was associated with decreased birth weight, length, and head circumference, although only among infants of women over age 30. Thus, postnatal environment and maternal characteristics apparently exacerbate the effects of prenatal alcohol exposure.

Morphologic Abnormalities

Another criterion of FAS is the presence of the specific group of facial anomalies mentioned previously (short palpebral fissures, a flattened nasal bridge, an absent or elongated philtrum, and a thin upper lip). From embryological studies, investigators know that these morphologic abnormalities occur when the midline of the face is formed during the first trimester. A significant correlation between first-trimester alcohol exposure and the rate of these physical anomalies was found in the MHPCD project. As noted in other studies of FAS, however, the relationship between prenatal alcohol exposure and the characteristic facial features associated with FAS diminished as the children matured.

CNS Deficits

Both animal and human studies have demonstrated that brain structures, including the hippocampus, frontal lobes, corpus callosum, and basal ganglia, are important sites of alcohol's action on the fetal brain. Indeed, researchers have documented anomalies of brain structure and function among children with FAS. Evidence of CNS deficits in FAS children also appears in their tendency to have delayed motor and speech development and speech and hearing impairments. In prenatally exposed children who do not have FAS, researchers have identified neurologic effects at birth that reflect abnormalities in sleep patterns and in the newborn's ability to respond and adapt, as measured by the Brazelton Neonatal Behavioral Assessment Scale.

One way to gauge CNS functioning is to use neuropsychological measures designed to assess brain functioning. Using such measures, one group of researchers found that 5- to 16-year-old children with FAS had significant verbal learning and memory deficits. Similarly, another study reported memory deficits in 13-year-old children with FAS, and other investigators found that children with FAS had deficits in problem-solving, information processing and storage, and visual and spatial skills.

The neuropsychological findings are similar for children who were exposed to alcohol during gestation but do not have FAS. In a study, 14-year-old children who had been prenatally exposed to alcohol had difficulty performing tasks that required processing information in order to make complex decisions. Researchers also have found that prenatally exposed children have particular difficulty in mathematical tasks. In another study, researchers compared the cognitive performance of children whose mothers drank an average of 11.8 ounces of absolute alcohol (approximately 24 drinks) per week throughout pregnancy and children whose mothers stopped drinking in the second trimester or did not drink at all during pregnancy. The researchers found that the children exposed throughout gestation performed more poorly than children in the other two groups, exhibiting deficits in short-term memory and encoding (sequential processing) and overall mental processing at an average age of 5 years and 10 months.

People with FAS often are mentally retarded, although the degree of deficit varies. In a 1996 study, researchers reported IQ scores of FAS patients ranged from 29 (severely retarded) to 120 (high average). Like other exposure-related effects, the impact of prenatal alcohol exposure on cognitive development demonstrates a continuum. Although study results are not completely consistent, alcohol exposure is related to decreased cognitive abilities even at lower levels of exposure.

People with FAS commonly exhibit behavioral problems as well. These problems can include poor concentration and attention, lack of independent living skills, stubbornness, and social withdrawal. In addition, children with FAS exhibit higher rates of conduct problems (for example, lying, cheating, and stealing).

Behavior problems also have been reported among offspring prenatally exposed to alcohol but without FAS. In one study, 4-year-old children whose mothers drank one to five drinks per day during pregnancy were less attentive and more active when observed in the home, compared with children of control mothers who drank less. At age 7 1/2, the children were less attentive and took a longer time to react to a stimulus on a Continuous Performance Task. In children ages 7 and 14, researchers demonstrated the effects of prenatal exposure to alcohol on both attention and memory. These effects were linear (the extent of the effect was directly correlated with the amount of alcohol exposure), implying that no "safe" threshold of alcohol exposure exists.

Summary and Conclusions

Given that alcohol is a teratogen, an appropriate goal would be to eliminate drinking during pregnancy. This means finding effective methods to help women who are alcoholic abstain during pregnancy and to motivate other drinking women to abstain from levels of alcohol consumption that would be insignificant outside of pregnancy. Clinicians need to ask pregnant women about their alcohol consumption, even at a "social drinking" level, and have appropriate tools available to intervene when necessary. Little research has been conducted on the effectiveness of alcohol treatment during pregnancy or the treatment of pregnant alcoholics, although these women are at greatest risk for having an FAS child.

Chapter 39

Life-Long Effects of Prenatal Exposure to Alcohol

Maternal alcohol consumption can affect the development of both the body and the brain of the fetus, with consequences that may persist throughout life. Only recently have researchers begun to evaluate the effects of prenatal alcohol exposure on performance in school and the workplace as the patient passes through childhood and adulthood. This chapter describes some types of structural brain damage that occur in humans and animals prenatally exposed to alcohol, reviews ways in which cognitive functioning can be impaired by fetal alcohol exposure, and discusses treatment strategies.

Nomenclature and Diagnostic Criteria

Many labels have been used to describe the effects of significant intrauterine alcohol exposure. Fetal alcohol syndrome (FAS) is a medical diagnosis initially defined as a specific pattern of facial and other physical deformities occurring in conjunction with growth retardation. Researchers refined this definition in 1989 and suggested that to support the diagnosis, effects must be observable in all three of the following realms: overall growth retardation, structural or functional abnormalities of the brain, and a characteristic pattern of facial deformities. The brain abnormalities may include structural and

Excerpted from "Effects of Prenatal Exposure to Alcohol across the Life Span," by Paul D. Connor and Ann P. Streissguth, in *Alcohol Health and Research World*, Summer 1996, Vol. 20, No, 3, p. 170(5). A complete copy of this publication may be ordered from the U.S. Government Printing Office. Call (202) 512-1800 for information on price and availability.

cognitive defects, delayed brain development, and signs of neurological impairment.

The diagnosis of FAS identifies only a relatively small proportion of children prenatally affected by alcohol. Therefore, the terms "fetal alcohol effects" (FAE) and "possible fetal alcohol effects" (PFAE) have been used since the mid-1970's to describe patterns of birth defects following significant prenatal alcohol exposure that do not include all of the facial features or growth retardation seen in FAS. In addition, the category "alcohol-related birth defects" (ARBD) is used to focus primarily on the physical anomalies rather than the brain disturbances associated with severe prenatal alcohol exposure.

A recent report from the Institute of Medicine (IOM) suggests a new category of prenatal alcohol exposure that would essentially replace FAE. The classification, referred to as "alcohol-related neurodevelopmental disorder" (ARND), focuses specifically on brain dysfunctions in the presence of significant prenatal alcohol exposure. IOM suggests using this term for patients who have a documented prenatal exposure to alcohol and identifiable problems suggesting faulty brain development. Unlike FAS, ARND does not require the presence of facial or other physical anomalies.

The range of prenatal alcohol effects has been described as a continuum, with no effects at one end and full developed FAS at the other end. This view, however, can be misleading. Although patients with FAS have more physical deformities, such as heart malformations and facial anomalies, the brain dysfunctions of people with FAE/ARND are often as severe as—if not worse than—brain dysfunctions in patients with FAS.

Although no alcohol-dose threshold is known to differentiate between FAS and ARND, the time of alcohol ingestion appears to be important. Drinking relatively early in pregnancy may lead to many of the facial anomalies seen in children with FAS, whereas the deleterious effects of alcohol on the brain can occur at any time during pregnancy.

Structural Damage to the Brain

In seeking to understand the brain dysfunctions that occur in patients diagnosed with FAS or ARND, researchers have studied brain structures in both animal models and human patients. The structural changes observed through this research can be related to defects in brain function.

Animal Studies

Animal models of FAS and ARND demonstrate widespread damage to the brain following relatively high prenatal exposure to alcohol, as well as significant brain changes following even moderate alcohol exposure. These changes in brain structure also have been identified frequently in human patients with FAS/FAE. In general, alcohol-exposed rats have smaller and lighter brains. Specific brain structures affected by prenatal exposure include the basal ganglia and the cerebellum, which are small in cases of exposure. Increases in the size of the fluid-filled cavities in the brain (the ventricles) also have been observed. Other studies have reported an overall reduction in the number of cells in the cerebral cortex, damage to a particular type of cell (pyramidal cells) in the hippocampus, and damage to the main pathway for the sense of smell in rats.

Human Studies

Many of the structural changes detected through animal studies also have been found in studies on humans. For example, children diagnosed with FAS often have a smaller-than-expected brain size and a smaller head, as well as reduction in the size of the cerebellum and the structures involved in the sense of smell. Ventricles may be enlarged, small, or absent.

The basal ganglia also have been identified as a site of cellular damage and shrinkage in humans with FAS. The communication pathways interconnecting the brain's two hemispheres (the corpus callosum) have been found to be atrophied or absent in many of these patients. Microscopic changes have been reported in the location of cells within the brain, suggesting evidence of abnormal migration patterns. As the fetus develops, cells move from one part of the brain to another in a prespecified pattern. If this migration is in some way disrupted, as it can be with prenatal alcohol exposure, the cells may not reach their intended destination; as a result, these cells may not function properly.

Although animal studies have shown prenatal alcohol-related changes in some regions of the brain involved with memory functioning (for example, the hippocampus), little analogous literature exists for humans, perhaps because it has been difficult to measure these structures reliably. However, new imaging techniques may reveal alcohol-related damage to these brain structures as well.

Neuropsychological Deficits

Scientists have recently begun investigating neuropsychological deficits in subjects diagnosed with FAS/ARND. Most of these studies have focused on children and adolescents, although researchers are increasingly reporting the persistence of deficits into adulthood. Because prenatal alcohol exposure affects so many regions of the brain, patients exhibit a wide variety of disturbances. Problems occur in a number of important areas, including attention, intelligence, memory, motor coordination, complex problem-solving, and abstract thinking.

Studies of infants reveal tremors, difficulty "tuning out" redundant sensory stimuli, and a weak suckle. Infants and toddlers may be developmentally delayed and often are hyperactive. As the child grows, various tests can help researchers investigate cognitive and behavioral problems. These tests, which can take from one hour to one full day to conduct, may be developed from a standard battery of neuropsychological tests or tailored to the specific neuropsychological problems being studied.

Neuropsychological tests show that people with FAS and ARND often have a hard time focusing their attention. One study found that 5- to 12-year-old children with FAS/FAE exhibited attentional deficits similar to children diagnosed with attention deficit disorder. Attentional disturbances also were prominent in adolescents diagnosed with FAS. These adolescents made impulsive errors on vigilance tasks, which required focusing and sustaining attention. In a study of caretaker reports about subjects with FAS/FAE, 60 percent of the subjects who were 6 to 11 years old and 60 percent of those who were 12 to 20 years old were reported to have had attention deficit problems in their lives. Caretakers in this study were defined as biological, adoptive, or foster parents; other people who were closely involved in the care of the subject; or those who reported a strong familiarity with the subject's history. For the adults with FAS or FAE, attentional problems were reported at some time in their lives by more than 40 percent of the caretakers. (This figure may be misleadingly low, because some informants had not known the subjects as children.) Patients who have difficulty focusing and maintaining attention may function poorly in work and in school. They may become distracted by extraneous events, losing track of the task at hand. For example, 70 percent of the subjects in one study had recurring problems paying attention at school.

Intellectual functioning, as measured by standardized IQ tests, is often below average in children and adolescents with FAS or FAE. In one study, researchers found that 68 percent of FAS/FAE subjects in the three age groups studied (children, adolescents, and adults) had received services for learning problems in school.

Performance in arithmetic is especially poor in patients with FAS/FAE. In a recent study, adolescent and adult patients with FAS and

FAE had significant difficulty performing tasks involving the calculation and estimation of numerical concepts, although they could read and write numbers. This deficit could make tasks that are important for independent living, such as managing finances, difficult. In a recent study, more than 80 percent of adult subjects with FAS/FAE were reported as sometimes or frequently needing help managing money.

Subjects with FAS/ARND often have problems with memory. Researchers found that patients with FAS had difficulty recalling a list of words even after hearing the list five times. These patients often failed to cluster words into categories (for example, tools or fruit), a strategy that facilitates recall. They also made more "intrusive" responses, adding words that were not on the original list. Some researchers hypothesized that patients with FAS performed on list-learning tasks similarly to patients with Huntington's disease. (Huntington's disease is a degenerative brain disorder that affects the basal ganglia, producing movement abnormalities and dementia.)

The difficulties in memory functioning that have been observed suggest that people with FAS/FAE may often forget their obligations at school or work, possibly resulting in disruptions of education or termination of employment. They also may forget medical appointments and thus may not receive timely medical care. Because of this problem, people with FAS/FAE often require someone else to remind them of appointments. Researcher found that children diagnosed with FAS experienced significant difficulty in remembering objects and produced many more spatial distortions when drawing than did control subjects. The researchers concluded that the difficulties in object memory were similar to the performance of patients who had undergone removal of the right temporal lobe of the brain, including the right hippocampal formation, to help control epilepsy. The authors therefore speculated that patients with FAS may have right hippocampal dysfunction.

Problem-solving, concept formation, and verbal fluency have been subjects of recent study in children and adolescents with FAS or ARND. Studies have found that FAS children and adolescents have difficulty solving problems and shifting attention between tasks and tend to make perseverative responses. These subjects also complete fewer categories on a test that measures these abilities (the Wisconsin Card Sorting Test) than do normal children. Several studies have found that subjects with FAS/FAE have decreased verbal fluency (naming as many words as possible in a given time) and nonverbal fluency (drawing as many designs as possible in a given time). They also have difficulty with cognitive estimation, a category of tasks that require the subject to estimate sizes, weights, amounts, and lengths of items to which they may not know the exact answer, such as "What is the height of the tallest tree in the world?" or "What is the age of the world's oldest woman?" People with FAS/FAE tend to give more extreme answers to many of these types of questions than may be expected. For example, they may report the length of a dollar bill as five feet. Deficits in these areas may make it difficult for the person with FAS/FAE to understand and learn complicated activities that require abstract reasoning to help them cope in complicated work and school environments.

Treatment Strategies

Although there have been no systematic studies of the benefits of early intervention for infants and young children with FAS/FAE, some approaches may be helpful. First, it is imperative that interventions include the whole family. Parents of children with FAS/FAE must be helped to understand that the behavioral and cognitive problems that arise are not something that the child is consciously choosing to do. Intervention also includes assisting the family in gaining access to special education, vocational training, and other services. Hand-in-hand with early intervention is early diagnosis. Parents report that an early diagnosis has been helpful to them in setting appropriate expectations for their child's performance.

So far, no empirical research provides insight on how to ameliorate the specific cognitive disturbances accompanying FAS and ARND. However, research addressing rehabilitation strategies for other neuropsychologically impaired populations may be relevant. For example, cognitive rehabilitation approaches (the use of compensation strategies for areas of deficit and attempts to ameliorate the deficit directly) are frequently used for patients with traumatic brain injury and may benefit people with FAS/FAE. In addition, anecdotal reports suggest that behavioral strategies using high levels of structure, concrete (rather than abstract) rules and consequences, and close caretaker supervision may help the FAS patient.

Behavioral approaches that assist children with FAS/ FAE in learning more adaptive ways of communicating their needs or feelings may help minimize the negative, immature, and attention-getting behaviors that are frequently observed in such children. One of these approaches, positive behavioral management, involves bringing about behavioral change through systematic management of the behavioral consequences. Although positive behavioral management strategies have been systematically applied to hundreds of autistic children, no analogous scientific literature exists on children with FAS/FAE.

Some researchers suggest that integration and coordination of the family, schools, and other community services can be beneficial in working with the child. These investigators include anecdotal reports from parents and teachers about strategies that have helped children with FAS. Other similar guides have been developed that suggest tactics that may be helpful when working with younger children. Finally, medications are another avenue of intervention that needs to be systematically examined, particularly in terms of the high frequency of attentional problems in children with FAS/ARND and the significant levels of depression noted in adolescents and adults.

Conclusions

Prenatal exposure to alcohol can have many deleterious effects throughout the life span. Patients with FAS show evidence of structural changes both facially as well as in the brain. Of primary concern are the changes in the brain that lead to deficits in cognitive functioning, including memory and learning problems, attention problems, coordination problems, and difficulties with problem-solving. Unlike the facial features, which tend to become more normal as the affected child grows to adulthood, the cognitive deficits persist, creating long-standing problems in many spheres of life. Affected individuals experience difficulties in work, school, and social functioning. Further study is needed to address the persistence of cognitive and emotional problems throughout the life span of people with FAS, particularly for adults with FAS/ARND, because many of the infants that were first diagnosed in the early 1970's are now adults. Finally, systematically examining various treatment and intervention strategies that have been used for other populations is vitally important in helping to tailor home, school, and community treatment programs to the problems that are commonly found in people with FAS and ARND.

Chapter 40

The Hormonal Effects of Alcohol Use on the Mother and Fetus

The endocrine (hormonal) system plays a critical role in maintaining the body's internal equilibrium (homeostasis). Through the release of hormones, the endocrine system regulates functions as diverse as reproduction, stress response, metabolism, growth, and behavior. Two structures—(1) a brain region called the hypothalamus and (2) the pituitary gland, which is attached to the base of the brain through the pituitary stalk—work together to control the activity of most endocrine glands in the body, including the adrenal glands, gonads (ovaries and testes), and thyroid gland. In turn, each of those glands produces one or more hormones (for example, cortisol, estrogen, testosterone, and thyroid hormone) that control various physiological activities in the body. Alcohol can alter the activities of all components of the endocrine system by acting either directly on the endocrine glands and/or on the hypothalamus or pituitary.

In a pregnant woman, alcohol-induced alterations in endocrine activity may affect not only her health but also her ability to maintain a successful pregnancy. Moreover, alcohol consumption during pregnancy can directly affect fetal development because alcohol readily crosses the placenta. Finally, alcohol consumed during pregnancy may

---

Excerpted from "The Hormonal Effects of Alcohol Use on the Mother and Fetus," by Kara Gabriel, M.A., Candace Hofmann, M.A., Maria Glavas, B.Sc., and Joanne Weinberg, Ph.D. in *Alcohol Health and Research World*, Summer 1998, Vol. 22, Issue, 3, p. 170(8). A complete copy of this publication may be ordered from the U.S. Government Printing Office. Call (202) 512-1800 for information on price and availability.

alter fetal development indirectly by disrupting the normal hormonal interactions between the mother and the fetus. This chapter reviews the multiple hormonal effects of alcohol use during pregnancy on the mother and fetus.

The Role of the Placenta

During pregnancy, the placenta plays a pivotal role in maintaining pregnancy and affecting fetal development. Until the fetal endocrine system is functional, the placenta acts as a miniature endocrine system, producing hormones such as human chorionic gonadotropin, chorionic thyrotropin, and chorionic corticotropin. Through its hormone production, the placenta regulates fetal growth, maturation, and nutrient utilization. In addition to its endocrine activity, the placenta acts as a partial barrier, or filter, between the maternal and fetal blood, allowing the transfer of some maternal hormones and other substances (such as alcohol) from the mother to the fetus while preventing the transfer of others. As a result of these placental functions, the fetus is exposed to three sets of hormones: (1) those secreted by the placenta, (2) those produced by the mother, and (3) the fetus's own hormonal secretions.

Alterations in placental functioning, including the production and activity of placental hormones, may affect fetal growth and development and increase the risk of spontaneous abortion. To date, little information is available on the direct effects of alcohol on the placental hormones in humans.

Alcohol's Impact on Endocrine Functioning in Pregnant Women

Historically, alcohol research in humans has been conducted primarily in men. Only during the past two decades have researchers begun to analyze alcohol's effects on women.

Even fewer studies have investigated the consequences of alcohol consumption during pregnancy on women's physiological (including endocrine) functions. The maternal endocrine system undergoes numerous changes that are geared toward maintaining the pregnancy and providing support for the fetus. Any disruption of the maternal hormone balance can lead to poor pregnancy outcome, including fetal birth defects. As the following sections describe, alcohol can interfere with maternal endocrine functions through numerous mechanisms.

Effects on the Hypothalamic-Pituitary-Adrenal Axis

The hypothalamic-pituitary-adrenal (HPA) axis is a hormone system that plays an essential role in the body's response to stressful events. During periods of stress, the hypothalamus secretes corticotropin-releasing hormone (CRH), which, in turn, stimulates the release of adrenocorticotropic hormone (ACTH) from the pituitary gland. ACTH regulates the growth and activity of the outer layer of the adrenal glands (the adrenal cortex) and induces the secretion of adrenal hormones called glucocorticoids—cortisol (in humans). As the glucocorticoid levels increase in the blood, they act on the pituitary, hypothalamus, and other brain regions to inhibit further activation of the HPA axis. This process of inhibiting further hormonal activation is called negative feedback.

Researchers have investigated alcohol's impact on HPA activity in both pregnant and nonpregnant females. Studies of pregnant rodents found that alcohol consumption further stimulated an already activated HPA axis. Thus, compared with pregnant females on non-alcohol-containing diets, pregnant females receiving an alcohol-containing diet exhibited increases in adrenal gland weight, resting glucocorticoid levels, and the HPA response to stress. This alcohol-induced activation of the HPA axis occurred early during pregnancy and persisted throughout gestation, regardless of whether the alcohol-containing diet included high or low alcohol concentrations. Because the hormones of the HPA axis play numerous roles in energy distribution, metabolism, and immune function, alcohol-induced HPA activation may produce widespread physiological changes during pregnancy.

Effects on the Hypothalamic-Pituitary-Gonadal Axis

The hormones of the hypothalamic-pituitary-gonadal (HPG) axis control reproductive functions and behavior. The HPG axis is activated by the secretion of gonadotropin-releasing hormone (GnRH) from the hypothalamus. GnRH, in turn, stimulates the release of luteinizing hormone (LH) and follicle-stimulating hormone (FSH) from the pituitary. Both LH and FSH regulate the development, growth, maturation, and reproductive functions of the gonads and stimulate the production of sex hormones, including estrogens and androgens (women also secrete small amounts of androgens, such as testosterone). Both estrogens and androgens activate numerous processes in the maturing organism, such as the onset of puberty, the development of secondary sex characteristics, and the behaviors associated with reproduction.

In the developing fetus, androgens also have an organizing function, affecting not only the testes and ovaries but also the size and function of different brain regions.

Studies of alcohol's effects on HPG activity in pregnant women found that alcohol use altered the levels of sex hormone-binding globulin (SHBG), a protein that binds to and temporarily inactivates androgens, thereby regulating the balance between biologically active and inactive androgens. During a normal pregnancy, SHBG levels increase with advancing gestational age. One study demonstrated that in heavy-drinking women whose alcohol abuse resulted in fetal damage, SHBG levels increased less than in nondrinking women. The heavy-drinking women exhibited elevated levels of active testosterone between weeks 16 and 22 of gestation. These findings indicate that alcohol may affect androgen levels most strongly during the first half of pregnancy.

Effects on the Hypothalamic-Pituitary-Thyroid Axis

The hypothalamic-pituitary-thyroid (HPT) axis regulates the rate of metabolism in the body and is essential for the normal growth and development of almost every organ system. The HPT axis is activated by the secretion of thyrotropin-releasing hormone (TRH) from the hypothalamus, which stimulates the release of thyroid-stimulating hormone (TSH) from the pituitary. Reductions in thyroid hormone levels, a condition called hypothyroidism, can result in serious consequences, the extent of which depends on the time during the person's life when thyroid function becomes impaired. In adults, hypothyroidism is marked by reductions in metabolic rate and energy expenditure, resulting in widespread changes in tissue function as well as in drowsiness and listlessness.

Research in pregnant animals has shown that alcohol consumption may reduce the levels of TSH in the blood but not in the pituitary, suggesting that alcohol alters maternal HPT activity. The functional significance of such alterations for both the pregnant female and the fetus, however, is still unknown.

Effects on Growth Hormone (GH) and Insulin-Like Growth Factors (IGF)

As the name implies, growth hormone promotes the body's growth and activity as well as the storage of energy in various tissues, including fat (adipose), liver, muscle, bone, heart, and lungs. In the absence of growth hormone, both animals and humans show stunted growth. Conversely, the hormone's presence results in increased growth as well as enhanced organ size and function. Growth hormone is produced in the pituitary gland. Secretion of the hormone is stimulated primarily by growth hormone-releasing hormone (GHRH), which is released from the hypothalamus. An inhibiting hormone that is also secreted by the hypothalamus—somatostatin—cooperates with GHRH to regulate growth hormone secretion. In addition, estrogens and androgens promote and glucocorticoids inhibit growth hormone release, demonstrating the interactive nature of the endocrine system.

Animal research has shown that pregnant alcohol-consuming rats exhibit reduced growth hormone levels. In addition, several animal studies have indicated that alcohol consumption may alter IGF levels in pregnant females. These alterations may contribute to overall changes in metabolism and other effects on both maternal and fetal systems.

Alcohol's Impact on Endocrine Functioning in the Fetus and Infant

Maternal alcohol consumption during pregnancy can produce devastating effects on the fetus. The most severe consequence is fetal alcohol syndrome (FAS), which is associated with characteristic patterns of abnormal facial structures, growth retardation, and developmental abnormalities of the central nervous system (CNS).

The type and extent of the alcohol-induced fetal damage is partly related to the level and pattern of fetal alcohol exposure. For example, lower levels of prenatal alcohol exposure are required to induce neurodevelopmental effects than to induce physical or growth effects. Maternal binge drinking (consumption of five or more standard drinks per occasion) during pregnancy is one of the strongest predictors of later neurodevelopmental deficits in children with alcohol-induced damage. Possibly, the effects of binge drinking are particularly severe because this drinking pattern results in high BALs in both mother and fetus, followed by repeated withdrawal episodes. Moreover, the fetus cannot metabolize alcohol effectively, because its immature liver does not produce the necessary enzymes.

Prenatal alcoho l exposure may adversely affect the fetal endocrine system and, consequently, the functioning of numerous organ systems. The endocrine activities of both mother and fetus change throughout gestation. For example, whereas the transfer of maternal hormones across the placenta and/or placenta/hormone production is essential during early pregnancy, the activity of the fetal endocrine system becomes more pronounced and important later in gestation. Consequently, alcohol's impact on fetal endocrine activity may occur through different avenues at different time periods. Because of their numerous effects on physiological processes, alcohol-induced alterations in hormone levels likely mediate some of the effects of prenatal alcohol exposure.

Effects on the HPA Axis

The HPA axis is essential for life because it affects the metabolism and activity of numerous systems (for example, the nervous system and the immune system) and ensures homeostasis in response to stress. In the fetus, the first cells to become functional in the pituitary are those that release ACTH. By 9 weeks of gestation, the human fetal pituitary gland contains measurable ACTH levels. Because maternal ACTH cannot cross the placenta into the fetal circulation, the fetal HPA system is controlled by a placental hormone called human chorionic corticotropin until the fetal hypothalamus and pituitary have fully matured. Maternal glucocorticoids (for example, cortisol), however, can cross the placenta and enter the fetal circulation.

Alcohol consumption activates the HPA axis and stimulates glucocorticoid release. Therefore, alcohol consumed during pregnancy will activate the maternal HPA axis and result in increased glucocorticoid levels. Those glucocorticoids can cross the placenta, resulting in elevated glucocorticoid levels in the fetal blood, thereby signaling the fetal HPA axis to decrease its activity. At the same time, however, alcohol in the maternal blood also crosses the placenta and directly activates the fetal HPA axis. Such conflicting messages may alter the development of the fetal HPA axis by disrupting communication among the CNS, hypothalamus, pituitary, and adrenal glands.

A recent study in human infants whose mothers drank heavily at conception found greater increases in cortisol levels in response to stress (for example, having blood drawn) compared with control infants. Furthermore, children prenatally exposed to alcohol are known to be hyperactive, uninhibited, and impulsive in behavior, particularly in challenging or stressful situations. Because the hormones of the HPA axis act on the CNS to alter behavior and performance in stressful situations, altered HPA activity may underlie some of the behavioral problems seen in children prenatally exposed to alcohol.

Effects on the HPG Axis

During gestation, the HPG axis influences not only the development of the reproductive system but also the organization of the CNS. (In humans, the external genitalia of both sexes begin to develop at 9 to 10 weeks after conception, and the gender-specific differentiation of the brain occurs throughout gestation.) Under the influence of testosterone (and, possibly, estrogen), certain brain areas develop differently in males and females.

Limited data are available on the association between prenatal alcohol exposure and HPG activity in humans. The available information indicates that prenatal alcohol exposure may slightly delay puberty in males, although the time of onset of puberty still is generally within normal limits in those adolescents. More extensive investigations regarding the effects of prenatal alcohol exposure on HPG activity and sexual development and behavior in humans are needed.

Effects on the HPT Axis

Normal functioning of the HPT axis is critical for growth and development as well as for regulation of the body's overall metabolic rate. Reductions in thyroid hormones during the first 2 years of life may be particularly devastating, because those hormones play a crucial role in CNS development. Accordingly, untreated hypothyroidism in infancy results in growth retardation (short stature) and mental retardation. During the first weeks of gestation, the transfer of maternal thyroid hormones to the fetus may play an important role in fetal development. By 11 to 12 weeks of gestation, however, the thyroid of the human fetus can produce and secrete its own hormones. Maternal alcohol consumption may reduce the availability of thyroid hormones to the fetus either indirectly, by inhibiting the transport of maternal hormone across the placenta, or directly, by interfering with the function of the fetal thyroid once it is active.

Effects on Growth Hormone (GH) and Insulin-Like Growth Factors (IGF)

Growth hormone and IGFs play a central role in promoting body growth and development. Accordingly, alcohol-induced impairment of this hormone system during fetal development could have severe consequences. Animal studies have shown that newborn animals prenatally exposed to alcohol had reduced growth hormone levels compared with control animals. More recently, researchers have shown that the activity of IGFs, which play an essential role in fetal development, may be affected by prenatal alcohol exposure.

Growth hormone normally is released from the pituitary periodically throughout the day. Growth hormone release increases in response to various factors, such as changes in blood sugar or insulin levels, fasting, or exercise. In children with FAS, growth hormone responses to stimulation by such factors were normal, as were growth hormone levels during sleep. In contrast to those results from growth hormone stimulation tests, the estimated rate of spontaneous 24-hour growth hormone secretion in children with FAS was lower than in children of normal stature and similar to that of children who were born small for their gestational age. In addition, the concentrations of IGF- 1 and of one component of IGF-binding protein in the blood of children with FAS were at the lower end of the normal range. These observations suggest that subtle alterations in growth hormone or IGF levels may contribute to alcohol-induced growth retardation.

Conclusions

Alcohol consumption during pregnancy disrupts the normal functioning of both the maternal and the fetal endocrine systems and may disturb the normal maternal-fetal endocrine balance. Those alterations may adversely affect the development and organization of multiple systems in the fetus and likely mediate some commonly observed effects of prenatal alcohol exposure. The exact mechanisms underlying alcohol-induced fetal damage have not been fully delineated. The tremendous impact of prenatal alcohol exposure on fetal development is not surprising, however, considering the interrelationship of the maternal and fetal endocrine systems, the complex role of the placenta, and the numerous direct and indirect effects of maternal alcohol consumption on both the mother and the fetus. Thus, although numerous factors likely play a role in alcohol-induced fetal damage, the disruption of hormonal influences on the developing fetus may explain at least some of the effects of prenatal alcohol exposure. An increased understanding of endocrine function during pregnancy; of the development of the fetal endocrine system; and of the processes influenced by maternal, placental, and fetal hormones may offer new insights into the adverse effects of prenatal alcohol exposure and possible methods of attenuating those effects.

Chapter 41

Assessing the Impact of Maternal Drinking during and after Pregnancy

Recent findings from longitudinal follow-up studies of adolescents and adults with fetal alcohol syndrome (FAS) indicate that the deficits associated with this disorder are long lasting and pervasive. In addition, follow-up data from several large, prospective studies of cohorts representing a broad range of alcohol exposure levels have confirmed that although FAS represents the severe end of a continuum of birth defects, moderate levels of alcohol intake produce physical and neurobehavioral deficits that are similar to, but less severe than, FAS. (A "moderate" level of alcohol intake usually refers to an average daily consumption of 0.5 to 0.99 ounce of absolute alcohol or the equivalent of 1 to 1.99 standard drinks.)

Accumulating evidence shows that many FAS deficits can be detected at infancy and remain through adolescence into adulthood. In particular, an abnormally small head circumference (microcephaly) and intellectual problems persist as an affected child matures, whereas behavioral, emotional, and social problems can become more pronounced. In addition, the long-term clinical consequences in terms of psychopathology and social maladjustment are only recently being recognized and persist even in people with FAS who were raised in a stable, supportive environment. Incidences of maladaptive behaviors,

---

Excerpted from "Assessing the Impact of Maternal Drinking during and after Pregnancy," by Sandra W. Jacobson, Ph.D. in *Alcohol Health and Research World*, Summer 1997, Vol. 21, No, 3, p. 199(5). A complete copy of this publication may be ordered from the U.S. Government Printing Office. Call (202) 512-1800 for information on price and availability.

such as poor judgment, failure to consider the consequences of one's actions, and difficulty perceiving social cues, are common, as are legal problems resulting from sexual misconduct, drunk driving, shoplifting, and other socially inappropriate behaviors.

In a recent long-term follow-up study of a Seattle cohort of adolescents and adults with FAS, Streissguth and colleagues (Streissguth, A.P.; Barr, H.M; Kogan, J.; and Bookstein, F.L. Understanding the Occurrence of Secondary Disabilities in Clients With Fetal Alcohol Syndrome (FAS) and Fetal Alcohol Effects (FAE): Final Report. Seattle: University of Washington School of Medicine, Fetal Alcohol and Drug Unit, 1996.) distinguished between prenatal, or "primary," disabilities, which reflect central nervous system (CNS) dysfunctions inherent in the FAS diagnosis, and "secondary" disabilities, with which a person is not born and which presumably could be ameliorated through intervention. Examples of secondary disabilities include mental health problems, disrupted schooling (for example, dropping out or being suspended or expelled), trouble with the law (for example, being charged with or convicted of a crime), inappropriate sexual behavior (for example, promiscuity), alcohol or drug problems, dependent living as an adult (for example, an inability to manage money), and problems with employment (for example, trouble holding a job). Streissguth and colleagues concluded that legal problems and other secondary disabilities occur frequently in adolescents and adults with FAS, with incidences ranging from approximately 30 to 94 percent for various types of secondary disabilities among the study sample.

Prenatal Versus Postnatal Effects

This chapter aims to demonstrate the need to differentiate the impact of prenatal drinking from the impact of the environment in which the child is raised when assessing neurobehavioral and other outcomes in children whose mothers drank both during and after pregnancy. In the 20 years since FAS was first identified, a major body of research has been compiled on the effects of prenatal alcohol exposure as well as the impact of being raised by an alcoholic parent. (The terms "alcoholism" and "alcoholic" as used in this chapter are summary terms for the diagnoses of alcohol abuse and alcohol dependence. The term "alcohol abuse" refers to abnormal patterns of drinking that result in detrimental effects on health, social problems, or both.) Distinguishing between the effects of prenatal exposure and the effects of postnatal environment often presents a major methodological challenge to researchers, however, because women frequently drink both during and after pregnancy (prenatal and postnatal drinking are moderately related).

An association between drinking during pregnancy and neurobehavioral function in infants and children normally is interpreted as teratogenic (attributable to a direct effect of alcohol exposure on fetal CNS development). The specific body systems affected by alcohol exposure and the resultant outcomes depend on when exposure occurs during the prolonged period of CNS sensitivity to alcohol. For example, first-trimester exposure is related to craniofacial anomalies, whereas the effects on growth particularly postnatal growth are related to alcohol exposure later in pregnancy. Experimental studies with laboratory animals have demonstrated the role of timing of binge-like alcohol exposure in inducing specific structural and behavioral deficits. However, little is known about the timing of exposure for many important neurobehavioral effects in humans, such as deficits in attention span or information-processing speed.

One alternative explanation—that an observed deficit is attributable to the socioenvironmental consequences of being raised by a drinking mother—can be evaluated by examining the relationship of the deficit to postnatal maternal alcohol use. In cases where the mother drinks both during and after pregnancy, however, it may not always be possible to determine the degree to which observed deficits are attributable to teratogenic versus socioenvironmental factors. Statistical analyses that include variables related to both prenatal and postnatal drinking behavior may sometimes obscure true prenatal effects and result in the failure to recognize a true effect or in an understatement of the magnitude of the effect (type II error).

Two Approaches to Assessment

Two analytical approaches have been used to assess the impact of prenatal versus postnatal drinking on the child. One approach was used in a prospective longitudinal study conducted in Detroit, Michigan, that investigated the effects of prenatal and postnatal alcohol exposure on infant neurobehavioral outcomes. Infants were assessed on the Bayley Scales of Infant Development, a complexity of play measure, and three infant information-processing tests:

1. The Fagan Test of Infant Intelligence
2. A test of cross-modal transfer
3. The Visual Expectancy Paradigm

Infants with moderate prenatal alcohol exposure performed more poorly than less-exposed infants on most of these tests, even after controlling for potential confounding variables. For example, prenatally exposed infants received lower scores on the mental development scale of the Bayley Scales of Infant Development and on a test of play complexity. Prenatal alcohol exposure also was associated with slower response times on the Visual Expectancy Paradigm, which directly assessed the infants' reaction time as they shifted their gaze back and forth at an image flashed on a screen. This result suggests slower information processing in prenatally exposed infants. Similarly, these infants demonstrated slower processing speed measured in terms of the length of their gaze (visual fixation) as they studied an object or picture on both the Fagan Test of Infant Intelligence and the cross-modal transfer test. Short looks, which are associated with more rapid information processing, have been found to predict a higher childhood IQ.

None of the neurobehavioral deficits detected during infancy was significantly related to postpartum drinking by the mother or caregiver, suggesting that these deficits were related specifically to prenatal alcohol exposure. Because postpartum drinking levels were unrelated to infant outcomes, they could not be potential confounding variables. (Confounding variables are those variables that can cause or prevent the outcome of interest—in this case, neurobehavioral deficits. Adjustments must be made for confounding variables in order to distinguish their effects from those of the variable under investigation—in this case, drinking during pregnancy). Therefore, postpartum drinking levels were not included in analyses assessing the impact of prenatal exposure on outcome, even though mothers who drank during pregnancy were likely to drink afterward as well (prenatal and postnatal drinking were moderately correlated.

A second analytical approach for assessing the effects of drinking during and after pregnancy was used in a longitudinal study conducted in Atlanta, Georgia. The deficits in intellectual functioning seen in children heavily exposed to alcohol throughout pregnancy continued to be evident even after the analyses statistically controlled for current drinking reported by the mothers or caretakers. Children exposed throughout pregnancy also were more often described as showing higher levels of negative externalizing behaviors, including destructive, inattentive, aggressive, and nervous or overactive behaviors; inappropriate social behavior; and poor social competence. These deficits likewise persisted after current caregiver drinking was controlled. In contrast, the impact of prenatal alcohol exposure on the child's internalizing behavior (specifically, depression) was no longer significant when the caretaker's current drinking was controlled. Thus, the child's depression was attributed at least in part to problems in the postnatal environment.

A similar pattern of results was seen when Brown and colleagues (Brown, R.T.; Coles, C.D.; Smith, I.E.; Platzman, K.A.; Silverstein, J.; Erickson, S.; and Falek, A. Effects of prenatal alcohol exposure at school age: II. Attention and behavior. *Neurotoxicology and Teratology* 13(4):369-376, 1991) examined sustained attention. They noted that a formerly significant deterioration of attention span detected in the children of mothers who drank heavily throughout pregnancy was no longer significant when current alcohol use was held constant. Thus, the researchers concluded that this effect derived from the consequences of the current caretaking environment. Alternatively, however, the prenatal and postnatal alcohol exposure measures in these instances could have been too confounded to determine which was the true predictor of the outcomes. The effects on attention cannot be conclusively attributed to the current caretaking environment, unless the impact of current drinking persists after controlling statistically for the influence of the prenatal exposure.

The data from these studies are consistent with findings demonstrating that cognitive performance is less affected by alcohol exposure in infants and children whose mothers stop drinking in early pregnancy, despite the mothers' resumption of alcohol use after giving birth. Thus, these studies show that although some secondary psychopathology or deficits are attributable to being raised by a mother whose alcohol abuse problems may prevent her from providing an optimal and stable home environment, several specific cognitive and behavioral deficits linked to prenatal alcohol exposure appear to reflect CNS damage.

Conclusions

The impact of being raised by an alcoholic parent has been examined extensively in the research on children of alcoholics (COAs), but few studies have compared the effects of being raised by an alcoholic father versus an alcoholic mother. Most COA research has focused on children whose fathers have problems with alcohol abuse or alcoholism, but whose mothers do not, in order to exclude the effects of alcohol exposure attributable to maternal drinking during pregnancy. Little is known about the impact of these nonalcoholic mothers' drinking habits on their children. As previously noted, however, recent findings have detected prenatal alcohol effects at moderate levels of alcohol consumption (between 3.5 and 7.0 ounces of absolute alcohol or the equivalent of 7 to 14 standard drinks per week) by pregnant women not considered to have a serious drinking problem. Thus, even though a mother is not an alcoholic, her child may not be spared the effects of prenatal alcohol exposure. Most likely, however, the pattern of neurobehavioral deficits will differ when such deficits result from direct fetal exposure rather than when they are paternally transmitted or postnatally incurred.

Chapter 42

Alcohol Withdrawal during Pregnancy

A woman who drinks alcoholic beverages during pregnancy exposes not only herself but also her fetus to alcohol. Alcohol readily crosses the placenta; consequently, the blood alcohol levels (BALs) of the fetus are similar to those of the mother. Likewise, if the woman suddenly abstains from alcohol, both she and her fetus may undergo withdrawal. This chapter briefly describes the withdrawal symptoms observed in pregnant women and newborns, discusses the birth defects associated with prenatal alcohol exposure, and explores the possibility that alcohol withdrawal (AW) may contribute to the adverse effects of prenatal alcohol exposure on fetal brain function and behavioral development.

Withdrawal Symptoms in Pregnant Women and Newborns

Pregnant Women

Despite warning labels on alcoholic beverages and an increased awareness among the general population of alcohol's deleterious effects on the developing fetus, the women who are the heaviest alcohol abusers frequently do not change their drinking practices during pregnancy. Such women are at the greatest risk for giving birth to a

---

Excerpted from " Fetal alcohol syndrome: does alcohol withdrawal play a role?," by Jennifer D. Thomas and Edward P. Riley, in *Alcohol Health and Research World*, Winter 1998, Vol. 22, No, 1, p. 47(7). A complete copy of this publication may be ordered from the U.S. Government Printing Office. Call (202) 512-1800 for information on price and availability.

child with alcohol-related problems. In the United States, approximately 3.3 percent of pregnant women are estimated to consume two or more drinks per day.

One of the consequences of heavy alcohol use is the potential for experiencing withdrawal symptoms during periods of abstinence. Symptoms of mild to moderate withdrawal from alcohol may include tremors, sweating, stomach pain, anxiety, and sleep disturbances. Severe withdrawal symptoms may include delirium tremors and violent agitation (seizures). These effects may begin within hours of the last drink and may persist for several days. Various tranquilizers and sedatives, including alcohol itself, have been used to manage these symptoms.

Newborns

When a pregnant woman undergoes AW, so does her fetus. To date, no studies have analyzed the symptoms and effects of withdrawal on fetuses in utero. However, researchers have studied withdrawal in newborns whose mothers were intoxicated during delivery.

The onset of withdrawal symptoms in newborns may be delayed compared with adults, because alcohol metabolism in newborns is slower than in adults. Neonatal AW typically manifests itself as hyperexcitability of the central nervous system (CNS) and gastrointestinal symptoms. CNS hyperexcitability results in symptoms such as tremors, excessive muscle tension, irritability, increased respiratory rate, poor sleeping patterns, and increased sense of hearing (hyperacusis). These infants also may exhibit spontaneous seizures accompanied by cessation of breathing (apnea) and arching of the back (opisthotonos). Gastrointestinal symptoms may include abdominal distention and, in a few cases, vomiting.

Newborns undergoing AW are best treated by being placed in a calm environment with decreased sensory stimulation. Pharmacological treatment with sedatives or tranquilizers has been used only for infants with the most serious symptoms (for example, seizures and vomiting).

The observations described here leave little doubt that newborns can undergo AW, and similar effects may occur in the fetus. The effects of maternal or fetal withdrawal (and its treatment) on the developing fetus, however, remain unknown.

Consequences of Prenatal Alcohol Exposure

Women who drink alcohol during pregnancy place their fetuses at risk for numerous developmental problems, ranging from prenatal mortality to disruptions in physical and behavioral development. The most serious consequence of heavy maternal drinking is a cluster of characteristic anomalies termed fetal alcohol syndrome (FAS). Symptoms of FAS include prenatal and postnatal growth retardation, characteristic facial abnormalities, and CNS anomalies. The distinct facial characteristics of children with FAS include such features as a flat midface, thin upper lip, and small eye openings. CNS anomalies associated with FAS include an abnormally small head (microcephaly) and behavioral problems, such as attention deficits, hyperactivity, motor dysfunction, mental retardation, and learning and social skills deficits. Although some of the physical characteristics of FAS become less pronounced as the child matures into adulthood, many of the behavioral problems persist.

Even if they do not meet all the criteria for a diagnosis of FAS, children exposed to alcohol in utero may exhibit a wide range of developmental problems, particularly behavioral disorders. These developmental problems often are referred to as fetal alcohol effects or alcohol-related birth defects. The identification of the factors that place a fetus at risk for the harmful effects of prenatal alcohol exposure and the elucidation of the mechanisms by which alcohol causes CNS dysfunction and subsequent behavioral alterations are among the challenges that researchers currently face.

Can Alcohol Withdrawal Damage the Fetus or Newborn?

There is little doubt that alcohol interferes with normal fetal development (is a teratogenic agent). Fetal alcohol exposure can adversely affect numerous developmental processes, such as the multiplication (proliferation), migration, and survival of cells, as well as the cells' development into specific cell types (differentiation). The mechanisms by which alcohol disrupts these processes have yet to be fully elucidated. Given alcohol's ubiquitous distribution throughout all body regions, however, it likely interferes with development through many direct and indirect actions.

Like alcohol itself, withdrawal from alcohol initiates a cascade of physiological events that might also affect the developing organism. Although there is no direct evidence that withdrawal contributes to alcohol's adverse effects on development, the possibility demands further investigation.

The clearest indications that withdrawal from drugs can have long-term adverse effects on the developing fetus have come from animal studies examining the teratogenic effects of narcotics. For example, a series of studies evaluating the effects of prenatal opiate exposure have shown that withdrawal contributes considerably to the adverse effects of these agents, increasing mortality and morbidity in fetal and newborn rat pups.

These studies also indicate that withdrawal can contribute to behavioral alterations associated with early narcotic exposure. For example, rats that have been prenatally exposed to opiates generally are more sensitive to aversive stimuli, such as heat, compared with normal rats.

Just as opiate withdrawal exacerbates the effects of opiate exposure, withdrawal from alcohol might contribute to alcohol's teratogenicity. To date, only a few studies have examined this possibility. For example, some researchers found that alcohol-treated rats exhibited more severe cognitive deficits if the alcohol exposure was stopped abruptly than if the alcohol levels were tapered off slowly. Because withdrawal would have been more severe following the abrupt removal of alcohol than following its gradual reduction, these observations suggest that the cognitive deficits were at least in part affected by withdrawal.

In addition, both animal and human studies suggest that maternal consumption of a large amount of alcohol in a short period of time (binge drinking) produces more severe brain damage and behavioral alterations in the developing organism compared with more chronic alcohol consumption. Maternal binge drinking also predicts cognitive variables (for example, IQ, attention, vigilance, and academic achievement) in prenatally exposed children and adolescents to a greater extent than does frequency of drinking.

Binge drinking produces a cyclical pattern of high BALs followed by withdrawal. Accordingly, these results have been used primarily to illustrate the importance of peak BALs as a risk factor for alcohol's effects on the fetus. However, withdrawal—particularly repeated episodes of withdrawal—possibly contributes to the increased severity of alcohol's effects on children whose mothers were binge drinkers during pregnancy.

Researchers are only beginning to address the question of how withdrawal from alcohol could damage the fetus or newborn. Several mechanisms that are related either to maternal or fetal withdrawal could conceivably play a role in these processes. For example, acute AW is associated with changes in many of the hormones related to stress. The possibility exists that the stress to the mother and/or the fetus associated with a withdrawal episode could damage the fetus. Episodes of stress during the prenatal period can reduce birth weight, disrupt brain development, decrease immune function, and induce behavioral alterations (for example, hyperactivity and cognitive deficits). These consequences of prenatal stress all are commonly observed following alcohol exposure during gestation. In addition to this indirect pathway, AW may directly affect the fetal CNS. The following sections explore this possibility. Because only few published studies have examined the contribution of withdrawal to alcohol's effects on the fetus, this hypothesis remains speculative.

Alcohol Withdrawal and the NMDA Receptor

Recently, researchers have been increasingly interested in the direct interaction of alcohol with proteins in the membranes of nerve cells (neurons) that contribute to the symptoms associated with AW. Some of these proteins form receptors, molecules that interact with the chemicals released by neurons for neuronal communication (neurotransmitters). Activation of these receptors can either excite the cell, making it more likely to transmit information to other neurons, or inhibit the cell, making it less likely to transmit information. One receptor in particular has received much attention in the analysis of alcohol's effects on the brain. This receptor, which interacts with the neurotransmitter glutamate—an amino acid that excites certain neurons during normal neurotransmission—can also be specifically activated by N-methyl-D-aspartate (NMDA) and is therefore referred to as the NMDA receptor.

In adult rats, acute alcohol treatment inhibits NMDA receptors, thereby producing an overall inhibitory effect. With continued alcohol exposure, however, the CNS attempts to offset this inhibitory effect by increasing the number and/or activity of NMDA receptors. This process is called neuro-adaptation. During abstinence, as alcohol is eliminated from the body, alcohol's inhibitory action decreases. As a result, the cells with elevated NMDA receptor levels are much more excited than under normal conditions, a phenomenon called rebound excitability. This hyperexcitability may contribute to the symptoms associated with AW, such as tremors, agitation, and seizures. This hypothesis is supported by findings that agents which block activation of NMDA receptors reduce withdrawal symptoms, whereas agents that activate these receptors exacerbate withdrawal symptoms.

During normal neurotransmission, activation of the NMDA receptor excites the neuron. If this receptor becomes overactivated, however, a cascade of intracellular events may occur, resulting ultimately in cell death. This process is called excitotoxicity. Excitotoxicity may result from several different types of insult, including lack of oxygen (hypoxia), interrupted blood supply (ischemia), low blood sugar levels (hypoglycemia), and epilepsy. Excitotoxicity also may occur in several chronic neurodegenerative diseases, such as Alzheimer's disease and Huntington's disease.

NMDA receptor-mediated excitotoxicity also may occur during AW, possibly leading to cell loss in various brain regions, including the cortex, hippocampus, and striatum. (The cortex, the outer layer of neurons covering the brain, contains areas for processing sensory information and controlling motor functions, speech, and higher cognitive functions. The hippocampus is a brain region thought to play a role in learning and memory. The striatum is a brain region below the cortex that is thought to be involved in motor function and some cognitive functions.)

The NMDA Receptor in Fetal Development and Alcohol Withdrawal

Mechanisms similar to those described in the previous section may play a role in alcohol's effects on the fetus, particularly because the developing organism is more vulnerable to NMDA receptor-related excitotoxicity compared with the adult. This vulnerability appears to result from the role that NMDA receptor activation plays during neuronal development. Both NMDA and glutamate promote neuronal growth and regulate the formation of connections among neurons (neuronal circuits). For example, NMDA receptor activation has the following effects:

- Promotes survival of the neuron whose receptors are activated
- Stimulates the outgrowth of dendrites, the branch-like extensions of neurons where signals from other neurons are received
- Affects the pattern of dendrite branching
- Influences the formation of synaptic connections that allow neurons to communicate with each other.

Through these functions, NMDA receptors play a critical role in the ability of neurons to alter their structure or function (neuronal plasticity), a process that is essential for brain development.

During fetal development, NMDA receptor activity must be tightly controlled to maintain a balance between the receptor's neuronal growth-promoting effects and its excitotoxic effects. Accordingly, both underactivation and overactivation of this receptor could be damaging to the developing organism. Thus, alcohol exposure could disrupt neuronal development by directly inhibiting NMDA receptors, whereas AW could interfere with development by overactivating NMDA receptors.

Conclusions

Prenatal alcohol exposure can have devastating effects on the growth and development of the fetus. Although alcohol can disrupt development through many mechanisms, both direct and indirect, little research has addressed the issue of whether withdrawal contributes to alcohol's deleterious effects. Researchers are now beginning to understand the role of neurotransmitter receptors in excitotoxic brain damage and in the development of withdrawal symptoms. The consequences of alcohol's actions at these receptors are highly complex in the dynamic context of development, because the neurotransmitters that react with these receptors also play important roles in neural development. For example, NMDA receptor activation can result in both neuronal growth-promoting and excitotoxic effects, and its activity therefore must be finely balanced. Consequently, both inhibition of the NMDA receptor after alcohol exposure and activation of the receptor during withdrawal could interfere with neuronal development. Future research on the direct and indirect effects of withdrawal on the fetus and newborn may result in more effective treatment strategies to reduce the long-term consequences of prenatal alcohol exposure.

Part Four

Alcohol and the Brain

Chapter 43

Actions of Alcohol on the Brain

Introduction

The mechanisms by which alcohol produces intoxication, reinforcement of continued drinking, dependence, and withdrawal upon cessation of drinking are based chiefly in the brain. Recent progress in neuroscience research has yielded information critical to characterizing the cellular and molecular processes that occur in the central nervous system (CNS) in response to alcohol and has helped associate these processes with the behavioral and physiological manifestations of alcohol use and abuse.

Actions of Alcohol on the Central Nervous System

Although alcohol ingestion initially induces a pleasurable state of mind, excessive drinking leads to confusion, incoordination, sedation, and sometimes coma. Alcohol has known reinforcing effects that may explain why some people seek repeated exposure to alcohol despite these and other adverse consequences. Prolonged drinking results in tolerance to alcohol's effects and may lead to craving for alcohol and to physical dependence. In alcohol-dependent individuals, cessation of drinking produces symptoms of withdrawal, such as tremors, hallucinations, and seizures. A fundamental challenge to alcohol researchers

---

Excerpted from *Ninth Special Report to the U.S. Congress on Alcohol and Health,* U.S. Department of Health and Human Services, National Institute on Alcohol Abuse and Alcoholism, June 1997.

is to understand the brain structures and CNS activities involved in intoxication, reinforcement, tolerance, and dependence.

Intoxication

Consumption of alcohol leads to a dose-dependent, transient elevation of blood alcohol concentration (BAC). In an inexperienced drinker, low BACs (25-45 milligrams/deciliter [mg/dL], or one to two drinks containing one-half of an ounce of ethyl alcohol) produce increased sociability, euphoria, and mild motor incoordination. (BACs produced by any given number of drinks differ according to various factors, including a person's genetic makeup, weight, lean body mass, gender, age, health, and the rate of alcohol intake.) BACs of 80-100 mg/dL correspond to legal limits set by states to enforce safe driving and are associated with changes in gait, concentration, and reaction time. Episodes of short-term amnesia (alcoholic blackouts) may occur with BACs at and above 80 mg/dL. BACs of 100-150 mg/dL can produce more overt signs of intoxication, including gait ataxia (inability to walk straight), nystagmus (rhythmic movements of the eyes), impaired mental and motor skills, sedation, and confusion. In nonalcoholic individuals, BACs above 400-500 mg/dL are commonly fatal.

Behavioral and physiologic changes observed with intoxication reflect effects of alcohol in various structures and functions of the brain. Motor incoordination observed in intoxicated individuals may result from actions of alcohol in the cerebellum, which participates in the control of movement. Alcohol has been shown to suppress nerve impulses released by Purkinje cells, cerebellar neurons that send sensory and movement-related messages to various parts of the body. The euphoric and anxiolytic (anxiety-reducing) effects of alcohol may be mediated by networks of nerve cells in various brain regions that subserve emotion, including the hypothalamus, septal area, amygdala, ventral tegmental area, nucleus accumbens, and cingulate gyrus. Sedation, confusion, and impaired cognition suggest widespread effects of alcohol on the cerebral cortex, which controls higher mental functions, perception, and behavioral reactions, and its functionally related structures in the pons. In addition, the sedative hypnotic properties of alcohol result in part from the drug's ability to enhance the inhibitory effects of GABA and inhibit the excitatory actions of glutamate. Alcoholic blackouts likely represent disruption of function in the hippocampus, a structure critical to consolidating new memories. Death after excessive drinking results from suppression of brain stem activities that control respiration.

Table 43.1. Brain-Related Terminology (continued on next page)

Amygdala: An almond-shaped structure in the temporal lobe, thought to contribute to alertness.

Antagonist: An agent that blocks or reverses the actions or effects of another agent.

ATP: Adenosine triphosphate; an energy-producing compound.

Cerebellum: Connected to the brain stem; it helps coordinate movement.

Cerebral cortex: Controls higher mental functions, perception, and behavioral reactions; considered to be the center of higher consciousness and the seat of all intelligent behavior.

Cingulate gyrus: Part of the structure that connects the two hemispheres of the brain.

CNS: central nervous system; the brain and the spinal cord.

Dopamine: A neurotransmitter.

Excitotoxicity: The processes by which excessive influx of calcium into the cell leads to cell death.

5-HT: 5-hydroxytryptamine; serotonin.

GABA: Gamma-aminobutyric acid; an amino acid in the central nervous system that inhibits neurotransmission.

Glutamate: An excitatory neurotransmitter.

Hippocampus: A brain structure critical to consolidating new memories.

Hypothalamus: Associated with thirst, hunger, and heightened emotional drives.

Ion channels: Proteins that span the cell membrane, forming pores that regulate the flow of specific charged particles into and out of the cell.

Isozymes: Multiple forms of the same enzyme.

Neuron: A nerve cell.

Neuropharmacologic effects: Effects of drugs on the nervous system.

Neurotransmitters: Chemical messengers released by excited or stimulated nerve cells. After being released, neurotransmitters travel across a synapse and then bind to a receptor on an adjacent nerve cell, usually triggering a series of chemical and electrical changes in the second cell.

Table 43.1. Brain-Related Terminology (continued)

Neurotrophin: A factor that promotes the survival, growth, and differentiation of certain nerve cells.

NMDA: N-methyl-D-aspartate; the NMDA receptor interacts with glutamate.

Nucleus accumbens: A brain structure affected by many drugs of abuse and implicated in the rewarding properties of addictive drugs.

Opioid: A substance in the body that acts in the brain to decrease the sensation of pain.

Phosphorylation: A chemical reaction resulting in the formation of a phosphate derivative of a molecule; these reactions are often critical to the regulation of receptor activity and the functions of other proteins.

PKC: Protein kinase C; an enzyme critical for many intracellular functions.

Pons: A broad mass of nerve fibers that forms the central portion of the brain stem. The pons participates in control of respiration and coordination of muscular activity.

Purkinje cells: Neurons in the cerebellum that send sensory and movement-related messages to various parts of the body.

Receptor: A complex protein structure that recognizes and binds neurotransmitters or interacts with specific enzymes.

Septal area: A region stretching as a thin sheet within the cerebral hemisphere that has functional connections with the hypothalamus and the hippocampus.

Serotonin: A neurotransmitter; important in cycles of waking and sleeping; helps regulate functions such as food and water intake, sexual response, and aggression.

Synapse: The site of connection between neurons.

VACC: Voltage-activated calcium channel; VACCs regulate neuronal excitability.

Ventral tegmental area: The midbrain region containing dopamine cell bodies that project to the nucleus accumbens.

Note: A glossary of alcohol-related terminology is presented in Chapter 69.

Reinforcement

Alcohol's reinforcing properties are those that increase the likelihood of future alcohol consumption, a behavior thought to contribute to the development of chronic drinking, dependence, and craving. Alcohol may have positive reinforcing effects, as exemplified by its pleasant euphoric actions, or negative reinforcing effects, as exemplified by its anxiolytic properties.

Researchers are exploring the neuropharmacologic effects that reinforce alcohol-seeking behavior and the specific brain pathways involved. Brain regions implicated in alcohol reinforcement include areas of the hypothalamus associated with thirst, hunger, and heightened emotional drives. Key neurotransmitters that appear to play a role in alcohol's reinforcing effects include GABA, dopamine, and serotonin.

Tolerance

Tolerance is a general term applied to compensatory adaptations. The brain and body adapt to chronic alcohol exposure. As a result, higher BACs are required to produce a state of intoxication, and BACs that would prove lethal in people who are not alcoholics may produce no discernible intoxication in alcoholics. For example, alcoholics who have developed tolerance appear to remain sober even at BACs of 230-460 mg/dL and can survive with BACs that exceed 1,000 mg/dL. Because more alcohol is required to achieve the same effect and because higher BACs are maintained for longer periods of time, the development of tolerance allows and may encourage increased alcohol intake and contributes to alcohol-induced organ damage, including damage to the brain.

Metabolic, behavioral, and neuronal mechanisms contribute to the development of tolerance. Chronic alcohol consumption increases levels of liver enzymes that metabolize alcohol, effectively increasing the ability of the liver to break down alcohol so that a larger dose is needed to achieve the same blood and brain alcohol levels. Behavioral tolerance describes the learned ability of a person or laboratory animal to function under the influence of alcohol or other drugs. Behavioral manifestations of tolerance are thought to involve adaptive, or plastic, CNS processes similar to learning and memory. Underlying these behavioral changes may be alcohol-induced changes in neuronal function. Chronic alcohol exposure can produce adaptive responses in neurons and can result in not only tolerance to alcohol's effects but also a requirement for the presence of the drug for normal nerve function. These adaptive responses appear to involve alterations to neural cell membranes, functions of ion channels, and responses to neurotransmitters such as GABA and glutamate.

Physical Dependence and Withdrawal

In addition to tolerance, chronic alcohol consumption may result in physical dependence, a state in which alcohol is required to maintain normal CNS function. Like tolerance, physical dependence involves adaptive changes in CNS activities. In alcohol-dependent persons, cessation of drinking may lead to craving for alcohol and symptoms of alcohol withdrawal syndrome. Withdrawal symptoms develop because adaptive changes that render CNS function normal in the presence of alcohol become maladaptive when alcohol intake is abruptly discontinued.

Symptoms of alcohol withdrawal include tremulousness, agitation, and autonomic hyperactivity (characterized by sweating, increased blood pressure, and rapid heart rate) that contrast sharply with the sedative effects typical of acute intoxication. Alcohol withdrawal syndrome evolves gradually over hours to days after the cessation of drinking. Tremulousness appears after 8-12 hours, followed in some instances by generalized seizures. Delirium tremens, a state of autonomic hyperactivity, agitation, and hallucinations, typically begins within 2 days after alcohol withdrawal and may last several days, a week, or more.

The cellular and molecular mechanisms responsible for these adaptive CNS responses, as well those involved in the intoxicating and reinforcing properties of alcohol, are areas of active investigation. Neuroscientists have begun to understand responses to alcohol in terms of its long- and short-term impact on nerve cell membranes; functions of neurotransmitters, their receptors, and related intracellular signaling molecules; and intracellular activities such as gene expression.

Summary

A fundamental goal of alcohol research is to define, at a cellular and molecular level, how alcohol produces intoxication, tolerance, dependence, withdrawal, and other short- and long-term behavioral and physiologic changes. Advances in neuroscience research have brought about remarkable progress toward this goal. Newly developed research techniques have allowed examination of alcohol's effects on the proteins and genes that control CNS functions. These approaches have characterized many of the molecular actions of alcohol in relation to the behavioral manifestations of its use and abuse and have provided clues toward developing new pharmacologic strategies for the prevention and treatment of alcoholism.

Unlike other psychotropic drugs, alcohol does not act through a single receptor. Rather, it may interact with and alter the function of many different cellular components, including cell membranes, neurotransmitter receptors, intracellular signaling enzymes, and genes. As a result, alcohol may have diverse and profound effects on nerve cell function.

The chemical and structural nature of cell membranes render them readily permeable to alcohol. Thus, alcohol has access to and may directly perturb the function of proteins outside the cell, in the cell membrane, or within the cell. Alcohol can alter the fluidity and electrical properties of membranes; with long-term alcohol exposure, significant reorganization of membrane components is observed. Changes in membrane properties may, in turn, alter the shape, interactions, and functions of membrane proteins. In addition, alcohol may interact directly with proteins to disrupt their normal functions.

Primary protein targets of alcohol's actions are the ligand-gated ion channels that serve as receptors for GABA, glutamate, serotonin, and ATP. Many of the intoxicating properties of alcohol result from its effects on receptors that interact with GABA, the brain's major inhibitory neurotransmitter, and glutamate, the brain's major excitatory neurotransmitter. The combined actions of GABA and glutamate through their respective receptors produce short-term changes in membrane electrical potential, firing of nerve impulses, and release of many neurotransmitters. Alcohol stimulates GABA receptor function and inhibits glutamate receptor function, yielding potentially profound effects on these various nervous system activities.

One type of GABA receptor, the $GABA_A$ receptor, is widely distributed in brain tissues. However, alcohol sensitivity of $GABA_A$ receptors is observed only in certain brain regions, possibly as a result of variation in the different subunit combinations that make up $GABA_A$ receptors. Phosphorylation of $GABA_A$ receptors by PKC increases their sensitivity to alcohol's effects, as shown in cultured cells and studies of knockout mice that lack functional genes encoding this enzyme. Deletion of PKC in these animals abolished alcohol-induced enhancement of GABA-gated chloride flux and reduced alcohol-induced anesthesia. $GABA_A$ receptors also play a role in tolerance to alcohol's intoxicating properties: With chronic alcohol exposure, $GABA_A$ receptors become less responsive to alcohol stimulation, an effect that may result from changes in the expression of receptor subunits.

Like GABA receptors, glutamate receptors may be composed of different subunit combinations that vary in sensitivity to alcohol. For the NMDA subfamily of glutamate receptors, observed variations in receptor subunit combinations may explain variations in alcohol responsiveness of different brain regions. As for GABA receptors, PKC may play a role in alcohol's acute inhibitory actions on NMDA receptor functions. Possible effects of acute alcohol exposure on NMDA receptor function include interference with brain processes critical to the consolidation of new memories, suggesting a role for NMDA receptors in alcoholic blackouts and other alcohol-associated memory disorders. Chronic alcohol exposure increases numbers of NMDA receptors in brain tissues, an adaptive response that may compensate for alcohol-induced inhibition of NMDA receptor function. However, this increase in NMDA receptor expression also may contribute to the development of seizures during alcohol withdrawal and may tender neurons more vulnerable to excitotoxic cell death.

Other alcohol-sensitive ligand-gated ion channels include serotonin 5-HT_3 receptors and ATP receptors. Alcohol appears to enhance activities of 5-HT_3 receptors but suppresses activities of ATP receptors. The 5-HT_3 receptor has been implicated in the intoxicating and reinforcing properties of alcohol, and 5-HT_3 receptor antagonists can decrease craving for alcoholic beverages in humans. Although pharmacologic studies indicate that alcohol acts directly on these ligand-gated ion channels to alter their functions, the role of 5-HT_3 receptors and ATP receptors in intoxication and other responses to alcohol require further investigation.

Alcohol may produce intoxication and dependence in part through direct or indirect effects on opioid receptors. Treatment of cells with alcohol in vitro increases the expression of one type of opioid receptor, the delta opioid receptor. In addition, alcohol causes the release of opioids, such as enkephalins and endorphins, in the brain. Binding of opioids to delta opioid receptors promotes dopamine release in the nucleus accumbens, an effect that may contribute to the euphoric and other pleasant feelings experienced with intoxication. These brain activities have been implicated in the reinforcing properties of alcohol. The opioid receptor antagonist naltrexone is thought to block dopamine release and has proven therapeutic efficacy in reducing craving for alcohol.

Activities of PKC, another crucial participant in intracellular signaling reactions, are also influenced by acute and chronic alcohol exposure. With chronic alcohol exposure, observed increases in PKC isozymes may mediate several adaptive responses to alcohol, including increased levels of VACCs and enhancement of neurite outgrowth by neurotrophins. Alcohol-induced increases in VACCs are associated with increased neurotransmitter release, increased neuronal excitability, and development of alcohol withdrawal seizures, and calcium channel antagonists have been shown to reduce alcohol withdrawal convulsions in both humans and animals. Neurite outgrowth may contribute to alcohol-associated brain injury by disturbing the development and organization of the CNS. The extensive role of PKC in regulating diverse cellular functions, including the activity of various other membrane proteins as well as DNA transcription and protein synthesis, suggests that increases in PKC activity may contribute to many other alcohol-associated adaptive responses of the CNS.

Effects of alcohol on gene transcription and protein synthesis may be responsible for some of the more enduring alcohol-associated changes in nerve cell function. Numerous alcohol responsive genes have been identified, and some have been cloned and characterized. Further research to characterize alcohol-responsive genes will provide clues about persistent CNS changes associated with alcohol use.

Through its actions on many different cellular components and activities, alcohol produces a diverse array of immediate and long-term alterations in CNS function. Continued research to identify and characterize molecular targets and cellular processes affected by alcohol will help reveal the mechanisms behind alcohol-induced intoxication, tolerance, dependence, and withdrawal and will aid in the development of agents that can offset or alleviate the harmful consequences of alcohol use.

Chapter 44

Alcohol and Brain Impairments

Alcohol consumption can damage the nervous system, including the brain. Consequently, alcoholics and chronic heavy drinkers can suffer abnormalities in their mental functioning and changes in behaviors associated with brain impairment. (The term "alcoholism" as used in this chapter refers to the criteria for alcohol dependence defined in the American Psychological Association's *Diagnostic and Statistical Manual of Mental Disorders, Fourth Edition*). The neurological effects of alcohol can occur directly, because alcohol is a toxic substance, or they can occur indirectly, through damage to other body organs (for example, the liver) that subsequently interferes with the workings of nerve cells in the brain.

Images of the brain created with modern neuroradiological techniques, such as magnetic resonance imaging (MRI) and computed tomography (CT), generally show a relationship between prolonged alcohol consumption and changes in the brain's structure. For example, MRI and CT images have shown brain shrinkage and tissue damage (brain lesions) in some alcoholics. These changes can cause poor temperature regulation, muscle weakness, and alterations in sleep patterns.

Excerpted from "Impairments of Brain and Behavior: The Neurological Effects of Alcohol," by Marlene Oscar-Berman, Ph.D. Barbara Shagrin, Ph.D., Denise L. Evert, Ph.D., and Charles Epstein, Ph.D. in *Alcohol Health and Research World*, Winter 1997, Vol. 21, No, 1, p. 65(11). A complete copy of this publication may be ordered from the U.S. Government Printing Office. Call (202) 512-1800 for information on price and availability.

Common Effects of Alcohol on the Nervous System

Alcohol has effects on both major components of the nervous system—the central nervous system (the brain and the spinal cord) and the peripheral nervous system (the nerves in the rest of the body).

Alcohol can have a negative effect on certain neurological processes, such as temperature regulation, sleep, and coordination. For example, moderate amounts of alcohol lower body temperature. Severe intoxication in a cold environment may produce massive, life-threatening declines in temperature (hypothermia).

In addition to its effect on body temperature, alcohol interferes with normal sleep patterns. Relatively small doses of alcohol can cause early sedation or sleepiness, awaking during the night, and suppression of rapid-eye-movement (REM) sleep. REM sleep is the dreaming stage of sleep; when REM sleep occurs near wakefulness, it often produces vivid hallucinations.

Another prominent effect of chronic alcohol consumption is harm to the pan of the brain called the cerebellum, resulting mainly in the loss of muscular coordination. This damage appears as imbalance and staggering, although other problems also may occur.

A peripheral nervous system disorder commonly seen in alcoholics is numbness and weakness in the hands and feet (peripheral neuropathy). This condition is thought to be largely a consequence of malnutrition in severe alcoholics. One type of peripheral nerve damage known as Saturday night palsy can occur when an alcoholic puts pressure on vulnerable nerves in the arm while lying in an intoxicated stupor, leaving him or her unable to extend the wrist for days to weeks.

Abnormalities in Neuropsychological Functions

In addition to changes in temperature regulation, sleep, and coordination, alcoholism-related brain changes can cause abnormalities in mental functioning that are detectable using specialized neuropsychological tests. Behavioral neurologists and neuropsychologists use these sensitive tests to measure both the obvious and the subtle consequences of brain damage. Results of the tests often show changes in emotions and personality as well as impaired perception, learning, and memory (cognitive abilities) after damage to particular brain systems.

Korsakoff's Syndrome

One of the most severe consequences of long-term alcoholism on mental functioning is Korsakoff's syndrome (KS), a devastating memory disorder in which a person appears to forget the incidents of his or her daily life as soon as they occur. Because of this dramatic loss of short-term memory (also called anterograde amnesia), patients with KS virtually live in the past. For example, someone who developed KS in the 1960's might believe that the President of the United States is Dwight Eisenhower or John Kennedy. Some alcoholics may have a genetic component or predisposition to develop this amnesic condition: These patients may have an enzyme deficiency that prevents their bodies from using thiamine (a B vitamin) efficiently. This deficiency, coupled with a diet high in alcohol and low in thiamine (along with other nutrients), may lead to brain damage causing the amnesia.

Although KS destroys short-term memory, it typically spares most long-term memories (memories formed or knowledge gained before the

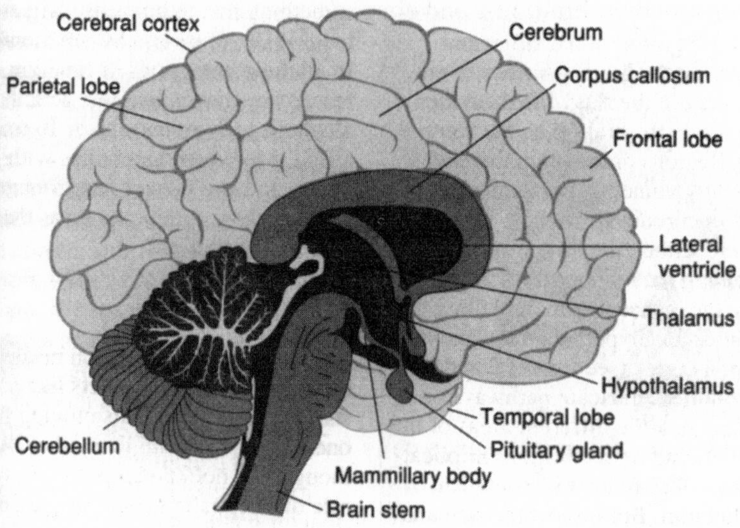

Figure 44.1. *Schematic of a lengthwise cross-section through the human brain. Brain structures that most frequently have been implicated in alcohol-related neurological disorders include parts of the diencephalon (the mammillary bodies of the hypothalamus and the dorsomedial nucleus within the thalamus), the cerebral cortex, and several central neurotrasmitter (nerve cell communication) systems.*

onset of prolonged heavy drinking). Thus, overall intelligence, as measured by standardized IQ tests, does not necessarily deteriorate, because the types of information and abilities tapped by these tests usually involve long-term memory.

Another disorder, Wernicke's encephalopathy, frequently occurs with KS, leading to a diagnosis in the patient of Wernicke-Korsakoff syndrome. Patients with Wernicke's encephalopathy, exhibit confusion, uncoordinated gait, and abnormal eye movements. Like KS, Wernicke's encephalopathy is thought to be caused by a thiamine deficiency.

Other Neuropsychological Problems

Within the past 25 years, clinical and experimental observations of patients with and without KS have revealed many other neuropsychological dysfunctions associated with alcoholism. Alcoholics demonstrate poor attention to what is going on around them; need extra time to process visual information; have difficulty with abstraction, problem-solving, and learning new materials; exhibit emotional abnormalities and disinhibitions; and show reduced visuospatial abilities (the capacity to deal with objects in two-dimensional or three-dimensional space). The once-common view that alcoholics without Korsakoff's syndrome are cognitively intact has been abandoned in light of accumulating evidence that cognitive impairments (and associated changes in brain structure) can occur in alcoholics who do not exhibit obvious clinical signs of anterograde amnesia.

Alcoholism-Related Brain Damage and Associated Neuropsychological Changes

The type and extent of structural damage to brain tissue can be determined by autopsy (post mortem) examination of the brain's components and individual nerve cells (neuropathological evidence). In addition, neuroradiological techniques, such as MRI and CT scans, allow the brain to be viewed inside the skull of a living person. Other neuroimaging techniques (functional neuroimaging) measure active brain functioning. Functional neuroimaging can reveal changes in the blood flow in and around the brain, brain metabolism, and brain electrical activity generated by nerve impulses (neurophysiological measures). One type of neurophysiological measure, event-related potentials (ERPs), consists of brain waves recorded from scalp electrodes while a person is presented with specific pieces of information or stimuli.

Scientists use computers to translate the information obtained from ERPs and other functional neuroimaging measures into meaningful pictures that, in turn, make it possible to view brain functioning while a person is thinking or performing a task.

When applied to alcohol research, neuropathological and imaging techniques have helped to provide cumulative evidence of brain abnormalities in alcoholics, such as atrophy of nerve cells (neurons) and brain shrinkage. Brain shrinkage appears as abnormal widening of the grooves (sulci) and fissures on the brain's surface or enlargement of the fluid-filled cavities deep inside the brain (the ventricles). Regions of the brain that are especially vulnerable to damage after years of chronic alcoholism include the cerebellum, the limbic system (including the hippocampus and amygdala), the diencephalon (including the thalamus and hypothalamus), and the cerebral cortex.

Countless intricate pathways of neurons link the different areas of the brain, including the regions implicated in alcohol-related neurological dysfunction. Because of the size and complexity of this network, the consequences of damage to one structure or system often can resemble the consequences of damage to another.

Neurotransmitters and Alcoholism

At the cellular level, alcohol appears to affect brain function in a variety of ways. For example, alcohol can alter the action of the chemicals that allow neurons to communicate (neurotransmitters). Specialized proteins on the surface of neurons, known as receptors, recognize neurotransmitters and initiate the cell's response. Neurotransmitters and receptors cluster where nerve cells come into close contact; these contacts are called synapses. Some neurotransmitters stimulate (excite) a response from the neurons that receive them; others inhibit neuronal response. Over periods of days and weeks, the levels of receptors change in response to chemical and environmental influences (for example, drugs and synaptic activity) on the neurons. Genes in the neuron's DNA are turned on or off, increasing or decreasing the synthesis of receptors. Over time, drugs that excite a given receptor generally lead to a reduction in (down-regulate) the numbers or activity of that receptor type. Drugs that inhibit a receptor eventually tend to lead to an increase in (up-regulate) that type of receptor. Up- and down-regulation are means by which the nervous system maintains a functional balance of neurotransmitters and receptors; when imbalances occur, effects can include seizures, sedation, depression, agitation, and other mood and behavioral disorders.

Glutamate

The major excitatory neurotransmitter in the human brain is glutamate, an amino acid. Glutamate has a fundamental role in a cellular adaptation called long-term potentiation, which is a persistent increase in the efficiency of a neuron's response to a neurotransmitter. Long-term potentiation may be an important mechanism in learning and memory.

Extremely small amounts of alcohol have been shown to interfere with glutamate action. This interference could affect multiple brain functions, including memory, and it may account for the short-lived condition referred to as "alcoholic blackout." Because of its inhibitory effect on glutamate, chronic consumption of alcohol leads to up-regulation of glutamate receptor sites in the hippocampus, an area that is crucial to memory and often involved in epileptic seizures. During alcohol withdrawal, glutamate receptors that have adapted to the continual presence of alcohol may become overactive. Glutamate overactivity has been linked repeatedly to cell death in situations ranging from strokes to seizures. Deficiencies of thiamine and magnesium, which are common in alcoholics as a result of malnutrition, may contribute to this potentially destructive overactivity.

GABA

Gamma-aminobutyric acid (GABA) is the major inhibitory neurotransmitter in the central nervous system. Evidence suggests that alcohol initially potentiates GABA effects; in other words, it increases inhibition, and often the brain becomes mildly sedated. But over time, chronic alcohol consumption reduces the number of GABA receptors through the process of down-regulation. When alcohol is eventually withdrawn, the loss of its inhibitory effects, combined with a deficiency of GABA receptors, may contribute to overexcitation throughout the brain. This effect, in turn, can contribute to withdrawal seizures within 1 or 2 days.

Other Neurotransmitters

Alcohol directly stimulates release of the neurotransmitter serotonin as well as natural substances related to opioids (endorphins) that may contribute to the "high" of intoxication. Serotonin helps regulate functions such as food and water intake, sexual response, and aggression. Changes in other neurotransmitters, such as acetylcholine (which underlies key cardiovascular mechanisms, including dilation of blood vessels) and the catecholamines (the decreased transmission of which has been linked to the memory deficits of patients with KS), have been less consistently observed.

Alcohol disrupts neuron activity in various other ways, For example, over several weeks, alcohol reduces the level of nerve growth factors, proteins important for cellular adaptation and survival. In addition, alcohol may cause long-term adaptive changes in membrane lipids.

Vulnerabilities to the Neurological Effects of Alcoholism

Alcoholism is a multidimensional disorder, and no simple answers exist to questions such as: "What are the neurological consequences of alcoholism?"; "What makes alcoholism affect different people in different ways?"; or even "What causes someone to become an alcoholic in the first place?" Widespread individual differences occur in the manifestation of alcoholism. For example, according to one estimate, 50 to 85 percent of non-KS alcoholics exhibit signs of cognitive decline. Thus, anywhere from 15 to 50 percent of such alcoholics may not exhibit any obvious signs of cognitive impairment. In general, the greater the consumption of alcohol, the worse the performance on cognitive tasks. However, among those alcoholics who exhibit neurological problems, researchers have found that measures of previous alcohol consumption (for example, duration, frequency, and quantity consumed) do not correlate consistently with the degree of neuropsychological dysfunction. This finding suggests that variables other than the presumed direct neurotoxic effects of alcohol may play a role in determining alcohol-related cognitive decline. In response to the variability in the consequences of alcoholism, researchers have looked for common elements that might help explain why certain alcoholics develop specific neurological symptoms or mental changes. Factors that may influence the neurological consequences of alcoholism include coexisting health problems, such as malnutrition and liver disease; the age at which problem drinking begins; the gender of the alcoholic; and a family history of alcoholism.

Common Alcohol-Related Medical Problems

Two common health problems occurring with alcoholism are vitamin deficiency and liver disease, both of which can result in neurological disorders. As mentioned previously, prolonged drinking with improper diet and associated malnutrition can lead to thiamine deficiency, a possible factor in KS-related brain damage. Several investigators have stressed the idea that damage in the diencephalon of KS patients is caused by thiamine deficiency, whereas cortical abnormalities, most notably in the frontal lobes, are caused by alcohol neurotoxicity or other conditions frequently associated with alcoholism (for example, liver disease or head trauma).

Thiamine Deficiency

Researchers differ in their explanations of how and why particular neuropsychological deficits are displayed in alcoholics. One theory proposes that alcoholics may fall into subgroups distinguished by whether their brains are vulnerable to the direct neurotoxic effects of alcohol, to thiamine deficiency, or to both factors. According to this viewpoint, alcoholics who are susceptible to alcohol toxicity alone may develop permanent or transient cognitive deficits associated with cortical shrinkage. Those alcoholics who are susceptible to thiamine deficiency alone will develop a mild or short-lived KS state with anterograde amnesia as a salient feature. Alcoholics who suffer from a combination of alcohol neurotoxicity and thiamine deficiency (have dual vulnerability) will experience widespread damage to large regions of the cerebral cortex as well as to structures deep within the brain. These people will exhibit severe anterograde amnesia as well as other cognitive impairments.

Liver Disease

Alcohol-related liver disease also contributes to neurological disturbances associated with heavy drinking. The risk of alcoholic liver damage depends on factors such as the drinker's nutrition, gender, and quantity and pattern of alcohol consumption. Recent research has focused on biological factors involved in protecting liver cells during metabolism; in some alcoholics, these protective mechanisms appear to be impaired. One condition associated with advanced liver disease, including alcoholic liver disease, is hepatic encephalopathy (also called portal-systemic encephalopathy—PSE). PSE is a progressive metabolic liver disorder that affects intellectual functioning. Alcoholics with PSE have livers so damaged by cirrhosis that the flow of venous blood into the liver is obstructed, allowing toxic substances and metabolic by-products to enter the bloodstream. These toxins, which can include ammonia and manganese, circulate to the brain, where they interfere with the actions of neurotransmitters. The effects of PSE can be reversed to some extent with liver transplantation.

Other Influences on Alcohol-Related Brain Injury

Age

When researchers first began to study the effects of alcohol on the brain, they observed structural brain changes in alcoholics similar to those seen in nonalcoholic subjects as a result of normal chronological aging. These observations gave rise to the "premature aging hypothesis." Two versions of the hypothesis exist, each with different propositions concerning the period in an alcoholic's life during which premature aging begins. According to the accelerated aging version of the hypothesis, aging starts to accelerate at whatever age problem drinking begins. This version predicts that young alcoholics will become old before their time and that neuropsychological and brain changes in alcoholics will mimic those found in chronologically older nonalcoholics. According to the increased vulnerability version of the premature aging hypothesis, vulnerability to alcohol-related brain damage is hastened only in people over age 50, in whom the normal manifestations of aging already have begun. This version suggests that because of the increased vulnerability of their brains to alcohol-related damage, older alcoholics will suffer more age-related symptoms and impairment than their nonalcoholic peers and younger alcoholics.

Regardless of alcohol's role in aging, older alcoholics, by virtue of their chronological age, may be particularly susceptible to the effects of alcohol. For example, elderly alcoholics have an increased risk of accidents, deleterious side effects, and overt toxicity resulting from alcohol intake. Treatment for medical conditions common among the elderly (for example, chronic pain and heart disease) also may increase alcohol-related problems in this group. For example, alcohol-medication interactions can have neuropsychological consequences ranging from drowsiness to disorientation; physical effects can include hemorrhage, malnutrition, and liver damage, which also can lead to neuropsychological problems.

Gender

Controversy exists over whether and to what extent chronic alcoholism affects women's brains differently from men's brains. Results of studies using the same techniques to measure brain structure and function in men and women have been inconsistent. However, researchers have found evidence of similar degrees of brain shrinkage and impairment on tests of mental functioning in men and women, even though the women participating in the study had shorter drinking histories than the men. Such evidence has led investigators to hypothesize that women's brains may differ from men's brains in their susceptibility to alcohol-related damage.

Family History

Researchers have found that adolescent and adult children of alcoholics who do not drink alcohol nevertheless show deficits in neuropsychological functioning. Evidence suggests that children of alcoholics have difficulty regulating their own behavior, organizing and remembering information, and learning tasks that involve two- and three dimensional space. In other studies, abnormal brain electrical activity, measured as a reduced peak in amplitude in one of the electrical components of the ERP (the P300 wave), has been observed in nondrinking sons of alcoholics who were performing cognitive tasks. Because the electrophysiological abnormalities in the children of alcoholics are similar to those displayed by abstinent alcoholics, researchers have inferred that brain waves may provide an observable marker for potential alcoholism in children of alcoholics even before the initiation of drinking behavior.

Family history of alcoholism has been associated with other notable results. In one study, intoxicated alcoholics, both with and without a family history of alcoholism, had problems on cognitive tests sensitive to temporal lobe functions (for example, memory). On tests sensitive to frontal lobe functions (for example, planning and judgment) however, only alcoholics with a positive family history of alcoholism performed poorly.

Recovery and Treatment

Studies suggest that slow recovery of cognitive functioning occurs in alcoholics who remain abstinent for at least 4 weeks, and certain indicators of impairment (CT and MRI images and brain glucose metabolism) have been shown to improve with prolonged abstinence. Although numerous pharmacological treatments have been given to alcoholics to improve neuropsychological functioning, none has proved entirely successful. Researchers have not established whether recovery is complete in most alcoholics (or what constitutes complete recovery), and they have not yet determined the typical length of the recovery period. With abstinence, some alcoholics show a slow reversal of neuropsychological impairment. Other alcoholics, however, display apparently irreversible deficits on specific tasks of cognitive function.

For example, in a study of cognitive recovery over a 14-month period, alcoholics who remained abstinent performed better than relapsers, but abstainers did not perform as well as nonalcoholic control subjects. In another study, drinkers with a positive family history of alcoholism who had been abstinent for up to 4 months showed poorer performance on tests of cognition than either drinkers with a negative family history of alcoholism or abstainers with a positive family history. However, alcoholics both with and without a positive family history of alcoholism showed significant improvement with abstinence. Hence, a positive family history of alcoholism did not impede recovery of cognitive function among abstinent alcoholics. In most studies of neuropsychological deficits, length of abstinence typically has approximated 4 weeks. It is possible that past research may have overestimated permanent neuropsychological deficits related to chronic alcoholism by examining alcoholics whose mental functioning continued to improve following the studies' conclusion.

Summary and Conclusions

Several hypotheses have been proposed to explain the diversity of neuropsychological abnormalities shown by chronic alcoholics: (1) In patients with KS, alcoholism can selectively interfere with short-term memory, emotion, and other functions associated with damage to limbic system and diencephalic structures; and (2) alcoholics can also suffer diffuse cortical damage that affects the functioning of both brain hemispheres (for example, abstracting and problem-solving abilities, poor attention, disinhibition, and perseverative responding). No definite relationships have been established, however, between damage to specific cortical regions and concurrent cognitive impairments, although findings from neuroimaging and neuropathology studies point to increased susceptibility of frontal brain systems.

Factors that contribute to differences among people in the neurological consequences of alcoholism are numerous and include nutritional deficiencies, liver disease, the age and gender of the drinker, and family history of alcoholism. The notion that neurological disorders result from the prolonged consumption of alcohol by certain vulnerable alcoholics is a plausible hypothesis, but identifying what makes certain alcoholics "vulnerable" remains a problem for further investigation.

Chapter 45

Structural Brain Alterations Associated with Alcoholism

The neuroimaging techniques of computed tomography (CT) and magnetic resonance imaging (MRI) provide noninvasive ways to examine the structure of the living brain. Using these techniques, investigators have shown that many people with histories of heavy alcohol consumption have brain structures that differ markedly from people without such histories. These structural changes may affect the higher brain functions of heavy drinkers, such as short-term memory and problem-solving.

Structural Brain Changes in Alcoholism

Early Pathological Studies

Pathological studies were the first to demonstrate an association between heavy alcohol consumption and structural changes in the brain. In contrast to CT and MRI studies, pathological studies examine the brain after death (post mortem). Early studies of patients with histories of heavy alcohol consumption showed a generalized shrinkage of the brain, sometimes more pronounced in the frontal lobes. Post mortem studies measuring the amount of different tissue types on individual slices of the brain showed that of the two primary types of

---

Excerpted from "Structural Brain Alterations Associated with Alcoholism," by Margaret J. Rosenbloom, Adolf Pfefferbaum, and Edith V. Sullivan, in *Alcohol Health and Research World*, Fall 1995, Vol. 19, No, 4, p. 266(7). A complete copy of this publication may be ordered from the U.S. Government Printing Office. Call (202) 512-1800 for information on price and availability.

brain tissue, the fiber-containing white matter, but not the gray matter (which is made up mainly of nerve cell bodies), is reduced in volume in alcoholics. Thinning of the corpus callosum, the bundle of white-matter fibers connecting the left and right cerebral hemispheres, is an example of white-matter reduction in alcoholics. Although post mortem studies have not shown a general reduction in gray-matter volume, some microscopic post mortem research has demonstrated reductions in the size of individual gray-matter cells, loss of cells, and less branching of fibers off the cells in some brain areas.

Subjects used in pathological studies who had had specific neurological illnesses frequently associated with excessive alcohol use, such as Korsakoff syndrome (a condition involving the inability to remember new information), also showed reduced size or other abnormalities in specific brain structures beneath the cortex (subcortical structures) that are involved in memory and motor activities. These structures include the mammillary bodies, the thalamus, and the cerebellar vermis, which lies between the two cerebellar hemispheres. Other pathological studies also have demonstrated a loss of cell bodies as well as a reduction in size of the hippocampus, a part of the brain that plays an important role in memory.

Structural Changes Seen through Imaging

Brain structures measured post mortem do not necessarily reflect how those structures appeared when the person was still alive. Investigators have therefore used in vivo imaging techniques—first CT and more recently MRI—to examine the brain in living subjects. CT technology yields images showing vertical slices of the brain as if they were cut from the bottom to the top (in an axial plane) and in which the cerebrospinal fluid (CSF) appears dark and the tissue appears light. In contrast, magnetic resonance images of the brain can be obtained from different angles, allowing axial views (like CT) as well as views from side to side and back to front. Magnetic resonance images discriminate not only between CSF and tissue but also between white and gray matter. Another advantage of MRI is that images can be acquired in three dimensions and then sliced to display specific internal brain structures or processed to display the brain's exterior surface. Images of both internal slices and the external surface can be created from any angle.

New advances in image processing have enabled magnetic resonance brain images of each member of a study group to be adjusted to the same scale and angle and then combined to form a composite, or "average," brain for that group. This technique can be used, for example, to visually compare a group of healthy men with a group of alcoholic men and to identify brain areas that differ between the two groups. Areas appearing to be different may then be measured separately on each subject's brain image and statistically compared to determine whether the variation is significant.

Accounting for Individual Difference

Both CT and MRI studies have shown that, on average, patients who meet the criteria for alcohol dependence show larger volumes of CSF and smaller volumes of brain tissue when measured against control groups of healthy people who abstain or are very light social drinkers. Individual differences do exist, however, and some alcoholics may be indistinguishable from many control subjects. In fact, some alcoholic subjects may even have larger brain-tissue volumes than do some control subjects. Only by testing many subjects and making statistical comparisons that take individual variability into account can the particular differences attributable to the disease be identified.

Findings Using CT and MRI

CT studies have shown that CSF-filled spaces in the middle and lower parts of the brain (the lateral and third ventricles) are often enlarged in chronic alcoholics, as are the fissures (sulci) located on the surface of both the brain (the cerebrum) and the cerebellum, or "little brain," which lies at the back of and below the cerebrum. The enlargement of CSF-filled spaces has been viewed as evidence of shrinkage or atrophy of the adjacent brain tissue. MRI technology has confirmed findings seen with CT. In addition, MRI has shown that cortical volumes of both gray and white matter are reduced in alcoholics and has confirmed structural changes previously only seen in post mortem studies. These alterations include reduced volumes of sections of the brain involved with muscle control, balance, and coordination, such as the cerebellar hemispheres and the cerebellar vermis. Researchers also have detected reductions in subcortical structures involved in memory, such as the front (anterior) portion of the hippocampus and the mammillary bodies. In previous pathological studies, damage to the mam millary bodies has been found typically in alcoholic patients with severe memory loss associated with Korsakoff syndrome. In vivo MRI studies, however, have demonstrated that these structures are compromised even in alcoholic patients who do not exhibit severe memory problems. Finally, MRI recently has confirmed pathological studies showing reduced corpus callosum size in alcoholics.

Summary

CT and MRI observations of the brains of chronic alcoholics indicate widespread loss of brain tissue. Older men are more vulnerable to the toxic effects of alcohol on the brain, particularly in the frontal lobes, than are younger men, and women may be more vulnerable than men, although systematic studies of women are only beginning. Withdrawal seizures, nutritional deficiencies, and other medical conditions associated with alcoholism appear to exacerbate some of these structural brain changes. Detailed imaging of the brain has revealed size and other deficits in a number of specific structures deep in the brain (for example, the mammillary bodies, the hippocampus, and the corpus callosum). Deficits in the size of certain brain structures are found even in alcoholics without extreme symptoms, such as Korsakoff syndrome, to which such structural loss previously had been linked. Although researchers have not linked changes throughout the cortex and in the hippocampus to cognitive behavioral function using current testing strategies, structural deficits in other areas (the cerebellum) are related to difficulties with balance. Likewise, deficits in the thalamus are correlated with an impaired sense of smell.

Studies of alcoholic patients conducted over the course of their illnesses have indicated that after relatively brief periods of abstinence (for example, 4 weeks), certain areas of the brain will recover. Longer periods of abstinence (for example, more than 3 months) are associated with additional recovery in brain structures (reduction of third-ventricle volume). White matter appears to be especially vulnerable to damage incurred by the resumption of drinking after a period of abstinence. Although investigators do not know whether recovery of gray-matter volume stemming from abstinence signals restoration of cognitive function, this relationship may yet be documented.

Chapter 46

Alcohol-Induced Sleepiness

What Is Sleepiness

Like hunger and thirst, sleepiness is considered a basic physiological drive state. It reflects the organism's need or pressure for sleep. Like other physiological drive states, the level of sleepiness is difficult to assess. Despite a general tendency toward increasing sleepiness after sleep loss, most sleep deprivation studies find some inconsistencies in the subjects' personal assessment of how sleepy they are.

Research has shown that people's ability to accurately judge their degree of sleepiness depends on several factors, such as internal point of reference, environmental demands, and time of day. For example, a person not getting enough sleep for an extended period will lose the internal reference to the experience of full alertness and therefore may underestimate his or her level of sleepiness. Similarly, people often judge their level of sleepiness to be higher in boring, nonstimulating situations in which environmental demands to stay alert or to pay attention are reduced. Finally, most people experience a circadian fluctuation with increased sleepiness over the midday and increased alertness in the early evening.

Excerpted from "Alcohol-Induced Sleepiness and Memory Function," by Thomas Roth, Ph.D., and Timothy Roehrs, Ph.D., in *Alcohol Health and Research World*, Fall 1995, Vol. 19, No, 2, p. 130(8). A complete copy of this publication may be ordered from the U.S. Government Printing Office. Call (202) 512-1800 for information on price and availability.

To assess sleepiness or alertness or the sedative effects of drugs, such as alcohol, scientists have asked people to self-rate their sleepiness or have used standard laboratory tests of performance. However, for the reasons stated above, self-ratings of sleepiness or sedative drug effects may be inaccurate. Similarly, performance tests sometimes are insensitive to the effects of small doses of sedative drugs or low breath alcohol concentrations.

A method to assess sleepiness objectively has been developed, however. This method conceptually is based on an observation originating in the 19th century that as sleep loss progresses over time, people increasingly experience uncontrollable brief naps, or microsleeps. In the Multiple Sleep Latency Test (MSLT), researchers quantify sleepiness by giving subjects repeated opportunities to fall asleep. Typically, four to five tests are conducted at 2-hour intervals in a sleep-conducive environment. Physiological recordings of the subject's brain waves and eye movements determine the exact moment of sleep onset. The time between lying down and sleep onset (the latency) is a measure of the subject's level of sleepiness.

People with a high degree of sleepiness (for example, because they are totally deprived of sleep, have had insufficient sleep relative to their biological needs, or are suffering from sleep disorders) fall asleep rapidly when given the opportunity to sleep. These people have a short latency on the MSLT. For example, limiting sleeping time by limiting time-in-bed (TIB) to 5 hours for several consecutive nights progressively decreases the subjects' sleep latency over the test days. In people with longer TIBs or people who are treated successfully for a sleep disorder, sleep latency increases on the MSLT (they are more alert).

The MSLT also can measure the effects of stimulant and depressant drugs on sleepiness. Stimulant drugs increase and depressant drugs decrease sleep latency in a dose-dependent manner. For example, increasing doses of depressant drugs lead to systematic increases in sleepiness as measured by the MSLT. Thus, the reliability and validity of the MSLT have been established under different experimental conditions.

Sleepiness and Memory Impairment

Memory development encompasses several processes, or phases, that occur when information is stored in the brain. One old and rather simplistic—but in this context, sufficient—model of memory processing distinguishes three phases of memory development. The first phase is the stimulus registration or acquisition phase, in which information is entered into short-term memory. The second phase is the consolidation of information from short-term into long-term memory (memory for more than 30 seconds). The third phase includes the retrieval of information from long-term memory.

Sleepiness can interfere with all three phases of memory development. In 1974 researchers assessed sleepiness effects on the acquisition phase by studying sleep-deprived subjects who experienced uncontrollable microsleeps (sleep episodes of less than 15 seconds). During microsleeps, the subjects did not respond to a given stimulus, suggesting that they did not register the stimulus.

Other studies found that the process of sleep onset or increasing sleepiness also disrupts memory consolidation. In a study subjects were presented with a stimulus at 1-minute intervals as they were falling asleep. Even when stimulus registration was ascertained, the subjects' memory when they were awakened 10 minutes later decreased as the stimulus occurred closer to sleep onset. Other studies found a general slowing of cognitive functions as a consequence of sleep loss. This may reflect a reduced information consolidation or impaired retrieval of information from long-term memory.

Alcohol-Induced Sedation and Memory Impairment

Alcohol's Sedative Effects

Laboratory studies evaluating alcohol's stimulating and sedative effects have found a biphasic response by the test subjects. At low alcohol doses and while the blood alcohol concentration (BAC) is ascending, alcohol's stimulating effects prevail. In contrast, at high alcohol doses and while the BAC is descending, alcohol primarily has sedative effects. Recently, researchers confirmed the biphasic effects of alcohol using the MSLT method. An alerting effect (increased sleep latency) was found over the first hour during the ascending phase of the BAC curve and at peak alcohol concentration; subsequently, a sedating effect (decreased latency) was observed.

Other studies have focused on alcohol's sedative effects throughout the descending phase of the BAC curve and beyond. Alcohol's sedative effects as measured by the MSLT are dose dependent. With increasing amounts of alcohol (the doses are equivalent to two to six beers), sleep latency decreases drastically, indicating an increasing sedative effect. Furthermore, sedation continues for at least 2 hours after the BAC has returned to 0.

Alcohol's Memory-Impairing Effects

Alcohol's amnestic effects have been studied extensively. Researchers reported that the degree of amnesia increased with larger doses of alcohol. Most studies report that alcohol impairs the acquisition of new information but does not affect the retrieval of previously memorized information.. The acquisition impairment occurs both at the attention phase and at the consolidation phase of memory processing. This amnestic effect has been described as a failure to process information "deeply" or as a "slowing of the processing rate." Alcohol affects several memory systems. Semantic memory and episodic memory clearly are altered. In addition, there are indications that perceptual memory is impaired.

The Link between Alcohol-Induced Sedation and Amnesia

So far, no studies have established the correlation between alcohol's sedative and amnestic effects by simultaneously assessing memory impairment and objective sleepiness (for example, with the MSLT). However, several studies provide indirect evidence for such a correlation.

Researchers simultaneously studied alcohol's sedative and performance-disruptive effects. The subjects received 0.75 gram of alcohol per kilogram of body weight. The sedative effects of this alcohol dose were measured by the MSLT. Performance-disruptive effects were assessed in two ways: (1) with a divided attention task, in which subjects tracked a moving target on a video screen while simultaneously responding to other stimuli appearing on the screen, and (2) with an auditory vigilance task, in which subjects detected long tones against the background of shorter tones. The subjects responded more slowly on both tasks but did not omit any responses, suggesting that alcohol leads to the cognitive slowing described in the sleep loss literature. Subjects with a higher degree of sleepiness tended to show a higher degree of performance impairment. The alcohol effects observed on a divided attention task or an auditory vigilance task likely predict a memory-impairing effect. This is suggested by studies of the sedative effects of different benzodiazepines that included divided attention and auditory vigilance tasks as well as memory tasks.

Researchers also have measured alcohol-induced memory impairment and self-rated sleepiness. One study found comparable dose dependence for both measures: The increase in memory impairment after larger alcohol doses was paralleled by a similar increase in sedation.

The researchers obtained similar results when they analyzed the effects of the benzodiazepine triazolam. Other studies, in contrast, suggest that alcohol's amnestic and sedative effects are independent of each other. Some of the inconsistencies among the studies may be due to the relatively unreliable self-reports used to assess sedation. Therefore, studies objectively measuring alcohol-induced sedation and concurrently assessing alcohol's amnestic effects are needed to resolve these discrepancies.

Preexisting Sleepiness and Alcohol-Induced Performance Impairment

Another strategy to establish a link between sleepiness and performance impairment—and, by inference, memory impairment—is to first manipulate subjects' level of sleepiness by reducing or extending their TIB for one or more nights. The subjects then receive alcohol, and alcohol's sedative and performance-disruptive effects are assessed.

Reducing TIB increases the level of sleepiness the following day; the increased sleepiness enhances the sedative and performance-disruptive effects of alcohol. For example, an alcohol dose of 0.4 gram per kilogram of body weight has a lower sedative effect than an alcohol dose of 0.8 gram per kilogram of body weight if all subjects have had the same TIB the previous night. However, if subjects receiving the low alcohol dose have had only 5 hours TIB for 5 consecutive days and subjects receiving the high alcohol dose have had 8 hours TIB, both alcohol doses have the same sedative effect.

In a similar experiment, simulated driving and psychomotor performance were assessed in subjects who received an alcohol dose of 0.6 gram per kilogram of body weight producing breath ethanol concentrations of 50 milligram-percent (half the legal intoxication level in most States) and who had either 8 or 4 hours TIB. Subjects with 4 hours TIB exhibited significantly greater impairment than subjects with 8 hours TIB. The increased alcohol effect was not due to differences in alcohol metabolism after reduced TIB, because breath alcohol levels were not affected by the TIB manipulation.

In contrast, longer TIB reduces the level of sleepiness (increases alertness) and leads to an attenuation of some of alcohol's effects. Subjects receiving an alcohol dose of 0.75 gram per kilogram of body weight after 8 hours TIB exhibited sedation and performance impairment, compared with subjects receiving a placebo after 8 hours TIB. However, after 7 nights of 10 hours TIB, the subjects experienced no effects from the same alcohol dose. Again, breath alcohol levels did not change as a result of the TIB manipulation.

Impact of Alertness-Enhancing Measures

Alcohol's sedative and performance-disruptive effects can be attenuated by enhancing the basal level of alertness after alcohol consumption, for example, with daytime naps. Researchers assessed the effects of a 0.5 gram per kilogram of body weight alcohol dose after the subjects did or did not have a 60-minute nap. The nap completely reversed the sedative effect and attenuated the performance-disruptive effects of the alcohol.

Another study examined the capacity of a 60-minute nap to reverse the sedative and performance-disruptive effects of alcohol, a benzodiazepine, and an antihistamine. The effectiveness of the nap to reverse the sedative effects of the drugs tested was inversely related to the extent of sedation initially produced by the drugs. For example, the benzodiazepine had the strongest sedative effect, which was least reversible by the nap. Alcohol, in contrast, had the smallest sedative effect. This effect was almost completely reversed by the nap.

Mechanisms of Alcohol-Induced Sedation and Amnesia

Alcohol affects some neurotransmitter systems in the same way that sedative drugs do. For example, alcohol facilitates GABA-mediated inhibition (acts as a GABA agonist) and reduces the release of acetylcholine (acts as an acetylcholine antagonist). Consequently, alcohol could mimic the actions of other sedative drugs. Alcohol additionally affects two other neurotransmitters that regulate sleep and wakefulness. One is serotonin, a neuromodulator of sleep; the other is glutamate, an excitatory neurotransmitter promoting wakefulness. Interaction with these neurotransmitter systems may contribute to alcohol's sedative effects.

Conclusions and Implications

Independent experiments have shown that alcohol causes memory impairment and that alcohol causes sedation. This chapter has reviewed information suggesting that the two effects may be linked, that is, that alcohol's amnestic effects are related to its sedative effects. Evidence supporting this hypothesis comes from sleep deprivation studies in healthy people, studies of patients with sleep disorders, studies of drugs with sedative effects, and studies of the interaction between alcohol's sedative and performance-disruptive effects.

From a clinical standpoint, the interaction between alcohol's sedative and amnestic effects would imply that alcohol consumption combined with any condition or drug producing sleepiness could increase the risk for alcohol-induced memory impairment. For example, subgroups of the general population are known to be sleepier than average. People who shift their sleep schedule frequently (for example, night workers or shift workers) are much sleepier than are people with a regular nighttime sleep schedule. Older people, who experience more fragmented sleep and who are more likely to have undetected sleep disorders, are sleepier than are younger people. In these risk groups, lower alcohol doses than predicted could induce memory impairment. Younger people who periodically sleep less (for example, when studying for exams) similarly may experience memory problems after consuming alcohol in amounts they usually tolerate.

In addition, drugs with sedative effects could lead to amnesia when combined with alcohol, even at doses normally considered safe. Benzodiazepines, which often are used for patients undergoing alcoholism treatment, could contribute to amnesia if the patients relapse. A brief report in the late 1980's described three clinical cases of global amnesia (total amnesia for recent events) associated with the concurrent use of the benzodiazepine triazolam and alcohol. Many over-the-counter cold medications and many antidepressants have anticholinergic and/or antihistaminic ingredients that could contribute to amnesia after alcohol consumption, even in social drinkers. In addition, recovering alcoholics with coexisting depression often are treated with antidepressants. If a relapse occurs, the sedating side effects of these medications could increase the risk for amnesia.

Chapter 47

Alcoholism and Memory Function

The development of modern imaging techniques makes it possible to examine the brains of subjects who are at different stages of alcoholism and whose medical and mental status can be ascertained at the time of imaging. Thus it is possible to examine directly the relationship between brain abnormalities and cognitive impairment and to screen patients carefully for other medical conditions that may contribute to such impairment.

This chapter summarizes research on memory deficits in alcoholics, emphasizing evidence obtained using brain imaging methods. Recent neurological theories about human memory are outlined, and relevant evidence is presented from brain imaging studies of alcoholics in which damage to specific brain structures is linked to particular aspects of memory performance.

Brain Imaging

The past two decades have witnessed the development of increasingly refined techniques for viewing the living brain. Computed tomography (CT) uses rotating x-ray beams to measure differences in tissue density across thin sections of brain tissue. CT provides excellent images of fluid-filled spaces in the brain, enabling researchers

---

Excerpted from "When Alcoholism Affects Memory Functions," by Terry L. Jernigan, Ph.D. and Arne L. Ostergaard, Ph.D., in *Alcohol Health and Research World*, Fall 1995, Vol. 19, No, 2, p. 104(4). A complete copy of this publication may be ordered from the U.S. Government Printing Office. Call (202) 512-1800 for information on price and availability.

to determine the overall degree of brain tissue shrinkage associated with alcoholism or other disorders. Although CT is more sensitive to gradations of tissue density than a conventional skull X-ray, it does not distinguish clearly between white and gray matter. Therefore it cannot delineate individual anatomical structures within the brain.

Increased size of fluid-filled brain structures, such as the cerebral ventricles and cortical sulci, is evidence of brain degeneration. However, this finding alone reveals little about the specific brain structures that are affected by this degeneration. The size of individual brain structures can be determined using magnetic resonance imaging (MRI). In MRI, the patient is placed in a chamber and exposed to radio waves in the presence of a powerful magnetic field. Different types of tissue produce different energy signals in response to this procedure. MRI scanners translate the signals into three-dimensional images that depict specific anatomical structures in fine detail. MRI is therefore a very sensitive tool for detecting and localizing small abnormalities of brain tissue. Measurements obtained from MRI images of patients can then be compared to those from normal controls.

Alcohol and Memory

One of the most common forms of severe amnesia associated with alcohol abuse is Wernicke-Korsakoff syndrome. The acute phase of the syndrome (Wernicke's encephalopathy) is characterized by mental confusion, eye movement abnormalities, and poor muscular coordination. When patients are treated with the B vitamin thiamine, their neurologic symptoms generally improve. However, most patients who recover from Wernicke's encephalopathy are left with a severe residual memory impairment called Korsakoff syndrome. The hallmark of this syndrome is a striking loss of the ability to learn new things. Although patients appear to comprehend what is going on around them, they may forget events moments after they have occurred. These symptoms are associated with anatomical damage to the limbic system, a brain region comprising several structures on the mesial (inner) surface of the temporal lobe, and to structures in the midline of the diencephalon.

Mental Processes That Support Memory

Learning a new telephone number, recalling the right word to use in conversation, recognizing a face, and finding one's way in a familiar neighborhood are generally considered functions of memory. However, these tasks all are assisted by information processing functions that are not memory processes per se. Among these information processing functions are the ability to focus and maintain attention and perception, and the ability to recognize and identify stimuli such as objects, figures, and words. Memory processes include learning and retrieving data.

This distinction is important because long-term alcoholism is associated not only with learning and retrieval deficits, but also with moderate declines in the ability to process information to be remembered. Thus, poor performance on memory tests may reflect deficits in memory, attention, or comprehension. Only when a patient has difficulty learning and retrieving information that is disproportionate to his or her ability to attend to, recognize, and identify the information does the psychologist infer a memory deficit per se.

Priming

Despite disabling memory problems, alcoholic amnesics learn some things well. For example, many of these patients can acquire new motor skills (for example, tracking a moving object) as quickly as nonamnesics. This suggests that motor skill learning may employ neural mechanisms different from learning of facts and events. Some evidence suggests that alcoholic amnesics also can learn certain cognitive skills (for example, a mirror reading task) normally.

Perhaps most surprisingly, memory for words and pictures may be normal in amnesics, although at an unconscious level. This phenomenon of unconscious remembering can be demonstrated by priming experiments. Priming in this context refers to the effect of previous exposure on the processing of a stimulus. In a typical priming test, a subject must read aloud different words that appear sequentially on a screen. The experimenter measures the time between each word's appearance and the subject's response. Subjects generally respond more quickly to words previously presented (primed words) compared with words not previously presented (novel words). The priming effect appears to occur whether the subject consciously remembers having seen the words before or not. Priming studies show that the processing of stimuli by alcoholic amnesics is significantly improved by recent prior exposure and that this effect is similar in magnitude to that obtained in subjects with normal memory.

Theory of Multiple Memory Systems

Evidence exists that dementing illnesses like Alzheimer's disease, which destroy limbic and neocortical structures, often result in impaired priming but normal skill learning. On the other hand, illnesses like Huntington's disease, which destroy basal ganglia (for example, striatal structures) are associated with impaired skill learning but normal priming.

All these findings have been integrated into a comprehensive neurological theory of human memory that posits the existence of multiple, independent memory systems in the brain. This theory attributes explicit memory to the mesial temporal lobe and diencephalic brain structures, skill learning to the striatum, and priming to the neocortex.

This model, combined with the pattern of memory performance observed in alcoholic amnesics, makes certain predictions about the sites of brain abnormality in these patients. Given the severe explicit memory deficits they experience, damage is expected in the system that includes the mesial temporal lobe structures and related structures in the midline diencephalon. However, because previous research has emphasized how learning skills are spared and the occurrence of priming, the striatum and neocortex are expected to be unaffected. In the following discussion, the direct anatomical evidence will be summarized and compared to these predictions.

Anatomical Correlates of Alcoholic Amnesia

In a study of 28 male nonamnesic alcoholics, MRI images of the brain were subjected to detailed anatomical analysis. Results were compared with those from a group of 36 matched nonalcoholic men. The amount of cerebrospinal fluid in the cerebral ventricles and in the cortical sulci was significantly increased in the alcoholic subjects, indicating loss of brain tissue. Individual brain structures were examined to determine whether the volume loss was generalized or limited to specific regions. The diencephalon, the caudate nucleus (a component of the striatum), and parts of the cerebral cortex and the limbic system (including the mesial temporal lobe) were significantly smaller in alcoholic subjects. Subjects exhibited mild deficits on attentional and perceptual-motor tasks. However, they did not have significant memory deficits of the type observed in alcoholic amnesics (for example, recalling ideas from a story after a 30-minute delay).

A second study, using the same MRI methods, compared a group of eight alcoholic amnesics to matched nonamnesic alcoholics. The alcoholic amnesics demonstrated a very similar pattern of brain volume losses to the nonamnesic alcoholics. However, the amnesics had significantly greater losses in specific midline diencephalic structures, the mesial temporal region, and the forward portion of the cortex above the eyes. The more severe memory problems afflicting these patients may therefore be attributable to damage in some of the structures within these regions.

These anatomical studies of subjects with alcoholic amnesia are in some ways consistent with predictions based on the multiple systems theory of human memory. Subjects exhibited damage in both the diencephalic and mesial temporal lobe components of the brain system thought to control explicit memory. Thus it is not surprising that these patients have severe deficits on tests of recognition and recall. However, if the multiple systems theory is correct, it is surprising that impairments in skill learning and priming rarely have been observed in alcoholic amnesics, because these patients do seem to have damage in striatal and neocortical structures as well. Therefore, the observation of striatal and cortical damage in alcoholic amnesics is inconsistent with the multiple systems model used to explain their memory performances. On the other hand, such damage is consistent with the evidence, described earlier, of alcohol-related deficits in stimulus processing and perceptual-motor function because these functions also have been associated (like priming and skill learning) with neocortical and striatal brain systems.

The results of a recent study of priming and explicit memory function in memory-impaired subjects may help to reconcile these inconsistencies. A group of 30 subjects with explicit memory performance ranging from normal to severely impaired was examined with tests of word priming and word recognition. Priming was measured as an improvement in the ability to identify words presented very briefly. Word identification performance for previously studied words was compared to performance for unstudied words. The difference in performance was taken as the measure of priming, or implicit memory. Explicit memory was measured by mixing studied with unstudied words and asking the subjects to state whether or not each word had been presented earlier in the test. Of this group, some of the subjects were alcoholic a mnesics, some had amnesias attributable to other causes, some had dementing illnesses, and some were healthy controls. Concurrent to the behavioral testing, MRI was performed and the anatomical methods described previously were applied.

As expected, within this group of subjects, the greater the damage to the mesial temporal lobe structures the greater the impairment of recognition memory. However, the magnitude of the priming effect was not correlated with the degree of neocortical damage. Instead, striatal and mesial temporal lobe damage both appeared to affect priming, but in opposite ways. That is, striatal damage was associated with larger priming effects, whereas mesial temporal damage was associated with smaller priming effects. Subjects with both striatal and mesial temporal damage exhibited intermediate priming effects.

To a large extent, the observed relationship between striatal damage and increased priming effects may be an artifact—a reflection of the experimental design rather than the subjects' inherent priming abilities. Some of the test items may be so easy to process that priming does not improve performance scores, even if prior exposure to the item did produce a strong memory. Thus, measurements of priming alone may not adequately represent memory, especially when the subject already is performing well on the task without being primed.

Within this context, the results of the anatomical study of memory impairment make more sense. Because subjects without striatal damage processed new (nonprimed) words efficiently, their priming scores were misleadingly low. Because subjects with striatal damage processed new words inefficiently, they had more room for improvement; thus, their priming scores more closely reflected the strength of the memory that resulted from the prior exposure. If the patients with striatal damage had normal memory, their priming scores were higher than the priming scores of subjects without striatal damage. If they had poor memory, their priming scores approached, or were even lower than, those of subjects without striatal damage.

If the above explanation is correct, the results of studies of priming in patients with alcohol-related memory impairment should be reconsidered; the distinction between the kind of memory measured as priming and the kind measured in explicit tasks may be spurious. Alcoholic amnesics may appear to perform normally on priming tasks largely because the priming scores of normal control subjects, used for comparison, are misleadingly low.

If the above explanation is accepted, the observation of normal priming in the context of impaired explicit memory no longer requires the existence of an independent memory mechanism for priming. It is suggested that priming, like recognition memory, is affected by damage to the mesial temporal lobe/diencephalic system. However, on many priming tasks, measured priming also will be related to proficiency at the baseline task, which may be reduced by striatal damage and perhaps by damage to other structures as well. Dissociation between priming and explicit memory is therefore likely to occur in alcoholic amnesics because they suffer from damage to both striatal and limbic structures in the brain. Damage in these two sites appears to affect two separate processing components, both of which are required in most priming tasks: One is a stimulus processing component and the other is a memory processing component.

Chapter 48

Wernicke-Korsakoff Syndrome (Alcohol-Related Dementia)

Definition

Wernicke-Korsakoff Syndrome (WKS) is a neurological disorder. Wernicke's Encephalopathy and Korsakoff's Psychosis are the acute and chronic phases, respectively, of the same disease.

WKS is caused by a deficiency in the B vitamin thiamine. Thiamine plays a role in metabolizing glucose to produce energy for the brain. An absence of thiamine therefore results in an inadequate supply of energy to the brain, particularly the hypothalamus (which regulates body temperature, growth, and appetite and has a role in emotional response. It also controls pituitary functions including metabolism and hormones) and mammillary bodies (where neural pathways connect various parts of the brain involved in memory functions). The disease is typically associated with chronic alcoholism, but may be associated with malnutrition or other conditions which cause nutritional deficiencies.

Facts

WKS has a relatively low prevalence (0.4% to 2.8% of reported autopsies). However, it is likely that the disease is under-reported and under-diagnosed. An estimated 25% of WKS cases were missed where the brains were not examined microscopically. Another study found that only 20% of clinical WKS diagnoses were made correctly in life when compared to autopsy results. Moreover, WKS appears to be only one distinct disease that causes alcohol-related dementia. Based on clinical research studies, between 22% to 29% of individuals with dementia were found to be heavy drinkers or alcoholics and 9% to 23% of elderly alcoholics in alcoholism treatment were found to also have dementia.

An estimated 1.1 to 2.3 million older Americans have problems with alcohol. Medical researchers are still grappling with how to more fully define the association between heavy alcohol use and symptoms of dementia.

Symptoms

WKS symptoms may be long-lasting or permanent and should be distinguished from the acute affects of alcohol consumption or from a period of alcohol "withdrawal." The disease is characterized by mental confusion, amnesia (a permanent gap in memory), and impaired short-term memory. An estimated 80% of persons with WKS continue to have a chronic memory disorder. Individuals often appear apathetic and inattentive and some may experience agitation. In addition, WKS tends to impair the person's ability to learn new information or tasks. Individuals with WKS are known to "confabulate" (make up or invent information to compensate for poor memory). Other symptoms include ataxia (weakness in limbs or lack of muscle coordination, unsteady gait), slow walking, rapid, tremor-like eye movements or paralysis of eye muscles. Fine motor function (for example, hand or finger movements) may be diminished and sense of smell also may be affected. In the advanced stages, coma can occur. Although treatable if caught early enough, the death rate from WKS is relatively high, about 10% to 20%.

Diagnosis

WKS is often missed as a diagnosis. In the acute phase, a physical examination may reveal skin changes and a red "beefy" tongue. In addition, blood count, electrolytes and liver function tests should be conducted. Even in the chronic phase, an MRI may show shrunken mammillary bodies and other changes in the brain. CT scans have showed enlarged ventricles and diencephalic lesions.

It is important that a full medical history include information about the person's daily drinking habits, both present and past. Family, friends and past medical records should be consulted to obtain the most complete information possible on the person's history with alcohol. Proposed criteria for diagnosing alcohol-related dementia (not strictly WKS) suggest that the diagnosis be made at least 60 days after the last exposure to alcohol and that a "significant" alcohol history would include an average of 35 drinks per week for men (28 for women) for at least five years. Typically, the period of significant drinking must be within three years of the onset of dementia.

Recent medical research also suggests that the genetic marker ApoE4 is a significant predictor of global intellectual deficits in people with WKS. Individuals with the ApoE genotype may experience a certain interaction with heavy alcohol use which could predispose them to WKS. Concerns about an inherited susceptibility to WKS should be discussed with a genetic counselor.

In cases of suspected non-alcohol related WKS, the physician may investigate anorexia nervosa, hyperemesis gravidarum, severe malnutrition and other disorders or surgical procedures which impair intestinal absorption of thiamine.

Treatment

If caught early enough, WKS is a preventable, treatable disease. Treatment consists of thiamine replacement therapy, sometimes along with other vitamins. Dosages may vary and should be monitored closely by a physician. If alcoholic consumption stops and treatment is properly administered, individuals with early-stage WKS can expect a marked recovery and may be capable of learning simple, repetitive tasks.

However, the person's confusion may take some time to subside and even incomplete recovery of memory can take up to a year. In the later stages, if damage to the brain is irreversible, individuals are likely to have lasting problems with memory and gait (for example, lack of muscle coordination and numbness or weakness in limbs).

Family Issues

Caring for a family member who has WKS or alcohol-related dementia presents multiple challenges for family caregivers. Lasting symptoms of dementia and other neurological problems are difficult conditions under even the best circumstances. Bizarre behaviors may be interpreted by the family as a continuation of "binge" drinking, even if the person has stopped drinking.

Individuals with a history of alcohol abuse have often isolated themselves from their families and loved ones. Strained relationships are common in families of alcoholics. As a caregiver, you may feel resentful of caring for a parent or spouse with a life-long history of alcohol abuse. In addition, it may be hard to convince the impaired person to give up drinking, since most WKS-affected individuals have been long-term alcoholics. Discuss with a physician or mental health professional effective strategies for preventing a loved one from drinking. Ironically, people with WKS can be quite apathetic and seldom demand alcohol, yet are likely to accept it if offered.

Families should enlist the help and support of mental health professionals or case workers who have experience in working with alcoholism. Family meetings or support groups also may be helpful in bringing together additional family members to assist the WKS person. A case manager or family counselor can help the family sort through issues and help arrange appropriate support services. In severe cases or when the family is unable to provide appropriate care, a residential facility may be sought. Nursing homes which provide special dementia care should be considered for a confused WKS patient.

Research indicates that alcoholism often runs in families. Having additional family members who are alcoholic increases the burden of care. Some research has shown that a person whose parent has a history of alcoholism may have an inherited susceptibility to alcohol addiction and alcohol-related neurological problems (peripheral neuropathies). Such findings suggest that people in alcoholic families need to take special precautions to avoid excessive use of alcohol in order to reduce their own risk of alcohol-related health problems.

Caring for the Person with WKS

It is important to ensure that the affected person continues to abstain from drinking alcohol and that the person maintains a balanced diet with adequate thiamine intake. However, even if the person stops drinking and replenishes thiamine, symptoms of the disease (for example, problem behaviors, agitation, lack of coordination, learning deficits) may continue. In an abstinent (sober) WKS patient, these symptoms must be recognized as part of the disease caused by irreversible damage to the brain and nervous system.

Family caregivers should take precautions to ensure the safety of the person with WKS, as well as others in the household. The confused or disoriented individual should not be left alone. Supervision is required to ensure that the person does not wander away from home, leave the stove on or the water running.

Short-term memory problems mean that the confused person may repeat the same question again and again. Coping with frequent repetition often involves a trial and error approach and a combination of strategies. First, be patient and deliver responses in a calm manner. The confused person will pick up on your mood and may become more frustrated if your voice is loud or angry. In addition, place reminders in the house to help the person feel more secure. Label inside doors and drawers with words or pictures. Write notes (for example, dinner is at 6:00 p.m.). Another strategy is to distract the person with another topic or activity (for example, a short walk, reminiscing over an old photo, etc.)

If the person continues to be agitated, symptoms should be discussed with a physician, neurologist or psychiatrist. Medications may be available to help control outbursts or anxiety.

Just as important, it is essential that the caregiver get some support and time off from constant caregiving demands. Make sure you leave some time to attend to your own needs, including eating well, getting enough sleep and getting regular medical check-ups. A home care worker, friend or family member may be needed to provide periodic respite assistance to help your loved one and to relieve the stress on you, the family caregiver.

Resources

Family Caregiver Alliance
690 Market Street, Suite 600
San Francisco, CA 94104
Phone: (415) 434-3388
Toll Free: (800) 445-8106 (in CA)
Fax: (415) 434-3508
E-Mail: info@caregiver.org
Web site: http://www.caregiver.org

Family Caregiver Alliance supports and assists caregivers of brain-impaired adults through education, research, services and advocacy. FCA's Information Clearinghouse covers current medical, social, public policy and caregiving issues related to brain impairments. For residents of the greater San Francisco Bay Area, FCA provides direct family support services for caregivers of those with Alzheimer's disease, stroke, head injury, Parkinson's and other debilitating brain disorders that strike adults.

Other Resources

American Association for Marriage and Family Therapy
1133 15th St., NW Ste. 300
Washington, DC 20005
Phone: (202) 452-0109
Web site: http://www.aamft.org

National Association of Professional Geriatric Care Managers
1604 N. Country Club Rd.
Tucson, AZ 85716
Phone: (520) 881-8008
Web site: http://www.caremanager.org

National Eldercare Locator
1112 16th St., NW, Suite 100
Washington, DC 20036
Toll Free: (800) 677-1116
Web site: http://www.aoa.dhhs.gov/aoa/dir/91.html

National Institute on Alcohol Abuse and Alcoholism (NIAAA)
National Institutes of Health
Willco Building
6000 Executive Boulevard
Bethesda, MD 20892-7003
Phone: (301) 443-0786
Web site: http://www.niaaa.nih.gov

National Organization for Rare Disorders
P.O. Box 8923
New Fairfield, CT 06812
Toll Free: (800) 999-6673
Phone: (203) 746-6518
Web site: http://www.rarediseases.org

Part Five

Treatment and Recovery

Chapter 49

How to Cut Down on Your Drinking

Steps to Follow

If you are drinking too much, you can improve your life and health by cutting down. How do you know if you drink too much? Read these questions and answer "yes" or "no":

- Do you drink alone when you feel angry or sad?
- Does your drinking ever make you late for work?
- Does your drinking worry your family?
- Do you ever drink after telling yourself you won't?
- Do you ever forget what you did while you were drinking?
- Do you get headaches or have a hang-over after you have been drinking?

If you answered "yes" to any of these questions, you may have a drinking problem. Check with your doctor to be sure. Your doctor will be able to tell you whether you should cut down or abstain. If you are alcoholic or have other medical problems, you should not just cut down on your drinking—you should stop drinking completely. Your doctor will advise you about what is right for you. If your doctor tells you to cut down on your drinking, these steps can help you:

National Institute on Alcohol Abuse and Alcoholism (NIAAA), NIH Pub. No. 96-3770, March 1996. Printed copies of this publication may be ordered from NIAAA by calling (301) 443-3860; or it may be downloaded from http://www.niaaa.nih.gov.

1. Write your reasons for cutting down or stopping.

Why do you want to drink less? There are many reasons why you may want to cut down or stop drinking. You may want to improve your health, sleep better, or get along better with your family or friends. Make a list of the reasons you want to drink less.

2. Set a drinking goal.

Choose a limit for how much you will drink. You may choose to cut down or not to drink at all. If you are cutting down, keep below these limits:

- *Women:* No more than one drink a day
- *Men:* No more than two drinks a day

A drink is:

- a 12-ounce bottle of beer;
- a 5-ounce glass of wine; or
- a 1 1/2-ounce shot of liquor.

These limits may be too high for some people who have certain medical problems or who are older. Talk with your doctor about the limit that is right for you.

Now—write your drinking goal on a piece of paper. Put it where you can see it, such as on your refrigerator or bathroom mirror. Your paper might look like this:

My drinking goal:

I will start on this day ___________.
I will not drink more than ______ drinks in 1 day.
I will not drink more than ______ drinks in 1 week.

or

I will stop drinking alcohol.

3. Keep a "diary" of your drinking.

To help you reach your goal, keep a "diary" of your drinking. For example, write down every time you have a drink for 1 week. Try to keep your diary for 3 or 4 weeks. This will show you how much you drink and when. You may be surprised. How different is your goal from the amount you drink now? Use the "drinking diary" shown in Table 49.1 to write down when you drink.

Table 49.1. Drinking Diary.

Week #______

	# of drinks	type of drinks	place consumed
Mon.			
Tues.			
Wed.			
Thurs.			
Fri.			
Sat.			
Sun.			

Working toward Your Goal

Now you know why you want to drink less and you have a goal. There are many ways you can help yourself to cut down. Try these tips:

- *Watch it at home.* Keep a small amount or no alcohol at home. Don't keep temptations around.
- *Drink slowly.* When you drink, sip your drink slowly. Take a break of 1 hour between drinks. Drink soda, water, or juice after a drink with alcohol.
- *Do not drink on an empty stomach!* Eat food when you are drinking.

- *Take a break from alcohol.* Pick a day or two each week when you will not drink at all. Then, try to stop drinking for 1 week. Think about how you feel physically and emotionally on these days. When you succeed and feel better, you may find it easier to cut down for good.
- *Learn how to say NO.* You do not have to drink when other people drink. You do not have to take a drink that is given to you. Practice ways to say no politely. For example, you can tell people you feel better when you drink less. Stay away from people who give you a hard time about not drinking.
- *Stay active.* What would you like to do instead of drinking? Use the time and money spent on drinking to do something fun with your family or friends. Go out to eat, see a movie, or play sports or a game.
- *Get support.* Cutting down on your drinking may be difficult at times. Ask your family and friends for support to help you reach your goal. Talk to your doctor if you are having trouble cutting down. Get the help you need to reach your goal.
- *Watch out for temptations.* Watch out for people, places, or times that make you drink, even if you do not want to. Stay away from people who drink a lot or bars where you used to go. Plan ahead of time what you will do to avoid drinking when you are tempted. Do not drink when you are angry or upset or have a bad day. These are habits you need to break if you want to drink less.

Do Not Give Up!

Most people do not cut down or give up drinking all at once. Just like a diet, it is not easy to change. That is okay. If you do not reach your goal the first time, try again. Remember, get support from people who care about you and want to help. Do not give up!

Chapter 50

Alcohol-Related Problems: Recognition and Intervention

Although two thirds of American men and one half of American women drink alcohol,[1] three fourths of drinkers experience no serious consequences from alcohol use.[2] Among those who abuse alcohol, many reduce their drinking without formal treatment after personal reflection about negative consequences.[3] Physicians can help prevent the serious effects of alcohol-related problems by stimulating such reflection and moving patients toward a healthier lifestyle.[4] The purpose of this text is to encourage family physicians to prevent serious consequences of alcohol-related problems by using simple screening and brief intervention strategies.

Rationale for Early Screening

Preventive efforts on the part of family physicians are important because: (1) alcohol-related problems are prevalent in patients who visit family practices; (2) heavy alcohol use contributes to many serious health and social problems; and (3) physicians can successfully influence drinking behaviors. In the United States, the one-year prevalence of alcohol-use disorders, including alcohol abuse and alcohol dependence, is about 7.4 percent in the adult population.[5] In

---

Excerpted and used with permission from the January 15, 1999, issue of *American Family Physician*. Although the text in this chapter is written for family physicians, general readers will find useful information about how doctors identify possible alcohol-use disorders.

patients who visit family practices, the prevalence is higher. One study of 17 primary care practices found a 16.5 percent prevalence of "problem drinkers,"[4] and another study found a 19.9 percent prevalence of alcohol-use disorders among male patients.[6]

Heavy alcohol use can affect nearly every organ system and every aspect of a patient's life. Table 50.1 lists many direct and indirect effects of alcohol-related problems. Alcohol causes diseases such as cirrhosis of the liver and exacerbates symptoms in existing conditions such as diabetes.[1,7,8] In addition, alcohol is implicated in many social and psychologic problems, including family conflict, arrests, job instability, injuries related to violence or accidents, and psychologic

Table 50.1. Consequences of Alcohol Abuse or Dependence

System/category	Early consequences
Liver disease	Elevated liver enzyme levels
Pancreatic disease	
Cardiovascular disease	Hypertension
Gastrointestinal problems	Gastritis, gastroesophageal reflux disease, diarrhea, peptic ulcer disease
Neurologic disorders	Headaches, blackouts, peripheral neuropathy
Reproductive system	Fetal alcohol effects, fetal alcohol syndrome
Cancers	
Psychiatric comorbidities	Depression, anxiety
Legal problems	Traffic violations, driving while intoxicated, public intoxication
Employment problems	Tardiness, sick days, inability to concentrate, decreased competence
Family problems	Family conflict, erratic child discipline, neglect of responsibilities, social isolation
Effects on children	Over-responsibility, acting out, withdrawal, inability to concentrate, school problems, social isolation

symptoms related to depression and anxiety.[2,8] These problems take an enormous emotional toll on individuals and families, and are a great financial expense to health care systems and society.

Many of these problems may be avoided by early screening and intervention by family physicians. Several studies of early and brief physician interventions have demonstrated a reduction in alcohol consumption and improvement in alcohol-related problems among patients with drinking problems.[9,10] A 40-percent reduction in alcohol consumption in nondependent problem drinkers has been demonstrated following physician advice to reduce drinking.[4]

Table 50.1. Consequences of Alcohol Abuse or Dependence (continued)

System/category	Late consequences
Liver disease	Fatty liver, alcoholic hepatitis, cirrhosis
Pancreatic disease	Acute pancreatitis, chronic pancreatitis
Cardiovascular disease	Cardiomyopathy, arrhythmias, stroke
Gastrointestinal problems	Esophageal varices, Mallory-Weiss tears
Neurologic disorders	Alcohol withdrawal syndrome, seizures, Wernicke's encephalopathy, dementia, cerebral atrophy, peripheral neuropathy, cognitive deficits, impaired motor functioning
Reproductive system disorders	Sexual dysfunction, amenorrhea, anovulation, early menopause, spontaneous abortion
Cancers	Neoplasm of the liver, neoplasm of the head and neck, neoplasm of the pancreas, neoplasm of the esophagus
Psychiatric comorbidities	Affective disorders, anxiety disorders, antisocial personality
Legal problems	Motor vehicle accidents, violent offenses, fires
Employment problems	Accidents, injury, job loss, chronic unemployment
Family problems	Divorce, spouse abuse, child abuse or neglect, loss of child custody
Effects on children	Learning disorders, behavior problems, emotional disturbance

Definitions

Table 50. 2 lists diagnostic criteria for alcohol dependence specified by the *Diagnostic and Statistical Manual of Mental Disorders, 4th ed. (DSM-IV).*[11] Alcohol abuse is manifested by recurrent alcohol use despite significant adverse consequences of drinking, such as problems with work, law, health or family life.

The diagnosis of alcohol dependence is based on the compulsion to drink. The dependent drinker devotes substantial time to obtaining alcohol, drinking and recovering, and continues to drink despite adverse social, psychologic or medical consequences. A physiologic dependence on alcohol, marked by tolerance or withdrawal symptoms, may or may not be present. Note that quantity and frequency of drinking are not specified in the criteria for either diagnosis; instead, the key elements of these diagnoses include the compulsion to drink and drinking despite adverse consequences.

Clinical Presentation

Alcohol-use disorders are easy to recognize in patients with longstanding problems, because these persons present to the family physician with diseases such as cirrhosis or pancreatitis (Table 50.1). Patients in the earlier stages of alcohol-related problems may have few or subtle clinical findings, and the physician may not suspect a high consumption of alcohol. Certain medical complaints, such as headache, depression, chronic abdominal or epigastric pain, fatigue, and memory loss, should alert the family physician to consider the possibility of alcohol-related problems.

The first signs of heavy drinking may be social problems. The compulsion to drink causes persons to neglect social responsibilities and relationships in favor of drinking. Intoxication may lead to accidents, occasional arrest, or job loss. Recovering from drinking can decrease job performance or family involvement. Social problems that indicate alcohol-use disorders include family conflict, separation or divorce, employment difficulties or job loss, arrests and motor vehicle accidents.

History

The most effective tool for diagnosing alcohol-related problems is a thorough history of the drinking behavior and its consequences. The National Institute on Alcohol Abuse and Alcoholism (NIAAA) has

Table 50.2. *DSM-IV* Criteria For Alcohol Dependence

A maladaptive pattern of alcohol use, leading to clinically significant impairment or distress, as manifested by three (or more) of the following, occurring at any time in the same 12-month period:

1. Tolerance, as defined by either of the following:

    (a) A need for markedly increased amounts of alcohol to achieve intoxication or the desired effect

    (b) Markedly diminished effect with continued use of the same amount of alcohol

2. Withdrawal, as manifested by either of the following:

    (a) The characteristic withdrawal syndrome several hours to a few days following cessation (two or more of the following): autonomic hyperactivity (e.g., sweating or pulse rate greater than 100), increased hand tremor, insomnia, nausea or vomiting, transient visual, tactile or auditory hallucinations or illusions, psychomotor agitation, anxiety or grand mal seizures

    (b) Alcohol or other substances are taken to relieve or avoid withdrawal symptoms

3. Alcohol is taken in larger amounts or over a longer period than was intended

4. There is a persistent desire or unsuccessful efforts to cut down or control drinking

5. A great deal of time is spent to obtain alcohol, drink alcohol, or recover from its effects

6. Important social, occupational or recreational activities are given up or reduced because of drinking alcohol

7. Alcohol use is continued despite knowledge of having a persistent or recurrent physical or psychologic problem that is likely to have been caused or exacerbated by alcohol

Specify if:

With physiological dependence: evidence of tolerance or withdrawal (i.e., either item 1 or item 2 is present) Without physiological dependence: no evidence of tolerance or withdrawal (i.e., neither item 1 nor item 2 is present)

Adapted with permission from American Psychiatric Association. *Diagnostic and statistical manual of mental disorders. 4th ed.* Washington, D.C.: American Psychiatric Association, 1994:181. Copyright 1994.

published *The Physician's Guide to Helping Patients with Alcohol Problems*, which presents a brief model for screening and assessing problems with alcohol.[12] NIAAA recommends screening for alcohol-related problems during routine health examinations, before prescribing a medication that interacts with alcohol, and in response to the discovery of medical problems that may be related to alcohol use.

NIAAA recommends using the CAGE[13] questionnaire to screen patients for alcohol use (Table 50.3). The CAGE questions are widely used in primary care settings and have high sensitivity and specificity for identifying alcohol problems.[14] Among patients who screen positive for alcohol-related problems, additional questions should include the family history of alcohol abuse as well as family, legal, employment and health problems related to drinking.

Other screening questionnaires are available and may perform better than the CAGE questionnaire. A recent study demonstrated the superiority of the AUDIT instrument in a Veterans Administration population (Table 50.4).[15] The TWEAK and AUDIT questionnaires performed better than the CAGE questionnaire in women (Table 50.5).[16]

Physical Examination

In the early stages of alcohol-related problems, the physical examination provides little evidence to suggest excessive drinking. Patients who abuse alcohol may have mildly elevated blood pressure but few other abnormal physical findings. Later, patients may develop significant and obvious signs of alcohol overuse, including gastrointestinal findings such as an enlarged and sometimes tender liver; cutaneous findings such as spider angiomata, varicosities and jaundice; neurologic signs such as tremor, ataxia or neuropathies; and cardiac arrhythmias. When patients arrive at the doctor's office inebriated, one should suspect a long-standing drinking problem.

Table 50.3. CAGE Questionnaire: One or more "yes" responses constitute a positive screening test.

1. Have you ever felt you ought to **C**ut down on your drinking?
2. Have people **A**nnoyed you by criticizing your drinking?
3. Have you ever felt bad or **G**uilty about your drinking?
4. Have you ever had a drink first thing in the morning to steady your nerves or get rid of a hangover (**E**ye-opener)?

Table 50.4. The AUDIT(Alcohol Use Disorders Identification Test) Questionnaire

The following questions pertain to your use of alcoholic beverages during the past year. A "drink" refers to a can or bottle of beer, a glass of wine, a wine cooler, or one cocktail or shot of hard liquor.

1. How often do you have a drink containing alcohol? (Never, 0 points; less than monthly, 1 point; 2 to 4 times per month, 2 points; 2 to 3 times per week, 3 points; greater than 4 times per week, 4 points)
2. How many drinks containing alcohol do you have on a typical day when you are drinking? (1 to 2 drinks, 0 points; 3 to 4 drinks, 1 point; 5 to 6 drinks, 2 points; 7 to 9 drinks, 3 points; 10 or more drinks, 4 points)
3. How often do you have 6 or more drinks on 1 occasion? (Never, 0 points; less than monthly, 1 point; monthly, 2 points; weekly, 3 points; daily or almost daily, 4 points)
4. How often during the past year have you found that you were not able to stop drinking once you had started? (Scoring same as question No. 3)
5. How often during the past year have you failed to do what was normally expected from you because of drinking? (Same as question No. 3)
6. How often during the past year have you needed a first drink in the morning to get yourself going after a heavy drinking session? (Same as question No. 3)
7. How often during the past year have you had a feeling of guilt or remorse after drinking? (Same as question No. 3)
8. How often during the past year have you been unable to remember what happened the night before because you were drinking? (Same as question No. 3)
9. Have you or someone else been injured as a result of your drinking? (No, 0 points; yes, but not in the past year, 2 points; yes, during the past year, 4 points)
10. Has a relative or friend, or a doctor or other health care worker, been concerned about your drinking or suggested you cut down? (Same as question No. 9)

Scoring: sum all points; total, 0 to 40 points; for complete scoring information, see reference 15.

Diagnosis and Classification

An accurate diagnosis of alcohol abuse or dependence requires a thorough medical history. A CAGE questionnaire with three or more positive responses is 100 percent sensitive and 81 percent specific for current alcohol dependence.[18]

NIAAA categorizes heavy drinkers into three groups: at-risk drinkers, problem drinkers (parallel to the *DSM-IV* diagnosis of "alcohol abuse"), and alcohol-dependent drinkers (parallel to the *DSM-IV* diagnosis of "alcohol dependence"). Table 50.6 describes the NIAAA assessment of alcohol-related problems.[12]

At-Risk Drinkers

In the absence of medical, social or psychologic consequences of drinking, men who have more than 14 drinks per week or more than four drinks per occasion are considered "at risk" for developing problems related to drinking. Similarly, women who have more than 11 drinks per week or more than three drinks per occasion are "at risk." Because some drinkers significantly underreport their alcohol use,

Table 50.5. The TWEAK Questionnaire.

Tolerance:	How many drinks can you hold ("hold" version; greater than 6 drinks indicates tolerance), or how many drinks does it take before you begin to feel the first effects of the alcohol? ("high" version; greater than 3 indicates tolerance)
Worried:	Have close friends or relatives worried or complained about your drinking in the past year?
Eye openers:	Do you sometimes take a drink in the morning when you first get up?
Amnesia:	Has a friend or family member ever told you about things you said or did while you were drinking that you could not remember?
Kut down:	Do you sometimes feel the need to cut down on your drinking?

Scoring: 2 points each for tolerance or worried; 1 point each for eye opener, amnesia, or kut down; sum all points; total, 0 to 7 points; for complete information about scoring, see reference 16.

physicians should define patients as "at risk" when they have a positive CAGE score or a personal or family history of alcohol-related problems.

Problem Drinkers

Patients who have current alcohol-related medical, family, social, employment, legal or emotional problems are considered "problem drinkers" regardless of their drinking patterns or responses to the CAGE questions. Typically, these patients score 1 or 2 on the CAGE questionnaire and drink above "at-risk" levels.

Table 50.6. Assessment of Risk for Alcohol-Related Problems

Severity of problem	Criteria
At risk	Men: greater than 14 drinks per week, greater than 4 drinks per occasion
	Women: greater than 11 drinks per week, is greater than 3 drinks per occasion, or
	CAGE score of 1 or higher for past year, or
	Personal or family history of alcohol problems
Current problem	CAGE score of 1 or 2 for past year, or
	Alcohol-related medical problems, or
	Alcohol-related family, legal or employment problems
Alcohol dependent	CAGE score of 3 or 4 for past year, or
	Compulsion to drink, or
	Impaired control over drinking, or
	Relief drinking, or
	Withdrawal symptoms, or
	Increased tolerance

Information from *The Physicians' Guide to Helping Patients with Alcohol Problems.* U.S. Department of Health and Human Services, Public Health Service, National Institutes of Health, National Institute on Alcohol Abuse and Alcoholism, 1995; NIH Publication No. 95-3769.

Alcohol-Dependent Drinkers

Patients drinking above the "at-risk" level who have CAGE scores of 3 or 4 should be questioned about their drinking compulsions, tolerance to alcohol, and withdrawal symptoms. Those who display these traits are considered "alcohol-dependent."

Primary Care Interventions

The physician should direct intervention efforts based on consideration of two important factors: the severity of the alcohol problem and the patient's readiness to change the drinking behavior.

Severity of the Alcohol Problem

In patients who show evidence of alcohol dependence, the therapeutic end points should be abstinence from alcohol and referral to a specialized alcohol treatment program. Decisions about inpatient or outpatient treatment depend on the patient's likelihood of alcohol withdrawal, resources, employment status, family support system, access to treatment programs, and motivation. Patients who resist formal treatment may prefer peer-directed groups, such as those offered by Alcoholics Anonymous, in conjunction with physician counseling and support. Al-Anon groups are available for adult family members of alcohol-dependent individuals. Abstinence is also indicated for non-alcohol-dependent patients who are pregnant, have comorbid medical conditions, take medications that interact with alcohol or have a history of repeated failed attempts to reduce their alcohol consumption.[12]

In patients who are at risk for developing alcohol-related problems or who have evidence of current problems, the therapeutic end point should be drinking at low-risk limits: for men, no more than two drinks with alcohol per day; for women or older persons (over 65) no more than one drink per day.[12]

Readiness to Change

A rare patient will present to the physician with the request for help in giving up alcohol. When persons change lifestyle behaviors such as tobacco or alcohol use, they typically move through stages of change: precontemplation (not ready for change), contemplation (ambivalence about change), preparation (planning for change), action (the act of change) and maintenance (maintaining the new behavior).[19]

This model of change can be pictured as a continuum, with a person moving back and forth among the stages, depending on the personal day-to-day costs and benefits of that behavior. Relapse is common and does not indicate a "failed" intervention. Contemplation (ambivalence) is the most common stage of change. One study found that 29 percent of hospitalized patients with alcohol disorders were uninterested in changing, 45 percent were ambivalent and 26 percent were ready to change their drinking behavior.[20]

Some experts consider precontemplation to be a synonym for alcoholic denial, that is, a refusal to acknowledge problems. However, others[21] do not find the concept of denial useful when working with patients with alcohol disorders. They note that direct or confrontational counseling strategies are likely to evoke resistance in patients, which, in turn, will be labeled "denial." Furthermore, their work demonstrates that even patients who do not admit to an alcohol problem can change their behaviors. Personal decisions about lifestyle changes evolve slowly over time, requiring much reflection, with repeated attempts at change and repeated setbacks. Patients will not leap from the precontemplation stage into the action stage after one clinic visit, no matter how insightful or aggressive the practitioner. The goal of each visit should be to help the patient move along the continuum of change toward a reduction in alcohol use.

Intervention Strategies

With the stage-of-change continuum in mind, physicians should tailor interviews according to the patient's stage.[20] In clinical settings, a good assessment is itself an intervention, stimulating patients to reflect on their drinking behavior. Well-intentioned advice, a familiar tool among physicians, works best with patients who are preparing for change. A physician who tries direct persuasion with an ambivalent patient risks pushing the patient toward resistance. However, at any stage, urgent persuasion is appropriate in patients requiring immediate change: a pregnant woman who drinks heavily or patients with severe medical, psychologic, or social problems related to alcohol use. Even in these circumstances, resistance to direct advice is likely. When giving advice, physicians should avoid prescriptive directions. Instead, physicians can educate patients about the consequences in an objective manner: "Drinking affects the fetus in this way...." This information is most effective when it addresses issues that directly concern the patient.

Rollnick and colleagues[18] have developed a menu of brief strategies for the primary caregiver, based on a model of counseling called

Table 50.7. A Menu of Interviewing Strategies for Patients with Alcohol-Related Problems

Strategies	**Stage of change**
Lifestyle, stresses and alcohol use	Precontemplation
Health and alcohol use	Precontemplation
A typical day	Precontemplation
"Good" things and "less good" things	Contemplation
Providing information	Contemplation
The future and the present	Contemplation
Exploring concerns	Preparation or action
Helping with decision-making	Preparation or action
Strategies	**Description**
Lifestyle, stresses and alcohol use	Discuss lifestyle and life stresses: "Where does your use of alcohol fit in?"
Health and alcohol use	Ask about health in general: "What part does your drinking play in your health?"
A typical day	"Describe a typical day, from beginning to end. How does alcohol fit in?"
"Good" things and "less good" things	"What are some good things about your use of alcohol? "What are some less good things?"
Providing information	Ask permission to provide information; deliver information in a nonpersonal manner: "What do you make of all this?"
The future and the present	"How would you like things to be different in the future?"
Exploring concerns	Elicit the patient's reasons for concern about alcohol use; list concerns about changing behavior
Helping with decision-making	"Given your concerns about drinking, where does this leave you now?"

Information from Rollnick S, Heather N, Bell A. Negotiating behavior change in medical settings: the development of brief motivational interviewing. *J Ment Health* 1992; 1:25-37.

"motivational interviewing" (Table 50.7).[20] In all patients, the physician should begin by directing the interview toward understanding the drinking behavior and how it fits into patients' lives. Among patients in the precontemplation stage, this assessment is the complete intervention. In the contemplation stage, the physician should explore patients' ambivalence toward change, including reasons to quit and reasons to continue drinking. At this point, patients may be receptive to information about the effects of alcohol. In the later stages, the physician may acquaint patients with helpful community resources such as Alcoholics Anonymous or formal treatment programs, and help them anticipate and prepare for temptations and setbacks.

The goal of these strategies is to help patients develop their own rationale for change and to nudge them in the direction of a healthier lifestyle. This nondirective approach removes the element of resistance because the patient does the work: the patient reflects on the ways alcohol fits into his or her life, weighs the personal costs and benefits of drinking, provides the arguments for change and makes the decision to quit drinking. The physician's job is simply to elicit information, encourage patients to reflect, and support their movement toward healthy change.

Final Comment

Excessive alcohol use can affect every part of a person's life, causing serious medical problems, family conflict, legal difficulties and job loss. Family physicians, with training in biomedical and psychosocial issues and access to family members, are in a good position to recognize problems related to alcohol use and to assist patients with lifestyle change. NIAAA provides simple guidelines for alcohol screening, based on a thorough drinking history and a sound understanding of the pattern of consequences. Physicians who are sensitive to these issues will find alcohol-use disorders easier to diagnose, and physicians who motivate their patients to reflect on their drinking will encourage recovery.

References

1. *Eighth special report to the U.S. Congress on alcohol and health from the Secretary of Health and Human Services*. Rockville, Md.: Department of Health and Human Services, National Institutes of Health, National Institute on Alcohol Abuse and Alcoholism, 1994; DHHS Publication No. 94-3699.

2. Regier DA, Farmer ME, Rae DS, Locke BZ, Keith S J, Judd LL, et al. Comorbidity of mental disorders with alcohol and other drug abuse. Results from the Epidemiologic Catchment Area (ECA) Study. *JAMA* 1990;264:2511-8.

3. Sobell LC, Sobell MB, Toneatto T, Leo GI. What triggers the resolution of alcohol problems without treatment. *Alcohol Clin Exp Res* 1993;17:217-24.

4. Fleming MF, Barry KL, Manwell LB, Johnson K, London R. Brief physician advice for problem alcohol drinkers. A randomized controlled trial in community-based primary care practices. *JAMA* 1997: 277:1039-45.

5. Grant BF, Harford TC, Dawson DA, Chou P, Dufour M, Pickering R. NIAAA's Epidemiologic Bulletin no. 35: prevalence of DSM-IV alcohol abuse and dependence, United States, 1992. *Alcohol Health Res World* 1994;18:243-8.

6. Burge SK, Amodei N, Elkin B, Catala S, Andrew SR, Lane PA, et al. An evaluation of two primary care interventions for alcohol abuse among Mexican-American patients. *Addiction* 1997;92:1705-16.

7. Dufour MC, Caces ME Epidemiology of the medical consequences of alcohol. *Alcohol Health Res World* 1993;17:265-71.

8. O'Connor PG. The general internist. Supplement 1: Identification and treatment of substance abuse in primary care settings. *Am J Addict* 1996;5:59-519.

9. WHO Brief Intervention Study Group. A cross-national trial of brief interventions with heavy drinkers. *Am J Public Health* 1996;86:948-55.

10. Richmond R, Heather N, Wodak A, Kehoe L, Webster I. Controlled evaluation of a general practice-based brief intervention for excessive drinking. *Addiction* 1995;90:119-32.

11. *American Psychiatric Association. Diagnostic and statistical manual of mental disorders. 4th ed.* Washington, D.C.: American Psychiatric Association, 1994.

12. *The physicians' guide to helping patients with alcohol problems*. U.S. Department of Health and Human Services, Public Health Service, National Institutes of Health, National Institute

on Alcohol Abuse and Alcoholism, 1995; NIH publication no. 95-3769.

13. Ewing JA. Detecting alcoholism. The CAGE questionnaire. *JAMA* 1984;252:1905-7.

14. Girela E, Villanueva E, Hernandez-Cueto C, Luna JD. Comparison of the CAGE questionnaire versus some biochemical markers in the diagnosis of alcoholism. *Alcohol* 1994;29:337-43.

15. Bradley KA, Bush KR, McDonnell MB, Malone T, Fihn SD. Screening for problem drinking. Comparison of CAGE and AUDIT. *J Gen Intern Med* 1998;13:379-88.

16. Bradley KA, Boyd-Wickizer J, Powell SH, Burman ML. Alcohol screening questionnaires in women. A critical review. *JAMA* 1998;280:166-71.

17. Hoeksema HL, de Bock GH. The value of laboratory tests for the screening and recognition of alcohol abuse in primary care patients. *J Fam Pract* 1993; 37:268-76.

18. Magruder-Habib K, Stevens HA, Ailing WC. Relative performance of the MAST, VAST, and CAGE versus *DSM-III-R* criteria for alcohol dependence. *J Clin Epidemiol* 1993;46:435-41.

19. Prochaska JO, Velicer WF, Rossi JS, Goldstein MG, Marcus BH, Rakowski W, et al. Stages of change and decisional balance for 12 problem behaviors. *Health Psychol* 1994;13:39-46.

20. Rollnick S, Heather N, Bell A. Negotiating behavior change in medical settings: the development of brief motivational interviewing. *J Ment Health* 1992;1:25-37.

21. Miller WR, Rollnick S, eds. *Motivational interviewing: preparing people to change addictive behavior*. New York: Guilford, 1991.

Chapter 51

Outpatient and Inpatient Detoxification

Alcohol detoxification can be defined as a period of medical treatment, usually including counseling, during which a person is helped to overcome physical and psychological dependence on alcohol. The immediate objectives of alcohol detoxification are to help the patient achieve a substance-free state, relieve the immediate symptoms of withdrawal, and treat any comorbid medical or psychiatric conditions. These objectives help prepare the patient for entry into long-term treatment or rehabilitation, the ultimate goal of detoxification. The objectives of long-term treatment or rehabilitation include the long-term maintenance of the alcohol-free state and the incorporation of psychological, family, and social interventions to help ensure its persistence.

Alcohol detoxification can be completed safely and effectively in both inpatient and outpatient treatment settings. This chapter describes the advantages and disadvantages of inpatient and outpatient detoxification programs and considers the influence that the detoxification setting may have on long-term treatment outcomes.

Outpatient and Inpatient Detoxification

Patients receiving outpatient detoxification treatment usually are expected to travel to a hospital or other treatment facility daily (excluding

Excerpted from "An Overview of Outpatient and Inpatient Detoxification," by Motoi Hayashida, in *Alcohol Health and Research World*, Winter 1998, Vol. 22, No, 1, p. 44(3). A complete copy of this publication may be ordered from the U.S. Government Printing Office. Call (202) 512-1800 for information on price and availability.

weekends) for treatment sessions. The sessions may be scheduled for daytime or evening hours, depending on the program. The initial assessment, including intake history, physical examination, ordering of laboratory studies, and the initiation of detoxification treatment, usually takes 1 to 2 hours on the first day of outpatient detoxification. Subsequent sessions may range from 15 to 30 minutes. If the detoxification program is combined with a day hospital program, sessions can last several hours per day. The duration of treatment may range from 3 to 14 days. In one study, the average duration of treatment for outpatients was 6.5 days, significantly shorter than the average duration for inpatient detoxification (9 days). Patients receiving inpatient care are admitted to a hospital or other facility, where they reside for the duration of treatment, which may range from 5 to 14 days.

The process of detoxification in either setting initially involves the assessment and treatment of acute withdrawal symptoms, which may range from mild (for example, tremor and insomnia) to severe (for example, autonomic hyperactivity, seizures, and delirium). Medications often are provided to help reduce a patient's withdrawal symptoms. Benzodiazepines (for example, diazepam and chlordiazepoxide) are the most commonly used drugs for this purpose, and their efficacy is well established. Benzodiazepines not only reduce alcohol withdrawal symptoms but also prevent alcohol withdrawal seizures, which occur in an estimated 1 to 4 percent of withdrawal patients.

Anticonvulsant medications are necessary in addition to benzodiazepines for patients with a history of seizures unrelated to alcohol withdrawal. Additional components of alcohol detoxification may include education and counseling to help the patient prepare for long-term treatment, attendance at Alcoholics Anonymous meetings, recreational and social activities, and medical or surgical consultations.

Advantages of Outpatient Detoxification

For patients with mild-to-moderate alcohol withdrawal syndrome, characterized by symptoms such as hand tremor, perspiration, heart palpitation, restlessness, loss of appetite, nausea, and vomiting, outpatient detoxification is as safe and effective as inpatient detoxification but is much less expensive and less time consuming. In addition, patients who enroll in long-term outpatient rehabilitation treatment following detoxification in an outpatient setting may benefit by attending the same treatment facility for both phases of treatment. Most outpatients experience greater social support than inpatients, with the exception of outpatients in especially adverse family circumstances or job situations. Outpatients can continue to function relatively normally and maintain employment as well as family and social relationships. Compared with inpatients, those patients in outpatient treatment retain greater freedom, continue to work and maintain day-to-day activities with fewer disruptions, and incur fewer treatment costs.

Disadvantages of Outpatient Detoxification

Among the drawbacks associated with outpatient detoxification is the increased risk of relapse resulting from the patient's easy access to alcoholic beverages. In addition, outpatients can more easily choose not to keep their detoxification appointments and, consequently, fail to complete detoxification. In one study of 164 patients randomly assigned to either inpatient or outpatient detoxification, significantly more inpatients than outpatients completed detoxification. The higher completion rate among inpatients should not be interpreted as an indicator of long-term sobriety, however. Inpatients who successfully completed detoxification might have either dropped out of treatment or returned to drinking had they been treated in the outpatient setting. Thus, although inpatients may be more likely to complete detoxification, they may be arbitrarily postponing the chance to resume drinking after discharge.

Outpatient detoxification is not appropriate for all patients. Most alcohol treatment programs find that fewer than 10 percent of patients with alcohol withdrawal symptoms will need admission to an inpatient unit. Outpatient detoxification is not safe for alcoholics at risk for potentially life-threatening complications of withdrawal, such as delirium tremens, or those with associated medical conditions such as pancreatitis, gastrointestinal bleeding, or cirrhosis. In addition, outpatient detoxification is not appropriate for suicidal or homicidal patients, those with severe or medically complicated alcohol withdrawal, patients in adverse or disruptive family or job situations, or patients who would not be able to travel daily to the treatment facility.

Advantages of Inpatient Detoxification

Patients for whom outpatient detoxification is not appropriate become candidates for inpatient detoxification. Inpatient settings offer the advantages of constant medical care and supervision provided by a professional staff and the easy availability of treatment for serious complications. In addition, such settings prevent patient access to alcohol and offer separation from the substance-using environment.

Disadvantages of Inpatient Detoxification

The primary disadvantage of inpatient detoxification is its relatively higher cost compared with outpatient alternatives. In addition, inpatient care may relieve patients of personal responsibilities and encourage unnecessary dependence on hospital staff.

Detoxification and Overall Treatment Outcome

A number of factors should be considered in determining the appropriate detoxification setting for a particular patient. An important consideration is how the setting might influence overall treatment outcome. For each case, treatment professionals must consider whether inpatient or outpatient treatment would contribute more positively to an alcoholic's recovery process. Little research has been conducted in this area, however, and the studies that have been conducted do not suggest that one detoxification mode is preferable to another for achieving long-term treatment outcomes. In fact, no significant differences in overall treatment effectiveness, as measured by comprehensive outcome measures such as the Addiction Severity Index (ASI), have been reported between inpatient and outpatient programs. In one study, about one-half of all patients randomly assigned to either inpatient or outpatient detoxification remained abstinent 6 months later, irrespective of the program to which they were assigned. In addition, there was no significant difference in the percentage of each group that enrolled in long-term treatment following detoxification. However, one-third to one-half of patients who enter detoxification treatment, whether as inpatients or outpatients, return to alcohol abuse within 6 months.

Treatment outcome may have more to do with patient characteristics than with detoxification settings. Some researchers found that among alcoholics assigned to six different substance abuse treatment programs, patients with low psychiatric severity (as measured by the ASI) at treatment intake improved on outcome measures (medical condition, alcohol use, other drug use, employment, legal status, family relations, and psychiatric status) in every treatment program, whereas patients with high psychiatric severity showed virtually no improvement in any program. Another study found that patients who had three or four symptoms (for example, a history of alcohol-related seizures, a history of delirium tremens, current unemployment, and intoxication at the initial visit) had a 30-percent chance of completing outpatient detoxification, whereas the patients with none of those symptoms had a 95-percent chance of completion.

A significant number of alcoholics do not respond to treatment beyond detoxification. They "dry out" and then return to alcohol abuse. Many alcoholics repeat this cycle a few times and eventually enter long-term rehabilitation treatment. Some, however, continue to repeat this cycle as "detox-loopers" and exhibit the so-called "revolving-door" phenomenon.

Transition from Detoxification to Rehabilitative Treatment

Interventions used in rehabilitative treatment can be introduced during detoxification to help the alcoholic complete the process and make the transition to long-term treatment. It is important that the interventions be introduced as early as possible. Such interventions can include treatment for psychological, physical, family, and other needs as well as cue exposure—the repeated exposure to the sight, smell, and taste of alcohol without attendant intoxication effects, which diminishes the physiological and subjective responses originally associated with the alcohol cues.

Conclusion

The respective advantages and disadvantages of inpatient and outpatient detoxification may make one setting more appropriate than the other for a particular patient, but the detoxification setting does not appear to influence overall treatment outcome. A number of questions remain unanswered concerning how to determine when a particular setting will be advantageous for a patient. For example, the greater freedom provided patients in outpatient detoxification may have positive as well as negative consequences. More research is needed before treatment professionals will be able to discriminate between those patients for whom such freedom would be beneficial and those for whom such freedom would be detrimental.

Chapter 52

Alcohol Withdrawal

Every year more than one-and-a-half million people in the United States either enter alcoholism treatment or are admitted to a general hospital because of medical consequences resulting from alcohol dependence. These patients, as well as a substantial number of other people who stop drinking without seeking professional treatment, experience alcohol withdrawal (AW). AW is a clinical syndrome that affects people accustomed to regular alcohol intake who either decrease their alcohol consumption or stop drinking completely. In these people, the central nervous system (CNS) has adjusted to the constant presence of alcohol in the body and compensates for alcohol's depressive effects on both brain function and the communication among nerve cells (neurons). Consequently, when the alcohol level is suddenly lowered, the brain remains in a hyperactive, or hyper-excited, state, causing withdrawal syndrome.

AW syndrome varies significantly among alcoholics in both its clinical manifestations and its severity. These manifestations can range from mild insomnia to severe consequences, such as delirium tremens (DTs) and even death. (Clinicians generally distinguish between signs and symptoms of a disorder or syndrome. "Signs" are changes in the patient's condition that can be objectively observed by an examiner—temperature, a rash, or high blood pressure. Conversely, symptoms

---

Excerpted from "Introduction to Alcohol Withdrawal," by Richard Saitz, in *Alcohol Health and Research World*, Winter 1998, Vol. 22, No, 1, p. 5(8). A complete copy of this publication may be ordered from the U.S. Government Printing Office. Call (202) 512-1800 for information on price and availability.

are changes that are subjectively perceived by the patient—irritability or craving for alcohol. The term "manifestations of alcohol withdrawal," which is used in this chapter, can refer to either signs or symptoms.) Substantial variability also exists in the incidence with which symptoms occur in various drinkers. Some people who regularly consume alcohol never experience any withdrawal symptoms. Conversely, in some alcoholics withdrawal symptoms can occur at blood alcohol concentrations (BACs) that would be intoxicating in non-alcohol-dependent people but which for the dependent patients represent a decline from their usual BACs.

Mechanisms of Alcohol Withdrawal

Regular alcohol intake affects numerous excitatory and inhibitory neurotransmitter systems in the brain. Similarly, many neurotransmitters and mechanisms probably are involved in AW. Of these neurotransmitters, scientists best understand the roles of GABA and glutamate. For example, researchers have demonstrated that alcohol enhances GABA's inhibitory effects on signal-receiving neurons, thereby suppressing neuronal activity. With chronic alcohol exposure, however, GABA receptors become less responsive to the neurotransmitter, and higher alcohol concentrations are required to achieve the same level of suppression. This clinically observed adaptation is referred to as tolerance.

When alcohol is removed from this adapted system, the GABA receptors remain less responsive, leading to an imbalance in favor of excitatory neurotransmission. This imbalance is enhanced further by an alcohol-induced increase in the number of one type of receptor for the excitatory neurotransmitter, glutamate. Even when alcohol is removed, the number of these receptors remains elevated, leading to enhanced excitatory neurotransmission. Both of these mechanisms contribute to the neuronal hyperexcitability that is characteristic of AW.

Clinical Features of Alcohol Withdrawal

Despite this current understanding of the mechanisms underlying AW syndrome, some controversies still exist regarding the risk, complications, and clinical management of withdrawal. These controversies likely arise from the varied clinical manifestations of the syndrome in alcoholic patients and from the diverse settings in which these patients are encountered. For example, some alcoholic patients who cut down or stop drinking may experience no withdrawal symptoms, whereas others experience severe manifestations. In fact, even in clinical studies of patients presenting for alcohol detoxification, the proportion of patients who developed significant symptoms ranged from 13 to 71 percent.

Despite the variability in the type and severity of symptoms that a person can experience, the clinical syndrome of AW has been well defined. Its symptoms generally appear within hours of stopping or even just lowering alcohol intake and, thus, BAC. The most common symptoms include tremor, craving for alcohol, insomnia, vivid dreams, anxiety, hypervigilance ("hypervigilance" refers to a state of being overly concerned with everything, of being "on edge"; this state manifests itself, for example, by continually looking around and moving one's head in abrupt, jerky movements), agitation, irritability, loss of appetite (anorexia), nausea, vomiting, headache, and sweating. Even without treatment, most of these manifestations will usually resolve several hours to several days after their appearance. The most severe manifestations of AW include hallucinosis, seizures, and DTs.

Hallucinosis, which may occur within 1 or 2 days of decreasing or abstaining from alcohol intake, is a complication distinct from DTs. Patients with alcohol hallucinosis see, hear, or feel things that are not there even though they are fully conscious and aware of their surroundings. Moreover, hallucinosis is not necessarily preceded by various physiological changes (autonomic signs).

AW seizures also can occur within 1 or 2 days of decreased alcohol intake, even in the absence of other withdrawal signs and symptoms. The patient usually experiences only one generalized convulsion, which involves shaking of the arms and legs and loss of consciousness. If a second convulsion occurs, it generally happens within 6 hours of the first seizure. Although multiple seizures are not common, AW is one of the most common causes in the United States of status epilepticus—a medical emergency characterized by continuous, unrelenting seizures.

DTs, which last up to 3 or 4 days, are characterized by disorientation and are usually accompanied by autonomic signs resulting from the activation of the nerves responsible for the body's response to stress. Those signs include severe agitation, rapid heartbeat (tachycardia), high blood pressure, and fever. (Thus, DTs are a much more serious condition than the "shakes," which often are also colloquially referred to as DTs.) DTs can develop between 1 and 4 days after the onset of withdrawal and are generally preceded by additional autonomic signs, such as sweating and tremors. About five percent of the patients who experience DTs die from metabolic or cardiovascular complications, trauma, or infections.

Risk Factors for DTs and Seizures

Given the wide range of potential manifestations associated with withdrawal, is it possible to predict their development in individual patients? Currently, the answer is "no." To date, most studies of predictors of severe or complicated withdrawal have been too limited methodologically to allow clinically accurate prognoses for individual patients. Based on current understanding of the withdrawal syndrome, as well as on some clinical research results, however, clinicians have identified some patient characteristics that likely confer a risk of more severe withdrawal symptoms, prolonged symptoms, or withdrawal-specific complications, such as DTs or seizures. These factors include the following:

- More severe alcohol dependence, including prior development of withdrawal symptoms
- Higher levels of alcohol intake, resulting in higher BACs
- Longer duration of alcoholism
- Abnormal liver function
- Prior detoxification
- Past experience of seizures or DTs
- Intense craving for alcohol
- Concomitant acute illness
- Older age
- Use of other drugs in addition to alcohol
- More severe withdrawal symptoms when presenting for treatment.

Management of Alcohol Withdrawal

Assessment

The symptoms of withdrawal are not specific and easily can be confused with other medical conditions. Consequently, the clinician's initial assessment also serves to exclude other conditions with symptoms similar to those of AW. Examples of such conditions include subdural hematoma (the collection of blood in the space between the membranes surrounding the CNS), pneumonia, meningitis, and other infections. Similarly, seizures and DTs may be confused with other conditions that should be excluded during initial assessment. For example, DTs, which represent an acute confusional state, can mimic delirium from other medical causes, such as encephalitis, meningitis, adverse effects of some medications, or Wernicke's encephalopathy. (Wernicke's encephalopathy is an acute condition characterized by general confusion, abnormal eye movements, and difficulty walking or keeping one's balance.) Likewise, AW seizures must be distinguished from seizures resulting from other causes, such as mineral or electrolyte abnormalities, strokes, brain tumors, epilepsy, or subdural hematoma. Thus, a diagnosis of DTs and AW seizures should be made only after other reasonable causes for these complications have been excluded.

Treatment of Alcohol Withdrawal

For all patients, especially those experiencing severe withdrawal symptoms, proven benefits of treatment include amelioration of symptoms, prevention of both seizures and DTs, and treatment of DTs. Treatment also may prevent increasing severity of withdrawal during subsequent withdrawal episodes and encourage the patient to enter alcoholism treatment for relapse prevention.

Patients with mild withdrawal symptoms and no increased risk for seizures can be managed without specific pharmacotherapy. Successful nonpharmacological treatments include frequent reassurance and monitoring by treatment staff in a quiet, calm environment. Most patients with mild withdrawal symptoms, whether they are treated or not, do not develop complications.

Many patients who experience mild withdrawal symptoms do not seek treatment at all. Nevertheless, even those patients may benefit from treatment in the long term, because repeated withdrawal episodes may enhance the brain's susceptibility to the hyperexcitability that occurs during AW. This process is known as kindling. Clinical studies have found that patients with a history of multiple withdrawal episodes have a higher risk of seizures than do patients experiencing their first withdrawal episode. The results of these clinical studies are confounded by differences among the subjects in the severity of dependence, duration of dependence, and quantity of alcohol consumed. The findings are consistent, however, with information obtained using animal research. Thus, prompt appropriate treatment of withdrawal, even in patients with mild symptoms, may conceivably prevent the development of complicated, more severe withdrawal during subsequent episodes.

Pharmacotherapy of Alcohol Withdrawal Symptoms

Patients who experience more severe withdrawal should receive pharmacotherapy to treat their symptoms and reduce their risk of seizures and DTs. The medications with the best efficacy and safety are the benzodiazepines. Like alcohol, these agents enhance the effect of the neurotransmitter GABA on the brain. Because of their similar effects, benzodiazepines and alcohol are cross-tolerant—in other words, a person who is tolerant to alcohol also is tolerant to benzodiazepines. Cross-tolerance also implies that when a person experiences a deficiency of one agent (for example, alcohol during withdrawal), the other agent (for example, a benzodiazepine) can serve as a substitute, thereby easing the withdrawal symptoms.

Benzodiazepines not only improve the symptoms of AW but also reduce the incidence of DTs and seizures. In addition, they generally are safe and can be administered repeatedly over several hours. The best-studied benzodiazepines for AW treatment are diazepam, chlordiazepoxide, and lorazepam. These agents all are relatively long acting (for up to several days) and therefore can provide a smooth course of treatment without the risk of rebound symptoms (for example, seizures) that occur late during withdrawal. Lorazepam should be used in patients with severe liver dysfunction and in patients who are at high risk of experiencing serious medical consequences following sedation, such as people with severe lung disease or elderly patients. Short-acting (for several hours) benzodiazepines probably are efficacious as well but are associated with a greater risk of rebound symptoms. To prevent recurrence of withdrawal symptoms, these agents must be given in increasingly smaller doses (require tapering) before they can be discontinued.

Many agents other than benzodiazepines have been used for managing AW. For example, other cross-tolerant medications, such as barbiturates, would be expected to relieve withdrawal symptoms and prevent withdrawal seizures and DTs. In fact, a few studies have demonstrated that long-acting barbiturates can ease withdrawal symptoms. However, controlled studies have not provided sufficient data to demonstrate that these agents can prevent seizures or DTs. Furthermore, barbiturates have a narrow therapeutic index—that is, the difference between the minimum dose required for a therapeutic effect and the dose at which the agents become toxic is small.

Alcohol itself also would be expected to improve withdrawal symptoms, and alcoholic patients know that alcohol consumption can relieve their symptoms. Alcohol should not be used, however, to treat withdrawal for several reasons. First, using alcohol as a treatment would promote its acceptability to the alcoholic. Second, alcohol has known toxic effects (for example, impairing the function of the liver, pancreas, and bone marrow) that are not shared by the safer benzodiazepines. Third, in one clinical study, alcohol was inferior to the benzodiazepine chlordiazepoxide.

Clonidine—an antihypertensive medication—also may have a role in the management of withdrawal symptoms, although it has not been shown to affect the occurrence of withdrawal-specific complications. Another agent that has shown promise for managing AW is the anticonvulsant carbamazepine. Animal studies have demonstrated that the medication may prevent seizures. Moreover, it does not interfere with mental processes, such as learning, whereas other agents (for example, benzodiazepines) can cause amnesia, mental dullness, and sleepiness (somnolence).

Carbamazepine also does not potentiate alcohol-induced depression of the CNS, nor does it affect respiratory function. In addition, unlike the benzodiazepines, carbamazepine does not have the potential for abuse. Finally, carbamazepine may prevent kindling. This agent has not been shown, however, to prevent withdrawal-specific complications, and it can cause substantial side effects, including nausea and dizziness.

Other medications can serve as effective adjuncts to care. For example, beta-blockers (such as propranolol and atenolol) can ameliorate some manifestations of withdrawal, such as tachycardia, high blood pressure, and even anxiety, but they increase the likelihood of delirium when used by themselves (as monotherapy). Consequently, these agents should be used only in combination with benzodiazepines. In general, the use of beta-blockers for treating withdrawal should be considered primarily for patients with coexisting coronary artery disease. Antipsychotic medications such as haloperidol can treat hallucinations and agitation that are unresponsive to adequate doses of benzodiazepines. Because antipsychotic medications can increase the risk of seizures, however, these agents should be used only in combination with benzodiazepines.

Management of Withdrawal-Specific Complications

AW seizures generally can be prevented by medications that are cross-tolerant with alcohol. For example, benzodiazepines have been shown to prevent both initial and recurr ent seizures. Similarly, carbamazepine and the barbiturate phenobarbital probably can prevent AW seizures, although insufficient data exist in humans to confirm this hypothesis. In contrast, phenyotin, an anticonvulsant medication used for treating seizures caused by epilepsy and other disorders, is ineffective for treating AW seizures. Because a diagnosis of AW-related seizures may require further evaluation, however, the agent is sometimes administered until other causes of seizures have been ruled out.

Benzodiazepines also prevent DTs. However, no known treatments exist to shorten the course of DTs once this complication has been established. Nonetheless, diazepam can improve outcome by rapidly inducing a calm, awake state, thereby avoiding the traumatic complications associated with severe agitation. Constant monitoring is essential for patients experiencing this serious complication.

Chapter 53

Delirium Tremens

What is delirium tremens?

Delirium tremens (the DTs) is a disorder that occurs in a small percentage of alcoholics and is caused by the withdrawal of alcohol. It is a serious medical disorder that includes severe memory disturbances, agitation, hallucinations, and other symptoms of alcohol withdrawal, such as headache and nausea. Delirium tremens usually starts 24 to 72 hours after a chronic alcoholic either stops drinking or severely limits drinking alcohol. Delirium tremens is potentially fatal.

How does it occur?

Chronic drinking changes the biochemical functioning of the body. When you start drinking less or completely stop drinking, your body chemistry changes again. While the body is going through this change, you suffer severe reactions.

What are the symptoms?

The symptoms of the DTs include:

- nightmares (accompanied by the sense of not being able to breathe)
- anxiety

- panic attacks
- restlessness and inability to sleep
- delusions and hallucinations (hearing or seeing things that are not there)
- disturbed behavior
- major memory disturbances
- dizziness
- rapid heartbeat
- fever
- dilated pupils
- convulsions
- sweating

How is it diagnosed?

A doctor will take your medical history, perform a physical exam, and may order blood tests and x-rays.

How is it treated?

Do not try to withdraw from heavy, prolonged use of alcohol without help. If you experience symptoms of the DTs, someone should take you to the emergency room at a hospital.

In the hospital, you will be closely watched and sedated if necessary to prevent injury to yourself and others. The doctor will monitor your blood pressure, pulse, and breathing. You will be given a nutritious diet and intravenous (IV) fluid supplements. You may receive vitamin supplements as well.

You will stay in a well-lighted room. A staff member will come in and talk with you and check on you several times a day. Family support will be welcomed. The staff will monitor your anxiety, delusions, and hallucinations, and help you through these events.

The doctor may prescribe sedatives and other medications to keep you calm and prevent seizures. The doctor will gradually reduce your dosage as your withdrawal ends.

How long will the effects last?

The symptoms of delirium tremens usually last 1 to 5 days. However, they can last for as long as 10 days.

How can I take care of myself?

You can help take care of yourself by following these guidelines:

- If you are in the hospital, keep the caregivers informed about how you are feeling. Report any auditory (voices) or visual (small bugs, animals) hallucinations.
- Rest.
- Eat and drink healthy foods and fluids as much as possible.
- Abstain from alcohol as recommended by your doctor.
- **Do not** drink alcohol while you are taking drugs to aid your withdrawal.
- Follow your doctor's advice for treatment of any other medical problems.

How can I stop the effects of alcohol dependence?

Coming to terms with alcohol dependence before it becomes a chronic, life-threatening problem is the best prevention.

Alcoholism is a treatable problem. If treated in its early stage by abstinence from alcohol you can avoid medical complications such as DTs.

If you are hospitalized for a reason other than alcoholism and you are a chronic drinker, inform your doctor and caregivers so they can prepare for delirium tremens. If you keep this information from your doctor, you may have serious complications that could result in death.

Alcoholics Anonymous (AA) meetings are open to all at no cost. In many cities there are several meetings a day at various locations to fit your schedule. Look up the phone number in the business section of your phone book to get more information on AA (for alcoholics) or Al-Anon (for families of alcoholics).

Chapter 54

Complications of Alcohol Withdrawal

Abrupt reduction or total cessation of long-term alcohol consumption produces a well-defined cluster of symptoms called acute alcohol withdrawal (AW). Although some patients experience relatively mild withdrawal symptoms, disease processes or events that accompany AW can cause significant illness and death. After acute withdrawal has subsided, a poorly defined syndrome of protracted withdrawal may ensue. The persistent alterations in physiology, mood, and behavior associated with protracted withdrawal may motivate the patient to relapse to heavy drinking. This chapter describes the acute withdrawal syndrome and its complications, including seizures, delirium tremens, Wernicke-Korsakoff syndrome, neuropsychiatric disturbances, and cardiovascular complications as well as the protracted withdrawal syndrome.

Acute Alcohol Withdrawal Syndrome

Alcohol withdrawal is a distinctive clinical syndrome with potentially serious consequences. Symptoms begin as early as 6 hours after the initial decline from peak intoxication. Initial symptoms include tremor, anxiety, insomnia, restlessness, and nausea. Particularly in

Excerpted from "Complications of Alcohol Withdrawal: Pathophysiological Insights," by Louis A. Trevisan, Nashaat Boutros, Ismene L. Petrakis, and John H. Krystal, in *Alcohol Health and Research World*, Winter 1998, Vol. 22, No, 1, p. 61(6). A complete copy of this publication may be ordered from the U.S. Government Printing Office. Call (202) 512-1800 for information on price and availability.

mildly alcohol-dependent persons, these symptoms may comprise the entire syndrome and may subside without treatment after a few days. More serious withdrawal symptoms occur in approximately 10 percent of patients. These symptoms include a low-grade fever, rapid breathing, tremor, and profuse sweating. Seizures may occur in more than 5 percent of untreated patients in acute alcohol withdrawal. Another severe complication is delirium tremens (DTs), which is characterized by hallucinations, mental confusion, and disorientation. The mortality rate among patients exhibiting DTs is 5 to 25 percent.

Seizures

Withdrawal seizures usually consist of generalized convulsions alternating with spasmodic muscular contractions (tonic-clonic seizures). Seizures that begin locally (for example, with twitching of a limb) suggest the presence of a co-occurring disorder, which should be fully investigated.

More than 90 percent of alcohol withdrawal seizures occur within 48 hours after the patient stops drinking. Fewer than 3 percent of such seizures may occur 5 to 20 days after the last drink. Clinical data suggest that the likelihood of having withdrawal seizures, as well as the severity of those seizures, increases with the number of past withdrawals. The correlation between the number of alcohol detoxifications and the development of alcohol withdrawal complications, including seizures, has been ascribed to cumulative long-term changes in brain excitability.

Delirium Tremens

DTs are a serious manifestation of alcohol dependence that develops 1 to 4 days after the onset of acute alcohol withdrawal in persons who have been drinking excessively for years. Signs of DTs include extreme hyperactivity of the autonomic nervous system, along with hallucinations. Women experiencing DTs appear to exhibit autonomic symptoms less frequently than men. Co-occurring medical problems may obscure the diagnosis and treatment of DTs or worsen the outcome. Such medical problems include altered blood chemistry, certain infections, and Wernicke's syndrome. Death may occur in up to 5 percent of patients with DTs. The risk of death is reduced, however, in patients receiving adequate medication and medical support.

Alcoholics who are awaiting surgical or medical treatment often exhibit DTs when their alcohol consumption is abruptly interrupted by hospitalization. Therefore, hospital staff must remain vigilant for signs and symptoms of alcohol withdrawal, even in patients not known to be alcoholic. In addition, clinicians must learn to differentiate DTs from other possible causes of delirium.

The prediction of complicated alcohol withdrawal is an important part of alcoholism treatment to ensure that appropriate therapies may be planned in advance. Risk factors for prolonged or complicated alcohol withdrawal include lifetime or current long duration of alcohol consumption, lifetime prior detoxifications, prior seizures, prior episodes of DTs, and current intense craving for alcohol. Certain clinical and biochemical findings have been associated with high risk for the development of DTs, including specific alterations of blood chemistry, elevated liver enzymes, and certain nervous system disturbances, including muscular incoordination.

Wernicke-Korsakoff Syndrome

The combination of Wernicke and Korsakoff syndromes is not a complication of AW but rather of a nutritional deficiency. Nevertheless, the syndromes usually occur during AW. Wernicke's syndrome is a disorder of the nervous system caused by thiamine deficiency, and alcoholics account for most cases in the Western world. The syndrome is characterized by severe cognitive impairment and delirium, abnormal gait (ataxia), and paralysis of certain eye muscles. A majority of patients are profoundly disoriented, indifferent, and inattentive; some exhibit an agitated delirium related to alcohol withdrawal. Ocular signs improve within hours to days; ataxia and confusion improve within days to weeks. A majority of patients are left with an abnormal gaze, persistent ataxia, and a potentially disabling memory disorder known as Korsakoff's syndrome. Although fewer than 5 percent of patients initially exhibit a depressed level of consciousness, the course in untreated patients may progress through stupor, coma, and death. Nutritional status should be closely monitored during treatment of acute AW to prevent Wernicke-Korsakoff syndrome.

Approximately 80 percent of alcoholic patients recovering from Wernicke's syndrome exhibit the selective memory disturbance of Korsakoff syndrome. Symptoms of Korsakoff syndrome include severe amnesia for past events, along with impaired ability to commit current experience to memory. The patient often recites imaginary experiences to fill gaps in his or her memory. Although the patient may be apathetic, intellectual abilities other than memory are relatively preserved. Korsakoff syndrome can occur in the absence of alcohol use; however, the disease rarely follows Wernicke syndrome in nonalcoholics. This observation has lead to speculation that the neurotoxicity of alcohol is an important contributing factor in the memory disorders of alcoholics.

Disturbances of Mood, Thought, and Perception

Withdrawing alcoholics exhibit psychiatric difficulties that may be related to the process of withdrawal itself or to co-occurring conditions. The major psychiatric problems associated with acute and protracted withdrawal are anxiety, depression, and sleep disturbance. Less frequently, psychotic symptoms, including delusions and hallucinations, may be associated with withdrawal.

Anxiety

Anxiety disorders are manifested by extreme fear and anxiety, accompanied by heart palpitations; shallow, rapid breathing (hyperventilation); sweating; and dizziness. Alcohol has antianxiety properties that promote its use to self-medicate anxiety. However, prolonged alcohol use—and especially acute AW states—can increase anxiety levels. Marked signs of anxiety commonly appear between 12 and 48 hours after cessation of alcohol consumption.

Hyperventilation may occur during acute withdrawal, leading to disturbed blood chemistry and resulting in symptoms that may be indistinguishable from those that occur in anxiety disorders. Some researchers have hypothesized that repeated AW may predispose alcoholics to certain anxiety disorders through the process of kindling.

Depression

Depressive symptoms often are observed in patients who are intoxicated or undergoing alcohol detoxification. As many as 15 percent of alcoholics are at risk for death by suicide, and recent consumption of alcohol appears to increase the danger of a fatal outcome from self-harm. This finding may be attributable to the release of behavioral inhibition associated with alcohol intoxication or with the depressive feeling states that accompany the decline from peak intoxication. Depressive disorders commonly emerge during AW; in addition to the depressive feeling states associated with alcohol consumption and withdrawal, the social, psychological, and physical problems associated with alcoholism may contribute to the development of depressive disorders.

Sleep Disturbances

Sleep disturbances—including frequent awakening, restless sleep, insomnia, and night terrors—are among the most common complaints of alcoholics. Sleep problems persist into AW, with pronounced insomnia and marked sleep fragmentation. In addition, alcoholics show increased incidence of interrupted breathing during sleep compared with the general population. These sleep disturbances can cause daytime drowsiness, reducing the efficiency of performance of daytime tasks and increasing the risk of car crashes.

Hallucinations and Perceptual Disturbance

Visual, auditory, and tactile hallucinations are frequently experienced in acute, complicated AW or DTs. Hallucinations that are not connected with DTs occur in 3 to 10 percent of patients during severe AW from 12 hours to 7 days after cessation or reduction of alcohol consumption.

In one study, 10 percent of 532 male patients admitted to a Veterans Affairs Hospital for AW developed hallucinations. Patients who hallucinated tended to be younger at the onset of their alcohol problems, consumed more alcohol per drinking occasion, developed more alcohol-related life problems, and had higher rates of other drug use than patients who did not hallucinate.

Cardiovascular Complications

The heart is a major site of alcohol-induced organ damage, including disturbances of heartbeat rhythm. For example, the "holiday heart syndrome" consists of episodes of abnormal cardiac rhythms following a bout of drinking. Because arrhythmia generally occurs after a binge, rather than during intoxication, AW may be a contributing factor to the occurrence of alcohol-related arrhythmia. Further study is required to elucidate the possible connection between AW and increased sudden cardiac death.

Protracted Withdrawal Syndrome

Data appear to indicate that a protracted withdrawal syndrome (PWS) may develop following AW and may persist for at least 1 year. Some manifestations of PWS include symptoms associated with AW that persist beyond their typical time course. These symptoms include tremor, sleep disruption, anxiety, depressive symptoms, and increased breathing rate, body temperature, blood pressure, and pulse. Other symptoms of PWS appear to oppose symptoms of AW. These symptoms of PWS include decreased energy, lassitude, and decreased overall metabolism.

The significance of this cluster of symptoms has been debated. For example, PWS could reflect the brain's slow recovery from the reversible nerve cell damage common in alcoholism. Clinically, the symptoms of PWS are important, because they may predispose abstinent alcoholics to relapse in an attempt to alleviate the symptoms.

Reproductive Hormones and Alcohol Withdrawal

Declines in the levels of neurosteroids may contribute to AW. Neurosteroids are substances involved in the metabolism of reproductive hormones that also have potent and specific effects on various functions of the brain. Because decreases in neurosteroids may contribute to AW symptoms, these compounds may have potential as medications for alleviating withdrawal.

Researchers have investigated the role of the male reproductive hormone testosterone on withdrawal symptoms. Long-term alcohol consumption causes failure of the reproductive system in men. In addition, testosterone levels decrease during alcohol consumption and increase after withdrawal. Low levels of testosterone during AW are associated with psychological symptoms, such as indecision, excessive worrying, fatigability, and lassitude. Researchers suggest that testosterone be administered during detoxification to determine whether a causal relationship exists.

Antiseizure Medications

For many years, seizures and other symptoms of AW have been treated with a class of sedating medications called benzodiazepines (for example, Valium®). Several studies have demonstrated that the antiseizure medications carbamezapine (Tegretol®) and valproic acid (Depakene®) are as effective as benzodiazepines for this purpose. Moreover, unlike the benzodiazepines, these antiseizure medications are not potential drugs of abuse.

Alcohol withdrawal seizures and PWS have been linked to both GABA and NMDA dysregulation. [GABA and NMDA are neurotransmitters, playing an important role in the communication between nerve cells.] Although the mechanisms of action of carbamezapine and valproic acid are not entirely understood, both medications appear to increase GABA levels in the brain in patients with seizure disorders. In addition, valproic acid at therapeutic levels appears to be effective at inhibiting seizures induced by the stimulatory effect of NMDA receptors.

Laboratory studies suggest that valproic acid may inhibit GABA metabolism and activate GABA synthesis. In addition, data indicate that carbamezapine decreases the flow of glutamate into the hippocampus, a part of the brain involved in seizures. Therefore carbamezapine and valproic acid prevent alcohol withdrawal seizures and kindling.

The antianxiety and mood-stabilizing actions of these anticonvulsants may enhance their efficacy in treating withdrawal symptoms. These actions also may help relieve the constellation of symptoms associated with PWS, perhaps resulting in fewer and more mild relapses during the period following acute withdrawal.

Summary

AW and its complications are among the most visible consequences of alcoholism. Those syndromes arise directly from adaptations made within nerve cell communication systems that are targets of alcohol in the brain. Among its actions, alcohol acutely facilitates the activity of $GABA_A$ receptor function and blocks NMDA receptor activity. The adaptations within these systems contribute to withdrawal-related symptoms, seizures, and neurotoxicity. Repeated AW episodes appear to increase the risk of future AW seizures.

Acute withdrawal symptoms and complications, including seizures, hallucinations, and DTs, represent medical emergencies. Some complications, including Wernicke-Korsakoff syndrome, may be permanently disabling. In addition, the distress associated with acute and protracted withdrawal presents an ongoing motivation to relapse to alcohol use in recently detoxified patients. Thus, the early stages of sobriety represent a period of risk at many levels.

Available treatments suppress many symptoms and complications of AW. Consequently, greater emphasis may now be placed on developing strategies to facilitate long-term sobriety. An important step in this direction may be the development of medications that lack the addiction potential of the benzodiazepines. The antiseizure medications meet these criteria and have the added capacity to suppress kindling.

AW represents a period of significant clinical risk that requires attentive medical management. However, AW also provides an opportunity to initiate treatments that may lead to extended sobriety. As such, it is a critical component of the long-term treatment strategy for every patient with alcoholism.

Chapter 55

Project MATCH (Matching Alcoholism Treatments to Client Heterogeneity)

NIAAA Reports Project MATCH Main Findings

In 1996, the National Institute on Alcohol Abuse and Alcoholism (NIAAA) announced main findings from the largest and most statistically powerful clinical trial of psychotherapies ever undertaken. Designed to test whether different types of alcoholics respond differently to specific therapeutic approaches, the eight-year, multisite trial confirmed one hypothetical "match" and did not confirm ten others, leading researchers to conclude that patient-treatment matching does not substantially alter outcomes.

"The hypothesis that patients who are appropriately matched to treatments will show better outcomes than those who are unmatched or mismatched is well founded in medicine, behavioral science, and alcoholism treatment," according to NIAAA Director Enoch Gordis, M.D. "These findings challenge the notion that patient-treatment matching is necessary in alcoholism treatment."

About nine percent of U.S. adults meet diagnostic criteria for alcohol dependence (alcoholism) and the less severe medical disorder alcohol abuse. Of these, more than 500,000 Americans were treated in 1993 in more than 8,000 inpatient and outpatient alcohol treatment

---

This chapter contains text from "NIAAA Reports Project MATCH Main Findings," National Institute on Alcohol Abuse and Alcoholism (NIAAA), December 17, 1996; and "What NIAAA's Project MATCH Really Found," by Richard L. Peck, in *Behavioral Health Management*, September-October 1997, Vol. 17, No. 5, p. 32(3),

programs in the United States. While some of these patients have experienced or eventually will experience lasting remission, authoritative studies report relapse rates of more than 50 percent or more at two to four years after treatment. A recent meta-analysis of past alcohol treatment outcome studies estimates that more than 50 percent of treated patients relapse within the first 3 months after treatment.

Researchers during the 1980s saw promise for improving alcohol treatment outcomes in reports from more than 30 small-scale studies indicating that patient characteristics interact with behavioral treatments to affect results. At the end of the decade, when the National Academy of Science's Institute of Medicine (IOM) recommended further research on patient-treatment matching, potential benefits were seen not only as improved treatment outcomes but also as increased cost-effectiveness and improved resource utilization.

NIAAA initiated "Matching Alcoholism Treatments to Client Heterogeneity" (Project MATCH) in 1989 to provide a rigorous test of the most promising hypothetical matches.

Project MATCH investigators selected three behavioral treatments that differed markedly in philosophy and practice: 12-step facilitation therapy (based on the principles of Alcoholics Anonymous but an independent treatment designed to familiarize patients with the AA philosophy and to encourage participation), cognitive-behavioral therapy (based on social learning theory and designed to provide skills for avoiding relapse), and motivational enhancement therapy (based on motivational psychology and designed to help patients mobilize personal resources to effect change). The treatments were selected in part for their distinctiveness and in part because each had demonstrated effectiveness, the potential to reveal matching effects, and the potential to be incorporated into standard alcoholism treatment programs. Many patients in the three treatments also participated in community meetings of Alcoholics Anonymous, a mutual support fellowship rather than a formal treatment.

Patient characteristics, chosen on the basis of research and theory, included severity of alcohol involvement, cognitive impairment, psychiatric severity, conceptual level, gender, meaning-seeking, motivational readiness to change, social support for drinking versus abstinence, sociopathy, and typology of alcoholism. The Project MATCH research group predicted 16 contrasts in patient responses to the treatments, to be measured as percentage of abstinent days and average number of drinks per drinking day during the year following treatment.

The researchers recruited 1,726 patients for two parallel study arms—one with alcohol dependent patients who received outpatient therapy and one with patients who received aftercare therapy following inpatient or day hospital treatment—that involved identical matching hypotheses and identical randomization, assessment, and follow-up procedures. Twenty-five therapists administered the therapies over a 12-week period in individual counseling sessions that adhered strictly to manuals developed for the trial.

The single confirmed match reported was between patients with low psychiatric severity and 12-step facilitation therapy. Such patients had more abstinent days than those treated with cognitive-behavioral therapy.

Overall, Project MATCH participants showed significant and sustained improvement in increased percentage of abstinent days and decreased number of drinks per drinking days, with few clinically significant outcome differences among the three treatments in either treatment arm. For example, there was no difference in sustained abstinence among treatments in the aftercare arm. However, outpatients who received 12-step facilitation were more likely to remain completely abstinent in the year following treatment than outpatients who received the other treatments.

Patients who participated in Project MATCH also showed decreased use of other drugs, depression, and alcohol-related problems as well as improved liver function—improvements that were maintained throughout the 12 months following treatment, the period during which most relapses typically occur.

The Project MATCH patients probably did well because the treatments were of high quality and well delivered, according to Thomas F. Babor, Ph.D., Department of Psychiatry, University of Connecticut Health Center and principal investigator for the Project MATCH Coordinating Center: "The striking differences in drinking from pretreatment levels to all follow-up points suggest that participation in any of the MATCH treatments would be associated with marked positive change."

Gerard Connors, Ph.D., chairperson of the Project MATCH Steering Committee and principal investigator at the Research Institute on Addictions in Buffalo, New York, noted that the findings did not rule out the possibility that other patient-treatment matching effects may be clinically important. "The MATCH data do not speak at all to matching patients types to different treatment settings, therapists, psychotherapies other than those studied, or pharmacological treatments," he said.

"A logical next step for alcoholism treatment research is to test our quite excellent behavioral treatments in conjunction with promising pharmacological treatments for alcoholism," said Richard K. Fuller, M.D., Director of NIAAA's Division of Clinical and Prevention Research, which oversaw Project MATCH.

The Project MATCH findings may surprise but should not dismay those who foresaw a revolution in alcohol treatment delivery based on patient-treatment matching, said Dr. Gordis. "These findings are good news for treatment providers and for patients who can have confidence that any one of these treatments, if well-delivered, represents the state of the art in behavioral treatments."

"Research attention now must focus full force on illuminating the complex biochemical mechanisms of alcoholism, including the abnormal appetite for alcohol that leads to impaired control over intake, tolerance—drinking ever greater amounts to achieve a desired effect—and the discomfort of abstinence known as craving. Our best pharmacologic and behavioral treatments await that understanding."

What NIAAA's Project MATCH Really Found

At first glance the message to managed behavioral care decision makers seemed to be this: It doesn't matter which type of treatment alcohol-abusing clients use, they'll do equally well with any of them—and thus the managed-care-friendly conclusion that the "cheapest" was good enough. Even less careful readers might find a hint that a simple referral to Alcoholics Anonymous was about as good as anything. What's more, all of this was based on a massive five-year study by the National Institute on Alcohol Abuse and Alcoholism called "the largest clinical trial of psychotherapies ever undertaken."

Those interpretations, as it turned out, were grossly oversimplified and misleading. True, the study—called Project MATCH did involve a sample of 1,726 patients throughout the United States and did scrupulously compare the outcomes of three common therapies: cognitive behavioral therapy (CBT), motivational enhancement therapy (MET) and an approach called "12-step facilitation" (TSF). The goal was to attempt to confirm studies indicating that specific patients could be matched to specific anti-alcoholism treatments for best outcomes—and, true, no particularly significant matches were found . But translating this to the treatment population in general is another matter. To clarify what all of this means, NIAAA's Chief of Treatment Research, John P. Allen, Ph.D., recently fielded questions from *Behavioral Health Management* Editorial Director Richard L. Peck.

Peck: To begin with, would you summarize the key finding(s) of Project MATCH?

Dr. Allen: First, it is important that people get into treatment, such as one of the three therapies we investigated; however, the exact assignment of patients to specific treatments is not as important as we would have predicted. Second, all three treatments worked quite well. When patients were compared in terms of the number of days drinking and number of drinks per day, between the start of treatment and 15 months after, the reductions were quite dramatic—for example, a reduction in drinking days from 25 before treatment to 6 after. Third, these treatment gains were maintained as long as 39 months post-treatment.

Peck: Still, didn't the absence of treatment matching factors surprise you?

Dr. Allen: Yes, many smaller-scale studies had found matching effects, but these were not confirmed in this much larger-scale trial. We were also surprised that patients did as well as they did, even with one of the treatments—motivational enhancement therapy—using only four sessions over 12 weeks. (12-step facilitation and cognitive behavioral therapy each used 12 sessions over that time period.) All in all, over two-thirds of appointments were kept and more than 90% of the patients participated in the one-year follow-up, despite literature indicating a much higher drop-out rate among ambulatory patients.

Peck: How, though, did the treatments the study patients received compare with the typical treatment they would find in the community?

Dr. Allen: There was a considerable difference. For each of the three treatments the NIAAA investigators developed a manual guiding counselors on how the treatment should be conducted, what its "active ingredients" were, what sorts of "homework" should be assigned, and so forth. These manuals have proven to be quite popular in the field, by the way, and we've distributed about 40,000 of them so far. (For free photocopies of any or all of the manuals, write: NIAAA, P.O. Box 10686, Rockville, MD 20849-0686.) Another difference was that the investigators trained, monitored and critiqued the counselors before the trial began. They had videotaped "practice sessions" on which they received feedback (and, for study purposes, their actual sessions were videotaped as well, with patients' permission). Counselors also had such credentialing requirements as a master's degree, Certified Alcoholism Counselor (CAC) certification and at least two years' field experience. Still another important consideration was that the patients received a thorough initial assessment lasting six to eight hours—probably quite a bit more extensive than they would typically receive in the field. Finally, all treatment was provided on an individual basis, rather than in group format, which is the predominant approach today.

Peck: How, then, does all of this bear on interpreting the findings?

Dr. Allen: The truly key finding of this study is that treatment, of any of the three types we investigated, works well when structured in this way.

Peck: In line with this, would you elaborate on the difference between the study's approach to "12-step facilitation" and simple referral to AA?

Dr. Allen: Yes, the 12-step facilitation approach is a formal treatment, involving a one-to-one relationship with a professional counselor guided by a manual specifically prepared for this. There is not the emphasis on peer support that you have with AA. I will say, however, that the philosophical basis of this approach is similar to AA's; that is, based on the disease concept of alcoholism, addressing spiritual issues and working the first five steps.

This was not a study of the efficacy of AA. We did find that patients who had attended AA did better on follow-up than those who hadn't, but it wasn't clear whether this was because they were more motivated by the treatment experience to benefit from AA, or because AA attendance was in itself a contributing factor.

Peck: What did you learn about cognitive behavioral therapy and motivational enhancement therapy?

Dr. Allen: Aside from the fact that both treatments worked well—and MET in particular did better than might have been expected with only four sessions—we were intrigued by some other possibilities, which will need further study. For example, CBT is frequently used in treating depression, and it is possible that the reduced frequency of drinking observed was related to a reduction in depression. With MET, the primary purpose of which is to enhance a person's sense of self-efficacy in dealing with problems, the question is whether it produced additional effects to reduced drinking. There were also questions about whether increasing the number or frequency of sessions for all three therapies would have improved the results. None of these issues has as yet been analyzed, but they should be.

Peck: What about the question so key to decision makers in managed care: cost? Were there any findings in terms of relative cost-effectiveness of these treatments?

Dr. Allen: These are undergoing actuarial analysis and are awaiting publication, but I can say that in a general sense, the costs involved were comparable.

Peck: So what is the real "take home" message of all this for managed behavioral care decision makers?

Dr. Allen: If I were in a position to decide on reimbursement for alcoholism treatment services, I would reimburse for services similar to the ones given in Project MATCH—that is to say, treatment approaches clearly defined in a manual format, counselors well trained, and patients comprehensively assessed and receiving considerable encouragement to continue attending sessions. We now know with some certainty that this general approach to treatment of alcohol abuse works, and works well.

The Next Big Study

NIAAA is in the process of launching another major study, of similar size and organization to Project MATCH, but investigating a quite different question: What combination of anti-alcoholism medications and psychosocial interventions works best with which patients? The medications involved will likely be naltrexone (ReVia) and acamprosate (not yet FDA-approved). The interventions have not as yet been specified but, according to Dr. Allen, will probably vary in intensity from brief therapy to moderately more intense approaches. The varying combinations—eight in all—will be investigated at each of the study sites to achieve across-the-board comparability. The study is scheduled for completion in 2002.

Reference

"Matching Alcoholism Treatments to Client Heterogeneity: Project MATCH Post-treatment Drinking Outcomes" appears in the January 1997 issue of the *Journal of Studies on Alcohol*, the oldest journal in the field of alcohol research.

Chapter 56

Diagnosis and Assessment of Alcohol Use Disorders among Adolescents

Adolescent alcohol problems are an important public health issue. Research has indicated an increasing prevalence of adolescent alcohol use disorders (AUDs—alcohol abuse and alcohol dependence) over recent decades. Approximately 40 percent of people with an AUD developed their first symptoms between the ages of 15 and 19. People with an earlier age of onset of AUDs tend to experience more severe alcohol problems and are more likely to have other psychiatric disorders. At the same time, longitudinal research has shown that drinking status and the presence of alcohol-related problems can change considerably across adolescence and into young adulthood. Much remains to be learned about the nature and development of alcohol problems during the teenage years.

The diagnostic criteria for AUDs have largely been developed based on research and clinical experience with adults. This chapter summarizes the role of diagnostic classification in the treatment and research of AUDs and describes the current diagnostic criteria for AUDs as defined in the *Diagnostic and Statistical Manual of Mental Disorders, Fourth Edition* (*DSM-IV*) (American Psychiatric Association 1994) and some of the diagnostic interviews and screening tools that can be used to assess AUDs among adolescents.

Excerpted from, "Diagnosis and Assessment of Alcohol Use Disorders among Adolescents," by Christopher S. Martin, Ph.D., and Ken C. Winters, Ph.D., in *Alcohol Health & Research World*, Spring 1998, Vol. 22, No. 2, p. 95(9). A complete copy of this publication may be ordered from the U.S. Government Printing Office. Call (202) 512-1800 for information on price and availability.

The Diagnosis of AUDs among Adolescents

For any type of medical or psychiatric disorder, a valid diagnostic system is necessary to advance both treatment and research. Psychiatric disorders, including AUDs, are best viewed as evolving constructs that organize and describe a constellation of symptoms and behaviors. An accurate diagnostic system informs the clinician about course, prognosis, and the most effective treatment approaches. For researchers, diagnostic classification allows identification of subgroups and developmental pathways to the disorder. The standardized definitions provided by specific diagnostic criteria facilitate communication among and between researchers and clinicians. Although alcohol problems occur along a continuum of severity, specific diagnostic boundaries must be defined to guide both research and the allocation of limited health care resources.

DSM-IV *Diagnostic Criteria for AUDs*

The *DSM-IV* describes two primary AUDs: alcohol abuse and alcohol dependence. A person receives a diagnosis of alcohol abuse if he or she experiences at least one of four abuse symptoms (role impairment, hazardous use, legal problems, and social problems) that lead to "clinically significant impairment or distress." These symptoms reflect either pathological patterns of alcohol use, psychosocial consequences, or both.

The framework for the diagnosis of alcohol dependence in the *DSM-IV* was influenced by the concept of the Alcohol Dependence Syndrome (ADS) developed by Edwards and Gross (Edwards, G., and Gross, M.M. Alcohol Dependence: Provisional Description of a Clinical Syndrome. *British Medical Journal* 1:1058-1061, 1976). In the ADS, alcohol dependence is defined rather broadly—that is, as a constellation of symptoms related to physical dependence as well as compulsive and pathological patterns of alcohol use. To qualify for a *DSM-IV* diagnosis of alcohol dependence, a person must exhibit within a 12-month period at least three of the following seven dependence symptoms:

1. tolerance,
2. withdrawal or drinking to avoid or relieve withdrawal,
3. drinking larger amounts or for a longer period than intended,
4. unsuccessful attempts or a repeated desire to quit or to cut down on drinking,

5. much time spent using alcohol,
6. reduced social or recreational activities in favor of alcohol use, and
7. continued alcohol use despite psychological or physical problems.

No single criterion is necessary or sufficient for an alcohol dependence diagnosis. Alcohol dependence is subtyped in *DSM-IV* as with or without physiological features, defined by tolerance or withdrawal symptoms.

In contrast to previous versions of the *DSM*, the symptoms of alcohol abuse and alcohol dependence are mutually exclusive in *DSM-IV*. Moreover, the diagnoses of alcohol abuse and alcohol dependence are arranged hierarchically, such that a dependence diagnosis precludes an abuse diagnosis. Although not stated explicitly in *DSM-IV*, this hierarchical design implies that compared with alcohol dependence, alcohol abuse should be relatively mild and should onset at an earlier age.

The *DSM-IV* diagnostic criteria for AUDs are similar to the *DSM-IV* criteria for other drug use disorders (although some important differences do exist). Although this chapter focuses on adolescent AUDs, many of the diagnostic and assessment issues that are discussed apply to other drug use disorders as well. Because adolescent drinking and AUDs are strongly associated with other drug use and drug use disorders, both alcohol and other drug use behaviors should be assessed in research and clinical settings.

Limitations of the DSM-IV *Criteria for AUDs in Adolescents*

In general, the *DSM-IV* criteria for AUDs have shown some validity in adolescents, in that groups classified as having alcohol dependence, alcohol abuse, and no diagnosis tend to differ on measures of alcohol use, other drug use, and independent measures of alcohol problem severity. However, the available data also suggest potential limitations of the *DSM-IV* criteria for AUDs when applied to adolescents. Some of these limitations may apply to adults as well.

One potential limitation is that the *DSM-IV* criteria appear to include several symptoms that are not typically experienced by adolescent problem drinkers. Some symptoms have a very low prevalence, even in clinical samples, and thus may have only limited utility. Those symptoms include withdrawal and alcohol-related medical problems, which generally emerge only after years of heavy drinking. Other symptoms may have limited utility because they tend to occur only in particular subgroups of adolescents. For example, the alcohol abuse symptom of hazardous use, which is usually assigned due to driving while intoxicated, is rare in early adolescence and then increases after age 16, although presumably only in youths with access to automobiles. Some researchers reported that among adolescents, the symptoms of hazardous use and alcohol-related legal problems were highly related to male gender, increased age, and symptoms of conduct disorder.

Another limitation is that some *DSM-IV* symptoms may have low specificity for adolescents—that is, their presence does not clearly distinguish among adolescents with different levels of drinking problems. For example, the development of some tolerance to alcohol's effects is likely a normal developmental phenomenon that occurs in most adolescent drinkers. The *DSM-IV* criteria define tolerance, in part, as the need to increase consumption by 50 percent or more to achieve the same effects. Thus, a need to consume three drinks to produce the same effect previously produced by two drinks would qualify as "tolerance" according to *DSM-IV*. Such a change in consumption at these relatively moderate drinking levels, however, likely occurs in most adolescent drinkers. Researchers found that tolerance was highly prevalent in adolescent drinkers with and without AUDs, even though this symptom was assigned only in subjects who consumed an average of five or more standard drinks per drinking occasion. Although marked tolerance to alcohol is an important aspect of alcohol dependence, difficulty in specifying and measuring this phenomenon makes it a problematic symptom for adolescents.

Other limitations of the *DSM-IV* criteria are related to the alcohol abuse category. The one-symptom threshold for the *DSM-IV* diagnosis of alcohol abuse, combined with the broad range of problems covered by the abuse symptoms, produces a great deal of heterogeneity among persons in this diagnostic category. A related issue is the lack of an accepted conceptual definition of alcohol abuse. Furthermore, the mutually exclusive *DSM-IV* categories of alcohol abuse and alcohol dependence symptoms are not clearly distinguished either conceptually or empirically. Some of the abuse and some of the dependence symptoms measure impaired control over drinking in the face of negative consequences. Some researchers found that measures of sensitivity, specificity and predictive power did not support the diagnostic distinction between abuse and dependence symptoms. Other investigators, however, have found results more supportive of the *DSM-IV*'s categorization of alcohol abuse and alcohol dependence symptoms.

A similar limitation of the *DSM-IV* and criteria among adolescents involves sequencing in the age of onset of alcohol abuse and alcohol dependence symptoms. Because alcohol abuse is usually considered as a relatively mild category relative to alcohol dependence, the onset of abuse symptoms would be expected to precede the onset of dependence symptoms. A study of sequencing in the age of symptom onset among adolescents, however, did not support the *DSM-IV* system. The results suggested that *DSM-IV* alcohol symptoms developed in three distinct stages among adolescents, with some dependence symptoms occurring before some abuse symptoms, as follows:

- The first stage was characterized by three dependence symptoms (tolerance, drinking larger amounts or for a longer period of time than intended, and much time spent using alcohol) and two abuse symptoms (role impairment and social problems).
- The second stage was characterized by three dependence symptoms (unsuccessful attempts or a persistent desire to quit or cut down on drinking, reduced activities because of alcohol use, and continued use despite physical or psychological problems) as well as two abuse symptoms (hazardous use and alcohol-related legal problems).
- The third stage, which had the longest time to symptom onset, was characterized by the dependence symptom of withdrawal.

Finally, another apparent limitation of the *DSM-IV* criteria for AUDs is the existence of "diagnostic orphans" —that is, persons who exhibit one or two alcohol dependence symptoms and no alcohol abuse symptoms, who therefore do not qualify for a *DSM-IV* AUD.

The Assessment of AUDs among Adolescents

Clinicians and researchers use various approaches to assess alcohol problems in adolescents. The comprehensiveness of the assessment depends upon the purposes of the evaluation. One approach is the use of brief screening instruments—most commonly self-report questionnaires—to determine the possible presence of alcohol problems. If an initial screening indicates the need for further assessment, clinicians and researchers can employ diagnostic interviews to assign

AUDs and to measure the nature and severity of alcohol problems. While this chapter emphasizes alcohol, most of these screening instruments and diagnostic interviews assess consumption patterns, problems and/or diagnoses for both alcohol and other drugs.

Commonly Used Diagnostic Interviews for Adolescents

A number of diagnostic interviews can be used to assess adolescent alcohol and other drug use disorders. Some of those instruments focus primarily on alcohol and other drug use disorders, whereas others are general psychiatric interviews that contain specific sections for assessing those disorders. The following descriptions summarize some of those diagnostic interviews. The list emphasizes interviews that have been adapted for *DSM-IV* criteria and are widely used in the United States.

Interviews Focusing on Alcohol and Other Drug Use Disorders

Adolescent Diagnostic Interview (ADI). The ADI assesses the symptoms of alcohol and other drug use disorders as defined in both the *DSM-III-R* and *DSM-IV*. The ADI also measures sociodemographic information; alcohol and other drug use history; and psychosocial functioning, including mental health. The ADI's reliability and validity are moderate to high.

Customary Drinking and Drug Use Record (CDDR). The CDDR is a structured interview that measures alcohol and other drug use for both recent (past 3 months) and lifetime periods, the presence of *DSM-III-R* and *DSM-IV* dependence symptoms for alcohol and other drug use disorders, and several negative consequences that are similar to *DSM-III-R* and *DSM-IV* alcohol and other drug abuse symptoms. The CDDR has high reliability across all major content domains and good concurrent validity. The CDDR has been found to discriminate between youth in the general population and those in treatment and produces results consistent with those of other diagnostic instruments.

Screening Instruments for Adolescent Alcohol Use Disorders

In contrast to diagnostic interviews, which serve to establish a diagnosis of an alcohol use disorder (AUD), the aim of screening tools is to identify the possible presence of an alcohol problem or AUD. Thus, screening tools are used to determine whether a more complete assessment of a person's condition and treatment needs is appropriate.

Screening tools are typically self-report questionnaires that employ scoring cutoffs. The use of screening tools requires caution. A score above the cutoff point does not necessarily indicate the presence of an AUD but merely suggests that a more detailed assessment should be performed. Similarly, a score below the cutoff point does not necessarily indicate the absence of an AUD, but merely suggests that this is likely.

The following descriptions summarize some of the available screening tools that have been used widely with adolescents. Some of these instruments assess both alcohol and other drug use and problems, whereas others are specific to alcohol.

Screening Tools for Alcohol and Other Drug Use Disorders

Client Substance Index Short (CSI-S). The CSI-S was developed and evaluated as part of a larger drug abuse screening protocol through the National Center for Juvenile Justice. The instrument is a 15-item yes/no questionnaire that is designed to identify juveniles within the court system who need additional assessment for alcohol and other drug problems. The CSI-S has shown good reliability. Scores on the CSI-S are consistent with other measures of adolescent alcohol and other drug problems, and the instrument discriminates among adolescent groups defined according to the severity of their criminal offenses.

Drug and Alcohol Problem (DAP) Quick Screen. This 30-item questionnaire has been tested in a pediatric practice setting. Studies have indicated that these items measure overall alcohol and other drug problem severity. The reliability and validity of the DAP Quick Screen, however, have not been evaluated.

Drug Use Screening Inventory—Revised (DUSI-R). The adolescent version of the DUSI-R assesses alcohol and other drug use patterns as well as psychosocial functioning in different life areas using 159 true/false questions. This tool, which was developed from the same initial pool of items as was the Problem Oriented Screening Instrument for Teenagers, yields scores on 10 functional adolescent problem areas: alcohol and other drug use, physical health, mental health, family relations, peer relationships, educational status, vocational status, social skills, leisure and recreation, and aggressive behavior/delinquency. The DUSI-R also includes a lie scale and has lifetime, past-year, and past-month versions. The adolescent version of the DUSI-R has shown good reliability and validity. For example, the scores on certain DUSI-R subscales are related to alcohol and other drug use disorder diagnoses among adolescents.

Perceived Benefit of Drinking and Drug Use. This 10-item questionnaire, which asks questions about the perceived benefits of alcohol and other drug use, was developed as a nonthreatening problem severity screen. It is based on the approach that beliefs about drug use, particularly the expected personal benefits of using alcohol and other drugs, tend to be associated with actual alcohol and other drug use. The validity of this instrument is supported by findings that in both school samples and adolescent psychiatric inpatient samples, test scores are related to other measures of alcohol and other drug use and associated problems.

Personal Experience Screening Questionnaire (PESQ). The PESQ is a 40-item questionnaire that provides measures of overall problem severity, alcohol and other drug use history, certain psychosocial problems, and response-distortion tendencies (the tendency to exaggerate or minimize responses about alcohol and other drug use behaviors). Cutoff scores indicating the need for further assessment have been established and validated for normal adolescents, juvenile offenders, and adolescents in addiction treatment.

Problem Oriented Screening Instrument for Teenagers (POSIT). This 139-item yes/no questionnaire is part of the Adolescent Assessment and Referral System developed by the National Institute on Drug Abuse. The POSIT was developed from the same pool of initial items as the DUSI-R (described previously). It addresses 10 areas of adolescent functioning (for example, alcohol and other drug use, mental health, family relations, educational status, and aggressive behavior/delinquency). Cutoff scores indicating the need for further assessment have been established. Several investigators have reported evidence supporting the validity of the POSIT.

Substance Abuse Subtle Screening Inventory (SASSI). The adolescent version of the SASSI consists of 81 questions pertaining to the severity of alcohol and other drug problems. The SASSI yields scores for alcohol problems, other drug problems, and defensiveness (the tendency to minimize or deny problems). Validity data indicate that the SASSI cutoff score suggesting "chemical dependency" corresponds highly with diagnoses of alcohol and other drug use disorders obtained upon treatment entry.

AUD-Specific Screening Tools

Adolescent Alcohol Involvement Scale (AAIS). The AAIS is a 14-item questionnaire that examines current and past alcohol consumption, drinking context, short- and long-term effects of drinking, and perceptions about drinking. An overall score describes the degree of alcohol involvement. The AAIS scores are significantly related to and diagnoses, independent clinical assessments of severity, and parental reports. Cutoff scores have been established for 13- to 19-year-olds from both clinical and nonclinical samples.

Adolescent Drinking Index (ADI). The ADI measures adolescent problem drinking using 24 items addressing alcohol problems related to psychological, physical, and social functioning, as well as impaired control over drinking behavior. The instrument yields an overall severity score as well as two subscale scores reflecting self-medicating drinking and rebellious drinking. Studies have confirmed the reliability and validity of this tool. Scores on the ADI are associated with alcohol consumption levels and differ significantly among adolescents with different levels of alcohol problem severity.

Rutgers Alcohol Problem Index (RAPI). The RAPI is a 23-item questionnaire that focuses on consequences of alcohol use pertaining to family life, social relations, psychological functioning, delinquency, physical problems, and neuropsychological functioning. Positive responses to the RAPI questions were found to correlate with AUD diagnoses.

Summary

Any diagnostic system applied to adolescent alcohol problems should reflect current knowledge of the nature and development of those problems. The diagnostic criteria for AUDs in the *DSM-IV*, however, were developed largely from research and clinical experience with adults. Although the number of studies is small, the available data suggest important limitations of the *DSM-IV* AUD criteria when applied to adolescents. More research is needed to evaluate potential changes in diagnostic criteria that may better represent the nature and development of adolescent alcohol problems. It is an open question whether future changes in diagnostic criteria for AUDs can provide a unified system that is equally valid for both adults and adolescents, or whether adolescent-specific clinical and research criteria for AUDs should be developed.

Chapter 57

Alcoholism in the Elderly Requires Tailored Screening and Treatment

Alcoholism among the elderly is a serious and frequently undiagnosed problem, according to the Council Report of the American Medical Association, published in a recent issue of the *Journal of the American Medical Association*.

According to the report, physicians are far more likely to make a diagnosis of alcoholism in young patients than in elderly patients, possibly because they are reluctant to take responsibility for such patients—or perhaps, the report suggests, because of denial "among some physicians who may have their own drinking problems."

The Council Report notes that epidemiological studies have found rates of alcoholism among people age 60 and older ranging from 2% to 10%—rates similar to those found among the general population. There are two types of elderly alcoholics: "those whose alcoholism occurred relatively early in life and those whose onset occurred at 60 years of age or older."

Elders who start drinking late in life may do so because of situational factors—for example, the death of a spouse and/or friends, retirement, and social isolation. They may also, the authors say, "have had undetected and undiagnosed alcoholism or a pattern of heavy alcohol consumption for years" that becomes obvious with stressful life events.

In general, late-onset alcoholics tend to have higher incomes and to be better educated than early-onset elderly alcoholics.

Physical/Psychological Effects

Heavy drinking can take a serious medical toll on elderly alcoholics. Elderly drinkers are more likely to develop cirrhosis of the liver than young alcoholics with liver disease. They are also subject to other disorders, such as:

- cancers of the mouth, larynx and esophagus;
- ulcers;
- respiratory disease;
- high blood pressure;
- strokes; and
- heart attacks.

Alcohol also may play a significant role in falls and fractures among people older than 65. The Council Report cites studies that have found a "greater decrease in bone density ... in elderly alcoholic patients compared with elderly nonalcoholic patients."

Finally, alcohol may interact adversely with medications taken by the elderly, affecting their sexuality, sensory functions, and sleep.

In addition to the physical effects, alcoholism has psychological effects on elders, as well. Heavy drinking may be associated with dementia and depression later in life, as well as with increasing risk of suicide attempts.

Treatment Problems

Despite the serious consequences of alcoholism in the elderly, there "can be formidable obstacles to identification, diagnosis, and treatment." The denial typical of alcoholism may cause elderly patients to put off treatment "until problems caused by their drinking become severe."

Even when they do seek treatment, physicians may be reluctant to deal with them. Studies suggest that physicians are less likely to diagnose alcoholism in elderly patients, and when they do identify it, they are uncertain of how to treat it. Unless elders are diagnosed in hospitals and physician offices, "there will be relatively few opportunities for the diagnosis to be made elsewhere."

Recommendations for Detection and Treatment

In assessing elders for alcoholism, the report suggests:

- Performing a complete physical examination, laboratory tests, and a mental status evaluation.
- Recording carefully the history of the patient's alcohol, tobacco, and other drug use, including over-the-counter medications.
- Checking the patient's medical history for many falls, bruises, and emergency room visits.
- Looking for certain medical problems including hypertension, gastrointestinal disturbances, insomnia, malnutrition, and unstable diabetes.

Some screening instruments can be useful, with slight modifications, in detecting elderly alcoholics.

For treatment, the physician should:

- Plan detoxification for elderly alcoholics in a hospital due to medical risks.
- Work with the patient and family to develop a treatment plan.
- Refer elders to inpatient or outpatient programs, to a halfway house, or to Alcoholics Anonymous or other self-help groups.

Treatment programs that emphasize social relationships and positive aspects of a "patient's life" have tended to be more successful for elderly drinkers, as opposed to "programs using traditional confrontation and focusing on past failures."

The goal of treatment should be abstinence, since even occasional drinking can lead to relapse or to medical problems for elders. However, some clinicians "advise against using disulfiram" to enforce abstinence in the elderly because of "the possibility of adverse cardiovascular effects."

Physicians also should practice prevention, says the report; watch for early warning signs of problem drinking, even if signs are absent, and "provide education on the adverse effects of alcohol with age," as well as alternative coping skills in the face of losses in old age.

Suggested Readings

Fredriksen, K.I. North of market: Older women's alcohol outreach program. *Gerontologist*, 32:270-272, 1992.

Kofoed, L.L., Tolson, R.L., et al. Treatment compliance of older alcoholics: An elderly-specific approach is superior to mainstreaming. *Journal of Studies on Alcohol*, 48:47-51, 1987.

Maypole, D.E. Alcoholism and the elderly: Review of theories, treatment and prevention. *Activities Adapt Aging*, 13:43-54, 1989.

Council on Scientific Affairs, American Medical Association. Alcoholism in the elderly. *Journal of the American Medical Association*, 275(10):797-801. Reprint requests to: Group on Science Technology and Public Health, Council on Scientific Affairs, American Medical Association, 515 N. State St., Chicago, IL 60610.

Advice from The Brown University Digest of Addiction Theory and Application*'s Editor*

More than any other age group, the elderly are susceptible to the "moral trap" of alcoholism. Since many lived through prohibition, the elderly often view alcohol dependence as a character flaw or moral weakness—an alcoholic is a "bad person." It's easy for health care providers to buy into this attitude and collude with their elderly alcoholics thus ignoring, disregarding, or not asking about the unique signs and symptoms of alcoholism in the elderly. After all, we don't want to tell our patients they are "bad people." But alas they are not bad, just suffering from a complicated illness that needs detection, diagnosis, treatment, and follow up like most complicated illnesses.

—by Timothy I. Mueller, M.D.

Chapter 58

Neuroscience: Implications for Treatment

Recent advances in neuroscience have stimulated the search for medications to treat alcoholism. Medications development relies on both preclinical and clinical investigations. Preclinical research studies the effects of experimental chemicals on the physiology and behavior of laboratory animals or on the function of cells grown in culture. Results of such research provide the basis for clinical studies of specific medications in humans.

Preclinical research has established that alcohol affects brain function by interfering with communication among nerve cells (neurons). Researchers have identified specific neural communication systems that contribute to the rewarding effects of alcohol consumption, thereby promoting alcoholism. Preexisting defects in such systems also may underlie vulnerability to excessive alcohol consumption.

Neurons communicate by synthesizing and releasing chemicals called neurotransmitters, which bind to specific receptor molecules on the surface of other neurons. Scientists can investigate this process using natural or synthetic chemicals that affect specific neurotransmitter systems. These experimental chemicals can influence neurotransmission by directly affecting the synthesis or release of a neurotransmitter, by affecting the rate of removal of a neurotransmitter after its

---

Excerpted from "Neuroscience: Implications for Treatment," by Ismene Petrakis, M.D. and John Krystal, M.D. in *Alcohol Health and Research World*, Spring 1997, Vol. 21, No, 2, p. 157(4). A complete copy of this publication may be ordered from the U.S. Government Printing Office. Call (202) 512-1800 for information on price and availability.

release, or by binding to a receptor and either activating or inactivating it. The linking of these neurotransmitter systems to behavior and even to psychiatric disorders has greatly influenced clinical research and has contributed to the development of novel pharmacotherapies for a number of psychiatric disorders, including alcoholism.

Clinically, medications can be used to treat alcoholism or its effects by (1) decreasing symptoms associated with the initial stages of recovery, such as anxiety or depression; (2) decreasing a person's desire to consume alcohol; (3) blocking a component of the addictive process (alcohol's reinforcing effects); (4) treating psychiatric disorders that might coexist with alcoholism; and (5) improving alcohol-related intellectual impairment. Although some of these treatment goals are not directed against alcoholism per se, amelioration of disorders associated with alcoholism may enable the patient to participate more effectively in his or her treatment.

The Opioid Antagonists

Endogenous opioids (those that originate in the body) are neurotransmitters whose actions in the brain are similar to that of morphine or heroin (which do not occur naturally in the body). Behavioral and pharmacological data in animals and humans suggest a link between the endogenous opioid system and alcohol consumption. For example, administration of alcohol induces the release of endogenous opioids in the hypothalamus, a region of the brain involved in the regulation of various physiological states, including mood, sleep, and appetite. This effect is especially pronounced in animals bred for high alcohol preference. Overall alcohol consumption is decreased by the opioid antagonists naltrexone and naloxone.

Naltrexone—a medication used to treat heroin addiction—blocks opioid receptors by competing for neurotransmitter binding sites. Two clinical trials established the efficacy of naltrexone in treating alcoholism. In a 12-week, double-blind, placebo-controlled trial, investigators found that only 23 percent of alcoholic subjects who were administered naltrexone relapsed to heavy drinking, compared with 54 percent of subjects taking a placebo. Treatment with naltrexone was associated with a decreased number of drinks per drinking day and a lower relapse rate among subjects who sampled alcohol after achieving abstinence. In another large, double-blind, placebo-controlled clinical trial, both naltrexone- and placebo-treated subjects were randomly assigned to one of two psychosocial treatments. One-half of each group of patients (the placebo-treated subjects and the naltrexone-treated subjects) received coping-skills training, a form of psychotherapy that teaches patients how to handle problems without resorting to alcohol. The remaining subjects received supportive counseling that emphasized abstinence. Naltrexone-treated subjects exhibited a higher rate of abstinence and better employment records than the placebo-treated patients, regardless of the type of psychotherapy provided. Psychotherapy interacted with the effect of medication, however. Overall, the highest rate of abstinence occurred in patients treated with both naltrexone and supportive therapy. Among subjects who sampled alcohol after abstinence, those receiving naltrexone and coping-skills treatment combined were less likely than other subjects to experience a relapse to heavy drinking. Based in part on these findings, the U.S. Food and Drug Administration approved naltrexone for the treatment of alcohol dependence.

Despite the promise of naltrexone, some questions have emerged that were not predicted by preclinical studies. For example, a small percentage of patients taking naltrexone develop nausea, which is thought to reflect an exacerbation of alcohol withdrawal symptoms. This raises the possibility that the timing of initiation of pharmacotherapy may influence the clinical outcome. If naltrexone precipitates symptoms of withdrawal, it may not be tolerated by patients if it is initiated during the early states of recovery. Another factor requiring additional study is the appropriate matching of psychotherapy to a course of naltrexone treatment. Naltrexone's long-term efficacy and cost-effectiveness also are unknown.

Medications That Affect Serotonin Function

The neurotransmitter serotonin (5-HT) affects multiple actions in the brain, including the regulation of mood states, appetite, and sleep. This diversity of function has been linked to the existence of several specific serotonin receptor subtypes as well as variability in the mechanisms whereby receptor activation is translated into neuronal function.

Preclinical studies suggest a relationship between serotonin function and alcohol consumption. For example, serotonin administration causes a decrease in alcohol consumption in animals selectively bred for alcohol preference as well as in animals that are genetically heterogeneous. This effect may not be specific to alcohol, because an increase in the availability of brain serotonin also may decrease consumption of food and nonalcoholic liquids. Other studies suggest that serotonin helps regulate reinforcement, because disturbances in the serotonin system may selectively affect consumption of rewarding substances such as alcohol, other drugs, and sweet-tasting substances.

Laboratory studies have found abnormalities in serotonin activity associated with alcohol use, alcoholism, and impulsivity. These abnormalities are more prominent in type II alcoholics, a group characterized by early onset of drinking and significant detrimental social consequences related to alcoholism.

The exact nature of the relationship between serotonin and alcoholism is unknown. One theory suggests that alcoholics are naturally deficient in brain serotonin. According to this view, alcoholism may represent an attempt to increase brain serotonin levels. Another theory suggests that serotonin either directly influences the reinforcing effects of alcohol and other drugs or exerts an indirect influence, through an effect on the neurotransmitter dopamine. A third suggestion is that low levels of serotonin lead to impulsive behavior, including an inability to modulate alcohol intake. Serotonergic abnormalities also may contribute to anxiety, potentially leading to the "self-medication" of anxiety symptoms with alcohol. Finally, serotonergic activity may affect general appetitive behaviors.

Among the medications evaluated for alcoholism treatment are several selective serotonin reuptake inhibitors (SSRI's) prescribed to treat depressive disorders. SSRI's increase the activity of serotonin by preventing its reabsorption into the neuron that released it. In several clinical trials, researchers evaluated the effects of three different SSRI's—zimelidine, fluoxetine, and citalopram—on alcohol consumption by heavy drinkers. Although each medication decreased alcohol consumption, its effect was small. Two more recent clinical trials showed no effect of fluoxetine or citalopram on alcohol consumption by alcoholics. These studies suggest that SSRI's have limited utility for treating alcoholism. However, some evidence suggests that they may benefit alcoholics who experience co-occurring depression.

Amino Acid Neurotransmitters

The amino acid glutamate is the most prevalent excitatory neurotransmitter in the brain, where it modulates arousal by making neurons more sensitive to further neurotransmission. Alcohol is a glutamate antagonist, blocking the NMDA receptor, a glutamate receptor subtype so named because it responds to the agonist N-methyl-D-aspartate. The NMDA receptor is involved in learning, memory, and seizure activity, functions known to be influenced by alcohol consumption.

In animal models, alcohol has been shown to manifest several of its behavioral effects (for example, impaired motor skills and cognition) through the NMDA receptor. Studies in humans provide evidence that NMDA antagonists produce alcohol-like properties in humans and can modulate the effects of alcohol intoxication, including euphoria, a "high" feeling, and sedation. In addition, evidence suggests that alcohol's reinforcing properties may be related in part to its effects on the NMDA receptor, possibly through glutamate's influence on dopamine activity.

Upon long-term alcohol exposure, NMDA receptors undergo increased activity (up-regulation) to help compensate for alcohol's continued antagonistic effect. At the end of a drinking bout, the now hyperactive glutamate system is no longer balanced by the presence of alcohol, leading to tremor, high blood pressure, sweating, and seizures (withdrawal syndrome). Administration of NMDA antagonists is one form of treatment that can suppress withdrawal-induced seizures in animals. Persistent alteration in NMDA receptor function in alcoholics may increase the risk of seizures and contribute to the development of alcohol-related organic brain disease. Thus, abnormalities of glutamate function may be involved in effects of alcoholism ranging from acute intoxication and addiction to long-term nervous system effects. This possibility suggests the recent hypothesis that alcoholism may be understood as a glutamate-related neuropsychiatric disorder.

These preclinical and clinical studies have suggested that glutamatergic medications may reduce alcohol consumption. The leading candidate in this area is acamprosate. Preclinical research suggests that acamprosate may block glutamate reuptake. A series of placebo-controlled European studies have indicated that detoxified alcoholics treated with acamprosate were less likely to drop out of treatment and achieved higher rates of abstinence than those on placebo. It has been hypothesized that acamprosate may help patients achieve abstinence at least in part by diminishing withdrawal symptoms. Additional clinical trials are required to answer questions raised about the use of acamprosate as a medication for alcoholism treatment, including the following: Does acamprosate decrease drinking in alcoholics? If so, for w hat population is it appropriate? Should it be paired with a psychosocial treatment, and if so, which one?

Future Directions

Because alcoholism is a complex disorder, its treatment should be multifaceted. Effective treatment must target the extensive social, psychological, and medical complications of alcoholism. Medications can play various, complementary roles in alcoholism treatment. For example, acamprosate may decrease symptoms associated with early recovery, naltrexone may decrease the desire to drink or may block the reinforcing aspects of alcohol, and medications such as fluoxetine or buspirone may help in treating co-occurring psychiatric disorders. Clinicians can use medications to ease patients into psychosocial treatments or to enhance the effect of psychosocial treatments in decreasing alcohol consumption. The optimal clinical applicability for these medications has yet to be fully examined. Clinical and neuroscience research will continue to increase our understanding of the applications and limitations of proposed treatments while stimulating the development of new medications.

Chapter 59

Medications Used to Help Maintain Abstinence

Overview

The pharmacotherapy for alcohol dependence was selected as an evidence report topic by the Agency for Health Care Policy and Research (AHCPR) because of its timeliness, the severity and impact of the disease, and the need for careful evaluation of new therapeutic modalities for its treatment. Alcoholism is a prevalent disease that will affect on the order of 10 percent of the adult population of the United States. An estimated 100,000 Americans die each year from alcohol-related disease or injury. The serious financial and nonfinancial impact of this disease extends to family members and society in general, and its annual dollar cost to the country has been estimated (as of 1995) to exceed $166 billion.

The treatment of alcohol dependence requires a two-step approach that includes withdrawal and detoxification followed by further interventions to maintain abstinence. There is considerable uncertainty about the best treatment strategies for patients in the post-detoxification stage. Some advocate a "drug-free" 12-step approach developed by Alcoholics Anonymous (AA), while others assert that the 12-step approach or other psychosocial approaches combined with appropriate nonaddictive pharmacotherapies may improve treatment outcomes.

Excerpted from "Pharmacotherapy for Alcohol Dependence. Summary, Evidence Report/Technology Assessment: Number 3," January 1999, Agency for Health Care Policy and Research, Rockville, MD. http://www.ahcpr.gov/clinic/alcosumm.htm.

Reporting the Evidence

This summary is drawn from an evidence report that focuses on the pharmacotherapies used for the treatment of alcohol dependence. The report is organized around a series of major clinical questions on the pharmacotherapy for alcohol dependence. They involve pharmaceutical agents that have been historically or are presently used in the treatment of alcoholism: disulfiram, the opiate antagonists naltrexone and nalmefene, serotonergic agents such as ondansetron, buspirone, and the selective serotonin reuptake inhibitors (SSRIs, such as citalopram, fluoxetine, paroxetine, sertraline, etc.), and lithium. Disulfiram and naltrexone, in particular, are mainstream agents in use in the United States today. However, it is important to recognize that the field of pharmacotherapy for alcohol dependence has evolved substantially over the past 5 years, especially with the emergence of data on the opiate antagonists.

Concomitantly, there is one promising pharmaceutical agent currently in use in Europe—acamprosate (calcium acetyl homotaurinate)—for preventing alcohol relapse. An investigational new drug (IND) application is on file for this drug at the United States Food and Drug Administration (FDA), and it is in Phase III trials in this country.

Much of the literature examined for the evidence report was designed to establish efficacy: Does the medication reduce alcohol intake in a well-controlled study setting? Examination of potential harms associated with treatment is equally important. The evidence on treatment harms was sometimes found within randomized controlled trials (RCTs) but was also identified through prospective cohort studies or secondary data sources, although the latter sources were not systematically searched.

Key Clinical Questions

Five questions were addressed relevant to the pharmacotherapy for treating the core symptoms of alcohol dependence such as craving, loss of control (relapse), abstinence, and total drinking or nondrinking days. The first three questions relate to three agents used primarily for the treatment of alcohol dependence: disulfiram, the opiate antagonists naltrexone and nalmefene, and acamprosate. These agents have been in use for different periods of time, and the amount of evidence available for each agent differs substantially.

Disulfiram inhibits aldehyde dehydrogenase and leads to increased levels of acetaldehyde when alcohol is consumed, with subsequent adverse physical effects such as nausea, headache, and weakness. Disulfiram has been in use for approximately 50 years. The opiate antagonists (naltrexone and nalmefene), which block opioid receptors leading to a hypothesized reduction in the rewarding properties of alcohol, have been in use in the United States for only a few years. Acamprosate, whose mechanism of action has not been clearly established as yet, is not available in the United States but has been used in Europe for a few years. The first three questions are:

1. What is the efficacy of disulfiram relative to placebo in treating alcohol dependence?
2. What is the efficacy of naltrexone relative to placebo in treating alcohol dependence?
3. What is the efficacy of acamprosate relative to placebo in treating alcohol dependence?

The fourth and fifth questions relate to drugs that have been approved by the FDA for conditions other than alcohol dependence such as depression and bipolar disease:

4. What is the efficacy of serotonergic agents relative to placebo in the treatment of alcohol dependence?
5. What is the efficacy of lithium relative to placebo in the treatment of alcohol dependence?

Animal studies indicate that alcohol intake can be reduced by SSRIs and other serotonergic agents such as buspirone and ondansetron. A moderate literature has examined the efficacy of these agents in maintaining remission in humans.

Finally, lithium has been used to treat alcoholism. Lithium has been a mainstay of treatment for bipolar affective disorder, although the literature in the area of alcohol dependence is limited. Nonetheless, clinical issues remain.

The efficacy of each of these agents was determined by an assessment of the following factors: reduction in the number of standard drinks of alcohol, reduction in the number of drinking days (or increase in the number of nondrinking days), reduction in relapse rates defined as time to first drink or development of an a priori defined relapse, overall resumption of drinking over the course of the study, number of episodes of heavy drinking, severity of side effects, and compliance with drug therapy.

Multiple other agents have been used to assist in the maintenance of remission from active drinking. These include agents that directly affect brain dopaminergic systems (bromocriptine) or gamma-amino butyric acid (GABA) systems (gamma-hydroxy butyrate). Evaluating the role of all agents that have been tried in the treatment of alcohol dependence would be of interest to the alcohol treatment professional but is outside the scope of the evidence report.

Findings

Findings are presented in bullet format for the five major drugs or drug classes reviewed.

Disulfiram

- A substantial literature has been generated on the use of disulfiram in alcoholism, but the number of controlled clinical trials is limited.
- Controlled clinical trials of disulfiram reveal mixed findings. There is little evidence that disulfiram enhances abstinence, but there is evidence that disulfiram reduces drinking days. When measured, compliance is a strong predictor of outcome.
- Studies of disulfiram implants are methodologically weak and generally without good evidence of bioavailability.
- Studies of supervised disulfiram administration are provocative but limited.

Naltrexone

- Trials of naltrexone in the treatment of alcoholism are recent and of generally good quality.
- There is good evidence that naltrexone reduces relapse and number of drinking days in alcohol-dependent subjects.
- There is some evidence that naltrexone reduces craving and enhances abstinence in alcohol-dependent subjects.
- There is good evidence that naltrexone has a favorable harms profile.

Acamprosate

- Trials of acamprosate in alcohol dependence are large but limited to European populations.

- There is good evidence that acamprosate enhances abstinence and reduces drinking days in alcohol-dependent subjects.
- There is minimal evidence on the effects of acamprosate on craving or rates of severe relapse in alcohol-dependent subjects.
- There is good evidence that acamprosate is reasonably well tolerated and without serious harms.

Serotonergic Agents

- There are several controlled clinical trials of serotonergic agents in primary alcoholics without comorbid mood or anxiety disorders.
- There is minimal evidence on the efficacy of serotonergic agents for treatment of the core symptoms of alcohol dependence.
- There is some evidence on the efficacy of serotonergic agents for the treatment of alcohol-dependent symptoms in patients with comorbid mood or anxiety disorders, although the data are limited.

Lithium

- There are limited studies on the effects of lithium in primary alcoholics without comorbid mood disorders.
- There is evidence that lithium is not efficacious in the treatment of the core symptoms of alcohol dependence.
- There is minimal evidence for efficacy of lithium for the treatment of alcohol-dependent symptoms in patients with comorbid depression.

Future Research

Although the quality of the research on pharmacotherapies for alcohol dependence has improved substantially since the 1960s, numerous difficulties were encountered in developing the evidence report. These difficulties involved both reviewing the available literature and developing concrete conclusions or drawing appropriate inferences about the efficacy of these drugs in treating the different patient populations suffering from alcoholism. To address some of these drawbacks and deficiencies in the empirical knowledge base, several significant areas have been identified for attention in future research. The topics and/or methodologic issues deserving high priority include:

- Pharmacotherapies shown to have efficacy in the treatment of alcoholism should be studied over longer time periods to establish their efficacy as maintenance treatments. These trials should probably last several years. Extending the length of follow-up once active treatment has ended, perhaps as long as 5 to 10 years, would also provide information on whether efficacy is still evident beyond active treatment. Lack of efficacy beyond active treatment would then raise the question of the value of very-long-term maintenance.
- Combination therapies (therapeutic regimens that involve two or more medications given simultaneously) should be examined for efficacy.
- Psychosocial co-interventions used within pharmacotherapy trials require more standardization, better compliance assessment, and better reporting in future publications. These include psychosocial interventions provided outside specialized treatment programs and in primary care settings.
- Effectiveness studies are needed to establish the benefit of these treatments in various settings (outside the specialized centers typically used in RCTs (randomized controlled trials) to date and, by implication, in patient populations encountered in all types of settings) once efficacy for alcohol dependence has been established.
- Common outcome measures need to be determined by standardizing the definition of outcomes and how they are assessed and using broader sets of endpoints that include clinical and health-related quality-of-life indicators.
- High dropout rates warrant attention, including identifying reasons for (differential) dropout, improving the reporting of baseline characteristics of different groups, and designing innovative ways to overcome significant dropout, especially for long-term studies.
- Research on the pharmacokinetics of these medications includes evaluating the relationship of drug blood levels and of drug metabolites to therapeutic or toxic outcome.
- All RCTs should include pharmacotherapy compliance assessment and enhancement for all treatment groups.

- The relationship of pharmacotherapy to patient heterogeneity needs to be better understood, including effects related to the patient's sex, severity of dependence, co-existing mental disorders, and the interactions among these factors.

Availability of the Full Report

The full evidence report from which this summary was taken was prepared for the Agency for Health Care Policy and Research by the Research Triangle Institute (RTI) and the University of North Carolina (UNC) at Chapel Hill, under contract No. 290-97-0011. Printed copies may be obtained free of charge from the AHCPR Publications Clearinghouse by calling 1-800-358-9295. Requesters should ask for Evidence Report/Technology Assessment Number 3, Pharmacotherapy for Alcohol Dependence (AHCPR Publication No. 99-E004). Online, the Evidence Report is at: http://www.ahcpr.gov/clinic/index.html#evidence.

Chapter 60

Alleviating Symptoms of Depression Improves Remission of Alcoholism

Investigator Deborah S. Hasin, Ph.D., and colleagues from the NIMH Collaborative Depression Study examined the 5-year course of illness in a sample of 127 patients diagnosed with RDC alcoholism and affective disorders. They found that, in patients with major depression (MDD), remission in the depression was often linked with remission of alcoholism.

All subjects were recruited from medical school treatment facilities at the Collaborative Study sites in Boston, Chicago, Iowa, New York, and St. Louis. Shortly after admission to treatment, investigators interviewed the subjects using the Schedule for Affective Disorders and Schizophrenia (SADS). They then followed up the subjects every six months for the five-year study period with the Longitudinal Interval Follow-Up Evaluation (LIFE), which tracks the status of patient symptoms and screens for the onset of new disorders.

The investigators defined remission from RDC alcoholism as "26 weeks or more with no evidence of any RDC alcohol symptoms." Subjects were considered to have relapsed into alcoholism if any RDC symptoms recur after 26 weeks. Remission from major depression was defined as "at least 8 weeks without experiencing anything more than one or two mild symptoms of depression." Patients were considered

---

"Alleviating symptoms of depression improves remission of alcoholism," in *The Brown University Digest of Addiction Theory and Application*, February 1997, Vol. 16, No. 2, p. 7(2),

to have relapsed into depression if two consecutive weeks of depressive symptoms occurred.

Analyses of the concurrent course of alcoholism and affective disorders indicated that remission of major depression and of alcoholism were linked.

The likelihood of remission of alcoholism was "clearly lower for those whose depression never remitted," the investigators say. Even among subjects who recovered from and then relapsed back into depression, there was a greater likelihood of recovery from alcoholism.

Further analyses indicated that subjects who experienced stable, ongoing remission of their depression "had the lowest cumulative probability of relapse in alcoholism."

Besides remission of depression, only two other predictors were associated with likelihood of remission of alcoholism. Subjects with bipolar II disorder were likely to remit, and subjects with greater severity of alcoholism dependence were less likely to remit. Age, gender, primary/secondary distinction, and Antisocial Personality Disorder were not predictive of remission of alcoholism. Conversely, only remission in depression predicted (positively) subsequent relapse in alcoholism in those who did remit.

Study Limits

The authors note that while this study examines the course of alcoholism, it does not examine "drinking per se." Alcoholism and alcohol consumption are, the authors say, "related but distinct phenomena." In addition, as this was a naturalistic study, "treatment was not randomly assigned and treatment status was not included" in the analyses. Thus, patients in the study "had a wide variety of treatment experiences for their alcohol problems, ranging from none to multiple hospitalizations."

Authors' Conclusions

In spite of these limitations, the authors conclude that "in this sample of patients with serious affective disorders and comorbid alcoholism, the status of the affective disorder had a relationship to the alcohol use disorder," and that "remission in MDD significantly improved the outlook for a remission in RDC alcoholism in these patients and significantly reduced the chances of an alcoholism relapse."

Suggested Readings

O'Sullivan, K., Rynne, C., et al. A follow-up study on alcoholics with and without co-existing affective disorder. *British Journal of Psychiatry*, 152:813-819, 1988.

Powell, B., Penich, E., et al. Outcomes of comorbid alcoholic men: A one-year follow-up. *Archives of Clinical and Experimental Research*, 16:131-138, 1992.

D.S. Hasin, W-Y Tsai, J. Endicott, T.I. Mueller, W. Coryell, M. Keller. The effects of major depression on alcoholism. Five year course. *The American Journal on Addictions*, 5: 144-155, 1996.

Part Six

Prevention

Chapter 61

Preventing Alcohol Abuse and Related Problems

Prevention measures aim to reduce alcohol abuse and its consequences. Such measures include policies regulating alcohol-related behavior on the one hand and community and educational interventions seeking to influence drinking behavior on the other. Researchers use scientific methods, such as randomized controlled trials, time-series analysis, and computer simulation, to determine the effectiveness of prevention initiatives. The resulting data may both inform policy and guide community and educational prevention efforts. This chapter summarizes research on the effectiveness of selected initiatives in each of these areas.

Policy Interventions

Alcohol Taxes. Researchers find that alcohol taxes and prices affect alcohol consumption and associated consequences. Studies demonstrate that increased beer prices lead to reductions in the levels and frequency of drinking and heavy drinking among youth. Higher taxes on beer are associated with lower traffic crash fatality rates, especially among young drivers, and with reduced incidence of some types of crime. Research suggests that the heaviest-drinking 5 percent of

---

Excerpted from *Alcohol Alert*, National Institute on Alcohol Abuse and Alcoholism (NIAAA), No. 34, PH 370, October 1996. The full text of this document, including references, is available on NIAAA's website at http://www.niaaa.nih.gov. Copies of the *Alcohol Alert* are also available free of charge from: NIAAA Publications, P.O. Box 34443, Washington, DC 20043.

drinkers do not reduce their consumption significantly in response to price increases, unlike drinkers who consume alcohol at lower levels. In one study, heavy drinkers who were unaware of the adverse health consequences of their drinking were less responsive to price changes than either moderate drinkers or better informed heavy drinkers.

Raising the Minimum Legal Drinking Age (MLDA). MLDA legislation is intended to reduce alcohol use among those under 21, to prevent traffic deaths, and to avoid other negative outcomes. Raising the MLDA has been accompanied by reduced alcohol consumption, traffic crashes, and related fatalities among those under 21. A nationwide study found a significant decline in single-vehicle nighttime (SVN) fatal crashes—those most likely to involve alcohol—among drivers under 21 following increases in the MLDA.

Zero-Tolerance Laws. The National Highway Systems Act provides incentives for all States to adopt "zero-tolerance laws" that set maximum blood alcohol concentration (BAC) limits for drivers under 21 to 0.02 percent or lower beginning October 1, 1998. An analysis of the effect of zero-tolerance laws in the first 12 States enacting them found a 20-percent relative reduction in the proportion of SVN fatal crashes among drivers under 21, compared with nearby States that did not pass zero-tolerance laws.

Other BAC Laws. Fourteen States have lowered BAC limits from 0.10 to 0.08 percent to reduce alcohol-related fatal motor vehicle crashes. One study found that States with the reduced limit experienced a 16-percent decline in the proportion of fatal crashes involving fatally injured drivers whose BACs were 0.08 percent or higher, compared with nearby States that did not reduce their BAC limit. In a separate analysis, this study found that States that lowered their BAC limit also experienced an 18-percent decline in the proportion of fatal crashes involving fatally injured drivers whose BACs were 0.15 or higher, relative to comparison States.

Administrative License Revocation Laws. Laws permitting the withdrawal of driving privileges without court action have been adopted by 38 States to prevent traffic crashes caused by unsafe driving practices, including driving with a BAC over the legal limit. These laws were associated with a 5-percent decline in nighttime fatal crashes in some studies. Other studies observed six- to nine-percent reductions in nighttime fatal crashes following their adoption.

Server Liability. Alcohol servers are increasingly held liable for injuries and deaths from traffic crashes following the irresponsible selling and serving of alcohol. Researchers assessed the effect of potential server liability on the rates of alcohol-related fatal crashes in Texas. SVN fatal traffic crashes decreased 6.5 percent after the filing of a major server-liability court case in 1983 and decreased an additional 5.3 percent after a 1984 case was filed. However, before concluding that server liability is effective, these results need replication.

Warning Labels. The mandated warning label on containers of alcoholic beverages aims to inform and remind drinkers that alcohol consumption can result in birth defects, impaired ability to drive a car or operate machinery, and health problems. Research indicates that public support for warning labels is extremely high; that awareness of the label's content has increased substantially over time; that perception of the described risks was high before the label appeared and has not generally increased; and that the label has not had important effects on hazardous behavior, although certain effects may be indicative of the early stages of behavioral change. One study of pregnant women found that after the label appeared, alcohol consumption declined among lighter drinkers but not among those who drank more heavily.

Community and Educational Interventions

The Saving Lives Program. The Saving Lives Program in six communities in Massachusetts was designed to reduce drinking and driving and to promote safe driving practices. Saving Lives involved the media, businesses, schools and colleges, citizens' advocacy groups, and the police in activities such as high school peer-led education, college prevention programs, increased liquor-outlet surveillance, and other efforts. Participating communities reduced fatal crashes by 25 percent during the program years compared with the rest of Massachusetts. The decline in alcohol-related fatal crashes was 42 percent greater in Saving Lives communities than in comparison cities during the program years. The proportion of drivers under 21 who reported driving after drinking in the month before being interviewed also declined in participating communities.

Life Skills Training (LST). LST teaches students in grades seven to nine skills to resist social influences to use alcohol and other drugs and to enhance general competence and self-esteem. LST has been found to increase students' knowledge of the negative consequences of drinking and to promote realistic, not inflated, perceptions of drinking prevalence. A study of LST's long-term effects among 12th grade students who had received a relatively complete version of the program showed significantly lower rates of weekly drinking, heavy drinking, and getting drunk than did control students. The full sample exposed to the program also showed significantly lower rates of drunkenness than did the controls.

Project Northland. Project Northland is a multicomponent, school- and community-based intervention to delay, prevent, and reduce alcohol use and related problems among adolescents. It includes social-behavioral curricula, peer leadership, parental involvement/education, and community-wide task force activities. The first 3 years of intervention, conducted in grades six through eight, resulted in significantly lower prevalence of past-month and past-week alcohol use among students in intervention communities compared with controls. These beneficial effects were particularly notable among students who had not yet begun experimenting with alcohol when the program began.

Alcohol Misuse Prevention Study (AMPS). The AMPS curriculum, for students in grades five through eight, focuses primarily on teaching peer-resistance skills and on clarifying students' misperceptions of their peers' alcohol use. Among adolescents at greatest risk for escalating alcohol misuse—those who engaged in early unsupervised use of alcohol—the AMPS intervention had a modest, but lasting, statistically significant effect of slowing the increase in alcohol misuse through grade 8 and into grade 12. Replication of this research again showed a significant effect for the highest risk subgroup.

Project STAR. Project STAR—involving schools, mass media, parents, community organizations, and health policy components in two sites in the Midwest—attempts to delay the onset and decrease the prevalence of alcohol and other drug use among students beginning in sixth grade. Project STAR teaches skills to resist alcohol use and educates students about the actual, as opposed to the perceived, prevalence of alcohol use among their peers. Early follow-up studies showed that the program had little effect on alcohol use. However, in a 6-year follow-up in Kansas City, students in program schools showed lower rates of increase in alcohol use and episodes of drunkenness over time than did students in control schools. Similar but smaller effects were observed at 3.5-year follow-up in Indianapolis.

Drug Abuse Resistance Education (DARE). DARE, typically taught to 10- and 11-year-old students in grades five and six by police officers, aims to inform about alcohol and other drugs and to teach social and decision-making skills to help students resist their use. Studies have found that DARE essentially has no impact on alcohol use.

Informational Programs. Programs attempting to persuade students not to use alcohol by arousing fear do not work to change behavior. Emphasizing the dangers of alcohol may attract those who tend to be risk-takers. Programs providing information about the pharmacological effects of alcohol may arouse curiosity and lead to drinking.

Server Training. Server training, mandatory in some States, educates alcohol servers to alter their serving practices, particularly with underage customers and those who show obvious signs of intoxication. Server training explains the effects of alcohol, applicable laws, how to refuse service to obviously intoxicated patrons, and how to assist customers in obtaining transportation as an alternative to driving. Some, but not all, studies report more interventions with customers after server training than before. One evaluation of the effects of Oregon's mandatory server-training policy indicates that it had a statistically significant effect on reducing the incidence of SVN traffic crashes in that State.

A Commentary by NIAAA Director Enoch Gordis, M.D.

Prevention encompasses activities or actions ranging from those affecting the whole population through social and regulatory controls to those affecting specific groups, such as adolescents, or the individual. Many of these activities overlap. For example, health warning labels, a product of legislation (social and regulatory control), also are educational. In this text, we have tried to give a "flavor" of this broad spectrum; the prevention areas described are by no means exhaustive, and some areas described in one category could well be in others.

The good news is that, using contemporary tools of science, prevention can be rigorously studied. Currently, research evidence shows that some prevention efforts are effective and others have little or no effect. This knowledge will help local communities, the States, and others who have made significant investments in prevention activities develop or refine existing programs to achieve their desired objectives.

Chapter 62

Why It's Important to Prevent Kids from Drinking

Too many kids are drinking. Just look at the most recent government statistics: by the time they're seniors in high school, 62% of our children report they have been drunk at least once in their lives. Among other drugs (excluding tobacco), only use of marijuana comes even close, with 45% of kids saying they have smoked pot.

Yet many people refuse to take the problem of underage drinking as seriously as they should. After all, they say, isn't getting drunk with your friends part of growing up in America?

Unfortunately, while the majority of kids who drink do grow up to become healthy adults, use of alcohol greatly increases the chances that they will be involved in a car crash, homicide, or suicide—the leading causes of death for teenagers and young adults. In fact, a 16-year-old is more likely to die of alcohol-related causes than any other.

Adults also may be ambivalent about underage drinking because they think kids are drinking to relax or have a good time with their friends. What's the harm, they ask, if they're not drinking and driving?

Kids, however, aren't "social drinkers" who enjoy a glass of wine with their meal or go to cocktail parties. Nearly 60% say they drink when they're upset and nearly 40% drink alone. By the time they get to college 40% of them have become "binge drinkers" which means they have had five or more drinks in a row during the past two weeks.

This chapter contains text from "Why It's Important to Prevent Kids from Drinking," and "How to Tell If Your Child May be In Trouble with Alcohol," the National Council on Alcoholism and Drug Dependence, Inc. (NCADD); reprinted with permission.

Kids typically begin using alcohol around the age of 13, long before their minds and bodies are mature enough to handle the effects of a powerful drug. Research shows that the earlier kids start drinking the more likely they will be to develop a problem with alcohol or other drugs later in life. This risk is especially high for the 10% of eighth graders who say they have been drunk at least once during the past month.

Once kids start drinking, their world suddenly becomes a more dangerous place. Girls are more likely to be forced into unwanted sexual activity, which can result in pregnancy. Boys get into more fights and commit acts of vandalism that may escalate into more serious crimes. The academic and athletic performances of both sexes can suffer.

In short, if we care about the health of our children, we must do everything we can to discourage them from drinking for as long as possible.

How to Tell If Your Child May Be in Trouble with Alcohol

- Smell of alcohol on breath, or sudden, frequent use of breath mints.
- Abrupt changes in mood or attitude.
- Sudden decline in attendance or performance at school.
- Losing interest in school, sports, or other activities that used to be important.
- Sudden resistance to discipline at school.
- Uncharacteristic withdrawal from family, friends, or interests.
- Heightened secrecy about actions or possessions.
- Associating with a new group of friends whom your child refuses to discuss.

If you believe your child may have a problem with alcohol, call the National Council on Alcoholism and Drug Dependence's HOPE-LINE at 800-NCA-CALL using a touch tone phone. They can provide the phone number of NCADD Affiliates or a state agency who can provide you with referral to local services.

Chapter 63

Preventing Alcohol Problems during Adolescence

Throughout the history of the United States, public opinion concerning alcohol use has oscillated from toleration to disapproval, and the average annual consumption of alcohol has risen and fallen in accordance with this pattern. Current annual per person alcohol consumption among adults in the United States is only about one-third of what it was in the early 19th century. Along with other indications, a 15-percent drop in adult alcohol consumption since its most recent peak around 1980 suggests that a third era of temperance may be under way. Additional evidence to support this shift in American attitudes toward alcohol includes the reinstatement of age 21 as the legal drinking age in all States by the mid-1980s and ongoing public activism, beginning in the mid-1970s, supporting tougher drunk-driving laws.

Despite overall lower alcohol consumption in the United States, American youth drink more at younger ages. One study found that only 9 percent of respondents born between 1919 and 1929 reported first using alcohol ("you first had a glass of beer or wine, or a drink of liquor such as whiskey, gin, scotch, etc.") at age 15 or younger, compared with 33 percent of those surveyed who were born between 1971 and 1975. Many youth drink alcohol regularly. In a 1995 survey, 25

Excerpted from, "Lessons from Project Northland: Preventing Alcohol Problems during Adolescence," by Carolyn L. Williams, Ph.D., and Cheryl L. Perry, Ph.D., in *Alcohol Health & Research World*, Spring 1998, Vol. 22, No. 2, p. 107. A complete copy of this publication may be ordered from the U.S. Government Printing Office. Call (202) 512-1800 for information on price and availability.

percent of 8th graders, 39 percent of 10th graders, 51 percent of 12th graders, and 68 percent of college students reported drinking at least once during the 30 days prior to being surveyed. In addition, the survey results suggest that many young drinkers consume multiple drinks per drinking occasion. Fifteen percent of 8th graders, 24 percent of 10th graders, 30 percent of 12th graders, and 40 percent of college students reported consuming five or more drinks in a row at least once in the 2 weeks before the survey.

The widespread and often heavy alcohol use by adolescents are associated with significant morbidity and mortality that are not confined to the group of more extreme users. In fact, because the general population includes more light and moderate drinkers than heavy drinkers, the former experience more alcohol-related problems as a group, even though as individuals they are at less risk than heavier drinkers. This finding has tended to shift the focus of prevention efforts away from the identification of problem drinkers toward the prevention of alcohol use during adolescence.

Project Northland is the largest community trial in the United States to focus on the prevention of alcohol use and alcohol-related problems among adolescents. Using the example of Project Northland, this chapter describes a comprehensive approach that combines individual-based strategies to encourage adolescents not to use alcohol with community-based strategies to both reduce alcohol availability and modify community attitudes regarding underage drinking.

Epidemiologic studies demonstrate the importance of delaying the onset of drinking and reducing alcohol use during adolescence. Data from the 1992 National Longitudinal Alcohol Epidemiologic Survey of 27,616 drinkers and former drinkers found that people who started drinking before age 15 were four times more likely to become alcohol dependent at some point during their lives, compared with those who had initiated drinking at age 20 or older (40 percent versus 10 percent). Similarly, the number of people who experienced alcohol abuse in their lifetime increased as the age of drinking onset decreased. (Lifetime alcohol dependence and abuse were defined using standard criteria from the American Psychiatric Association's (APA's) *Diagnostic and Statistical Manual of Mental Disorders, Fourth Edition* (APA 1994).) An earlier British study that followed a sample of young people from ages 16 to 23 found that those youth who drank the most in quantity and frequency at age 16 were the most likely to drink heavily at age 23. More specifically, 16-year-old males who reported drinking the week prior to the survey were nearly four times more likely to report heavy drinking (more than 50 drinks of alcohol in 1 week) at age 23, compared with those who reported being abstinent at age 16 (15 percent versus 4 percent).

A recent behavioral genetics study suggests that social and environmental factors are more important than genetic influences in delaying drinking until age 16. Researchers who conducted a population-based study that was able to identify all the twins born in Finland between 1975 and 1979 and to enroll them sequentially in the study when they reached age 16. The study included 2,711 total pairs of twins born over the 5-year period and demonstrated that remaining abstinent from alcohol until age 16 was clearly linked to nongenetic influences. Abstinence rates were influenced by sibling interaction effects, parental drinking patterns, and contextual features of the region. The study suggested that regional features may include variables such as local alcohol sales, ease of underage access to alcohol, and exposure to public drinking or intoxication, issues that have been identified as intervention targets by prevention researchers.

Adolescent's Social Environment: Targets for Comprehensive Prevention

Current prevention efforts tend to be comprehensive and to target factors in the adolescents' social environment that are known to affect underage drinking. The most immediate social environment for a given adolescent generally consists of parents, siblings, and best friends. The next ring includes larger peer groups, which may vary by setting (for example, friends at school, on sports teams, or at religious institutions); teachers; other relatives; and other important adults in an adolescent's life (for example, coaches, religious advisors, or other youth group leaders). The outer ring includes the broader community of business (for example, alcohol merchants, including neighborhood merchants, and major employers in the region) and community leaders as well as local and national government leaders (ranging from school superintendents and police chiefs to mayors and the governor), with the top of the outer ring reserved for mass media and advertising. Project Northland targeted each ring of the adolescents' social environment.

Much of the popular youth culture—frequently cited by parents, other adults, and youth as among the primary reasons for an adolescent's use of alcohol, tobacco, and other drugs—is developed primarily in the outermost ring of a young person's social environment (mass media, advertising, and businesses that target peer-group identity to encourage youth to engage in various behaviors). For example, advertisements, rock music videos, radio, and youth-oriented publications are adult-created aspects of youth culture that model ways to seek independence and define identity, including sexuality and attractiveness, both of which are crucial developmental issues for adolescents. Popular youth culture influences young peoples' preferences for clothing, hairstyles, and music within their peer groups. Recent studies document the persuasive and pervasive health-compromising messages in the youth culture promoted by mass media and advertising. For example, research indicates that sporting events and music videos, which are especially appealing to adolescents, expose youth to extensive alcohol and tobacco use by people they view as positive role models. In sporting events, beer commercials predominate and include images or themes that portray activities which are dangerous when combined with drinking (for example, boating).

Table 63.1. The Social Environment of Adolescents.

Ring	**Includes**
First/Inner	Parents, Siblings, Best Friends
Second/Middle	Peer Groups, Teachers, Relatives, Other Adults
Third/Outer	Business/Community Leaders, Mass Media and Advertising, Government Leaders

Until recently, prevention efforts concentrated on changing only family, school, peer, and other immediate interpersonal influences. Even then, interventions with families have been limited. Interventions aimed at the outer ring of a young person's social environment, however, are beginning to show promising results. A conceptualization of adolescents' social environment has guided intervention development for Project Northland. The project is being conducted in 24 school districts and communities in northeastern Minnesota and is following a cohort of 2,351 adolescents from sixth grade to high school graduation. Project Northland has two distinct phases: early adolescence (Phase 1), which began when the students entered sixth grade (1991) and was completed during their eighth grade school year (1993-1994), and the students' last 2 years of high school (Phase 2), to be completed in 1999. An interim phase occurred during funding transition, when the students were in the 9th and 10th grades; during that time, they received less intensive interventions.

Project Northland is one of six promising alcohol and other drug prevention programs listed in an independent review as having demonstrated effectiveness. Key components of effective prevention programs and how they are used in Project Northland are listed below.

Key Components of Effective Prevention Programs and Their Use in Project Northland

The key components of effective programs were identified by Dusenbury and Falco (Dusenbury, L., and Falco. M. "Eleven components of effective drug abuse prevention curricula," *Journal of School Health* 65(10):420-25, 1995.).

Research based/theory driven. Social learning theory was used to develop interventions to decrease alcohol use and related problems among adolescents through strategies to encourage adolescents not to drink, reduce alcohol availability, and modify community attitudes concerning youth drinking.

Developmentally appropriate information about alcohol and other drugs. Early adolescent programs began in sixth grade with education for parents to develop and communicate family guidelines discouraging underage drinking. Peer leadership training was introduced in seventh grade. Community-level influences on underage drinking were gradually introduced by 8th grade, culminating in peer action teams during high school and a more complex curriculum in 11th grade. The name and content of Project Northland programs changed annually to mark developmental changes in the cohort.

Social resistance skills training. An 8-week curriculum in seventh grade focused on developing skills to resist peer pressure as well as opportunities for peer leaders to plan alcohol-free activities until the students graduated from high school.

Normative education. Changes in norms concerning underage drinking were a major goal of the Project Northland interventions from 6th through 12th grades.

More broadly based skills training and comprehensive health education. Project Northland maintained a strong focus on alcohol but within that context taught youth leadership skills and ways to achieve developmental milestones of adolescence (for example, autonomy and identity formation) without alcohol. Skills to identify and interpret unhealthy messages in the mass media also were taught.

Interactive teaching techniques. Peer leaders, role plays (including production of an improvisational theater piece in eighth grade), comics, fun games, alternative activities, and small-group projects were among the interactive teaching strategies used each year.

Teacher training and support. Part-time field staff were available at each intervention school. Teachers were given leave to attend half- or full-day training sessions before classroom implementation.

Adequate coverage and sufficient follow-up. Project Northland programs covered 6th through 12th grades and were successfully implemented with high participation rates each year.

Cultural sensitivity. People of color were represented in program materials, which included content specific to northern Minnesota Indian tribes and were sensitive to rural and small-town life in a northern climate. Programs were offered to a small school located on an Indian reservation outside the intervention districts when some of the cohort began transferring in and out of the study schools.

Additional components (for example, family, community, and mass media initiatives). Parent training and community-wide initiatives were part of Project Northland from sixth grade onward. Print media were used extensively throughout the program. (Radio and television could not be used because broadcasts could be received in reference communities.)

Evaluation. Project Northland was a randomized community trial using a cohort design beginning with sixth graders from 24 northern Minnesota school districts. School districts were randomly assigned to either the intervention or the reference condition. Interventions were assessed using outcome measures that included an annual student survey; parent telephone interviews; observational studies of alcohol-purchase attempts by youthful buyers without age identification; and surveys of merchants, police, school principals, and community leaders.

Interventions for Project Northland

The Phase 1 interventions for Project Northland included 3 years of behavioral curricula, peer leadership, parental involvement, and task forces to initiate community-level changes. At the end of Phase 1, the intervention group, compared with a control group, demonstrated statistically significant reductions in the onset and prevalence of drinking (among all students there was a 29-percent reduction in past-week alcohol use and a 19-percent reduction in past-month use). The reductions were attributed primarily to changes in peer norms (young peoples' views of the acceptability of underage drinking) and peer drinking behavior, parent-child communication that reinforced abstention, increased negative perceptions about the consequences of alcohol use (for example, "it would hurt my reputation," "using alcohol could threaten my eligibility to participate in sports," and "I would be breaking school rules and policies"), and increased resistance skills, according to students' survey responses. The greatest program benefits were found for students who had not yet started drinking when the intervention began in 1991.

Although the Phase 1 interventions did not change the broader social environment (for example, youth access to alcohol in the community), the results suggest that Project Northland not only affected the targeted alcohol and other drug use behaviors but also influenced a number of their predictive factors, which are generally considered more resistant to change. For example, after Phase 1, students in the intervention group scored significantly lower than the control group did on the Minnesota Multiphasic Personality Inventory-Adolescent (MMPI-A) Alcohol/Drug Problem Proneness Scale. The MMPI-A Proneness Scale measures risk factors for adolescent alcohol and other drug use, such as negative peer group influences, reduced involvement with parents, rule breaking, stimulus seeking, and lowered achievement orientation.

Challenges for Prevention during High School

The positive outcomes of Phase 1 of Project Northland have attenuated. This finding is consistent with other successful prevention programs with the rates of past-week alcohol use for students who reported no lifetime alcohol use at the sixth-grade baseline. During the interim period from 9th to 10th grade, when interventions were minimal, no statistically significant differences were found between students in the intervention and control communities on any of the alcohol use measures. As the interventions resumed their level of intensity in 11th grade, the differences in past-week alcohol use for intervention and control group students who were nondrinkers at the start of the study approached significance. At the time this text was written, data collection had not been completed to determine program effects at the 12th-grade endpoint of the study. Statistics suggest that alcohol use during adolescence is a complex, ingrained social behavior, the prevention of which requires long-term interventions. Without such interventions, gains made during early adolescence may be lost.

Phase 2 of Project Northland included new strategies for the intervention students' last years of high school that built on the interventions in early adolescence. Whereas Phase 1 emphasized strategies to encourage adolescents not to use alcohol, Phase 2 emphasized changing six community norms about adolescent alcohol use along with stimulating community action to reduce the availability of alcohol among high school students.

Community-Level Norms for the High School Phase of Project Northland

1. It is unacceptable for high school students to drink.
2. It is unacceptable for anyone (for example, parent, older teen, merchant, or other adult) to provide alcohol to high school students.
3. Adults and high school students should take action when high school students are drinking.
4. Parents do have influence on their high school students' drinking. Parents can provide social support, set clear expectations, monitor and supervise, and avoid inconsistent or excessively severe punishment.
5. Community events and public places are opportunities for modeling healthy behaviors for high school students.
6. High school students can have fun, establish their maturity and independence, and relieve stress and boredom without alcohol.

Although widespread acceptance existed during Phase 1 for the norm that drinking by sixth graders was undesirable (based on anecdotal and survey data from parents and students), no universal support was evident for norm 1, that drinking by high school students was unacceptable. In addition, we routinely heard that parents and other adults violated norm 2 (that it is unacceptable for anyone to provide alcohol to high school students) by providing alcohol for high school students' parties or by purchasing alcohol for adolescents who could not purchase it for themselves. Norm 3 (that adults and high school students should take action when high school students are drinking) attempted to shift the focus away from the notion that underage drinking was an individual adolescent's problem to the recognition that adults and high school students can intervene to reduce drinking during the high school years. Parents were encouraged (see prevention strategies below) to increase "protective factors" that reduced the likelihood that their child would drink (to provide social support, set clear expectations, monitor and supervise adolescents' behavior, and avoid inconsistent or excessively severe punishment). Community members were educated (see prevention strategies below) to recognize that community events, such as summer festivals, and public places, such as parks, provided opportunities for adults to model healthy behaviors for high school students (norm 5). Norm 6 identified key issues of adolescence (to have fun, establish maturity and independence, and relieve stress and boredom) that advertisers and mass media often model as reasons for using alcohol. Those characteristics were successfully influenced in Phase 1 (young adolescents recognized that they did not need alcohol to have fun, establish their identity, and so forth). Phase 2 also addressed these issues, because we recognized that counter messages from the youth culture became more intense as the students progressed through high school.

Five Prevention Strategies for High School

Phase 2 of Project Northland used five major strategies to reduce alcohol availability among youth and reinforce the norms listed above. The strategies were community organizing, parent education, youth participation, media campaigns, and school curriculum. Seven local field staff were responsible for implementing the community organizing component in the 11 communities where the intervention students lived. The specific techniques used for community organizing, aimed at the outer ring (see Table 63.1), included the following:

- One-on-one interviews with local citizens representing a broad spectrum of the community (averaging about 100 interviews per community)

- Formation of local action teams interested in implementing strategies to reduce underage access to alcohol in their geographical area and regional training sessions for team members on how to develop policy solutions to underage drinking in their geographical area
- Participation in community festivals (for example, booths at fairs and distribution of petitions)
- Adoption of community policies (for example, "gold card" programs, in which local businesses provided discounts to students who pledged to remain free of alcohol and other drugs and provide community service)
- Responsible beverage server (RBS) training sessions for retail outlets and bars (held by all communities to emphasize ways to reduce youth access)
- Compliance checks of age-of-sale laws (coordinated with local police or sheriffs' departments).

Action teams initiated ordinances designed to reduce youth access to alcohol (for example, youth curfews; mandatory RBS training; penalties to establishments for failure to check age identification; and noisy-assembly laws, which prohibit loud parties at certain hours), and three communities adopted at least one such ordinance during the 2 years of community organizing.

Parent programs have been a part of Project Northland since the first year. Therefore, it was a challenge during the last 2 years of the project to initiate new and developmentally appropriate programs for parents with considerable experience with the interventions. Some parents participated on action teams. In addition, short written materials were used to reach all parents of the intervention students. A postcard campaign of 11 cards, mailed at 6-week intervals, encouraged specific actions that parents could take to keep adolescents alcohol-free during high school (for example, "The next time your teen goes to a party, call ahead to make sure there will be an adult chaperone."). During the students' senior year, materials were sent to all intervention parents and students encouraging them to communicate about alcohol by answering discussion questions and returning their answers to be eligible for a drawing of $500 per school. The discussion topics for the "Sound-OFF!" program included the minimum drinking age, adults providing alcohol to adolescents, and community responses to underage drinking. This program was widely publicized in the local media, and 20 percent of all intervention students and parents participated.

Youth participation has been a key component of Project Northland since its inception. Youth action teams were formed in 17 of the 18 intervention schools. Part-time, local, adult coordinators were hired to assist the teams, which met after school. Teams were brought together for two regional training sessions and to testify before the Minnesota legislature in support of a bill to reduce youth access to alcohol. These regional events underscored to the students that they were part of a larger, positive peer group in northeastern Minnesota that supported the Project Northland norms. The youth action teams not only targeted the first two rings of adolescents' social environments but also worked for change in the broader social environment. More specifically, youth action teams were active in the following:

- Planning alcohol-free activities
- Planning safe homecoming, prom, or graduation activities
- Participating in community events, such as festivals and fairs
- Developing activities for "chemical health weeks" (for example, mock crashes and "ghost-out" activities, in which a number of students would be identified as "victims" of alcohol-related crashes and act as ghosts throughout the school day)
- Decreasing underage access to alcohol by working to change local policies related to alcohol sales at community festivals and promoting family policies, such as providing safe and alcohol-free activities for youth in the home.

Several print-media campaigns during Phase 2 reinforced the efforts of the adult community organizing and the youth action teams by highlighting their activities. (The use of radio and television was not feasible, because those broadcasts also could be received in the reference communities.) Youth and adult community members were trained separately in media advocacy (for example, writing and distributing press releases, contacting reporters, and pitching story ideas) to increase newspaper coverage of both the problems associated with underage alcohol use and solutions to those problems. Project staff developed media kits for each community and distributed Project Northland newsletters during the intervention period to highlight successes in the various communities. In addition, they distributed calendars to merchants licensed to sell alcohol in the intervention communities to assist clerks in calculating a buyer's age. Over a 6-month period during the students' senior year, project staff mailed monthly educational messages for insertion in bulletins to religious organizations in the intervention communities.

Although 18- to 20-year-olds cannot legally purchase alcohol themselves, they are likely to provide it to younger adolescents. Thus, a "Don't Provide" campaign was developed with the assistance of an advertising agency to communicate to young adults (ages 18 to 22) that providing alcohol to high school students was unacceptable. (The Martin Williams advertising firm provided pro bono work in developing the "Don't Provide" campaign.) The campaign included three posters for distribution to liquor and convenience stores, restaurants, bars, schools, and clinics; two corresponding postcards for the students' parents; four postcards mailed to the target population of young adults; and mylar stickers for stores' cooler doors. Messages were developed based on focus-group responses from young adults about what would be attention-getting and compelling. The messages included warnings about potential legal consequences (for example, "Buy a minor a drink, and you could end up in the clink.") as well as appeals to adolescents' social responsibility and greater maturity ("Don't provide alcohol to anyone under 21; they're just kids for crying out loud."). Local adult or youth action teams distributed the posters and stickers throughout the communities. Local newspapers provided campaign coverage, and one community developed a corresponding T-shirt.

The final media effort was a celebration and thank-you poster, entitled "Celebrating Success: How Project Northland Became a Prevention Model for the Nation," which was mailed to approximately 5,500 community members (for example, parents and students, police, merchants, community leaders, schools, and faith organizations). The poster included pictures of eight Project Northland volunteers, selected by nomination, to represent students, parents, police, school representatives, and members of the broader community.

During Phase 2 less reliance was placed on classroom curricula, which were the core of Phase 1 interventions. A classroom-based program was used only in 11th grade. That program involved a mock trial that emphasized the social and legal consequences of underage drinking. Although delivered within the classroom environment, the curriculum focused on the outer ring of the social environment. It reinforced that underage drinking is a community-wide problem and gave students the opportunity to debate the legal intricacies of alcohol-related cases in six class sessions. The cases were developmentally appropriate and included the following:

- Personal injury or property damage resulting from the provision of alcohol to minors at home
- Use of alcohol by a pregnant adolescent
- Commercial alcohol sale to a minor and the resulting violence
- Drinking by minors at a community festival
- Lack of enforcement by a coach of the State athletic association's rules against alcohol use
- Rape resulting from alcohol use at a party.

Why Harm Reduction Is Not Used in Project Northland

Project Northland does not use a harm-reduction approach. Harm reduction suggests that because alcohol and other drug use is prevalent during adolescence, a more effective prevention strategy would be to reduce the harm associated with use or promote "responsible use," rather than emphasize "no use" prevention messages. However, alcohol use is illegal for all high school and most college students. Consequently, any harm-reduction approach would condone illegal behavior, which at best conveys a problematic message to adolescents.

As discussed earlier in this article, research has indicated the following:

- Historical evidence exists that adolescence has not always been a time of heavy alcohol use.
- Significant morbidity and mortality are associated with underage drinking.
- With earlier alcohol use, a significant increase occurs in the risk of developing an alcohol dependency or abuse disorder.

These findings, as well as others, suggest the need for consistent, simple messages advocating no alcohol use during adolescence. When delivered and reinforced in multiple ways, these messages may be the most effective alcohol prevention approach with the least amount of harm associated with it.

Remaining Challenges for the Prevention of Alcohol-Related Problems during Adolescence

Although findings are still unclear on whether Project Northland has achieved its long-term goals of reducing alcohol use and alcohol-related problems in its cohort of adolescents, the achievement of several short-term goals is apparent. For example, outcomes show that community members will work with researchers to implement extensive programs targeting adolescents' social environment over an extended time period. In addition, considerable support can be organized to reinforce community norms regarding the unacceptability of underage drinking and the value of healthy alternatives to adolescent alcohol use. Community leaders, including merchants, city council members, school officials, and parents, can be mobilized to provide sustained and consistent "no use" messages to students throughout their high school years. Those messages can emphasize appropriate consequences, as well as workable alternatives for meeting adolescents' needs, without resorting to more ambiguous messages about "responsible use." The effect of community-level interventions can be evaluated and policy decisions made on the basis of empirical findings. As analyses are initiated on the outcomes of Project Northland, information will be forthcoming about the challenges involved in fostering change at the community level.

The findings from the early adolescent phase of Project Northland are consistent with those of other researchers who have demonstrated lower alcohol use rates using similar strategies based on social learning theory. Unfortunately, those types of programs are not used widely in U.S. schools, even though information is available on the types of programs most likely to be effective. Whether and how those programs can be implemented on a large scale, how much it would cost (and who would pay), and how the interventions can affect the smaller group of adolescents who have already initiated drinking by sixth grade are questions that remain.

One area that Project Northland has not fully addressed is the role that mass media and advertising play in defining a youth culture that directs American youth to accomplish developmental tasks, such as autonomy and identity formation, by using tobacco and alcohol. The Minnesota tobacco trial has finally allowed public access to formerly internal documents indicating how the tobacco industry effectively marketed cigarettes to youth while deflecting responsibility by attributing youth smoking to peer pressure, parents, and a youth culture that they helped create through pervasive and potent advertising and promotional activities. Parallels in the alcohol industry are evident. In addition, alcohol advertising has been found to include images or themes at odds with former Surgeon General Koop's 1989 recommendations that alcohol advertising not portray activities that are dangerous when combined with drinking (for example, driving and being near water) or that feature celebrities who are particularly appealing to youth. Although research has not clearly substantiated the potential influence of advertising on youth drinking, recent studies suggest that alcohol advertising may predispose young people to drink. Even modest viewing of popular music video stations or televised sports may result in substantial exposure to glamorized depictions of alcohol and tobacco use.

The pervasiveness of media messages about tobacco and alcohol, the potency of the messages for adolescent audiences, and the placement of the messages where youth will see them (for example, on billboards near schools) need to be better understood as potential contributors to adolescent drinking, rates of which are growing while the rest of the population is decreasing its alcohol consumption. Comprehensive community efforts that include interventions designed to reduce media and advertising targeting of youth are fruitful areas for further prevention research.

Acknowledgements

The authors are grateful for the multidisciplinary team of collaborators and their numerous contributions to this research program and for the involvement of students, parents, school districts, and community members from northeastern Minnesota who have been active participants over an 8-year period.

Chapter 64

Prevention and Intervention with Children of Alcoholics

Children of alcoholics (COAs) are at increased risk for a wide range of behavioral and emotional problems, including addiction to alcohol and other drugs (AODs), depression, anxiety, school failure, and delinquency. Prevention and intervention efforts attempt to reduce this risk by modifying risk-associated factors. In general, prevention programs target children because of the behavior of an adult caregiver, rather than because of the child's own behavior. Intervention programs, however, usually target children who have begun to exhibit symptoms themselves, such as depression, poor academic performance, or problems getting along with their peers.

Prevention Models

Primary prevention focuses on children who have not exhibited specific problems but who may be at risk because of genetic or environmental factors or both. Secondary prevention (intervention) is targeted toward children who already exhibit behaviors predictive of later AOD use. Finally, the goal of tertiary prevention (which is analogous to

---

Excerpted from "Breaking the Cycle of Addiction: Prevention and Intervention with Children of Alcoholics," by Ann W. Price, M.A., and James G. Emshoff, Ph.D., in *Alcohol Health and Research World*, Summer 1997, Vol. 21, No, 3, p. 241(6). A complete copy of this publication may be ordered from the U.S. Government Printing Office. Call (202) 512-1800 for information on price and availability.

treatment) is to help children who are already involved with AODs and to prevent further deterioration of their behavior.

Some research suggests that the risk for behavioral problems is increased by exposure to stress and reduced by social support, social competency (social skills), and self-esteem. Therefore, the goals of primary prevention with COAs should include stress reduction and the development of self-esteem, social competence, and a strong social support system.

Other primary prevention models take a different approach. For example, the "distribution of consumption" model proposes to reduce the general public's consumption of alcohol by limiting its availability. This theoretically would reduce the number of problem drinkers and consequently the number of children exposed to alcohol problems in the family. This strategy involves raising the drinking age, limiting "happy hours," and increasing the price of alcoholic beverages or limiting the hours of their sale. This approach will not be discussed here, however, because it does not specifically target COAs.

Another model, called the "sociocultural model," focuses on education and on enhancing children's competencies through information, values clarification (examining values regarding alcohol), and skill-building techniques. The goal of this approach is to teach children to moderate their drinking and avoid later alcohol problems. Sociocultural programs can be implemented throughout the community or may be targeted via schools, recreational activities, or physicians' offices.

Screening and Identification

Many COAs never receive intervention services. COAs are usually identified incidentally when the child's parent enters alcoholism treatment. This type of identification is ineffective in reaching the majority of COAs, because most alcoholics never receive treatment. In addition, few children seek help voluntarily, because family denial puts pressure on the child to keep the family's secret.

Identification of COAs, therefore, requires a process of active screening. Certain behavior patterns suggest a child may have an alcoholic parent. Some of these behaviors may reflect lack of parental supervision, such as frequent tardiness or absence from school or carelessness in dress or personal hygiene. Other possible indicators of COA status include emotional instability, immaturity, conflict with peers, isolation from other children, academic problems, or physical complaints (for example, headaches and stomach aches). Many people who work with children are not trained to recognize these subtle signs; in addition, these signs are not specific to COAs. Therefore, researchers have developed questionnaires to identify COAs who do not display obvious behavior problems.

One commonly used screening instrument is the CAGE, a set of four questions regarding the respondent's concern over his or her own drinking behavior. The Family CAGE is slightly reworded to reflect a respondent's concern for the drinking habits of a relative. This questionnaire is intended to screen for, not diagnose, family alcoholism: a positive finding on the Family CAGE should be followed by a complete diagnostic assessment.

The Family CAGE

The CAGE is perhaps the most widely used screening test for alcoholism. This tool has been adapted to reflect concern for a parent's drinking through the following four questions:

1. Do you think your parent needs to **C**ut down on his/her drinking?
2. Does your parent get **A**nnoyed at comments about his/her drinking?
3. Does your parent ever feel **G**uilty about his/her drinking?
4. Does your parent ever take a drink early in the morning as an **E**ye opener?

Children of Alcoholics Screening Test (CAST)

Another useful questionnaire is the Children of Alcoholics Screening Test (CAST) (see: Jones, J. *Preliminary Test Manual: The Children of Alcoholics Screening Test*. Chicago: Family Recovery Press, 1982; and Sheridan, M.J. "A psychometric assessment of the Children of Alcoholics Screening Test (CAST)," *Journal of Studies on Alcohol* 36:117-126, 1995). The CAST is designed to identify both young and adult children of alcoholics. The 30-item instrument probes the respondent's attitudes, feelings, perceptions, and experiences related to the drinking behavior of the respondent's parents. A shorter version of CAST has also been developed. Because of time constraints and the fact that many school-based programs are run by teachers rather than psychologists, such measures are not routinely used to identify COAs in the school environment.

Prevention Groups

Most programs for COAs are delivered in group settings. Group programs reduce COAs' feelings of isolation, shame, and guilt while capitalizing on the importance to adolescents of peer influence and mutual support. Groups may be structured and closed-ended, with a specific beginning and end-point, or open-ended, with participants joining and leaving the group as they feel the need.

Groups may be directed at the general population of COAs, as in broad-based community prevention programs, or targeted at specific high-risk groups, such as abused or neglected children as well as youth with academic problems or gang affiliations. These groups are readily identified and contain a large percentage of COAs. Prevention and intervention services can be offered to high-risk COAs as part of comprehensive social service programs aimed at those populations.

Alateen

Alateen is an example of a community-based self-help program for COAs based on the 12-Step approach of Alcoholics Anonymous. Alateen generally meets in public settings, such as churches or community centers. Little data exist on the effectiveness of Alateen. In one study, COAs participating in Alateen had more positive scores than nonparticipating COAs on a scale measuring mood and self-esteem, factors affecting risk for behavioral problems, including alcohol misuse. Conversely, in a study of 4- to 16-year-old sons of alcoholics, investigators found that group counseling had more positive effects than did Alateen in improving self-worth. Unfortunately, not enough empirical evidence exists to draw any firm conclusions about the effectiveness of Alateen.

School-Based Groups

Children are available at schools for long periods of time and in large numbers; therefore, educational institutions are logical settings for intervention efforts. Behavior problems potentially indicating parental alcoholism can be most readily recognized in school. An added benefit is that COA programs within schools have ready access to needed information and services. Finally, children and adolescents may find it embarrassing to attend programs at an outside agency or treatment center, particularly in settings that may have a negative stigma attached (for example, mental health centers).

School curricula often include information about AODs and their impact on the family. These AOD education classes provide a valuable opportunity for teachers to observe possible signs of parental alcoholism. For example, COAs may be extremely negative or apprehensive about alcohol and drinking or may exhibit changes in attendance patterns or interest levels during AOD education. Although schools appear to be logical prevention settings, few school-based programs designed specifically for COAs have been described. Therefore, the types and prevalence of such programs are not known.

Program Content

Although there are several types of intervention programs, some strategies are common to most programs. Among these strategies are training in social competency and coping skills, as well as providing information, social support, and alternatives to AOD use. These strategies have been developed for prevention efforts with diverse populations, but are applied (and sometimes adapted or customized) to groups of COAs.

The content of COA prevention and intervention programs is often based on social cognitive theory. The goals of such programs are to reduce children's stress, increase their social support system, provide specific competencies and skills, and provide opportunities for increased self-esteem. Social cognitive theory emphasizes techniques such as role playing, modeling, practice of resistance skills, and feedback. Role playing allows the child to rehearse common situations such as riding in the car with a drunk parent. Through modeling, participants learn appropriate behavior (for example, effective communication skills) by observing group leaders and peers. Resistance skills help children cope with peer pressure to drink. Both the group leader and participants provide the child with positive feedback to reinforce and encourage newly acquired skills. These techniques have contributed to significant reductions in the use of cigarettes, alcohol, and marijuana in general prevention programs that target wider groups rather than COAs specifically. More research is needed to test these techniques with COAs.

The influence of the child's developmental stage must be considered during program design. For example, elementary school-aged children do not always have realistic perceptions of relationships and causal links and may believe that they are the cause of their parents' drinking problem. During the middle school years, COAs, as well as other children, often make decisions about using AODs themselves.

In addition, the emergence of emotional or mental health problems is not unusual for many adolescents, including COAs. Therefore, prevention efforts should focus on the preteen years.

Many COAs who appear to be coping well are actually in a self-protective state of denial. Group facilitators should exercise patience and sensitivity as children adjust to their changing awareness about their parents' drinking. Group leaders should also recognize that COAs may become overly dependent on them and should be sensitive to the feelings of abandonment that children may experience when the group terminates.

Information and Education

Most programs provide information about alcohol and alcoholism to help correct false expectancies. For example, COAs often overestimate the positive effects of alcohol consumption on cognitive and social performance, thereby increasing their risk for excessive drinking.

Most programs promote the concept of alcoholism as a disease to help the child put the behavior of the alcoholic parent in perspective. For example, understanding the biological basis of alcoholism manifestations such as tolerance, blackouts, and withdrawal helps the child overcome misplaced self-blame and guilt about parental drinking. Finally, COAs must learn that they are at risk for a variety of psychosocial problems, especially alcoholism. Research shows that COAs who are aware of their risk status drink significantly less than COAs who are unaware of their risk status.

Competencies and Coping Skills

Competencies are skills that help children cope with stress, thereby reducing their risk for alcoholism and other psychosocial problems. Most programs teach specific emotion-focused and problem-focused coping skills. Emotion-focused coping is a process by which the child seeks social support or uses strategies such as distancing or reframing the negative aspects of the situation to emphasize the positive aspects. For example, the child's inability to control parental drinking may be offset by the knowledge that sources of help are available.

Problem-focused coping emphasizes the problems of living in an alcoholic home, such as having to explain unusual parental behavior to friends. In addition, this approach attempts to enhance decision-making, problem-solving, and communication skills, as well as the ability to resist peer pressure to drink, as discussed earlier under "Program Content." Emotion-focused and problem-focused skills are not mutually exclusive, and children who learn both skills are better equipped to manage their lives.

Personal-Social Competencies

Personal-social competencies can improve COA functioning despite exposure to stress. Such competencies include the ability to establish and maintain intimate relationships, express feelings, and solve problems. These skills can be enhanced by buttressing the COAs self-esteem and self-efficacy (the belief that one can perform a particular task).

Social support arises naturally out of participation in group treatment. In the group setting, children often learn for the first time that other children have problems similar to theirs. Many children benefit from sharing their experiences and emotions in a safe environment with other children. Through mutual exchange, children learn survival skills from the experiences of their peers, gain practice in expressing feelings, and build their social support networks.

Many COAs attempt to achieve perfection in everything they do as a means of acquiring self-esteem. This sets the stage for inevitable failure. Therefore, interventions often emphasize alternative ways to acquire self-esteem and self-efficacy, as discussed next.

Alternative Activities

Alternative activities provide opportunities for COAs to participate in activities that exclude alcohol, tobacco, and other drugs. Healthy alternative activities (for example, sports, peer leadership training institutes, and programs such as Outward Bound) may help children build a sense of self-efficacy; increase self-esteem; provide a positive peer group; and increase life skills, such as problem-solving and communication. Programs may focus exclusively on alternative activities but preferably are part of a comprehensive prevention program.

Conclusions

Despite their risk status, most COAs are remarkably well adjusted. Nevertheless, many children exhibit emotional and behavioral problems as a result of parental drinking. Improved research methods can guide intervention to prevent adverse outcomes from developing.

Results of evaluation research suggest several appropriate levels of intervention and basic prevention program components. Basic AOD education should be included in public school curricula. Parental and family training are promising areas that have been shown to reduce child and adolescent risk factors. Comprehensive community programs that target social norms regarding AODs are another promising, yet underutilized, area. Preventive intervention programs should include the basic components of information and education, skill building in the areas of coping and social competence, social support, an outlet for the safe expression of feelings, and healthy alternative activities.

Chapter 65

Alcoholism: Taking a Preventive, Public Health Approach

Although its exact prevalence has not been established, alcoholism affects about 5% to 10% of the general population, 10% to 20% of ambulatory patients, and 20% to 40% of patients in hospital settings.[1,2] This common disorder has serious health consequences and is responsible annually for a large number of deaths from alcohol-related diseases, accidents, and homicides. It is also a factor in numerous social problems, including domestic violence. Because of the problem's enormity, alcohol abuse merits the attention of primary care physicians.

The etiology of alcoholism is unknown, but strong evidence exists for a genetic origin.[3] Given the inherited risk, a variety of psychological and environmental factors (for example, depression, broken home, and alcohol misuse by other family members) appear to influence the expression of that risk in the individual.[4] Once begun, alcoholism typically progresses over 10 to 20 years. Because the progression is gradual, however, it is difficult to determine the exact time when a person becomes an alcoholic.

People without a genetic risk for alcoholism or a previous history of alcohol abuse can also have an alcohol problem (for example, a recently bereaved person) or experience negative consequences from drinking (for example, a teenager who drinks and drives). Thus all patients, not just those with a diagnosis of alcoholism, are candidates for primary prevention efforts by the primary care physician in the

"Alcoholism: Taking a Preventive, Public Health Approach," by Richard D. Blondell, MD, Robert L. Frierson, MD, and Steven B. Lippmann, MD, in *Postgraduate Medicine*, Vol. 100, No. 1, July 1996; reprinted with permission.

office setting. These efforts can reinforce and support substance abuse education and interventions that take place within the home, at school or work, and in the community.

The most effective way for the physician to reduce alcoholism (and other substance abuse) is by taking a positive, public health approach combining medical, psychological, and social interventions.[5] When early alcoholism or risk factors for alcohol abuse are detected, the physician acts either to prevent alcohol abuse from beginning or to halt any further progression of the disease. Since alcohol problems and their solutions differ significantly according to the age, sex, and ethnicity of the individual,[6] it is important for physicians to be "culturally sensitive" and avoid imposing their own personal norms upon their patients. Simply passing judgment usually proves to be counterproductive.

Primary Prevention: Before It Starts

The goal of primary prevention is to identify those patients at risk for alcohol abuse and to educate them in order to stop the disease before it starts. Persons at risk for alcohol abuse (Table 65.1) often present to their doctor for routine healthcare. To inform them of their increased vulnerability for addictions, the physician needs to take a thorough history to uncover risk factors for alcoholism.[7] Sometimes drawing a genogram (medical family tree) helps uncover important information about family dynamics, major life events, and other aspects of the environment that the patient may not otherwise volunteer.

Table 65.1. Risk Factors for Alcoholism

Extreme poverty	Learning disability
Family dysfunction	Peers who abuse alcohol
Family history of alcoholism	Personal history of alcohol abuse

Low-risk patients who drink at all should be told to drink only in moderation (no more than two standard-sized drinks per day) and never at work, before driving, or when operating machinery. For high-risk patients (for example, those with a strong family history of alcohol problems), recommend that they consider total abstinence as the best way to prevent alcoholism. These patients also need to be encouraged to learn more about alcoholism by attending meetings of Alcoholics

Anonymous (AA) as an observer and by reading AA literature or similar publications.

Advise total abstinence for adolescents, women who are pregnant or trying to conceive, persons with alcohol-sensitive conditions (for example, pancreatic or liver disease, congestive heart failure, hypertriglyceridemia), those taking certain medications (for example, warfarin sodium, metronidazole), recovering alcoholics, and patients with past alcohol-related problems.

To be prepared for talking with patients about alcohol use and abuse, have on hand some brochures on alcoholism, responsible drinking, and warning signs and perhaps a list of recommended books. By keeping in mind the potential for alcohol abuse by any patient, physicians can assist patients in preventing alcohol problems from beginning.

Secondary Prevention: Intervene Early

Secondary prevention aims to identify patients with early disease and halt disease progression. In its early stages, alcoholism has few specific signs or symptoms, but clinicians can prevent progression if they recognize alcoholism early and intervene.

Before they exhibit overt alcoholism, alcoholic patients typically present to healthcare facilities for a variety of difficulties over a 5- to 15-year period. Physicians with a high degree of suspicion can recognize combinations of certain conditions (Table 65.2) that are suggestive of alcoholism as the root cause.

When alcoholism is being considered in the differential diagnosis for a presenting symptom or combination of symptoms, questioning the patient about the quantity and frequency of alcohol use is usually

Table 65.2. Symptoms and Signs of Early-Stage Alcoholism

Anxiety	Intermittent diarrhea
Depressed mood	Labile or refractory hypertension
Drunk driving arrests	Macrocytosis
Dyspepsia, gastritis	Marital and other family problems
Elevated liver enzyme levels	Recurrent minor injuries
Frequent job changes	Sleep disturbance
Glucose intolerance	Vague abdominal complaints
Hyperlipidemia	Victim or perpetrator of violence
Impotence	

unproductive, since many patients underreport consumption. However, two simple questions have been shown to be useful for screening: "Have you ever had a drinking problem?" and "When was your last drink?" (yes and less than 24 hours ago are positive responses).[8] If the patient gives negative responses to both questions, yet responds defensively or shows signs of discomfort with the topic, that may be a clue that there is in fact an alcohol problem.

Further information can be obtained with the CAGE questionnaire. These questions may be modified to suit the individual patient's circumstances but should address the same four areas: (1) recognition by the patient of alcohol excess or the need to "control" drinking, (2) negative effects on others, (3) adverse consequences, (4) evidence of tolerance, actual chemical dependence, or the need to manage a withdrawal syndrome.

When the physician determines that alcohol abuse caused the presenting condition, positive intervention is clearly indicated. The patient must hear an unambiguous message, such as "Your drinking habits are causing your problem." This approach may seem bold, but decisive action is necessary if the physician hopes to overcome the patient's denial, the main defense mechanism against recognition of the problem and acceptance of treatment.

The next step, even if the patient does not accept the diagnosis, is to negotiate a treatment strategy consistent with the patient's circumstances and with the physician's health concerns for the patient. For example, the patient might agree to limit drinking to a specified quantity and frequency ("controlled drinking") or to avoid alcohol altogether. You might also talk about ways to cope with the urge to drink and encourage the patient to attend AA meetings. It helps to be prepared with the phone numbers of an AA group or a chemical dependency counselor and suggestions of relevant books, tapes, or videos.

The main objective is to be sure that the patient adheres to the plan of action, so always schedule a return office visit to monitor the outcome. Family members, friends, or coworkers can also be contacted to verify the patient's compliance.

If a patient does not keep the return appointment or fails to adhere to the plan of action, the physician may want to consult with an alcoholism treatment expert for advice about what to do next. A serious alcohol problem may require further steps, including a formal intervention, counseling, or an inpatient treatment program.

It is not clear which type of substance abuse treatment works best. Researchers comparing inpatient programs with various other methods seldom find differences in outcome.[9] However, outcomes are better with employer-mandated inpatient approaches than with outpatient alternatives.[10]

Tertiary Prevention: Chronic Disease

The goal of tertiary prevention is to treat and rehabilitate patients with chronic alcoholism to prevent disease progression (Table 65.3). Typically, 10 to 20 years of active drinking are needed to reach this stage, although in some persons alcoholism proceeds more rapidly. Patients often require hospitalization for an acute medical problem, related or unrelated to alcohol.

Table 65.3. Symptoms and Signs of Chronic Alcoholism

Alienation from friends and family	Pancreatitis
Arrests for intoxication, incarcerations	Parotid swelling
Cardiomyopathy	Periodontal disease
Financial problems	Recurrent trauma (especially from falls)
Hepatitis or cirrhosis	Seizures, delirium tremens
Job loss	Testicular atrophy
Malnutrition	Wernicke-Korsakoff syndrome

The first step in treatment is to assess the risk for a withdrawal syndrome by obtaining information about the quantity and frequency of alcohol consumption. This information often can be obtained from the patient and supplemented with data from family members or medical records. Explain to the patient the benefits of stopping alcohol abuse and what to expect during withdrawal (for example, "Your health will improve if you avoid drinking," "You may get very nervous during detoxification, but we will give you medicines that will help").

Detoxification is the medical care that safely carries the patient through withdrawal to rehabilitation or other definitive treatment.[11] Benzodiazepines are widely used for the withdrawal syndrome, but phenobarbital is also effective. These drugs should not be given on an arbitrary schedule but should be given only in response to objective hyperadrenergic signs (for example, tachycardia, hypertension, diaphoresis).[12] Magnesium sulfate, also used routinely, reduces neuromuscular irritability. Multivitamins, especially those including thiamine, must always be given. Treat malnutrition and other medical problems as indicated.

Once the patient's condition is clinically stable, plan together for his or her rehabilitation. Physicians who maintain a nonjudgmental, concerned attitude have greater effectiveness with patients who abuse alcohol. Thus, you might say to the patient, "You are really ill right now because of your drinking, and I want to help you get better. I know some people who could help. Would you be willing to talk to them?" Then you can provide the phone numbers of AA or a chemical dependency counselor or program and have the patient call directly from the hospital bed or the office.

This preparation and immediate action can help break through the denial that is so much a part of alcoholism. You might also enlist the support of family members or friends to help persuade the person to begin treatment and quit drinking.

Dual Diagnosis

Patients who have a diagnosis of both alcoholism and a psychiatric disorder present a special challenge. Psychiatric problems may be secondary to alcoholism, as is often the case with depression, or they could represent a separate primary diagnosis (for example, schizophrenia). These patients may require treatment in a mental health setting, where treatment of both disorders can be integrated. Unless mental illness was known to precede the abuse of alcohol, the patient's alcoholism often is treated first, after which the patient is reevaluated for a separate psychiatric diagnosis.

Depressive symptoms may resolve when the patient abstains from alcohol and is involved with psychotherapy and self-help groups. However, if pharmacotherapy is required, most experts recommend prescribing selective serotonin reuptake inhibitors, rather than other types of antidepressants, because of their low abuse potential.

Patients in Recovery

Since there is no cure for alcoholism, even sober alcoholics are said to be "in recovery," a lifelong process.

Abstinence. Total abstinence from alcohol and other sedatives (including prescription drugs) is the cornerstone of management. Relapses are so common that they should be expected and planned for. Discussion of temptations, means of coping, support systems, and nondrinking lifestyle (for example, healthful diet, walking, or other exercise) is often helpful.

Aftercare. This is a follow-up program to assist in maintaining sobriety. It may include group therapy, individual psychotherapy, employer-mandated or other monitoring programs, and self-help groups such as AA. Patients are often advised to obtain an AA sponsor and attend 90 AA meetings in the first 90 days after treatment.

Family members can be profoundly affected by the alcoholic's illness and may benefit from Al-Anon or Alateen (for adolescent children of alcoholics) meetings. Books for recovering alcoholics and their family members are also valuable aids.[13]

Medications. Medications have also been used to help prevent a return to drinking. Disulfiram (Antabuse) causes the patient to experience unpleasant sensations (occasionally fatal) when alcohol is ingested, but it has not always proven to be clinically effective. It works best in patients who are motivated to take it every day.[14] A typical maintenance dose is between 125 and 500 mg per day.

Naltrexone hydrochloride (ReVia®) is a new medication that appears to prevent relapses by reducing the craving for alcohol. The dose must be individualized, so the product information should be carefully reviewed before this drug is prescribed. Indications are that this medication may be most effective when prescribed in the context of formal psychological and social therapies.[15,16]

Predicting relapses. Patients who are "in good recovery" do not drink or use drugs. They attend self-help meetings regularly, take care of their physical health (including not "forgetting" or canceling appointments), get along socially, function well at school or on the job, and obey the law. If, at the time of a scheduled return visit, a patient reports failing at one or more of these tasks, a relapse may be imminent.

To help prevent a relapse, advise the patient to increase attendance at AA meetings and to call his or her AA sponsor. Consultation with an experienced substance abuse clinician may also be helpful, especially if the patient is experiencing overt psychiatric symptoms. Addictive medications should not be prescribed. It is helpful for patients in recovery to get some positive reinforcement; for example, the physician might say that he or she is proud of the patient's efforts and note the many rewards to living a healthful lifestyle.

Summary

Alcoholism is a common, chronic, often progressive disorder that has negative effects on a patient's health and severe consequences for society as well. A positive, public health approach that integrates medical, psychological, and social therapies can lead to improved outcomes for patients who abuse alcohol.

Physicians can play an important role by educating patients to prevent alcohol abuse from starting, being alert to the risk factors, recognizing the signs of alcoholism (especially during its early stages), and initiating interventions designed to halt progression of this disease.

Doctors should maintain a therapeutic stance with patients who have continued to abuse alcohol, even after frequent relapses. Consultation with alcoholism experts may be helpful when treatment is difficult or there is the possibility of a dual diagnosis.

References

1. Maly RC. Early recognition of chemical dependence. *Prim Care* 1993;20(1):33-50 [Erratum, Prim Care 1993;20(2):x].
2. Moore RD, Bone LR, Geller G, et al. Prevalence, detection, and treatment of alcoholism in hospitalized patients. *JAMA* 1989;261(3):403-7.
3. Devor EJ, Cloninger CR. Genetics of alcoholism. *Annu Rev Genet* 1989;23:19-36.
4. Coleman P. Overview of substance abuse. *Prim Care* 1993;20(1):1-18.
5. Center for Substance Abuse Prevention. *Prevention primer: an encyclopedia of alcohol, tobacco, and other drug prevention terms*. Rockville, Md: National Clearinghouse for Alcohol and Drug Information, 1993.
6. Seale JP, Muramoto ML. Substance abuse among minority populations. *Prim Care* 1993;20(1):167-80.
7. Pearson TA, Terry P. What to advise patients about drinking alcohol: the clinician's conundrum (Editorial). *JAMA* 1994;272(12):967-8.
8. Cyr MG, Wartman SA. The effectiveness of routine screening questions in the detection of alcoholism. *JAMA* 1988;259(1):51-4.
9. Frances R, Franklin JE. Addiction medicine. *JAMA* 1992;268(3):330-2.

10. Walsh DC, Hingson RW, Merrigan DM, et al. A randomized trial of treatment options for alcohol-abusing workers. *N Engl J Med* 1991;325(11):775-82.

11. Cross GM, Hennessey PT. Principles and practice of detoxification. *Prim Care* 1993;20(1):81-93.

12. Saitz R, Mayo-Smith MF, Roberts MS, et al. Individualized treatment for alcohol withdrawal: a randomized double-blind controlled trial. *JAMA* 1994;272(7):519-23.

13. Mooney AJ, Eisenberg A, Eisenberg H. *The recovery book.* New York: Workman, 1992.

14. Fuller RK, Branchey L, Brightwell DR, et al. Disulfiram treatment of alcoholism: a Veterans Administration cooperative study. *JAMA* 1986;256(11):1449-55.

15. Volpicelli JR, Alterman AI, Hayashida M, et al. Naltrexone in the treatment of alcohol dependence. *Arch Gen Psychiatry* 1992;49(11):876-80.

16. O'Malley SS. Integration of opioid antagonists and psychosocial therapy in the treatment of narcotic and alcohol dependence. *J Clin Psychiatry* 1995;56(Suppl 7):30-8.

Chapter 66

Alcohol Abuse Prevention Strategies

Prevention

While there is no single definition of prevention there is general agreement among prevention practitioners on the overall goal of prevention. It is to foster a climate in which:

- Alcohol use is acceptable only for those of legal age and only when the risk of adverse consequences is minimal;
- Prescription and over-the-counter drugs are used only for the purposes for which they were intended;
- Other abusable substances (for example, gasoline or aerosols) are used only for their intended purposes; and
- Illegal drugs and tobacco are not used at all.

The Center for Substance Abuse Prevention (CSAP) has been charged since its inception in 1986 with providing guidance and leadership in the Nation's prevention efforts. As a result of CSAP's efforts, some basic premises regarding prevention have been established:

- Prevention strategies must be comprehensively structured to reduce individual and environmental risk factors and to increase resiliency factors in high-risk populations.

This chapter includes text from "Prevention," and "Prevention Strategies," excerpted from the Center for Substance Abuse Prevention's *Prevention Primer: An Encyclopedia of Alcohol, Tobacco, and Other Drug Prevention Terms,* Rockville, MD: National Clearinghouse for Alcohol and Drug Information, 1993.

- Community involvement is a necessary component of an effective prevention strategy; a shared relationship among all parties is essential in the promotion of alcohol, tobacco, and other drug prevention efforts.
- Prevention must be intertwined with the general health care and social services delivery systems and it must provide for a full continuum of services.
- Prevention approaches and messages that are tailored to differing population groups are most effective.

Current prevention strategies reflect a relatively new approach that was introduced in the 1970s and expanded in the 1980s. Prevention research has become more sophisticated, with improved evaluation techniques resulting in the development of a scientific basis for prevention efforts. Prevention strategies are evolving as new scientific findings shed light on promising approaches to reducing alcohol, tobacco, and other drug problems.

Since the mid-1980s, the prevention field has developed sophisticated information dissemination and networking systems. A centralized information source is available through CSAP's National Clearinghouse for Alcohol and Drug Information (NCADI). [See "A Directory of Resources" in the end section of this book for contact information.] By calling NCADI's toll-free telephone number, prevention practitioners can get answers to their questions and access publications and literature searches. CSAP's RADAR Network Centers operate as an interactive communication system among people at the national, State, and community levels. The RADAR Network allows members around-the-clock access to information, publications, funding source referrals, and audiovisual materials developed by Federal agencies, Network members, and other organizations.

In summary, prevention has developed into a respected, organized discipline. Prevention offers communities an opportunity to stop alcohol, tobacco, and other drug problems before they start, and provides hope for effecting community change to support healthy behaviors.

Prevention Strategies

Prevention strategies targeting youth have evolved over the past 20 years as evaluation research reveals more about what works. Several strategies are used effectively, especially in combination:

- *Information dissemination.* This strategy provides awareness and knowledge of the nature and extent of alcohol, tobacco, and other drug use, abuse, and addiction and their effects on individuals, families, and communities, as well as information to increase perceptions of risk. It also provides knowledge and awareness of prevention policies, programs, and services. It helps set and reinforce norms (for example, underage drinking and drug dealers will not be tolerated in this neighborhood).
- *Prevention education.* This strategy aims to affect critical life and social skills, including decision making, refusal skills, critical analysis (for example, of media messages), and systematic and judgmental abilities.
- *Alternatives.* This strategy provides for the participation of targeted populations in activities that exclude alcohol, tobacco, and other drug use by youth. Constructive and healthy activities offset the attraction to, or otherwise meet the needs usually filled by, alcohol, tobacco, and other drug use.
- *Problem identification and referral.* This strategy calls for identification, education, and counseling for those youth who have indulged in age-inappropriate use of tobacco products or alcohol, or who have indulged in the first use of illicit drugs. Activities under this strategy would include screening for tendencies toward substance abuse and referral for preventive treatment for curbing such tendencies.
- *Community-based process.* This strategy aims to enhance the ability of the community to provide prevention and treatment services to alcohol, tobacco, and other drug use disorders more effectively. Activities include organizing, planning, enhancing efficiency and effectiveness of services implementation, interagency collaboration, coalition building, and networking. Building healthy communities encourages healthy lifestyle choices.
- *Environmental approach.* This strategy sets up or changes written and unwritten community standards, codes, and attitudes—influencing incidence and prevalence of alcohol, tobacco, and other drug use problems in the general population. Included are laws to restrict availability and access, price increases, and community-wide actions.

Chapter 67

Changing Environments that Contribute to Alcohol-Related Problems

Environmental approaches to prevention are an important part of comprehensive responses to alcohol, tobacco, and other drug problems. Contemporary strategies to prevent alcohol, tobacco, and other drug problems are often based on a public health model. This model, derived from the communicable disease model, stresses that problems arise through a reciprocal relationship among the agent, the host, and the environment.

In the case of alcohol, tobacco, and other drug problems, the agent is the alcohol, tobacco, or drug, the host is the individual drinker or user, and the environment is the social and physical context of drinking or use. Of particular importance to prevention are the environmental influences on drinking and other drug use.

Environmental approaches for reducing alcohol problems reflect a relatively recent change in how we as a society view alcohol, tobacco, and other drug problems. Until recently the principal prevention strategies focused on education and early treatment. In this view education was intended to inform society about the disease of addiction and to teach people about the early warning signs so that they could initiate treatment as soon as possible. Now efforts focus on "high risk" populations and attempt to correct a suspect process or flaw in

---

This chapter includes text from "Environmental Approaches to Prevention," excerpted from the Center for Substance Abuse Prevention's *Prevention Primer: An Encyclopedia of Alcohol, Tobacco, and Other Drug Prevention Terms,* Rockville, MD: National Clearinghouse for Alcohol and Drug Information, 1993.

individuals, such as low self esteem or lack of social skills. The belief is that the success of education and treatment efforts in solving each individual's problems will solve society's alcohol, tobacco, and other drug problems as well.

Prevention researchers generally agree that the most effective approach to reducing alcohol, tobacco, and other drug problems is through a public health systems approach that acknowledges the complexity of the interactions contributing to the development of problems.

This view is disputed by the alcoholic beverage industry, which seeks to attribute societal alcohol problems solely to the misuse of its product by a deviant subpopulation of problem drinkers or alcoholics. Current environmental messages regarding alcohol consumption are strongly influenced by the marketing and promotional activities of the alcohol industry, and are little driven by health and welfare concerns. Those messages are:

- Drinking is encouraged in virtually all situations. Example: Advertising slogans like "Put a little weekend in your week."
- Potential risks of drinking are downplayed. Examples: Alcoholic beverage sponsorship of racing cars or speedboats, proliferation of gas station mini-marts selling chilled single cans of beer to go.
- Abstinence is actively discouraged. Examples: The brandy advertisements that declare "I assume you drink"; frequent drinking on TV programs unrelated to plot development.
- Heavier consumption is actively encouraged. Example: Happy hour two-drinks-for-the-price-of-one promotions, or packaging to encourage larger purchases like 12 packs of beer or liters of wine coolers.
- Individual-focused prevention efforts deny the role of environmental factors. Example: Alcoholic beverage industry-sponsored prevention campaigns tell individuals to "Know when to say when" or "Friends don't let friends drive drunk."

It is within this environmental context that drinking patterns of the general population are shaped and problems develop. Contemporary prevention activities seek to change that environment through a range of activities, from raising community awareness to enacting regulatory measures to control how, where, and when alcoholic beverages are marketed, served, and sold. Often these prevention measures are opposed by the alcoholic beverage industry, which usually opposes regulatory measures and uses its considerable influence to lobby policymakers who have the power to enact environmental change measures.

The key to environmental approaches is the acknowledgment that alcohol, tobacco, and other drug problems are the result of complex interactions over time. As problems vary from place to place and time to time, no set of specific strategies will be appropriate for every instance. Thus, effective prevention must be integrated into community life and operate in complex social and economic environments to assist community members with the difficult decisions necessary to effect social change.

The development of problems is not individually based but rather the result of behaviors influenced by factors occurring in a variety of environments that contribute to an array of community level problems. For example, within this model efforts to reduce problems associated with drinking and driving might include an intervention directed at high risk contexts and environments such as server training for reducing the likelihood of drinking to intoxication by patrons in licensed establishments. For other drugs, environmental interventions might seek to change the economic lure of the illicit drug trade by developing jobs for inner city youth, or providing opportunities for success in alternative activities, such as sports or cultural endeavors.

In a public health approach to prevention emphasis is placed on system-level changes in those social, cultural, and economic environments most likely to yield desired reductions in alcohol, tobacco, and other drug problems.

Chapter 68

Community-Based Prevention Efforts

Community Partnerships

Through the early 1980s, preventing alcohol, tobacco, and other drug problems was viewed as primarily an educational effort, with a focus on efforts to change individual behavior, usually through classroom lessons. But both experience and evaluation studies have shown that a "systems approach" can be significantly more effective.

A systems approach views the community and the environment as interconnected parts, each affected by the others and needing to work together. Because the individual parts have the potential either for supporting or undermining prevention efforts of other parts, the goal of any community serious about prevention is to make the parts work together. Cooperation and support through a systems approach move communities closer to creating environments for youths that consistently discourage involvement with alcohol, tobacco, and other drugs.

In 1992, the Center for Substance Abuse Prevention (CSAP)'s Division of Community Prevention and Training accepted a new responsibility to provide national leadership in efforts that initiate, promote, and support the development of worksite prevention policies that focus on alcohol, tobacco, and other drug abuse, as well as HIV/AIDS issues in the workplace. Current efforts include assisting Community

---

This chapter includes text from "Community Partnerships," "Community Action Groups," and "Resources for Prevention," excerpted from the Center for Substance Abuse Prevention's *Prevention Primer: An Encyclopedia of Alcohol, Tobacco, and Other Drug Prevention Terms,* Rockville, MD: National Clearinghouse for Alcohol and Drug Information, 1993.

Partnership Program grantees to increase their business commitment and participation in workplace prevention activities. In addition the CSAP Drug-Free Workplace Helpline (1-800-843-4971) provides guidance to private sector business, industry, and labor on effective workplace substance abuse prevention policies and programs.

Another organization working for community collaboration is the Community Anti-Drug Coalitions of America (CADCA), which fosters networking and regional cooperation among coalitions, helping them share information and expertise. Created at the recommendation of the President's Drug Advisory Council and funded in part by a grant from The Robert Wood Johnson Foundation, CADCA provides training, technical assistance, and resource referral to assist community coalition efforts.

Community Action Groups

In the last decade nonprofit groups known as community action groups or community-based coalitions have formed to bring about large-scale prevention efforts in their communities. Typically, community action groups are initiated by civic-minded private citizens. For instance, in Jackson, Mississippi, a father started STIK (Stop the Teen Intoxication Kick) when his 14-year-old son's best friend was caught with alcohol. In Kensington, Maryland, an automobile dealership owner started DADD (automobile Dealers Against Drunk Driving) after reading that crashes were the leading killer of young people.

While community action groups typically start with one person, their success depends on enlisting others with skills and resources to achieve their objectives. For example, the Washington, DC, Regional Alcohol Program (WRAP) began with a few citizens in 1982 and has succeeded through infusions of new people, ideas, and resources over time.

The founding members of WRAP began the community action group with a news conference announcing their formation. The publicity drew volunteers and donations to support activities. With no paid staff, WRAP decided to undertake four multimedia campaigns each year along with a youth seminar to encourage local teens to form safety clubs in their schools. They held news conferences to launch each campaign, and placed prevention messages on donated posters, t-shirts, pins, pens, milk cartons, and gas pumps, and in tuxedo pockets, flower boxes, package liquor bags, restaurant windows, office elevators, paycheck envelopes, and grocery bags.

Several years after the formation of WRAP there were substantial changes in the Washington, DC, area. Alcohol-related deaths dropped by more than 17 percent. In 4 of the 6 years of WRAP's Operation Prom Graduation, which involved 175 high schools, there were no alcohol-related fatalities among high school seniors. Although it is not possible to prove that these changes were a direct result of WRAP's activities, the outcome is encouraging.

Perhaps one of the most well-known community action groups is Mothers Against Drunk Driving (MADD). Started in 1980 by Candy Lightner after her daughter was killed by an alcohol-impaired driver with prior convictions for driving under the influence, MADD had some 357 chapters nationwide by 1985. MADD's purpose is to both secure justice for those who have been harmed by alcohol-impaired driving and to prevent future alcohol-impaired driving.

Forming a Community Action Group

The key to starting a successful community action group is to enlist the active support of opinion-makers, advocates, and volunteers.

- *Opinion-makers* are those in leadership positions who are considered to be influential in the community, such as the mayor and other political leaders; presidents of community organizations, service clubs, and business or professional organizations; newspaper editors and publishers, and local TV and radio personalities; and professional athletes. Because of their status in the community, opinion-makers are often effective spokespersons for prevention issues. They can also provide access to those who shape the laws and opinions of the community and be a valuable asset in fund-raising.

- *Advocates* are those who, in the course of their professional lives, can have an impact on the audiences for community action initiatives. They may include doctors, dentists, nurses, other medical personnel, teachers, coaches, school administrators, treatment professionals, social workers, psychologists, nutritionists, police, clergy, retailers, media representatives, and opinion-makers. They help build credibility for a community action group by their active support and participation in educating the community.

- *Volunteers* can be either individuals or members of a group, such as auxiliaries, parents' groups, senior citizens' groups, or local volunteer bureaus. The role of volunteers is central to the success of a community action group. Volunteers can perform all the tasks needed for a successful community action group, including program administration, grant writing, activities development, community organizing, and public education.

Community action groups are emerging across the Nation. Their numbers are predicted to increase during the next decade as community members seek to develop local responses to alcohol, tobacco, and other drug problems.

Many community members who are concerned about alcohol, tobacco, and other drug problems want to do something about them but don't know where to begin. Help is available. The end section of this book includes directories of information resources as well as federal and state government agencies able to offer assistance.

Resources at the community level range from county health departments mandated to administer local alcohol, tobacco, and other drug prevention and recovery services to task forces or committees of local residents to coordinate prevention initiatives and advise policy makers on how resources should be allocated. Local law enforcement agencies can also serve as prevention resources, providing such services as presentations to parents and youth, school-based programs such as Drug Awareness and Resistance Education (DARE) programs, and neighborhood watch programs.

Other local government agencies that can support prevention efforts are parks and recreation departments, that can assist in the development of alcohol, tobacco, and other drug-free events and recreation; departments of mental health, that can provide information and early intervention services; and alcohol beverage control boards, that can help with programs to prevent sales of alcohol to minors.

Nongovernment Resources

Many national organizations are actively involved in efforts to reduce alcohol, tobacco, and other drug use and related problems. These organizations develop prevention materials, disseminate programs, conduct national media campaigns, lobby for legislation, and provide training and technical assistance. Some provide financial resources to local initiatives. In addition, many have chapters that are active in prevention initiatives in local communities.

Local businesses also have an important role to play in prevention. Businesses can provide support for local efforts in the form of donated materials and services (for example, printing, art work, paper supplies, reproduction) and by encouraging their employees to act as volunteers.

Part Seven

Additional Help and Information

Chapter 69

Glossary of Alcohol-Related Terms

5-HT: 5-hydroxytryptamine; serotonin.

A

Abstainer: A person who drinks less than 0.01 fl. oz. of alcohol per day (i.e., fewer than 12 drinks in the past year).

Access: The extent to which an individual who needs care and services is able to receive them. Ease of access depends on several factors, including insurance coverage, availability and location of appropriate care and services, transportation, hours of operation, and cultural factors, including languages and cultural appropriateness.

Acid-base balance: Normal body fluid pH (i.e., hydrogen ion concentration), which must be narrowly regulated for proper body functioning.

Acidosis: A condition in which body fluids become too acidic.

This glossary includes terms excerpted from *Alcohol Health & Research World*, Volume 19, No. 2, Spring 1995, Volume 21, No. 2, Spring 1996, and Volume 23, No. 3, Summer 1999; from *Ninth Special Report to the U.S. Congress on Alcohol and Health,* U.S. Department of Health and Human Services, National Institute on Alcohol Abuse and Alcoholism, June 1997; and from "Workplace Managed Care: Working Glossary of Terms," Center for Substance Abuse Prevention (CSAP), April 1999.

Active transport: The transfer of substances (i.e., molecules or ions) across a cell membrane from a lower to a higher concentration, thus requiring energy expenditure.

Acute care: Medical treatment rendered to individuals whose illnesses or health problems are of a short-term or episodic nature. Acute care facilities are those hospitals that mainly serve persons with short-term health problems.

Adduct: A molecule formed by one molecule attached to another; for example, by attachment of acetaldehyde to a protein.

Adhesion: The property of remaining close or attaching to a cell or tissue.

Affect: An outward manifestation of a person's feelings or emotions.

Agonist: A chemical substance that can bind to a receptor and initiate a reaction.

Alcohol dehydrogenase (ADH): The primary enzyme responsible for the breakdown of alcohol. ADH catalyzes the formation of acetaldehyde from alcohol.

Alcoholic dementia: Dementia resulting from prolonged, heavy alcohol consumption.

Aldehyde dehydrogenase (ALDH): An enzyme that breaks down acetaldehyde formed from alcohol by alcohol dehydrogenase (ADH).

Aldehyde oxidase: An enzyme that breaks down aldehydes to acids and generates superoxide anion as a byproduct.

Alkalosis: A condition in which body fluids become too alkaline.

Allele: One of two or more different forms of the same gene.

Ambulatory Care: All types of health services provided on an outpatient basis, in contrast to services provided in the home or to persons who are inpatients. While many inpatients may be ambulatory, the term ambulatory care usually implies that the patient must travel to a location to receive services that do not require an overnight stay.

Amino acids: The building blocks of proteins. Some amino acids also function as neurotransmitters.

Ammonia: A neurotoxic chemical compound that is formed in the body primarily as a product of protein metabolism.

Amnesia: Memory loss.

Amygdala: An almond-shaped structure in the temporal lobe, thought to contribute to alertness.

Anemia: A blood condition in which the number of functional red blood cells is below normal.

Antagonist: An agent that blocks or reverses the actions or effects of another agent.

Anterior: Toward the front of the body.

Anterior pituitary: A small gland at the base of the brain that is controlled by the hypothalamus and which manufactures hormones influencing many organs in the body.

Anterograde amnesia: Inability to remember new information for more than a few seconds.

Antibody: A protein that is produced by B cells in response to, and which interacts with, an antigen.

Antidiuretic hormone (ADH): A hormone produced in the hypothalamus and released from the posterior pituitary gland in response to dehydration; plays an important role in regulating fluid excretion.

Antigen: Any substance that is recognized by B cells or T cells and stimulates them to initiate an immune response.

Antioxidants: Chemicals (for example, glutathione and vitamins A and E) that prevent certain destructive chemical processes in cells.

Apoptosis: A series of chemical reactions within a cell that are induced by various events and which result in the cell's death.

Asterixis: Also called flapping tremor. A neurological disorder that is characterized by involuntary jerking movement, especially of the hands. It frequently is seen in patient with impending hepatic coma.

Atherosclerosis: A disease of the arteries in which fatty plaques accumulate on the arteries' inner walls, usually leading to narrowing and "hardening of the arteries and eventually obstructing blood flow.

ATP (Adenosine triphosphate): An energy-producing compound.

Atrial fibrillation: A loss of coordinated contraction that occurs in one or both of the upper chambers of the heart resulting in rapid and irregular heart and pulse rates.

Atrophy: Wasting away, or shrinkage, of tissue; caused by cell death rather than shrinkage of individual cells.

Attributions: Inferences on the causes and effects of behavior.

Autonomic responses: Physiological responses that are controlled by the autonomic nervous system (e.g., heart rate, blood pressure, and sweat gland activity). These responses are not under conscious control.

B

B lymphocyte (B cell): A type of white blood cell that originates in the bone marrow and is distributed throughout the blood and lymphoid tissues. B cells produce antibodies when stimulated by the appropriate antigens.

Basal ganglia: A group of nerve cell structures at the base of the cerebral hemisphere that are involved in motor control.

Behavioral health: A managed care term that applies to the assessment and treatment of problems related to mental health and substance abuse. Substance abuse includes abuse of alcohol and other drugs.

Behavioral healthcare: A continuum of services of individuals at risk of or suffering from mental, addictive or other behavioral disorders.

C

Case management: The monitoring and coordination of treatment rendered to patients with a specific diagnosis or requiring high-cost or extensive services.

Catalyst: Any substance that facilitates a chemical reaction and which does not undergo a permanent chemical change itself.

Catecholamines: A group of physiologically active substances with various roles in the functioning of the sympathetic and central nervous systems.

Cell-mediated immune response: An immune response provided by the direct actions of immune system cells (primarily T cells), as opposed to an immune response mediated by antibodies (i.e., humoral immune response).

Cellular toxin: A toxin that is released from a cell; also called endotoxin.

Cerebellum: The brain structure at the base of the brain that is involved in the control of muscle tone, balance, and sensorimotor coordination.

Cerebral cortex: The intricately folded outer layer of the brain, composed of nerve-cell bodies and gray matter, that covers the cerebrum. The cerebral cortex contains areas for processing sensory information and for controlling motor functions, speech, higher cognitive functions, emotions, behavior, and memory.

Cerebrospinal fluid (CSF): The clear fluid that fills the cavities within the brain and that surrounds the brain and spinal cord.

Cerebrum: The largest portion of the brain; includes the cerebral hemispheres (see cerebral cortex and basal ganglia).

Chemokines: Small proteins secreted by immune cells that can attract other immune cells to the tissue site where the chemokines are produced. Chemokines play a role in chemotaxis.

Chemotaxis: The directed movement of a cell in response to a stimulus, such as a chemokine.

Cholesterol: A fat-like substance that is an important component of cell membranes and is the precursor of many steroid hormones and bile salts. High cholesterol levels are associated with coronary artery disease.

Cholesteryl ester: The product of a reaction between cholesterol and an organic acid.

Cholesteryl ester transfer protein (CETP): A compound that transports cholesteryl esters from high density lipoproteins to low density lipoproteins for eventual removal from the blood.

Cingulate gyrus: Part of the structure that connects the two hemispheres of the brain.

Cirrhosis: A disease characterized by fibrosis, nodules, and loss of the normal structure of the liver accompanied by decline in liver function.

Claims review: The method by which an enrollee's healthcare service claims are reviewed prior to reimbursement. The purpose is to validate the medical necessity of the provided services and to be sure the cost of the service is not excessive.

Classical conditioning: A concept first developed by the Russian scientist Pavlov positing that when a neural stimulus (e.g., the sound of a bell) is repeatedly paired with a nonconditioned stimulus (e.g., food) which includes a certain reaction (e.g., salivation), the neural stimulus eventually becomes a conditioned stimulus that elicits the same reaction as the nonconditioned stimulus with which it was initially paired.

CNS: Central nervous system.

Coinsurance (Copayment): Percentage of covered expenses the insured party must pay for healthcare services above and beyond the deductible.

Collagen: The major protein constituent of connective tissue.

Conditioned withdrawal syndrome: The experience of physiological symptoms (e.g., sweating, tremors, and anxiety) of withdrawal from alcohol and other drugs that is not caused by the actual withholding of the drug but by stimuli that have been associated with previous withdrawal episodes.

Consumer: An individual who receives care, who purchases care directly, or who selects among health plans purchased on his or her behalf by an employer or another entity; an individual who receives behavioral healthcare services. Preferable to the terms "client" and "patient."

Coordination of Benefits (COB): Provisions and procedures used by third-party payers to determine the amount payable to each payer when a claimant is covered under two or more group plans.

Corpus callosum: The tract of myelin-coated nerve fibers connecting the two cerebral hemispheres.

Corpus striatum: One of the basal ganglia; located deep in the cerebral hemispheres and upper brain stem and involved in the programming of movement.

Cortisol: A glucocorticoid produced by the adrenal gland that helps regulate metabolism.

Cost-sharing: Health insurance practice that requires the insured person to pay some portion of covered expenses (e.g., deductibles, coinsurance, and copayments) in an attempt to control utilization.

Credentialing: The process of reviewing a practitioner's credentials, i.e., training, experience, or demonstrated ability, for the purpose of determining if criteria for clinical privileging are met.

Cultural competence: Actions that indicate an awareness and acceptance of the importance of addressing cultural factors while providing care; ability to meet the needs of clients and patients from diverse backgrounds.

Cytochrome: An enzyme that detoxifies foreign compounds.

Cytochrome p450 2E1: A microsomal enzyme that plays an important role in alcohol metabolism but also produces free radicals.

Cytokine: A substance that regulates cellular interactions and cellular functions. Cytokines are produced by a variety of cell types throughout the body.

Cytosol: The fluid substance within a cell.

Cytotoxic: Toxic to cells.

D

Dementia: A global intellectual impairment that includes loss of abstract thinking and memory functions, personality changes, breakdown of social skills, and other disturbances of higher brain functions.

Diencephalon: The area of the brain consisting of the thalamus, which is the brain's relay center to the cerebral cortex, and the hypothalamus.

Differentiation: A developmental process during which cells become increasingly specialized and acquire new characteristics and functions.

Diuresis: Increased urine production.

Diuretic: An agent that increases urine production.

DNA: The abbreviation for deoxyribonucleic acid, a molecular component of chromosomes that encodes the genetic information in all organisms except some viruses. DNA molecules usually consist of two strings of nucleotides.

Dopamine: A neurotransmitter that is involved in motor activity and which is believed to be associated with the sensations of reward induced by alcohol and certain drugs of abuse.

Down-regulation: A decrease in the number or sensitivity of receptors as a regulatory mechanism to compensate for increased activation of the receptors.

Drink: In the United States, the U.S. Department of Health and Human Services (DHHS) and the U.S. Department of Agriculture (USDA) have developed a commonly used definition of a standard drink that has been published in *Nutrition and Your Health: Dietary Guidelines for Americans* (DHHS and USDA 1995). According to that definition, a standard drink contains approximately 0.5 fl oz (or approximately 12 grams) alcohol and corresponds to the following beverage amounts:

- 12 fluid ounces regular beer
- 5 fluid ounces wine
- 1.5 fluid ounces 80-proof distilled spirits.

Dual Diagnosis: Identification of dual diseases, disorders, or injuries, commonly used to described individuals diagnosed with both mental disorders and addictive diseases.

E

Eicosanoids: The physiologically active substances derived from arachidonic acid (i.e., the prostaglandins, leukotrienes, and thromboxanes).

Electroencephalogram (EEG): A record of electrical brain activities measured with electrodes placed on different areas of the scalp.

Electrolyte: A substance that breaks down into electrically charged ions when dissolved in solution. Electrolytes are essential to physiological functioning.

Embolism: The obstruction of a blood vessel by a blood clot or other substance (e.g., a fat droplet) that has been transported through the bloodstream from another part of the body.

Employee Assistance Program (EAP): Programs to assist employees, their family members, and employers in finding solutions for workplace and personal problems.

Encephalopathy: Any disease of the essential tissues of the brain.

Endothelin: An extremely potent vasoconstrictor (i.e., agent that causes narrowing of the blood vessels).

Endothelium: The layer of cells that lines the blood vessels.

Endotoxin: A potent toxin contained in the cell walls of bacteria found in the intestine; it is released when a bacterium dies and is broken down.

Enzyme: A protein that directs and accelerates (i.e., catalyzes) chemical reactions in the body, such as the breakdown of complex molecules into simpler ones, but does not itself undergo permanent change.

Epithelium: The cell layer(s) covering the body's organs and lining the vessels, body cavities, glands, and organs. The epithelia of different organs consist of different types of cells.

Epithelium: The covering or lining tissue of the body.

Excitotoxicity: The processes by which excessive influx of calcium into the cell leads to cell death.

Expectancies: Expectations regarding the effects of a behavior or drug.

Extracellular fluid: All fluids outside the cells, including the noncellular portion of blood (i.e., plasma).

F

Fatty acid: Long-chain organic acid found in lipids (fats and oils). Unsaturated fatty acids have no double bonds in their structure; polyunsaturated fatty acids have two or more double bonds.

Ferritin: An iron-containing compound that regulates the storage and transport of iron in the cells.

Fibrin: An insoluble protein that forms the basis of a blood clot by linking with similar molecules in a fibrous meshwork. It is the ultimate product in the process of coagulation.

Fibrinolysis: Dissolution of a blood clot through digestion of fibrin by plasmin.

Fibrosis: The formation of fibrous tissue in the liver.

Folic acid: A vitamin of the B group that is essential for cell growth, cell division, and the absorption of nutrients from the intestines.

Free radicals: A group of short-lived, electrically charged, highly reactive atoms incapable of existing in a free state for a prolonged period.

Frontal lobe: The anterior region of the cerebral cortex.

G

GABA: Gamma-aminobutyric acid; an amino acid in the central nervous system that inhibits neurotransmission.

Gatekeeper model: A situation in which a primary care provider, the "gatekeeper," serves as the consumer's contact for healthcare and referrals. Also called closed access or closed panel.

Gene: A string of nucleotides that directs the synthesis of a protein.

Genotype: The genetic makeup of an individual organism.

Glial cells: Cells in the brain that are interspersed among and support neurons.

Glomerulus: A tiny ball or tuft of capillaries projecting into the capsule at the "head" of each nephron (kidney) tubule.

Glutamate: An amino acid that serves as the major excitatory neurotransmitter in the brain.

Glutamine: The major transport amino acid for ammonia.

Glutathione: A sulfur-containing compound found in high concentrations in liver cytosol and mitochondria. Glutathione is an antioxidant.

H

Heavy Drinker: Someone who drinks more than 1.00 fl. oz. alcohol per day (i.e., more than 2 drinks per day) or who reports having five or more drinks on five or more occasions in the past 30 days.

Hematopoiesis: The production and development of all blood cells.

Hemisphere: Two halves of the forebrain; refers mainly to the hemispheres of the cerebral cortex. Each hemisphere controls the sensory input and motor functions of the opposite half of the body. The left hemisphere primarily controls speech, language, reading, writing, and arithmetic calculations. The right hemisphere mainly controls nonlinguistic functions (e.g., complex patterns of sensory recognition, spatial abilities, and intuition).

Hemodynamics: The forces and mechanics involved in blood circulation (as through the kidney or another body part).

Hemoglobin: The oxygen-carrying molecule in red blood cells.

Hemolysis: The destruction of red blood cells and the associated release of hemoglobin.

Hepatic coma: Prolonged unconsciousness that occurs as a consequence of severe liver disease, such as cirrhosis or hepatitis.

Hepatic encephalopathy (Portal-systemic encephalopathy, or PSE): A progressive metabolic liver disorder that affects intellectual functioning.

Hippocampus: A region of the temporal lobe that is thought to play a role in learning and memory as well as in alcohol withdrawal seizures.

Homeostasis: The maintenance of a constant internal environment of the body, achieved through the body's regulation of body temperature, blood pressure, heart rate, respiration. levels of minerals in the blood, and so forth.

Humoral immune response: An immune response provided by antibodies circulating in the body's fluids, primarily the blood and lymph, as opposed to an immune response provided by the direct actions of immune cells.

Hyperplastic: Pertaining to hyperplasia, an abnormal multiplication or increase in the number of normal cells in normal arrangement in a tissue.

Hypertension: High blood pressure.

Hypothalamus: A region of the brain that is involved with basic behavioral and physiological functions; associated with thirst, hunger, and heightened emotional drives.

Hypoxia: Below-normal levels of oxygen in inspired gases, arterial blood, or tissue.

I

IGF-1: A protein produced by the liver in response to growth hormone (GH) that carries out some of the effects of GH at tissue level.

In vitro: Observable in a test tube or other artificial environment.

In vivo: Within the living body.

Indicated prevention: A strategy designed for persons who are identified as having minimal but detectable signs or symptoms or precursors of some illness or condition, but whose condition is below the threshold of a formal diagnosis of the condition.

Indicator: A defined, measurable variable used to monitor the quality or appropriateness of an important aspect of patient care. Indicators can be activities, events, occurrences, or outcomes for which data can be collected to allow comparison with a threshold, a benchmark, or prior performance.

Inflammatory response: Redness, swelling, heat, and pain produced in response to tissue injury or infection as the result of increased blood flow and an influx of white blood cells and cytokines to the affected site.

Integrated delivery system: A system of providers and diverse organizations working collaboratively to coordinate a full range of care and services within a community.

Interleukin: A group of cytokines with various immune system functions.

International Classification of Diseases, Ninth Revision (ICD-9): The *ICD-9* system is a classification system that groups related disease entities and procedures for the reporting of statistical information. Responsibility for maintenance of the classification system is shared between the National Center for Health Statistics (NCHS) which handles diagnosis classification, and the Health Care Financing Administration (HCFA) which handles procedure classification.

Interstitial fluid: Fluid between cells.

Intracellular fluid: Fluid within cells.

Ion: An electrically charged atom or group of atoms.

Ion channels: Proteins that span the cell membrane, forming pores that regulate the flow of specific charged particles into and out of the cell.

Isoenzymes: Variants of one enzyme that perform the same function but may have different properties.

J

Jaundice: A yellowish staining of the skin, whites of the eyes, and deeper tissues produced by an accumulation of metabolic end products in the blood; often a symptom of liver disease.

K

Korsakoff syndrome: See Wernicke-Korsakoff syndrome.

Kupffer cells: Specialized immune cells in the liver that filter bacteria and other foreign organic substances from the blood.

L

Lecithin-cholesterol acyl transferase (LCAT): An enzyme that transforms cholesterol to cholesteryl esters.

Lesion: A wound, injury, or pathological change in a body tissue.

Leukocytes: See white blood cells.

Leukocytosis: A blood condition in which the number of white blood cells is higher than normal.

Leukotrienes: A class of biologically active compounds that occur in white blood cells and induce allergic and inflammatory reactions.

Ligand: Any substance binding to a receptor.

Light drinker: A person who drinks 0.01 to 0.21 fl. oz. of alcohol per day (i.e., 1 to 13 drinks per month).

Limbic system: Parts of the cerebral cortex, hippocampus, hypothalamus, and other brain structures that together function in the expression of emotional behavior.

Lipid peroxidation: The destructive metabolism of fatty substances in cells.

Lipids: A family of complex molecules, including fats and fat-like molecules (e.g., fatty acids, steroids, or glycosides) that, among other functions, serve as an energy source and constitute part of the cell membrane.

Lipopolysaccharide: A compound or complex of lipids and carbohydrates.

Lipoprotein lipase: An enzyme involved in the breakdown of substances such as very low density lipoproteins.

Lipoproteins: Complexes consisting of proteins and fats or other lipids that are important for transporting lipids throughout the body.

Liver lobules: The functional units of the liver. Each lobule is composed of plates of hepatic cells arranged, spoke-like, around a central vein. Plates of hepatic cells are separated by blood vessels feeding from branches of the hepatic artery to the central vein and vessels that accept bile produced by hepatic cells and transport it to bile ducts.

Liver sinusoids: Small, irregular blood vessels found in the liver.

Low density lipoprotein: A type of molecule found in the bloodstream that has a lower protein-to-lipid ratio compared with high density lipoproteins.

Lymphoid tissues: The tissues in which B cells and T cells develop and congregate to initiate an immune response, including the bone marrow, thymus, lymph nodes, spleen, and tonsils.

M

Macrophage: An immune cell that has left the bloodstream and resides in the tissues and which is responsible for consuming foreign bodies such as bacteria. Macrophages also process and present antigen to T cells and secrete cytokines and complement proteins.

Mammillary body: A brain structure located near the hypothalamus that is involved in memory and in the control of autonomic (i.e., involuntary) body functions.

Managed Behavioral Health Care: Any of a variety of strategies to control behavioral health (i.e., mental health and substance abuse) costs while ensuring quality care and appropriate utilization. Cost-containment and quality assurance methods include the formation of preferred provider networks, gatekeeping (or precertification), case management, relapse prevention, retrospective review, claims payment, and others. In many health plans, behavioral health care is separated from care available in the rest of the health plan for the separate management of costs and quality of care.

Managed Behavioral Health Care Organizations (MBHO): An organized system of behavioral healthcare delivery, usually to defined population or members of HMOs, PPOs, and other managed care structures; also known as a behavioral health carve-out.

Mean corpuscular volume (MCV): A measure of the average size of a sample of red blood cells.

Medical necessity: The evaluation of healthcare services to determine if they are: medically appropriate and necessary to meet basic health needs; consistent with the diagnosis or condition and rendered in a cost-effective manner; and consistent with national medical practice guidelines regarding type, frequency and duration of treatment.

Mesial: Toward the middle.

Messenger ribonucleic acid (mRNA): A type of RNA molecule that carries the information from a gene and serves as a template for the production of proteins.

Metaplasia: A change in type of cells in a tissue to another type of cells that are not normal for that tissue.

Microcirculation: The blood flow throughout the system of small blood vessels in the body.

Microsomal enzymes: Detoxifying enzymes associated with microsomes.

Microsomes: Fragments of the endoplasmic reticulum, an intracellular organelle that functions to transport materials through cells.

Mitochondria: Cell components that generate energy.

Moderate drinker: A person who drinks 0.22 to 1.00 fl. oz. alcohol per day (i.e., 4 to 14 drinks per week).

Monocyte: A phagocyte that originates in the bone marrow and circulates in the bloodstream. Monocytes also enter the tissues, where they mature into macrophages.

Morbidity: An actuarial determination of the incidence and severity of sicknesses and accidents in a well-defined class or classes of persons.

Mortality: An actuarial determination of the death rate at each age as determined from prior experience.

Motility: Spontaneous and involuntary movement (e.g., of muscles involved in the gastrointestinal tract).

Motivational state: A psychological state that initiates or modifies a certain behavior (e.g., seeking and consuming alcohol or other drugs).

Mucosa: A thin tissue layer that lines cavities or canals of the body that open to the outside (e.g., regions of the gastrointestinal tract or the nose). The mucosa secretes mucus and absorbs water, salts, and other substances.

Mucosal barrier: The ability of the epithelium to prevent the transfer of substances from the gastric or intestinal cavity into the mucosa.

Myelin: A cell coating that facilities conduction of nerve impulses along the nerve fiber.

N

Natural killer (NK) cell: A type of white blood cell that kills tumor cells and virus-infected cells.

Necrosis: Death of one or more cells or of a portion of tissue or organ resulting from irreversible damage.

Nephron: The functional unit of the kidney, each consisting of a glomerulus surrounded by a capsule that connects to a long, looping tubule system.

Neuroadaptation: Changes in the function of certain brain cells that occur in response to long-term changes in the body's internal and external environment (e.g., prolonged presence of alcohol in the brain).

Neuromodulator: A substance that modifies the function or effects of a neurotransmitter.

Neuron: A nerve cell.

Neuropharmacologic effects: Effects of drugs on the nervous system.

Neurotoxic: Toxic to nerve cells.

Neurotransmitter: A chemical messenger released by a neuron to carry a signal to (e.g., excite or inhibit) adjacent neurons; causes a reaction in nerve, muscle, or gland cells.

Neurotrophin: A factor that promotes the survival, growth, and differentiation of certain nerve cells.

Neutropenia: A blood condition in which the number of neutrophils is lower than normal.

Neutrophil: A type of white blood cell that performs phagocytic and degradative functions similar to those of macrophages.

NMDA: N-methyl-D-aspartate, a synthetic amino acid capable of activating certain glutamate receptors.

Nucleotide: The building block of DNA or RNA. Specific strings of DNA nucleotides make up genes.

Nucleus accumbens: A brain structure affected by many drugs of abuse and implicated in the rewarding properties of addictive drugs.

O

Opioid: A substance in the body that acts in the brain to decrease the sensation of pain.

Organelle: Membrane-surrounded structures found within cells that contain enzymes and other components for performing specialized cell functions.

Osmosis: The movement of water across a membrane from the more dilute side to the more concentrated side.

Oxidation: A type of chemical reaction involving the loss of electrons. See also peroxidation.

Oxidative stress: An imbalance between increased production of free radicals and decreased availability of antioxidants.

P

Pallidum: Also called globus pallidus; one of the basal ganglia. A brain structure at the base of the cerebral hemispheres involved in motor control.

Pancreatitis: Inflammation of the pancreas.

Pancytopenia: A blood condition in which the numbers of red blood cells, white blood cells, and platelets are lower than normal.

Paradigm: A set of related theories or models.

Parenchyma: A general term designating the functional elements of an organ.

Parietal lobe: The region of the cerebral cortex that mainly receives somatosensory information (i.e., not from the sensory organs but from receptors in or near the body surface.)

Parotid glands: The largest salivary glands, which lie just below and in front of the ears.

Permeability: The degree to which a membrane allows various molecules to pass through it.

Peroxidation: Enzymatic oxidation of organic substrates, such as lipids, in the presence of hydrogen peroxide.

Phagocyte: A white blood cell capable of ingesting (i.e., phagocytosing) foreign particles and microorganisms. Phagocytes include monocytes, macrophages, and neutrophils.

Phenotype: The observable characteristics of an organism; the product of genetic makeup.

Phosphorylation: A chemical reaction resulting in the formation of a phosphate derivative of a molecule; these reactions are often critical to the regulation of receptor activity and the functions of other proteins.

PKC: Protein kinase C; an enzyme critical for many intracellular functions.

Plasma: The watery portion of the blood, in which the blood cells are suspended; the plasma contains minerals, nutrients, regulatory substances, gases, and proteins.

Plasma cell: A B cell that has been activated by antigen to produce and secrete large amounts of antibodies.

Plasmin: An enzyme that digests the protein fibrin in the dissolution of blood clots; normally present in the blood in the form of its inactive precursor, plasminogen.

Plasminogen activators: A protein that activates the precursor plasminogen to its active form, plasmin, to initiate the dissolution of a blood clot.

Platelets: Disk-shaped components of blood that aggregate to stop bleeding during the clotting process.

Polymorphism: For a specific gene, the presence of two or more gene variants (i.e., alleles) in a population.

Polymorphism: The occurrence of two or more different forms of the same genetic trait in a population.

Pons: A broad mass of nerve fibers that forms the central portion of the brain stem. The pons participates in control of respiration and coordination of muscular activity.

Portal systemic encephalopathy (PSE): The most common form of hepatic encephalopathy. This cerebral complication of liver cirrhosis disrupts consciousness regulation of emotions, and mental efficiency and can lead to hepatic coma.

Positively reinforcing effects: The effects of a drug (e.g., alcohol) that increases the probability that a person will attempt to consume more of that drug.

Posterior: Toward the back of the body.

Practice guidelines: Systematically developed statements on healthcare practice that assist providers and consumers in making decisions about appropriate healthcare for specific situations or conditions. Managed care organizations frequently use these guidelines to evaluate appropriateness and medical necessity of care.

Prefrontal cortex: The most anterior sections of the frontal lobes; involved in memory processes, specifically in delayed response tasks.

Preventive care: Comprehensive care emphasizing priorities for prevention, early detection and early treatment of conditions, generally including risk assessment appraisals, routine physical examination, immunizations, and well-baby care.

Primary care: Basic or general healthcare, traditionally provided by family practice, pediatrics, and internal medicine.

Primary Care Provider (PCP): A term used to denote a family practitioner, general internist, pediatrician, and sometimes an ob/gyn. Generally, under managed care, a PCP supervises, coordinates, and provides initial ambulatory medical care, acting as a "gatekeeper" for the initiation of all referrals for nonurgent specialty care.

Primary prevention: Strategies designed to decrease the number of new cases of a disorder or illness (incidence).

Prostaglandins: A class of biologically active compounds that affect many physiologic activities, including blood pressure, muscle contraction, and body temperature.

Protein: The product of the genetic information encoded in a gene. Proteins are made up of chains of amino acids, whose order and synthesis are dictated by the gene's nucleotide sequence. Enzymes are one type of protein.

Proteinase: One of a group of enzymes that break down proteins.

Psychomotor functions: Motor functions as a consequence of mental activity.

Purkinje cells: Neurons in the cerebellum that send sensory and movement-related messages to various parts of the body.

R

Receptor: A protein in the wall or interior of a neuron or other cell that recognizes and binds to neurotransmitters or other chemical messengers.

Retrograde amnesia: The inability to remember events that occurred before the trauma or disorder causing the amnesia.

RNA: The abbreviation for ribonucleic acid, a DNA-like molecule that plays a role in using genetic information (i.e., DNA) to produce proteins.

S

Sarcoplasmic reticulum: A system of interconnected tubules within heart muscle cells with functions related to the transmission of nervous excitation to the contractile parts of the heart muscle.

Secondary prevention: Strategies designed to lower the rate of established cases of a disorder or illness in the population (prevalence).

Selective prevention strategy: A strategy designed for individuals who are members of population subgroups whose risk of the development of an imminent or lifetime disease or disability is significantly above average.

Sensorimotor functions: Functions involving perception of information from the senses and physical reactions of muscles (e.g., a reaction to touching a hot surface).

Septal area: A region stretching as a thin sheet within the cerebral hemisphere that has functional connections with the hypothalamus and the hippocampus.

Serotonin: A neurotransmitter that affects mood, consummatory behavior, and the development of tolerance to alcohol; important in cycles of waking and sleeping.

Solute: The substance dissolved in solution (e.g., salt is the solute in the solution known as salt water).

Stellate cell: A star-shaped fibroblastic cell derived from an Ito cell, a fat-storing cell in the liver. Stellate cells have lost the high levels of vitamin A associated with Ito cells and have gained an ability to contract in response to endothelin, a vasoconstrictor.

Striatum: See corpus striatum.

Stroke: Any condition during which the blood supply to the brain or regions of the brain is suddenly interrupted.

Substance abuse: There are many definitions of substance abuse. The American Psychiatric Association's *Diagnostic and Statistical Manual of Mental Disorders, 4th ed. (DSM-IV)* defines substance abuse as the maladaptive pattern of substance use leading to clinically significant impairment or distress, as manifested by one or more of the following occurring within a 12 month period:

- recurrent substance use resulting in a failure to fulfill major role obligations;
- recurrent substance use in situations in which it is physically hazardous;
- recurrent substance-related legal problems; and
- continued substance use despite having persistent or recurrent social or interpersonal problems caused by or exacerbated by the effects of the substance.

Substrate: The specific compound acted upon by an enzyme.

Sulci: The grooves or furrows on the surface of the brain.

Superoxide anion: A free radical that is an oxygen atom with an extra electron.

Sympathetic nervous system: The division of the nervous system that coordinates the body's response to stress.

Synapse: A microscopic gap separating adjacent neurons; where neurotransmitters and receptors cluster.

Synergistic: Describing the property of one agent to enhance the effect of another agent.

T

T lymphocyte (T cell): A type of white blood cell that originates in the bone marrow and matures in the thymus. T cells are activated by contact with antigen to mount a cell-mediated immune response and secrete important cytokines.

Temporal lobe: The region of the cerebral cortex forming part of the sides and bottom of the brain on each side. This region is involved in sensory processing, language functions, and emotions.

Tertiary prevention: Strategies designed to decrease the amount of disability associated with an existing disorder or illness.

Thalamus: A mass of gray matter that forms the lateral walls of the diencephalon and which is involved in the transmission and integration of certain sensations.

Thiamine: Vitamin B_1; essential for growth and for the health of the cardiovascular and nervous systems; required for normal brain functioning.

Thrombocytopenia: A blood condition in which the number of platelets is below normal.

Thromboxane A_2: A compound that strongly stimulates platelet aggregation and activation in the process of blood clot formation.

Thrombus: A clot of blood within the heart or blood vessels. If a detached thrombus is carried in the blood and lodges at a later point, it is called an embolus.

Thymus: A lymphoid organ, located near the base of the neck, where T cells mature.

Tolerance: The need of a chronic drinker to consumer increasing amounts of alcohol over time in order to achieve the same effect (e.g., euphoria) that the drinker initially experienced from smaller quantities.

Transcription: The enzymatic process of protein synthesis whereby genetic information encoded in one strand of DNA is used to specify a complementary sequence of nucleic acids in a messenger RNA (mRNA) chain.

Triglyceride: A lipid or neutral fat that serves as a metabolic energy source.

Tumor necrosis factor (TNF): A cytokine produced by macrophages that has anticancer effects.

U

Universal prevention: Prevention designed for everyone in the eligible population, both the general public and for all members of specific eligible groups.

Up-regulation: An increase in the number or sensitivity of receptors as a regulatory mechanism to compensate for decreased activation of the receptors.

V

VACC: Voltage-activated calcium channel; VACCs regulate neuronal excitability.

Vasoconstrictor: A substance that causes constriction of blood vessels.

Ventral tegmental area: The midbrain region containing dopamine cell bodies that project to the nucleus accumbens.

Ventricle: A normal cavity-for example, in the brain or heart.

Ventricular fibrillation: Rapid and uncoordinated contraction of the lower chambers of the heart, most often resulting from restriction or interruption of the heart muscle's blood supply. The heart then ceases to pump blood.

Very low density lipoprotein (VLDL): A type of molecule formed primarily in the liver to transport cholesterol and triglycerides in the blood to body tissues.

Visuospatial abilities: Functions such as reading maps, solving jigsaw puzzles, or performing motor skills that involve spatial perception.

W

Wernicke-Korsakoff syndrome (WKS): A neurological disorder thought to be caused by thiamine deficiency. WKS is characterized by cognitive impairments in memory (e.g., anterograde amnesia) as well as deficits in abstraction and problem-solving. Wernicke's encephalopathy is an acute condition characterized by general confusion and incoherent speech. It may or may not precede Korsakoff syndrome, the chronic condition characterized by anterograde amnesia.

White blood cell: Immune cells that make up the first line of defense against infection and toxic agents; also called leukocytes.

Withdrawal: The physiological (e.g., tremors) and psychological (e.g., anxiety) effects that occur if a chronic drinker suddenly abstains from alcohol use.

Chapter 70

Resources for Recovery and Support

Al-Alon Family Group Headquarters, Inc.
1600 Corporate Landing Parkway
Virginia Beach, VA 23454-5617
Phone: (757) 563-1600
Toll Free: (888) 4AL-ANON (for meeting information, M-F, 8a-6p ET; except holidays)
Fax: (757) 563-1655
Web site: www.al-anon-alateen.org
E-mail: wso@al-anon.org

Alcoholics Anonymous
P.O. Box 459
Grand Central Station
New York, NY 10163
Phone (212) 870–3400
Web site: www.alcoholics-anonymous.org

Family Empowerment Network
(Support Group for Fetal Alcohol Syndrome)
313 Lowell Hall
610 Langdon St.
Madison, WI 53703-1195

Information in this chapter was compiled from many sources. All contact information was verfied and updated in March 2000. Inclusion does not constitute endorsement.

Family Empowerment Network (continued)
Toll-Free: (800) 462-5254
E-mail: fen@mail.dcs.wisc.edu
Web site: http://www.dcs.wisc.edu/pda/hhi/family.htm

Moderation Management
P.O Box 1752
Woodinville, WA 98072
Phone: (732) 295-0949
Toll Free: (888) 561-9843
Web site: http://moderation.org
E-mail: moderation@moderation.org

Rational Recovery Systems, Inc.
Box 800
Lotus, CA 95651
Phone: (530) 621-4374 or (530) 621-2667
Fax: (530) 622-4296
Web site: www.rational.org/recovery
E-mail: mailto:icc@rational.org

Recovery, Inc.
802 North Dearborn St.
Chicago, IL 60610
Phone: (312) 337-5661

Smart Recovery (Self Management and Recovery Training)
7537 Mentor Avenue, Suite #306
Mentor, Ohio 44060
Phone: (440) 951-5357
Fax: (440) 951-5358
Web site: www.smartrecovery.org
E-mail: SRMail1@aol.com

Secular Organizations for Sobriety/Save Our Selves (SOS)
LifeRing Secular Recovery
1440 Broadway, Suite 1000
Oakland, CA 94612-2029
Phone: (510) 763-0779
Fax: (510) 763-1513
Web site: www.unhooked.com
E-mail: service@lifering.com

Women for Sobriety
P.O. Box 618
Quakertown, PA 18951-0618
Toll Free: (800) 333-1606
Phone: (215) 536-8026
E-mail: newlife@nni.com
Web site: http://www.womenforsobriety.org/body.html

Chapter 71

A Directory of Information Resources

Association for Medical Education and Research in Substance Abuse (AMERSA)
125 Whipple Street
Third Floor
Suite 300
Providence, RI 02908
Phone: (401) 785-8263
Fax: (401) 418-8774
E-Mail: doreen@amersa.org
Web site: www.amersa.org

American Society of Addiction Medicine
4601 North Park Avenue
Arcade Suite 101
Chevy Chase, MD 20815
Phone: (301) 656-3920
Fax: (301) 656-3815
E-Mail: Email@asam.org
Web site: http://www.asam.org

Information in this chapter was compiled from many sources. All contact information was verified and updated in March 2000. Inclusion does not constitute endorsement.

Center for Alcohol Studies, Rutgers
607 Allison Road
Piscataway, NJ 08854-8001
Phone: (732) 445-2190
Fax: (732) 445-3500
E-mail: chrouse@rci.rutgers.edu
Web site: http://www.rci.rutgers.edu/~cas2/

Center for Substance Abuse Prevention (CSAP)
5600 Fishers Lane, Rockwall II
Rockville, MD 20857
Phone: (301) 443-0365
E-Mail: nnadal@samhsa.gov
Web site: www.samhsa.gov/csap/index.htm

Connecticut Clearinghouse
334 Farmington Avenue
Plainville, CT 06062
Toll Free: (800) 232-4424
Fax: (860) 793-9813
E-Mail: info@ctclearinhouse.org
Web site: www.ctclearinghouse.org

The Core Institute
Center for Alcohol and Other Drug Studies
Southern Illinois University at Carbondale
Carbondale, IL 62901
Phone: (618) 453-4366
E-Mail: coreinst@siu.edu
Web site: www.siu.edu/~coreinst

FACE—Truth and Clarity on Alcohol
105 West Fourth Street
Clare, MI 48617
Toll Free: (888) 822-3223
Fax: (517) 386-3532
E-Mail: face@glccomputers.com
Web site: http://wwww.faceproject.org

Family Caregiver Alliance
690 Market Street, Suite 600
San Francisco, CA 94104
Phone: (415) 434-3388
Toll Free: (800) 445-8106 (in CA)
Fax: (415) 434-3508
E-Mail: info@caregiver.org
Web site: http://www.caregiver.org

The FAS Family Resource Institute
P.O. Box 2525
Lynwood, WA 98036
Phone: (253) 531-2878
Toll Free in Washington: (800) 999-3429
E-mail: delindam@accessone.com
Website: http://www.accessone.com/~delindam/index.html

Hazelden Foundation
P.O. Box 11
Center City, MN 55012-0011
Toll Free (800) 257-7800; or 1-651-257-4010 outside the U.S.
E-mail: info@hazelden.org
Web site: http://www.hazelden.org

The Higher Education Center for Alcohol and Other Drug Prevention
Education Development Center, Inc.
55 Chapel Street
Newton, MA 02158-1060
Toll Free: (800) 676-1730
Fax: (617) 928-1537
E-Mail: HigherEdCtr@edc.org
Web site: http://www.edc.org/hec/

Mothers Against Drunk Driving (MADD)
PO Box 541688
Dallas, TX 75354-1688
Toll Free: (800) GET-MADD (800-438-6233)
Web site: http:// www.madd.org

National Association of Alcoholism and Drug Abuse Counselors (NAADAC)
1911 North Fort Myer Drive, Suite 900
Arlington, VA 22209
Toll Free: (800) 548-0497
Phone: (703) 741-7686
Fax: (800) 377-1136 or (703) 741-7698
E-Mail: naadac@naadac.org
Web site: http://www.naadac.org

The National Association of State Alcohol and Drug Abuse Directors (NASADAD)
808 17th Street NW., Suite 410
Washington, DC 20006
Phone: (202) 293-0090
Fax: (202) 293-1250
E-Mail: dcoffice@nasadad.org
Web site: http://www.nasadad.org

National Clearinghouse for Alcohol and Drug Information (NCADI)
P.O. Box 2345
Rockville, MD 20847-2345
Toll Free: (800) 729-6686
Toll Free: (800) 487-4889 (TDD)
Fax: (301) 468-6433
Web site: http://www.health.org

National Commission Against Drunk Driving
1900 L Street NW., Suite 705
Washington, DC 20006
Phone: (202) 452-6004
Fax: (202) 223-7012
E-Mail: KWilli2636@aol.com
Web site: http://www.ncadd.com

National Council on Alcoholism and Drug Dependence, Inc.
12 West 21 Street, Seventh Floor
New York, New York 10010
Toll Free: (800) NCA-CALL (800-622-2255) (24-hour affiliate referral)

Phone: (212) 206-6770
Fax: (212) 645-1690
E-mail: national@ncadd.org
Web site: http://www.ncadd.org

National Group Rides and Designated Drivers (GRADD)
P.O. Box 2116
Goldenrod, FL 32733-2116
Phone: (407) 671-2409
Fax: (407) 671-2476
E-Mail: info@saferide.org
Web site: http://www.saferide.org

National Highway Traffic Safety Administration (NHTSA)
U.S. Department of Transportation
Impaired Driving Program, NTS-11
400 Seventh Street SW.
Washington, DC 20590
Phone: (202) 366-9581
Fax: (202) 366-2766
Web site: http://www.nhtsa.dot.gov

National Institute on Alcohol Abuse and Alcoholism (NIAAA)
National Institutes of Health
Willco Building
6000 Executive Boulevard
Bethesda, MD 20892-7003
Phone: (301) 443-0786
Web site: http://www.niaaa.nih.gov

National Organization on Fetal Alcohol Syndrome
418 'C' Street North East
Washington, DC 20002
Phone: (202)785-4585
Fax: (202) 466-6456
E-mail: nofas@erols.com
Web site: http://www.nofas.org

Prevention Online (PREVLINE)
E-Mail: webmaster@health.org
Web site: http://www.health.org

Promising Practices: Campus Alcohol Strategies
550 South Hope Street, Suite 1950
Los Angeles, CA 90071
Phone: (703) 993-3697
E-mail: caph@gmu.edu
Web site: http://www.promprac.gmu.edu

Remove Intoxicated Drivers (RID)
P.O. Box 520
Schenectady, NY 12301
Phone: (518) 372-0034
Fax: (518) 370-4917
E-mail: mlutz@voyager.net
Web site: http://www.crisny.org/not-for-profit/ridusa

Research Institute on Addictions (RIA)
1021 Main Street
Buffalo, NY 14203
Phone: (716) 887-2566
Fax: (716) 887-2252
Web site: http://www.RIA.org

Students Against Drugs and Alcohol (SADA)
7443 East 68th Street
Tulsa, OK 74133
Phone: (918) 249-1315
Fax: (918) 249-1315
E-Mail: sada@sada.org
Web site: http://www.sada.org

Web of Addictions
Web site: http://www.well.com/user/woa

Chapter 72

Federal Resources for Information on Underage Drinking

The use of alcohol by minors has terrible consequences. When juveniles drink, they are indulging in behavior that is both illegal and dangerous. Alcohol has been shown to play a part in teen assaults, rapes, murders, thefts, and suicides, and it is a major factor in automobile crashes and fatalities involving teens. Recognizing the magnitude of the problem of underage drinking, Congress appropriated $25 million in fiscal year (FY) 1998 to establish the Combating Underage Drinking Program and another $25 million in FY 1999 to continue it, under the title of the Enforcing the Underage Drinking Laws Program. The Office of Juvenile Justice and Delinquency Prevention administers the program and assists States and other jurisdictions in their efforts to keep youth from drinking alcoholic beverages and to see that they avoid the lethal mixture of drinking and driving. Prevention of underage drinking and its attendant ills would have innumerable and long-lasting benefits for every American.

Center for Substance Abuse Prevention (CSAP)
5600 Fishers Lane, Rockwall II
Rockville, MD 20857
Phone: (301) 443-0365
E-Mail: nnadal@samhsa.gov
Web site: www.samhsa.gov/csap/index.htm

Excerpted from *Enforcing the Underage Drinking Laws Program: A Compendium of Resources*, U.S. Department of Justice, Office of Juvenile Justice and Delinquency Prevention, May 1999.

CSAP provides national leadership in the Federal effort to prevent alcohol, tobacco, and illicit drug problems, which are linked to other serious national problems. CSAP connects people and resources to innovative ideas and strategies and encourages efforts to reduce and eliminate alcohol, tobacco, and illicit drug problems in the United States and abroad. CSAP is sponsoring a teleconference initiative with a series of broadcasts in substance abuse prevention, including helping youth stay drug free. These programs include The Girl Power! campaign (www.health.org/promos/youth.htm). CSAP supports the National Clearinghouse for Alcohol and Drug Information (NCADI) as a resource to share activities from CSAP and other agencies and organizations on substance abuse education and prevention.

Centers for Disease Control and Prevention (CDC)
Division of Adolescent and School Health (DASH)
1600 Clifton Road NE
Atlanta, GA 30333
Phone: (404) 639-3311
E-Mail: netinfo@cdc.gov
Web site: www.cdc.gov

CDC established DASH in its National Center for Chronic Disease Prevention and Health Promotion in 1988. DASH pursues four strategies: identifying and monitoring highest priority risks, synthesizing and applying research, implementing national programs to prevent these risks, and evaluating and improving those programs. One of the highest priority risk behaviors is underage drinking.

Drug Enforcement Administration (DEA)
U.S. Department of Justice
Information Services Section (CPI)
700 Army-Navy Drive
Arlington, VA 22202
Web site: www.usdoj.gov/dea

The mission of the Drug Enforcement Administration is to enforce the controlled substances laws and regulations of the United States; to bring to the criminal and civil justice system of the United States or any other competent jurisdiction those organizations and principal members of organizations involved in the growing, manufacture, or distribution of controlled substances appearing in or destined for illicit traffic in the United States; and to recommend and support nonenforcement programs aimed at reducing the availability of illicit controlled substances on the domestic and international markets.

Juvenile Justice Clearinghouse (JJC)
P.O. Box 6000
Rockville, MD 20849-6000
Toll Free: (800) 638-8736
Fax: (301) 519-5212
E-Mail: askncjrs@ncjrs.org
Web site: www.ojjdp.ncjrs.org

The component of the National Criminal Justice Reference Service sponsored by OJJDP, JJC offers easy access to information on all topics of delinquency prevention and juvenile justice, including underage drinking. Currently available is the video *Beyond the Bench,* which encourages and instructs judges in becoming involved in community-wide efforts to address juvenile drug-impaired driving. The Clearinghouse is also the source for information, application kits, and other resources related to OJJDP funding opportunities, including the Underage Drinking Laws program.

National Clearinghouse for Alcohol and Drug Information (NCADI)
P.O. Box 2345
Rockville, MD 20847-2345
Toll Free: (800) 729-6686
Toll Free: (800) 487-4889 (TDD)
Fax: (301) 468-6433
E-Mail: info@health.org
Web site: www.health.org

Supported by CSAP, NCADI is the world's largest resource for current information and materials concerning substance abuse. Resources on underage drinking include videotapes, brochures, publications, articles such as "The Effects of Alcohol Abuse in the Health of Adolescents" and "Adolescent Alcohol Decisions," and customized searches in the form of annotated bibliographies on underage drinking. Other publications include *Guidelines and Benchmarks for Prevention Programming* and *The Young and Restless: Generation X and Alcohol Policy.*

National Highway Traffic Safety Administration (NHTSA)

U.S. Department of Transportation
Impaired Driving Program, NTS-11
400 Seventh Street SW
Washington, DC 20590
Phone: (202) 366-9588
Fax: (202) 366-2766
Web site: www.nhtsa.dot.gov

NHTSA's mission is to save lives, prevent injuries, and reduce traffic-related health care and other economic costs. The goal of NHTSA's Impaired Driving Program is to reduce alcohol-related fatalities to 11,000 by the year 2005. Technical assistance targeting underage drinking and driving includes Youth Assessments, the Cross-Age Peer Mentoring Program, and many other youth-targeted programs. Another project, Strides for Safety, is conducted state by state to provide visibility and support for student efforts to promote youth safety. National Organizations for Youth Safety (NOYS) State affiliates plan and implement a march or rally by students in April of each year in support of youth safety issues deemed important to that State. In 1997, more than 20 States participated in NOYS. In Connecticut, for example, a student rally was instrumental in convincing the Governor to sign a zero-tolerance law. A March 1998 brochure, *Youth Motor Vehicle Fatalities 1992–1996,* which is available from NHTSA, highlights statistics, including trends, on impaired-driving fatal crashes from 1982 to 1996 involving young people ages 15 through 20.

National Institute on Alcohol Abuse and Alcoholism (NIAAA)

National Institutes of Health
Willco Building
6000 Executive Boulevard
Bethesda, MD 20892-7003
Phone: (301) 443-0786
Web site: www.niaaa.nih.gov

NIAAA supports and conducts biomedical and behavioral research on the causes, consequences, treatment, and prevention of alcoholism and alcohol-related problems. NIAAA also provides leadership in the national effort to reduce the severe and often fatal consequences of these problems. Available publications include *Alcohol Alert* (No. 29

focuses on college students and drinking and No. 37 deals specifically with teenage drinking) and a variety of brochures, special reports, and research papers. A previous issue of *Alcohol Health & Research World,* Volume 20, November 3, 1996, was devoted to drinking throughout one's lifespan and included an article titled "Drinking During Adolescence." NIAAA also analyzed the relationship between the age of drinking onset and the prevalence of lifetime alcohol abuse and dependence. Volume 22, Number 2, Spring 1998 was devoted to topics concerning alcohol and youth.

National Institute on Drug Abuse (NIDA)

National Institutes of Health
6001 Executive Boulevard
MSC 9561
Rockville, MD 20892
Phone: (301) 443-1124
Toll Free: (888) 644-6432
Toll Free: (888) 889-6432 (TTY)
E-Mail: Information@lists.nida.nih.gov
Web site: www.nida.nih.gov

NIDA brings the full power of science to bear on drug abuse and addiction. To do this, NIDA supports and conducts research across a range of disciplines and ensures rapid and effective dissemination and use of research results to improve prevention, treatment, and policy. NIDA prevention programs include the Adolescent Alcohol Prevention Trial and the Reconnecting Youth Program.

Office of Juvenile Justice and Delinquency Prevention (OJJDP)

Office of Justice Programs
U.S. Department of Justice
810 Seventh Street NW
Washington, DC 20531
Phone: (202) 307-5911
Fax: (202) 307-2093
E-Mail: askjj@ojp.usdoj.gov
Web site: www.ojjdp.ncjrs.org

OJJDP provides Federal leadership on juvenile justice and delinquency prevention efforts, which include alcohol and other substance use and abuse. In response to a congressional mandate, OJJDP is administering the Underage Drinking Laws program, which includes State grant and discretionary funds and training and technical assistance. These efforts are in addition to other OJJDP-related initiatives, which include teen courts, many of which handle alcohol-related offenses, and the Enforcing the Underage Drinking Laws Program.

Office of National Drug Control Policy (ONDCP)
Executive Office of the President
Washington, DC 20503
Phone: (202) 395-6618
Fax: (202) 395-6730
E-mail: ondcp@ncjrs.org
Web site: www.whitehousedrugpolicy.gov

The principal purpose of ONDCP is to establish policies, priorities, and objectives for the Nation's drug control program, the goals of which are to reduce illicit drug use, manufacturing, and trafficking; drug-related crime and violence; and drug-related health consequences, including drug, alcohol, and tobacco use among youth.

Office of National Drug Control Policy (ONDCP)
Drug Policy Information Clearinghouse
P.O. Box 6000
Rockville, MD 20849-6000
Toll Free: (800) 666-3332
Fax: (301) 519-5212
E-Mail: ondcp@ncjrs.org
Web site: www.whitehousedrugpolicy.gov

The ONDCP Drug Policy Information Clearinghouse is a single source of statistics, data, research, and referrals useful for developing or implementing drug policy. The Clearinghouse distributes ONDCP publications, including the *National Drug Control Strategy,* the first goal of which is to educate and enable America's youth to reject illegal drugs and alcohol and tobacco. The Clearinghouse also produces and distributes fact sheets, including *Alcohol and Crime*.

Safe and Drug-Free Schools Program
U.S. Department of Education
600 Independence Avenue SW
Portals Building, Room 604
Washington, DC 20202-6123

Phone: (202) 260-3954
Fax: (202) 260-7767
Toll Free: (800) 624-0100 (Publications)
E-Mail: safeschl@ed.gov
Web site: www.ed.gov/offices/OESE/SDFS/

The Safe and Drug-Free Schools Program is the Federal Government's primary vehicle for reducing drug, alcohol, and tobacco use and violence, through education and prevention activities in our Nation's schools. Initiatives include funding opportunities through State grants and national programs, collaborations with other Federal agencies, and publications and videotapes such as *Creating Safe and Drug Free Schools: An Action Guide* and *Teaching Children Affected by Substance Abuse*.

Chapter 73

State Substance Abuse Agencies

Alabama
Department of Mental Health/Retardation
Substance Abuse Division
P.O. Box 301410
Montgomery, AL 36130-1410
Phone: (334) 242-3961
Fax: (334) 242-3759

Alaska
Department of Health and Social Services
Division of Alcoholism and Drug Abuse
P.O. Box 110607
Juneau, AK 99811-0607
Toll Free: (800) 478-2072
Phone: (907) 465-2071
Fax: (907) 465-2185
Web site: http://health.hss.state.ak.us/

Arizona
Department of Health Services
Bureau of Substance Abuse and Mental Health
2122 East Highland Street
Phoenix, AZ 85016

Excerpted from *Enforcing the Underage Drinking Laws Program: A Compendium of Resources*, U.S. Department of Justice, Office of Juvenile Justice and Delinquency Prevention, May 1999.

Arizona (continued)
Phone: (602) 381-8999
Fax: (602) 553-9142
E-mail: alelatr@hs.state.az.us
Web site: http://www.hs.state.az.us/

Arkansas
Department of Health
Bureau of Alcohol and Drug Abuse Prevention
Freeway Medical Center
5800 West 10th Street, Suite 907
Little Rock, AR 72204
Phone: (501) 280-4511
Fax: (501) 280-4532
Web site: http://health.state.ar.us/

California
Department of Drug and Alcohol Abuse
1700 K Street
Sacramento, CA 95814
Phone: (916) 445-1943
Fax: (916) 323-5873
E-mail: sjantz@adp.cahwnet.gov
Web site: http://www.adp.cahwnet.gov

Colorado
Department of Human Services
Alcohol and Drug Abuse Division
4055 S. Lowell Blvd.
Denver, CO 80236
Phone: (303) 866-7480
Fax: (303) 866-7481
Web site: http://www.cdhs.state.co.us/ohr/adad/index.html

Connecticut
Division of Community Based Regulations
P.O. Box 340308
410 Capitol Avenue
Hartford, CT 06134-0308
Phone: (860) 509-8045
Fax: (860) 509-7541
Web site: http://www.state.ct.us

Delaware

Division of Alcoholism, Drug Abuse, and Mental Health
Department of Health and Social Services
1901 North DuPont Highway
New Castle, DE 19720
Phone: (302) 577-4461
Fax: (302) 577-4486
Web site: http://www.state.de.us/dhss

District of Columbia

Department of Human Services
Addiction Prevention and Recovery Administration
1300 First Street NE.
Washington, DC 20002
Phone: (202) 727-0715
Fax: (202) 535-2028
Web site: http://www.dchealth.com

Florida

Department of Children and Families
Alcohol, Drug Abuse and Mental Health Program Office
1317 Winewood Boulevard, Building 3
Tallahassee, FL 32399-0700
Phone: (850) 487-2920
Fax: (850) 487-2239
Web site: http://www.state.fl.us/cf_web/

Georgia

Substance Abuse Services
Division of Mental Health, Mental Retardation and Substance Abuse
2 Peachtree Street NW.
Atlanta, GA 30303
Phone: (404) 657-6419
Fax: (404) 657-2160
E-mail: blhoopes@dhr.state.ga.us
Web site: http://www2.state.ga.us/Departments/DHR/mhmrsa.html

Hawaii

Department of Health
Alcohol and Drug Abuse Division
601 Kamokila Blvd.
Kapolei, HI 96707

Hawaii (continued)
Phone: (808) 692-7506
Web site: http://www.hawaii.gov/doh/

Idaho
Department of Health and Welfare
Division of Family and Community Services
P.O. Box 83720
Boise, ID 83720-0036
Phone: (208) 334-5700
Fax: (208) 334-6699
Web site: http;//www2.state.id.us/dhw

Illinois
Department of Alcoholism and Substance Abuse
James R. Thompson Center
100 West Randolph, Room 5-600
Chicago, IL 60601
Phone: (312) 814-3840
Fax: (312) 814-2419

Indiana
Bureau of Chemical Addictions
Division of Mental Health
Family and Social Services Administration
402 West Washington Street, Room W353
Indianapolis, IN 46204-2739
Phone: (317) 232-7800
Fax: (317) 233-3472
Web site: http://www.state.in.us

Iowa
Division of Substance Abuse and Health Promotion
Lucas State Office Building, Third Floor
321 East 12th Street
Des Moines, IA 50319
Phone: (515) 281-4404
Fax: (515) 281-4535
Web site: http://idph.state.ia.us/sa.htm

Kansas

Department of Social and Rehabilitative Services
Alcohol and Drug Abuse Services
Biddle Building
300 Southwest Oakley
Topeka, KS 66606
Phone: (913) 296-3925
Fax: (913) 296-0494
Web site: http://www.state.ks.us/public/srs/

Kentucky

Department of Mental Health/Mental Retardation Services
Division of Substance Abuse
100 Fair Oaks Lane, 4th Floor
Frankfort, KY 40621
Phone: (502) 564-3487
Fax: (502) 564-6533
Web site: http://dmhmrs.chr.state.ky.us/

Louisiana

Department of Health and Hospitals
Office for Addictive Disorders
P.O. Box 2790-BIN #18
Baton Rouge, LA 70821
Phone: (225) 342-6717
Fax: (225) 342-3875
Web site: http://www.dhh.state.la.us/

Maine

Office of Substance Abuse
AMHI Complex
Marquardt Building, #159
State House Station
Augusta, ME 04333-0159
Phone: (207) 287-2595
TTY: (207) 287-4475
Fax: (207) 287-4334
Web site: http://www.state.me.us/dmhmrsa/osa/

Maryland
Governor's Crime Control and Prevention Commission
300 East Joppa Road, Suite 1105
Baltimore, MD 21286-3106
Phone: (410) 321-3521
Fax: (410) 321-3116
E-mail: info@goccp-state-md.org
Web site: http://www.cesar.umd.edu/goccp/goccp.htm

Massachusetts
Department of Public Health
Bureau of Substance Abuse Services
250 Washington Street
Boston, MA 02108
Phone: (617) 624-5111
TTY: (617) 536-5872
Fax: (617) 624-5185
Web site: http://www.state.ma.us/dph/

Michigan
Department of Community Health
Center for Substance Abuse Services
3423 North Martin Luther King Boulevard
P.O. Box 30195
Lansing, MI 48909
Phone: (517) 335-8810
Fax: (517) 335-8837
Web site: http://www.mdmh.state.mi.us/

Minnesota
Department of Human Services
Chemical Dependency Program Division
444 Lafayette Road
St. Paul, MN 55155-3823
Phone: (651) 296-3933
Fax: (612) 297-1862
Web site: http://www.dhs.state.mn.us/

Mississippi
Department of Mental Health
Division of Alcohol and Drug Abuse
1101 Robert E. Lee Building
Jackson, MS 39201

Phone: (601) 359-1288
Fax: (601) 359-6295
Web site: http://www.dmh.state.ms.us/

Missouri

Department of Mental Health
Division of Alcohol and Drug Abuse
1706 East Elm Street
P.O. Box 687
Jefferson City, MO 65102
Phone: (573) 751-4942
Fax: (573) 751-7814
E-mail: mailto:dmhmail@maildmh.state.mo.us
Web site: http://www.modmh.state.mo.us/

Montana

Addictive and Mental Disorders Division
P.O. Box 202951
1400 Broadway
Helena, MT 59620-2951
Phone: (406) 444-3964
Fax: (406) 444-4435
E-mail: rmena@mt.gov
Web site: http://www.dphhs.mt.gov/whowhat/amdd.htm

Nebraska

Division of Alcoholism and Drug Abuse
Department of Public Institutions
P.O. Box 94728
Lincoln, NE 68509-4728
Phone: (402) 471-2851
Fax: (402) 479-5145
E-mail: hhsinfo@hhs.state.ne.us
Web site: http://www.hhs.state.ne.us/beh/dadaas.htm

Nevada

Bureau of Alcohol and Drug Abuse
505 East Third Street
Carson City, NV 89713
Phone: (702) 687-4790
Fax: (702) 687-6239
Web site: http://www.drug-abuse.com/usa/nevada

New Hampshire
Department of Health and Human Services
Office of Alcohol and Drug Abuse Prevention
State Office Park South
105 Pleasant Street
Concord, NH 03301
Phone: (603) 271-6104
Fax: (603) 271-6116
Web site: http://www.dhhs.state.nh.us/

New Jersey
Department of Health
Division of Addiction Services
129 East Hanover Street
CN 362
Trenton, NJ 08625-0362
Phone: (609) 292-5760
Fax: (609) 292-3816
Web site: http://www.state.nj.us/health/as/admin.htm

New Mexico
Department of Health
Division of Substance Abuse
1190 St. Francis Drive
P.O. Box 26110
Santa Fe, NM 87502-6110
Phone: (505) 827-2601
Fax: (505) 827-0097
Web site: http://www.health.state.nm.us/website.nsf/frames

New York
Office of Alcoholism and Substance Abuse Services
1450 Western Avenue
Albany, NY 12203-8200
Phone: (518) 457-2061
Web site: http://www.oasas.state.ny.us

North Carolina
Department of Human Resources
Division of Mental Health, Developmental Disabilities, and Substance Abuse Services

3001 Mail Service Center
Raleigh, NC 27699-3001
Phone: (919) 733-7011
Web site: http://www.dhhs.state.nc.us/docs/rclist.htm#dmh

North Dakota
Department of Human Services
Division of Mental Health, Alcohol and Drug Abuse
600 South Second Street
Suite 1E
Bismarck, ND 58504-5729
Phone: (701) 328-8920
Fax: (701) 328-8969
E-mail: soerhk@state.nd.us
Web site: http://lnotes.state.nd.us/dhs/dhsweb.nsf

Ohio
Department of Alcohol and Drug Addiction Services
Drug Addiction Services
280 North High Street, 12th Floor
Columbus, OH 43215-2537
Phone: (614) 466-3445
Fax: (614) 752-8645

Oklahoma
Department of Mental Health and Substance Abuse Services
P.O. Box 53277
Oklahoma City, OK 73152-3277
Phone: (405) 522-3908
Fax: (405) 522-3650
Web site: http://www.odmhsas.org/agencyoverview.htm

Oregon
Office of Alcohol and Drug Abuse Programs
500 Summer Street NE., Third Floor
Salem, OR 97310-1016
Phone: (503) 945-5763
TTY: (503) 945-5893
Fax: (503) 378-8467
E-mail: oadap.info@state.or.us
Web site: http://www.oadap.hr.state.or.us/

Pennsylvania
Office of Drug and Alcohol Programs
P.O. Box 90, Room 933
Harrisburg, PA 17108
Phone: (717) 787-8200
Fax: (717) 772-6285
Web site: http://www.health.state.pa.us/

Rhode Island
Rhode Island Department of Health
Canon Building
3Capitol Hill
Providence, RI 02908-5097
Phone: (401) 222-2231
TTY: (800) 745-5555
Fax: (401) 222-6548
Web site: http://www.health.state.ri.us

South Carolina
Department of Alcohol and Other Drug Abuse Services
3700 Forest Drive, Suite 300
Columbia, SC 29204
Phone: (803) 734-9553
Fax: (803) 734-9663
Web site: http://www.daodas.state.sc.us/

South Dakota
Department of Human Services
Division of Alcohol and Drug Abuse
Hillsview Plaza
500 East Capitol Avenue
Pierre, SD 57501-5070
Phone: (605) 773-3123
Fax: (605) 773-7076
E-mail: info@dada
Web site: http://www.state.sd.us/dhs/dhs.html

Tennessee
Department of Health
Alcohol and Drug Abuse Services
Cordell Hall Building
425 Fifth Avenue North, Third Floor
Nashville, TN 37247-0101

Phone: (615) 741-1921
Fax: (615) 532-2419
E-mail: Ddenton@mail.state.tn.us
Web site: http://www.state.tn.us/hh.html

Texas

Commission on Alcohol and Drug Abuse
9001 North IH 35, Suite 105
Austin, TX 78753-5233
Phone: (512) 349-6600
Fax: (512) 837-0998
Web site: http://www.texas.gov/agency/517.html

Utah

Department of Human Services
Division of Substance Abuse
120 North 200 West, Room 201
Salt Lake City, UT 84103
Phone: (801) 538-3939
Toll Free Hotline: (888) 918-8500
Fax: (801) 538-4696
Web site: http://www.hsdsa.state.ut.us/

Vermont

Agency of Human Services
Office of Alcohol and Drug Abuse Programs
108 Cherry Street
Burlington, VT 05402-0070
Phone: (802) 651-1560
Fax: (802) 651-1573
E-mail: mlaplan@vdh.state.vt.us
Web site: http://www.state.vt.us/adap/

Virginia

Office of Substance Abuse Services
Department of Mental Health, Mental Retardation, and Substance Abuse Services
P.O. Box 1797
Richmond, VA 23218
Phone: (804) 786-3906
Fax: (804) 371-0091
Web site: http://www.dmhmrsas.state.va.us

Washington
Department of Social and Health Services
Division of Alcohol and Substance Abuse
P.O. Box 45330
Olympia, WA 98504-5060
Phone: (360) 438-8200
Fax: (360) 438-8078
Web site: http://www.wa.gov/dshs

West Virginia
Department of Health and Human Resources
Office of Behavioral Health Services
Division of Alcoholism and Drug Abuse
350 Capital St., Rm. 350
Charleston, WV 25301-3702
Phone: (304) 558-20627
Fax: (304) 558-1008
E-mail: obhs@wvdhhr.org
Web site: http://www.uacdd.wvu.edu/obhs

Wisconsin
Department of Health and Family Services
Division of Community Services
Bureau of Substance Abuse Services
P.O. Box 7851
1 West Wilson Street
Madison, WI 53707-7851
Phone: (608) 267-7164
Fax: (608) 266-1533
E-mail: langejb@dhfs.state.wi.us
Web site: http://www.dhfs.state.wi/us/substabuse/index.htm

Wyoming
Department of Health
Division of Behavioral Health
Substance Abuse Program
451 Hathaway Building
2300 Capitol Avenue
Cheyenne, WY 82002-0480
Phone: (307) 777-7094
Fax: (307) 777-5580
Web site: http://www.wdbh.state.wy.us/services/psa/index.html

American Samoa
Department of Human Resources
Government of American Samoa
Pago Pago, AS 96799
Phone: 011-684-1371/1372/1373
Web site: http://www.government.as/medical.htm

Guam
Department of Mental Health and Substance Abuse
790 Governor Carlos G. Gamacho Road
Tamuning, GU 96911
Phone: 011-671-647-5400
Fax: 011-671-649-6948
Web site: http://mail.admin.gov.gu/pubhealth/

Puerto Rico
Department of Health
Mental Health and Anti-Addiction Services Administration
P.O. Box 21414
San Juan, PR 00928-1414
Phone: (809) 764-3670
Fax: (809) 765-5895

Virgin Islands
Department of Human Services
Knud Hansen Complex, Building A 1303
Hospital Ground
St. Thomas, US VI 00802
Phone: (340) 774-0930
Fax: (304) 774-3466
E-mail: humanservice@usvi.org
Web site: http://www.usvi.org/humanservices/index.html

Index

Index

Page numbers followed by 'n' indicate a footnote. Page numbers in *italics* indicate a table or illustration.

A

B

C

E

F

G

H

I

J

M

N

O

P

Q

R

S

T

U

V

W

X

Y

Z

Health Reference Series

COMPLETE CATALOG

AIDS Sourcebook, 1st Edition

Basic Information about AIDS and HIV Infection, Featuring Historical and Statistical Data, Current Research, Prevention, and Other Special Topics of Interest for Persons Living with AIDS

Along with Source Listings for Further Assistance

Edited by Karen Bellenir and Peter D. Dresser. 831 pages. 1995. 0-7808-0031-1. $78.

"One strength of this book is its practical emphasis. The intended audience is the lay reader . . . useful as an educational tool for health care providers who work with AIDS patients. Recommended for public libraries as well as hospital or academic libraries that collect consumer materials."
—*Bulletin of the Medical Library Association, Jan '96*

"This is the most comprehensive volume of its kind on an important medical topic. Highly recommended for all libraries." —*Reference Book Review, '96*

"Very useful reference for all libraries."
—*Choice, Association of College and Research Libraries, Oct '95*

"There is a wealth of information here that can provide much educational assistance. It is a must book for all libraries and should be on the desk of each and every congressional leader. Highly recommended."
—*AIDS Book Review Journal, Aug '95*

"Recommended for most collections."
—*Library Journal, Jul '95*

■

AIDS Sourcebook, 2nd Edition

Basic Consumer Health Information about Acquired Immune Deficiency Syndrome (AIDS) and Human Immunodeficiency Virus (HIV) Infection, Featuring Updated Statistical Data, Reports on Recent Research and Prevention Initiatives, and Other Special Topics of Interest for Persons Living with AIDS, Including New Antiretroviral Treatment Options, Strategies for Combating Opportunistic Infections, Information about Clinical Trials, and More

Along with a Glossary of Important Terms and Resource Listings for Further Help and Information

Edited by Karen Bellenir. 751 pages. 1999. 0-7808-0225-X. $78.

"Highly recommended."
—*American Reference Books Annual, 2000*

"Excellent sourcebook. This continues to be a highly recommended book. There is no other book that provides as much information as this book provides."
—*AIDS Book Review Journal, Dec-Jan 2000*

"Recommended reference source."
—*Booklist, American Library Association, Dec '99*

"A solid text for college-level health libraries."
—*The Bookwatch, Aug '99*

Cited in *Reference Sources for Small and Medium-Sized Libraries, American Library Association, 1999*

■

Alcoholism Sourcebook

Basic Consumer Health Information about the Physical and Mental Consequences of Alcohol Abuse, Including Liver Disease, Pancreatitis, Wernicke-Korsakoff Syndrome (Alcoholic Dementia), Fetal Alcohol Syndrome, Heart Disease, Kidney Disorders, Gastrointestinal Problems, and Immune System Compromise and Featuring Facts about Addiction, Detoxification, Alcohol Withdrawal, Recovery, and the Maintenance of Sobriety

Along with a Glossary and Directories of Resources for Further Help and Information

Edited by Karen Bellenir. 650 pages. 2000. 0-7808-0325-6. $78.

SEE ALSO *Drug Abuse Sourcebook, Substance Abuse Sourcebook*

■

Allergies Sourcebook

Basic Information about Major Forms and Mechanisms of Common Allergic Reactions, Sensitivities, and Intolerances, Including Anaphylaxis, Asthma, Hives and Other Dermatologic Symptoms, Rhinitis, and Sinusitis

Along with Their Usual Triggers Like Animal Fur, Chemicals, Drugs, Dust, Foods, Insects, Latex, Pollen, and Poison Ivy, Oak, and Sumac; Plus Information on Prevention, Identification, and Treatment

Edited by Allan R. Cook. 611 pages. 1997. 0-7808-0036-2. $78.

■

Alternative Medicine Sourcebook

Basic Consumer Health Information about Alternatives to Conventional Medicine, Including Acupressure, Acupuncture, Aromatherapy, Ayurveda, Bioelectromagnetics, Environmental Medicine, Essence Therapy, Food and Nutrition Therapy, Herbal Therapy, Homeopathy, Imaging, Massage, Naturopathy, Reflexology, Relaxation and Meditation, Sound Therapy, Vitamin and Mineral Therapy, and Yoga, and More

Edited by Allan R. Cook. 737 pages. 1999. 0-7808-0200-4. $78.

"A great addition to the reference collection of every type of library."
—*American Reference Books Annual, 2000*

Alzheimer's, Stroke & 29 Other Neurological Disorders Sourcebook, 1st Edition

Basic Information for the Layperson on 31 Diseases or Disorders Affecting the Brain and Nervous System, First Describing the Illness, Then Listing Symptoms, Diagnostic Methods, and Treatment Options, and Including Statistics on Incidences and Causes

Edited by Frank E. Bair. 579 pages. 1993. 1-55888-748-2. $78.

"Nontechnical reference book that provides reader-friendly information."
—*Family Caregiver Alliance Update, Winter '96*

"Should be included in any library's patient education section." —*American Reference Books Annual, 1994*

"Written in an approachable and accessible style. Recommended for patient education and consumer health collections in health science center and public libraries." —*Academic Library Book Review, Dec '93*

"It is very handy to have information on more than thirty neurological disorders under one cover, and there is no recent source like it." —*Reference Quarterly, American Library Association, Fall '93*

SEE ALSO *Brain Disorders Sourcebook*

■

Alzheimer's Disease Sourcebook, 2nd Edition

Basic Consumer Health Information about Alzheimer's Disease, Related Disorders, and Other Dementias, Including Multi-Infarct Dementia, AIDS-Related Dementia, Alcoholic Dementia, Huntington's Disease, Delirium, and Confusional States

Along with Reports Detailing Current Research Efforts in Prevention and Treatment, Long-Term Care Issues, and Listings of Sources for Additional Help and Information

Edited by Karen Bellenir. 524 pages. 1999. 0-7808-0223-3. $78.

"Provides a wealth of useful information not otherwise available in one place. This resource is recommended for all types of libraries."
—*American Reference Books Annual, 2000*

"Recommended reference source."
—*Booklist, American Library Association, Oct '99*

■

Arthritis Sourcebook

Basic Consumer Health Information about Specific Forms of Arthritis and Related Disorders, Including Rheumatoid Arthritis, Osteoarthritis, Gout, Polymyalgia Rheumatica, Psoriatic Arthritis, Spondyloarthropathies, Juvenile Rheumatoid Arthritis, and Juvenile Ankylosing Spondylitis

Along with Information about Medical, Surgical, and Alternative Treatment Options, and Including Strategies for Coping with Pain, Fatigue, and Stress

Edited by Allan R. Cook. 550 pages. 1998. 0-7808-0201-2. $78.

". . . accessible to the layperson."
—*Reference and Research Book News, Feb '99*

■

Asthma Sourcebook

Basic Consumer Health Information about Asthma, Including Symptoms, Traditional and Nontraditional Remedies, Treatment Advances, Quality-of-Life Aids, Medical Research Updates, and the Role of Allergies, Exercise, Age, the Environment, and Genetics in the Development of Asthma

Along with Statistical Data, a Glossary, and Directories of Support Groups and Other Resources for Further Information

Edited by Annemarie S. Muth. 650 pages. 2000. 0-7808-0381-7. $78.

■

Back & Neck Disorders Sourcebook

Basic Information about Disorders and Injuries of the Spinal Cord and Vertebrae, Including Facts on Chiropractic Treatment, Surgical Interventions, Paralysis, and Rehabilitation

Along with Advice for Preventing Back Trouble

Edited by Karen Bellenir. 548 pages. 1997. 0-7808-0202-0. $78.

"The strength of this work is its basic, easy-to-read format. Recommended."
—*Reference and User Services Quarterly, American Library Association, Winter '97*

■

Blood & Circulatory Disorders Sourcebook

Basic Information about Blood and Its Components, Anemias, Leukemias, Bleeding Disorders, and Circulatory Disorders, Including Aplastic Anemia, Thalassemia, Sickle-Cell Disease, Hemochromatosis, Hemophilia, Von Willebrand Disease, and Vascular Diseases

Along with a Special Section on Blood Transfusions and Blood Supply Safety, a Glossary, and Source Listings for Further Help and Information

Edited by Karen Bellenir and Linda M. Shin. 554 pages. 1998. 0-7808-0203-9. $78.

"Recommended reference source."
—*Booklist, American Library Association, Feb '99*

"An important reference sourcebook written in simple language for everyday, non-technical users."
—*Reviewer's Bookwatch, Jan '99*

Brain Disorders Sourcebook

Basic Consumer Health Information about Strokes, Epilepsy, Amyotrophic Lateral Sclerosis (ALS/Lou Gehrig's Disease), Parkinson's Disease, Brain Tumors, Cerebral Palsy, Headache, Tourette Syndrome, and More

Along with Statistical Data, Treatment and Rehabilitation Options, Coping Strategies, Reports on Current Research Initiatives, a Glossary, and Resource Listings for Additional Help and Information

Edited by Karen Bellenir. 481 pages. 1999. 0-7808-0229-2. $78.

"Belongs on the shelves of any library with a consumer health collection." —*E-Streams, Mar '00*

"Recommended reference source."
—*Booklist, American Library Association, Oct '99*

SEE ALSO *Alzheimer's, Stroke & 29 Other Neurological Disorders Sourcebook, 1st Edition*

■

Breast Cancer Sourcebook

Basic Consumer Health Information about Breast Cancer, Including Diagnostic Methods, Treatment Options, Alternative Therapies, Help and Self-Help Information, Related Health Concerns, Statistical and Demographic Data, and Facts for Men with Breast Cancer

Along with Reports on Current Research Initiatives, a Glossary of Related Medical Terms, and a Directory of Sources for Further Help and Information

Edited by Edward J. Prucha. 600 pages. 2000. 0-7808-0244-6. $78.

SEE ALSO *Cancer Sourcebook for Women, 1st and 2nd Editions, Women's Health Concerns Sourcebook*

■

Burns Sourcebook

Basic Consumer Health Information about Various Types of Burns and Scalds, Including Flame, Heat, Cold, Electrical, Chemical, and Sun Burns

Along with Information on Short-Term and Long-Term Treatments, Tissue Reconstruction, Plastic Surgery, Prevention Suggestions, and First Aid

Edited by Allan R. Cook. 604 pages. 1999. 0-7808-0204-7. $78.

"This key reference guide is an invaluable addition to all health care and public libraries in confronting this ongoing health issue."
—*American Reference Books Annual, 2000*

"This is an exceptional addition to the series and is highly recommended for all consumer health collections, hospital libraries, and academic medical centers." —*E-Streams, Mar '00*

"Recommended reference source."
—*Booklist, American Library Association, Dec '99*

SEE ALSO *Skin Disorders Sourcebook*

Cancer Sourcebook, 1st Edition

Basic Information on Cancer Types, Symptoms, Diagnostic Methods, and Treatments, Including Statistics on Cancer Occurrences Worldwide and the Risks Associated with Known Carcinogens and Activities

Edited by Frank E. Bair. 932 pages. 1990. 1-55888-888-8. $78.

Cited in *Reference Sources for Small and Medium-Sized Libraries, American Library Association, 1999*

"Written in nontechnical language. Useful for patients, their families, medical professionals, and librarians."
—*Guide to Reference Books, 1996*

"Designed with the non-medical professional in mind. Libraries and medical facilities interested in patient education should certainly consider adding the *Cancer Sourcebook* to their holdings. This compact collection of reliable information . . . is an invaluable tool for helping patients and patients' families and friends to take the first steps in coping with the many difficulties of cancer."
—*Medical Reference Services Quarterly, Winter '91*

"Specifically created for the nontechnical reader . . . an important resource for the general reader trying to understand the complexities of cancer."
—*American Reference Books Annual, 1991*

"This publication's nontechnical nature and very comprehensive format make it useful for both the general public and undergraduate students."
—*Choice, Association of College and Research Libraries, Oct '90*

■

New Cancer Sourcebook, 2nd Edition

Basic Information about Major Forms and Stages of Cancer, Featuring Facts about Primary and Secondary Tumors of the Respiratory, Nervous, Lymphatic, Circulatory, Skeletal, and Gastrointestinal Systems, and Specific Organs; Statistical and Demographic Data; Treatment Options; and Strategies for Coping

Edited by Allan R. Cook. 1,313 pages. 1996. 0-7808-0041-9. $78.

"An excellent resource for patients with newly diagnosed cancer and their families. The dialogue is simple, direct, and comprehensive. Highly recommended for patients and families to aid in their understanding of cancer and its treatment."
—*Booklist Health Sciences Supplement, American Library Association, Oct '97*

"The amount of factual and useful information is extensive. The writing is very clear, geared to general readers. Recommended for all levels."
—*Choice, Association of College and Research Libraries, Jan '97*

Cancer Sourcebook, 3rd Edition

Basic Consumer Health Information about Major Forms and Stages of Cancer, Featuring Facts about Primary and Secondary Tumors of the Respiratory, Nervous, Lymphatic, Circulatory, Skeletal, and Gastrointestinal Systems, and Specific Organs

Along with Statistical and Demographic Data, Treatment Options, Strategies for Coping, a Glossary, and a Directory of Sources for Additional Help and Information

Edited by Edward J. Prucha. 1,069 pages. 2000. 0-7808-0227-6. $78.

■

Cancer Sourcebook for Women, 1st Edition

Basic Information about Specific Forms of Cancer That Affect Women, Featuring Facts about Breast Cancer, Cervical Cancer, Ovarian Cancer, Cancer of the Uterus and Uterine Sarcoma, Cancer of the Vagina, and Cancer of the Vulva; Statistical and Demographic Data; Treatments, Self-Help Management Suggestions, and Current Research Initiatives

Edited by Allan R. Cook and Peter D. Dresser. 524 pages. 1996. 0-7808-0076-1. $78.

". . . written in easily understandable, non-technical language. Recommended for public libraries or hospital and academic libraries that collect patient education or consumer health materials."

—*Medical Reference Services Quarterly, Spring '97*

"Would be of value in a consumer health library. . . . written with the health care consumer in mind. Medical jargon is at a minimum, and medical terms are explained in clear, understandable sentences."

—*Bulletin of the Medical Library Association, Oct '96*

"The availability under one cover of all these pertinent publications, grouped under cohesive headings, makes this certainly a most useful sourcebook."

—*Choice, Association of College and Research Libraries, Jun '96*

"Presents a comprehensive knowledge base for general readers. Men and women both benefit from the gold mine of information nestled between the two covers of this book. Recommended."

—*Academic Library Book Review, Summer '96*

"This timely book is highly recommended for consumer health and patient education collections in all libraries." —*Library Journal, Apr '96*

SEE ALSO *Breast Cancer Sourcebook, Women's Health Concerns Sourcebook*

Cancer Sourcebook for Women, 2nd Edition

Basic Consumer Health Information about Specific Forms of Cancer That Affect Women, Including Cervical Cancer, Ovarian Cancer, Endometrial Cancer, Uterine Sarcoma, Vaginal Cancer, Vulvar Cancer, and Gestational Trophoblastic Tumor; and Featuring Statistical Information, Facts about Tests and Treatments, a Glossary of Cancer Terms, and an Extensive List of Additional Resources

Edited by Edward J. Prucha. 600 pages. 2000. 0-7808-0226-8. $78.

SEE ALSO *Breast Cancer Sourcebook, Women's Health Concerns Sourcebook*

■

Cardiovascular Diseases & Disorders Sourcebook, 1st Edition

Basic Information about Cardiovascular Diseases and Disorders, Featuring Facts about the Cardiovascular System, Demographic and Statistical Data, Descriptions of Pharmacological and Surgical Interventions, Lifestyle Modifications, and a Special Section Focusing on Heart Disorders in Children

Edited by Karen Bellenir and Peter D. Dresser. 683 pages. 1995. 0-7808-0032-X. $78.

". . . comprehensive format provides an extensive overview on this subject."

—*Choice, Association of College and Research Libraries, Jun '96*

". . . an easily understood, complete, up-to-date resource. This well executed public health tool will make valuable information available to those that need it most, patients and their families. The typeface, sturdy non-reflective paper, and library binding add a feel of quality found wanting in other publications. Highly recommended for academic and general libraries."

—*Academic Library Book Review, Summer '96*

SEE ALSO *Healthy Heart Sourcebook for Women, Heart Diseases & Disorders Sourcebook, 2nd Edition*

■

Communication Disorders Sourcebook

Basic Information about Deafness and Hearing Loss, Speech and Language Disorders, Voice Disorders, Balance and Vestibular Disorders, and Disorders of Smell, Taste, and Touch

Edited by Linda M. Ross. 533 pages. 1996. 0-7808-0077-X. $78.

"This is skillfully edited and is a welcome resource for the layperson. It should be found in every public and medical library." —*Booklist Health Sciences Supplement, American Library Association, Oct '97*

Congenital Disorders Sourcebook

Basic Information about Disorders Acquired during Gestation, Including Spina Bifida, Hydrocephalus, Cerebral Palsy, Heart Defects, Craniofacial Abnormalities, Fetal Alcohol Syndrome, and More

Along with Current Treatment Options and Statistical Data

Edited by Karen Bellenir. 607 pages. 1997. 0-7808-0205-5. $78.

"Recommended reference source."

—*Booklist, American Library Association, Oct '97*

SEE ALSO *Pregnancy & Birth Sourcebook*

■

Consumer Issues in Health Care Sourcebook

Basic Information about Health Care Fundamentals and Related Consumer Issues, Including Exams and Screening Tests, Physician Specialties, Choosing a Doctor, Using Prescription and Over-the-Counter Medications Safely, Avoiding Health Scams, Managing Common Health Risks in the Home, Care Options for Chronically or Terminally Ill Patients, and a List of Resources for Obtaining Help and Further Information

Edited by Karen Bellenir. 618 pages. 1998. 0-7808-0221-7. $78.

"Both public and academic libraries will want to have a copy in their collection for readers who are interested in self-education on health issues."

—*American Reference Books Annual, 2000*

"The editor has researched the literature from government agencies and others, saving readers the time and effort of having to do the research themselves. Recommended for public libraries."

—*Reference and User Services Quarterly, American Library Association, Spring '99*

"Recommended reference source."

—*Booklist, American Library Association, Dec '98*

■

Contagious & Non-Contagious Infectious Diseases Sourcebook

Basic Information about Contagious Diseases like Measles, Polio, Hepatitis B, and Infectious Mononucleosis, and Non-Contagious Infectious Diseases like Tetanus and Toxic Shock Syndrome, and Diseases Occurring as Secondary Infections Such as Shingles and Reye Syndrome

Along with Vaccination, Prevention, and Treatment Information, and a Section Describing Emerging Infectious Disease Threats

Edited by Karen Bellenir and Peter D. Dresser. 566 pages. 1996. 0-7808-0075-3. $78.

Death & Dying Sourcebook

Basic Consumer Health Information for the Layperson about End-of-Life Care and Related Ethical and Legal Issues, Including Chief Causes of Death, Autopsies, Pain Management for the Terminally Ill, Life Support Systems, Insurance, Euthanasia, Assisted Suicide, Hospice Programs, Living Wills, Funeral Planning, Counseling, Mourning, Organ Donation, and Physician Training

Along with Statistical Data, a Glossary, and Listings of Sources for Further Help and Information

Edited by Annemarie S. Muth. 641 pages. 1999. 0-7808-0230-6. $78.

"This book is a definite must for all those involved in end-of-life care." —*Doody's Review Service, 2000*

■

Diabetes Sourcebook, 1st Edition

Basic Information about Insulin-Dependent and Noninsulin-Dependent Diabetes Mellitus, Gestational Diabetes, and Diabetic Complications, Symptoms, Treatment, and Research Results, Including Statistics on Prevalence, Morbidity, and Mortality

Along with Source Listings for Further Help and Information

Edited by Karen Bellenir and Peter D. Dresser. 827 pages. 1994. 1-55888-751-2. $78.

". . . very informative and understandable for the layperson without being simplistic. It provides a comprehensive overview for laypersons who want a general understanding of the disease or who want to focus on various aspects of the disease."

—*Bulletin of the Medical Library Association, Jan '96*

■

Diabetes Sourcebook, 2nd Edition

Basic Consumer Health Information about Type 1 Diabetes (Insulin-Dependent or Juvenile-Onset Diabetes), Type 2 (Noninsulin-Dependent or Adult-Onset Diabetes), Gestational Diabetes, and Related Disorders, Including Diabetes Prevalence Data, Management Issues, the Role of Diet and Exercise in Controlling Diabetes, Insulin and Other Diabetes Medicines, and Complications of Diabetes Such as Eye Diseases, Periodontal Disease, Amputation, and End-Stage Renal Disease

Along with Reports on Current Research Initiatives, a Glossary, and Resource Listings for Further Help and Information

Edited by Karen Bellenir. 688 pages. 1998. 0-7808-0224-1. $78.

"This comprehensive book is an excellent addition for high school, academic, medical, and public libraries. This volume is highly recommended."

—*American Reference Books Annual, 2000*

"An invaluable reference." —*Library Journal, May '00*

Selected as one of the 250 "Best Health Sciences Books of 1999." —*Doody's Rating Service, Mar-Apr 2000*

"Recommended reference source."
—*Booklist, American Library Association, Feb '99*

". . . provides reliable mainstream medical information . . . belongs on the shelves of any library with a consumer health collection." —*E-Streams, Sep '99*

"Provides useful information for the general public."
—*Healthlines, University of Michigan Health Management Research Center, Sep/Oct '99*

■

Diet & Nutrition Sourcebook, 1st Edition

Basic Information about Nutrition, Including the Dietary Guidelines for Americans, the Food Guide Pyramid, and Their Applications in Daily Diet, Nutritional Advice for Specific Age Groups, Current Nutritional Issues and Controversies, the New Food Label and How to Use It to Promote Healthy Eating, and Recent Developments in Nutritional Research

Edited by Dan R. Harris. 662 pages. 1996. 0-7808-0084-2. $78.

"Useful reference as a food and nutrition sourcebook for the general consumer." —*Booklist Health Sciences Supplement, American Library Association, Oct '97*

"Recommended for public libraries and medical libraries that receive general information requests on nutrition. It is readable and will appeal to those interested in learning more about healthy dietary practices."
—*Medical Reference Services Quarterly, Fall '97*

"An abundance of medical and social statistics is translated into readable information geared toward the general reader." —*Bookwatch, Mar '97*

"With dozens of questionable diet books on the market, it is so refreshing to find a reliable and factual reference book. Recommended to aspiring professionals, librarians, and others seeking and giving reliable dietary advice. An excellent compilation." —*Choice, Association of College and Research Libraries, Feb '97*

SEE ALSO *Digestive Diseases & Disorders Sourcebook, Gastrointestinal Diseases & Disorders Sourcebook*

■

Diet & Nutrition Sourcebook, 2nd Edition

Basic Consumer Health Information about Dietary Guidelines, Recommended Daily Intake Values, Vitamins, Minerals, Fiber, Fat, Weight Control, Dietary Supplements, and Food Additives

Along with Special Sections on Nutrition Needs throughout Life and Nutrition for People with Such Specific Medical Concerns as Allergies, High Blood Cholesterol, Hypertension, Diabetes, Celiac Disease, Seizure Disorders, Phenylketonuria (PKU), Cancer, and Eating Disorders, and Including Reports on Current Nutrition Research and Source Listings for Additional Help and Information

Edited by Karen Bellenir. 650 pages. 1999. 0-7808-0228-4. $78.

"This reference document should be in any public library, but it would be a very good guide for beginning students in the health sciences. If the other books in this publisher's series are as good as this, they should all be in the health sciences collections."
—*American Reference Books Annual, 2000*

"Recommended reference source."
—*Booklist, American Library Association, Dec '99*

SEE ALSO *Digestive Diseases & Disorders Sourcebook, Gastrointestinal Diseases & Disorders Sourcebook*

■

Digestive Diseases & Disorders Sourcebook

Basic Consumer Health Information about Diseases and Disorders that Impact the Upper and Lower Digestive System, Including Celiac Disease, Constipation, Crohn's Disease, Cyclic Vomiting Syndrome, Diarrhea, Diverticulosis and Diverticulitis, Gallstones, Heartburn, Hemorrhoids, Hernias, Indigestion (Dyspepsia), Irritable Bowel Syndrome, Lactose Intolerance, Ulcers, and More

Along with Information about Medications and Other Treatments, Tips for Maintaining a Healthy Digestive Tract, a Glossary, and Directory of Digestive Diseases Organizations

Edited by Karen Bellenir. 335 pages. 1999. 0-7808-0327-2. $48.

"Recommended reference source."
—*Booklist, American Library Association, May '00*

SEE ALSO *Diet & Nutrition Sourcebook, 1st and 2nd Editions, Gastrointestinal Diseases & Disorders Sourcebook*

■

Disabilities Sourcebook

Basic Consumer Health Information about Physical and Psychiatric Disabilities, Including Descriptions of Major Causes of Disability, Assistive and Adaptive Aids, Workplace Issues, and Accessibility Concerns

Along with Information about the Americans with Disabilities Act, a Glossary, and Resources for Additional Help and Information

Edited by Dawn D. Matthews. 616 pages. 2000. 0-7808-0389-2. $78.

■

Domestic Violence & Child Abuse Sourcebook

Basic Information about Spousal/ Partner, Child, and Elder Physical, Emotional, and Sexual Abuse, Teen Dating Violence, and Stalking, Including Information about Hotlines, Safe Houses, Safety Plans, and Other Resources for Support and Assistance, Community Ini-

tiatives, and Reports on Current Directions in Research and Treatment

Along with a Glossary, Sources for Further Reading, and Governmental and Non-Governmental Organizations Contact Information

Edited by Helene Henderson. 600 pages. 2000. 0-7808-0235-7. $78.

■

Drug Abuse Sourcebook

Basic Consumer Health Information about Illicit Substances of Abuse and the Diversion of Prescription Medications, Including Depressants, Hallucinogens, Inhalants, Marijuana, Narcotics, Stimulants, and Anabolic Steroids

Along with Facts about Related Health Risks, Treatment Issues, and Substance Abuse Prevention Programs, a Glossary of Terms, Statistical Data, and Directories of Hotline Services, Self-Help Groups, and Organizations Able to Provide Further Information

Edited by Karen Bellenir. 600 pages. 2000. 0-7808-0242-X. $78.

SEE ALSO *Alcoholism Sourcebook, Substance Abuse Sourcebook*

■

Ear, Nose & Throat Disorders Sourcebook

Basic Information about Disorders of the Ears, Nose, Sinus Cavities, Pharynx, and Larynx, Including Ear Infections, Tinnitus, Vestibular Disorders, Allergic and Non-Allergic Rhinitis, Sore Throats, Tonsillitis, and Cancers That Affect the Ears, Nose, Sinuses, and Throat

Along with Reports on Current Research Initiatives, a Glossary of Related Medical Terms, and a Directory of Sources for Further Help and Information

Edited by Karen Bellenir and Linda M. Shin. 576 pages. 1998. 0-7808-0206-3. $78.

"Overall, this sourcebook is helpful for the consumer seeking information on ENT issues. It is recommended for public libraries."

—*American Reference Books Annual, 1999*

"Recommended reference source."

—*Booklist, American Library Association, Dec '98*

■

Endocrine & Metabolic Disorders Sourcebook

Basic Information for the Layperson about Pancreatic and Insulin-Related Disorders Such as Pancreatitis, Diabetes, and Hypoglycemia; Adrenal Gland Disorders Such as Cushing's Syndrome, Addison's Disease, and Congenital Adrenal Hyperplasia; Pituitary Gland Disorders Such as Growth Hormone Deficiency, Acromegaly, and Pituitary Tumors; Thyroid Disorders Such as Hypothyroidism, Graves' Disease, Hashimoto's Disease, and Goiter; Hyperparathyroidism; and Other Diseases and Syndromes of Hormone Imbalance or Metabolic Dysfunction

Along with Reports on Current Research Initiatives

Edited by Linda M. Shin. 574 pages. 1998. 0-7808-0207-1. $78.

"Omnigraphics has produced another needed resource for health information consumers."

—*American Reference Books Annual, 2000*

"Recommended reference source."

—*Booklist, American Library Association, Dec '98*

■

Environmentally Induced Disorders Sourcebook

Basic Information about Diseases and Syndromes Linked to Exposure to Pollutants and Other Substances in Outdoor and Indoor Environments Such as Lead, Asbestos, Formaldehyde, Mercury, Emissions, Noise, and More

Edited by Allan R. Cook. 620 pages. 1997. 0-7808-0083-4. $78.

"Recommended reference source."

—*Booklist, American Library Association, Sep '98*

"This book will be a useful addition to anyone's library." —*Choice Health Sciences Supplement, Association of College and Research Libraries, May '98*

". . . a good survey of numerous environmentally induced physical disorders . . . a useful addition to anyone's library."

—*Doody's Health Sciences Book Reviews, Jan '98*

". . . provide[s] introductory information from the best authorities around. Since this volume covers topics that potentially affect everyone, it will surely be one of the most frequently consulted volumes in the *Health Reference Series*." —*Rettig on Reference, Nov '97*

■

Ethical Issues in Medicine Sourcebook

Basic Information about Controversial Treatment Issues, Genetic Research, Reproductive Technologies, and End-of-Life Decisions, Including Topics Such as Cloning, Abortion, Fertility Management, Organ Transplantation, Health Care Rationing, Advance Directives, Living Wills, Physician-Assisted Suicide, Euthanasia, and More; Along with a Glossary and Resources for Additional Information

Edited by Helene Henderson. 600 pages. 2000. 0-7808-0237-3. $78.

Family Planning Sourcebook

Basic Consumer Health Information about Planning for Pregnancy and Contraception, Including Traditional Methods, Barrier Methods, Permanent Methods, Future Methods, Emergency Contraception, and Birth Control Choices for Women at Each Stage of Life

Along with Statistics, Glossary, and Sources of Additional Information

Edited by Amy Marcaccio Keyzer. 600 pages. 2000. 0-7808-0379-5. $78.

SEE ALSO *Pregnancy & Birth Sourcebook*

■

Fitness & Exercise Sourcebook

Basic Information on Fitness and Exercise, Including Fitness Activities for Specific Age Groups, Exercise for People with Specific Medical Conditions, How to Begin a Fitness Program in Running, Walking, Swimming, Cycling, and Other Athletic Activities, and Recent Research in Fitness and Exercise

Edited by Dan R. Harris. 663 pages. 1996. 0-7808-0186-5. $78.

"A good resource for general readers."

—*Choice, Association of College and Research Libraries, Nov '97*

"The perennial popularity of the topic . . . make this an appealing selection for public libraries."

—*Rettig on Reference, Jun/Jul '97*

■

Food & Animal Borne Diseases Sourcebook

Basic Information about Diseases That Can Be Spread to Humans through the Ingestion of Contaminated Food or Water or by Contact with Infected Animals and Insects, Such as Botulism, E. Coli, Hepatitis A, Trichinosis, Lyme Disease, and Rabies

Along with Information Regarding Prevention and Treatment Methods, and Including a Special Section for International Travelers Describing Diseases Such as Cholera, Malaria, Travelers' Diarrhea, and Yellow Fever, and Offering Recommendations for Avoiding Illness

Edited by Karen Bellenir and Peter D. Dresser. 535 pages. 1995. 0-7808-0033-8. $78.

"Targeting general readers and providing them with a single, comprehensive source of information on selected topics, this book continues, with the excellent caliber of its predecessors, to catalog topical information on health matters of general interest. Readable and thorough, this valuable resource is highly recommended for all libraries."

—*Academic Library Book Review, Summer '96*

"A comprehensive collection of authoritative information." —*Emergency Medical Services, Oct '95*

Food Safety Sourcebook

Basic Consumer Health Information about the Safe Handling of Meat, Poultry, Seafood, Eggs, Fruit Juices, and Other Food Items, and Facts about Pesticides, Drinking Water, Food Safety Overseas, and the Onset, Duration, and Symptoms of Foodborne Illnesses, Including Types of Pathogenic Bacteria, Parasitic Protozoa, Worms, Viruses, and Natural Toxins

Along with the Role of the Consumer, the Food Handler, and the Government in Food Safety; a Glossary, and Resources for Additional Help and Information

Edited by Dawn D. Matthews. 339 pages. 1999. 0-7808-0326-4. $48.

"This book takes the complex issues of food safety and foodborne pathogens and presents them in an easily understood manner. [It does] an excellent job of covering a large and often confusing topic."

—*American Reference Books Annual, 2000*

"Recommended reference source."

—*Booklist, American Library Association, May '00*

■

Forensic Medicine Sourcebook

Basic Consumer Information for the Layperson about Forensic Medicine, Including Crime Scene Investigation, Evidence Collection and Analysis, Expert Testimony, Computer-Aided Criminal Identification, Digital Imaging in the Courtroom, DNA Profiling, Accident Reconstruction, Autopsies, Ballistics, Drugs and Explosives Detection, Latent Fingerprints, Product Tampering, and Questioned Document Examination

Along with Statistical Data, a Glossary of Forensics Terminology, and Listings of Sources for Further Help and Information

Edited by Annemarie S. Muth. 574 pages. 1999. 0-7808-0232-2. $78.

"There are several items that make this book attractive to consumers who are seeking certain forensic data. . . . This is a useful current source for those seeking general forensic medical answers."

—*American Reference Books Annual, 2000*

"A wealth of information, useful statistics, references are up-to-date and extremely complete. This wonderful collection of data will help students who are interested in a career in any type of forensic field. It is a great resource for attorneys who need information about types of expert witnesses needed in a particular case. It also offers useful information for fiction and nonfiction writers whose work involves a crime. A fascinating compilation. All levels."

—*Choice, Association of College and Research Libraries, Jan 2000*

Gastrointestinal Diseases & Disorders Sourcebook

Basic Information about Gastroesophageal Reflux Disease (Heartburn), Ulcers, Diverticulosis, Irritable Bowel Syndrome, Crohn's Disease, Ulcerative Colitis, Diarrhea, Constipation, Lactose Intolerance, Hemorrhoids, Hepatitis, Cirrhosis, and Other Digestive Problems, Featuring Statistics, Descriptions of Symptoms, and Current Treatment Methods of Interest for Persons Living with Upper and Lower Gastrointestinal Maladies

Edited by Linda M. Ross. 413 pages. 1996. 0-7808-0078-8. $78.

". . . very readable form. The successful editorial work that brought this material together into a useful and understandable reference makes accessible to all readers information that can help them more effectively understand and obtain help for digestive tract problems."

—*Choice, Association of College and Research Libraries, Feb '97*

SEE ALSO *Diet & Nutrition Sourcebook, 1st and 2nd Editions, Digestive Diseases & Disorders Sourcebook*

■

Genetic Disorders Sourcebook, 1st Edition

Basic Information about Heritable Diseases and Disorders Such as Down Syndrome, PKU, Hemophilia, Von Willebrand Disease, Gaucher Disease, Tay-Sachs Disease, and Sickle-Cell Disease, Along with Information about Genetic Screening, Gene Therapy, Home Care, and Including Source Listings for Further Help and Information on More Than 300 Disorders

Edited by Karen Bellenir. 642 pages. 1996. 0-7808-0034-6. $78.

"Recommended for undergraduate libraries or libraries that serve the public."

—*Science & Technology Libraries, Vol. 18, No. 1, '99*

"Provides essential medical information to both the general public and those diagnosed with a serious or fatal genetic disease or disorder."

—*Choice, Association of College and Research Libraries, Jan '97*

"Geared toward the lay public. It would be well placed in all public libraries and in those hospital and medical libraries in which access to genetic references is limited." —*Doody's Health Sciences Book Review, Oct '96*

■

Genetic Disorders Sourcebook, 2nd Edition

Basic Consumer Information about Hereditary Diseases and Disorders, Including Cystic Fibrosis, Down Syndrome, Hemophilia, Huntington's Disease, Sickle Cell Anemia, and More

Along with Facts about Genes, Gene Therapy, Genetic Screening, Ethics of Gene Testing, Genetic Counseling, a Glossary of Genetic Terminology, and a Resource List for Help, Support, and Further Information

Edited by Kathy Massimini. 650 pages. 2000. 0-7808-0241-1. $78.

■

Head Trauma Sourcebook

Basic Information for the Layperson about Open-Head and Closed-Head Injuries, Treatment Advances, Recovery, and Rehabilitation

Along with Reports on Current Research Initiatives

Edited by Karen Bellenir. 414 pages. 1997. 0-7808-0208-X. $78.

■

Health Insurance Sourcebook

Basic Information about Managed Care Organizations, Traditional Fee-for-Service Insurance, Insurance Portability and Pre-Existing Conditions Clauses, Medicare, Medicaid, Social Security, and Military Health Care

Along with Information about Insurance Fraud

Edited by Wendy Wilcox. 530 pages. 1997. 0-7808-0222-5. $78.

"Particularly useful because it brings much of this information together in one volume. This book will be a handy reference source in the health sciences library, hospital library, college and university library, and medium to large public library."

—*Medical Reference Services Quarterly, Fall '98*

Awarded "Books of the Year Award"

—*American Journal of Nursing, 1997*

"The layout of the book is particularly helpful as it provides easy access to reference material. A most useful addition to the vast amount of information about health insurance. The use of data from U.S. government agencies is most commendable. Useful in a library or learning center for healthcare professional students."

—*Doody's Health Sciences Book Reviews, Nov '97*

■

Health Resources Sourcebook

Basic Consumer Health Information about Sources of Medical Assistance, Featuring an Annotated Directory of Private and Public Consumer Health Organizations and Listings of Other Resources, Including Hospitals, Hospices, and State Medical Associations

Along with Guidelines for Locating and Evaluating Health Information

Edited by Dawn D. Matthews. 500 pages. 2000. 0-7808-0328-0. $78.

Healthy Aging Sourcebook

Basic Consumer Health Information about Maintaining Health through the Aging Process, Including Advice on Nutrition, Exercise, and Sleep, Help in Making Decisions about Midlife Issues and Retirement, and Guidance Concerning Practical and Informed Choices in Health Consumerism

Along with Data Concerning the Theories of Aging, Different Experiences in Aging by Minority Groups, and Facts about Aging Now and Aging in the Future; and Featuring a Glossary, a Guide to Consumer Help, Additional Suggested Reading, and Practical Resource Directory

Edited by Jenifer Swanson. 536 pages. 1999. 0-7808-0390-6. $78.

SEE ALSO *Physical & Mental Issues in Aging Sourcebook*

■

Healthy Heart Sourcebook for Women

Basic Consumer Health Information about Cardiac Issues Specific to Women, Including Facts about Major Risk Factors and Prevention, Treatment and Control Strategies, and Important Dietary Issues

Along with a Special Section Regarding the Pros and Cons of Hormone Replacement Therapy and Its Impact on Heart Health, and Additional Help, Including Recipes, a Glossary, and a Directory of Resources

Edited by Dawn D. Matthews. 336 pages. 2000. 0-7808-0329-9. $48.

SEE ALSO *Cardiovascular Diseases & Disorders Sourcebook, 1st Edition, Heart Diseases & Disorders Sourcebook, 2nd Edition, Women's Health Concerns Sourcebook*

■

Heart Diseases & Disorders Sourcebook, 2nd Edition

Basic Consumer Health Information about Heart Attacks, Angina, Rhythm Disorders, Heart Failure, Valve Disease, Congenital Heart Disorders, and More, Including Descriptions of Surgical Procedures and Other Interventions, Medications, Cardiac Rehabilitation, Risk Identification, and Prevention Tips

Along with Statistical Data, Reports on Current Research Initiatives, a Glossary of Cardiovascular Terms, and Resource Directory

Edited by Karen Bellenir. 612 pages. 2000. 0-7808-0238-1. $78.

SEE ALSO *Cardiovascular Diseases & Disorders Sourcebook, 1st Edition, Healthy Heart Sourcebook for Women*

Immune System Disorders Sourcebook

Basic Information about Lupus, Multiple Sclerosis, Guillain-Barré Syndrome, Chronic Granulomatous Disease, and More

Along with Statistical and Demographic Data and Reports on Current Research Initiatives

Edited by Allan R. Cook. 608 pages. 1997. 0-7808-0209-8. $78.

■

Infant & Toddler Health Sourcebook

Basic Consumer Health Information about the Physical and Mental Development of Newborns, Infants, and Toddlers, Including Neonatal Concerns, Nutrition Recommendations, Immunization Schedules, Common Pediatric Disorders, Assessments and Milestones, Safety Tips, and Advice for Parents and Other Caregivers

Along with a Glossary of Terms and Resource Listings for Additional Help

Edited by Jenifer Swanson. 600 pages. 2000. 0-7808-0246-2. $78.

■

Kidney & Urinary Tract Diseases & Disorders Sourcebook

Basic Information about Kidney Stones, Urinary Incontinence, Bladder Disease, End Stage Renal Disease, Dialysis, and More

Along with Statistical and Demographic Data and Reports on Current Research Initiatives

Edited by Linda M. Ross. 602 pages. 1997. 0-7808-0079-6. $78.

■

Learning Disabilities Sourcebook

Basic Information about Disorders Such as Dyslexia, Visual and Auditory Processing Deficits, Attention Deficit/Hyperactivity Disorder, and Autism

Along with Statistical and Demographic Data, Reports on Current Research Initiatives, an Explanation of the Assessment Process, and a Special Section for Adults with Learning Disabilities

Edited by Linda M. Shin. 579 pages. 1998. 0-7808-0210-1. $78.

Named "Oustanding Reference Book of 1999."
—*New York Public Library, Feb 2000*

"An excellent candidate for inclusion in a public library reference section. It's a great source of information. Teachers will also find the book useful. Definitely worth reading."
—*Journal of Adolescent & Adult Literacy, Feb 2000*

"Readable . . . provides a solid base of information regarding successful techniques used with individuals who have learning disabilities, as well as practical sug-

gestions for educators and family members. Clear language, concise descriptions, and pertinent information for contacting multiple resources add to the strength of this book as a useful tool."

—*Choice, Association of College and Research Libraries, Feb '99*

"Recommended reference source."

—*Booklist, American Library Association, Sep '98*

"This is a useful resource for libraries and for those who don't have the time to identify and locate the individual publications."

—*Disability Resources Monthly, Sep '98*

■

Liver Disorders Sourcebook

Basic Consumer Health Information about the Liver and How It Works; Liver Diseases, Including Cancer, Cirrhosis, Hepatitis, and Toxic and Drug Related Diseases; Tips for Maintaining a Healthy Liver; Laboratory Tests, Radiology Tests, and Facts about Liver Transplantation

Along with a Section on Support Groups, a Glossary, and Resource Listings

Edited by Joyce Brennfleck Shannon. 591 pages. 2000. 0-7808-0383-3. $78.

■

Medical Tests Sourcebook

Basic Consumer Health Information about Medical Tests, Including Periodic Health Exams, General Screening Tests, Tests You Can Do at Home, Findings of the U.S. Preventive Services Task Force, X-ray and Radiology Tests, Electrical Tests, Tests of Blood and Other Body Fluids and Tissues, Scope Tests, Lung Tests, Genetic Tests, Pregnancy Tests, Newborn Screening Tests, Sexually Transmitted Disease Tests, and Computer Aided Diagnoses

Along with a Section on Paying for Medical Tests, a Glossary, and Resource Listings

Edited by Joyce Brennfleck Shannon. 691 pages. 1999. 0-7808-0243-8. $78.

"A valuable reference guide."

—*American Reference Books Annual, 2000*

"Recommended for hospital and health sciences libraries with consumer health collections."

—*E-Streams, Mar '00*

"This is an overall excellent reference with a wealth of general knowledge that may aid those who are reluctant to get vital tests performed."

—*Today's Librarian, Jan 2000*

Men's Health Concerns Sourcebook

Basic Information about Health Issues That Affect Men, Featuring Facts about the Top Causes of Death in Men, Including Heart Disease, Stroke, Cancers, Prostate Disorders, Chronic Obstructive Pulmonary Disease, Pneumonia and Influenza, Human Immunodeficiency Virus and Acquired Immune Deficiency Syndrome, Diabetes Mellitus, Stress, Suicide, Accidents and Homicides; and Facts about Common Concerns for Men, Including Impotence, Contraception, Circumcision, Sleep Disorders, Snoring, Hair Loss, Diet, Nutrition, Exercise, Kidney and Urological Disorders, and Backaches

Edited by Allan R. Cook. 738 pages. 1998. 0-7808-0212-8. $78.

"This comprehensive resource and the series are highly recommended."

—*American Reference Books Annual, 2000*

"Recommended reference source."

—*Booklist, American Library Association, Dec '98*

■

Mental Health Disorders Sourcebook, 1st Edition

Basic Information about Schizophrenia, Depression, Bipolar Disorder, Panic Disorder, Obsessive-Compulsive Disorder, Phobias and Other Anxiety Disorders, Paranoia and Other Personality Disorders, Eating Disorders, and Sleep Disorders

Along with Information about Treatment and Therapies

Edited by Karen Bellenir. 548 pages. 1995. 0-7808-0040-0. $78.

"This is an excellent new book . . . written in easy-to-understand language." —*Booklist Health Sciences Supplement, American Library Association, Oct '97*

". . . useful for public and academic libraries and consumer health collections."

—*Medical Reference Services Quarterly, Spring '97*

"The great strengths of the book are its readability and its inclusion of places to find more information. Especially recommended." —*Reference Quarterly, American Library Association, Winter '96*

". . . a good resource for a consumer health library."

—*Bulletin of the Medical Library Association, Oct '96*

"The information is data-based and couched in brief, concise language that avoids jargon. . . . a useful reference source." —*Readings, Sep '96*

"The text is well organized and adequately written for its target audience." —*Choice, Association of College and Research Libraries, Jun '96*

". . . provides information on a wide range of mental disorders, presented in nontechnical language."

—*Exceptional Child Education Resources, Spring '96*

"Recommended for public and academic libraries."

—*Reference Book Review, 1996*

Mental Health Disorders Sourcebook, 2nd Edition

Basic Consumer Health Information about Anxiety Disorders, Depression and Other Mood Disorders, Eating Disorders, Personality Disorders, Schizophrenia, and More, Including Disease Descriptions, Treatment Options, and Reports on Current Research Initiatives

Along with Statistical Data, Tips for Maintaining Mental Health, a Glossary, and Directory of Sources for Additional Help and Information

Edited by Karen Bellenir. 605 pages. 2000. 0-7808-0240-3. $78.

■

Mental Retardation Sourcebook

Basic Consumer Health Information about Mental Retardation and Its Causes, Including Down Syndrome, Fetal Alcohol Syndrome, Fragile X Syndrome, Genetic Conditions, Injury, and Environmental Sources

Along with Preventive Strategies, Parenting Issues, Educational Implications, Health Care Needs, Employment and Economic Matters, Legal Issues, a Glossary, and a Resource Listing for Additional Help and Information

Edited by Joyce Brennfleck Shannon. 642 pages. 2000. 0-7808-0377-9. $78.

■

Obesity Sourcebook

Basic Consumer Health Information about Diseases and Other Problems Associated with Obesity, and Including Facts about Risk Factors, Prevention Issues, and Management Approaches

Along with Statistical and Demographic Data, Information about Special Populations, Research Updates, a Glossary, and Source Listings for Further Help and Information

Edited by Wilma Caldwell. 400 pages. 2000. 0-7808-0333-7. $48.

■

Ophthalmic Disorders Sourcebook

Basic Information about Glaucoma, Cataracts, Macular Degeneration, Strabismus, Refractive Disorders, and More

Along with Statistical and Demographic Data and Reports on Current Research Initiatives

Edited by Linda M. Ross. 631 pages. 1996. 0-7808-0081-8. $78.

■

Oral Health Sourcebook

Basic Information about Diseases and Conditions Affecting Oral Health, Including Cavities, Gum Disease, Dry Mouth, Oral Cancers, Fever Blisters, Canker Sores, Oral Thrush, Bad Breath, Temporomandibular Disorders, and other Craniofacial Syndromes

Along with Statistical Data on the Oral Health of Americans, Oral Hygiene, Emergency First Aid, Information on Treatment Procedures and Methods of Replacing Lost Teeth

Edited by Allan R. Cook. 558 pages. 1997. 0-7808-0082-6. $78.

"Unique source which will fill a gap in dental sources for patients and the lay public. A valuable reference tool even in a library with thousands of books on dentistry. Comprehensive, clear, inexpensive, and easy to read and use. It fills an enormous gap in the health care literature." —*Reference and User Services Quarterly, American Library Association, Summer '98*

"Recommended reference source."
—*Booklist, American Library Association, Dec '97*

■

Osteoporosis Sourcebook

Basic Consumer Health Information about Primary and Secondary Osteoporosis, Juvenile Osteoporosis, Related Conditions, and Other Such Bone Disorders as Fibrous Dysplasia, Myeloma, Osteogenesis Imperfecta, Osteopetrosis, and Paget's Disease

Along with Information about Risk Factors, Treatments, Traditional and Non-Traditional Pain Management, and Including a Glossary and Resource Directory

Edited by Allan R. Cook. 600 pages. 2000. 0-7808-0239-X. $78.

SEE ALSO *Women's Health Concerns Sourcebook*

■

Pain Sourcebook

Basic Information about Specific Forms of Acute and Chronic Pain, Including Headaches, Back Pain, Muscular Pain, Neuralgia, Surgical Pain, and Cancer Pain

Along with Pain Relief Options Such as Analgesics, Narcotics, Nerve Blocks, Transcutaneous Nerve Stimulation, and Alternative Forms of Pain Control, Including Biofeedback, Imaging, Behavior Modification, and Relaxation Techniques

Edited by Allan R. Cook. 667 pages. 1997. 0-7808-0213-6. $78.

"The text is readable, easily understood, and well indexed. This excellent volume belongs in all patient education libraries, consumer health sections of public libraries, and many personal collections."
—*American Reference Books Annual, 1999*

"A beneficial reference." —*Booklist Health Sciences Supplement, American Library Association, Oct '98*

"The information is basic in terms of scholarship and is appropriate for general readers. Written in journalistic style . . . intended for non-professionals. Quite thorough in its coverage of different pain conditions and summarizes the latest clinical information regarding pain treatment."
—*Choice, Association of College and Research Libraries, Jun '98*

"Recommended reference source."
—*Booklist, American Library Association, Mar '98*

Pediatric Cancer Sourcebook

Basic Consumer Health Information about Leukemias, Brain Tumors, Sarcomas, Lymphomas, and Other Cancers in Infants, Children, and Adolescents, Including Descriptions of Cancers, Treatments, and Coping Strategies

Along with Suggestions for Parents, Caregivers, and Concerned Relatives, a Glossary of Cancer Terms, and Resource Listings

Edited by Edward J. Prucha. 587 pages. 1999. 0-7808-0245-4. $78.

"A valuable addition to all libraries specializing in health services and many public libraries."

—*American Reference Books Annual, 2000*

■

Physical & Mental Issues in Aging Sourcebook

Basic Consumer Health Information on Physical and Mental Disorders Associated with the Aging Process, Including Concerns about Cardiovascular Disease, Pulmonary Disease, Oral Health, Digestive Disorders, Musculoskeletal and Skin Disorders, Metabolic Changes, Sexual and Reproductive Issues, and Changes in Vision, Hearing, and Other Senses

Along with Data about Longevity and Causes of Death, Information on Acute and Chronic Pain, Descriptions of Mental Concerns, a Glossary of Terms, and Resource Listings for Additional Help

Edited by Jenifer Swanson. 660 pages. 1999. 0-7808-0233-0. $78.

"Recommended for public libraries."

—*American Reference Books Annual, 2000*

"This is a treasure of health information for the layperson." — *Choice Health Sciences Supplement, Association of College & Research Libraries, May 2000*

"Recommended reference source."

—*Booklist, American Library Association, Oct '99*

SEE ALSO *Healthy Aging Sourcebook*

■

Plastic Surgery Sourcebook

Basic Consumer Health Information on Cosmetic and Reconstructive Plastic Surgery, Including Statistical Information about Different Surgical Procedures, Things to Consider Prior to Surgery, Plastic Surgery Techniques and Tools, Emotional and Psychological Considerations, and Procedure-Specific Information

Along with a Glossary of Terms and a Listing of Resources for Additional Help and Information

Edited by M. Lisa Weatherford. 400 pages. 2000. 0-7808-0214-4. $48.

Podiatry Sourcebook

Basic Consumer Health Information about Foot Conditions, Diseases, and Injuries, Including Bunions, Corns, Calluses, Athlete's Foot, Plantar Warts, Hammertoes and Clawtoes, Club Foot, Heel Pain, Gout, and More

Along with Facts about Foot Care, Disease Prevention, Foot Safety, Choosing a Foot Care Specialist, a Glossary of Terms, and Resource Listings for Additional Information

Edited by M. Lisa Weatherford. 600 pages. 2000. 0-7808-0215-2. $78.

■

Pregnancy & Birth Sourcebook

Basic Information about Planning for Pregnancy, Maternal Health, Fetal Growth and Development, Labor and Delivery, Postpartum and Perinatal Care, Pregnancy in Mothers with Special Concerns, and Disorders of Pregnancy, Including Genetic Counseling, Nutrition and Exercise, Obstetrical Tests, Pregnancy Discomfort, Multiple Births, Cesarean Sections, Medical Testing of Newborns, Breastfeeding, Gestational Diabetes, and Ectopic Pregnancy

Edited by Heather E. Aldred. 737 pages. 1997. 0-7808-0216-0. $78.

"A well-organized handbook. Recommended."

—*Choice, Association of College and Research Libraries, Apr '98*

"Reecommended reference source."

—*Booklist, American Library Association, Mar '98*

"Recommended for public libraries."

—*American Reference Books Annual, 1998*

SEE ALSO *Congenital Disorders Sourcebook, Family Planning Sourcebook*

■

Public Health Sourcebook

Basic Information about Government Health Agencies, Including National Health Statistics and Trends, Healthy People 2000 Program Goals and Objectives, the Centers for Disease Control and Prevention, the Food and Drug Administration, and the National Institutes of Health

Along with Full Contact Information for Each Agency

Edited by Wendy Wilcox. 698 pages. 1998. 0-7808-0220-9. $78.

"Recommended reference source."

—*Booklist, American Library Association, Sep '98*

"This consumer guide provides welcome assistance in navigating the maze of federal health agencies and their data on public health concerns."

—*SciTech Book News, Sep '98*

Rehabilitation Sourcebook

Basic Consumer Health Information about Rehabilitation for People Recovering from Heart Surgery, Spinal Cord Injury, Stroke, Orthopedic Impairments, Amputation, Pulmonary Impairments, Traumatic Injury, and More, Including Physical Therapy, Occupational Therapy, Speech/ Language Therapy, Massage Therapy, Dance Therapy, Art Therapy, and Recreational Therapy

Along with Information on Assistive and Adaptive Devices, a Glossary, and Resources for Additional Help and Information

Edited by Dawn D. Matthews. 531 pages. 1999. 0-7808-0236-5. $78.

"Recommended reference source."
—*Booklist, American Library Association, May '00*

■

Respiratory Diseases & Disorders Sourcebook

Basic Information about Respiratory Diseases and Disorders, Including Asthma, Cystic Fibrosis, Pneumonia, the Common Cold, Influenza, and Others, Featuring Facts about the Respiratory System, Statistical and Demographic Data, Treatments, Self-Help Management Suggestions, and Current Research Initiatives

Edited by Allan R. Cook and Peter D. Dresser. 771 pages. 1995. 0-7808-0037-0. $78.

"Designed for the layperson and for patients and their families coping with respiratory illness. . . . an extensive array of information on diagnosis, treatment, management, and prevention of respiratory illnesses for the general reader." —*Choice, Association of College and Research Libraries, Jun '96*

"A highly recommended text for all collections. It is a comforting reminder of the power of knowledge that good books carry between their covers."
—*Academic Library Book Review, Spring '96*

"A comprehensive collection of authoritative information presented in a nontechnical, humanitarian style for patients, families, and caregivers."
—*Association of Operating Room Nurses, Sep/Oct '95*

■

Sexually Transmitted Diseases Sourcebook

Basic Information about Herpes, Chlamydia, Gonorrhea, Hepatitis, Nongonoccocal Urethritis, Pelvic Inflammatory Disease, Syphilis, AIDS, and More

Along with Current Data on Treatments and Preventions

Edited by Linda M. Ross. 550 pages. 1997. 0-7808-0217-9. $78.

Skin Disorders Sourcebook

Basic Information about Common Skin and Scalp Conditions Caused by Aging, Allergies, Immune Reactions, Sun Exposure, Infectious Organisms, Parasites, Cosmetics, and Skin Traumas, Including Abrasions, Cuts, and Pressure Sores

Along with Information on Prevention and Treatment

Edited by Allan R. Cook. 647 pages. 1997. 0-7808-0080-X. $78.

". . . comprehensive, easily read reference book."
—*Doody's Health Sciences Book Reviews, Oct '97*

***SEE ALSO** Burns Sourcebook*

■

Sleep Disorders Sourcebook

Basic Consumer Health Information about Sleep and Its Disorders, Including Insomnia, Sleepwalking, Sleep Apnea, Restless Leg Syndrome, and Narcolepsy

Along with Data about Shiftwork and Its Effects, Information on the Societal Costs of Sleep Deprivation, Descriptions of Treatment Options, a Glossary of Terms, and Resource Listings for Additional Help

Edited by Jenifer Swanson. 439 pages. 1998. 0-7808-0234-9. $78.

"This text will complement any home or medical library. It is user-friendly and ideal for the adult reader."
—*American Reference Books Annual, 2000*

"Recommended reference source."
—*Booklist, American Library Association, Feb '99*

"A useful resource that provides accurate, relevant, and accessible information on sleep to the general public. Health care providers who deal with sleep disorders patients may also find it helpful in being prepared to answer some of the questions patients ask."
—*Respiratory Care, Jul '99*

■

Sports Injuries Sourcebook

Basic Consumer Health Information about Common Sports Injuries, Prevention of Injury in Specific Sports, Tips for Training, and Rehabilitation from Injury

Along with Information about Special Concerns for Children, Young Girls in Athletic Training Programs, Senior Athletes, and Women Athletes, and a Directory of Resources for Further Help and Information

Edited by Heather E. Aldred. 624 pages. 1999. 0-7808-0218-7. $78.

"Public libraries and undergraduate academic libraries will find this book useful for its nontechnical language." —*American Reference Books Annual, 2000*

"While this easy-to-read book is recommended for all libraries, it should prove to be especially useful for public, high school, and academic libraries; certainly it should be on the bookshelf of every school gymnasium." —*E-Streams, Mar '00*

Substance Abuse Sourcebook

Basic Health-Related Information about the Abuse of Legal and Illegal Substances Such as Alcohol, Tobacco, Prescription Drugs, Marijuana, Cocaine, and Heroin; and Including Facts about Substance Abuse Prevention Strategies, Intervention Methods, Treatment and Recovery Programs, and a Section Addressing the Special Problems Related to Substance Abuse during Pregnancy

Edited by Karen Bellenir. 573 pages. 1996. 0-7808-0038-9. $78.

"A valuable addition to any health reference section. Highly recommended."

—*The Book Report, Mar/Apr '97*

". . . a comprehensive collection of substance abuse information that's both highly readable and compact. Families and caregivers of substance abusers will find the information enlightening and helpful, while teachers, social workers and journalists should benefit from the concise format. Recommended."

—*Drug Abuse Update, Winter '96/'97*

SEE ALSO *Alcoholism Sourcebook, Drug Abuse Sourcebook*

■

Traveler's Health Sourcebook

Basic Consumer Health Information for Travelers, Including Physical and Medical Preparations, Transportation Health and Safety, Essential Information about Food and Water, Sun Exposure, Insect and Snake Bites, Camping and Wilderness Medicine, and Travel with Physical or Medical Disabilities

Along with International Travel Tips, Vaccination Recommendations, Geographical Health Issues, Disease Risks, a Glossary, and a Listing of Additional Resources

Edited by Joyce Brennfleck Shannon. 650 pages. 2000. 0-7808-0384-1. $78.

■

Women's Health Concerns Sourcebook

Basic Information about Health Issues That Affect Women, Featuring Facts about Menstruation and Other Gynecological Concerns, Including Endometriosis, Fibroids, Menopause, and Vaginitis; Reproductive Concerns, Including Birth Control, Infertility, and Abortion; and Facts about Additional Physical, Emotional, and Mental Health Concerns Prevalent among Women Such as Osteoporosis, Urinary Tract Disorders, Eating Disorders, and Depression

Along with Tips for Maintaining a Healthy Lifestyle

Edited by Heather E. Aldred. 567 pages. 1997. 0-7808-0219-5. $78.

"Handy compilation. There is an impressive range of diseases, devices, disorders, procedures, and other physical and emotional issues covered . . . well organized, illustrated, and indexed."

—*Choice, Association of College and Research Libraries, Jan '98*

SEE ALSO *Breast Cancer Sourcebook, Cancer Sourcebook for Women, 1st and 2nd Editions, Healthy Heart Sourcebook for Women, Osteoporosis Sourcebook*

■

Workplace Health & Safety Sourcebook

Basic Information about Musculoskeletal Injuries, Cumulative Trauma Disorders, Occupational Carcinogens and Other Toxic Materials, Child Labor, Workplace Violence, Histoplasmosis, Transmission of HIV and Hepatitis-B Viruses, and Occupational Hazards Associated with Various Industries, Including Mining, Confined Spaces, Agriculture, Construction, Electrical Work, and the Medical Professions, with Information on Mortality and Other Statistical Data, Preventative Measures, Reproductive Risks, Reducing Stress for Shiftworkers, Noise Hazards, Industrial Back Belts, Reducing Contamination at Home, Preventing Allergic Reactions to Rubber Latex, and More

Along with Public and Private Programs and Initiatives, a Glossary, and Sources for Additional Help and Information

Edited by Chad Kimball. 600 pages. 2000. 0-7808-0231-4. $78.

■

Worldwide Health Sourcebook

Basic Information about Global Health Issues, Including Nutrition, Reproductive Health, Disease Dispersion and Prevention, Emerging Diseases, Health Risks, and the Leading Causes of Death

Along with Global Health Concerns for Children, Women, and the Elderly, Mental Health Issues, Research and Technology Advancements, and Economic, Environmental, and Political Health Implications, a Glossary, and a Resource Listing for Additional Help and Information

Edited by Joyce Brennfleck Shannon. 500 pages. 2000. 0-7808-0330-2. $78.

■

Health Reference Series Cumulative Index 1999

A Comprehensive Index to the Individual Volumes of the Health Reference Series, Including a Subject Index, Name Index, Organization Index, and Publication Index;

Along with a Master List of Acronyms and Abbreviations

Edited by Edward J. Prucha, Anne Holmes, and Robert Rudnick. 990 pages. 2000. 0-7808-0382-5. $78.